JESUS BECO[

A Theological Interpretation of the Synoptic Gospels

Thomas G. Weinandy, OFM, Cap.

Foreword by John C. Cavadini

The Catholic University of America Press • Washington, D.C.

Library of Congress Cataloging-in-Publication Data

Names: Weinandy, Thomas G. (Thomas Gerard), author.

Title: Jesus becoming Jesus : a theological interpretation of the
Synoptic Gospels / Thomas G. Weinandy, OFM, Cap. ;
foreword by John C. Cavadini.

Description: Washington, D.C. : The Catholic University of America
Press, 2018. | Includes bibliographical references and index.

Identifiers: LCCN 2017056272 | ISBN 9780813230450 (pbk. : alk. paper)

Subjects: LCSH: Bible. Gospels—Criticism, interpretation, etc. |
Synoptic problem. | Jesus Christ—Biography.

Classification: LCC BS2555.52 .W44 2018 | DDC 226/.06—dc23

LC record available at https://lccn.loc.gov/2017056272

"Father Thomas Weinandy reads the Synoptic Gospels synoptically. And his optic is an explicitly theological one. He illuminates the theological premises and claims of the Gospels themselves. In addition he brings into clear relief that the narratives of Matthew, Mark, and Luke narrate a Trinitarian drama, and that the church's Trinitarian doctrine discloses the very logic of the Gospel account. Weinandy shows that doctrine is not extrinsic to the evangelists' narrative. It provides the key to its proper interpretation."

—Robert Imbelli, author of *Rekindling the Christic Imagination*

"The author's aim is to read Scripture within the theological tradition. Reading Thomas Weinandy's new book is like reading a medieval biblical commentary. The experience requires patience, as the author moves slowly and carefully, line by line through the Synoptic Gospels, gathering their metaphysical and theological implications. The experience is rewarded with intermittent explosions, as the results of the author's meditation come together and ignite, lighting up the text like fireworks."

—Francesca Aran Murphy, University of Notre Dame

"Weinandy's work brings new insight and theological vibrancy to the study of the gospels. I am not aware of any other contemporary source that manages to capture in one volume such an extensive theological exposition of the gospels. The author's creative approach to "Jesus becoming more and more Jesus in act through his saving grace" imparts a delightful freshness to the study of the gospels today, adapting traditional theological concepts to a modern context in order to help readers better see the face of Jesus who is true man and son of the Father."

—Matthew Ramage, author of *Jesus, Interpreted* and *Dark Passages of the Bible* (CUA Press)

JESUS BECOMING JESUS

To Matthew, Mark, and Luke

CONTENTS

Foreword by John C. Cavadini   ix

Preface   xv

PART I
THE INFANCY NARRATIVES AND
THE BAPTISM OF JESUS
1

1. The Conception of Jesus: The Salvific Act of
   the Incarnation   3

2. The Birth of Jesus: The Epiphany of the Salvific Act   31
   of the Incarnation

3. The Baptism and Temptation of Jesus   70

PART II
JESUS' PUBLIC MINISTRY
111

4. Jesus' Priestly Salvific Acts: Initiating the   113
   Kingdom of God

5. Jesus' Prophetic Salvific Acts: Promulgating the Law of   146
   the Kingdom of Heaven

6. Jesus' Filial Relationship with His Father   179

PART III
PREFIGUREMENTS OF JESUS' PASSION,
DEATH, AND RESURRECTION
207

7. Peter's Profession of Faith and the Transfiguration   209

8. Jesus' Triumphal Entry into Jerusalem   243

PART IV

THE PASSION NARRATIVES

281

9. The Anointing of Jesus and the Last Supper   289

10. Jesus' Agony, Arrest, and Trials   319

11. Jesus' Crucifixion and Death   357

12. Jesus' Resurrection and Ascension   412

Conclusion: The Theological Foundation of   465
Jesus' Salvific Acts

Suggested Further Reading   475

Index   477

John C. Cavadini

There may be no more cited line in *Dei Verbum,* the Second Vatican Council's Constitution on Divine Revelation, than this: "The study of the sacred page is, as it were, the soul of sacred theology" (*DV* 24). Not only is the study of the sacred page the soul of theology, but it is also equally important for the training of preachers. Accordingly, we also read that "Catholic exegetes and other students of sacred theology ... should devote their energies ... to an exploration and exposition of the divine writings ... so that as many ministers of the divine word as possible will be able effectively to provide the nourishment of the Scriptures for the People of God ... in order to set [their] hearts on fire with the love of God" (*DV* 23). Passages such as these are used to justify the prominence of Bible courses in seminary and undergraduate curricula, and yet there is almost nothing rarer than a course which actually studies the sacred page *as* the sacred page, that is, as inspired Scripture, rather than simply as a text, perhaps of special significance for Western culture and the Church, but yet simply a text to be studied just like any other textual artifact left to us from Antiquity. The above cited passages from *Dei Verbum* clearly regard the study of Scripture, insofar as it is the "soul" of sacred theology and "nourishment" for the People of God, as irreducibly theological—for *DV* talks of "Catholic exegetes and *other* students of sacred theology." And yet, ironically, there is almost nothing rarer than a constitutively theological required Scripture course; most are constitutively historical and essentially secular. But if they are not already theological, how can they provide the "soul" or essential living breath, of theology, let alone of preaching?

What would a constitutively theological exegesis look like? *Dei Verbum* provides some answers. First of all, as already noted, it would be the study of the "sacred page," that is, Scripture *as* Scripture. *DV* comments that this means the books of the Bible, both Old and New Testaments (so named), are, "in their entirety, with all their parts, sacred and canonical because, written under the inspiration of the Holy Spirit, they have God as their author" (*DV* 11). Further, the inspiration of the Holy Spirit, we learn, does not replace human authorship, but in fact precisely inspires and one might even say liberates it, "so that with God acting in them and through them," the human authors of Scripture "as true authors, consigned to writing everything and only those things which he wanted" (ibid.).

Treating Scripture as the "sacred page" means paying equal attention to both of these authorships, to God as author, and to the human authors. Treating the latter as "true authors" means paying attention to "literary forms," to the situation of the writer's own "time and culture," to "customary and characteristic" styles of narration and communication. It seems fair to say that this half of the exegete's job is amply represented in Scripture courses in seminaries and universities. *DV* goes on to comment, however, that, "since Holy Scripture must be read and interpreted in the same spirit in which it was written, no less serious attention must be given to the content and unity of the whole of Scripture if the meaning of the sacred texts is to be correctly worked out," the meaning, that is, that "God wanted to manifest by means of [the human authors'] words" (*DV* 12).

Can we really say that we have lived up to this half of the exegete's job? That our courses generally give *no less* serious attention to the "content and unity of the whole of Scripture?" Especially where this is taken to mean that "[t]he living Tradition of the whole Church must be taken into account along with the harmony which exists between elements of the Faith"? I think it is fair to say that this side of the study of the "sacred page" has been almost wholly untouched, and that we have not, therefore, lived up to the challenge of *Dei Verbum* to develop a Scriptural exegesis and pedagogy that respects and receives both "authorships" equally and therefore discovers anew the truly incarnational character of the sacred text, the uniquely self-emptied Divine Word, emptied, as it is, precisely into "human language" (see *DV* 13). In fact, more often than not, we teach Scripture as though the *only* relevant considerations for exegesis are the considerations relevant to the human authorship, and considerations of the living Tradition of the Church and of the unity of the whole of Scripture are seen almost as elements guaranteeing a misleading and anachronistic interpretation, a *mis*interpretation, and, not to mince words, "eisegesis."

Thomas Weinandy's superb new book, the first of a planned series, is intended to help us to think about, to try on (as it were), and at once to recover, re-imagine and re-create, the side of the exegesis of the "sacred page" that is concerned with God as author, so that we might learn to give *more* attention—and even *"no less"* attention—to the divine authorship of Scripture. Weinandy does this precisely by following the suggestions of *DV*, by taking into account the "living Tradition of the Church and the harmony that exists between the elements of faith," and the "content and unity of the whole of Scripture." He works "according to these rules" precisely as *DV* specifies. Because we are not used to imagining how a full bodied approach to Scriptural exegesis might look if we were taking *DV—all of DV*—seriously, some of Weinandy's moves may strike some readers as odd.

For example, he freely uses the language of "hypostasis," "nature," and "person" to interpret biblical passages regarding the relation between Jesus and the Father and regarding the identity of Jesus Christ Himself. Of course the application of this language to the Trinity (including the precise use of the word "Triad" or "Trinity") was not developed until some three to four centuries after the Gospels were written, and so Weinandy's use of these terms may strike some readers as "anachronistic," as offending against the historical enterprise, and intruding later categories upon the text. But this would be true only if the employment of these expressions, as the Church uses them, did not itself arise from a genuine process of interpreting the "content and unity of the whole of Scripture" which yielded true results regarding "what God wanted to manifest by means of the sacred writers' words" — precisely as was claimed by exegetical theologians such as Athanasius and Gregory Nazianzus and by the Ecumenical Councils who approved their insights. This "living Tradition of the whole Church must be taken into account" precisely because it has been accepted as truly clarifying and genuinely articulating the meaning of Scripture.

That this should be true is not a surprise if we understand the relationship between Scripture and Tradition, and this is true not only on the strictest Catholic reading of "Tradition" but on a reading of "Tradition" that many other Christians can and do buy. Scripture is "Scripture" because it was believed, by those receiving it as canonical, to present Apostolic teaching as such could be summarized by the "Rule of Faith." Irenaeus made the point long ago that it is a hallmark of the Gnostic and Valentinian hermeneutic to oppose Tradition against Scripture, alleging a secret inheritance of teaching from the Apostles as necessary to interpret Scripture against what would otherwise seem its obvious meaning, for example, that the Creator is the only and highest God (see *Adv. haer.*3.2.2; 1.10.3, and 2.27.2). "Tradition" is not simply the name of the "Rule of Faith" for Irenaeus, but rather the name for what *DV* calls "the content and unity of the whole of Scripture" precisely *as* Scripture and not just as a collection of (now) ancient writings. Irenaeus calls it the "hypothesis" of Scripture, that is, what makes it hold together as Scripture, as God's Word. Perhaps we could call it the "narrative grammar" of Scripture which can be summed up in the Creed, or the Rule of Faith, but which as such never replaces Scripture but simply is a guide to interpreting it properly (see the famous example at *Adv. haer.* 1.9.4). In turn, then, Scripture arises from Tradition (see *Adv. haer.*3.1.1), and can therefore never succeed in displacing it without displacing itself. Augustine echoes Irenaeus when he comments that ambiguities in Scripture that cannot be clarified simply on the basis of a knowledge of grammar and culture, even ambiguities of punctuation and phrasing, are to be settled by an appeal to the Rule of Faith (*De doct.* 3.3.6).

Scripture *as Scripture* is "Traditional," and Tradition is "Scriptural." By contrast with Gnosticism and Valentinianism, Tradition is the friend of Scripture—if by Scripture you mean the inspired Word of God, the "sacred page," and not just a series of loosely held together cultural artifacts of Antiquity. Weinandy's book is one extended performance of the search for the meaning of Scripture *as* Scripture by connecting it to its "hypothesis" and by using the exegetical connections that have been developed and definitively accepted by the Church already. This is just as "scientific" as historico-critical practice, if by "scientific" one means pertaining to a "science" or a "scientia," only the *scientia* here in question is Theology. The search for an "objective" meaning of Scripture *as Scripture* by constitutive appeal to another "science," that is, for example, history, can never succeed. The idea that it is "objective" ("scientific" in that sense) has been demonstrated to be an illusion in any event, for example, Josef Ratzinger's/Pope Benedict XVI's repeated demonstration that the results of such "scientific" analysis have generally simply reflected scholarly trends (while not at the same time wishing to deny genuine results that could be taken up into a theological account).

Weinandy's book is an extended exegetical reflection, steeped in his vast knowledge of the Tradition of the Church and of Catholic theology, which brilliantly makes a claim to showing one way that the study of the sacred page can serve as the "soul" of sacred theology, and, perhaps even more importantly, one kind of exegesis of the Scripture that can "provide the nourishment of the Scriptures for the People of God … in order to set [their] hearts on fire with the love of God." Thereby, as a corollary side effect, he shows how we can begin to think about kinds of exegesis that would truly justify the number of courses that are required in seminary and Catholic university curricula for Scripture courses. Weinandy does not claim that his reading demonstrates the only way to recover a Scriptural exegesis that takes the divine authorship seriously. He makes no such claim, but offers his own reading as a resource and an inspiration and an example of the recovery of a hermeneutic that takes "equally seriously" the divine authorship as it is evident in "the content and unity of the whole of Scripture," as that has been clarified and continues to be clarified "by the living Tradition of the whole Church" and "the harmony that exists between elements of the faith," elements, that is, of the "hypothesis" of Scripture itself. I recommend careful study of Weinandy's book to anyone who wants to think not only about "Jesus becoming Jesus," but, in an analogous way, about "Scripture becoming Scripture" ever more and ever more deeply in our minds and in our hearts.

PREFACE

This is not the book I intended to write. Almost twenty years ago, John Webster, then the Lady Margaret Professor of Divinity at the University of Oxford (now sadly deceased), encouraged me to write a one-volume systematic theology. At the time I was busy with other writing projects, and then my formal academic life was interrupted for nine years while I worked for the United States Conference of Catholic Bishops. Upon leaving the bishops' conference in August 2013, I was granted a sabbatical by my Capuchin provincial, and I spent six months of it in the Holy Land. There I first undertook writing what I thought would be the fulfillment of Professor Webster's suggestion. My plan was to treat the major doctrines or mysteries of the faith: Creation, God, Trinity, Incarnation, and so on. The structure I conceived was to make a respectful nod to Scripture and then move quickly on to the Fathers of the Church, the teachings of St. Thomas Aquinas, and, in conclusion, contemporary theological issues. But as I began writing the initial chapter, on the Incarnation with my supposed deferential bow to the infancy narratives, I found myself becoming engrossed in the theological narrative contained within them. My theological interpretation became longer and longer as I became more enthused about what I was finding. While obviously well acquainted with the texts on one level, I discovered that the more I examined and contemplated the texts, the more their theological and doctrinal richness came to light, and so came to life. About six weeks or so into my project, I asked myself: What is becoming of my one-volume systematic theology? It was not taking the direction that I had supposed and intended. I was not sure what to do. But after some deliberation and prayer, I thought the Lord told me: *Just stay with the Scriptures. Simply write a theological or doctrinal interpretation of the New Testament.* This book is the result of that resolution.

A Theological Interpretation
of the New Testament

My interest in and love of Scripture has grown immensely over many years, yet I am not technically, in the academic sense, a Scripture scholar. I am a systematic theologian trained in historical theology. Being such, my exclusive focus on the Bible, specifically the New Testament, may seem to be a disadvantage, if not something that should be forbidden. Yet I considered my being a systematic theologian a liberating strength. Not being a Scripture scholar as such meant that I need not—because I could not and therefore should not—take up all the issues that Scripture scholars normally address. Not being professionally and academically fully versed in the historical critical method, I rarely touch upon the concerns that surround such a method. Nor do I examine matters surrounding Form Criticism, though, at some points, the interests of redaction criticism do come into play. This book, then, is not what many might consider a typical scripture commentary. But one should not conclude that this book is not a scholarly academic work. Rather, the academic strength of this book lies in my being a systematic theologian, which allows me the freedom and scholarly tools to interpret the New Testament in accordance with my own scholarly discipline, one that brings its own creativity and resourcefulness. My hope is that my theological or doctrinal interpretation offers a new scriptural freshness and a deeper theological understanding to the Gospels of Matthew, Mark, and Luke than is generally found within contemporary New Testament commentaries.

In writing my theological interpretation of the Gospels of Matthew, Mark, and Luke, I have attempted to follow the teaching of the Second Vatican Council's *Dogmatic Constitution on Divine Revelation, Dei Verbum*. Thus I did not intend my theological interpretation to be idiosyncratic—that is, not simply my personal insights or pious reflections—but rather a theological interpretation that would be founded upon and flow from the Church's faith as expressed within both Scripture and tradition. The Scriptures, particularly the New Testament, embody and express the preaching and teaching of the apostolic church, and therefore the sacred written text must always be interpreted and understood from within that living and ever present apostolic tradition. As *Dei Verbum* states:

> Sacred Tradition and sacred Scripture, then, are bound closely together, and communicate with the other. For both of them, flowing out from the same di-

vine well-spring, come together in some fashion to form one thing, and move towards the same goal. Sacred Scripture is the speech of God as it is put down in writing under the breath of the Holy Spirit. The Tradition transmits in its entirety the Word of God which has been entrusted to the apostles by Christ the Lord and the Holy Spirit. (*DV* 9)

The divinely revealed realities, which are contained and presented in the text of sacred Scripture, have been written down under the inspiration of the Holy Spirit. For Holy Mother Church relying on the faith of the apostolic age, accepts as sacred and canonical the books of the Old and the New Testaments, whole and entire, with all their parts, on the grounds that, written under the inspiration of the Holy Spirit (cf. Jn 20:31; 2 Tm 3:16; 2 Pt 1:19-21; 3:15-16), they have God as their author, and have been handed on as such to the Church herself. (*DV* 11)

Sacred Tradition, then, is not something detached from Scripture but is rather the reading of Scripture from within the living apostolic faith that gave rise to the written inspired text. Being a systematic theologian in communion with the Church, I have attempted to read and interpret the New Testament, particularly the Gospels of Matthew, Mark, and Luke, from within that living apostolic tradition. I have also, in accordance with *Dei Verbum*, approached the divinely inspired texts from within the doctrinal context of the Church's magisterial teaching, particularly in the light of the first four Ecumenical Councils, and within the received living theological tradition that resides within the Church. I did so believing that such authoritative teaching, especially regarding the Trinity and Incarnation, rose out of and gave expression to the apostolic faith that is fully and already contained within the sacred text itself, and so it can presently be employed as the living interpreter of the sacred texts in which such teaching is sacredly enshrined. As *Dei Verbum* underscores, sacred Tradition and sacred Scripture are bound closely, and together they nurture the Church's understanding of the one Gospel. There is a hermeneutical interrelationship between Scripture and the Church's magisterial and theological tradition, each illuminating the other and so together fostering fuller life and understanding within both.

As I have attempted to implement *Dei Verbum*'s declaration that "sacred Tradition and sacred Scripture make up a single sacred deposit of the Word of God, which is entrusted to the Church" (*DV* 10), I have also ardently endeavored to take seriously *Dei Verbum*'s other admonition:

Sacred theology relies on the written Word of God, taken together with sacred Tradition, as on a permanent foundation. By this Word it is most firmly strengthened and constantly rejuvenated, as it searches out, under the light of the faith, the full truth stored up in the mystery of Christ. Therefore, the "study of the sacred page" should be the very soul of sacred theology. (*DV* 24)

As a systematic theologian, I am concerned principally with the doctrines of the faith, and in this study I show how these saving mysteries reside within the sacred texts, and how sacred Scripture is the "soul of sacred theology." In so doing, I have not only provided new insight and understanding to the sacred mysteries, but also engendered a new theological vibrancy within and fuller doctrinal appreciation of the sacred texts themselves. If Scripture is the soul of theology, theology is the ever-living expression of Scripture.

Although I have, over the course of my academic life, read many biblical commentaries, especially New Testament commentaries, I did not read any biblical commentaries or studies while preparing or writing this book. I avoided them because I did not want to become engaged with various opinions and sundry issues that would distract and lead me away from what I was attempting to do. I soon realized that to engage other authors would significantly expand an already burgeoning text. So there are no footnotes to secondary literature within the following study, except to a number of theological studies of my own, where one can find a fuller or separate theological exposition of the scriptural topic at hand. In the actual composing of this book, there were simply three components: (1) the text of the Bible itself, (2) me with my theological and academic history, and, hopefully, (3) the light of the Holy Spirit.

The Major Theme: A Theology of Saving Acts

In my originally intended systematic theology, I wanted to stress and develop the importance of "acts," for example, those constituting the divine persons within the Trinity or the act of the Incarnation. Throughout my academic life, beginning with my undergraduate philosophical study of Étienne Gilson and Thomas Aquinas, I have often focused on the philosophical and theological importance of the notion of "act" and what it means to be "in act" in various ways (see my *Does God Change? The Word's Becoming in the Incarnation*, *Does God Suffer?*, and *The Father's Spirit of Sonship: Reconceiving the Trinity*). I thought this notion would be lost as I began to focus exclusively on the Bible. But to my surprise, the importance of "act" almost immediately became the major theme of my theological interpretation of the Gospels of Matthew, Mark, and Luke. When writing the opening chapters on the infancy narratives, I realized, to a fuller degree than I had ever before imagined, the centrality of divine and human actions within the Gospels. Divine revelation comes primarily and foundationally through divine actions—the act of the Father's Son becoming incarnate by the Holy Spirit being the supreme revelatory and culminating divine act. I likewise became aware of the importance of Jesus' actions: the human acts of the Father's Son, human acts performed in communion with the Holy Spirit. I also perceived, again more fully, the causal nature of Jesus' actions. In the act of becoming man and through his subsequent human acts, Jesus was to bring about—cause—humankind's salvation. This in turn gave rise to the central overarching theme of this theological study of the Synoptic Gospels: Jesus (YHWH-Saves) through his saving acts was becoming Jesus (YHWH-Saves). The Gospels tell of Jesus enacting his name. Jesus more and more becomes Jesus in act through his saving acts; he becomes more and more the Savior. He definitively becomes Jesus-in-act within the actions of his saving death and resurrection, which will find their completion when Jesus comes in glory at the end of time, when all the faithful will achieve the fullness of salvation, when Jesus becomes Jesus-fully-in-act. Thus readers will find in this book a great deal of discussion of Jesus' actions and the causal nature of these saving acts.

Because my emphasis is on Jesus' saving acts, my theological interpretation of the Synoptic Gospels examines, almost exclusively, the major events in Jesus' life: his birth, baptism, transfiguration, triumphal entry into Jerusalem, passion, death, and resurrection. There is little sustained treatment of Jesus' teaching, such as his parables. Even when I treat his Sermon on the Mount, I do so emphasizing that Jesus enacts the Beatitudes and in so doing he is the primary initial and so foundational recipient of their blessings. Thus my study does not cover the entirety of what is contained within the Gospels of Matthew, Mark, and Luke. In treating the saving events within the life of Jesus, I examine them as they are narrated within all three Synoptic Gospels; for example, I treat all three accounts of the Transfiguration together. Although each of the Gospels, in accordance with each author's theological emphasis and intent, may narrate the saving events in Jesus' ministry somewhat differently, it is theologically important to realize that it is only in considering all three narratives that one obtains a comprehensive theological appreciation of what is being revealed. The three accounts complement one another and so together enhance our theological understanding. I also found that in comparing and contrasting the events of Jesus' life as they are narrated in Matthew, Mark, and

Luke, the reading and the interpreting of these events becomes much more theologically interesting and fruitful and even fun.

I also highlight the importance of the Old Testament. Evident within the Gospel accounts of Jesus' saving acts is the fulfilling of previous divine revelations, the previous prefiguring saving acts, contained within the Old Testament. Jesus can only be truly known in relationship to what has gone before, and only in Jesus does what has gone before obtain its full saving theological significance.

Lastly, while this volume exclusively examines the Gospels of Matthew, Mark, and Luke, I do reference, within the footnotes, the Gospel of John and other New Testament writings. I have done so to bring out theological similarities, differences, and developments. I also wanted to demonstrate that the whole of the New Testament is formative of the complete Gospel. The writings of the New Testament may have been written in different genres and for different ends, yet they all treat of the same saving mystery, and so they all enhance our understanding of the entire mystery that is Jesus Christ.

Gratitude

During the years of writing this book, I have received the gracious and generous help of many people. I first want to thank the Capuchin friars at Holy Spirit Friary in Jerusalem, particularly Fr. Stefano Giulio Dubinie and Fr. Joseph Mindling, who offered me fraternal hospitality when I first began this writing adventure. My former provincial, Fr. David Nestler, and my present provincial, Fr. Thomas Betz, deserve my gratitude for allowing me to pursue my academic interests. I am also grateful to the many friars with whom I live at Capuchin College in Washington, D.C. Not only did they offer prayers on my behalf, but they, especially the student friars, often encouragingly asked over the years how close I was to completing my book, only to hear me say that there was much yet to do. Then there are the many academic colleagues and friends who read the draft chapters and corrected typos, offered insightful scriptural and theological suggestions, and helped me clarify my positions and so sharpen their expression. I especially want to acknowledge Dr. Mary Healy, Dr. Daniel Keating, Dr. John Yocum, and my good Capuchin confrere and ever faithful friend, William Fey, D.Phil. Oxon, Bishop of Kimbe, Papua New Guinea. I particularly want to acknowledge Fr. Peter Hocken, who also faithfully commented on all of the chapters but unfortunately died before this book was published. Those who knew him knew him to be a holy priest and, in many ways, a prophet in our time. I must also express my thanks to those beloved laywomen who prayed for me during this academic venture—Mrs. Judith Virnelson, Mrs. Kathleen Jones and Mrs. Doris Ferlmann—and to my brother, Robert, who always asked how "it" was coming along. I am grateful to the Catholic University of America for publishing this book, especially to John Martino and my copy editor, Ashleigh McKown, with whom it was a joy to work. I finally want to thank all the Saints whose intercession I daily requested. I could name "a great cloud of witnesses" (Heb 12:1), but I will limit myself to four: Thomas Aquinas, Lawrence of Brindisi, Kateri Tekakwitha, and above all Mary, the Mother of Jesus.

Professor Webster encouraged me to write a *one*-volume systematic theology. Instead I have now written the first of a *multivolume* theological interpretation of the New Testament, presuming I will complete the remaining volumes. I do not think John would mind, since I have hopefully furthered our understanding and nurtured our love of the marvelous mysteries of our Christian faith, by pondering their principal inspired written expression within the New Testament. The writing of all books takes work and what I have come to call stick-to-it-iveness, but it was nonetheless a joy and a delight to contemplate Jesus becoming Jesus.

Thomas G. Weinandy, OFM, Cap.
The Feast of Pope St. Leo the Great, 2016

PART I

ᨆ

THE INFANCY NARRATIVES AND
THE BAPTISM OF JESUS

W ITHIN this opening section, chapters 1 and 2 examine the doctrinal or theological content of the infancy narratives in the Gospels of Matthew and Luke. Although the infancy narratives are considered a later addition to
the initial proclamation of the basic Gospel message (e.g., as found
in the Gospel of Mark), they are foundational to the subsequent
Gospel narrative: the person and work of Jesus. Within his public
ministry, Jesus had manifested the uniqueness of who he is and
the singularity of his saving acts. In this light, the infancy narratives are a historical look back at the beginning to provide a prophetic anticipation, a proleptic prophetic prolegomenon, of Jesus'
subsequent revealing of his divine identity and saving ministry.
Who Jesus revealed himself to be, the infancy narratives tell us,
is ontologically constituted in the manner of his conception, and
what he salvifically accomplished, because of who he is, equally
springs from the manner of his coming into being. Thus the act by
which Jesus is conceived in the womb of Mary is the hermeneutical key for understanding the doctrinal prophetic content within
the infancy narratives. Within his subsequent public ministry and
through his passion, death, and resurrection, Jesus will fulfill—he
will enact—what was prophetically proclaimed within the infancy
narratives, confirming those prophecies. Thus the infancy narra

tives prophetically both anticipate and confirm the later Gospel narrative: who Jesus is and his salvific deeds.

To disregard the full doctrinal content inherent within the infancy narratives is a failure to appreciate the irreplaceable truth revealed within these narratives. And to discount the infancy narratives as a mere theological anticipatory footnote to the central Gospel proclamation is to deprive the body of the Gospels of their proper doctrinal interpretive light. Apart from the infancy narratives, who Jesus is and the salvific manner of his life, death, and resurrection possess no doctrinal ontological foundation. Thus the infancy narratives are of the utmost doctrinal importance not only in themselves but for the whole of the subsequent Gospel narrative.

Chapter 3 examines Jesus' baptism and ensuing temptations. Within the baptism of Jesus, the prophecies of the infancy narratives begin to be fulfilled. In the act of being baptized, Jesus is revealed to be the Spirit-anointed Servant-Son of God who will take up his Father's work of salvation—the work for which he was first conceived and became incarnate. The temptations that Jesus experiences immediately following his Father's commission to inaugurate his saving activity are direct challenges to that charge: will Jesus be faithful to his Father as the Father's Son, and will he be the Father's faithful anointed Suffering Servant? With these observations in mind, we can now proceed to study the infancy narratives.

1 · THE CONCEPTION OF JESUS

The Salvific Act of the Incarnation

To grasp the significance of Jesus' conception within the Gospel of Luke, we need to treat first the conception of John the Baptist. Because John's ministry is the revelational anticipation of the coming of Jesus' ministry, his conception and birth are the precursors of Jesus'.

The Gospel of Luke

The Conception of John the Baptist

In his introductory remarks, Luke informs us that while others have compiled other narratives about Jesus and his ministry in accordance with "eyewitnesses," he, "having followed all things closely for some time past," will now also "write an orderly account" so that Theophilus "may know the truth concerning the things of which you have been informed."[1]

Unsurprisingly, given Luke's desire to be accurate, he begins his narrative of John's and Jesus' conception by placing both accounts within their historical, political, and religious context. "In the days of Herod, king of Judea, there was a priest named Zechariah, of the division of Abijah; and he had a wife of the daughters of Aaron, and her name was Elizabeth." In providing this historical detail, Luke deprives both conceptions of any mythological interpretation—a symbolic tale about an ahistorical ethereal realm. Although the conception of John the Baptist was miraculous in that Elizabeth was barren, and both she and her husband Zechariah were advanced in years it took place within a specific place at a specific time. And though Jesus' conception was not

---

1. All quotations are taken from Lk 1:1-25 unless otherwise noted. All biblical quotations throughout this study are taken from the Revised Standard Version (Catholic edition) unless otherwise noted.

of human origin and so not effected by human causality, it involved real human beings within a specific geographical location and within a definite historical setting. As in the Old Testament narration of the Lord's divine acts, it is imperative, for Luke, that God, who exists distinct from the world, is nonetheless capable of acting within the world, and thus his actions are historical events. The terminal effect of his actions inheres within this historical world while the cause of the action is found in the Lord God alone. For Luke, just as the ministry of John the Baptist is historically prior to and a preparation for the ministry of Jesus, John's conception is historically prior to and a preparation for the conception of Jesus.

Having provided the historical setting, Luke proceeds to narrate the events that took place therein. Even though Zechariah and his wife Elizabeth "were both righteous before God, walking in all the commandments and ordinances of the Lord blameless," "they had no child because Elizabeth was barren, and both were advanced in years." When Zechariah was performing his priestly duties of offering incense in the temple and "the whole multitude of the people were praying outside at the hour of incense ... there appeared to him an angel of the Lord." Even though he was in the most holy sanctum of the temple, and thus in the presence of the most holy Lord God, Zechariah became "troubled ... and fear fell upon him" when the Lord's angel appeared, which alerted Zechariah that he was in God's presence. Yet the angel assured him that he need not be afraid, "for your prayer is heard, and your wife Elizabeth will bear you a son, and you shall call his name John."

The setting of this proclamation is significant. The angel of the Lord appeared not only during a time of prayer for Zechariah and all the people, but also within the temple, the most sacred and holiest place. The temple is the fruit of the Lord's covenant with his people. He would be their God, and they would be his people, so he would dwell in their midst. The temple is a historical sacramental expression, a tangible sign of that covenantal divine presence, for here daily prayers and sacrifices were offered to the abiding Lord. It is also the living expression of the Lord's past mighty deeds and the living hope of the future fulfillment of the Lord's promises. Here the Passover was annually commemorated and here all the people pray daily for the coming of the anticipated Messiah. In this temple, which embodies the totality of past revelation, a revelation that fundamentally looks to a future fulfillment; when the people are gathered in worship, a people who are the present living embodiment of the past and the present living expectation of the future; when incense is being offered up to God, at this time and in this place, the angel of Lord appears to Zechariah. He informs Zechariah that his prayer "is heard." But the present hearing of Zechariah's prayer is the hearing of all past and present prayers of "the whole multitude," for from the seemingly barren and lifeless womb of venerable Elizabeth a son will be born to him, a son called John. The angel of the Lord immediately and prophetically proclaims the future significance of this child's birth for both Zechariah and for the whole of Israel.

Recall that the infancy narratives are a look back at the beginning, the conceptions of John the Baptist and Jesus, but they look back not simply to what took place in the past but also as perceiving the past as the prophetic anticipation of the future. This past prophetic anticipation of the future the apostolic church now believes to be fulfilled. Thus what the angel of the Lord is about to prophetically proclaim to Zechariah concerning his future son must be understood not so much as he might have understood it at the time, but as it would be understood by the later apostolic church, which would interpret the angel's prophecy concerning John as fulfilled in his relationship to Jesus. Only in hearing the angel's proclamation with the ears of the apostolic church do we discern its full revelatory doctrinal truth.

Not only will Zechariah "have joy and gladness," but also "many will rejoice at his birth." The reason for such joy is that "he will be great before the Lord." In the context of John's future fulfilling his greatness, which the apostolic church believed had been fulfilled, "the Lord" before whom he will be great is not simply God as such but Jesus as well, for it is in the presence of Jesus and his Father, specifically at Jesus' baptism, that his greatness will be manifested before both.[2] In not drinking "wine nor strong drink" he will be separated from all others, for he will be solely dedicated to the Lord God (see Nm 6:1-8). Thus "he will be filled with the Holy Spirit, even from his mother's womb." Precisely because John is filled with the Spirit, he will bring many sons of Israel "to the Lord God, and he will go before him in the spirit and power of Elijah" (see Mal 4:5). As it was foretold that Elijah was to come "before the great and terrible day of the Lord comes" (Mal 4:5), so John will now

---

2. Jesus declares that John is even "more than a prophet" because he fulfills the prophecy of Malachi 3:1: "Behold I send my messenger before your face, who shall prepare your way before you" (Lk 7:27). John is more than a prophet because he does not merely foretell the coming of the Lord but prepares his way and identifies him upon his arrival. For doing so, Jesus declares that "among those born of women none is greater than John," and yet "he who is least in the kingdom of God is greater than he" (Lk 7:28). In preparing for the coming of Jesus, John is preparing for the coming of God's kingdom and so is yet to reside in it, and thus the least in the kingdom is greater than he. Ultimately, John, who is the greatest born of women, will also be great within the kingdom of God.

assume and fulfill that prophetic role. In fulfilling that role, John will "turn the hearts of fathers to their children [Malachi adds: "and the hearts of children to their fathers"], and the disobedient to the wisdom of the just." In bringing reconciliation and peace within families and turning disobedient hearts to God's just wisdom, John will "make ready for the Lord a people prepared." Again, the context in which the angel of the Lord's prophecy will be fulfilled, "the Lord" for whom John will prepare a way, in the spirit of Elijah, is Jesus. Thus the angel of the Lord's prophecy concerning John is also a prophetic proclamation that Jesus, as "the Lord," is truly divine and so is the wisdom and justice of God.

Here we grasp the full significance of this prophetic declaration taking place within the temple. The angel of the Lord was foretelling that the son to be born of Zechariah and Elizabeth, both righteous and yet without offspring, would become the preparatory herald of a new coming of the Lord God of Israel, and so the fulfillment of all that the temple presently signified (God's ancient covenantal presence with his people) and anticipated (God's future new life-giving covenantal presence with his people), and thus the answer to all the prayers and sacrifices that were offered therein. John, then, will assume the whole revelatory and prophetic history of Israel in his future ministry as the preparatory precursor for the Lord's coming, and thus become more than a prophet (see Lk 7:24-28). The Lord God in hearing Zechariah's personal petition for a son was simultaneously hearing the prayers of "the multitude of the people," from ages past and present, for their long-awaited Messiah.

Because Zechariah, given his and Elizabeth's advanced age, did not believe "this good news" that Gabriel (now identified) was sent by God to deliver, he will be silent "because you did not believe my words, which will be fulfilled in their time." Zechariah's lack of faith led to silence, which would only be broken upon the birth of his son, whose voice would prepare a people for the coming of the Messiah and call for repentance and faith. At this time, the words spoken by Gabriel, words that Zechariah refused to believe, will be fulfilled.

Those waiting outside "wondered at his delay in the temple." Unable to speak, the people perceived that Zechariah had a vision. When he completed his time of service in the temple, Zechariah returned home, and in "these days his wife Elizabeth conceived." Hiding herself, she proclaimed, "Thus the Lord has done to me in the days when he looked on me, to take away my reproach among men." The Lord had not forgotten ancient Israel in her waiting but had constantly looked upon her (Israel and Elizabeth) and was now taking away her seeming reproach not simply through the conception of John but through another conception, the one of whom John will be his herald. The conception of John is a prophetic act, for his conception only finds its anticipated fulfillment, only obtains its voice, in the conception of the one he was to herald. Without the ensuing conception of Jesus, John's voice, as was his father's, would have remained silent.

The Conception of Jesus

As in the case of the conception of John the Baptist, Luke informs us of all the historical particulars concerning Jesus' conception: "In the sixth month, the angel Gabriel was sent from God to a city of Galilee, named Nazareth, to a virgin betrothed to a man whose name was Joseph, of the house of David; and the virgin's name was Mary."[3] Within this specific historical, geographical, and personal setting, God sends the angel Gabriel. Significantly, the same angel, Gabriel, whom God sent to Zechariah while he was in the temple, is now sent by God to the town of Nazareth in Galilee, thus establishing that the same Lord God of Israel is responsible for both "sendings." There is therefore a necessary interrelated continuity between Gabriel's message to Zechariah and the message he will now proclaim in Nazareth. Gabriel is God's personal living link, by which he binds together his past saving presence and deeds, tangibly symbolized in the temple with his new saving presence, deeds that are about to be inaugurated in Nazareth.[4]

Gabriel declares, "Hail, full of grace, the Lord is with you!" Notably, Gabriel does not address Mary by name. Rather, his greeting is by way of a declaration—she is hailed as, and so decreed to be, the one "full of grace." Being full of grace entails a reciprocal relational causality. Because Mary is full of grace, "the Lord is with" her, and because the Lord is with her, she is full of grace. The act by which Mary is full of grace, the indwelling presence of the Lord *within* her, is the same act by which the Lord is *with* her. The Lord is not simply present "to" Mary, as two persons are present to one another, but the Lord resides fully within her, for she interiorly possesses the fullness of grace, which is the full interior presence of God. Although "Mary" is her name, who she actually is, as declared by Gabriel, is the one who possesses the fullness of

3. All quotations in this section are from Lk 1:26–38 unless otherwise noted.
4. Gabriel is the bond between the Old and New Testaments, for his first message within the temple was the last message to the old Israel, personified in Zechariah and Elizabeth, and his second message is the first message that announces the inauguration of the new Israel, in the person of Mary, which will be found in Jesus, the new saving presence of God.

grace, the one in whom resides the fullness of the Lord's presence. Thus being full of grace assumes the status of a title or even a name and so entails the
defining characteristic of who Mary is. The woman called "Mary" can rightly
and simply be addressed as "full of grace."[5]

Mary's was "greatly troubled" by the possible meaning of this greeting.
But Gabriel assures her that she should not be afraid, "for you have found favour with God." The full gracious presence of the Lord entails that Mary has
equally "found favour with God." The act of bestowing within Mary his very
own full gracious presence, the act of finding favor with God, is the wellspring
from which naturally flows the following culminating act: "And behold, you
will conceive in your womb and bear a son, and you shall call his name Jesus."

Because of his name, YHWH-Saves, Jesus will be "great" and he will be
"called the Son of the Most High." Moreover, "the Lord God will give him the
throne of his father David, and he will reign over the house of Jacob forever;
and of his kingdom there will be no end." Mary, then, is to bear a human son,
but this son, as prophetically decreed, "will be" so great and his saving deeds
so significant that "he will," at a future time, be acclaimed as "the Son of the
Most High" God, for he could only do what he did if he were such. Being who
he is and doing what he has done, the Lord God "will" fulfill in him the promise made to his father David (his human kingly ancestor) and bestow on him
an everlasting kingdom, and thus he "will" reign over the Lord's chosen people forever.

Gabriel's message is entirely prophetic, but now viewed by the apostolic
church as having been fulfilled, having been subsequently confirmed by Jesus'
life, death, and resurrection. All that Gabriel had prophetically proclaimed to
Mary has come to pass. And here at the moment of Jesus' conception there
is already a prophetic anticipation of his coming in glory—his eschatological
kingly presence—for only then will his kingly Davidic reign find its "forever-
ness." The doctrine concerning Jesus' conception, his first coming in lowliness, contains the doctrine of his second coming, his coming in glory.

Mary responds, "How can this be, since I have no husband?" Traditionally understood, Mary's response is not one of doubt (like Zechariah, when
told that Elizabeth would bear a son in her old age), but rather an enquiry as
to the nature of the causality. (Mary was obviously not a philosopher, but as a
rational human being, she nonetheless knew that effects require causes.) If all

---

5. This is not the place to argue for the Immaculate Conception. Nonetheless, we find in
Gabriel's greeting the revelational basis for such a doctrine.

that Gabriel has prophesied is to find fulfillment in the son she is to bear, and since she has no husband, what is to take place cannot be achieved through human causality. And if not through human causality, then how will the conception of her son be accomplished? This is the heart of the narrative. How is Mary to conceive her human son, who will be named Jesus and who will subsequently acquire his divine titles and attain all that Gabriel, the messenger of God, has foretold? "The Holy Spirit will come upon you, and the power of the Most High will overshadow you; therefore the child to be born will be called holy, the Son of God." Gabriel informs Mary of the nature and the effect of the divine causality. They constitute the principle doctrinal truth proclaimed within the infancy accounts. From this primordial truth flows all else that Gabriel prophetically revealed and that the apostolic church testifies has been confirmed and fulfilled. The cause of her son's conception will be the overshadowing power of the Most High, the Holy Spirit, and thus not a human cause. Because this conception will be of divine origin, the human son conceived, the effect of this divine causal act, will receive the very holiness of the one responsible for the act of conception—that is, the holiness of the Holy Spirit, the holiness of the Most High Lord God—"he will be called holy." Because he will be conceived by "the power of the Most High," her holy son will be "the Son of the Most High." That is, because of this divine causal act, "the child to be born" of Mary, he who is divinely conceived within her womb, will be called "the Son of God." Therefore the basis for Gabriel's earlier prophetic promises springs from the nature of the act of conception itself. The human son of Mary, Jesus, will come to be known as the Son of the Most High and inherit the everlasting throne of his father David, precisely because he who is conceived in her by the Holy Spirit, and so born of her, is none other than "the Son of God."

Luke informs us that Mary accepts and believes Gabriel's explanation as to how she is to conceive and bear a son without a husband and so professes: "Behold, I am the handmaid of the Lord; let it be to me according to your word." Being the handmaid of the Lord God of Israel, Mary willingly consents to Gabriel's prophecy being fulfilled in her. Her act of faith was not merely an acknowledgment of the truth that Gabriel spoke to which she gave assent. Rather, it was an allowing of herself to be drawn into the mystery of her son's conception and so into the mystery of who her son would be. This being drawn into the mystery of her son is the overshadowing of the Holy Spirit upon her by which her son would be conceived within her womb. In the Spirit, she is in living communion with her begotten son, and so in the Spirit she will be in living communion with him throughout his life. Before proceeding to Matthew's account, I want to accentuate more fully the theological significance of this annunciation scene.

Everything that Gabriel proclaimed to Mary finds its source within God's previous revelation to her ancestors: the Hebrew Scriptures and the Jewish tradition. This is precisely what makes Gabriel's message intelligible to Mary. As a devout Jewish woman, Mary knew "the Lord," and so she knew that he is "the Most High." She also knew God to be "holy," and so all whom he anoints with his "spirit" is made holy. Mary appreciated that God's glory "overshadowed" the temple for he dwelt therein. Mary knew that God promised an everlasting kingdom to David, and that Israel and the holy men of the past were known as sons of God.

Simultaneously, Mary realized that all the above, within the very act of Gabriel's intelligible proclamation, was now to take on unprecedented meaning. She also recognized that all that Gabriel proclaimed was to be accomplished through the son she was to conceive and bear. This is why she asked her question. Because she had no husband, how was all she was familiar with going to assume this radical new reality through her son? This acquisition of a new reality and meaning resides in Gabriel's declaring to Mary a fundamentally new act of the Lord, one that would give to all that was familiar within the Jewish religious tradition unparalleled novelty and so consummate significance. This new act is that the son to be born of Mary would be conceived by the Holy Spirit coming upon her and thus by the overshadowing of the Most High. This new divine causal act, which cannot be humanly fully grasped, thus carries within it all previous divine acts, and it does so by enacting their ultimate fulfillment within this very new act. Because Jesus will be conceived in the womb of Mary by the overshadowing of the Holy Spirit, by the power of the Most High, he, in a new and unprecedented singular manner, will assume the very holiness of the Lord God and so, in a new and unprecedented singular manner, will be the Son of the Most High. Thus the conceiving of Jesus by the power of the Holy Spirit will be the definitive act of the Lord God within history, for through it the man Jesus will be properly identified as the Son of God. Jesus, as the holy Son of God, will become, as his name implies, the definitive Savior. As the unique Savior-Son of God, the Lord God will give to Jesus, in an unanticipated manner, the throne of his father David, and so, in an unanticipated manner, his kingdom will have no end—it will be an eschatological kingdom. Thus Jesus, in his very person, ontologically binds together the Old and New Testaments and so, in his saving ministry, binds the saving deeds of the Old Testament to himself as the one who fulfills them, thus making himself "the New Testament."

There is also the theological significance of Mary's *fiat*. While Mary's act of faith was her intellectual acknowledgment of the truth that Gabriel spoke, it was also the allowing of herself to be personally drawn into the mystery of her son's conception and so into the mystery of who her son would be. This drawing in is the overshadowing of the Holy Spirit, by which her son would be conceived within her womb. In this overshadowing, Mary is inextricably and essentially joined to the mystery of the Incarnation, for in this very act the Son of God assumes flesh from her flesh and so becomes incarnate within her womb as her son. The Son of God *is* the son of Mary. In the Spirit she comes into living communion with her begotten S/son and so in the Spirit she will be in living communion with him throughout his life. As Mary was in communion with her son in his first saving act, his being conceived in her womb by the overshadowing of the Spirit, so, in the same Spirit, she will be in communion with him in all his future saving acts. This will find its ultimate expression in her presence beneath the cross.[6]

Because the mystery of her son begins with Mary's consenting to be taken into the mystery of who he is through the overshadowing of the Spirit, one can only properly know the mystery of Mary's son by properly knowing Mary, for in her the mystery literally comes to be. Here, then, we perceive the proper significance of Mary's virginity. Although Mary is understood to have virginally conceived Jesus in that his conception was not by way of human causality, the act of a human father, the maintaining of her virginity, is not for the sake her virginity; Mary's virginity was not important in and of itself. Mary's virginity is significant only in relation to her motherhood. The preserving of Mary's virginity within the act of her son's conception clearly manifests that the nature of the act by which Jesus is conceived is none other than an act of the Holy Spirit. Likewise, Mary's virginity is the prerequisite state that allows for and so confirms the identity of the one of whom she is the mother: the Son of God. To highlight that Mary remained a virgin in the act of

---

6. Jesus cannot be properly perceived to be the Son of God apart from Mary, for to have faith in her son as the Son of God, and so to be in communion with him through the indwelling Spirit, is to unite oneself within her faith, which gave consent to his being conceived within her womb by the overshadowing of the Holy Spirit. To acknowledge in faith that Jesus is the Son of God incarnate is but an echo of Mary's faith, by which he became the Son of God incarnate. Only in acknowledging that Mary is the Mother of God can one acknowledge, in communion with her faith, that her son is the Son of the Father.

conception highlights the singular nature of the act of conception, that of the Holy Spirit, and thus the singular nature of her motherhood. The singular nature of her motherhood highlights the singular identity of her son—"thus the child to be born of you will be called holy, the Son of God" (Lk 1:35). Mary's virginity is therefore exclusively the servant of her motherhood, for it testifies that her human child is the Son of God.

Furthermore, in seeing in the Spirit's act of conception the living union between Mary and her son who dwells within her womb, we also perceive her to be the new living temple—the new living presence of God in our midst. While Gabriel announced to Zechariah the birth of his son, the one who would prepare a way for the Lord, within the temple of old and thus within the ancient manner of God's holy presence, he now announces to Mary that she will conceive within her womb the ultimate expression of God's holy presence, the presence of whom John will proclaim. Thus the Holy Spirit, through his act of overshadowing of Mary, builds a living temple—a new Holy of Holies within which the living most holy God now newly dwells among his people, a dwelling that is most unprecedented and unanticipated. Mary, as the new living temple in whom the Son of God dwells bodily, then becomes the living prophetic image of the future church.

We can perceive within the communion of the Holy Spirit's incarnating act and Mary's act of assent the foundational act by which the church is also conceived. The Holy Spirit incarnates the Son of God within the womb of Mary in communion with her act of faith. Their co-inhering communion of acts engenders the conception of Jesus as the Son of God incarnate. It also engenders the communion between Mary and her conceived son. This Spirit-filled communion between Jesus and Mary, this living communion between Jesus' flesh and Mary's flesh, establishes her as the first member of the church and so fashions her as its living icon, for through her act of faith she conjoins herself to the very act of the Holy Spirit, by which her son is conceived within her womb. Thus, in becoming man within Mary's womb through the power of the Holy Spirit, the Son of God is enacting his primordial ecclesial act, for through this act he not only becomes man, but also, through his assumed humanity, he lives in communion with Mary, his mother. In becoming man within the womb of Mary, through the power of the Holy Spirit, the Son of God enacts his first human act, by which he initiates himself as Savior and Lord of his church. From the moment of his conception, Jesus, the Incarnate Son, never exists or lives apart from his church. All of his subsequent saving acts that will give birth to his church—calling his apostles; his public ministry; and especially his passion, death, and resurrection—are predicated upon his taking on flesh within the womb of Mary and so establishing a living salvific communion with another human being.⁷ Mary, through her act of faith, is a living image or personal icon and expression of the communion of salvific life between Jesus and his church. In the very act of becoming man, Jesus is enacting his name as YHWH-Saves, for this is his first saving act through which he comes into ecclesial salvific communion with another human being: Mary.⁸

7. Jesus can only fully become the Savior and Lord of his church through his death and resurrection, for only in those acts does the church come fully into existence, and only in these acts does Jesus fully become Jesus. Ultimately, this will find its completion in his second coming, when Jesus and his church will be united forever in the fullness of his risen glory.

8. Although the church would only gradually come to perceive Mary as the living icon or expression of the church, we clearly see here the foundational revelation for this doctrine. First, as Mary and her son, the incarnate Son of God, form one living communion within the unity of the Holy Spirit, so in the same Holy Spirit the church and Jesus form one living holy communion. To live in full communion with Jesus, one must be in living communion with the church. Within a Pauline context, the church, as reflected in Mary, is the living Body of Christ in communion with the living risen Christ her head through the mutual indwelling of the Holy Spirit.

Second, as Mary's faith pertains to and gives expression of the full mystery of her Son, so the church's faith pertains and gives expression to the full mystery of Jesus in all his saving acts. To profess the fullness of faith in the mystery of Jesus is to profess the fullness of the church's faith.

Third, as Mary is the living holy temple in whom the Lord Jesus dwells, so the church is the holy living temple in whom the Lord Jesus dwells. To dwell fully in the presence of Jesus, one must dwell fully within the church.

Fourth, as Mary is the one who bears Jesus, the Savior, into the world, so the church bears Jesus the Savior into the world through word and sacrament—through being the church in the fullness of its reality. To come to know Jesus through faith and to reap the full benefits of his saving deeds, the full life of the Holy Spirit, one must enter into communion with his church.

Fifth, as Mary is "full of grace" in anticipation of her son's holy presence within her, so the church is full of grace, because within the church Jesus is fully present. Thus through his church, Jesus is making holy, making full of grace, her members.

Sixth, as Mary is in communion with her son from conception to death and so participates in his saving deeds from conception to death, so too does the church share and so participate in his work of redemption.

Seventh, as Mary, as holy mother of her son and who participated in all his saving acts, was assumed into the glory of her risen son, so the church, made holy in Christ and which participates in and makes present his saving deeds, will ultimately be assumed into and share fully in the risen glory of Jesus Christ.

The church, then, is the visible living communion of all the faithful who, like Mary, live in communion with her son, the Lord Jesus Christ. Within the event of Mary conceiving Jesus, the incarnate Son of God, through the overshadowing of the Holy Spirit, we perceive, at least in embryo, the whole doctrinal significance of Mary and so the whole doctrinal significance of the Church.

Catholics believe that as Mary is the full living icon of the church so the Catholic Church

The Gospel of Matthew: The
Conception of Jesus

Matthew begins his Gospel, "The book of the genealogy of Jesus Christ, the son of David, the son of Abraham."[9] Matthew, on behalf of the apostolic church, is making a profession of faith. The genealogy that he is about to enumerate is that of a historical man, Jesus, who is professed to be the Christ, the anointed of God. So much is this the case that the apostolic church has ascribed this title to his very name. The Holy Spirit so interiorly imbued Jesus that he, in a singular manner, defines Jesus' being and persona—who he is. To say the name "Jesus" is to identify him simultaneously as "the Christ," and so to know rightly who this man is is to know him simply as "Jesus Christ." Matthew will shortly establish the grounds for such a twofold designation.

Matthew highlights Jesus' Jewish ancestry, emphasizing that he is the son of Abraham and the son of David. Jesus is, by birth, a member of the Lord's chosen people, sprung from the seed of Abraham the father of faith, and the one in whom all nations will be blessed. He is equally a member of the royal house of David, from whose progeny an everlasting kingdom will come. Jesus is thus placed within the living tradition of the Lord's covenantal relationship with his people, and thus his God, by right of birth, is the one Lord God of Abraham, Isaac, and Jacob. Moreover, the promise the Lord made to David, that from his seed would sprout an everlasting kingdom, now converges upon Jesus. Matthew, within his genealogy, knits Jesus into the whole fabric of the Old Testament revelation. Whatever newness he brings, it cannot be severed from all that God has done in the past through his revealing acts. In Jesus, the Old and New Testaments are integrally and permanently woven together.

Matthew sequentially delineates Jesus' genealogy through the use of the word "begat"—"Abraham was the father of (begat) Isaac, and Isaac was the father (begat) Jacob ... etc."—but, significantly, when the genealogy eventually arrives at Joseph, it reads: "Jacob was the father (begat) Joseph the husband of Mary, of whom Jesus was born, who is called Christ." With Jacob the begetting stops. Joseph is the last to be begotten, and he begets no one. The long ancestry of Abraham and David has ended abruptly. For Matthew, that is the

---

is the full living icon of Mary—the mother of the Church—for all the fullness of truth and life that resides in Mary in relation to her son through the Holy Spirit is found within the Catholic Church through her relationship with Jesus through the Holy Spirit.

9. All quotations in this section are from Mt 1:1-25 unless otherwise noted.

doctrinal or theological point. Joseph's importance, unlike all those who have gone before him, is not found in his begetting, but in his being the husband of Mary. He embodies and so carries into the marriage, and thus to her son, the Abrahamic and Davidic line. Mary's importance lies not in her conceiving a son from Joseph, but precisely that she is the mother of Jesus, who is not of Joseph. Jesus is important because he is the Christ. Evident in this final sequence of Jesus' genealogy is the work of the Holy Spirit. While Joseph is the Abrahamic and Davidic husband of Mary, the child born of her is of the Holy Spirit and thus the cause for why Jesus is the Christ—the anointed one.

The anointed history of the Jewish people comes to its fulfillment in the decisive anointing of the Holy Spirit—the birth not of a son conceived by man, but of a son conceived by the Holy Spirit.[10] The ancient history of the Jewish nation, starting with Abraham and proceeding through the centuries, bearing with it the cumulative revelation of God, has found its culmination in the Christ, who is Jesus, whose mother is Mary, the wife of Joseph. Therefore, for Matthew, this is "the book of the genealogy of Jesus Christ" encompassing three segments of fourteen generations, the third of which concludes simply with "the Christ." Matthew will immediately provide a descriptive historical narrative explaining how it is that Joseph is "the husband of Mary, of whom Jesus is born, who is called the Christ."

Just as he began his Gospel with the genealogy of "Jesus Christ," Matthew begins his birth narrative by stating, "Now the birth of Jesus Christ [or of the Christ] took place in this way." If Jesus was not begotten of Joseph, then how did he come to be? In narrating his birth, Matthew will simultaneously provide the foundational reason why Jesus is "Jesus Christ."

Significantly, Matthew does not say "when Mary had been betrothed to Joseph," but rather "when his mother Mary had been betrothed to Joseph." The focus, as at the climax of the genealogy, is on Jesus, and Mary's importance lies solely in being "his mother," who was "betrothed to Joseph." Now, "before they came together she was found to be with child of the Holy Spirit." But Joseph, having discovered that Mary was pregnant and not knowing the cause, "being a just man and unwilling to put her to shame, resolved to send her away quietly." Joseph was just because he knew he could not rightfully and lawfully wed a woman who was already pregnant, the child of which was

---

10. It should be noted however that while this is a decisive anointing, it cannot be separated from Jesus' baptismal anointing or his being anointed as Lord at his resurrection. The fullness of all these various anointings finds its ultimate fulfillment when Jesus returns in glory and the anointed history of Israel reaches its completion.

not his own. Yet he also refused to shame Mary, precisely because he could not in any way satisfactorily account for her pregnancy, so he decided that the best course of action was to discretely retract their betrothal bond. However this situation came to be, he feared that continuing the relationship would be inappropriate. What was perplexing to Joseph is that he could not establish the cause of Mary's pregnancy. Thus Mary and Joseph both had similar concerns. Mary wanted to know how she could conceive a son when she was not married, and Joseph was concerned, since the betrothed was pregnant and he was not the cause, how Mary became pregnant. Both, being rational human beings, wanted to know "the cause."

As Joseph continued to ponder this inexplicable situation, "behold, an angel of the Lord appeared to him in a dream, saying, 'Joseph, son of David, do not fear to take Mary your wife, for that which is conceived in her is of the Holy Spirit; she shall bear a son, and you shall call his name Jesus for he will save his people from their sins.'" As the angel Gabriel came to Mary, so now an angel appeared to Joseph in a dream and thus the message to Mary, as well as to Joseph, was of divine origin. There is a congruity between these messages. Not only are both messages divine in origin, but also the truth of each confirms the other—that Jesus is conceived by the act of the Holy Spirit. Thus both messages corroborate that the cause, the act of conception, is not human but divine.

Although the cause is divine, the Holy Spirit, the effect of the Spirit's action, as in Luke, terminates in conceiving a child within the womb of Mary and so within the reality of this world. Joseph is told that Mary "will bear a son," and because that son is conceived by the Holy Spirit, "you will call his name Jesus, for he will save his people from their sins." For Matthew, how Mary conceives her son determines the name that he will receive: Jesus, YHWH-Saves.

Similarly, we now perceive why Matthew is narrating "the birth of Jesus Christ." Jesus is the Savior because the Holy Spirit accrues to him in his very conception. The Holy Spirit, in the act of conception, ontologically imprints his identity as YHWH-Saves; it fashions him *to be* YHWH-Saves and so he simply *is* Jesus Christ. Jesus' identity (YHWH-Saves) is predicated upon his being the Christ (the Anointed of God), and so he will enact his saving deeds and name, as he who is completely imbued with the Holy Spirit. Jesus must become Jesus (YHWH-Saves) through his saving actions performed within the anointing of the Holy Spirit and so become fully Jesus Christ.

As Gabriel tells Mary that her son will inherit the throne of his father, David, so the angel refers to Joseph as "son of David." This infers that, because Joseph is about to assume his lawful status as Mary's husband and so be the lawful father of her son, so Mary's son will lawfully be of the lineage of David and so assume and ultimately fulfill the divine promises that accrue to his being a member of the household of David. Jesus the Christ will establish, as Savior, the everlasting kingdom divinely promised to his forefather David.

Matthew concludes by stating that Mary's conception "of the Holy Spirit" fulfills what "the Lord" prophetically spoke through Isaiah: "'Behold, a virgin shall conceive and bear a son, and his name shall be called Emmanuel [which means 'God with us']." Mary is the virgin who has now conceived a human son, who will be called Emmanuel because he was conceived "of the Holy Spirit." Here we find Matthew's proclamation of the Incarnation. Because it is by the Holy Spirit that Jesus is humanly conceived within the womb of Mary, the effect of his conception is that "God is with us" and thus that Jesus is divine, for if not, the prophecy would not have been fulfilled. Also, because it is "the Lord" who spoke the promise, because Jesus, as "God with us," is the fulfillment of the promise, and because it is "of the Holy Spirit" that the promise is fulfilled, we find in the human conception of Jesus the manifestation of the entire Trinity. To perceive correctly who the man Jesus is is to perceive the Father, the Son, and the Holy Spirit. Thus Jesus is the Christ, the one imbued with the Holy Spirit in his very conception, for he is God (YHWH) with us saving his people.

Matthew closes by telling us that when Joseph awoke, he obediently "took his wife, but knew her not until she had borne a son; and he called his name Jesus." That Joseph did not have sexual relations with Mary confirms, for Matthew, that she indeed conceived of the Holy Spirit. It also confirms Joseph to be a just and righteous man. Joseph, from the onset, did not want to intrude himself improperly or irreverently into a situation whose cause was unknown. Having learned that Mary conceived "of the Holy Spirit," he fearlessly took her as his wife and continued in his righteous reference toward her and her child. Joseph's rightful act as father was to name his son and he obediently did so: "and he called his name Jesus."

What we find here in both accounts of Luke and Matthew is the culmination of God's revelation of himself within the Old Testament. Within the Old Testament, God revealed himself to be the One Holy Savior who acts within time and history and so abides with his people making them holy. Jesus, as the Incarnate Son of that one God, will abide with his people as the definitive Holy Savior who will free them from all unrighteousness and make them holy as God is holy.

The Incarnating Act as the
Hermeneutical Key for Understanding
the Infancy Narratives

Before we examine the Visitation, it is imperative to see that the nature of the causal act by which Jesus is conceived is the absolute hermeneutical key for understanding the doctrinal content within both infancy narratives. This causal act determines who Jesus is, and who Jesus is, in turn, is the determinant upon which all of Gabriel's promises are or will come to be fulfilled. The ontological causal act by which Jesus will be conceived within the womb of Mary—that is, the act by which Jesus will ontologically come to be—is the overshadowing of the Holy Spirit, the power of the Most High. This overshadowing act of the Most High governs—that is, determines what is effected—both the manner of Jesus' existence and the identity of the one who is so conceived.

Importantly, although it is humanly impossible to grasp fully the nature of this divine act (the overshadowing of the Holy Spirit [Lk] or being conceived of the Holy Spirit [Mt]) and so the terminus of this divine act (precisely because the act that effects this end is itself incomprehensible), we can properly and rightly know what the mystery is that results from this divine act: the Son of God existing as man. Thus, we know, in faith, what the mystery is, even though we do not fully comprehend the nature of the act by which this mystery was effected, nor then the known mystery itself: the incarnation of the Son of God.[11] This is the revealed mystery of faith. Because it is *within Mary's womb* that Jesus is conceived by the Holy Spirit, he *exists in a human manner* as man. Because it is *by the Holy Spirit, by the power of the Most High,* that Jesus is conceived as man within the womb of Mary, *the identity* of Jesus, who it is who

---

11. Sometimes contemporary theology speaks of "mysteries" as that which cannot be known and thus cannot be conceived properly or articulated clearly. Our human conceptions and articulations are merely approximations of the truth but not the truth itself. This is a false understanding of the nature of the divinely revealed mysteries, such as the Trinity or Incarnation. Although the mysteries of the faith, like the Trinity and the Incarnation, cannot be fully comprehended and thus cannot be articulated in their entirety so as to make them fully understandable to the human mind, the mysteries of the faith can be known in that we know what the mysteries are. We know that the one God is the ontological communion of the Father, the Son, and the Holy Spirit. We know that Jesus is the Son of God existing as man. We know the truth contained within the mysteries of the faith even if we cannot comprehend fully the mystery that we know. The doctrines of the church are doctrines precisely because they conceive properly and express rightly the truth contained within the mysteries.

is conceived as man, *is that of the Son of God, the Son of the Most High.* It cannot be overstated that *only* the Holy Spirit, as the power of the Most High, could enact such an act. No human causal agent could enact an act such that the effect of that act is the Son of God, the Son of the Most High, existing as man.[12] Thus this act of Jesus' coming to be in the womb of Mary not only manifests that her human son is truly the Son of God, but also that the Holy Spirit, who enacts the act, is equally divine.

How Jesus is the Son of God therefore differs in kind and not in degree from how others are sons of God, such as those of the Old Testament, precisely because the act of the Holy Spirit differs in kind. The Holy Spirit did not simply anoint Jesus as an already existing man and so confer upon him the filial title "son of God." Rather, the act of the Holy Spirit is the very act by which the Son of God is conceived as man in the womb of Mary, and so the very identity of Jesus, *who he is,* is that of "the Son of God." Inherent within this act of the Holy Spirit is the notion that the Son of God and the Holy Spirit eternally exist. If the Son did not eternally exist, it would be impossible for the Holy Spirit to enact an act whereby the Son comes to exist as man within the womb of Mary. And if the Holy Spirit did not eternally exist, he could not enact the act whereby the eternal Son came to exist as man. For the Son to come to exist in time as man through the act of the Holy Spirit, both must first eternally exist as God.

Because it is by the Holy Spirit that the Son of God is conceived as man within the womb of Mary, Jesus' possession of the Holy Spirit likewise differs in kind from that of all others who have been, are, or will be anointed by Holy Spirit. Within the very incarnating act of the Holy Spirit, the Spirit comes to inhere within the humanity of the Son in accordance with who he

---

12. God could not even give a human agent the power, and so delegate a human agent, to enact this act for the very nature of the act ontologically demands a divine agent. There are certain acts that metaphysically demand a divine agent, for only a divine agent possesses the necessary power to perform such acts, for example, the act of creation. The act of creation ontologically demands that he who brings something into being exist in and of himself—be "being itself" (*ipsum esse*). Thus it is metaphysically impossible for a being who is not *ipsum esse* to create, and therefore God could not empower or delegate a being to create for no other being other than himself is *ipsum esse*. The act of the Incarnation is likewise such an act.

God can empower human beings to work miracles in his name. But miracles are acts that affect what already exists—the healing of a blind man, the growing of food, or even the raising of someone from the dead—that is, to natural human life. Such miracles are far different acts from those that bring something into being or by which the Son of God comes to exist as man, or an act that raises someone incorruptibly and gloriously from the dead and so humanly exists in a new manner.

ontologically is: the Son of God existing as man. The Spirit resides within the humanity of Jesus, then, not as an anointing bestowed from without, but as an anointing that flows necessarily from within his coming to be and so existing as the incarnate Son. In the Spirit's one act of overshadowing Mary, by which the Son of God is conceived within her womb, the Holy Spirit uniquely anoints the humanity of the Son of God with the Spirit of divine Sonship. Jesus is imbued, in the same act of his conception, with the singular Spirit of Sonship because he is the Son, and thus this anointing of the Spirit of Sonship is peculiar to Jesus. In turn, this singular anointing of the Spirit of Sonship, in the same act of his conception, distinguishes Jesus by identifying him as the Son of God, for only as the divine Son could he be so anointed.

This anointing of the Spirit of Sonship equally defines and so identifies Jesus as the Messiah, the anointed one of God, and it is ultimately the basis upon which Matthew can speak of the genealogy and birth of "Jesus Christ." Again, his anointing as the Messiah is not that of the Spirit coming upon him at some later time within some later event, but from within the incarnating act itself, whereby he, as the Son, is imbued with the Spirit of Sonship, which singularly designates him the unique Messiah.[13] For Jesus to be "the Son" is for him to possess "the Spirit of Sonship" and as such be the Messiah, the singular anointed one of God.[14]

In how Jesus comes to be we also find the nascent revelation, the prophetic anticipation, of the full revelation of the Lord God of Israel as the Father, the Son, and the Holy Spirit. None other than "God" sent Gabriel to Mary to deliver his prophetic word concerning her son and the manner of his conception, and similarly an angel of God informs Joseph. None other than the action of "the Holy Spirit," "the power of the Most High," will bring this about. Mary's child is "of the Holy Spirit." Because of these specific divine causal actions, attributed to God and the Holy Spirit, Mary's son, Jesus, will be called none other than "the Son of God"—"God with us"—and thus the God who initiated this

13. When, in the Gospel of Mark, Peter declares of Jesus, "You are the Christ" (8:30), the anointed one, and Matthew in his Gospel, by way of elaboration, adds: "You are the Christ, the Son of the living God" (16:16). Luke more succinctly has "The Christ of God" (9:20), and all the evangelists have Peter make the same declaration. To be "the Christ" is to be "the Son of living God" or "the Christ of God," for to be the Christ demands that Jesus possess the Spirit as Son, the Spirit of Sonship, and thus be the Son of the living God, the Christ of God.

14. As we will see in chapter 6 the anointing of the Spirit of Sonship will also become manifest in how Jesus becomes humanly self-conscious of his divinity and so come to know himself to be the divine Son in relationship to the Father as well as through his future words and deeds.

event is none other than his Father. The one act of Jesus' conception forms a Trinitarian tableau, the intertwining threefold communion of acts that identify named actors: the Father, the Son, and the Holy Spirit. Here again we see that the causal act by which Jesus is conceived, the act of the Holy Spirit, is of the utmost importance, for that very causal act reveals the Trinity.

Within these historical accounts of Jesus' conception we also find the initial biblical expression of a doctrinal Trinitarian metaphysics. As one would expect, the hermeneutical key to this metaphysics is the nature of the causal act by which Jesus is conceived within the womb of Mary. The singular causal act of the Holy Spirit by which the Son of God comes to exist as man reveals the divine ontological identities of the Holy Spirit and the Son. Likewise, this same divine causal act, the coming to be of Jesus, that ontologically identifies the Son and the Holy Spirit simultaneously ontologically identifies the Father, for the ontological identity of the Son necessitates the ontological identity of the Father and vice versa. And the Father being the Father is, by necessity, the ontological source who initiates, fathers, the Holy Spirit's causal act, by which the Son becomes man, and so the Father is the eternal source from whom the Son and Holy Spirit derive their distinctive ontological divine identities. As the Father fathers his Son as man through the action of the Holy Spirit, so the Father eternally fathers his Son through the Holy Spirit. Only when one perceives this Trinitarian metaphysics does one apprehend, in faith, the fullness of what has been revealed. Within the infancy narratives, to know rightly this historical man Jesus, by way of the causal act through which he came to be, is to know, in keeping with the Old Testament revelation, the one Lord God of Israel—the Father, the Son, and the Holy Spirit.

Having perceived more fully the theological and doctrinal importance of Jesus' conception, we can now more fruitfully examine the Visitation.

The Visitation

Within the Visitation, the two pregnant mothers, Elizabeth and Mary, each having conceived in an extraordinary manner, meet one another. The manner of their conceiving, one in old age and the other by the overshadowing of the Holy Spirit, bears upon the future God-ordained ministry of each of their sons. Elizabeth bears he who will go before the Lord God to prepare his way, and Mary bears the Lord God himself. Thus the encounter between these two women, together with their respective sons, is a prophetic epiphany of who Jesus is as well as an anticipatory prelude to John's future prophetic ministry.

Moreover, Mary, in her *magnificat*, proclaims the great things the Lord God has done for her and in so doing simultaneously prophetically declares the future great saving deeds of her son.

Just prior to her consent to becoming the mother of Jesus, Gabriel informs Mary that her cousin Elizabeth has also conceived a son in her old age, thus demonstrating that nothing is impossible with God. Shortly thereafter, Mary hastened to a city in Judah "and entered the house of Zechariah and greeted Elizabeth."[15]

When Elizabeth heard the greeting of Mary, the babe leaped within her womb; Elizabeth was filled with the Holy Spirit, and she exclaimed with a loud cry, "Blessed are you among women and blessed is the fruit of your womb! And why is this granted me, that the mother of my Lord should come to me? For behold, when the voice of your greeting came to my ears, the babe in my womb leaped for joy. And blessed is she who believed that there would be a fulfillment of what was spoken to her from the Lord."

The effect of Mary's greeting is twofold. First, the babe within Elizabeth's womb leaped, and Elizabeth notes that it was with joy. Second, Elizabeth herself is filled with the Holy Spirit. Elizabeth provides the cause for such joyful leaping and for her own being filled with the Spirit. She cries out that Mary is blessed among women and the reason she is so blessed is that the fruit of her womb is blessed. Elizabeth's greeting echoes Gabriel's greeting: "Hail, full of grace, the Lord is with you!" (Lk 1:28). Elizabeth confirmed what Gabriel anticipated. Mary is full of grace because her womb is "full" of Jesus. The Lord is with Mary because he is the fruit of her womb. Elizabeth joyfully acknowledges that Mary is singularly blessed among women, for she realizes that she has been granted a singular privilege, she knows not why, of having "the mother of my Lord come to me." Thus Mary's greeting to Elizabeth heralded not only her own blessed presence but also that of the son within her womb. To be in the presence Mary, and thus in the presence of her son, filled Elizabeth with the Holy Spirit and so she perceived that Mary is blessed among women because the fruit of her womb is blessed, for that fruit is none other than the Lord himself. Elizabeth recognized that Mary's blessing, and now her own unmerited blessing upon Mary's visit, is that she is "the mother of my Lord."

Elizabeth is the first human being to proclaim the doctrine of the Incarnation and, significantly, she does so by identifying who Mary is: "the mother of my Lord." As Gabriel greeted Mary with the title "full of grace" because

15. All quotations in this section are from Lk 1:39–80 unless otherwise noted.

the Lord was with her, so Elizabeth greets Mary with the title "mother of my Lord" because the Lord dwells within her. To bear the title, to be named and identified, "full of grace" is simultaneously to bear the title, to be named and identified, "*Theotokos*—Mother of God." No other human being was, is, or will be full of grace as Mary is, for no one else is the Mother of God. Thus to name Mary "the mother of my Lord," and so to establish and profess her singular identity, necessitates that the singular fruit within Mary's womb, her human son, is none other than the one Lord—a title, name, and identity that were exclusively employed within the Jewish tradition for YHWH.[16] Importantly, Elizabeth ontologically anchors the doctrine of Incarnation to Mary, for he who is in her womb, his identity, is the Lord, and the manner in which he is in her womb, his manner of existence, is as man.

In designating Mary "the mother of my Lord," Elizabeth was likewise the first to articulate the doctrinal truth of the Incarnation in a way that is striking, concise, and memorable (a doctrinal "sound bite"), that is, to predicate of the Son/God/Lord what pertains to being human. If Mary is the mother of the Lord, then the Lord must be born, but the Lord as God cannot be born; therefore the Lord must have come to exist as man, for only as man can the Lord be born of a woman. The later patristic tradition, which continues to this day, would employ this manner of speaking, as did Elizabeth: to profess the doctrinal truth of the Incarnation in an arresting and succinct manner.[17]

16. Because the divine name revealed to Moses—YHWH—was considered so sacred, the Jewish people employed the term *Adonai* (Lord) to signify it. When the Old Testament was translated into Greek (the Septuagint), the word *Kyrios* (Lord) was used to translate *Adonai*. Thus to call Jesus "Lord" is equivalent to signifying that he is "YHWH."

17. Ignatius of Antioch (died c. 110 AD) would speak, within his seven letters, of "divine blood" (Ephesians 1), and of "the passion of my God" (Romans 5). This manner of speaking would later be termed "the communication of idiom," or the predicating of divine and human attributes to one and the same person, the divine Son of God. This manner of speaking would become the touchstone for doctrinal orthodoxy concerning the Incarnation. Some would later deny that Jesus is truly God precisely because he is born, suffers, and dies (e.g., Arius). Others would say that, because Jesus is truly God, he cannot be truly human because God cannot be born, suffer, and die (e.g., the Docetists). The Nestorian Controversy arose precisely because Nestorius, unlike Elizabeth, believed it was erroneous to call Mary the Mother of God (*Theotokos*). Cyril of Alexandria and the Council of Ephesus (431 AD) dogmatically declared that Mary was the Mother of God, thus assuring the truth, that the son born of her was none other the divine Son of God. While it is commonplace to say that Cyril of Alexandria was the victor at Ephesus, it actually was Elizabeth who won the day.

We also find here that Mary is the doctrinal guardian of the truth of the Incarnation. Because Mary's singular dignity and honor reside solely in relationship to her son Jesus, to denigrate that dignity and honor is not so much to insult her, but to denigrate her son—the Son of

Elizabeth has forever set in place, in her profession that Mary is the mother of the Lord, the threefold nonnegotiable ontological incarnational truths that are necessary for a proper conception and articulation of the Incarnation. To conceive and articulate properly who Jesus ontologically is, one must first uphold that the son of Mary is ontologically *truly the Lord God*; second, one must uphold that her son is ontologically *truly man*; third, one must uphold that her truly human son ontologically *truly is* the true Lord God. For Elizabeth, Mary's son is (1) truly the Lord God who (3) truly exists (2) as truly man. Jesus is one ontological existing being, and the one ontological existing reality that he is is the God/Son/Lord existing as man. Elizabeth's proclamation is utterly remarkable because it expresses clearly and emphatically the entire doctrine, the complete mystery, of the Incarnation.

John's leaping for joy also similarly expresses his cognizance of being in the presence of the Lord. In accord with his mother's own proclamation of Mary being the mother of her Lord, John's leaping is an expressive recognition of the Incarnation. As David joyfully "danced before the Lord with all of his might" in the presence of the ark of the covenant (the physical expression of God's covenantal dwelling place; 2 Sm 6:14), so now John leaps for joy at the arrival of Mary, the new physical ark of the covenant, the new living temple, in whom the Lord dwells. John's leaping for joy is prophetic, anticipating his future ministry of preparing for and announcing the joyful news that the kingdom of God is at hand. For John, the kingdom will be at hand because, as was the case when he was within his mother's womb, the Lord is at hand. John's ministry will culminate in his baptizing Jesus, which will identify Jesus as the Spirit-filled Son of the Father and initiate his own ministry of preaching the joyful news that the kingdom of God is at hand.

What is also of doctrinal significance is that Elizabeth, having professed that Mary is "the mother of *my Lord*," calls her blessed because she believed that what was "spoken to her from *the Lord*" would be fulfilled. The term "Lord" is employed to designate two distinct identifiable subjects. The identity of the one referred to in the first use of the term is different from the identity of the second. Because "Lord" was used exclusively to designate YHWH, both the Lord of whom Mary is the mother and the Lord who spoke to Mary, while possessing distinct identities, must both be God. Not only is Elizabeth the first

---

God incarnate. Mary, by her being the mother of the Lord, is the persistent and constant doctrinal guardian of the Incarnation. To have an erroneous understanding of Mary consequently means an erroneous understanding of her son.

to give expression to the doctrine of the Incarnation, but also she is the first to express the truth that both the Son, the one whose mother is Mary, is God, and that the one who spoke to Mary is God. And she has done so, in keeping with the Old Testament revelation of the one God, without implying that there are two existing gods, both of whom can be called "Lord." Elizabeth has implicitly confirmed that both God the Son, of whom Mary is the mother, and God the Father, who spoke to Mary through the angel Gabriel and so is the initiator of all that has taken place, are, while distinct in identity, the one God, for both are simply, in an unqualified manner, designated "Lord."

In addition, what Elizabeth proclaimed—that Mary is the mother of her Lord and that Mary believed what the Lord had spoken to her—is done so as one "filled with the Holy Spirit." Again we have before us a scene that embodies a Trinitarian tableau. Elizabeth, under the inspiration of the Holy Spirit, professed Mary to be the mother of her Lord, the Son of God, and Mary is such because she believed the word of the Lord, that of God the Father. Thus Elizabeth is the first to profess, by her words and actions, both the doctrine of the Incarnation and the doctrine of the Trinity.[18]

In response to Elizabeth's acclamation of praise of her and of her son, Mary proceeds to proclaim her own act of praise. She does so by echoing the words and sentiments of Hannah, who, like Elizabeth, conceived though she was barren. And Hannah promises to give her son, Samuel, to the Lord. Upon presenting her son to the Lord in the temple, she proclaimed, as Mary will now, the greatness of the Lord (see 1 Sm 2:1-10). Mary's *magnificat* is divided into two parts.

Mary first gives glory to the Lord for what he has done for her. Within her "soul" and "spirit," from within her heart and with all the strength of her very being, Mary "magnifies the Lord," the Lord God of Israel, and "rejoices in God my Savior," the holy and mighty God who saved her from sin and filled her with grace. The reason for such exultant praise is that Mary's Lord and Savior has regarded "his handmaid's" low estate, and in so doing has so raised her up so that "all generations will call me blessed," for "he who is mighty has done great things for me and holy is his name." The mighty work that God has done is to elect her, from among all women, to be the mother of his Son, and in so doing he has manifested the holiness of his name, not only insofar as he is God but also through the son born of Mary: "the child to be born of you will

---

18. Elizabeth could be considered the first Doctor of the Church. Another woman, Mary Magdalene, will first proclaim that Jesus, the Son of God incarnate, is the risen Lord of glory.

be called holy, the Son of God." Because of her motherhood, Mary magnifies the Lord and rejoices in God her Savior, and in so doing expresses her joy that her son is the Son of God, a son who will become her Lord and Savior. Mary acknowledges that what has been done to her is in accord with God's mercy, which he habitually gives "to those who fear him from generation to generation." Thus the first part of Mary's *magnificat* is entirely positive in tone and expression. It is a joyful affirmation of who the Lord God is and a grateful acclamation of his choosing her to be the mother of his Son through the power of the Most High.

If the first part of Mary's *magnificat* expresses what God mercifully does for those who humbly fear him, the second part expresses what he does to those who are arrogant in their might. To these he shows the "strength with his arm," and he scatters "the proud in the imagination of their hearts." He "puts down the mighty from their thrones." While he exalts "those of low degree" and fills "the hungry with good things," "the rich" he sends "empty away." Significantly, Mary is professing not simply what God has done in the past to the proud and the mighty and what he has done to the lowly and hungry, but more so what he is about to accomplish because of what he has done to her and what he is about to do through the son born of her. And what her son, Jesus, is about to do has eschatological significance in that while his mighty deeds will pertain to those who live here on earth within history, they will find their everlasting fulfillment at the end of time. Through her son, God will show the mighty the strength of "his arm" and so will forever scatter "the proud" and topple the mighty "from their thrones." Through her son, the Lord will forever exalt the lowly and fill the hungry. Mary, within her joyful canticle, gives voice to the new and final definitive and universal salvific act that God will accomplish through her son, Jesus (YHWH-Saves), for her son, again through the overshadowing of the Holy Spirit, is the Son of God incarnate and so specifically anointed to be as such the Savior. She is rejoicing that, through her son, those who perpetrate evil, the proud and the mighty, will be irrevocably condemned and forever vanquished, and that those who humbly fear the Lord God will be conclusively vindicated and eternally exalted. Mary's son will perform those saving acts befitting a righteous and holy warrior, for God has remembered "his mercy" and the promises he made to "our fathers" and "to Abraham and to his posterity forever."[19] Jesus will through his saving acts establish the kingdom of

19. Mary is often portrayed as being mild and meek, such that she loses all inner fortitude or outward expression of strength (grit), which otherwise would impel her to righteous anger

God and so prove his Father's supreme, just, and beneficent dominion over all, for his kingdom will be free of every evil and abounding in every good, and so Jesus will fulfill the ancient promises made by his Father.[20]

Having remained with Elizabeth for three months, Luke tells us that Mary returned to her home. This simple statement concludes the narrative of John's and Jesus' conception. Both conceptions are doctrinally woven together, for the conception of John anticipates and finds fulfillment in the conception of Jesus. John's conception is a prophetic foretelling, the initial precursoring, of Jesus' conception—the coming of the Lord. His leaping for joy within his mother's womb manifests his Spirit-inspired recognition that he is already in the presence of he who is to come and "who is mightier than I" (Lk 3:16)—the Son of the Most High God.

Conclusion

The doctrinal truths contained within the infancy narratives are foundational for understanding the whole of the remaining Gospel narratives (even Mark's), which they precede. We saw that the doctrinal truths within the infancy accounts are often prophetic in nature, that is, anticipatory of what Jesus will do and what others will come to believe concerning him. In fulfilling the prophecies contained within the infancy narratives, Jesus will unambiguously manifest and so confirm that what was prophetically ascribed to him, as to who he actually is and so what he is to accomplish, is actually true.

Thus, although the infancy narratives provide a metaphysical account of who the man Jesus is as the Son of God and in so doing reveal the divine identities of the Father and the Holy Spirit, they are prophetic in that the truth of these accounts must be confirmed within Jesus' subsequent salvific acts. The apostolic church believed that they had been confirmed, but the infancy narratives simply provide the prophetic basis for what later would be made ful-

---

at evil and injustice and to an appropriate rejoicing at their downfall. Mary's *magnificat* belies such a false mildness and meekness and rather shows her rejoicing at the downfall of evil and those who perpetrate such evil. Likewise, the traditional portrayal of Mary as crushing the head of the serpent (the devil) is not the mild act of a feeble woman, but the righteous act of a resolute woman (see Gn 3:15).

20. Although Hannah exalts and rejoices in God for the gift of her son, her canticle is more in accord with the second part of Mary's. It focuses on God destroying the perpetrators of evil, the mighty and the proud, and his raising up the poor and humble. In so doing, God manifests and proves that his will, authority, and power will prevail over the power and might of evildoers.

ly manifest, thus confirming what had been established and foretold at Jesus' conception—that he would be called the Son of God. Only within Jesus' saving acts, performed in communion with the same Holy Spirit by whom he was conceived, would he fully reveal that he is the Son of God and thus that God is his Father. The name given to Mary's son, then, is the initial divine indication to this subsequent revelation. In both Luke and Matthew, the angel messengers specify that Mary's son is to be called "Jesus," that is, "YHWH Saves." In light of what was just said immediately above, this prophetic naming must be enacted, for only in the enactment of his name does Jesus reveal that he is the Son of the Father acting in communion with the Holy Spirit.

Although the Son of God in becoming man and so becoming Jesus is his nascent saving act, Jesus must still become Jesus. In his conception, Jesus is, literally, Jesus (YHWH-Saves) in embryo. The son of Mary is prophetically named "Jesus," but at his naming the prophecy that lies within his name is not fulfilled, for Jesus is only potentially the one through whom the Lord God will save his people. The bestowal of the name "Jesus" prophetically decrees what Jesus must do for him to be truly Jesus. If Jesus, as his name testifies, actually is YHWH saving his people, he must live up to his name. The "Jesus" in potency must become the "Jesus" in act, for only through his earthly saving act—in his passion, death, and resurrection—does he truly become Savior and so truly become Jesus. This will culminate in the final saving act of his second coming in glory, for only then will Jesus fully save his people by empowering them to share fully in his resurrected divine life. Jesus achieves the fullness of who he is as Jesus only at the end of time. In the act of his coming in glory, all the faithful will share in the fullness of Jesus' glory, and so in that act Jesus will become fully YHWH-Saves.

Similarly, only in his enacting his name through his death and resurrection will Jesus rightfully and properly inherit "the throne of his father David" by establishing an everlasting kingdom—the kingdom of God. Again, Jesus' sovereignty will culminate only in his coming again in regal glory, for only then will he forever vanquish his enemies and usher his faithful subjects into the everlasting splendor and eternal life of his heavenly kingdom.

It is only in becoming the Savior, through his earthly saving acts and in glorious return from heaven, that Jesus will fully manifest that his salvific acts are done in the full anointing of the Holy Spirit, the Spirit of Sonship, thus revealing that he is truly the anointed divine Son of the Father, the Messiah. This will confirm that he was, from his conception, aptly and properly named: YHWH-Saves.

In the naming of Jesus and in the ensuing enactment of his name there likewise resides a threefold revelation concerning the Father, the Son, and the Holy Spirit. First, Jesus is named as the one through whom the Lord God "YHWH" will save his people, and through his saving acts Jesus will reveal, in accordance with Gabriel's prophecy, that he is truly the divine Son of the Most High and so is the holy Son of God. Thus Jesus, as Son, is "YHWH-Saves." Second, in the acts by which Jesus will fulfill his name as Savior, and so reveal that he is the Son of God, he will simultaneously, in the very enactment of his name, reveal that his Father is also Savior. The Father will save his people, for he will bring salvation through and in communion with Jesus, the Father's Son, and so the Father will equally be "YHWH-Saves." Thus Jesus reveals that the one Lord God (YHWH) is the Father and the Son, for together, in the person of Jesus, each in their own appropriate manner, is YHWH saving humankind—the Father in harmony with his Son. Third, Jesus will enact his saving deeds in and through the singular indwelling of the Spirit of Sonship and so manifest that he is indeed the Christ (the Messiah), the anointed Son of the Father. What makes Jesus' saving acts efficacious is not simply that he performed them as the Father's Son, but also that he performed them in communion with the Holy Spirit, the Spirit of Sonship. By enacting his Spirit-imbued saving deeds, through the Spirit of Sonship, Jesus is revealing not only that he and his Father together are bringing salvation, but also that the Holy Spirit, in communion with them, is also YHWH saving his people. Thus the Holy Spirit is "YHWH-Saves."

In Jesus, the YHWH-Father will save his people through the human salvific acts of his YHWH-Son, holy acts that will be performed in the communal power and love of YHWH-Holy Spirit. In the human salvific acts of Jesus, the Father, the Son, and the Holy Spirit are together enacting, each in accord with who they are, a threefold ontological perichoretic communal single salvific act as YHWH-Saves.[21] In addition, the enactment of Jesus' name as YHWH-Saves will testify to and so confirm that metaphysical understanding of the Trinity as found in the enactment in his conception. As in Jesus' conception, so throughout the whole of his salvific ministry, there will be a continual and ever present threefold communion of inhering acts, and within it the one God is revealed to be the Father, the Son, and the Holy Spirit. This in turn will

21. Maximus the Confessor (d. 662) first used the term *perichoresis*. Literally meaning "to dance around together," it expresses the ontological interweaving of the persons of the Trinity or the ontological interrelationship between the persons of the Trinity. A perichoretic act is performed by the persons of the Trinity, each person playing or performing his specific and distinctive subjective role in unison or communion with the others, by which the act is enacted.

again sanction the truth that to truly know Jesus, YHWH-Saves, is to know the Father, the Son, and the Holy Spirit.

Finally, evident throughout is the singular significance that Jesus is a man. It is by the overshadowing of the Holy Spirit that Jesus was humanly conceived in the womb of Mary so as to be the Son of the Father. The locus and terminus of this threefold divine perichoretic act constitute the coming to be of the man Jesus, for it is this human Jesus who is the divine Son of the Father, and this human Jesus is the divine Son of the Father because he was conceived by the power of the Holy Spirit so as to be the Father's Son existing as man. Thus all subsequent saving acts will be human acts that reveal that Jesus is the Son of God. This revelation will in turn testify that the Son's human saving acts are done in communion with the Father, for he will enact them in communion with the Holy Spirit. Therefore I will continue to emphasize that to know in truth the human Jesus is to know the Father, the Son, and the Holy Spirit.[22]

I noted above that the infancy narratives are the apostolic church's later look back to the beginning; that is, having come to believe in the Gospel, it wished to establish the initial historical events that account for who Jesus is and what he subsequently accomplished. The narration of the manner of Jesus' conception is not simply the telling of a past event for the sake of historical accuracy or the adding of a historical footnote to what is most central to the Gospel. Rather, although the infancy narratives concerning Jesus may postdate the earliest preaching of the Gospel, the early church inserted them into the Gospel narrative as a whole precisely because they viewed them as a prophetic anticipation and thus the historical confirmation of what they had come to believe. The salvific words that Jesus spoke and the salvific deeds that he enacted during his public ministry are the historical fulfillment anticipated in Gabriel's prophecy to Mary, that her son would be called the Son of God, and in the angel's prophetically informing Joseph to name the child "Jesus," for he would fulfill his name in saving God's people. This confirms that the human son conceived in Mary's womb is indeed the Son of God, our Savior, and so attests to the truth of the singular act by which he was conceived: the overshadowing of the Holy Spirit. This initial singular divine causal act is the foundational saving act of the whole subsequent Gospel story—the good news of Jesus the Christ, the Son of the Father.

22. Because of Jesus' saving deeds, to know Jesus in faith is to be in communion with him as Son and so to be in communion with the Father and the Holy Spirit.

2 · THE BIRTH OF JESUS

The Epiphany of the Salvific Act
of the Incarnation

The doctrinal heart of the Incarnation lies in the conception of John the Baptist and obviously in the conception of Jesus, but there are important doctrinal elements within their birth narratives. As John's conception is a theological prelude to the revelational significance of Jesus' conception, in this chapter we find that the narrative of John's birth theologically anticipates the doctrinal significance of Jesus birth.

The Birth of John the Baptist

Upon giving birth to her son, Elizabeth's "neighbors and kinsfolk heard that the Lord had shown great mercy to her, and rejoiced with her."[1] It is the initial fulfillment of Gabriel's promise to Zechariah: "And you will have joy and gladness, and many will rejoice at his birth" (Lk 1:14). Elizabeth's kinsfolk, the first of many, rejoice that the Lord removed Elizabeth's reproach and permitted her to conceive a child even in her old age, and also that her son has now been born.

What her kinsfolk did not fully appreciate was that it was not only Elizabeth's conception that was exceptional but also her son—unbeknownst to them they were rejoicing in the birth of the precursor of the Lord's coming. When they came together on the eighth day for the child to be circumcised, they wanted to call him Zechariah, after his father. Elizabeth resolutely countered their proposal. "Not so; he shall be called John." They rebutted, noting that no kindred were called by that name. Making signs to his father, Zecha-

---

1. All quotations in this section are from Lk 1:57-80 unless otherwise noted.

riah was called upon to adjudicate the matter. He wrote, "His name is John." Elizabeth's "shall" became Zechariah's "is." The matter now settled, the kinsfolk "marvelled," expressing their perception that John was exceptional both for being born of an elderly mother and also in himself. This was confirmed, for immediately Zechariah "opened his mouth and his tongue was loosed, and he spoke, blessing God." This act precipitated fear among the neighbors, and "all of these things were talked about through all of the hill country of Judea; and all who heard them laid them up in their hearts, saying: 'What then will this child be.' For the hand of the Lord was with him." The familial and communal scene surrounding the naming of John bespeaks the presence of the Lord God, his presence eliciting rejoicing, gladness, marvel, fear, and questioning as to what this all means for the future: What will this child be? While pondering these events in their hearts, they knew not the answer, but, judging from the to-do over his naming, they rightly judged that the hand of the Lord was upon him and that divine hand would determine who he would become. Within this context, Zechariah, "filled with the Holy Spirit," proclaimed what this child would come to be.

Like Mary's canticle, Zechariah's is divided into two parts. In the first part, Zechariah in a sense picks up where Mary left off, that is, blessing God for his redeeming presence.

> Blessed be the Lord God of Israel, for he has visited and redeemed his people,
> and has raised up a horn of salvation for us in the house of his servant David,
> as he spoke by the mouth of his holy prophets from of old, that we should be
> saved from our enemies and from the hand of all who hate us.

Although Zechariah first appears to speak as if this divine visitation and redemption have already taken place, he is actually speaking of what is taking place in the present, for he "has raised up a horn of salvation for us in the house of his servant David." This "horn of salvation," this mighty warrior-Savior, is such precisely because he is from the house of David and is the promised kingly warrior whose reign will be everlasting. This fulfills ancient prophecies, and so the Davidic warrior-Savior will bring freedom from those enemies who hate God's people. While the political allusions are evident, the past and present allusions symbolize the profounder and more fundamental need of salvation: freedom from sin and death. (This becomes more evident in what follows.) The horn of salvation will perform those acts of "mercy promised to our fathers," for God will remember "his holy covenant," and having been delivered from "the hand of our enemies, we might serve him without fear, in holiness and righteousness before him all the days of our lives." Those enemies and cause of fear are presently the Romans, but the crucial result of God's merciful acts in keeping his covenantal promise is not one of political freedom, but of being able to serve God freely in holiness and righteousness. True freedom resides in freedom from sin and so to come, freely and fearlessly, before God in holiness and righteousness.

Having blessed God for raising up a horn of salvation from the house of David, who will bring freedom and holiness, Zechariah now directs his prophecy to his son, and he does so by picking up where the angel Gabriel left off when he appeared to in the temple to inform him that his son would "make ready for the Lord a people prepared."

Zechariah says, "And you, child, will be called the prophet of the Most High." John will be a prophet, but not just another prophet as of old; he will be *the prophet of the Most High*. John will embody, in who he is and in what he will proclaim, the whole of the ancient prophetic tradition and so convey it into the present, where it will attain its ultimate fulfillment and completion, "for you will go before the Lord to prepare his ways." All that the Jewish tradition entailed—the revelatory deeds and words of God contained within Scripture and professed and lived from generation to generation—now converges upon John, for he is the one who will prepare the way for the immanent coming of all that has been promised and awaited, the coming of the Lord.

Significantly, as we saw above in Gabriel's address to Zechariah in the temple, John is "the prophet of the Most High" because he is preparing a way for "the Lord," and thus he is preparing a way for God's coming into the midst of his people. Again, for the apostolic church, "the Lord" for whom John, the prophet of the Most High, is preparing a way is Jesus, who was conceived by the power of the Most High, and thus Zechariah's prophetic declaration, similar to his wife's declaration that Mary is the mother "of my Lord," is a profession of faith in the Incarnation. The man Jesus is "the Lord," but he can only be authentically "the Lord" if "the Lord" exists as man. Moreover, Zechariah is distinguishing "the Most High," the one for whom John is the prophetic servant, and "the Lord," the one for whom he is preparing for as the prophet-servant of "the Most High." Just as Elizabeth's double-use of the divine title "Lord" for both God the Father (whose word Mary believed) and God the Son (of whom Mary is the mother) while distinguishing them professes their equality as God, her husband employs two distinct divine titles to distinguish God the Father (the Most High) and God the Son (the Lord), and in so doing professes that they are equally divine. Because Zechariah is making this prophetic declaration after being "filled with the Holy Spirit," we find within the whole of this event, like Elizabeth's, an acknowledgment of both the Incarnation and of the Trinity.

Zechariah, after his prophetic declaration that his son, as the prophet of the Most High, will prepare a way for the Lord, asserts what the Lord will do as Savior of God's people. He will "give knowledge of salvation to his people in the forgiveness of their sins, through the tender mercy of our God." Although Zechariah's words are prophetic, the nascent church knows them to be fulfilled in Jesus. Thus Jesus, as the Lord, will give knowledge of salvation not simply in words, but in the salvific acts through which his people will experience forgiveness. The knowledge of their forgiveness is founded upon Jesus' saving acts and their personal experience of the consequences those saving acts—the experience of divine forgiveness. What Jesus will do and what his people will know find their causal source in "the tender mercy of our God." Thus while Jesus, as the Lord, is the Savior, he is making present through his saving acts the tender mercy of God, and so what the people experience directly in and through Jesus is God's mercy. This prophetic declaration acknowledges, then, the communion of salvific acts shared by Jesus, as Lord, and the merciful God, and so their own inner divine communion with Jesus the Lord and with God his Father.

Zechariah spoke in terms of the peoples' earthly fears and enemies from which they will be saved, serving as symbols of the more fundamental enemies of sin and death of which they are afraid. This is confirmed not only in that the Lord will save his people from their sin by the mercy of God, but also because he will save them from death, allowing them to be at peace with God. The people will know their merciful forgiveness, "when the day shall dawn upon us from on high to give light to those who sit in darkness and in the shadow of death, to guide our feet into the way of peace." Presently, God's people sit in the darkness of sin and the shadow of death, but when the Lord from on high appears, a new day will dawn, and in the light of his saving deeds, he will guide his people in the path of righteous peace—with God and one another—dispelling the fearful darkness of sin and death. This prophecy will be fulfilled in Jesus, for he, as the incarnate Lord, is the dawn from on high, a light that all can see with their eyes, for it shines forth from the body of the Lord, and he, in his very person and saving deeds, is the light that vanquishes the fearful darkness of sin and dispels the terrifying shadow of death, for in communion with him all will be able to walk in righteous and holy peace. Zechariah's prophecy is thus a foretelling of the birth of the church, the *ecclesia,* for it will be composed of those who walk, in faith, in righteous holiness and in peaceful communion with Jesus, their Lord and Savior. Moreover, Zechariah's prophecy is eschatological, for only when Jesus returns in glory will he banish completely the scourge of sin and expel forever the curse of death.

Luke concludes the narrative of John's birth by informing us that he bodily grew and "became strong in spirit." He was also "in the wilderness till the day of his manifestation to Israel." This conclusion is a summary of his preparation—physical and spiritual growth. Physically it was a life hidden in the wilderness, where he grew strong in the Spirit so that, being physically and spiritually prepared, he could be manifested to God's people as the one to prepare the way for the Lord.

The Birth of Jesus in Luke's Infancy Narrative

In his concern for providing the historicity of his narrative, thus depriving it of any mythological interpretation, Luke again places the birth of Jesus within its historical, geographical, and Jewish context. Joseph and Mary were Jews during the reign of Caesar Augustus, who had called a census. Thus Joseph "went up from Galilee, from the city of Nazareth, to Judea, to the city of David, which is called Bethlehem, because he was of the house and lineage of David, to be enrolled with Mary his betrothed, who was with child."[2] Thus the human child to be born would be registered as a subject of the Roman Empire and placed within the setting of world history, the implication being that Jesus' birth is of universal historical significance. Specifically, he would be born within the *city of David* as member of the *house and lineage of David*. This triple emphasis (city, house, lineage), echoing the prophecies of Gabriel and Zechariah, carries with it an expectant fulfillment of God's promise to David: he would raise up a descendent whose reign would be everlasting. The narrative likewise looks not simply to the imminent birth of Jesus of David's royal line, but also to its eschatological fulfillment, when Jesus, the new David, reigns forever in glory.

Luke immediately then tells of the birth. "And while they were there, the time came for her to be delivered. And she gave birth to her first-born son and wrapped him in swaddling cloths, and laid him in a manger, because there was no room for them in the inn." After lengthy narratives about the conceptions of John and Jesus and details of John's birth, all imbued with revelational

2. All quotations in this section are from Lk 2:1-20 unless otherwise noted.

and doctrinal significance, Luke's simple and concise account of Jesus' birth is almost anticlimactic, seemingly devoid of theological importance. But Luke's matter-of-fact narrative is of doctrinal consequence.

Although Jesus' conception was miraculous in that he was conceived in the womb of Mary by power of the Most High and the overshadowing of the Holy Spirit, his birth was not miraculous. The absence of any extraordinary aspect concerning his birth underscores the authenticity of Jesus' humanness. Jesus was born as any other human being, and it is this fact that in turn accentuates the authenticity of the Incarnation, for the one who is born in a truly human manner is none other than the Son of God, the Son of the Most High. Likewise, that the Son of God was born of Mary in a truly human manner accentuates and guarantees that he was truly conceived as man, by the overshadowing of the Holy Spirit, in the womb of Mary. If the Son of God was not born as a man, then it would be difficult, if not impossible, to claim that he had been conceived as man, and so it would be difficult, if not impossible, to conclude that he truly is man.

This demands that Mary gave birth to her son in a natural manner, much as any other human mother would. To deny that Mary gave birth to her son naturally would remove all intelligible meaning to the concept of "giving birth," and so deprive her of her supreme grace and singular honor—the foundation of all her other graces and honors—that of being the Mother of God. To in any way threaten or endanger that Mary is truly the Mother of God is ultimately to threaten and endanger the truth of the Incarnation—that he who was conceived as man within her womb by the overshadowing of the Holy Spirit is the Son of God. The doctrinal significance of Luke's account of Jesus' birth lies in its simplicity and brevity—nothing extraordinary or miraculous happened because that is the point of the Incarnation. What is extraordinary is that the Son of God was born into our world as a Jewish child of the house and lineage of David in the small town of Bethlehem and wrapped, like all newborns, in swaddling cloths, and because there was no room in the inn, his mother Mary laid him in an animal's feeding box. That is what is doctrinally significant.[3]

3. If Jesus' birth was in some manner miraculous and therefore revelatory and of theological significance, Luke presumably would have included it in his narrative.

There arises the question of Mary's virginity. The theological tradition maintains that Mary was a virgin before, during, and after giving birth to Jesus. It also argues that Mary conceived without stain and gave birth without pain. Would not painful natural childbirth jeopardize Mary's virginity? I have treated this issue more extensively in relation to Mary being the

After his simple narrative of Jesus' birth, Luke swiftly moves on to the account of the angels revealing his birth to the shepherds. This could easily be considered Luke's epiphany. As in the Gospel of Matthew, Jesus is revealed to the gentile wise men, so here Luke narrates the revealing of Jesus to the Jewish shepherds.

As the shepherds were keeping the nightly watch of their sheep, "an angel of the Lord appeared to them," bringing with him "the glory of the Lord" that "shone around them." Fearful of being in such a divine presence, the shepherds are told not to be afraid, as in the cases of Zechariah and Mary: "for behold I bring you good news of great joy which will come to all people." The good news that will bring joy not only to them but to all peoples and nations is: "for to you is born this day in the city of David a Savior, who is Christ the Lord." The joy springs from the birth of a human baby in the city of David, and with this birth springs the joy of a hope fulfilled—the kingly heir to the throne of David. But the angel does not proclaim that a baby is born to them but that "a Savior" is born to them. The baby is a Savior because he is "Christ the Lord." The shepherds would not have fully grasped the significance of this angelic event with the angel's proclamation, but the apostolic church would have. The Savior that is joyfully announced, the babe born for the shepherds

---

New Eve. See "The Annunciation and Nativity: Undoing the Sinful Act of Eve," *International Journal of Systematic Theology* 14, no. 2 (2012): 217-32. This essay was reprinted in *Jesus: Essays in Christology* (Ave Maria, Fla.: Sapientia, 2014), 172-89. Here I can only make a few summary points.

First, if Jesus, as the New Adam, assumed a humanity of the sinful race of the first Adam and thereby experienced the effects of that fallen humanity—such as pain, suffering, and death—is it not proper that Mary, herself being of the sinful race of Adam, equally experience pain, suffering, and death? Second, if Jesus, in assuming a humanity from disobedient Adam, overcame such disobedience through his own obedience, even unto death on the cross, and so became the New Adam of a new human race, should not Mary, through her obedience, overcome the sin and curse of Eve—painful childbirth—thus becoming the New Eve? The ultimate issue is this: if Jesus was not immune from the effects of Adam's sin in becoming man, then Mary, from whom he received his humanity, ought not be immune from the effects of Eve's sin.

As to the maintaining of Mary's virginity while naturally giving birth to Jesus, the premiere title for Mary is that she is the Mother of God. She is a virgin mother in that she conceived her son by the Holy Spirit. The tradition argued for a miraculous birth in order to maintain Mary's virginity. I argue that it was not the birth that was miraculous, for such a miracle jeopardizes the Incarnation and so Mary being the Mother of God, but that, if such is necessary, then the preservation of Mary's virginity was miraculous. As I argued in chapter 1, Mary's virginity is the servant of her motherhood. Her virginity denotes that she conceived her son not by way of human causality but by way of the Holy Spirit. Her virginity defines the nature of her motherhood, and not that her motherhood defines the nature of her virginity. She is not a mother virgin. She is a virgin mother.

and all people, is Jesus, YHWH-Saves. Jesus is the saving presence of the Lord God of Israel because he is the one truly anointed one (the Christ/Messiah), from his conception with the Spirit of Sonship as the Son of God, and therefore truly the divine Lord. This babe, who is the Savior, Christ the Lord, will inherent the throne of David, for as the anointed Savior he will establish an everlasting kingdom and so be the Lord of all. This is who the newborn baby is—this is his identity. The angel has proclaimed the truth and reality of the Incarnation. Not surprisingly, the angel has also given partial expression to the Trinity. It is an angel "of the Lord" who came to the shepherds, it is the glory "of the Lord' that shone upon them, and the babe born is Christ "the Lord." As with Elizabeth, the term "Lord" has two referents: "the Lord" to whom belong the angels and the glory, and "the Lord" who is born and by implication references the Father and the Son.

The glory of the Lord is manifested in the heavens precisely because the Lord's Son resides on earth. The glory that resides upon earth, which is be heralded from heavens, is that of a newborn wrapped in swaddling cloths. The glory that heaven proclaims is the humility and poverty of the Incarnation—the Son of God existing as a child lying in a manger. This lowly estate of his Son is the catalyst for the Father's display of joyful glory in the heavens. In the Incarnation, in this babe, the Father is making manifest the glory of his Son.[4]

Thus the shepherds will find the Savior, Christ the Lord, by looking for a babe who "is wrapped in swaddling cloths and lying in a manger." This proclamation occasioned the glory of the Lord in the heavens, and this reality initiates the heavenly finale. "And suddenly there was with the angel a multitude of the heavenly host praising God and saying, 'Glory to God in the highest, and on earth peace among men with whom he is pleased!'" The heavenly angelic choir praises and glorifies God and announces peace upon earthly men and women because God is pleased with them—so pleased that he has given to them a Savior, Christ the Lord, the Davidic king of peace, who presently lies in manger.

4. This glory of the Son's incarnate lowliness finds it fulfillment on the cross, where Jesus, "Christ the Lord," will decisively enact his saving deeds as "Savior."

Within the Gospel of John, this same truth is professed in that the Word became flesh (*sarx*), that is, the weakness of human flesh. "And the Word became flesh and dwelt among us, full of grace and truth; we have beheld the glory, glory as of the only Son from the Father" (Jn 1:14). This finds its culmination on the cross, the hour of Jesus' glory, for in the humiliation of the cross the Father displays for all the world to see the true glory of his eternal Son (see Jn 13:31-32, 17:1).

After the angels returned to heaven, the shepherds act upon what was re-vealed to them: "Let us go over to Bethlehem and see this thing that has hap-pened, which the Lord has shown to us." Having arrived, they "found Mary and Joseph, and the babe lying in a manger." What they found was exactly what the angel told them: a mother and a father with a baby lying in a manger. Luke again narrates a simple family setting. Other than the mean circumstanc-es, nothing appears unusual or surprising. But after the shepherds "saw it they made known the saying which had been told to them concerning the child; and all who heard it wondered at what the shepherds told them." Luke's narra-tive here contains a reversal.

The "shepherd event" first begins with the appearance of an angel of the Lord accompanied by the glory of the Lord. Within the context of this divine glory and presence, the shepherds are then told of a newborn babe lying in a manger in Bethlehem. Here "heavenly glory" precedes "earthly reality." With the arrival of the shepherds, "earthly reality" precedes "heavenly glory." What the shepherds see is a baby with his father and mother. What they proclaim is what has been made known to them: "the saying which had been told them concerning the child." So, the shepherds declared to those in and around the city of David the following: We saw a babe that an angel of the Lord, who ap-peared in glory accompanied by a heavenly host glorifying God, told us was "a Savior, Christ the Lord." What the angels proclaimed from the heights of heav-en the shepherds now proclaim upon the lowliness of earth, and their message is the same. Although the shepherds would not have fully grasped the entire revelational content of their own proclamation (the apostolic church would have), it did cause them and those to whom they told it to "wonder." This won-der, reminiscent of John's kinsfolk, is not simply speculating as to the meaning of all that has been told, but more marveling at the sight (a babe in swaddling cloths lying in a manger) and the meaning that has been divinely revealed (a Savior, Christ the Lord). While Mary "kept all of these things [Jesus' con-ception and birth and now the angel's message to the shepherds], pondering theme in her heart," the shepherds "returned glorifying and praising God for all that they had heard and seen, as it had been told to them." As the heaven-ly messengers, the angels, returned praising and glorifying God, so now the earthly messengers, the shepherds, returned to their flock in the same man-ner, for both—heaven and earth—knew that a Savior is born in the city of Da-vid, Christ Lord. In communion with the heavenly host of angels, the earth-ly shepherds, though unbeknownst to them, are, in their wondering at what they had heard and seen, rejoicing in the Incarnation. This is why both heaven and earth are rejoicing—he who is of heaven, the Son of the Most High God, has come down to earth and now exists as man. This communion of heaven and earth, with its communion of rejoicing, finds its singular cause in a newborn—Jesus—who has, in his very person, conjoined all that is heavenly divine and all that is earthly human. Thus the heavenly hosts and the earthly shepherds are rejoicing in David's human kingly heir, Jesus (YHWH-Saves), the anointed Son of God, Christ the Lord.

The Circumcision

Before examining Matthew's account of Jesus' birth and the adoration of the magi, we must first consider Luke's account of Jesus' circumcision and his presentation/consecration in the temple as well as Mary's purification. The accounts of these events further contribute to our understanding of Jesus being the Son of God, his relationship to the Father and the Holy Spirit, and his vocation as the Savior.

To start, the prescribed Jewish liturgical acts of Jesus' circumcision and presentation commemorate past divine saving events. What we find is that Jesus, in fulfilling these liturgical acts, prophetically anticipates his fulfilling the saving acts that they commemorate. Jesus' participation within these acts contributes, then, to the ongoing revelation of who he is and what he is to achieve. Thus, in the prophetic anticipation of fulfilling saving acts, Jesus imparts to these liturgical acts and the saving acts that they commemorate their yet-to-be-revealed ancient meaning, their mature revelational significance, what they were really all about from their onset. Also, Jesus' earthly anticipated fulfillment of the events already directs our attention to their ultimate eschatological fulfillment at his coming in glory.

Luke is concise about the circumcision, noting that it occurred eight days after Jesus' birth and he was named "Jesus," "the name given by the angel before he was conceived in the womb" (Lk 2:21). Circumcision is the outward sign of the covenant that God made with Abraham, the father of the Jewish people. In making this covenant, God promised that he would make him "the father of a multitude of nations," from which "kings will come." "I will establish my covenant between me and you and your descendants after you throughout their generations for an everlasting covenant, to be God to you and to your descendants after you." As a sign of this everlasting covenant with God, Abraham and all his male descendants were to be circumcised when they are "eight days old." If a male is not circumcised, he "shall be cut off from his people; he has broken my covenant" (Gn 17:1-14). This law was subsequently inscribed in the Mosaic Law (Lv 12:3), and only those who were circumcised (including non-Jews) were permitted to participate in the Passover (Ex 12:43-49), the annual enacted remembrance of God's paramount saving deed: protecting them from the angel of death and freeing them from the slavery of Egypt. Circumcision, then, was the act that formally initiated or enrolled the Jewish male into God's covenanted chosen people, and thus placed upon him the responsibilities of the Jewish law as well as the right to participate actively in its liturgical prayer and customs. To be circumcised was therefore a sign of one's being marked as a member of God's holy people, as opposed to those who were uncircumcised and thus lived sinful and idolatrous lives. This outward sign bespoke of an interior circumcised heart, that one is to be cut free of stubbornness and disobedience and so live in humble submission to God (see Lv 26:41; Dt 10:16; Jer 4:4).

In fulfilling the Mosaic Law, Jesus' parents, by having him circumcised on the eighth day, authenticated his being a son of Abraham and so placed him within the living covenantal tradition of the Jewish people. He bore the responsibility of keeping the Law of Moses and possessed the right to share in all covenantal liturgical prayer. For the apostolic church, this physical circumcision prophetically gave expression to Jesus' being the true son of Abraham, interiorly circumcised of heart, who would be, unlike his often unfaithful ancestors, truly separated from evil. Likewise, the early church would have recognized that Jesus, as the Son of God, did obediently fulfill the law and the prophets; that is, he humbly did the will of his Father. Jesus' participation in the Jewish liturgical heritage, the first shedding of his blood, anticipated his definitive enactment of that heritage through his own prayerful sacrificial acts with their saving effects—the paschal liturgy of his own death, the full shedding of his blood, and in his resurrection. This future paschal liturgy of the cross and resurrection would be the true cutting free from sin, providing entrance into a new covenant with his Father so as to live truly holy lives in the Spirit.

This act of circumcision is also conjoined to the act of naming, the name "given by the angel before he was conceived in the womb": Jesus. These conjoining acts of circumcision and naming designate Jesus, YHWH-Saves, as the obedient son of Abraham, through whom God will save the children of Abraham and in whom, as a son of Abraham, all nations will be blessed (Gn 12:2; 22:15-18). He will be the true king sprung from the loins of his father Abraham, for he will establish God's kingdom, where all peoples will be blessed.

In Matthew, the angel tells Joseph that he is to name the son conceived in Mary's womb "Jesus" and in Luke Gabriel tells Zechariah to name his son

"John" and tells Mary to call her son "Jesus," but here Luke emphasizes that the name "Jesus" was given by Gabriel before his conception, thus accentuating that this present naming finds its eternal source in God himself. God as his Father, and not an earthly parent, properly and rightly is the one who names his incarnate Son, and he does so by designating him not as a savior but as the Savior, Jesus—as YHWH-Saves. In Jesus, YHWH the Father is saving his people through YHWH his Son. Again, the naming of Jesus entails the ontological communion of the Father and Son enacting conjointly in the work of salvation. Thus the circumcision and naming of Jesus were the prophetic enactments of God fulfilling his promise to Abraham, now known in faith to have been fulfilled: "So shall my covenant be in your flesh an everlasting covenant" (Gn 17:13). Jesus, having formally assumed the responsibilities and the rights of his people in being circumcised, will establish a new covenant by fulfilling his name, which he will do by offering his own flesh as the new Passover lamb of sacrifice, which will establish the new living and lasting covenantal communion with God his Father.

The Presentation of Jesus and the Purification of Mary

Luke immediately proceeds to the presentation of Jesus and the purification of Mary, an event that took place forty days after his birth. "And when the time came for their purification according to the law of Moses, they brought him up to Jerusalem to present him to the Lord (as it is written in the law of the Lord, 'Every male that opens the womb shall be called holy to the Lord') and to offer a sacrifice according to what is said in the law of the Lord, 'a pair of turtledoves, or two young pigeons.'"[5]

Luke has braided together two Mosaic ordinances that pertain to both Mary and Jesus. The first concerns Jesus being dedicated or consecrated to God as the first-born son. The Lord commanded Moses: "Consecrate to me all the first-born; whatever is the first to open the womb among the people of Israel, both of man and of beast is mine" (Ex 13:2; see also 13:12–13). While the Lord slew the first born of the Egyptians, both of man and beast, he spared the first born of the Israelites. In response to this saving act, each first-born male animal was to be consecrated and so given to the Lord by way of sacrifice, while each male child was to be redeemed by way of an animal sacrifice and

---

5. All quotations in this section are from Lk 2:22–40 unless otherwise noted.

so consecrated to God, as one belonging to him. When a future son asks what is the meaning of this, he learns that because of God's powerful act of salvation, "I sacrifice to the Lord all the males that first open the womb; but all the first-born of my sons I redeem" (Ex 12:13-16).

His parents, in accordance with God's command to Moses, presented Jesus in the temple and so, as Mary's first-born son who opened her womb, he was consecrated to God, thus becoming holy unto the Lord. Mary and Joseph would not have grasped the full significance of this act, but the apostolic church, which included Mary, would have perceived in this historical event a prophetic act, for this customary liturgical act was now seen as not just the dedicating of an ordinary Jewish first-born male to God, but the consecrating to God the one who did truly belong to him. Joseph and Mary consecrated their son to God and so dedicated him to God not only as their son but also as the incarnated Son of the Father. The Son of God existing as a human child was being consecrated to God, given over to his Father. Thus the Father could rightfully claim in a unique manner: "[He is] mine" (Ex 13:2). And as God's consecrated Son, Jesus would enact, in accordance with his Father's will, the Lord's new mighty deed of which the Exodus was the prefigured anticipation, and this liturgical act was a commemoration. The apostolic church would have perceived that this newly born and recently named Jesus, YHWH-Saves, would and did bring freedom from sin by inaugurating the authentic kingdom of God, the true land of promise, and he would have done so, as the holy consecrated Son incarnate, by being the new lamb of sacrifice, which would redeem all the children of Israel. Being marked with the blood of Jesus, the human blood of the Son of God, would forever ward off death and establish an everlasting communion of life with God. Jesus, in a true revelational sense, is the last first-born son to be consecrated to God and the last first-born son to be redeemed, for through his dedication to God, he, as the all-holy Son of God, in accord with the faith of the apostolic church, performed the act of redemption by which all would be redeemed in him, and in him all would be dedicated to God, and in him all would be made holy. In Jesus, God can now truly say: "all are mine." Luke is narrating a past event, yet the apostolic community would have perceived it as a prophetic event that has now been fulfilled, for Jesus has fulfilled, through his sacrificial death and resurrection, what this commemorative event itself prefigured and anticipated: God redeeming his people. Only in Jesus' fulfillment of this ancient liturgical commemorative act does it and the saving act it represents achieve their true revelational significance, which had laid hidden.

Mary, having given birth to Jesus, was considered, according to Jewish law, unclear for forty days (Lv 12:1-8), during which time the mother is not permitted to touch any "hallowed thing," nor is she permitted "into the sanctuary." After her time of purification, the mother was to stand at the door of the tent/sanctuary and give to the priest a year-old lamb as a "burnt offering" to God and a young pigeon or turtledove as a "sin offering." If she was poor, however, she could offer either two pigeons or two turtledoves, one as a burnt offering and one as a sin offering. The priest makes these offerings on her behalf, "and she shall be clean" (Lv 12:1-8).

In performing this prescribed liturgical action, Mary was not simply fulfilling the law, but also publicly acknowledging that she was the mother of her son, Jesus. This in turn testifies that her son is of Jewish origin and ancestry and, significantly theologically, that he is truly human and so born in a truly human manner. If such were not the case, Mary's act of giving birth would not have rendered her unclean and in need of purification. Thus, as Jesus must be consecrated to God and so made holy because he is the first-born son who opened the womb of his mother, so Mary confirms, by participating in the liturgical rite of purification, that such is indeed the case—that Jesus is her first-born son who did open her womb. Both Jesus' circumcision and Mary's act of purification liturgically verify that Jesus is a Jewish male, thus leaving no doubt as to his humanity.[6]

Although Mary, standing before the priest at the door of the temple, offered in her poverty not a lamb but either two pigeons or turtledoves, her son will become, in the humble richness of his incarnate poverty, the true lamb of sacrifice, offering himself as the priestly sacrifice and so gain entrance to the living heavenly temple, having purified all of their sin and making them holy. Mary stands literally as the representative—the icon—of the church. As she was purified through the offering of her lowly gift and so permitted to pass through the door of the temple and enter into its inner holy sanctum, so through Jesus' humble self-offering before his heavenly Father purified the church so as to allow the faithful to enter into inner holy sanctum of heavenly temple—into the presence of his all-holy heavenly Father. All the above is confirmed in the prophetic words of Simeon.

Luke next narrates that, in the course of Jesus being consecrated to God and

6. Again, these liturgical acts testify that Mary gave birth to Jesus, her first-born son, naturally. If, in being born, Jesus did not open her womb, then his presentation and dedication to God in the temple would be a mere pretense. If Mary did not give birth to Jesus in a natural manner, then her purification would have equally been a pretense. Yet Luke presents these events as truly and rightfully taking place in accordance with and in fulfillment of the Jewish Law.

Mary being purified, there was a man in Jerusalem, the place where God dwelt within the temple, whose name was Simeon. Being "righteous" and "devout," he was awaiting "the consolation of Israel." The Holy Spirit, being "upon him," revealed to him that "he should not see death before he had seen the Lord's Christ." Possessing the Spirit of righteous devotion toward God, Simeon yearned that all that God had promised to his people, by way of the covenants, law, and prophets, would be fulfilled. He embodied the prophetic expectancy of all past generations. Thus he was awaiting the Lord's anointed, the Messiah. Inspired by the Holy Spirit, he entered the temple, the dwelling place of God and thus the tangible symbol of Israel's sacred history, which intently anticipated the future. Here he found Mary and Joseph bringing their child Jesus into the temple, "to do for him according to the custom of the law." Simultaneous to or immediately after Jesus had been consecrated and dedicated to the Lord, Simeon beheld him, took him in his arms, and blessed God. He blessed God, for the promise made to him by the Holy Spirit was, in this seeing of Jesus, fulfilled. Having seen the Lord's Christ, he could now proclaim, "Lord, now let me your servant depart in peace, according to your word; for mine eyes have seen your salvation which you have prepared in the presence of all peoples, a light for the revelation to the Gentiles, and for the glory of your people Israel." Simeon did not grasp the full meaning and significance of his own prophetic message, and although his canticle caused Jesus's parents to marvel "at what was said of him," the apostolic church again recognized that Simeon's prophecy had been fulfilled.

In seeing the child, Simeon saw "the Lord's Christ," for he saw who was singularly anointed with the Spirit of Sonship from his conception and so is uniquely the divine Son of God. Simeon, in seeing the child before him, cast his eye to the future, which the apostolic church believed had now arrived, for in beholding the child named Jesus, his eyes saw the Lord's salvation, which God had prepared in the presence of all peoples so that all peoples would see. As Savior, Jesus is and will be "a light for revelation to the Gentiles," and as such he is and will be "for the glory to your people Israel." Within the temple, Jesus, as a circumcised son of Abraham, as the holy one dedicated to God, is the glory of Israel because, as God had promised Abraham, he is the salvation not only of the chosen people of Israel but also of all peoples. Having seen the face of Jesus, Simeon could now look into the face of death and so request that the Lord let him, the Lord's servant, depart in peace, for he instinctively grasped in the Spirit dwelling within him that death no longer need be feared. The apostolic church would hear in Simeon's prophetic declaration their own voice, for it knew, in a manner that Simeon did not, that in the Lord's Messiah death had been vanquished, and the risen life of the Holy Spirit, the Spirit whom Simeon himself knew, now shone in glory upon Jew and Gentile alike.

Simeon next blessed Jesus' parents and "said to Mary, his mother, 'Behold, this child is to set for the fall and rising of many in Israel, and for a sign that is spoken against [and a sword will pierce through your own soul also], that the thoughts out of many hearts may be revealed.'" This blessing is an acknowledgment of Mary and Joseph's unique parental vocation and thus the need of God's singular blessing in fulfilling that role. It is also a preparatory blessing, for their son, "this child," "is set for the fall and rising of many in Israel and a sign that will be spoken against." Although Simeon rejoiced at seeing the Lord's anointed and thus the Savior, he grasped in the Spirit that Jesus would be accepted by some as the Lord's Christ and so be the cause of their rising to newness of life, as well as being rejected by others and so be the cause of their falling into disbelief. On this division between those who arise in faith and those who fall in disbelief, Jesus "is set"; that is, Jesus, as the Lord's Christ, has been preordained and firmly established by God to be the cause of election through faith or the cause of condemnation through disbelief.

Simeon placed within this prophetic declaration an aside to Mary—"and a sword will pierce through your own soul also"—and thus the reason for Simeon's blessing: to prepare and strengthen her in the face of such an event. The word "also" is important. It denotes that a sword will primarily pierce the soul of Jesus and then also redound to a piercing of Mary's soul. The apostolic community knew well that Simeon's prophetic testimony had been fulfilled in their midst. It perceived that the disbelief of some within Israel, their rejection of him as the Lord's Christ, was the sword that brought Jesus immense suffering. This rejection not only precipitated the suffering of his unjust condemnation and death on the cross, the piercing of his physical heart, but also the suffering of extreme sadness, the piercing of his soul, knowing that their unbelief is the very act of their downfall. The early church would have also recognized that Mary's soul was pierced in communion with her son. She witnessed the growing animosity against her son and stood beneath his cross and so suffered, physically and emotionally, in communion with him. The rejection of her son as the Lord's Christ, the disbelief of her fellow Jews, would have been, as for Jesus, her deepest sorrow. The early church would have also identified with Mary, for they too now experienced persecution at the hands of those Jews who rejected Jesus as the Lord's Christ, and they too mourned over their lack of faith.[7]

7. Mary is also the representative icon of the church. The church still suffers over the disbelief of others as well as suffering the persecution that those who do not believe enact upon her.

The purpose of this acceptance in faith or rejection in disbelief is "that the thoughts out of many hearts may be revealed." Throughout all ages, what is hidden in the heart, what is secreted in the mind, is revealed and manifested in either faith or disbelief. Faith in Jesus as the Lord's Christ manifests a mind and heart that are humble before truth, eager for righteousness, and thirsting for holiness—a person of loving docility toward God. Disbelief in Jesus as the Lord's Christ manifests a mind and heart that are haughty before truth, callous toward righteousness, and spurning of holiness—a person of arrogant docility to his own will.

Luke concludes his account of Jesus' dedication and Mary's purification by noting that "there was a prophetess, Anna, the daughter of Phanuael, of the tribe of Asher; she was of great age, having lived with her husband seven years from your virginity, and as a widow till she was eighty-four."[8] Anna "did not depart from the temple, worshiping with fasting and prayer night and day." Like Simeon, Anna is described as a devout Jewish woman. That she did not depart from the temple indicates that she wished to live in God's presence, continually worshiping him day and night through prayer and ascetical practices. Her manner of life marks her as a prophetess, a holy woman who intimately knows the Lord and thus the custom of his ways. Again, like Simeon, Anna comes upon the scene of Joseph, Mary, and Jesus ("at that very hour") and "gave thanks to God." Luke does not say why she gave thanks, but the intimation is that it is for the same reason that Simeon, her cohort in the Spirit, gave thanks—she too in her old age, in seeing Jesus, is seeing the Lord's Christ. Because of this she "spoke of him to all who were looking for the redemption of Jerusalem." Fulfilling her prophetic vocation, she heralds her last word from the Lord by telling others about "him"—Jesus. Luke specifies that "all" to whom she spoke where those who eagerly awaited the redemption of Jerusalem, implying that there were many such people near the temple as well as others who were less concerned.

Elderly Simeon and Anna represent ancient Israel, but more specifically that ancient Israel that, in humble holiness, is prayerfully longing for the Lord's anointed. Their agedness, as Israel's, contrasts sharply to him whom they bear witness: a child. This child, Jesus the Lord's Christ, will be the new birth of Israel, for a new people of God through a new covenant will come to life in and through him.

---

8. Luke's detail concerning Anna lends credence to the historicity of the account. Because Luke notes that she was a widow until the age of eighty-four, one can presume that she had died and that Luke obtained his information from someone who knew her well.

Luke begins his narrative of Jesus' dedication and Mary's purification by noting that Jesus' parents "brought him up to Jerusalem." All the subsequent events are enacted within the temple and its precincts. Luke concludes these events by noting that Anna, within the temple, prophesied to all who were longing for "the redemption of Jerusalem." The whole of this prophetic narrative binds Jesus to Jerusalem and to the temple therein, and thus to the holy city of God and his holy dwelling. Jesus, now a babe, will fulfill the prophetic acts that took place in Jerusalem and within the temple in the concluding acts of his life. In this earthly holy city, through his sacrificial death and glorious resurrection—acts that he, as the infant incarnate Son, was dedicated to perform as the Lord's Christ—Jesus will redeem Jerusalem. He will do so not by renovating an old earthly city, but by establishing a heavenly Jerusalem of which the old earthly city is but an anticipatory sign. In his very person, he will become the living heavenly temple in whom and through whom all can enter into the presence of his Father, to worship and adore in communion with the Holy Spirit. While these prophetic acts anticipate Jesus's earthly salvific acts, they equally await their final fulfillment when Jesus comes in glory, bringing with him the heavenly Jerusalem in which he is the living everlasting temple.

Luke draws these events to a close by stating simply, "And when they had performed everything according to the law of the Lord, they returned into Galilee, to their own city, Nazareth. And the child grew and became strong, filled with wisdom; and the favour of God was upon him." Despite all that they had encountered, simply performing what was required of them in accordance with Jewish custom and law, Joseph and Mary did what was natural and normal. They returned with their child to their own region and city. Yet Luke hints that although the following years appeared to be uneventful, for Jesus physically grew as children do, he was "filled with wisdom" for "the favour of God was upon him." The apostolic community knew that this wisdom was unique, and this divine favor was singular because it marked, in a veiled manner, the youthful Jesus as the Son of God, the Lord's Christ.

The Birth of Jesus in Matthew's Infancy Narrative

Like Luke's account of Jesus' birth, Matthew's account is also sparse, giving no information other than the historical time and geographic place. "Now when Jesus was born in Bethlehem of Judea in the days of Herod the king."[9]

9. All quotations in this section are from Mt 2:1-23 unless otherwise noted.

Nonetheless, it situates the event within time and history and thus outside the realm of mythology.

Matthew is more interested in making known those who first recognized the significance of Jesus' birth. This is of soteriological significance that directly bears upon Jesus' divine identity as the Messiah-King. "Behold, wise men form the East came to Jerusalem, saying, 'Where is he who has been born king of the Jews? For we have seen his star in the East, and have come to worship him.'"[10] Matthew here emphatically alerts us to pay close attention to what we are about to read, for the narrative that is to unfold is of the utmost theological significance—the revealing of something new and unexpected. The principal actors are not Jews but wise men from the East. All that takes place revolves around them and in reaction to their presence. And all that they do is focused on Jesus—the prophetic revealing of who he is.

Fascinatingly, Matthew traced Jesus' linage back to Abraham, the father of the Jewish people, and so he is unlike Luke, who traced it back to "the Gentile" Adam. Yet Matthew, unlike Luke's Jewish shepherds, has the non-Jewish wise men from the East as the first seekers of Jesus. Even though the wise men are not of Abraham's seed, they are already experiencing the promised blessings that flow from him to all nations. And unlike the poor and uneducated Jewish shepherds, these Gentiles are rich and educated. Both Matthew and Luke, each in their own unique manner, perceive that Jesus is of ultimate significance to both Jew and Gentile, whether poor and uneducated or rich and learned.

Curiously, "Luke's" shepherds, being members of God's covenanted people, are told of Jesus' birth in a manner that is in keeping with that covenant. Their Lord God personally sends to them an angel with a heavenly host who tells them, in great detail, that "to you is born this day in the city of David a Savior, who is Christ the Lord," and cues them to look for a babe in swaddling cloths lying in a manger. Although the pagan Gentle seer, Belaam, prophesied that "a star shall come forth out of Jacob and a sceptre shall rise out of Israel" (Nm 24:17), "Matthew's" wise men are bereft of all such divinely revealed information, for they are not privy to what is revealed solely to God's chosen ones. They must fend for themselves. Within the ancient world, the appearance of a new star harbingered the birth of a new king, and so the wise men had to ascertain this by their own observance of the heavens. No angels ap-

---

10. I am not going to address the historical, geographical, and astrological issues related to this narrative, for that would take us far from our primary theological concerns. I accept that there is a historical basis for Matthew's account, for which he provides the revelational and theological significance.

peared in the wise men's night sky. Their own eyes had to observe the new star, and their own learned ability had to interpret properly this "natural" phenomenon. Their natural ability, their eyes, and their intellect could lead them close to the king of the Jews, to Jerusalem (five miles north of Bethlehem), but they had to ask the Jews about the exact location. For Matthew, human beings may be able to obtain some knowledge of God and so draw near to his presence, yet the fullness of such knowledge and his abiding presence can only be obtained through divine revelation, which, at present, only the Jews, as God's covenanted people, exclusively possessed.

The irony is that the Gentile wise men, merely by observing nature, were aware that the king of the Jews had been born, the star of the foretold scepter having arisen in Israel. The Jews, heirs of God's prophetic revelation, were completely oblivious to the event. Also, the resolute search of the wise men contrasts starkly to the anxious flustered response of the Jews. "When Herod the king heard this, he was troubled, and all of Jerusalem with him." Likewise, while the wise men came to worship the newborn Jewish king, the apprehensive agitation of the Jews would coalesce into fear, to the point that Herod would seek to kill the child. In this agitated state, Herod assembled the chief priests and scribes to ask "them where the Christ was to be born."

The wise men asked where "the king of the Jews" was born, but the Jews intuitively perceived that such an enquiry was not simply to locate some "ordinary" king but to find "the king" of the Jews and thus the one truly anointed: "the Christ." The king to be found is no mere earthly ruler, but the promised Messiah, and precisely because he is such that anointed kingship is divine in scope and power.

The wise men learned that the king would be born in Bethlehem, their knowledge exceeding that which is knowable by human reason. This prophetic knowledge must come from the Jews, for only they, as God's chosen people, possess such revealed knowledge. This alludes to the whole prophetic tradition foretelling that all nations will entreat the Jews to show them their God. "Many peoples and strong nations shall come to seek the Lord of hosts in Jerusalem, and to entreat the favour of the Lord" (Zec 8:20-23).

The wise men are told: "In Bethlehem of Judea; for it is written by the prophet: 'And you, O Bethlehem, in the land of Judah, are by no means least among the rulers of Judah; for from you shall come a ruler who will govern/ shepherd my people Israel.'" Though somewhat abbreviated, the first part of this passage is from Micah 5:2, and the last clause is from 2 Samuel 5:2. The Hebrew of Micah reads: "But you, O Bethlehem Ephrathah, who are little to

be among the clans of Judah, from you shall come forth for me one who is to
be ruler in Israel, whose origin is from of old, from ancient of days." "Bethlehem," as in Luke, calls to mind the birthplace of King David, the great king of
Judah and to whom God promised an everlasting kingdom. While the quote
in Matthew emphases that Bethlehem is "by no means least among the rulers
of Judah," the original Hebrew and Septuagint translations stress precisely the
opposite. Bethlehem is so small among the clans (literally thousands) of Judah that it is not worthy to be among them; it really should not be numbered
among the clans of Judah. Yet despite its meagre standing, from it God will
bring forth a ruler from the house of David. For Matthew, precisely because
Bethlehem has brought forth such a Davidic ruler, it is not "the least," though
it once may have been considered such. This ruler from Bethlehem will, according to Micah, "come forth for me one who is to be ruler in Israel." The
Christ-King will "come forth" from the Lord God ("me") and so rule on his behalf. Within the context of Matthew's narrative, this "coming forth" acquires
a unique and singular meaning, for the one who has come forth is none other
than the begotten Son of God who was "conceived ... of the Holy Spirit," and
as man, in the Spirit of Sonship, will govern Israel on behalf of his Father.

For Micah, this ruler's origin is "from of old, from ancient days." His ancestors do not simply go back many generations, even to the time of the re-
nowned David, but to "ancient days," that is, from within the eternity of God,
who is "ancient of days" (Dn 7:9). To God is presented "one like a son of man"
who is "given dominion and glory and kingdom, that all peoples, nations, and
languages should serve him; his dominion is an everlasting dominion, which
shall not pass away, and his kingdom one that shall not be destroyed" (Dn
7:13-14). This son of man, one who is truly human, assumes divine authority
and glory; thus his kingdom is of heavenly origin and so encompasses all peoples of every language.

In adding the clause from 2 Samuel 5:2, Matthew accentuates that the one
born in Bethlehem will be like David and so be a shepherd-king. The Lord said:
"You [David] shall be shepherd of my people Israel, and you shall be prince over
Israel." Unlike the present Herod and many former kings, the Messiah-King of
Bethlehem will not lord it over his people, but will lovingly shepherd them to
green pastures where they will thrive in peace and concord. According to Micah, Israel will continue to live in foreign servitude until "she who is in travail
has brought forth" (within the present context, this could refer to Mary giving
birth to Jesus), and then the new ruler from Bethlehem "shall stand and feed
his flock in the strength of the Lord, in the majesty of the name of the Lord his

God. And they shall dwell secure, for now he shall be great to the ends of the earth" (Mi 5:3-4). The apostolic community would have recognized that this prophecy has now been fulfilled because the son of man, Jesus the good shepherd who feeds his flock with the knowledge of his Father and the strength of the Holy Spirit, has received all glory and power. Through his death and resurrection, he has founded the everlasting kingdom of God, whose gates are forever open to all. These prophesies, while having their earthly fulfillment, also point once more to their ultimate eschatological end, when Jesus will exercise this everlasting authority and power and shepherd his people in heavenly pastures of peace and life.

Not only did the wise men now know where the Jewish king was born, but so did Herod. Within his "troubled" and now plotting mind, he "summoned the wise men secretly and ascertained from them what time the star appeared." Herod did not wish his plot to be known, lest it and the secret meeting be foiled, but he could not enact his plot without obtaining knowledge from the wise men. The irony is that the Jews provided the wise men the knowledge needed to fulfill their plans—"to come to worship him"—and they now provide Herod with the information needed to fulfill his plan—to come to kill him. Having obtained this knowledge, Herod "sent them to Bethlehem" as if they were now emissaries acting on his behalf, commissioning them "to search diligently for the child, and when you have found him bring me word, that I too may come and worship him." Herod's exhortation "to search diligently" was hardly an encouragement the wise men needed, since they had been doing so from the onset of their travels. It merely expresses Herod's own duplicitous anxiety that they may not find "the new born king of the Jews" and so frustrate his diabolic plan.

Only in departing the deceitful darkness of Herod did the wise men again see the star in whose light they were led to Jesus. Matthew says nothing about their emotional state upon leaving Herod, yet he notes that "when they saw the star, they rejoiced exceedingly with great joy." Matthew's account appears to enact here an axiom—the darkness of deceit and falsehood, especially in relation to God, gives birth to fear and hatred, while the light of truth, especially the truth of God, gives rise to joy and gladness.

With this exceeding joy the wise men entered "the house of Mary his mother, and they fell down and worshiped him. Then, opening their treasures, they offered him gifts, gold and frankincense and myrrh." The wise men's act of worship fulfills what was prayed in Psalm 71. The psalm petitions God to give to his king justice and righteousness, right judgment and deliverance, peace, and dominion. Not only may his enemies be conquered, but also "may the kings of Sheba and Seba bring gifts! May all kings fall down before him, and all nations serve him" (Ps 72:1-11). Likewise, Isaiah's prophecy in 49:23 is fulfilled: "Kings shall be your foster fathers and their queens your nursing mothers. With their faces to the ground they shall bow down before you." Although some Jews may reject a child of their race (Jesus), foreign nobility will care for him as one of their own. The wise men/kings, in fulfilling this petition and prophecy, first performed a twofold intertwining act that is of theological significance—the falling down and the worship. The act of worship is that of lying prostrate before Jesus and in that humility acknowledging being in the presence of someone who has divine Lordship over them; someone they acknowledge to be righteous and just has dominion over them. What is of the utmost importance is that before whom the wise men lie prostrate in worship is a human child, and it is this child who is the divine Messianic King of the Jews.

Likewise, Isaiah 60 declares that Israel should arise and shine, for "the glory of the Lord has risen upon you," thus dispelling all darkness. For this reason, "nations shall come to your light, and kings to the brightness of your rising." Through the guiding light of the star, the wise men have entered into the light of the Lord by entering the house of Mary and beholding her son. Likewise, they bring with them the wealth of the nations. "A multitude of camels shall cover you, and young camels of Median and Ephah; all those from Sheba shall come. They shall bring gold and frankincense and shall proclaim the praise of the Lord" (Is 60:1-6). Traditionally, these gifts bear a threefold significance: gold befitting a king, frankincense denoting worship (the rising prayer-filled smoke before the holy altar of God), and myrrh in anticipation of anointing a body after death. Although the significance of each gift is not theologically essential, the gifts do manifest the divine kingly messianic nature of the one receiving them. Nonetheless, while the Old Testament passages refer to gold and frankincense, Matthew also mentions myrrh, which may prophesize Jesus' death and the anointing of his body—a sacrificial death that would establish his heavenly kingdom and lead to his glorious kingly reign.[11]

11. In Matthew's Gospel, "Mary Magdalene and the other Mary" came to Jesus' tomb on the morning after the Sabbath, but nothing is mentioned of their bringing spices to anoint the body of Jesus (see Mt 28:1). In the Gospel of Mark, because the Sabbath was about to begin, there was no time to anoint the body of Jesus. Therefore on the morning after the Sabbath, "Mary Magdalene, and Mary the mother of James, and Salome, brought spices, so that they might go and anoint him" (Mk 16:1). Again, because of time restraints, Luke's Gospel narrates that "women from Galilee followed (to the tomb), and saw the tomb, and how his body was laid; (and) then re-

What we see, then, within the home of Mary is a liturgical act prophetically anticipating the heavenly fulfillment. There, as the Book of Revelation portrays in various ways, we find the heavenly Jerusalem paved in gold (see 21:18-21), and the heavenly temple where the slain lamb stands triumphantly upon a golden altar, around which the everlasting smoke of incense from golden bowls and censers bears the prayers of praise and glory and worship and honor of all saints from all peoples and nations (see 5:1-13, 8:1-4). "The Lamb"—the wise men's King-Messiah of Bethlehem, whose once slain body was anoint-

---

turned and prepared spices and ointments. But on the first day of the week, at early dawn, they went to the tomb, taking the spices which they had prepared. And they found the stone rolled away from the tomb, but when they went in they did not find the body" (Lk 23:55-24:3). The women in Mark and Luke came to the tomb to anoint Jesus' body, but they were unable to do so because Jesus was already raised from the dead. Thus, if the wise men's gift of myrrh was to symbolize Jesus' death and the need for anointing his body, this gift became superfluous. Although Jesus would die, no respectful anointing of his body was necessary because he would rise bodily in glory from the dead. The respect shown to Jesus' body does not reside in an earthly anointing administered by loyal and faithful holy women, but instead respect is shown to Jesus' body, his humanity, by the Father, through the anointing power of the Holy Spirit, raising him glorious from the dead. As the Holy Spirit anointed Jesus' humanity in the act of the Incarnation—the anointing of the Spirit of Sonship—so the Holy Spirit, the Spirit of Sonship, anointed his humanity in his resurrection by making him the glorious of God incarnate.

But the Gospel of John narrates that after Joseph of Arimathea received permission from Pilate, he "came and took the body. Nicodemus also came, bringing a mixture of myrrh and aloes, about a hundred pounds' weight. They took the body of Jesus, and bound it in linen cloths with spices, as is the burial custom of the Jews" (Jn 19:38-42). Mary Magdalene comes early to the tomb, but John makes no reference to her bringing spices to anoint Jesus' body.

While likely impossible to sort out this discrepancy, I could imagine, with a ting of humor, that because Joseph of Arimathea and Nicodemus probably hurriedly anointed Jesus' body to meet the time restraints of the approaching Sabbath, the women were not entirely satisfied that the men had done it properly and so prepared their own spices/myrrh to anoint the body after the Sabbath was over. More to the point, the actual anointing in John's Gospel fulfills the symbolism of myrrh seen within the gift of the wise men in that the sacred body of Jesus was rightly anointed, showing the respect it deserved, for through the sacrificial death of Jesus, the offering of his holy body/humanity, humankind was reconciled to the Father.

Of some significance, as Luke mentions that the wise men brought myrrh and John mentions that Jesus was anointed with myrrh, so both Luke and John narrate that the inscription on Jesus's cross echoes the words of the wise men. Luke states: "There was also an inscription over him, 'This is the King of the Jews'" (23:38). John states: "Pilate also wrote a title and put it on the cross; it read, 'Jesus of Nazareth, the King of the Jews'" (19:19). It is on the cross that Jesus fulfills the prophetic declaration of the wise men, for on the cross Jesus conquers sin and death and users in the Kingdom of God. On the cross one truly finds "the King of the Jews." Moreover, as the Gentile wise men recognized who Jesus is, so the Gentile Pilate equally proclaimed who Jesus is. As at the onset of Jesus' life, so at the end of Jesus' life Gentiles make prophetic proclamations, and they do so amid those Jews who refuse to accept that Jesus is their king.

ed with myrrh—now reigns in golden splendor amid the burning incense of praise and worship of all his holy faithful from every nation.

Given that the wise men were Gentiles, their act of worship before the Christ-King of the Jews reflects their perception of Jesus as being divine. They were not simply curious observers of something that exclusively bore upon the lives of others—the Jews—but not themselves. Rather, in entering Mary's home as uninvited guests and in the very act of worshiping her son, they were, as Gentile outsiders, deliberately inserting themselves, as if by right, into the kingdom of her anointed son. In so doing, they boldly declared themselves to be, and wanted to be acknowledged as such, equal members of God's chosen people. In the act of worshiping Jesus, the wise men were making a theological statement, one that they did not fully grasp but that the apostolic community, composed of Jews and Gentiles, would: "The anointed King of the Jews is our King too." Thus the worshiping by the wise men was a prophetic act that would find its fulfillment in the conversion of all nations—all peoples who acknowledge Jesus as their Lord and Savior and so echo the wise men: "My King too."[12]

The whole of Matthew's account of the wise men is soteriological in nature, and this soteriology is predicated upon the child, Jesus. The wise men did not know the name of "the new born king of the Jews"; nonetheless, who they found was "Jesus." In finding Jesus, they found the Savior—YHWH-Saves. In their very seeking and discovering of Jesus, they prophetically revealed that he was the Savior of not only the Jews but also the Gentiles. His name is of the utmost salvific significance to them and to all nations, of which they are the living representatives. Jesus, in the later fulfilling of his name on the cross and in the resurrection, would save the whole of humankind. Jesus is the Christ-King of the Jews and so rightly their promised anointed Savior, and is equally the Christ-King of the Gentiles and so their Savior as well. And in their very act of humble prostrate worship, they, and not the Jews, manifested and so revealed that Jesus, the Christ-King, is truly divine, thus confirming by their action the previous declaration. The son of Mary is conceived by the power of the Holy Spirit, and therefore he is Emmanuel—God with us. When Matthew alerted us at the onset to "behold," this is what he wanted us, revelationally and theologically, to see—in wonder and faith.

Matthew concludes his narrative of the wise men by stating simply, "And

12. The early church wondered whether Gentiles could become Christians. The matter was settled with the conversion of Cornelius (see Acts 10) and with the conversion of Paul as the Apostle to the Gentiles.

being warned in a dream not to return to Herod, they departed to their own country by another way." The wise men's foiling of Herod's craftily conceived plot leads directly to the swift nocturnal departure of the Holy Family into Egypt, and Herod's final frantic but determined attempt to kill "he who was born king of the Jews."

The wise men having departed, Joseph was warned by an angel in a dream to rise and flee with Mary and the child into Egypt and to stay there until told to return, "for Herod is about to search for the child to destroy him." Joseph obeyed and remained in Egypt until Herod had died. "This was to fulfill what the Lord had spoken by the prophet, 'Out of Egypt have I called my son.'"

The above interweaves multiple Old Testament images. Herod's attempt to kill the child is prophetically anticipated in the story of Moses. Pharaoh ordered that all the Israelite male babies be killed. Moses's mother saved him by sending him down the Nile in a basket, where he was discovered by Pharaoh's daughter. As Moses escaped the clutches of Pharaoh, so Jesus evaded the fury of Herod. And as Moses became the great anointed leader of the Israelites, whom the Lord God commissioned and empowered to lead his people from the slavery of Egypt into the Promised Land of freedom and plenty, so the young Jesus will reenact the life of Moses and in so doing prophesize what he would eventually accomplish: lead God's people from the slavery of sin and death and into the Promised Land of true freedom and everlasting life. Within this context, Matthew concludes by quoting Hosea 11:1. "When Israel was a child, I loved him, and out of Egypt I called my son." Jesus is not simply the new Moses reenacting the Exodus, but his being called out of Egypt as the new child whom God loves is a prophetic anticipation of his being the new Israel, which he literally embodies as the Father's beloved Son. Thus, although the child Jesus enacts the Exodus as the new Moses, he does so in a manner different from that of Moses. He is not merely the leader of God's people, but, as the Father's beloved Son, he will open, through his death and resurrection, a passage from this world of sin and death into a new communion with his heavenly Father. This new communion with the Father is in being in communion with his Son, the risen Jesus, which is to be a member of the new Israel.[13]

---

13. Matthew, in portraying him as the new Moses, is designating Jesus as the new prophet whom God had promised Moses that he would raise up. Moses told the Israelites that when they enter the Promised Land, "the Lord your God will raise up for you a prophet like me from among you, from your brethren—him you shall heed." While the Israelites rightly and fearfully knew that they could not see God's face and live, the Lord promised: "I will raise up for them a prophet like you [Moses] from among their brethren; and I will put my words in his mouth,

Once again, this fleeing to and returning from Egypt is a prophetic symbolic anticipation of Jesus' soteriological mission, which is predicated upon his being the new Moses—he who as the Son of God embodies within his own humanity the emergence of the new Israel—the new Israel that will mature upon his glorious return, when he leads his faithful into the everlasting Promised Land of heavenly glory.

Matthew again returns to the machinations of Herod. Having realized that he had been tricked by the wise men, "Herod was in a furious rage," and so he, evocative of Pharaoh, sent solders to kill all the boys in Bethlehem and its region aged two years old or younger. This was in keeping with what the wise men told him.[14] Herod's killing of "the Holy Innocents" is a foreboding of the child Jesus' fate. He may have escaped for now, but his kingly mission as the Christ entails his innocent death on the cross, and it will be perpetrated by those who, like Herod, refuse to acknowledge him as the Christ-King, whether they be Jews or Gentiles (the Romans). Thus the Holy Innocents, in their death, are privileged to enact a prophecy—the death of he who is supremely holy and wholly innocent.

Nonetheless, this atrocious act was done, Matthew tells us, in fulfillment of the words of the prophet Jeremiah: "A voice was heard in Ramah, wailing and loud lamentation, Rachel weeping for her children; she refused to be consoled, because they were no more" (Jer 31:15). Historically, this lament is situated at the time when Syria carried off the Hebrew exiles, in 587 BC. Rachel, the wife of Jacob, who traditionally is believed to have lived near Bethlehem and was buried in nearby Ephrath, is portrayed as weeping. So loud is her weeping that it can be heard in Ramah, nine miles north of Jerusalem and so approximately eighteen miles from Bethlehem. Rachel cannot "be consoled" because

---

and he shall speak to them all that I command him" (Dt 18:15-18). Unlike God's presence on Mt. Horeb, to be in the presence of Jesus, as the new Moses, is not a fearful experience, for as man, he can speak to other human beings face to face, simply as one of them, and yet the one who is speaking is none other than Emmanuel—God with us. Therefore he is *the* prophet promised of old, which is seen especially in Matthew's account of the Sermon on the Mount. Here Jesus ascends the mountain to promulgate the new law of God's kingdom, for here he is speaking God's words and speaking all that his Father has commanded him.

The Gospel of John also sees Jesus as the new Moses. Although John the Baptist is not "the prophet" (Jn 1:21), Jesus is (Jn 7:40). For a fuller treatment, see my "The Son's Filial Relationship to the Father: Jesus as the New Moses," *Nova et Vetera* 11, no. 1 (2013): 253-64, republished in *Jesus: Essays in Christology* (Ave Maria, Fla.: Sapientia, 2014), 21-33.

14. Although the church commemorates the three wise men twelve days after Christmas (the Epiphany), they must have arrived in Jerusalem considerably later.

her children are "no more." Rachel here becomes the personification of all Israel, especially those who have lost their children in Herod's butchery.

Rachel's lament within Jeramiah's prophecy is set within the context of joy. Chapter 31 begins with God reaffirming that he "will be the God of all of Israel, and they shall be my people." He has loved his people "with an everlasting love" and so will continue to be faithful. He will prosper them, and so all should "sing aloud with gladness for Jacob." All should "proclaim, give praise and say, 'The Lord has saved his people, the remnant of Israel.'" He will gather his people from all the nations to which they have been scattered and therefore they will rejoice and sing for joy. "I will turn their mourning into joy, I will comfort them, and give them gladness for sorrow." In this midst of the Lord's promises that will result in joy and prosperity comes Rachael's lament. Immediately following this lament, Jeramiah proclaims: "Thus says the Lord: 'Keep your voice from weeping, and your eyes from tears'" because "there is hope for your future … and your children shall come back to their own country. I have heard Ephraim bemoaning," and so the Lord will remember "Ephraim my dear son," "my darling child." The Lord continues to tell of the great things he will do for his people, all of which culminates in the greatest promise of all.

> Behold, the days are coming, says the Lord, when I will make a new covenant with the house of Israel and the house of Judah, not like the covenant which I made with their fathers when I took them by the hand to bring out of the land of Egypt, my covenant which they broke.... But this covenant which I will make with the house of Israel after those days, says the Lord; I will put my law within them, and I will write it upon their hearts; and I will be their God, and they shall be my people. And no longer shall man teach his neighbour and each his brother, saying "Know the Lord," for they shall all know me, from least of them to the greatest, says the Lord; for I will forgive their iniquity, and I will remember their sin no more. (Jer 31:1-34)

Here Matthew has pulled one verse (Rachel's lament) out of thirty-four and used it to interpret the killing of the Holy Innocents. But that lament cannot be understood without the fourteen verses that precede it or the eighteen that follow, all of which proclaim what the powerful Lord will do, culminating in his promise of a new covenant. Thus Bethlehem's weeping at the demise of her children is wrapped within the expectancy of God fulfilling his promises, and within that hope resides the expectancy of an even greater joy. In truth, Bethlehem is wrapped within the child Jesus, for he is the future fulfillment of the Lord's promises and future cause of joy. In, through, and with him, the Lord will establish the new covenant. Jesus, as the embodiment of the new covenant, is the Father's "dear son" and "darling child" in whom he will save "his people, "the remnant of Israel." Through Jesus the Father "will turn mourning into joy," and with Jesus the Father will provide "comfort" and "give them gladness for sorrow." Rachel's lament, then, is wrapped within a confident prophetic soteriological profession of future joy, for in Jesus the Lord God will become the God of Israel in a new way, and all of humankind will be his people in a new way.

Matthew closes his infancy narrative by summarizing the outcome of the drama that resulted from Jesus' birth, from the arrival of the wise men in Jerusalem to Herod's failed attempt to kill the child. Herod having died, an angel again appeared to Joseph in Egypt, telling him to arise and return the child to Israel, thus confirming what was said before: "Out of Egypt have I called my son." This would also imply, again, that Jesus is the new Moses. Moses, having been exiled, was told by God to return to his homeland: "Go back to Egypt; for all the men who were seeking your life are dead" (Ex 4:19). As Moses returned to Egypt to lead God's people into the Promised Land, so Jesus now returns to Israel to establish the Promised Land of the kingdom of God. On his arrival, however, Joseph heard that "Archelaus reigned over Judea in place of his father Herod" and became fearful. Once again, being warned in a dream, he proceeded to Galilee and "dwelt in a city called Nazareth," fulfilling what the prophets said: "He shall be called a Nazarene."[15]

Having come to the conclusion of Matthew's narrative, we can properly summarize it as the actual playing out of Psalm 2, which is a prophetic theological rendering of Jesus' future death and resurrection.

There is Herod and all similar earthly rulers. Why do the nations conspire and the peoples plot in vain? The kings of the earth set themselves, and rulers take council together, against the Lord and his anointed, saying, "Let us burst their bonds asunder, and cast their cords from us."

Although Herod and all that he stands for conspires and plots against the Lord and his anointed—the Father and his Son, Jesus the Christ-King of the Jews,

---

15. Scholars are not sure which prophets or what prophecies Matthew may be referencing, as the saying he quotes does not appear in the Old Testament. He may be suggesting Jgs 13:5-7. The significance would then mean that Jesus was one dedicated to God. Nazareth is never mentioned in the Old Testament. Jesus, by growing up in Nazareth, is entering into anonymity. His youth and maturing into adulthood are hidden.

He who sits in the heavens laughs, the Lord has them in derision. Then he will speak to them in his wrath, and terrify them in his fury, saying, "I have set my king on Zion, my holy hill."

Herod's "furious rage" provokes nothing more than God's mocking laughter and derisive scorn at his vain attempt to kill the child. The Lord God has set Jesus as king of Zion on his "holy hill," and from there he will not be moved. That hill will ultimately be Golgotha, where the rage against God's anointed finds its definitive expression. Yet the cross will echo the words of the wise men: Jesus of Nazareth, King of the Jews. Jesus' holy and loving sacrificial death will make that hill holy and with it the entire world, for his Father will backhandedly sweep away that rage by his joyful raising his "king" from the dead. In the resurrection, the Father "decrees":

You are my son, today I have begotten you. Ask of me, and I will make the nations your heritage, the ends of the earth your possession.

The Father has eternally begotten his Son. And "of the Holy Spirit" his Son is conceived as man upon earth. In the resurrection, he established his Son incarnate as the King of the Jews and the Lord of all nations. The wise men, unlike Herod, prophetically enact the psalm's conclusion.

Now therefore, O kings, be wise; be warned, O rulers of the earth. Serve the Lord with fear, with trembling kiss his feet, lest he be angry, and you perish in the way; for his wrath is quickly kindled.

The wise men took heed and adoringly prostrated themselves before the feet of the child—"the new born king of the Jews." In so doing, they represent all kings and their nations, all rulers and their peoples: "Blessed are all who take refuge in him" (the Lord's begotten anointed Son, the Christ-King).

Although Matthew's account of Jesus' birth is the prophetic playing out of Psalm 2, it has been and will continue to be enacted until Jesus comes in glory, when his Father places all of his enemies under his feet and he will reign forever supreme with all of God's holy people (see Heb 10:13). "They [Evil rulers and their followers] will make war on the Lamb and the Lamb will conquer them, for he is the Lord of lords and the King of kings, and those with him are called and chosen and faithful" (Rv 17:14).

Having examined the theological and doctrinal content of Matthew's narrative of Jesus' birth, we can now complete our study of Luke's infancy narrative.

Finding Jesus in the Temple

After narrating Jesus' dedication and Mary's purification in the temple, Luke gives us a "snapshot" of Jesus' life twelve years later. The Holy Family went from Nazareth down to Jerusalem to celebrate the Passover. Here we see "the lost boy" Jesus in the temple conversing with the teachers, before later being found by his parents. But this is not an isolated event; it is a theological and revelational bridge that spans the infancy narrative and the main body of the Gospel. This event reaches back to the angel Gabriel's prophecy that, because he is conceived by the Holy Spirit, he would be the Son of the Most High and will be called the holy Son of God. Likewise, it reaches into the future, when Jesus will reveal fully that he truly is the Son of the Most High and the holy Son of God. Jesus is himself the bridge, for here, at the age of twelve, he manifests his own youthful self-awareness as the Father's Son and his future mission in accordance with his Father's will. Thus this event is a glimpse of the conception prophecies beginning to be fulfilled and so is also anticipatory of their later fulfillment.

Luke informs us that, having celebrated the Passover, Joseph and Mary returned to Jerusalem only to discover that Jesus was not in the company of his kinsfolk. Instead, they found their son in the temple among the teachers "listening to them and asking them questions; and all were amazed at his understanding and his answers."[16] Although Jesus was doing the listening and the querying, what amazed the teachers was his understanding and his answers. Jesus, seemingly just an inquisitive young boy, asked questions and listened to the answers, and his answers to his own questions expressed such understanding that he caused amazement among the teachers.[17] Mary and Joseph were also amazed: "when they saw him were astonished." This temple "colloquy" anticipates the climax of this event.

Having "discovered" Jesus after a three-day search, Mary expresses her (sinless) consternation: "Son, why have you treated us so? Behold, your father and I have been looking for you anxiously." Here Mary refers to Jesus as her son and makes reference to his father, Joseph. On one level, it is a typical family muddle, especially for parents of a twelve-year-old boy. But Jesus, as he will often do within his future public ministry, raised the issue to a deeper level.

---

16. All quotations in this section are from Lk 2:41-52 unless otherwise noted.

17. The contrast between Jesus' wisdom and his being the son of Joseph and Mary can also be found in Lk 4:22, Mt 13:53-57, Mk 6:2-3, and Jn 6:42 and 7:15.

"How is it that you sought me? Did you not know that I must be in my Father's house?"[18] Mary and Joseph "did not understand the saying which he spoke to them."

Although Jesus, who lives with his parents in Nazareth, appears to be an ordinary boy of twelve, he already possesses knowledge of the Jewish Scriptures and tradition that amazes his teachers, who are knowledgeable on the topics discussed. This precociousness is explained in Jesus' (sinless) rebuke to his mother. His parents should have known from the start that he would be in the temple precisely because that was his "Father's house," where God dwells upon the earth. This earthly act of physically positioning himself within his Father's house, the act of physically placing himself in the earthly presence of his Father, reveals that Jesus is always in the presence of the Father, for the Father is *his* Father and thus he is singularly the Father's Son. This accounts for Jesus' possession of such amazing wisdom and knowledge—God being his Father, he received, as the incarnate Son, his Father's wisdom and knowledge. This physically positioning of himself within his Father's house is also an outward sign testifying to his human mental, emotional, and psychological wholehearted commitment to always do his Father's will as the Father's Son. Thus, as Son, Jesus is always physically in his Father's house because he is always in his Father's presence and so always doing his Father's business. This continual singular being in his Father's presence and this singular faithful doing of his Father's will is what will confirm that he is the Father's Son.

This twelve-year-old boy lived in his father's house in Nazareth and simultaneously resided with God his Father—manifested by his presence within his Father's house in Jerusalem—the temple. As Jesus abided with Mary and Joseph, he simultaneously abided with his Father. Jesus was the son of Mary and Joseph and was simultaneously the Son of his Father. This son of Mary and Joseph, this boy of twelve, was then humanly conscious of God being his Father, and in this recognition of his Father he was humanly conscious of himself as the Father's Son; the boy Jesus, the son of Mary and Joseph, humanly knew *who* he was, his divine identity, as the Father's Son.[19] It was this simultane-

18. Another translation is "I must be about my Father's business." Each translation expresses Jesus singular commitment to the Father whose Son he is.

19. Unsurprisingly, Jesus at twelve years of age knew that God was uniquely his Father, and thus his own self-identity as the Father's Son. (For a boy of twelve not to know *who* he was would be a cause for real concern.) Like all children, Jesus came to know who he was in the course of normal human development, the difference being that he humanly grew into his self-identity through his growing awareness of his Father. How this gradual growth in

ity that confounded Mary and Joseph. Ignorance of this simultaneity initiated the three-day search. If they had grasped this simultaneity, Mary and Joseph would have known immediately where *their son* was; that he would naturally, in accordance with who he is, be in *his* Father's house. It is "all of these things" that Mary, "his mother kept ... in her heart." Luke concludes by informing us that Jesus went down with his parents to Nazareth and "was obedient to them" (probably to their parental relief). In this setting of obediently residing in the home of Joseph and Mary the twelve-year-old boy, Jesus continued to grow and mature, within his human heart and mind, "in wisdom and in stature, and in favor with God and man" (Lk 2:41-52).[20] This maturing and growing found favor not only among those with whom Jesus lived in Nazareth and its environs but also with God.

Again, the focus of this story is the human boy, Jesus. No one—the temple

---

awareness of his Father came about is debatable, but I argue that it was through his daily praying with his parents from his earliest age and their teaching him the Scriptures and their Jewish religious heritage. As he grew, this would be reinforced by attending synagogue worship and hearing the Scriptures proclaimed and commented upon. Jesus' own growth in his life of prayer and contemplation would immensely affect his self-conscious awareness of his Father. Obviously, Jesus at the age of nine would possess greater clarity and understanding than at the age of four, but he was long aware that God was his Father and thus of his own self-identity as Son before he reached the age of twelve.

20. As noted above, Luke also provides a parallel story, though with a radically different ending that takes place at the onset of Jesus' public ministry in Nazareth, "where he was brought up." In the synagogue, he read Is 61:1-2 in a way that indicated that the passage was fulfilled in him. He read it as the one for whom it was intended. The Spirit of the Lord was upon him (Jesus) precisely because he was anointed by the Lord. He received the anointed commission to proclaim the good news to the poor and captives. Like the teachers in the temple, his fellow Nazareans "spoke well of him, and wondered at his gracious words which proceeded out of his mouth." They exclaimed, "Is not this Joseph's son?" This question not only expressed the rhetorical truth that this was indeed Joseph's son, but also the incredulity that, being Joseph's son, he could not possibly possess such wisdom and knowledge, much less that Isaiah's prophetic utterance could find fulfillment in him. In the face of such arrogance, they attempted to throw him off a cliff (Lk 4:16-30).

Matthew places this event within the broader context of Jesus' wisdom and mighty works and gives fuller details of his family background. He is not simply the son of Joseph, but more derisively "the carpenter's son." His mother is Mary, and many of his brethren are named. With this unimpressive lineage, not unlike their own, "they took offense at him" (Mt 13:53-58).

As Mary and Joseph failed to understand how "their son" must be in his "Father's house," so their fellow citizens could not grasp how one of their own could possess such wisdom and do such mighty works as the anointed one of the Lord, the Father's Son. Once again, the double simultaneity that confounded his parents now confounds Jesus' fellow townsmen. Although Mary prayerfully pondered the mystery of her son in her heart, the citizens of Nazareth cursorily concluded that one of their own, the son of the town carpenter, could not possibly be the Lord's anointed who, in the Spirit, would proclaim the good news of salvation.

teachers, Joseph, and Mary—doubts that what they see and hear is a normal youthful male. Yet what Jesus manifests in his answers and what he attempts to reveal to his human parents is that he is none other than the Father's Son and so properly and rightly resides in his Father's house. This event is an incarnational epiphany—Jesus, the human boy, is the Son of God—awaiting its later completion within Jesus' future ministry and finding its confirmation in the Father raising him gloriously from the dead.

The Infancy Narratives: Conclusion

I have contributed a substantial amount of time on the infancy narratives because they are not simply addendums to the body of their respective gospels but essential prophetic anticipations of all that would follow—Jesus' public ministry and his passion, death, and resurrection. In the light of Jesus' life, death, and resurrection, the early apostolic community would have recognized that the prophecies contained within the infancy narratives had been marvelously fulfilled and in a way that would never have been anticipated at their proclamation. With this in mind, I now provide a partial summary of what we have doctrinally ascertained within them.

Jesus' conception is the determinative act upon which the whole infancy narrative, both of Matthew and Luke, derives its meaning. Although the conception of John the Baptist anticipates Jesus', Jesus' conception gives meaning to John's conception. Without Jesus' conception, John's becomes pointless. Moreover, all the prophecies concerning John and his future ministry only find their focus and application in the conceiving of Jesus. Equally, all the prophecies concerning Jesus obtain their doctrinal import in the unique act of his conception. The way he is conceived governs the ontological import of who he will be and the singular soteriological significance of what he will achieve. In addition, all the initial epiphanies following Jesus' birth—that of the shepherds, the wise men, Simeon and Anna, the youthful Jesus in the temple—bear witness to the unique manner in which he was conceived, and so to the singular soteriological future that prophetically lies before him. The definitive act that determines everything is the act of the Holy Spirit coming upon Mary, the overshadowing power of the Most High (Luke), such that the one conceived within the womb of Mary is of the Holy Spirit (Matthew). This act ontologically determines who Jesus is and so ontologically determines all the salvific acts that he will subsequently perform. This act, then, is the hermeneutical key for properly interpreting all prophetic utterances and for rightly perceiving how they will be fulfilled.

Because Jesus is conceived in the womb of Mary, he will be her human son, and because he is conceived by the overshadowing of the Holy Spirit and the power of the Most High, her human son will be called holy, and as such he will thus be called the Son of the Most High and the Son of God. The act of the Holy Spirit within the womb of Mary is the defining act that ontologically determines who Jesus, the holy Son of God, is and simultaneously how the Son of the Most High exists as man. The conceiving act of the Holy Spirit is the definitional act of the Incarnation and is an act that only Jesus can divinely perform.

Because the Son of God comes to be man through the act of the Holy Spirit, the Son of God as man, inherently and integrally possesses as man the Spirit proper to himself as Son, after the manner of being the Son. Jesus, then, as the Son of God incarnate, possesses the Holy Spirit not as subsequent to his conception but as ontologically constitutive of his identity in the act of conception. This singular possession of the Holy Spirit, this precise possession of the Spirit as the Spirit of Sonship, ontologically defines him as the Son of God existing as man.

Because Jesus, as the Son of God, possesses the Spirit of Sonship, he is properly and uniquely the Christ/Messiah—the anointed one. Again, this anointing is not subsequent to Jesus' coming to be but is singularly constitutive of his coming to be, because it is by the Holy Spirit that he, as the Father's Son, comes to exist as man, and so possesses as man the Spirit in keeping with who he is as Son—the Spirit of Sonship. It is upon this basis that Matthew can simply and properly speak of "the genealogy of Jesus Christ" and "the birth of Jesus Christ." The designation "Christ" defines who Jesus is, for this anointing inheres within the very act of his coming to be. Thus it is not a title bestowed upon him but a personal name that wells up from within who Jesus is, and so characteristically defines who he is as the Son of God. This is why the angel heralds to the shepherds that the one born in Bethlehem is "Christ the Lord." Jesus was born "Christ the Lord" because he was conceived as such by the overshadowing of the Holy Spirit. And because it is in possessing the Spirit of Sonship that defines the singular manner in which Jesus is the Christ, the name "Christ" equally designates and defines that Jesus is the Son of God, for his anointing is that which only properly belongs to the Son alone.[21]

---

21. This is the ontological and incarnational basis upon which the apostolic church employs the title "Christ" as part of Jesus' proper name: Jesus Christ.

Because Jesus Christ is the Son of God incarnate, Matthew can profess that he is truly God-with-us—Emmanuel. Jesus is the Son of God and is with us is as man. Thus, for Matthew and the early Christian community, Isaiah's prophecy has been fulfilled in a most unprecedented and even literal manner.

In the light of the above, the designation "Lord" is employed within the infancy narratives in a radically new way that is of the utmost significance. On the one hand, the divinely revealed name "Lord" (the Greek equivalent of YHWH) is used to designate God (the Father). Various angels "of the Lord," in various ways, are sent to Mary, Joseph, Zechariah, and the shepherds. "The Lord God" will give to Jesus the throne of his father David. Mary is the handmaid "of the Lord." Elizabeth declares that Mary is blessed because she believed "the word of the Lord." The shepherds go to Bethlehem to see what "the Lord" had made known to them. Mary and Joseph go to Jerusalem to fulfill "the law of the Lord" so that their son could be dedicated "to the Lord." Simeon rejoices because he has seen "the Lord's Christ" and so can die in peace. All of these directly reference God (the Father). On the other hand, simultaneously during the same events, Zechariah proclaims that his son will turn many "to the Lord" because he will prepare a way for "the coming of the Lord." Mary is full of grace because "the Lord" (Jesus) is with her. Elizabeth rejoices that "the mother of my Lord" has come to visit her. Zechariah rejoices that the "Lord God of Israel" has visited his people (ultimately in the person of Jesus). Both Jesus and God can rightfully be called "the Lord" because Jesus is the Son of the Father and God is the Father of his Son. Thus the divine name YHWH can properly be attributed to them. The one God YHWH is now professed to be the Father of his Son. As the Father's Son, Jesus is both "Christ the Lord" and "the Lord's Christ."

Within the above doctrinal examination, we have therefore discerned the revelation of the Trinity. Within the act of Jesus' conception as man we perceive the Father, who divinely and actively authors the act of conception; the Son, who divinely and actively assumes his humanity in the act of conception; and the Holy Spirit, who divinely enacts the act of conception. The one incarnating act is, then, an intertwining act, a perichoretic act, that braids together the personal divine acts of the Father, the Son, and the Holy Spirit, the distinguishing acts that reveal who each is.

This perichoretic act founds the truth that Jesus is both "Christ the Lord" and "the Lord's Christ." Jesus came into being as the Son of God incarnate through the act of the Holy Spirit, the Spirit of Sonship, and so by nature is "Christ the Lord [Son]." Being "Christ the Lord" as the Son of God incarnate, he is "the Lord's [Father's] Christ," for the Lord (Father) is the one who authored the act by which his Son was conceived by the Holy Spirit, thus constituting him as his (the Lord's/the Father's) Christ. This divine incarnating perichoretic act within the created order of time and history manifests the perichoretic act that the trinity of persons are in themselves—the Father fathering his Son in and through the act of Holy Spirit so that the Son acts as the Father's Son in and through the act of the Holy Spirit.[22]

Mary's significance lies in the fact that it is within her womb that this perichoretic incarnational act occurs, thus guaranteeing that the act is incarnational—that the Father's Son has come to exist as her son, as man. Her virginity bears witness to this act, for her son's existence is not of human origin but of the Holy Spirit. Because the incarnate Son dwells within the womb of Mary, she is now the new living holy temple in which the Most High dwells. Likewise, the Son, in assuming flesh within the womb of Mary through the power of the Holy Spirit, enacts his foundational ecclesial salvific act: establishing his church. In this incarnational act, a Spirit-filled salvific communion is established between his flesh and Mary's flesh, and as such he dwells within her womb. This communion designates her as the living prophetic icon of the church, for she is the first human being to share in the saving and life-giving indwelling presence of Jesus as Savior and Lord of his church. Thus Jesus never lives apart from his church, for both are conceived simultaneously and will grow together as Jesus performs his saving acts. These acts will bring the church to full birth in his death and resurrection and his subsequent pouring out of the Holy Spirit upon the church as her Savior and Lord. Then, as Mary lived in Spirit-filled communion with her son as her Savior and Lord, so the whole church will live in Spirit-filled communion with her Savior and Lord.

Mary's significance also resides in being the wife of Joseph her husband. Being the wife of Joseph means that her son is of the house and lineage of David. So, born in Bethlehem and as the Son of God incarnate, he will inherit the throne of his father David by establishing an everlasting kingdom and will reign forever. He is the newborn king of the Jews and so is their anointed king—the Christ foretold.[23]

22. Placed within the Western doctrinal tradition, the Father fathers his Son within his paternal love of the Holy Spirit such that the Son loves the Father within his filial love of the Holy Spirit. Thus the Holy Spirit proceeds as the paternal love of Father in the begetting of his Son and proceeds from the Son as the filial love of the Son for the Father, the same love in which he was begotten. For a fuller presentation of this understanding, see my *The Father's Spirit of Sonship: Reconceiving the Trinity* (Edinburgh: T&T Clark, 1995).

23. There is an inherent relationship between Jesus establishing the kingdom of God and

All of this is focused on a human being: the child conceived and born. This holy child—who will be called and so rightly identified as the Christ, the Son of God, the Son of the Most High, Emmanuel, the Lord, the Davidic King— is Jesus, YHWH-Saves. This child assumes his name Jesus precisely because he is the Christ, the Son of God, Emmanuel, the Lord and King and precisely because he is the Christ, the Son of God, Emmanuel, the Lord and King that will be the Savior. As Jesus enacts his name, as Jesus becomes YHWH-Saves, through his salvific deeds, he will reveal that he is truly the Christ, the Son of God, and in so doing he will establish the everlasting kingdom of God promised to his father David.

As Jesus enacts his name, he will manifest that he is Savior as YHWH-Son. He will also be manifesting that his Father is Savior as YHWH-Father, for only as the Father's Son, in communion with him, is Jesus the Savior. Equally, in manifesting that he is Savior as YHWH-Son, he will also be manifesting that the Holy Spirit is Savior as YHWH-Holy Spirit, for only in communion with the Holy Spirit, the Spirit of Sonship, is Jesus the Savior. To perceive properly the human saving acts of Jesus is to perceive the distinct saving perichoretic acts of the Father, the Son, and the Holy Spirit. In Jesus we find YHWH, as the Trinity, saving his people.

We have discovered in the infancy narratives the entire doctrine of the Gospel literally in embryo. In the incarnating act, the whole previous salvific history of Israel is drawn into the womb of Mary, the wife of Joseph, and the child she carries will be the fulfillment of that salvific history—Jesus Christ, the Father's Son, the Lord and Savior. Through his life, death, and resurrection, he will assume his kingly everlasting reign, which will find its eschatological culmination in the final act by which Jesus will enact his name fully and completely: YHWH-Saves. In his coming in glory, Jesus will conclusively be Savior by ushering all the faithful into his Father's heavenly presence within the communion of the Holy Spirit. Thus what is presently in embryo will grow into the one mature man: Jesus and those who share with him, the Christ, the communion of the Spirit of Sonship and so dwell in his Father's everlasting heavenly kingdom as his sons and daughters.[24] To know the act by which Jesus is conceived is to know the whole of the Gospel—from beginning

---

his establishing the church, for the church will become the living Spirit-filled embodiment of the kingdom.

24. Paul develops this understanding. He speaks of all becoming "one new man" in Christ (Eph 2:15) and growing "to mature manhood, to the measure of the stature of the fullness of Christ" (Eph 4:13.)

to end—for as he humanly lies within Mary's womb as the Son of God, he literally embodies its whole.

As Mary enfolds within her womb the entire Gospel of salvation, to which she will give birth, so the church will continually enfold the whole of the Gospel of salvation and to which, to the end of the ages, she gives birth throughout the whole world—Jesus Christ. And as Jesus becomes fully Jesus in the everlasting saving act of his coming in glory, so the church, prefiguratively anticipated in Mary's assumption, will achieve its full expression—the glorious heavenly assembly of the Father's holy people—the mature body of Christ fully alive within the divine love of the Holy Spirit.

Finally, the infancy narratives, in a marvelous and creative manner, doctrinally knit together names, titles, and concepts, all of Old Testament origin, so that, founded upon the conceiving incarnational act of the Holy Spirit, they depict a new revelational tapestry that was previously unimaginable. The incarnating act of the Holy Spirit knits together persons and acts, with their corresponding names and titles, such that they become inseparable. The person in whom the Holy Spirit knits together all the various threads, and from whom the tapestry reveals its entire motif, is Jesus. To know the Christ, the Son of God, the Holy One of God, the Son of the Most High, the Lord, the Savior, the King of David—and so to know the Father, the Most High, the Holy One, the Lord, the source of all holiness and the author of all salvific promises and their fulfillment as well as to know the Holy Spirit, the Father's Spirit of Sonship, the one who anoints and makes holy, the one who empowers, and in whom all salvific deeds are done—is simply to know the man, Jesus.

3 · THE BAPTISM AND TEMPTATION
OF JESUS

Chapters 1 and 2 examined the Incarnation as it was professed within the infancy narratives of the Gospels of Matthew and Luke. These accounts, each in its own distinctive manner, were prophetic. Not only did they proclaim that Jesus Christ the Lord would be called the holy Son of God, but also that, because of who is, he would be the long-awaited Savior, the king of the Jews. We also saw that how Jesus came to be, the act by which he came to exist, simultaneously manifested the Father and the Holy Spirit—their intertwining acts that contributed to Jesus being the Son of God existing as man. This prophetic proclamation would be fulfilled as Jesus enacted his name—YHWH-Saves. The more Jesus becomes Jesus through his saving acts, the more he would manifest that he is truly the Son. In turn, the progressive procession of these acts would also reveal his Father, who is the author of all that Jesus does as Son, and manifest the Holy Spirit, who inwardly directs and interiorly empowers Jesus as Son to perform his saving deeds in communion with him. All the above is fulfilled within the body of the Gospels.[1] Within Jesus' public ministry, through his saving acts that inaugurate the Kingdom of God, we behold the only begotten Son from the Father, for these acts bear testimony that the fullness of the Holy Spirit abided and continues to abide in him.

This chapter examines the introductory verse of Mark's Gospel and then the baptism of Jesus, the act whereby he commits himself, in the Spirit, to be the faithful Son in whom the Father is well pleased. We then study briefly Jesus' genealogy as contained within the Gospel of Luke, because Luke, unlike

---

1. Although the body of the Gospels testifies to the fulfillment of the prophecies contained in the infancy narratives, these narratives were also written to confirm what the early Christian church believed concerning Jesus. The manner in which Jesus is conceived became the initial revelational foundation, the constitutive ontological endorsement, for what was later believed.

Matthew, who places Jesus' genealogy at the onset of his Gospel, places his genealogy immediately after Jesus' baptism. Both purposely located their genealogies for theological or doctrinal reasons. Finally, we doctrinally assess the various narratives concerning Jesus' temptations.

Mark's Introductory Proclamation

The Gospel of Mark, having no infancy narrative, begins with the ministry of John and the baptism of Jesus. His opening verse is of theological significance not only as a preface to Jesus' baptism but for the whole of his Gospel. He states: "The beginning of the gospel of Jesus Christ, the Son of God" (Mk 1:1). As Matthew speaks of "the genealogy of Jesus Christ," so Mark speaks of "the gospel of Jesus Christ." For Matthew, Jesus is the Christ, the anointed of God, because he is conceived "of the Holy Spirit." Similarly, for Mark, his being the Christ is predicated upon what immediately follows—the descent of the Holy Spirit upon Jesus at his baptism. Thus Jesus' baptism marks the beginning of his Gospel, and that beginning determines who Jesus is and the whole of what he will subsequently accomplish during his salvific ministry.

Just as Matthew simply referred to "Jesus Christ" so too does Mark, who identifies Jesus not only as "YHWH-Saves" but also as "YHWH-Saves-Anointed-One." This name defines precisely who he is: YHWH, the Spirit-anointed one, Savior, or, as Mark concludes, "the Son of God." Jesus is the Son of God because he is singularly anointed, as Christ, with the Spirit proper to him, the Spirit of Sonship, and in being so anointed he is, as Son, YHWH-Saves.

As in Matthew, the opening verse professes both the doctrine of the Incarnation and the doctrine of the Trinity. The man Jesus is the Son of God (of the Father), for he possesses the Holy Spirit both as ontologically constitutive of who he is as the Father's Son from all eternity and as ontologically constituted as the incarnate Son of God, Jesus Christ. For Mark, the initial good news that governs the entirety of his Gospel (the good news) is the historical person of Jesus Christ, whose identity is determined by his defining possession of the Holy Spirit as the Father's/God's Son.[2]

The truth of this introductory proclamation is confirmed for Mark within Jesus' baptism. For Matthew and Luke, this same truth is also confirmed, for

---

2. As Mark professes at the onset, this is the Gospel of Jesus Christ, the Son of God, so it culminates in the centurion's proclamation beneath the cross: "Truly, this man was the Son of God!" (Mk 15:39). Jesus' saving death enacts the truth of who Jesus is as the Christ, the Son of God.

Jesus' baptism testifies to his being conceived as the Christ, the Son of God, through the power of the Holy Spirit.

The Prophetic Ministry of John the Baptist

In John the Baptist's conception and birth we found that the prophecies concerning him clustered around his future vocational ministry. The child to be conceived would bring joy to many at his birth, for he would be "great before the Lord" and, "filled with the Holy Spirit," he would turn many "to the Lord," for "he will go before him in the spirit and power of Elijah," thus making "ready for the Lord a people prepared" (Lk 1:14-17). John "will be called the prophet of the Most High," for he "will go before Lord to prepare his ways" and will bring "knowledge of salvation" through "forgiveness" of sin and thus manifest "the tender mercy" of God and so bring "light" into "the shadow of death," which will guide all into "the way of peace" (Lk 1:76-79). Although found in Luke alone, these prophecies are fulfilled within all of the synoptic accounts of John's later ministry, culminating in Jesus' baptism. In fulfilling these prophecies, John reveals that Jesus is truly the divine savior—Christ the Lord.[3]

Mark prefaces his baptismal narrative (and so begins "the Gospel of Jesus Christ, the Son of God") with the prophetic passage "Behold, I send my messenger before your face, who shall prepare your way; the voice of one crying in the wilderness: Prepare the way of the Lord, make his paths straight."

Although Mark states that he is quoting Isaiah, he is actually quoting Malachi 3:1: "Behold, I send my messenger to prepare the way before me" and Isaiah 40:3: "A voice cries: 'In the wilderness prepare the way of the Lord, make straight in the desert a highway for our God.'"[4] For the sake of theological clarity, each passage is examined separately.

3. Luke notes that "the word of God came to John the son of Zechariah" (Lk 3:2). By recalling that John is Zechariah's son, Luke connects all the prophecies that attended his conception and birth to what is about to take place: the fulfillment of those prophecies. Thus John is now embarking on the fulfillment of his prophetic vocation, the sole purpose for which he was extraordinarily conceived.

Luke begins his narrative of Jesus' baptism, and thus the whole of Jesus' public ministry, by placing it, as is his custom, within its historical secular and religious context (see Lk 3:1-2). What follows, then, concerns a historical person who performs acts that are historical in nature, and so all the events narrated effect this historical world order and those living within it. All the doctrines that are revealed within the life and ministry of Jesus are thus ontologically grounded in the real world and are not ethereal events performed by godlike beings from or in another realm. For Luke, the historical anchor is the doctrine that Jesus is a historical man.

4. This accounts for why some ancient manuscripts have "prophets" rather than "Isaiah."

Within the Malachi passage, Mark adds "before your face" and changes "to prepare the way before me" to "to prepare your way." Thus we have an "I" (God) who is speaking not about himself ("me"), as in Malachi's original text, but we now have an "I" (God) speaking about someone other than himself ("your face"/"your way"). Instead of God sending a messenger to prepare a way for his own coming, Mark has God sending a messenger to prepare a way for someone else. Obviously, the messenger will immediately be identified as John the Baptist, and the "face" before whom he is coming and the way for whom he is preparing is Jesus. The doctrinal implication is that God (the Father) is sending John, his messenger, to prepare the way before his Son. (This in keeping with Mark's initial proclamation: "The beginning of the gospel of Jesus Christ, the Son of God.") And because the original speaker in both Malachi and Mark remains God and because within Malachi God tells of a messenger coming before "me," Mark's changing of "me" to "your" implies that the one for whom the way is now being prepared is equally God. If the referent to the "your" of Mark's Gospel is ontologically inferior (not God) to the "me" (God) in Malachi's prophecy, then the prophecy would not be fulfilled, for the one whose way is now being prepared for by God is not God. But Malachi states that God is sending a messenger to prepare for his own (God's) coming. In the light of this, we are to read Mark's quotation of Malachi as follows: "Behold, I [God the Father] send my messenger [John] before your face [Jesus], who shall prepare your [Jesus'] way." Because Mark changes "before me" to "before your face," the "your" designates that Jesus is God for the original "me" refers to God. Thus, for Mark, the prophecy is now being fulfilled in that God (the Father) has now sent the prophesied messenger (John the Baptist) who is now going before the face of God (Jesus) by way of preparation, and the God who is "sending" (the Father) and the God who is being "prepared for" (Jesus), while possessing distinct identities, are nonetheless both God—one is God the Father and the other is God the Son, who now actually possesses a

---

Also, in the Gospels of Matthew and Luke, the Malachi quote comes from the mouth of Jesus during his ministry. Jesus tells his disciples that John is more than a prophet, for he fulfills Malachi's prophecy: "Behold, I send my messenger before your face, who shall prepare your way before you" (Mt 11:10; Lk 7:27). Jesus, in quoting this prophecy, is not only identifying John as the messenger, but also identifying himself as the one for whom John is preparing. Because the "you" for whom John is preparing a way, according to Malachi, refers to God, Jesus is identifying himself as the coming of God, in whom the prophecy is fulfilled. Mark has apparently taken Jesus' designation of who John is and placed it at the beginning of his Gospel to identify who John is—the one who fulfills this prophecy.

human "face," that of Jesus. This is confirmed within the following allied passage taken from Isaiah.

It is set within the context of God "comforting my people," of his speaking "tenderly to Jerusalem," that "her iniquity is pardoned," that she has "received from the Lord's hand double for all her sins" (Is 40:1-2). In the light of God's forthcoming tender comforting mercy that will abound doubly more than Israel's sins, a voice is to cry out, "in the wilderness prepare the way of the Lord, make straight in the desert a highway for our God" (Is 40:3).[5] Mark abbreviates this passage as "the voice of one crying in the wilderness: 'Prepare the way of the Lord, make his paths straight,'" yet the content remains the same. Mark is alerting his readers that "the gospel of Jesus Christ" concerns the fulfilling of this prophecy, whereby God will speak tenderly to Jerusalem, comfort his people through the forgiveness of their sins, and more than double his benevolence upon them. The initial reason for perceiving this fulfillment lies in that God has sent a "voice" into the desert (John), who is preparing a way for the Lord (YHWH)—the highway for our God. Just as Mark, through Malachi, informs us that God has sent his messenger (John) before "your face" to prepare "your way"—"your" referring to Jesus (who is God's Son)—in Isaiah, the sent "voice" of God (John) is preparing a highway for "the Lord" (Jesus) who is "our God." Thus, for Mark, the fulfilling of the intertwining of Malachi's and Isaiah's prophecies testifies that Jesus is "the Lord" (YHWH) and so "God," for it is for him that "the messenger" is being sent and it is for him that the "voice" is preparing. Moreover, the "I" who sends the messenger (the Father), who gives "voice" to him who he sent (John), is distinct from him (Jesus) before whom the messenger is sent and whose "voice" for whom (Jesus) a way is being prepared. Again, the author of these fulfilled prophecies is God the Father, and the one in whom these prophesies are fulfilled is Jesus, the Lord. Both, while distinct in identity, are the one God.

All three Synoptic Gospels narrate that John the Baptist appeared in the wilderness of Judea, preaching a baptism of repentance for the forgiveness of sins. Matthew provides a summation of John's message: "Repent, for the

---

5. Historically, Isaiah's prophecy refers to God leading his people back to Jerusalem from Babylon. Thus the Israelites' pilgrimage is not simply their own return but God's as well, and so they are to prepare and make a way for him so that he might again dwell with them in the land that he has given to them from of old and so abide with them within the temple in Jerusalem. This event is now considered the prophetic prefiguring of Jesus, who as the Son of God will dwell with and lead humankind from the exile of sin and death to the heavenly Jerusalem, the true living land of promise.

kingdom of God is at hand" (Mt 3:1-2; see Mk 1:4 and Lk 3:2-3). The kingdom of God is immanent because of the presence of Jesus, who will enact and so embody the kingdom in his own person. At this juncture, Matthew and Luke, having previously introduced John and his ministry, place the prophecy from Isaiah 40:3, thus asserting, in consort with Mark, that Jesus is "the Lord" (YHWH) for whom John is preparing, and so acknowledging both his full divinity and his singular identity distinct from God (the Father).

Of some theological significance, Luke extends the Isaiah quotation to verse 5. Isaiah reads: "And the glory of the Lord shall be revealed, and all flesh shall see it together" (Is 40:5). Luke reads: "And all flesh shall see the salvation of God" (Lk 3:6). When the Lord comes, for whom John is preparing, "the glory of the Lord" will be revealed to all flesh because all will "see the salvation of God." Thus Jesus, as YHWH-Saves, will enact the saving deeds of God and in so doing manifest for all flesh to see the perichoretic glory of himself and his Father, for both, each in their own specific subjective manner, are the Lord—YHWH bringing salvation.

John's physical appearance is also a prophetic statement of Jesus as the one for whom he is preparing. Matthew and Mark note that John was dressed in camel hair and wore a leather girdle around his waist and ate locusts and honey (see Mt 3:4 and Mk 1:6). John's dress depicts him as the prophet Elijah (2 Kgs 1:8) of whom Malachi prophesied, "Behold, I will send you Elijah the prophet before the great and terrible day of the Lord's comes" (Mal 4:5; see Mt 17:11-12 and Mk 9:9-13). The great and terrible day of "the Lord" (YHWH) has come for Jesus (YHWH-Saves) has appeared.

This is theologically significant, for this great and terrible day is the Lord's judgment against sin. John, as Elijah, is preparing for this day by preaching a baptism of repentance and in so doing setting the baptized free from fear of this coming terrible day of God's judgment. Those baptized by John, having repented of their sins, are thus prepared for the coming of Jesus, in whom this terrible day of judgment will be realized. This is seen within Luke's Gospel where Luke comments on the reaction of those hearing Jesus declare that John is the messenger who has prepared the way for his coming and thus is the greatest of those born of woman: "When they heard this all the people and tax collectors justified God, having been baptized with the baptism of John; but the Pharisees and the lawyers rejected the purpose of God for themselves, not having been baptized by him" (Lk 7:27-30). Those baptized by John recognize in Jesus God's just condemnation of sin, but those who rejected John's baptism of repentance and so now reject Jesus find themselves outside the parameters of God's saving justice and thus face the terrible day of his judgment. Jesus, through his public ministry, will continue to preach repentance by way of preparing for the coming of God's kingdom and to allow those who believe in him to escape the pending judgment of God. While this terrible day of God's judgment initially appears with the coming of Jesus, it only finds definitive enactment on the cross, where Jesus, having assumed within his own humanity God's righteous condemnation of sin, vanquishes sin and its condemnation through his loving sacrificial offering of human life to his Father while freeing those who believe in him from divine condemnation. They need not fear the day of God's judgment, when Jesus comes in glory at the end of time to judge heaven and earth.[6] Thus John's appearance as the personification of Elijah is prophetic as to what is both immediately imminent and eschatologically pending. Jesus is about to appear before him for baptism, which will initiate his public ministry and culminate in his passion, death, and resurrection (the day of his judgment of sin and the day of his justifying the righteous). This in turn presages his future coming in glory, when he will effectuate the great and terrible day of the Lord, the day when all evildoers will be irrevocably condemned and the faithful will be wholly sanctified. With the coming of John comes Elijah, and with the coming of Elijah comes Jesus, and with his appearance the great and terrible day of Lord, the eschatological age, is at hand.

Matthew and Mark summarize that people came to John from Judea, Jerusalem, and around the Jordan confessing their sins and being baptized (see Mt 3:5 and Mk 1:5), and also provide some confrontational dialogue between John and the Pharisees and the Sadducees. John castigates them for their arro-

---

6. Jn 3:36 states: "He who believes in the Son has eternal life; he who does not obey the Son will not see life, but the wrath of God rests on him."

Peter, in his first Pentecost sermon, quotes Jl 2:28-32: "And in the last days it shall be, God declares, that I will pour out my Spirit upon all flesh." God will show "wonders in the heavens above and signs on the earth beneath ... before the great day of the Lord comes, the great and manifest day. And whoever calls on the name of the Lord shall be saved" (Acts 2:16-21). For Peter, the name that one must call upon to be saved on the great and manifest day of the Lord is Jesus, for he is the Lord.

Paul tells the Thessalonians that they need not fear "the day of the Lord," for "you are all sons of the light and sons of the day ... For God has not destined us for wrath, but to obtain salvation through Christ who died for us so whether we wake or sleep we might live with him" (1 Thes 5:1-11).

Paul also writes to the Romans, "There is therefore now no condemnation for those who are in Christ Jesus" because in coming in our sinful flesh, he has "condemned sin in the flesh." Those who live in Christ are thus free from such condemnation and empowered to live according to the Spirit (Rom 8:1-4).

gant assumption that they have no need of repentance because they have Abraham as their father, and if such be the case, they must "bear fruit that befits repentance," which is yet to be manifested. If they do not bear such good fruit, they, like a dead tree, will be cut down at its roots and cast into the fire (see Mt 3:7:10 and Lk 3:7-9). Luke, by way of contrast, also tells of those who humbly come to John (the multitudes, tax collectors, and soldiers) asking him what they must do to bear the fruit of repentance. John responds appropriately to each (see Lk 3:10-14). Luke is once more depicting the humble and lowly, as first exemplified in the shepherds, as those who are open to and eager for the appearance of the Savior, Christ the Lord. Here John's baptism prepares those who humbly repent of their sins. The repentant and baptized sinners come to faith in Jesus when he makes his appearance. Although John's baptism is not sacramental in the strict theological sense, it is nonetheless a sign, a symbolic act, that effects spiritual change in the lives of the baptized. They have turned away from sin and so have opened themselves to the truth of the Gospel found in the person of Jesus.

The Synoptics provide John's own self-conscious interpretation of who he is and what he is about. Luke notes that people, as at his circumcision and naming, questioned the significance of who he might be, "whether perhaps he were the Christ" (Lk 3:15). The Synoptics' presentation of John's words differs slightly, but the content is similar. Matthew, Mark, and Luke are in accord that John said that he baptizes with water for repentance, while the one coming after him will baptize with the Holy Spirit (Matthew and Luke, who adds "and with fire"). The reason is that he is mightier than John, and because of this John is not worthy to stoop down and untie his sandals or carry them (see Mt 3:11-12; Mk 1:7-8; Lk 3:15-16). John is fulfilling his prophetic vocation through his preaching of repentance and baptizing for the forgiveness of sin with water, which symbolizes purification from what is morally unclean. Those purified of sin are thus inwardly prepared in heart and mind to receive the one coming after him. The one coming after him (Jesus), who is yet to fulfill his prophetic vocation, is so mighty that he "will baptize with the Holy Spirit (and with fire)," an immersion into the very life of the Spirit such that one is actually, not merely symbolically, made holy. Here we find an allusion to and so the fulfillment of Ezekiel 36:25-27, where God professes:

> I will sprinkle clean water upon you, and you shall be clean from all your uncleanness and from all your idols I will cleanse you. A new heart I will give you, and a new spirit I will put within you; and I will take out of your flesh

the heart of stone and give you a heart of flesh. And I will put my spirit within you, and cause you to walk in my statutes and be careful to observe my ordinances.

This inner transformative cleansing in the Spirit, through which the Israelites are empowered to live holy lives, will result in their truly being God's people and God being their God (see Ezek 36:28). The further symbolism of fire accentuates the burning away of all contamination of inner evil, thus making the person entirely pure and unalloyed in his integral integrity, who he truly is (see Is 1:25, Zec 13:9, and Sir 2:5). This cleansing of fire will come when God sends his messenger before him, "the messenger of the covenant in whom you delight" (Mal 3:1-4).

The might of Jesus resides in his ability to baptize in the Holy Spirit, which bespeaks a divine power. Once again for John, the divine "I" of God within Ezekiel's prophecy now resides in Jesus, for he will be the one who is acting. He will cleanse the people of sin through his immersing them in the Holy Spirit, thus giving them hearts of flesh so as to keep the commandments. In so doing, they will truly be God's holy people and the holy God will truly be their God.

Although the people, in their expectancy, questioned whether John might be the Christ, John proclaims that the one coming after him (Jesus) is the Christ, for he properly possesses the Spirit as his own Spirit, by divine right, and thus possesses the divine capability of immersing others in his own divine Spirit. His being the Christ, the one inherently imbued with the Holy Spirit, is what makes Jesus mightier than John, the one whose sandals even John is unfit even to untie. This will be confirmed at Jesus' baptism, when the Father testifies that Jesus is his Son imbued with his own Holy Spirit, the Father's Spirit of Sonship.[7]

Also, in Jesus, Malachi's prophecy is coming to pass, for in him the great day of the Lord's fiery appearing is at hand, which will consume all evil, leaving only unalloyed goodness. All will delight in Jesus, for he is the harbinger of the new covenant. Matthew and Luke describe the nature of this purifying fire this way:

---

7. Although all the Synoptics narrate that John proclaimed that Jesus will baptize with the Holy Spirit, Luke's infancy narrative provides the foundational reason this is the case. Because Jesus was conceived by the Holy Spirit as the Son of God incarnate, he "naturally" possesses the Spirit as Son and thus rightly and properly possesses the literal inborn ability to baptize others with the Spirit. Nonetheless, only as Jesus enacts his saving deeds, particularly through his death and resurrection, will his ability to baptize in the Holy Spirit be activated, for only then will he be truly the Savior and Lord.

His winnowing fork is in his hand, and he will clear his threshing floor and gather his wheat into the granary, but the chaff he will burn with unquench-able fire. (Mt 3:12 and Lk 3:17)

In Isaiah, God tells the "worm Jacob, the men of Israel" that he, "the Lord," their "Redeemer ... the Holy One of Israel," will help them, for he will make a "threshing sledge" in which the mountains and hills will become chaff car-ried away by the wind. Then "you shall rejoice in the Lord; in the Holy One of Israel you shall glory" (Is 41:14-16; see Jer 15:7). For John, Jesus holds the win-nowing fork, he is the threshing floor, for in him will the pure grain (those immersed in the Holy Spirit) be gathered into the granary of God's kingdom, and the evil chaff (those not purified of evil) will be cast into never-ending fire. In so doing, Israel will know that their Redeemer Jesus has come to their aid, and so they will rejoice in the Lord, the Holy One of Israel. John's prophe-cies concerning baptism with the Holy Spirit and fire are the saving deeds that God promised within the Old Testament that he would perform. John none-theless predicates these divine saving deeds to the one who is mightier than he, whose appearance is immanent: Jesus. Thus Jesus is the divine Lord, the Holy One of Israel, the redeemer in whom all will rejoice.

Before proceeding to Jesus' actual baptism, a couple summary points can be made concerning John the Baptist's ministry. That John was calling people to repentance and baptizing them for the forgiveness of their sins as the way of preparing for the Lord and so the imminent coming of the kingdom of God alerts the audience that Jesus' impending public ministry is fundamentally salv-ific—the passing from the realm of sin into a holy life within God's kingdom.

For John, Jesus' forthcoming salvific public ministry is predicated upon who he is—the one mightier than himself who will baptize with the Holy Spirit—implying that Jesus is the Christ, the one who is divinely endowed and so inte-riorly imbued with the Holy Spirit and so capable of baptizing in the Holy Spir-it. Simply put, John has been sent by God to prepare for Jesus (YHWH-Saves), who is the anointed Christ and so the saving Lord (YHWH). John's proclama-tion embraces the Father, the Son, and the Holy Spirit: the *Father*, the one who sent him to prepare a way for the Lord; *Jesus*, the Lord for whom John is prepar-ing a way; and the *Holy Spirit*, for Jesus is the mighty Spirit-filled Christ.

Clearly, John's preparation and description of who he is preparing for are focused on the man Jesus. Once again, to know properly the man Jesus is to know the Trinity, for he is the one mightier than John, who, as the sav-ing Lord, possesses the Holy Spirit in such a singular manner so as to be the Christ capable of baptizing with the Holy Spirit. What is not evident thus far is how Jesus Christ the Lord will accomplish his salvific mission such that its achievement will result in the forgiveness of sins and his being able then to do what he came to do: baptize with the Holy Spirit and usher the saved into the holy kingdom of God. Jesus' baptism provides the initial clue as to how he will undertake his work of redemption.

The Baptism of Jesus

Jesus' baptism marks the inauguration of his public ministry, for the baptismal event is the Father actively commissioning him, in the anointing of the Holy Spirit, to establish his kingdom, and Jesus is actively embracing, in the same anointing of the Holy Spirit, that commission. This commissioning and embracing are predicated upon Jesus being, in communion with the Holy Spirit, the Son of the Father. This event was deemed so important within the apostolic church that all four Gospels and the Acts of the Apostles take account of it.

By way of a prolegomenon, Jesus' baptism must be considered one unique liturgical sacramental action. John's baptism was a symbolic act that signified the person's desire to be cleansed of sin and to turn more deeply to God, and so effected a change within the person by preparing him for the coming of the Messiah. Yet it did not effect an interior transformative sanctification by which a new relationship with God was established, one that differed in kind and not simply in degree from the one already present. Although Jesus' baptism will not establish a new kind of relationship with his Father, different from the one he already possessed through his conception by the Holy Spirit as the Son of God incarnate, it will effect an interior transformative change. The Holy Spirit will fashion him into the new high priest and the new Prophet, empowering him to perform his priestly and prophetic salvific acts by which he will establish the kingdom of God. In this sense, Jesus' baptism is sacramental in that the various symbolic acts contained within his baptism effected or caused what they symbolized, the whole of which brought about one inclusive, cumulative, transformative effect. Jesus received the Holy Spirit in a way that effected an interior change—the commissioning Spirit that empowered and so compelled him to undertake his salvific priestly and prophetic ministry. Jesus' baptism is also liturgical in that its various sacramental components were simultaneously visible acts of prayerful Spirit-filled communion between him and his Father. And within this prayerful sacramental communion that the Father bestowed upon him, in the descent of the commissioning Spirit, he grasped, in the same Spirit, his priestly and prophet salvific commission.

Jesus' baptism prophetically anticipates those priestly and prophetic salvific acts by which Jesus will establish the church's whole sacramental order and, in particular, the church's sacramental liturgical act of baptism. The Holy Spirit empowered Jesus, within the sacramental act of his baptism, to undertake his priestly and prophetic ministry, which will culminate in his death and resurrection. Thus the Holy Spirit empowered Jesus, within the sacramental act of his baptism, to enact those salvific acts that establish all the church's sacramental acts, by which Jesus, through the church's sacramental actions, cleanses the faithful of sin and makes them holy. Jesus' sacramental liturgical baptism specifically anticipates the church's sacramental liturgical baptism. Because Jesus' death and resurrection establish a new covenantal relationship with his Father, one that differs from the old covenant, the church's sacramental baptism, unlike John's, will establish a new kind of covenantal relationship between those baptized and the Father, for the Holy Spirit will be poured out upon those baptized in a manner that differs from the manner in which the Spirit came upon those baptized by John. Those baptized will now be interiorly sanctified by the indwelling of the Spirit so as to become adopted holy children of the Father after the manner of Jesus his Son.

The above prolegomenon will govern our entire exposition of Jesus' baptism. To grasp adequately the theological and doctrinal significance of this one simultaneous baptismal act, it is necessary to examine its various sequential facets.

Introductory Acts

John's ministry of repentance and baptism was the catalyst for Jesus' own baptism. The first symbolic act of the baptismal sequence is nonetheless performed by Jesus himself. Aware that John was preparing for his coming, Jesus actively steps forward for baptism. "Jesus came from Galilee *to* the Jordan *to* John, *to be* baptised by him" (Mt 3:13; see also Mk 1:9).[8] In this act, Jesus brings John's ministry to a close, for in being baptized by John, not only has John now fulfilled his prophetic commission, but Jesus has also now assumed his ministry, for which John was preparing. Also, in presenting himself to be baptized by John, Jesus identified himself and so embraced his full membership,

8. Only Mark notes that Jesus came "from Nazareth of Galilee." This could imply that he was aware that Jesus was raised in Nazareth by Mary and Joseph even though Mark does not have an infancy narrative, and thus that he may have also known the nature of Jesus' conception and birth.

an identity and membership that accrued to him at his conception, within his own Jewish people and their sinful history, as well as the whole race of sinful Adam—both of which need repentance.[9]

In Matthew, John perceives this and "would have prevented it," protesting that he should be baptized by Jesus rather than the other way around. John recognized on the one hand Jesus' Messianic holiness, but on the other hand failed to grasp that intrinsic to Jesus' Jewish Messianic mission is his assuming the sin of humankind as an actual member of Adam's race.[10] To John's protest Jesus responds, "Let it be so now; for thus it is fitting for us to fulfil all righteousness" (Mt 3:14-15). In presenting himself to be baptized, Jesus takes his ministry to those with whom he shares a common sinful lineage, both Jew and Gentile, and he is doing so by embracing the righteous acts of God, acts that he will fulfill. In this act of presenting himself for baptism and more so in the act of baptism, in this embracing the responsibility of fulfilling all righteousness, Jesus is performing that act of filial obedience manifesting that he is truly the Father's Son. Jesus' presenting himself finds its completion within the baptismal act, of which the Synoptics provide various detailed narrative accounts.

---

9. Mark stresses that the whole of Judea and all the people of Jerusalem came to John to be baptized, "confessing their sins." Jesus is numbered among them, the whole Jewish community, in need of repentance and thus also a member of the sinful race of Adam.

Luke notes that Jesus came to John "when all of the people were baptized." For Luke, only when John had fully prepared *all* the people for the coming of Jesus did Jesus present himself for baptism. Thus, having fulfilled his prophetically anticipated ministry, which finds its culmination in Jesus' baptism, John's ministry comes to an end. This is confirmed by Luke, having summed up John's ministry by stating, "So with many other exhortations, he preached good news to the people." He then says, "But Herod the tetrarch, who had been reproved by him for Herodias, his brother's wife, and for the evil things that Herod had done, added this to them, that he shut up John in prison" (Lk 3:19-20). Having completed his ministry, John's last witness to Jesus is his imprisonment and death—a testimony that prophetically anticipates the completion of Jesus' own ministry.

For a fuller study of Jesus assuming a humanity from the sinful race of Adam, see my *In the Likeness of Sinful Flesh: An Essay on the Humanity of Christ* (Edinburgh: T&T Clark, 1993).

10. By identifying with the whole sinful history of the Israelites as well as that of whole sinful history of humankind, Jesus is prophetically anticipating that the Jewish people and all nations will be blessed in him. In so doing, he will fulfill God's primordial promise made to Abraham that his descendants will be blessed, as will all nations. As a descendant of Abraham, Jesus will bless his own people as well as all the Gentile nations (see Gn 12:3, 18:18, 22:17-18, 26:4, 28:14).

The Sacramental Acts

Matthew narrates that "when Jesus was baptized he went up immediately from the water, and behold, the heavens were opened and he saw the Spirit of God descending like a dove and alighting on him; and lo, a voice from heaven, saying: 'This is my beloved Son, with whom I am well pleased'" (Mt 3:16-17). Mark also narrates that, having come up out of the water, Jesus "immediately saw the heavens opened and the Spirit descending upon him like a dove; and a voice came from heaven, 'You are my beloved Son; with you I am well pleased'" (Mk 1:10-11). Luke specifies that it was "when Jesus also had been baptized and was praying that the heaven was opened and the Holy Spirit descended upon him in bodily form as a dove, and a voice came from heaven, 'You are my beloved Son; with you I am well pleased'" (Lk 4:21-22).

John's physical act of baptizing Jesus is a sacramental liturgical causal act that simultaneously effects what it symbolizes. The symbolic acts of Jesus entering and coming up out of the waters immediately effect another set of symbolic physical heavenly signs: the concurrent physical tearing open of the heavens and the descent of the Holy Spirit in the (bodily) form of a dove. The accompanying voice from heaven interprets the meaning of these sacramental acts.

But what does the earthly sacramental act of immersion symbolize such that it effects the heavenly symbolic acts? The immersing in water, the going down into the water, and the rising up out of the water symbolically denote that Jesus has embraced a divine commission that demands that he must die so as to rise to a new life. Having presented himself as a sinful member of Adam's race and in the act of participating in John's baptism for the forgiveness of sin, Jesus, in this baptismal act, is laying hold of his salvific priestly ministry, which will culminate in his sacrificial death on the cross and in his resurrection—the putting to death of his sinful humanity inherited from Adam and the raising up, as the new Adam, of a new, re-created holy humanity that is free from sin and death.[11] These are the righteous acts that he is to perform. These earthly symbolic acts give rise to the heavenly symbolic acts.

11. Jesus would later explicitly interpret his baptism as such: "I came to cast fire upon the earth, and would that it were already kindled! I have a baptism to be baptized with; and how I am constrained until it is accomplished!" (Lk 12:49-50). This fire, as intimated in John's proclamation that the one coming after him would baptize with fire and the Holy Spirit, is the purifying fire of the Spirit and the true baptism that Jesus agonizingly awaits to enact in his death and resurrection, for then he will be free of Adam's sin and so free, as the glorious risen new

The symbolic opening of the heavens and the Spirit's descent in the (bodi-ly) form of a dove first testifies that Jesus has received the Holy Spirit that both commissions and empowers him to perform these priestly righteous acts. And they testify that, through Jesus' priestly self-sacrifice, the heavens will be truly torn opened and the risen priestly Jesus will pour forth from heaven the Holy Spirit upon the earth. In Jesus, the new high priest, the newly re-created race of Adam will once more have access to the heavenly Father. Thus, through Je-sus' priestly acts, the kingdom of God will be established, of which he will be the everlasting Davidic King.

Here we perceive the significance of Matthew's "behold." What Matthew wants the reader to behold is the "immediate" sacramental effect of Jesus' coming up out of the waters—the opening of the heavens and the descent of "the Spirit of God," and thus the act by which Jesus both willingly receives and obediently accepts the salvific priestly work that the Father has conferred upon him.[12] This opening of the heavens and the descent of the Spirit of God upon Jesus likewise gives rise to Matthew's "lo." This "lo" or "behold" (both English words translate the Greek word *idou*) accentuates the Father's unan-ticipated and astonishing definitive declaration that the one upon whom the heavens opened and the Spirit alighted is none other than his beloved Son, and he is well pleased precisely because his Son, through his paternal bestow-al of the Holy Spirit, has assumed the salvific task allocated to him.

That Luke accentuates the "bodily" form of the dove's descent through the opened heavens also highlights the sacramental effect of the baptismal act. The sacramental bodily form of the dove coming down out of the open heav-

---

Adam, to pour out the purifying fire and sanctifying power of the Holy Spirit, thus making all things anew.

Paul develops this theological understanding in his Letter to the Romans and his First Let-ter to the Corinthians. He portrays Jesus' death and resurrection as the putting to death of the human nature he inherited from Adam ("our old self") and the assuming of a new and glorious humanity in his resurrection and so becoming the new Adam. Christians, within baptism, are united to this dying and rising with Christ. In baptism, the sinful nature they inherited from Adam is put to death; they too are buried with Christ and rise to newness of life, sharing in his resurrected humanity (Rom 6:1-14; 1 Cor 15:20-24, 15:45). Romans 8 articulates the Spirit-filled life one is now able to live in Christ.

12. Unlike Mark and Luke, who speak of the Holy Spirit descending, Matthew employs the more common Old Testament designation: Spirit of God. In so doing, primarily for his Jewish audience, he is highlighting that the Spirit of God who came down upon those in the past is the same Spirit of God who is newly descending upon Jesus. Here Matthew is showing the conti-nuity of the present with the past and the fulfillment of the past in the present. The anointing of the Spirit of God in the past finds its completion in the Spirit of God descending upon Jesus at his baptism.

ens expresses the invisible particularity of this new coming of the Holy Spirit upon Jesus. Because the Holy Spirit descends in the symbolic bodily form of a dove from the symbolically opened heavens, his descent is his being sent by the Father, who resides symbolically above the heavens. Moreover, that the Spirit descends upon the waters of the Jordon in the bodily form of a dove recalls the Spirit hovering over the chaotic waters at creation and so bringing forth order and life, as well as the dove being sent forth by Noah from the ark at the receding of the flood waters to return with a newly grown olive shoot (see Gn 1:2 and 7:11). As in the past, at Jesus' baptism the hovering descent of the Holy Spirit bespeaks the coming of a new creation that is free from the chaos of sin and once more rightly ordered to the living God. Jesus, as the Father's beloved Son, possessing the creative and new power of the Holy Spirit, will accomplish this re-creation through his priestly sacrificial death and resurrection to the pleasure of his Father.

The terminating act within the whole liturgical sacramental event of Jesus' baptism is performed by the Father in his declaring that Jesus is his beloved Son, with whom he is well pleased. This act reveals that, although the Father "lay hidden" until this point within the baptismal accounts, he was actively present within the whole sacramental liturgical event. Being the Father, he is the source and culmination of the baptismal event. The Father sent John to prepare a way for the Lord, one that finds its terminus in Jesus' baptism and so in the recognition that he is the Lord. The Father, within the baptismal act, tears opens the heavens and sends the Holy Spirit upon Jesus, the Spirit that bears the Father's divine commission. The Father likewise empowers Jesus, in the sending of the Holy Spirit, to embrace his divine commission. The sacramental baptismal act, having accomplished all that it symbolized—Jesus' commissioning in the Holy Spirit and his embracing of that commission in the same Holy Spirit—the Father performs the act that is proper to him alone; that is, he interprets the whole of the sacramental baptismal event, an event in which he is the primary actor, by declaring: "This is my beloved Son, with whom I am well pleased." The Father has approved the whole baptismal sacramental liturgy in the revelation that Jesus is his obedient and so beloved Son who will enact his salvific plan.

In the light of the above, I want to accentuate the role of the Holy Spirit in relationship to the Father and to Jesus, his Son. The symbolic sacramental act of Jesus entering and rising out of the waters effects the symbolic opening of the heavens and the symbolic descent of the Holy Spirit in the (bodily) form of a dove upon Jesus, thus expressing the reality that Jesus is newly receiving the Holy Spirit. The new way in which Jesus receives the Holy Spirit is found within the twofold intertwining effect that the Spirit causes. The first effect of the Spirit's descent is the Father commissioning Jesus. The Father is newly conferring upon Jesus his commissioning Spirit. The second effect is that Jesus is obediently taking hold of his Father's commission within the same Spirit that his Father has bestowed upon him. The Holy Spirit is simultaneously both the Spirit of the Father's commissioning and the Spirit of the Son's embracing that commissioning. The Holy Spirit possesses both because he is the Father's Spirit of Sonship. The Holy Spirit, being the *Father's Spirit* of Sonship, imbues Jesus with the Father's will, which the Father desires for him as his beloved Son, conforming Jesus' filial will to the paternal will of the Father. Having done so, the Holy Spirit simultaneously, being the Father's *Spirit of Sonship*, prompts and compels Jesus to embrace freely and lovingly the will of his Father, thus attesting to his being the Father's beloved Son, which the Father confirms in his baptismal declaration.

But what is the full meaning of the Father's declaration? How do his words fully interpret the whole baptismal event? Do they define what is new in this baptismal descent of the Holy Spirit? The answer to these questions can be fully perceived within the liturgical nature of Jesus' baptism and within the Old Testament references within the Father's declaration; that is, in being the Father's beloved Son, the Father is anointing Jesus to be Prophet, Priest, and King.

The Prayerful Liturgical Acts

Jesus' baptism is a liturgical sacramental act and thus an act of prayer and worship. Matthew states, "the heavens were opened and he [Jesus] *saw* the Spirit of God descending like a dove and alighting upon him." Mark states that Jesus both "*saw* the heavens opened and the Spirit descending upon him like a dove." Luke says neither that Jesus saw the heavens open nor that he saw the Spirit descending upon him, but rather that "when Jesus was praying, the heaven was opened, and the Holy Spirit descended upon him in bodily form, as a dove." Thus Luke places the *seeing* of Matthew and Mark within the context of prayer. This implies that Jesus' seeing within Matthew and Mark is not simply an ocular physical experience. It is an experience of communion with what is beyond the opened heavens. It is a communion that is founded within the alighting communion of the Holy Spirit who descends from heaven. It is a communion with the heavenly Father in the love of the Holy Spirit and so an experience, in communion with the Spirit, of Jesus being the Father's beloved

Son. This seeing of the Father within the communion of the Holy Spirit is the experience that Luke describes simply as "when Jesus was praying." The sacramental act of baptism is a liturgical act that enacts and so manifests the unique mystical or prayerful union between the Father and Jesus, his Son, in the communion of the Holy Spirit. From within this prayerful communion, the Father declares that Jesus is his beloved Son, with whom he is well pleased. From within this prayerful communion, we are also able to perceive the answers to our questions.

First, within Luke's baptismal account, it is doctrinally significant that God the Father is the first to fulfill Gabriel's prophecy made at Jesus' conception. In answer to Mary's enquiry as to how her child will be conceived, Gabriel responds, "The Holy Spirit will come upon you, and the power of the Most High will overshadow you; therefore the child to be born will be called holy, the Son of God" (Lk 1:25). The Father confirms that Jesus is holy, having been conceived by the Holy Spirit, by being the first to declare publicly, in this new prayerful descent of the Holy Spirit upon him at his baptism: "You are my beloved Son." In being the first to call Jesus "the Son of God," the Father is identifying how this designation should be understood. The very nature of this singular prayerful communion between himself and his beloved Son provides the Father an opportunity to make a singular declaration concerning Jesus' identity. By sending forth his Spirit of Sonship upon Jesus, which uniquely binds them as Father and Son, the Father makes a singular metaphysical statement as to who Jesus truly is. If a human being were first to call Jesus "the Son of God," that could be understood merely as an honorific title, as in the Old Testament (see Jb 1:6, 2:1, 38:7; Hos 1:10). Because the Father, within this singular communion of the Holy Spirit, declares him to be "my beloved Son," that proclamation defines the divine ontological nature of Jesus' Sonship. Within Mark and Luke, the Father's directly addressing Jesus manifests that he is personally acknowledging and confirming his own paternal identity as Father in relationship to Jesus his Son, and in so doing equally acknowledging and confirming Jesus' own filial divine Sonship in relationship to him as Son. The words "my" and "beloved" designate the ontological particularity of the "you," which is that of being "my beloved Son." From within the ontological divine depths of the Father's eternal fatherhood, that which makes him *be* who he is as the Father, he reveals the eternal ontological divine depth of Jesus' identity, that which makes him *be* who he is: the Father's Son. For Jesus to be the beloved Son of the Father is for him to be God as the Father is God, precisely because the Father—acting as only the Father could act—pronounced him to be such.[13] The corroboration of this proclamation lies in the unique way the Holy Spirit, the Father's Spirit of Sonship, lovingly binds them together as the loving Father of the Son and the loving Son of the Father. As in the Incarnation, where Jesus was conceived by the overshadowing of the Holy Spirit and so possessed the Spirit of Sonship, at his baptism, in the hovering of the Holy Spirit, the Father pours out his Spirit of Sonship upon Jesus, attesting that he is his Son, who will now act in the Spirit on his behalf. It is this assuming the task of acting on the Father's behalf that Jesus manifests, in the Spirit of Sonship, that he is the beloved Son of the Father, for in his reciprocal love of Father, he will lovingly do his Father's will. This prayerful communion of the Father and the Son also testifies to their communion of wills, the paternal divine will of the Father and the human filial will of Jesus, the incarnate Son. Together, in the one Spirit, they will enact the righteous deeds of salvation on behalf of humankind.

Doctrinally, then, the Father's declaration at Jesus' baptism authenticates the singular manner of his conception and so his singular identity as his beloved Son, and in turn Jesus' conception by the power of the Holy Spirit becomes the ontological foundational act that authorizes the Father to make such an arresting proclamation at his baptism. Although the Father newly poured out his Holy Spirit on Jesus at his baptism, the commissioning Spirit through whom Jesus will enact his saving ministry, this baptismal anointing, is founded upon the Father's Spirit of Sonship, through whom Jesus was conceived as the Son of God incarnate. Thus, as Jesus was conceived by the Spirit of Sonship, and so singularly anointed as the Christ, in his baptism the alighting of the Spirit of Sonship confirms that he is the Christ, who singularly possesses the Spirit as the Father's Son. Again, the way Jesus is conceived by the Holy Spirit is the hermeneutical principle for grasping the full theological significance of the Father's declaration at his baptism. Both his conception and his baptism collaboratively authenticate that Jesus bears the Spirit of Sonship and so is ontologically the Father's Son.

Also, in the Father declaring, in the descent of the Holy Spirit, that Jesus is his beloved Son, we gain entrance and perceive beyond the torn heaven into the very mystery of the Trinity. The Father reveals himself as Father not by saying that he is the Father, but by revealing his Son by saying in the love of

13. The Gospels of Mark and Matthew do not contain Gabriel's prophecy that Jesus would be called the Son of God, but they do have the Father call him such. Thus the Father in their Gospels is equally making a metaphysical declaration as to the ontological status of Jesus' Sonship.

the Spirit, "You are my beloved Son." In this declaration the Father manifests himself as the loving Father of his Son. This is in keeping with who the Father is, for he is only the Father in that he fathers his Son, and so it is only proper that he reveal himself as the Son's Father. We perceive here that the Father is metaphysically incapable of revealing himself as Father apart from his Son, for he is defined as Father only in relationship to his beloved Son.[14] Thus, within the Trinity itself, although the Father knows himself to be "Father," he only does so in the fathering of his Son in the love of the Spirit, for his ontological identity as Father is entirely constituted and predicated upon his loving act of fathering his Son. The Father is, then, perfectly reflected in his Son, for the Son is, by definition, the perfect image of his Father. Thus, if the Father wishes to reveal himself to others, he must do so through his Son, for his Son is the perfect manifestation of himself. This is why, within the Synoptic Gospels, the Father never speaks of himself. He never says "Father." He only speaks of his Son and only in so doing reveals himself as the Son's loving Father. As the Father eternally speaks one Word—Son—within historical realm of the Incarnation, the Father speaks one Word—Son—and in it reveals himself.

In addition, Jesus, within the Synoptic Gospels, never speaks of himself as Son. He only speaks of himself in relation to his Father: "my Father." This is in keeping with who the Son is, for he is only the Son in that he is begotten of his Father, and so it is only proper that he reveal himself as the Father's Son. Again, we perceive here that the Son is metaphysically incapable of revealing himself apart from his Father, for he is defined as Son only in relation to his loving Father. Thus, within the Trinity itself, while the Son eternally knows himself as "Son," he knows himself as Son only in being begotten of the Father in the love of the Spirit, and so his ontological identity as Son is equally constituted and predicated upon his loving the Father in the same Spirit as the Father's Son. Thus the manner in which the Trinity exists determines the manner in which it reveals itself. In the love of the Holy Spirit, the Father eternally speaks one Word—Son—and so within the historical realm of the Incarnation he speaks, in the love of the Holy Spirit, one Word—Son. Equally, in the love of the Holy Spirit, the Son eternally speaks one Word—Father—and so within the Incarnation he speaks, in the love of the Holy Spirit, one Word—Father. Within the historically finite realm the Father, in the love of the Spirit, speaks

14. Although God does truly reveal himself with the Old Testament, especially in the revealing of his divine name, YHWH, his revelation as ontologically "Father" only takes place within and through the revelation of the person of Jesus, his incarnate Son.

and acts only to reveal his beloved Son, and the Son, in the same love of the Spirit in which he himself is loved, speaks and acts only to reveal his beloved Father.[15]

What we find in Jesus' baptism is the inauguration of this mutual reciprocal revelation. In the symbolic tearing open of the heavens, which had, since the last prophet, been shrouded in silence, the Father, through the descent of Spirit, breaks his silence by revealing to his Son: "You are my beloved Son." In this descent of the Holy Spirit, through the torn heavens, the Father is commissioning Jesus, his beloved Son, to speak and therefore break the silence of his hitherto silent hidden life in Nazareth. Only the Father can open the mouth of Jesus, for, as Son, his is the very mouth from which comes forth the Father's Word. Jesus, in assuming this commission in the Spirit, will reveal his Father through his priestly acts and prophetic words—the loving words and merciful acts of his Father. In so doing, he will establish the kingdom of God wherein humankind, in union with him, will be able to possess communion with his Father in the love of the Holy Spirit. Within that kingdom the faithful, in union with Jesus the Son, will hear the Father speak his Word—"You are my beloved sons"—and, in communion with Jesus, they, in the same love of the Spirit, will cry out "Abba," Father.[16]

Although Mark and Luke has the Father directly address Jesus—"You are my beloved Son, with you I am well pleased"—Matthew has the Father's words addressed to those present: "This is my beloved Son with whom I am well pleased" (Mt 3:16-17; Mk 1:10-11; Lk 3:21-22). For Matthew, the sacramental effect of Jesus' baptism is significant not only for Jesus, but also for those for whom he will now undertake his divinely commissioned saving ministry. They are to recognize that Jesus is the one who is imbued with the Father's Spirit and as such is the Father's beloved Son, in whom he is well pleased. Ultimately, for Matthew, this is what they are to "behold." They are to behold the man Jesus, for in beholding him they are seeing the Father's beloved Son, who singularly possesses the Father's Spirit of Sonship. Those who come to believe in Jesus must rightly recognize him to be the Son of God in accordance with the Father's declaration. Their profession of faith—in heart, mind, and voice— must echo the Father's revelatory confession—his heart, mind, and voice.

---

15. The above will be more fully developed in later chapters, especially chapter 7, which examines Jesus' filial relationship to his Father.

16. Paul later develops this notion. See Gal 4:6 and Rom 8:14-15.

Prophet, Priest, and King

The infancy narratives revealed that Jesus is of the linage of David because Joseph, his adopted father, is the "son of David" (Mt 1:20). Moreover, Gabriel declared to Mary that "the Lord God will give him [her son] the throne of his father David, and he shall reign over the house of Jacob forever; of his kingdom there will be no end" (Lk 1: 32-33). Within Jesus' baptism, we read, in the declarative words of his Father, that he will become the new Davidic King through his priestly and prophetic saving deeds. These prophetic words find their source within what he had prophetically declared previously within the Old Testament. They provide more specificity as to the newness of the descent of the Holy Spirit upon Jesus. They manifest that the Father, in the baptismal outpouring of the Holy Spirit, is anointing Jesus, commissioning him, so as undertake his priestly and prophetic ministry by which he will establish his Father's kingdom. Jesus, as the Spirit-anointed incarnate Son, becomes the new Prophet and the new high priest, and in so doing he becomes the everlasting King.

In declaring Jesus to be his beloved Son in whom he is well pleased, the Father is echoing the words that he spoke through Isaiah: "Behold my servant, whom I uphold, my chosen, in whom my soul delights; I have put my Spirit upon him, he will bring forth justice to the nations" (Is 42:1). The Father is likewise calling to mind the enthronement psalm, Psalm 2:7: "He said to me, 'You are my son, today I have begotten you.'" Within the Father's declaration, and thus within the interweaving of these texts and the prophetic contexts they bring with them, we find the Father's proclamation that Jesus is Prophet, Priest, and King.

The New Prophet

We can perceive within the Father's addressing Jesus as his beloved Son the inherent bestowal of Jesus' prophetic vocation. Although the Father's address to Jesus as "You are my beloved Son" within the concomitant sending for of his Spirit is a paternal declaration as to his divine identity, it is also a personal paternal directive mandating Jesus, as his beloved divine Son, to undertake the salvific cause that the Father intended from his conception. By anointing him with the Spirit of Sonship, the Father has singularly designated and appointed Jesus, and so in a real sense activated or quickened him as his beloved Son to speak and act on his behalf. Jesus' baptism is the Father's impelling

Jesus to undertake now his vocation as the new prophet and, as such, in a manner that differs in kind and not simply in degree from the prophets of old.[17] To be "the Son of the Father"—and so possessing, as the Christ, the Spirit of Sonship—not only designates the ontological divine identify of who Jesus is, but also determines his salvific mission as being the Father's prophetic voice. In his commissioning Spirit, the Father has unsealed the mouth of Jesus, his Son, to speak, to give voice, on his behalf. From this moment on, to hear the human voice of Jesus is not simply to hear the human voice of the Son, but it is also to hear equally the human voice of the Father within the very human voice of Jesus, his Son. For Jesus to be the Son is for him to be the voice of the Father. As Son, he has no voice other than that of the Father. In Jesus, the incarnate Son, the Father and the Son, within the communion of their mutually shared Spirit, speak with one and the same human voice.[18] The fact that, within the Father's descending Spirit, Jesus willingly assumes, in his reception of the Holy Spirit, his prophetic vocation is what elicits the Father's pleasure in him as his beloved Son.[19]

Here we can see the fulfillment of several Old Testament prophecies. God, speaking through Isaiah, declares:

> There shall come forth a shoot from the stump of Jesse, and a branch shall grow out of his roots. And the Spirit of the Lord shall rest upon him, the spirit of wisdom and understanding, the spirit of counsel and might, the spirit of knowledge and fear of the Lord. And his delight shall be in the fear of the Lord. (Is 11:1-3)

17. Jesus, as the new prophet, does not simply possess the assurance of "belief" or "faith" in what the Father reveals to him, but the assurance of "knowledge" in what the Father reveals. In his personal "knowing" of his Father, within the Spirit of Sonship, Jesus, as Son, "knows" what he will reveal.

18. Jesus implies this when he declares to his Apostles: "He who hears you hears me, and he who rejects you rejects me, and he who rejects me rejects him who sent me" (Lk 10:16; see Mt 10:40). To hear the Apostles is to hear Jesus, and to hear Jesus is to hear the Father who sent him. This is more explicit in John's Gospel: "He who rejects me and does not receive my sayings has a judge; the word that I have spoken will be his judge on the last day. For I have not spoken on my own authority; the Father sent me has himself given me commandment what to say and what to speak. And I know that his commandment is eternal life. What I say, therefore, I say as the Father has bidden me" (Jn 12:48-50; see also 5:24).

19. The Father will later confirm that Jesus is his anointed prophet. Within Jesus' Transfiguration, the Father, echoing his baptismal words, declares: "This is my beloved Son, with whom I am well pleased; listen to him" (Mt 17:5). "This is my beloved Son; listen to him" (Mk 9:7). "This is my Son, my Chosen; listen to him" (Lk 9:35). The Apostles are to listen to Jesus because he, as the Father's chosen prophet, speaks his Father's words, and therefore his Father is well pleased.

Being of the linage of David, the son of Jesse, Jesus is the "shoot" and the "branch" that have come forth from Jesse's decaying and withered stump. The reason for this outbreak of new life, we now perceive, is that God the Father has sent forth his Spirit so as to rest upon his Son, Jesus. In this Spirit, Jesus will now prophetically speak forth his Father's wisdom and counsel, for he, as Son, will possess the Father's knowledge. In his reverent fear of his Father, he will obediently speak with might, and his delight, within his reverent fear, will be in obediently doing his Father's will. In so doing, as Isaiah continues, Jesus will not see and judge with human wisdom, "but with righteousness he shall judge the poor, and decide with equity for the meek of the earth." Jesus also "shall smite the earth with the rod of his mouth, and with the breath of his lips he shall slay the wicked." The reason he can rightly judge those who are good—the poor and the meek—and condemn the wicked is that "righteousness shall be the girdle of his waist, and faithfulness the girdle of his loins" (Is 11:3-5). Within his public ministry, which flows directly from his baptismal commissioning, Jesus, through his prophetic words and righteous deeds, shows righteous mercy toward the humble, poor, and meek and righteous anger and condemnation toward the wicked. Within his prophetic words and actions, Jesus will initiate the Father's kingdom. This prophetic ministry will culminate in Jesus' sacrificial death, which speaks louder than words, and the Father's mercy toward sinners and condemnation of all evil. In this prophetic act, the Father will be well pleased and so raise his beloved Son, Jesus, to a new Spirit-filled life of everlasting glory. Thus we see the fulfillment of Isaiah 42:1, for by the Father "choosing" Jesus and "putting his Spirit upon him," Jesus "will bring justice to the nations" and so be king of all the nations.

It is not surprising that, within the Gospel of Luke, Jesus begins his public ministry by reading the passage of Isaiah 61:1-2 (see chap. 4).

> The Spirit of the Lord God is upon me, because the Lord has anointed me to bring good tidings to the afflicted; he has sent me to bind up the brokenhearted, to proclaim liberty to captives, and the opening of the prisons to those who are bound; to proclaim the year of the Lord's favor.

His Father has anointed Jesus with his paternal Spirit and has sent Jesus to bring the Father's good news (the Gospel) to the afflicted and downtrodden and so to set free those bound by sin and imprisoned by death. This is Jesus' prophetic ministry: to proclaim in word and deed his Father's year of favor. Again, through Jesus' death and resurrection, this year becomes an everlasting year of favor, for through his death and resurrection, Jesus rules over his everlasting kingdom.

What is now evident is the fulfilling of God's promise to Moses: "I will raise up for them a prophet like you [Moses] from among their [the Israelites'] brethren, and he shall speak to them all that I command him" (Dt 18:18). Here the Father appoints Jesus to be the new Mosaic prophet. His Father has chosen him from among his Jewish brethren and has commissioned him, within the baptismal anointing of his Spirit, to speak, as his incarnate beloved Son, all that he has commanded. Interestingly, God tells Moses how he can discern a false prophet from a true one. When what the prophet has prophesied comes to be, then one is able to judge that the prophet has spoken what is true and so has spoken what is truly of God. All that Jesus prophetically says and does within his public ministry will be actualized and so will prove him to be a true prophet, again, within his death and resurrection. Having seen, within Jesus' baptism, the Father anointing him to be his new Prophet, we can proceed to examine his equally anointing him to be the new high priest.

The New High Priest

Jesus' baptism sacramentally symbolizes his dying and rising, which in turn effects the opening of the heavens, through which the Spirit descends upon him. The Father's words, referencing Isaiah, confirm and specify the nature of Jesus' priesthood. Isaiah 42 begins the first of the four "suffering servant songs," and thus for Jesus to be his "chosen" one, the one in whom the Father "delights," is for him to embrace, in the Holy Spirit, the suffering deeds of righteousness, which "he will bring forth justice to the nations."[20] Jesus will reveal that he is truly the begotten Son of the Father by being the Spirit-anointed suffering servant. Within the Christian tradition, beginning within the apostolic church, the "suffering servant songs" define Jesus' priestly ministry and so confirm that he is the new high priest.[21]

20. The Father's proclamation that Jesus is his beloved Son alludes to God's commanding Abraham to sacrifice his son, Isaac: "Take your son, your only son Isaac, whom you love" (Gn 22:2). The act that God will ultimately not allow Abraham to do he will—sacrifice his only beloved Son for the forgiveness of sins.

21. Jesus three times predicts that he is going to suffer and die, and rise on the third day (see Mk 8:31, 9:31, and 10:33-34 and parallels). During the Last Supper, Jesus says of Judas: "For the Son of man goes as it is written of him, but woe to that man by whom the Son of man is betrayed" (Mk 14:21; see also Mt 26:24 and Lk 22:23). Luke, on two occasions, emphasized that the risen Jesus "opened" the minds of those to whom he appeared and of those for whom he interpreted the Scriptures so that they would understand "that it is written that the Christ should suffer and on the third day rise from the dead" (Lk 24:25-27, 24:44-47). Matthew interprets Jesus' healing as the fulfillment of Isaiah 53:4: "he took our infirmities and bore our diseases"

Within the Father's baptismal declaration we find the entirety of the "suffering servant songs." Jesus, as suffering Son-Servant, could rightfully say that "the Lord called me from my mother's womb, from the body of my mother he named my name," for his Father sent him into the world to take flesh from his mother, Mary, and his Father, through Gabriel, designated that he should be called Jesus, YHWH-Saves. Within his baptism, Jesus now recognizes that he is his Father's servant who is to "bring Jacob back to him" and gather "Israel" and in so doing he will "be honored in the eyes of the Lord," his Father.[22] Jesus will also become aware of the truth spoken by his Father: "I [God] will give you [Jesus, my Son] as a light to the nations that my salvation may reach to the end of the earth." Thus "the Redeemer of Israel [God the Father] and his Holy One [Jesus, his Son], [who is] deeply despised, abhorred by the nations, the servant of rulers" declares: "Kings shall see and arise; princes, and they shall prostrate themselves; because the Lord, who is faithful, the Holy One of Israel, who has chosen you" (Is 49:1-7).

Jesus is the one whom his Father has given a prophetic tongue so that he can teach the weary. At his baptism, the Father has "opened" his "ear," and Jesus, within his baptism, has not rebelled at his Father's word nor has he turned back. Rather, because Jesus has spoken his Father's word, "I gave my back to smiters, and my cheeks to those who pulled my beard; I hid not my face from shame and spitting." Because of this, God the Father will vindicate his Son and declare him innocent (Is 50:4-11).

Although God prophetically proclaimed "Behold, my servant shall prosper, he shall be exalted and lifted up, and shall be very high," Jesus would come to realize that, as the Father's Servant-Son, such high exaltation would only come through his being lifted high upon the cross, for only in his priestly sacrificial death would he truly prosper as the king within his Father's kingdom. In Jesus, his Servant-Son, the Father's words will be fulfilled: "As many were astonished at him—his appearance was so marred, beyond human semblance, and his form beyond that of the sons of men." His very upbringing stands against

---

(Mt 8:17). In the Acts of the Apostles, Peter tells his Jewish listeners that, while they, out of ignorance, handed Jesus over to be killed, this was still done so "what God foretold by the mouth of the prophets, that his Christ should suffer, he thus fulfilled" (Acts 3:18). The Ethiopian eunuch is reading Isaiah 53:7-8 when Philip meets him, and it is from this passage that Philip explains to him the whole of the Gospel (Acts 8:26-35). Peter also references the prophecies concerning Jesus's sacrificial death (see 1 Pt 1:10-11, 2:22-25). The Book of Revelation portrays Jesus as the Lamb who was slain and so looks back to Is 53:7 and Zec 4:10 (see 5:6).

22. This prophecy also speaks of the suffering servant being a prophet. From his mother's womb the Lord "made my mouth like a sharp sword" (Is 49:2).

him, for he was but a "young plant" rooted in "dry ground." Therefore he had no "comeliness that we should look at him, and no beauty that we should desire him." Because Jesus is an unremarkable man from Nazareth, he is "despised and rejected by men; a man of sorrows, and acquainted with grief; and as one from whom men hide their faces he was despised, and we esteemed him not." Yet it is upon such a man, Jesus, that the Father bestowed his Spirit and so appointed his Servant-Son to be the new high priest who would offer himself as the supreme sacrifice for the forgiveness of sin. Jesus is the priest who "has borne our griefs and carried our sorrow ... smitten by God, and afflicted. But he was wounded for our transgressions, he was bruised for our iniquities; upon him was the chastisement that made us whole, and with his stripes we are healed ... [for] the Lord had laid on him the iniquity of us all." Jesus would be the sacrificial "lamb" who would be judged worthy of death, "cut off from the land of the living, stricken for the transgression of the my (God's) people," and thus "they made his grave with the wicked and with a rich man in his death, although he had done no violence and there was no deceit in his mouth." But because Jesus, as high priest, "makes himself an offering for sin," his days will be prolonged and the Lord will prosper him, for "he will see the fruit of his travail of his soul and be satisfied; by his knowledge shall the righteous one my servant, make many to be accounted as righteous; and he shall bear their iniquities." Because Jesus will pour out "his soul to death" and so "numbered with transgressors," having "bore the sins of many" and making "intercession for the transgressors," his Father will raise him up to sit among "the great" and "the strong" as the Lord and King of an everlasting kingdom.

Although Jesus will only fulfill these prophecies during his public ministry and particularly within his passion and death, these yet unfulfilled prophesies were implanted within him at his baptism.[23] They were implanted when the Father poured out his Spirit upon him and so appointed him to be his suffering Servant-Son, who would take upon himself the sin of all humankind and through priestly self-sacrifice to his Father obtain forgiveness. Thus Jesus literally embodies both priest and victim, and the supreme efficacy of his priestly self-sacrifice will reside within his being, both as priest and victim,

---

23. To James and John's request to sit at his right and left within his kingdom, Jesus responds, "Are you able to drink the cup that I will drink, or be baptized with the baptism with which I am baptized?" (Mk 10:38). Here Jesus is explicitly conjoining his baptism with the cross, which is the fulfillment of the prophetic act of his baptism. Even more to the point, Jesus states: "I have a baptism to be baptized with; and how I am constrained until it is accomplished" (Lk 12:50). Jesus anxiously waits for the enactment of his real baptism (the cross), of which John's baptism was a prophetic prefigurement.

the Spirit-anointed and so holy Son of God. Jesus, as the Son of God incarnate, will be the supreme efficacious high priest because he will offer himself as the supreme efficacious sacrifice.[24] Jesus, in assuming, in the Spirit, the priestly responsibility of fulfilling these prophecies, elicited his Father's good pleasure. Moreover, in fulfilling these prophecies, Jesus will authenticate the Father's declaration that he is truly his beloved Son.

The King

In all the above, and thus the reason for its detailed description, we recognize that the Father, within Jesus' baptism, confers upon him, in the outpouring of the Spirit, the titles Prophet and Priest. And in enacting his prophetic and priestly vocation, throughout his public ministry and decisively in his death and subsequent resurrection, Jesus will establish his Father's kingdom and become its everlasting King. Here the Father's quoting from Psalms 2 takes on its theological import:[25] "I will tell of the decree of the Lord: He said to me, 'You are my son, today I have begotten you'" (Ps 2:7).[26] Kings and nations will plot "against the Lord's anointed," Jesus, the Son who was anointed by his Father at his baptism. Yet his Father is assuring Jesus, his anointed Son, that he will establish him as the everlasting king: "I have set my king on Zion, my holy hill" (Ps 2:6). This is the Father's decree: because of and through Jesus' prophetic and priestly ministry, he will "make the nations your heritage, and the ends of the earth your possession" (Ps 2:8). In this way, the Father will manifest his pleasure in he who is his beloved Son—Jesus, his Spirit-anointed Prophet and Priest and so King.

24. This is the major doctrinal theme of the Letter to the Hebrews.

25. We have already seen the significance of Ps 2 within our treatment of Luke's infancy narrative in relationship to Herod's plotting to kill the child, Jesus.

26. The Father does not actually quote the last phrase of Ps 2:7, "today I have begotten you." This "today" has multiple connotations. (1) It could refer to the eternal "today" of Jesus, as the Father's Son, being eternally begotten in the love of the Holy Spirit (see Heb 1:5). (2) It could refer to the day of Jesus' conception, when the Son is begotten, in the love of the Holy Spirit, as man. (3) As in the present case, it could refer to Jesus' baptism—the day on which Jesus is "begotten" by the Father, in the outpouring of the Spirit, as his kingly Prophet and high priest (see Heb 5:5). (4) It could be the day of his resurrection, when the Father begets Jesus as his risen Son—the Lord of glory (see Acts 13:30-33). (5) It could also refer to the everlasting day when the Father enthrones Jesus forever, having put all of his enemies under his feet, as the kingly Son of the new heaven and new earth (see 2 Pt 1:16-19; Peter is alluding back to Jesus' Transfiguration, where as the begotten Son of the Father he is revealed to be glorious Lord. See Mt 17:1-8, Mk 9:2-8, and Lk 9:28-26). In a sense, all these "todays" embody one "today"—when the Father establishes from and for all eternity the glory of his Son—Jesus Christ the Lord and King.

What we find in Jesus' baptism and in the Father's confirming proclamation is both the inauguration and the prefigurement of the entire Gospel. The sacramental act of Jesus' baptism initiates and anticipates the fullness of the Gospel as embodied in Jesus, the Father's Spirit-anointed Son. There is the earthly sacramental liturgical action of Jesus being immersed into the waters of the Jordan, symbolizing his death and resurrection. This sacramental action immediately gives rise to the symbolic physical heavenly action, the tearing open of the heavens and the descent of the Holy Spirit in the (bodily) form of a dove. These sacramental actions effect the reality of the Father's imbuing Jesus with the Holy Spirit so as to commission and so authorize and empower him to inaugurate his saving mission, which will culminate in the actual opening of the true heavenly realm with its outpouring of the Holy Spirit. Jesus, as the bearer of the prophetic Spirit, will accomplish his priestly ministry, which culminates in his death and the putting to death the sin-marred humanity he received from Adam. By his resurrection, he will become the new Adam in assuming of his new Spirit-filled and glorious humanity. His baptism symbolically and prophetically anticipated all of this in his descending into and rising out of the waters.

Having gained access to the heavenly realm of his Father, Jesus, as the risen Lord and Savior, will be empowered in the Spirit to baptize in the Holy Spirit, and in so doing fulfill John's prophecy prior to his baptism. Those whom Jesus baptizes in the Spirit will be cleansed of sin and made holy and so live within the kingdom of God. All of this anticipates the final eschatological opening of the heavens, from which the Spirit-filled resurrected Jesus will descend to gather all the Spirit-filled faithful into the heavenly presence of his Father. There, in union with their glorified Savior and Lord, they will reside with their Father within the communion of life and love of the Holy Spirit. All the above is contained within the Father's baptismal declaration, for in heaven he will everlastingly avow to Jesus "You are my beloved Son in whom I am well pleased" and declare to all "This is my beloved Son, in whom I am well pleased." There too the Father will forever affirm to all who now share, with and in and through Jesus, his paternal Spirit of Sonship: "You are my beloved son and daughters, in whom I am well pleased."

Concluding Theological Points

The baptism of Jesus is another testimonial act that reveals both the Trinity and the Incarnation. As within the act of Jesus' conception, the baptismal act is an interwoven threefold act—the act of the *Father* conferring upon Jesus his commission by sending the Holy Spirit and empowering him in the same Spirit to embrace that commission; the act of the *Holy Spirit*, through whom the Father's commission is bestowed upon Jesus and in whom Jesus embraces his Father's commission; and the act of *Jesus* welcoming and embracing his Father's divine commission in communion with the Holy Spirit. This threefold act is contained within the Father's declaration that Jesus is his beloved Son, in whom he is well pleased. He is pleased because Jesus, as his Son, has assumed, in the Holy Spirit, the mission he has conferred, in the Spirit, upon him. Of utmost importance is that this Trinitarian tableau is enacted upon the historical man: Jesus. To declare that the man Jesus is the Son is to declare that the Son exists as man (the Incarnation), and within this declaration the Father and the Holy Spirit are identified, for Jesus is the only beloved Son of the Father only in communion with the Holy Spirit (the Trinity). Thus, again, to know rightly the man Jesus is to know the Father, the Son, and the Holy Spirit.

The pleasure of the Father is predicated upon Jesus fulfilling the prophetic and priestly salvific work that the Father has given him to do. Although the Father has summoned him to present himself before John for baptism and has conferred upon him the Holy Spirit, through whom he will carry out his prophetic and priestly mission, Jesus has yet to accomplish it and so is yet to be king. The work of salvation still lies in the future. Thus, within the sacramental act of the baptism, in the Father sending forth of his Spirit upon Jesus, the Father is hastening Jesus to become Jesus. The Father has given to him anew the Spirit, by which he will be able to perform his saving prophetic and priestly work and so truly become who he is, Jesus (YHWH-Saves). The Father, then, has given to Jesus, within his baptism, the Spirit, whereby he is able to enact his name. Jesus will decisively enact his name in the power of the Spirit through his saving prophetic and priestly sacrificial death on the cross, and the Father, in the Spirit, will decisively express his pleasure in raising Jesus from the dead as the universal Savior and definitive Lord and King. As stated above, the Father's definitive expression of his pleasure will eternally echo in heaven when Jesus brings all the faithful to the fullness of glory.

I stressed when treating the infancy narratives that only as Jesus enacts his name, YHWH-Saves, does he reveal that he is truly the Son of God and so fulfill the prophecy within the narratives that such would he be called. In Jesus' baptism, the Father inaugurates this by empowering him to go forth in the power of the Holy Spirit. Only as Jesus fulfills his vocation that he initially embraced within his baptism is the declaration of the Father made manifest—that Jesus is his beloved Son. The evident point is that only as Jesus becomes who he is, only as he enacts, in and through the Spirit, his divinely given name, only as he becomes more fully the one who saves his people from their sins, does he express and make apparent his divine identity as the only Son of the Father. In enacting his name, as Jesus becomes Jesus, he confirms that he is "the Son."

Within the baptism, we perceive not only the present and future saving acts of Jesus as YHWH-Saves but also those of the Father and the Holy Spirit. The act of the Father sending forth his Spirit upon Jesus, which will continue throughout Jesus' entire saving ministry, is the enacting of his paternal name as Father-YHWH-Saves. The act of the Holy Spirit in empowering Jesus to be Jesus, which will continue throughout Jesus' entire saving ministry, is the enacting of the Spirit's "hidden" name as Spirit-YHWH-Saves. Within the one sacramental baptismal act we perceive in the man Jesus (YHWH-Saves) the perichoretic saving acts of the entire Trinity—the one God, YHWH.

In fulfilling his baptismal charge through his saving action, Jesus will not only demonstrate that he is the Son, but also simultaneously reveal the Father and the Holy Spirit. As the baptismal act is the threefold communal act of the Father, the Son, and the Holy Spirit, every saving act that Jesus will perform as Son will contain within it the distinct contributing saving acts of the Father and the Holy Spirit. The acts by which the Trinity is revealed are the same acts by which each contributes, in accordance with who they distinctively are, to humankind's salvation.[27] This will become clear when we treat Jesus' public ministry and his passion, death, and resurrection.

The baptism of Jesus will become the paradigm or template for the apostolic church's own liturgical sacramental baptismal practice because Jesus' own baptism is the foundational liturgical sacramental act that prophetically anticipates the efficacy of the future sacrament of Baptism. This sacrament will be instituted in Jesus' own death and resurrection. In his dying and rising, Jesus obtains his authority and power, as the risen Lord, to send forth his

---

27. The Trinity is not revealed through some proclamation—Jesus simply telling us that the one God is the Father, the Son, and the Holy Spirit. It is by their acts that we come to know them, for each acts to reveal who each one is. The Father performs those specific paternal salvific acts that reveal that he is the Father. The Son preforms those specific filial salvific acts that reveal that he is the Son. The Holy Spirit performs those specific Spirit-filled salvific acts that reveal that he is the Holy Spirit. Obviously, as seen above within the baptismal event, they perform their specific identifiable salvific acts in communion with one another and so concurrently reveal that they are the one God. All three persons, as the name "Jesus" declares, are "YHWH-Saves."

Spirit within the sacrament of baptism so that others can die and rise with and in him and so share in his glorified and risen humanity. Thus, within the sacrament of baptism, Jesus continues, until the end of time, to be Jesus—YHWH-Saves—for within this sacrament he continually brings the saving effects of his saving acts to bear upon those baptized, their dying to sin and rising to new life in the Holy Spirit. Jesus' liturgical action within his own baptism is nonetheless the same liturgical action emulated and signified within the Christian sacrament of baptism. Although the reality of baptism is founded within Jesus's death and resurrection, the baptismal liturgical sacramental action finds it source within Jesus' own baptism, as it is the very liturgical sacramental sign of what Jesus enacted in his death and resurrection. From this rather lengthy theological study of Jesus' baptism, we perceive its centrality within the life and ministry of Jesus. All that was prophesied concerning Jesus within the infancy narratives is confirmed, and all that Jesus will do after his baptism is prophetically revealed. Jesus of Nazareth is the Son of God, the anointed Spirit-filled Christ, who is the new Prophet and high priest and will become the universal Savior and so the everlasting King and definitive Lord.

Luke's Genealogy

Matthew began his Gospel with Jesus' genealogy and emphasized that Jesus is the Christ, "the son of David, the son of Abraham" (Mt 1:1). In so doing, Matthew highlights Jesus' Jewish ancestry and the promises made to Abraham (in him all nations will be blessed) and to David (his royal offspring will establish an everlasting kingdom over which he will reign forever). Jesus will be the Christ because he is not begotten of Joseph but of the Holy Spirit and so will fulfill these promises made from of old.

Luke, in contrast, provides his rendering of Jesus' genealogy immediately following Jesus' baptism. "Jesus, when he began his ministry, was about thirty years of age, being the son [as was supposed] of Joseph" (Lk 3:23). Why does Luke place his genealogy at this juncture? Why not, like Matthew, at the onset of his Gospel, which seems a more proper location? As Matthew placed his genealogy at the beginning for theological reasons, so Luke's positioning of his genealogy determines its doctrinal significance.

Luke sandwiches his genealogy between Jesus' baptism and "when he began his ministry." Jesus' public ministry finds its impetus in his baptism, for there, in the descent of the Holy Spirit, he, as the Son of God, embraced the commission given to him by his Father. He did so when he was "thirty years" old, and thus he is taking up in earnest what was already intimated when he was twelve. At that time, having commemorated the Passover covenant, his parents, Mary and Joseph, found him in the temple holding a colloquy with the teachers. After asking about his behavior, they were told: "Did you not know that I must be in my Father's house/about my Father's business?" Mary and Joseph "did not understand the saying which he spoke to them" (Lk 2:49-50). Mary and Joseph did not fully grasp the significance of Jesus' "twofold parenthood." As parents, they sought him out only to be told that he was in his Father's house transacting his Father's business. For Luke, what the young boy Jesus consciously perceived at twelve he now, as a mature man of thirty, fully embraces. Having been charged by his Father within the communion of the descending Spirit, the living divine communion symbolized in the temple, Jesus, the Father's Son, solemnly undertakes the completion of his Father's saving work—the establishing of a new covenant through his becoming the new Prophet and the new Priest, the suffering servant who will offer himself as the new Passover lamb of sacrifice.

In a more intense manner than Joseph and Mary, the people who will now be the recipients of Jesus ministry will be challenged by what is true and what they presume to be true. Joseph and Mary knew that Joseph was not the father of Jesus, though they did not fully perceive that he was the Father's Son. So ordinary was Jesus' childhood and maturing into manhood that everyone who knew him assumed that Mary was his mother and Joseph was his father. What is fascinating is that Luke states that the undisputed supposition is that Joseph was Jesus' father. Although it is true that Mary is his mother (that is no mystery), the mystery that will now be revealed during the course of Jesus' public ministry is who his father is—the mystery of the Incarnation. Those confronted with Jesus' teaching and actions will be forced to ask their own form of Mary's question. Mary asked, "How can this be, since I have no husband?" (Lk 1:34). Those from his hometown of Nazareth will shortly ask, "Is not this Joseph's son?" (Lk 4:22). For Luke, this is the doctrinal question that began with Mary and continues throughout the Gospel: Who is the father of Jesus? The answer to this question once more resides in the manner of his conception. Having been conceived within the womb of Mary by the overshadowing power of the Holy Spirit determines and so defines him as the Father's Son. To know Jesus' Father is to know Jesus. Having been baptismally commissioned in the same Spirit of Sonship in which he was conceived, Jesus is now eager to embark on his prophetic and priestly mission—the revealing of the Father and

in so doing revealing himself as the Father's Son—and he will do so by transacting his Father's business.

Luke, however, is not simply alerting us to Jesus' public ministry wherein
he will reveal his true Father. His proximate concern lies in the genealogy that
immediately follows. Although Matthew begins his genealogy with Abraham
and makes his way up to "Jacob, the father of Joseph," Luke begins his genealogy with Joseph, the supposed father of Jesus. Joseph is "the son of Heli, the
son of Matthat, the son of Levi ... [and concludes] the son of Seth, the son of
Adam, the son of God" (Lk 3:23-38).

The Father has just proclaimed Jesus to be his beloved Son, and Luke proceeds to trace his ancestry to the first human being, Adam, who does not
have a human father and is therefore "the son of God." Thus human history is
bookended by two sons of God, neither of whom has a human father: the first,
Adam, created at the dawn of time, and Jesus, begotten from all eternity. There
is, then, for Luke, a theological interlacing between these two sons.

Because all human beings spring from Adam's seed, they too, having been
begotten in Adam's image, were to be sons of God, because God is ultimately the father of Adam's race. But while Adam was created by God and so "the
son of God," the whole Jewish tradition bears witness that Adam sinned, and
so the children sprung from his seed are now marked by his sin—the sons of
Adam were no longer truly the sons of God. Sin now scarred their filial divine image, their minds and hearts deformed, having inherited their father's
sin-disfigured humanity. No longer did they share in the holiness of God and
so no longer did they enjoy their filial relationship with God their father. The
subsequent history of Adam's race is a history of sin and a history of God's
attempt, specifically and particularly in his covenantal relationship with the
Jews, to restore the original paternal and filial relationship between God and
Adam's race.

For Luke, Jesus, being a son of Adam, was born into this sinful history and
so bore the sinful birthmark of his father. He, like Adam's race, was not a son
of God. But for Luke, the offspring of sinful Adam culminated in Jesus, the Son
of God. The race of Adam that had no father other than God will now be restored to its primordial divine sonship by Jesus, the new Adam, who had no
father other than God. Thus Jesus is both a sin-tainted son of Adam and the
holy Son of the Father, and being such he is able, as God's Son, to re-create, as
Adam's son, the sons of Adam into holy sons of God. For Luke, the S/son of
God refashions the sons of God into "Sons" of God.

What we find in Luke's positioning of Jesus' genealogy immediately after his baptism is his narrative concerning the centrality and primacy of Jesus. The whole of human history, a history "of Adam, the son of God," finds its center in Adam's son, Jesus, the Son of God, and with this centrality his primacy is established. The entirety of Adam's history, from beginning to end, finds its apex and culmination in Jesus. All who have come forth from Adam before Jesus and all who come forth from Adam after Jesus are to be incorporated into Jesus, for, as the Adam-incarnate Son of God, he will re-create the whole of humankind through his death and resurrection and so be empowered to baptize the whole of humankind with the Holy Spirit, his Spirit of Sonship. In so doing, he will bring humankind into communion with himself as the resurrected, re-created Adam-incarnate Son and so into communion with his and now humankind's Father. For Luke, God, in creating Adam as his son and thus in the likeness of his divine Son, prophetically prefigured and anticipated the new Adam—Jesus, his beloved Son. Thus, from the onset of creation, from the creation of Adam, the son of God, God intended to send his eternal Son as the new Adam in whom all those created by God, the whole Adam, would find their consummate sonship and so filial communion with him, their true Father.[28]

The Temptations of Jesus

The Gospel of Mark tells us succinctly: "The Spirit immediately [after his baptism] drove [literally, thrust him forth forcibly] into the wilderness. And he was in the wilderness forty days, tempted by Satan; and he was with the wild beasts; and the angels ministered to him" (Mk 1:12-13). Matthew first states that Jesus "was led up by the Spirit into the wilderness to be tempted by the devil. And he fasted for forty days and forty nights and afterwards was hungry" (Mt 4:1-2). Luke emphasizes that Jesus "was full of the Holy Spirit" and that he "returned from the Jordon, and was led by the Spirit for forty days in the wilderness, tempted by the devil. And he ate nothing in those days" (Lk 4:1-2).

The baptism of Jesus took place at the Jordan River, a lush ecosystem (by Palestinian standards) surrounded by desert wilderness. Luke alludes to this

28. Although impossible to prove that Paul was aware of the Lucan tradition and so Luke's genealogy, the Pauline theology of Jesus as the new and second Adam is in accord with Luke's understanding (see 1 Cor 15:45-49; Rom 8:15-21).

A common patristic tradition is that, because God created man through his Word/Son and thus in the image of the Son, it is fitting that man be re-created in the image of the Son through the incarnated Son—Jesus. See, e.g., Athanasius, *De Incarnatione*.

by noting that Jesus "returned from the Jordan" back into the wilderness. Given that Jesus received the Holy Spirit, the Spirit of life, at the Jordan, the Jordan is symbolic of life and fruitfulness, a mini Garden of Eden, an oasis where the animals were tame. But the world after Adam's sin was no longer the verdant good garden that God created. Jesus returned into the barren wilderness of sin and death inhabited by wild beasts, and so into the domain of Satan. Thus the Spirit drove and thrust him into this wilderness because his mission, conferred upon him at baptism, was to transform, through the Spirit of life, the barren world of sin and death into the verdant garden of God's kingdom. Jesus' Spirit-filled task is to do battle with Satan, the author of sin and death, and re-create the desolate wilderness of the world into a garden of life. This will be seen later within Jesus' exorcisms, healings, and miracles, all of which involve the vanquishing of evil and the restoration of life. The ultimate expression of this will be in Jesus' burial and resurrection, where Jesus is buried in a garden of death only to rise in the resurrected Spirit, thus transforming it into a garden of life (see Jn 19:41).[29] This will result in the opening of all graves when the world will become a new creation free from death.

The forty days could be reminiscent of either the forty days Moses spent on Mt. Sinai (see Ex 24:18) or the forty years the Israelites sojourned in the wilderness, during which they often fell into temptation (see Dt 8:2). Within Matthew's Gospel especially, Jesus will become the new Moses, both as the new law giver and as the one who will lead humankind from the slavery of sin and death into the new and real promised land of God's kingdom. But Jesus' temptations would appear to reenact those of the wondering Israelites—the difference being that Jesus, unlike his forebears, did not succumb to temptation but, in the power of the Holy Spirit, remained faithful to God his Father.

Jesus fasted during these forty days to arm himself against the sinful allurements of this world, and thus he, in the freedom of the Spirit, would no longer, unlike his ancestors in the wilderness, long for the former flesh pots of Egypt, the slavery of sin (Ex 16:1-3). The fruit of his fasting is seen immediately at the conclusion of his forty-day fast when Jesus, in the Spirit, overcomes the devil's temptations to draw him back into the enslaving wilderness of sin.

Matthew implies that the Spirit led Jesus into the wilderness to tempt him by the devil, but the immediate causal context was Jesus' hunger, for it is this

29. Ironically, within John's Gospel, Mary Magdalene mistakes Jesus for the gardener, for in his death and resurrection he has re-created the world as the new and eternal Eden at his second coming (see Jn 20:15).

hunger that the devil first plays upon. The devil perceives that Jesus' immediate need and desire for food provides him with an ample opportunity for an apt and seductive temptation. Thus the devil declares to Jesus: "If you are the Son of God, command these stones to become loaves of bread."[30] In a sense, the devil has a long memory, for one of the first temptations to which the Israelites fell prey was that of hunger—they had no bread as they did in Egypt, where they had their fill (see Ex 16:1-3). Although Jesus is a member of unfaithful Israel, he will not succumb, as they did, to the wiles of the devil, and so he will be the true Israelite who will give birth to a new nation. Moreover, Jesus, despite the Israelites' failing, places this temptation within the light of God's humbling them to teach them that they do not live by bread alone. Jesus responds, "It is written, 'Man shall not live by bread alone, but by every word that proceeds from the mouth of God'" (Mt 4:4 quoting Dt 8:3; see also Dt 4:1-3). Unlike his ancestors, the humble Jesus learnt God's lesson and recognized the falsity of the devil's temptation. If he was to live rightly before his Father, he was to live not by the bread that he places within his mouth, but by the word that comes from the mouth of his Father. Although the devil was tempting Jesus by echoing the words that his Father addressed to him—"If you are the Son of God"—thus implying that, if he really is the Father's Son, he could easily turn stone into bread, Jesus did not recognize his Father's voice. For Jesus to be the Father's Son, to live as the Son, is not to obtain physical ease and pleasure, symbolized in earthly bread, but to consume and so be nourished on the Spirit-filled life-giving word of his Father. Thus Jesus will be faithful to his Father as the new Spirit-filled Prophet that his Father commissioned him to be.[31]

Following Matthew, the devil then "took him to the holy city, and set him on the pinnacle of the temple, and said to him, 'If you are the Son of God, throw yourself down; for it is written, "He will give his angels charge of you," and "On their hands they shall bear you up, lest you strike your foot against a stone"'" (Mt 4:5-6, quoting Ps 91:11-12).[32] The image is of the devil seeming

30. Interestingly, Matthew, who implies that the Spirit led Jesus into the desert to being tempted, does not say that "the devil tempted Jesus," but that "the tempter came and said to him" (Mt 4:3).

31. This will be more fully expressed in the Gospel of John, where Jesus as the Word, the Prophet, does only what his Father tells him.

32. Luke likely makes this the final temptation because Jesus' final temptation, the agony in the garden, will take place in Jerusalem across from the Temple Mount.

Ironically, while Satan quotes Ps 91:11-12 to tempt Jesus to manifest inappropriately his divine Sonship by having angels miraculously keep him from injury, the psalm itself proclaims how God will protect the man who is faithful to him. "He who dwells in the shelter of the Most High, who abides in the shadow of the Almighty," to him the Lord will be a "refuge" from all

to have control over Jesus since he "took him" and "set him." Jesus appears powerless before the devil's will and power. Yet Jesus refuses to play the devil's game of self-aggrandizement. Jesus rebukes the devil by saying, "Again it is written, 'You shall not tempt the Lord your God'" (Mt 4:6, quoting Dt 6:16). While human beings, in their pride, might be tempted to employ "their divinity" for the sake of enhancing their own glory, such a flattering ploy becomes an insult when suggested to God. Jesus, as "the Lord your God," will not permit his Sonship to be manipulated and abused by publicly performing a trivial spectacle for the mere sake of dazzling the crowds. Jesus, as the Father's faithful Son, will manifest his glory in Jerusalem on a new Temple Mount where he will be lifted high upon the cross as the new high priest and lamb of sacrifice. Here too it may appear that Satan is having his way with Jesus, tempting him again with the same words: "If you are the Son of God, come down from the cross" (Mt 27:40). But again, Jesus will not succumb to the temptation; he will not "throw [himself] down" to manifest demonstratively the stupidity of those who arrogantly mock him. Rather, he will now fulfill his Father's will, his priestly baptismal commitment, and offer his Spirit-filled life as a holy and innocent sacrifice, and in so doing vanquish the rule of Satan and reconcile to his Father all those under the devil's sinful dominion. This will be the cause for genuine astonishment, for here the faithful will recognize the truly humble divine love and beneficent divine power of the Son to the pleasure of God his Father. "Truly this was the Son of God" (Mt 27:54).

Matthew continues: "Again, the devil took him to a very high mountain, and showed him all the kingdoms of the world and the glory of them; and he said to him, 'All these I will give you, if you will fall down and worship me.' Then Jesus said to him, 'Begone, Satan! for it is written, "You shall worship the Lord your God and him only shall you serve"'" (Mt 4:8-10, quoting Dt 6:13). Luke emphasizes that Satan will give "all this authority and their glory" to Jesus because "all has been delivered to me" (Lk 4:6). This time, the devil does

---

harm and terror. Because the faithful man will "cleave to me [God] in love, I will deliver him; I will protect him, because he knows my name. When he calls to me, I will answer with him; I will be with him in trouble, I will rescue him and honor him. With long life I will satisfy him, and show him my salvation" (Ps 91). This is precisely what the Father does for Jesus. Because Jesus is faithfully cleaved to the Father and his will, because Jesus, as Son, knows his Father's name, because Jesus calls upon his Father in Gethsemane and upon the cross, the Father rescued him from death and honored him in his glorious resurrection and in so doing showed to Jesus his paternal salvation. Angels did "bear him up," but hardly in the manner that Satan imagined or desired. Satan may be able to quote Scripture, but he completely fails to grasp the significance of what he is quoting. This is because there is no truth in him.

not preface his temptation with the seductive appeal to Jesus' divine status: "If you are the Son of God." He simply vulgarly appeals to what most tempted him and to which he easily and willingly fell—raw power and the tyrannical authority and self-serving glory that accrues to it. Satan would nonetheless willingly and "happily" give up his entire worldly kingdom with its power and glory—the world's worship of him—if he could achieve his most frenzied desired diabolical goal—God's worship of him. Jesus responds with fed-up anger: "Begone, Satan! for it is written, 'You shall worship the Lord your God and him only shall our serve.'" (Mt 4:10, quoting Dt 6:13).[33] Jesus has had enough of Satan's games and brings Satan's temptations to an abrupt end by employing his power, as the Spirit-filled Son, to cast him away. Jesus also reaffirms his filial loyalty to his Father by declaring that he will worship him and serve him alone as his priestly Son. Moreover, Jesus will find himself on another "very high mountain," Golgotha, and from there, upon the cross, he will view not the kingdoms of the world in all their earthly splendor, glory, and power, but rather the demise of those kingdoms in all their earthly splendor, glory, and power, for he will be putting them to death. In Jesus' priestly sacrificial death, in this supreme act of his filial service to and worship of his Father alone, first promised at his baptism, all that Satan glories in will be destroyed, and in his resurrection the true splendor, glory, and power of the kingdom God will be manifested—a kingdom of life and love. Again, this will find its definitive end in Jesus' glorious coming at the end of time. Then all the faithful will enter the heavenly kingdom and will together with Jesus, their Lord and Savior, in the love of the Spirit, serve and worship the Father alone. Then Satan and all his minions will reap not the glory and adulation of the world but the fruit of the glory that this world has to offer: eternal damnation where no one worships anyone, not even Satan to his everlasting infuriation, but only themselves.

With the departure of Satan, Matthew and Mark tell us that angels came to minster to Jesus (see Mt 4:11 and Mk 1:13). The nature of this ministry is not specified, but one can surmise that they brought with them, within this wilderness of desolation, the consolation and love of the Father's Spirit, the Spirit of Sonship that the Father bestowed upon him at his baptism, for in that Spirit, Jesus just achieved his first triumph over evil, and he did so by being faithful as the Father's prophetic and priestly beloved Son in whom he is well pleased.[34]

33. The implication is that not only will Jesus not tempt the Lord his God, but that Satan should stop tempting Jesus who is God.

34. As Satan will return to tempt Jesus at appropriate times, so too will the angels return to comfort him at appropriate times, e.g., during his agony in the garden (see Lk 22:42).

What we perceive within Jesus' temptations is a prophetic living icon of his entire ministry. Throughout his ministry, Jesus will remain in the wilderness of sin and death, where he will be continually provoked by Satan and his temptations. As Luke tells us, the devil departed only to return at "an opportune time" (Lk 4:13). This battle to remain steadfast as the Father's Son and to stand firm against all that Satan embodies will be a battle of triumphs because, in being faithful to his Father through the Spirit of Sonship, Jesus will bestow freedom upon those who are demon possessed; he will dispel sin with forgiveness, confront sickness with healing, and triumph over death with life. He will preach the good news of the kingdom of God to the poor and lowly. This public ministry will be but a foretaste of his final confrontation with the devil and his cohorts, sin and death, in Gethsemane, at the foot of the cross, and from the cross Jesus will cry out, "Begone, Satan!" And in his death Jesus, the ever-faithful Spirit imbued Servant-Son, will breathe forth the Father's Spirit of Sonship upon the wilderness of the world, transforming it into a garden of life.

What we ultimately perceive within Jesus' temptations is Satan's attempt to have Jesus enact his name other than in the manner for which he was named. Satan tempted Jesus to make a name for himself as the Son of God—changing stones into bread, being caught by angels, and becoming the lord and king of the entire world. It all had to do with Jesus becoming consumed with himself and so becoming the image of Satan. But Jesus remained true to his name, for he remained faithful to his Father as the perfect filial image of his Father, and thus, in the power of the Spirit, Jesus, as the obedient Son, remained and will remain Jesus—YHWH-Saves—for he will be always and only enact his name for the salvation of all of humankind.

Conclusion

Jesus, in the act of being baptized, embraced his messianic vocation as the beloved prophetic and priestly Son of the Father and so will do the deeds of righteousness. His temptations are the immediate test of that event. Also, Jesus' temptations in the desert embody and so represent his continual internal conflict to fulfill his Spirit-empowered pledge to his Father. The whole of Jesus' public ministry is a ministry of being faithful, as the Son of the Father, to what he had committed himself to be within his baptism. It is a ministry in which Jesus ever becomes Jesus—YHWH-Saves. Within that same ministry lies the temptation not to be loyal to his baptismal commitment. To that prophetic and priestly ministry we now turn.

⁊⸾

JESUS' PUBLIC MINISTRY

*H*AVING EXAMINED the doctrinal significance of Jesus' conception and birth as well as his baptism and temptations, in this second part of the study I survey the theological significance of Jesus' public ministry. Chapter 4 considers Jesus' salvific acts that initiate the in-breaking of the kingdom of God, such as his miracles, exorcisms, and acts of forgiveness. Chapter 5 appraises the acts by which Jesus exercises his authority, such as his promulgating the new law of the kingdom of heaven, the Sermon on the Mount, and the authority he exercises over the lives of his followers. These two chapters complement and enhance one another. Chapter 6 investigates Jesus's relationship with his Father both as Jesus manifests this relationship and as others perceive this relationship. My selection of passages will not be exhaustive but nonetheless will illustrate the theological and doctrinal content of Jesus' public ministry. Within these chapters we find Jesus actualizing himself as Savior—that is, enacting his name—and so revealing that he was the Son of God. Because Jesus' salvific words and actions testify that he is the Son, they also reveal the Father and the Holy Spirit. The subsequent part of this study examines the immediate anticipation and prefigurement of Jesus' passion, death, and resurrection contained within his public ministry and the Passion Narratives.

4 · JESUS' PRIESTLY SALVIFIC ACTS

Initiating the Kingdom of God

The Beginning of Jesus' Ministry:
The Founding of the Church

After his temptations, Jesus returned to Galilee, Matthew and Mark noting that he did so after he had heard that John was arrested, an event that marks the end of his ministry.[1] He was divinely appointed to prepare for the coming of the Lord. Jesus, having been baptized, now undertook his own divinely appointed commission as the anointed Messiah.

Both Mark and Matthew tell us that Jesus began his public ministry by proclaiming: "The time is fulfilled, and the kingdom of God is at hand; repent and believe in the Gospel" (Mk 1:15; see also Mt 4:17). If the kingdom of God is at hand and if Jesus is the initiator of that kingdom, then the reality of that kingdom must be made present, for only then will there be any attraction or obligation to enter into that reality through repentance and faith.

But prior to providing Jesus' specific teaching concerning the kingdom and the acts that he performs that make present that kingdom, Matthew and Mark first tell of Jesus calling his first disciples. As Jesus was walking along the Sea of Galilee, he first met "Simon, who is called Peter, and Andrew his brother" who were fishing. Jesus tells them, "Follow me, and I will make you fishers of men." They immediately left their nets and followed him. In turn, Jesus called "James the son of Zebedee and John his brother." They too immediately left their boat and their father and followed Jesus (Mt 4:18-22; Mk 1:16-20).

What is striking here is not simply the immediacy with which these first

---

1. His death at the hands of Herod is John's final prophetic act, for it harbingers Jesus' own death. As the one sent to prepare the way for Jesus was killed for the sake of truth, so the one for whom he was preparing will also lay down his life for the sake of the truth—the Gospel.

disciples left their fishing careers and even their father. (Mark notes that the sons of Zebedee left their father "in the boat with the hired servants.") More striking is the new vocation (career) that Jesus promises them: fishers of men. But even this is not the primary theological or doctrinal point that Matthew and Mark wish to make. What is most striking is that these first four disciples seemingly follow Jesus prior to ever hearing him proclaim the Gospel and prior to ever seeing any of his works and presumably, then, to never even having met him. Their following Jesus seems contrary to reason and historical accuracy. Yet this, I propose, is the heart of the theological or doctrinal issue.

Matthew and Mark take for granted that these four men heard the Gospel because they already stated the summary of what Jesus was saying—the time has been fulfilled, the kingdom of God is at hand, repent and believe in the good news. The theological point that Matthew and Mark are making is that theologically (if not historically) prior, there must be "official witnesses" to what Jesus says and does before his actual saying and doing. In other words, there must be a "body" of committed followers who will be with Jesus from his baptism—that is, from the moment that he begins his public ministry—so that they can receive the fullness of Jesus' revelation and thus later testify to the fullness of that revelation.[2] Matthew and Mark are making an ecclesiological doctrinal statement. If the apostolic church is to possess the apostolic faith, there must be Apostles from the onset. In a sense, Jesus must first found his church, the hearers of the Gospel, before he can proclaim the Gospel, through which the church will come fully into being, so that when the Gospel does

---

2. Within the Acts of the Apostles, when the Apostles recognize the need to replace Judas, Peter sets the criteria for such a replacement. "So one of the men who have accompanied us during all the time the Lord Jesus went in and out among us, beginning from the baptism of John until the day when he was taken up from us—one of these men must become with us a witness of his resurrection" (Acts 1:21-22). Whoever the new Apostle is, he must have seen and heard all that Jesus did and said throughout the whole of his public ministry, from his baptism to his ascension, for only then would he be an authoritative witness to the whole of Jesus' salvific ministry and so bear witness to the fruit of his ministry—Jesus' own resurrection.

Similarly, when Peter preaches the Gospel to Cornelius and his household, he prefaces his sermon by wanting to tell them "the word which was proclaimed throughout all of Judea, beginning from Galilee after the baptism which John preached: how God anointed Jesus of Nazareth with the Holy Spirit and with power; how he went about doing good and healing all that were oppressed by the devil, for God was with him. And we are witnesses to all that he did both in the country of the Jews and in Jerusalem" (Acts 10:37-39). Cornelius can be assured of the truth of what he is about to hear, for Peter authoritatively witnessed it from beginning to end. The church is the authoritative apostolic witness, for she possesses the entirety of the Gospel of Jesus Christ.

come fully into being, the church can be the bearer of the Gospel to others. This accounts for why Matthew specifies that Simon is called Peter long before Jesus designates him as such (see Mt 16:18). Peter, the rock, and his fellow cohorts, must be, from the onset, the apostolic foundation, a foundation built upon their faith, upon which Jesus will build his church. Without them there would be no living foundational embodiment of the Gospel and so no foundational witnesses to the Gospel for that is what defines the church—the living reality that is imbued with and so testifies to the Gospel of Jesus, who he is and what he has salvifically accomplished and continues to achieve in communion with his church. Here, at the commencement of his ministry, we find Jesus inaugurating his church and manifesting the first doctrine at the heart of it—Jesus and the apostolic church are never separated but intimately and indissolubly united. To be in communion with the living Jesus, in the fullness of the salvific mystery that he forever embodies, one must be in living communion with his church, which is to be in communion with the living Jesus. According to Matthew and Mark, establishing this communion is Jesus' primordial act; thus it is the first salvific act by which Jesus becomes Jesus, and it will be his ultimate act by which he becomes Jesus, both in his death and resurrection, and when he comes again in glory. Jesus becomes Jesus only as he progresses in establishing his church, bringing it to full maturity at the end of time. This is why, though unbeknownst to them at the time, his first disciples immediately left everything, even their family, and followed Jesus, for to follow and be in communion with him is to be the church in communion with him. In addition, the church, prefigured in Jesus' first followers, is, in its totality, the fisher of men.[3]

3. Although I have emphasized, in accordance with Matthew and Mark, the theological priority of the church over the Gospel, historically they both come to be simultaneously. The church comes to be in the receiving of the Gospel. Jesus' first "Apostles" are called prior to the Gospel only so that they can be the church who hears the Gospel and so become the church.

Luke may provide a more historical setting and context for Jesus' calling his first disciples. Having taught in the synagogue in Capernaum, he entered Simon's house to find that his mother-in-law is sick. Having healed her and many others as the day was ending, Jesus spent the night at Simon's home. The next day, he first prayed in a lonely spot and then went forth to preach. Having preached to the people from one of the fishermen's boats, he told Simon to set out into the deep and to cast out his net. Simon protests that they had caught nothing all night but would comply with Jesus' command. Having filled two boats with fish, "Simon Peter" fell to his knees and proclaimed, "Depart from me, for I am a sinful man, O Lord." All were astonished at the catch, including James and John, the sons of Zebedee. Jesus responds, "Do not be afraid; henceforth you will be catching men." It is at this point that Luke tells us that "when they had brought their boats to land, the left everything and followed him"

The Beginning of Jesus' Ministry: Who Is Jesus?

Luke does not provide a summary of Jesus' initial teaching, but he does present an incident that manifests Jesus' self-perception and his understanding of what the Gospel entails. He does so by bringing forward what is more summarily contained later in Matthew and Mark (see Mt 13:52-58 and Mk 6:1-6).

Having been anointed with the Spirit at his baptism, Luke first narrates that Jesus, "full of the Holy Spirit," returned to the desert to be tempted by Satan. Luke says that Jesus, having rebuffed Satan by the power of the Spirit, "returned in the power of the Spirit into Galilee," where he taught in the synagogues to the acclaim of all (Lk 4:14-16). Similarly, Jesus "came to Nazareth, where he had been brought up" and entered the synagogue on the Sabbath, as was his custom. There he read a passage from Isaiah 61:1-2 and 58:6. (The actual text is slightly different in Luke's account, but the meaning is substantially the same.)

> The Spirit of the Lord is upon me, because he has anointed me to preach good news to the poor. He has sent me to proclaim release to the captives and recovering of sight to the blind, to set at liberty those who are oppressed, to proclaim the acceptable year of the Lord.

The reaction of the synagogue members was that of all fixing of their eyes upon him. This "fixing of their eyes" was not because they had never seen Jesus before, as if he were some stranger coming into their neighborhood pub, but because Jesus was not reading this passage as if it were speaking of some future prophet. Rather, Jesus read this passage as one to whom it applied. It is how he said "me" that caught the focused attention of the synagogue so that "the eyes of all in the synagogue were fixed on him." This ancient prophetic passage was written for only one person to read, and that person had just read it—Jesus! Jesus could rightly and singularly proclaim this passage because, at his baptism, the Holy Spirit came down upon him, and he did so that Je-

---

(Lk 4:31-5:11). Luke's narrative provides additional reasons than Matthew and Mark for why Simon and the others left everything and followed Jesus—they had heard him preach, they witnessed his healings and exorcisms, and they were personally involved in the miraculous catch of fish. Luke also refers to Simon as Simon Peter, and it is he who fell to his knees in worship before Jesus and proclaimed him to be Lord (Yahweh-God). Although a sinner and surely not fully aware of the significance of what he said and did, Peter is nonetheless the foundational rock of the church and so will be a fisher of men, for he and the others will witness what they have experienced, seen, and heard—they are the church who prayerfully acknowledge Jesus as Lord.

sus would be empowered to do all that the passage declares—preach the good news, release those captive in sin and death, heal the blind and the sick, and thus proclaim the Lord's favor.

That Jesus interpreted this passage as applying to himself is reinforced by what he states next. With all eyes fixed upon him, he declared: "Today this scripture has been fulfilled in your hearing." The reason that the passage is being fulfilled is because the one to whom it applies just read it. Jesus himself will fulfill this passage from Isaiah. But Jesus does not say that the passage is fulfilled in his reading; that is, the message is not fulfilled merely in his proclamation. Rather, he says that the Scripture is fulfilled in their hearing. Jesus will do all that this passage prophetically declares, but it will not be truly fulfilled unless those who see and hear do so with eyes and ears of faith and so believe that he is the one to whom it applies, that he is the one upon whom rests the Spirit of the Lord. The receiving of Jesus' words in faith fulfills the good news, for only then is the good news fulfilled in the hearers—the obtaining of the salvation that Jesus offers. This is the problem.

Although those who knew him from his youth "spoke well of him" ("He was always a very kind and courteous young man"), because they did know him so well, they "wondered at the gracious words which proceeded out of his mouth, and they said, 'Is not this Joseph's son?'" It is not the words that Jesus spoke from his mouth that disturbed his neighbors, for they were "gracious," but rather the one whose mouth spoke them, the son of Joseph. Those in the synagogue were moved by the words, but they refused to believe them to be true, for the one who spoke them could not possibly fulfill them because he, as they very well knew, was simply an ordinary man from their own home town. But this is the point of the Incarnation. The Son of God was conceived by the Holy Spirit in the womb of Mary, the wife of Joseph the carpenter, and it is upon him, like the people of Nazareth, whom the Father anointed with the Spirit so as to bring good news to the poor. But "the poor" of Nazareth were too "captive" in their "blindness" to be freed from their "oppression" and so rejoice in the Lord's "acceptable year." Once again, we find here a prophetic paradigm of Jesus' entire public ministry. People are scandalized not by what Jesus says and does, but by the fact that it is he who says and does them—Jesus cannot possibly be the one upon whom the Father's Spirit rests.[4] So Jesus

4. Although Matthew and Mark note only that Jesus taught in the synagogue on the Sabbath, they do narrate an even more negative response to his words. Those who knew Jesus "were astonished and said, 'Where did this man get this wisdom and these mighty works? Is not this the carpenter's son? Is not his mother called Mary? And are not his brothers James,

concludes by saying, "Truly, I say to you, no prophet is acceptable in his own country" (Lk 4:24). Matthew and Mark editorialize that it is because of their lack of faith that Jesus could not do many "mighty works there" (see Mt 13:57-58 and Mk 6:4-6). Jesus could not enact Isaiah's prophecy because it could not be fulfilled in their seeing and hearing.[5]

With the above in mind we can now proceed to Jesus' public ministry, wherein he will enact Isaiah's prophecy, and in so doing some will hear with conviction and see in faith and so the good news will be fulfilled in them, while others will hear with suspicion and see in disbelief and so the good news will be unfulfilled in them. The irony is that those who do not accept Jesus as the Son whom the Lord has anointed with the Spirit, and so ultimately put him to death as a blasphemer, make possible the definitive fulfillment of the passage from Isaiah, for on the cross the "good news to the poor" is fully manifested—those "oppressed" by sin and "captive" to death are "set free" and so are "acceptable" to "the Lord."

Jesus' Power and Authority over Evil

Establishing the kingdom of God is a twofold task: the conquering of evil and the inaugurating of what is good, holy, and righteous. Not surprisingly, the Gospel of Matthew summarizes the beginning of Jesus' public ministry by stating that he not only preached the Gospel of the kingdom, but also that he healed the sick and cast out unclean spirits (see Mt 4:23-25; Mk 1:32-34). Satan, the evil one, is the author of sin with its subsequent consequences of sickness and death and so is the great opponent of God's kingdom. He needs to be vanquished if that kingdom is to become a reality. In this light, Mark and Luke begin Jesus' public ministry with a series of healings and exorcisms.

Joseph and Simon and Judas? And are not all of his sisters with us? Where did he get all of this?' And they took offence at him" (Mt 13:54-56; see Mk 6:2-3).

5. By emphasizing that the passage from Isaiah is "fulfilled in your hearing," Jesus is making a point similar to one I made previously concerning Matthew and Mark. There I emphasized that Matthew and Mark had Jesus' first act be the calling of his disciples—he needed "hearers" of his Gospel before he could proclaim it. Jesus, in Luke's Gospel, emphasizes that the Isaiah passage is fulfilled not in the speaking but in the hearing. Only if they accept Jesus' words in faith is the passage fulfilled, for they will then know and experience the truth the passage contains. The problem is that there are no "hearers" in the synagogue at Nazareth—there is no church to hear the Gospel—because of the false presumption that the people think they know who Jesus is when in fact they do not. The church knows that Jesus is not the son of the earthly Joseph, the carpenter, but the Son of the heavenly Father, the Creator of all.

Power over Satan

Having gone down from Nazareth to Capernaum along the Sea of Galilee, as Mark and Luke narrate, Jesus taught in the synagogues and the people were astonished by his teaching, "for he taught them with authority, and not as the scribes" (Mk 1:21-22; see also Lk 4:31-32). Although the scribes taught by invoking the words of Scripture and so the authority of God, Jesus invoked no authority other than his own. This is theologically significant because the question arises as to where Jesus obtains this authority. It does not reside merely in his ability to teach but also in the power inherent within his authority. Thus Jesus, within the peoples' synagogue, first confronts evil in a man possessed by an unclean spirit (Mk 1:23-28; Lk 4:33-37). At the sight of Jesus, the unclean spirit cries out, "What have you to do with us, Jesus of Nazareth? Have you come to destroy us? I know who you are, the Holy One of God." What has this man from Nazareth to do with the kingdom of evil? The unclean spirit immediately intuits (significantly, he initiates the encounter) that Jesus has come to destroy those like himself, for he perceives that he is in the presence of the Holy One of God. Here at the onset of Jesus' ministry we have a confrontation, symptomatic of his entire ministry, between what is unclean and unholy, its literal embodiment in a human being, and what is clean and holy, its literal embodiment in Jesus, who has borne the holiness of God from his conception. Jesus rebuked the spirit and said, "'Be silent, come out of him!' And the unclean spirit, convulsing him and crying with a loud voice, came out of him."[6] Although Jesus simply commands the unclean spirit to come out, his act is nonetheless violent, for the spirit leaves only in convulsing the man and

---

6. Although evil spirits frequently know who Jesus actually is, as in the case above, he tells them to "be silent." This is especially so in Mark's Gospel: "And whenever the unclean spirits beheld him, they fell down before him and cried out, 'You are the Son of God.' And he strictly ordered them not to make him known" (Mk 3:11-12). Why? First, especially in Mark, Jesus refuses to allow others to proclaim who he is, even if they are in one sense correct, until he properly reveals who he is. This is referred to as "the Messianic Secret." Others may call him "the Christ" or "Son of God," but their understanding may not be in accord with what it truly and fully means for him to be "the Christ" or "the Son of God." (This will be evident even when we treat of Peter's own profession of faith—he did not comprehend that for Jesus to be the Christ meant that he must suffer and die.) Thus Jesus orders them to remain silent and not make him known for fear that such a proclamation would foment confusion and false impressions. Second, importantly, although Satan and the unclean spirits may know and acknowledge who Jesus is, they are hardly sanctioned as official ecclesial witnesses so as to testify as to who Jesus is. Only the Apostles and thus the church, as Jesus' divinely appointed by him, are sanctioned in the Holy Spirit to profess and proclaim authoritatively the Gospel. This is in keeping with

crying out, presumably, in agony. What is often not recognized or acknowledged, probably because of a misconceived notion of Jesus' kindness and gentleness, is the glaring fact that overcoming Satan and evil is not child's play but the actual violent conflict between two hostile powers—the malevolent power Satan and his legions and the holy power of God. Satan is the enemy of God and so the enemy of God's holy one and, like the warrior David, Jesus, if he is to assume everlastingly David's throne, must act in a Davidic manner—he must permanently overthrow the kingdom of Satan.[7] Also, in the act of casting out the unclean spirit, the man, Jesus of Nazareth, is enacting his name as the one who saves and revealing that he is the Holy One of God who brings into existence God's holy kingdom. Jesus embodies God's holy kingdom and so to live under his authority and power is to enjoy, as he enjoys, the freedom of God's children and so no longer live, as he does not live, under the dominion of Satan. Because he is the Holy One of God, Jesus uniquely possesses authority and power that differ in kind from that of the scribes. Jesus' authority and power reside within himself as the Holy Son of the Father, whereas the scribes must look to an authority outside themselves—the sacred text and tradition. The people perceive this nuance. "What is this? A new teaching! With authority he commands even the unclean spirits, and they obey him" (Mk 1:27-28; see also Lk 4:36-37).

Power over Sickness

Biblically, sickness and disease are consequences of sin, the result of evil infecting God's good creation, and so Jesus also confronted the uncleanness of not only Satan but also in the form of leprosy. A leper came to him and, kneeling, beseeched: "If you will, you can make me clean." Jesus stretched out his hand and touched the unclean leper, saying, "I will, be clean" (Mk 1:40-45; see also Mt 8:2-4 and Lk 5:12-16). Lepers were not permitted to have contact with

---

Mark first having Jesus call his original Apostles before he inaugurates his public ministry—only they testify authoritatively.

7. Through his cross and resurrection, Jesus will permanently overthrow Satan, and this will be finalized when all his enemies will be fully subject to him. The Letter to the Hebrews claims that Jesus' enemies will then become his footstool. See Heb 10:11-13 and Ps 110:1. This becomes a major theme in the Book of Revelation, within which the ongoing violent persecution by Satan and his earthly allies of Jesus and his earthly faithful saints is evident. This fierce harassment reaches its climax with the imminent coming of Jesus at the end of time, whereupon the glorious Jesus effortlessly but violently subdues Satan and those in league with him and brings down from heaven upon earth the new Jerusalem, wherein his faithful will dwell with him in peace (see Rv 17-21).

other human beings and, being socially and physically quarantined, they were outcasts. This leper, confident in faith that Jesus could heal him, discards this social and medical protocol and kneels before Jesus, a sign of abeyance, but here also a sign of worship. Pointedly, Matthew has the leper address Jesus as "Lord." For the apostolic church, the leper's confidence that Jesus could heal him resided in his faith that Jesus was the divine Lord, before whom he knelt in supplicatory worship. Jesus confirms the truth of the leper's faith. Jesus by his own personal authority and power heals the leper. By the act of his human will and by the act of his bodily touching, the leper is cleansed. Therefore this human act testifies that Jesus personally possesses, literally embodies, an authority and power that exceed the merely human and so testify that the man Jesus personally possesses an authority and power that is of divine origin.[8]

Of doctrinal importance, this healing act is a sacramental act for Jesus' human words and gesture (bodily touching) effect what they signify. The basis of this sacramental act is the Incarnation—the Son of God speaks and acts as man—that is, he wills, speaks, and acts humanly and therefore bodily—and in so doing effects what his words and acts denote. Jesus' words and actions do not simply mark the occasion or externally give expression to what he is doing solely as God apart from his humanity. Rather, because he exists as man, Jesus' word and actions define and determine what he, as the Son of God, is doing in and through the instrumentality of his humanity. This sacramental conjoining of Jesus' human words and acts through which his divine power brings about an effect are all theandric acts—divine deeds done humanly. As such, these sacramental acts are revelatory of the Incarnation, for these human words and acts manifest that he who is humanly speaking and humanly acting is the Son of God.

Matthew perceives the soteriological priestly sacramental significance in Jesus' healings and exorcisms. He recognizes that Jesus, within his ministry, was assuming unto himself, within his own humanity, the consequences of sin. Jesus' exorcisms and healings "fulfill what was spoken by the prophet Isaiah, 'He took our infirmities and bore our diseases'" (Mt 8:17; see Is 53:4). Jesus, through his exorcisms and healings, is expressing, within his own humanity, his divinely conferred vocation, that of being the Suffering Servant. This in turn highlights that Jesus is performing a priestly sacramental ministry, for he is taking upon himself, within his own humanity, the evils that

---

8. There are many instances where Jesus' healing involves touching. See, e.g., Mt 8:14-17, 9:27-31, 20:29-34, and parallels.

permeate human existence and in so doing likewise free humankind, through his sacramental human action, from the evil that inheres within and around them. Jesus' ministry of healing presages his ultimate exorcism and final sacramental priestly healing act—the cross upon which he will assume the entirety of human sin and its consequences and, through the sacrificial offering of his own holy life, will conquer all evil and destroy death through his glorious bodily resurrection.[9] This will culminate in his glorious return, when sickness and death forever cease and eternal life is everlastingly bestowed upon all the faithful.[10]

Power over Death

Human proneness to sickness finds its end in death. All three Synoptic Gospels narrate the story of Jesus raising the twelve-year-old daughter of Jairus, the synagogue ruler.[11] Within this account of Jesus healing Jairus' daughter is also the healing of the woman with a hemorrhage. Both acts are theologically significant, for they are sacramental in nature (Mt 9:18-26; Mk 5:21-43; Lk 8:40-56).

Like the leper, Jairus comes to Jesus and kneels before him in supplication. In Matthew, Jairus informs Jesus that his daughter has died, requesting that he "come and lay your hand on her" and asserting that if he does, "she will live." In Mark and Luke, Jairus informs Jesus that his daughter "is at the point of death" but requests that he "come and lay your hands on her, so that she may be made well, and live." Notably, Jairus does not simply request that Jesus employ his power to heal his daughter, but explicitly asks Jesus to lay his hands upon her—bodily touch is important for Jairus. Although Mark and Luke have the child die as Jesus and the throng make their way to Jairus' house, all three Gospels contrast the faith of Jairus with the those who believe that Jesus cannot undo the power of death. Jesus is impatient with their lack of faith, brusquely informing them that the child is "sleeping" and "not dead," to which the mourners "laughed at him, knowing that she was dead" (Lk 8:53). According to Mark and Luke, Jesus did not allow anyone to enter the house "except Peter and James and John the brother of James" and "the child's father and

---

9. Jesus can assume the sin of humankind because, within the Incarnation, he assumed not a generic or sterilized humanity but a humanity of the sinful race of Adam.

10. In the Book of Revelation within the new Jerusalem, which is the dwelling place of God, there will be no more sorrow, pain, death, or mourning, "for the former things have passed away" (Rv 21:3-4).

11. Luke also tells of Jesus raising the son of the widow of Nain (Lk 7:11-17).

mother" (Mk 5:40 and Lk 8:51). "Taking her by the hand he said to her '*Talitha cumi*'; which means, 'Little girl, I say to you, arise.' And immediately the girl got up and walked" (Mk 5:41-42). Jesus, through his human words and bodily touch, which form one priestly sacramental act, is able to give life to one who was dead. Again, being a sacramental act, this act bears witness to the Incarnation, for Jesus' human words and bodily actions bestow life and thus that he is the author of life as God's eternal Son. As noted above, because of the Incarnation, this is a divine act done humanly.[12]

That Jesus took Peter, James, and John into the little girl's room when he performed the miracle makes them the official ecclesial witnesses to the event. This may account for why Jesus makes the rather unreasonable, and in the end impossible, demand upon the parents, despite their amazement. "And he strictly charged them that no one should know this." (Mk 5:43). How did Jesus ever think her parents could keep quiet? Even if they did remain silent, was the little girl to go in hiding for the rest of her life? She would be bouncing out of the house immediately after her parents gave her something to eat, as Jesus requested! As Matthew, unlike Mark and Luke, states, "And the report of this event went through all the district." Of course it did! What Mark, and Luke too, wants the reader, and ultimately Jesus, to recognize is that Peter, James, and John represent the church. They are the believing eyes and ears who see and hear the Gospel, and so it is their testimony, and not the testimony of the parents, that is authoritatively apostolic.[13]

On Jesus' way to Jairus' house, a woman with a flow of blood for twelve years touched him, saying to herself: "If I only touch his garment, I shall be made well" (Mt). "And immediately the hemorrhage ceased; and she felt in her body that she was healed of her disease" (Mk). Simultaneously, Jesus, "perceiving in himself that power had gone forth from him, immediately turned about in the crowd, and said 'Who touched my garments?'" (Mk). In response, his bewildered disciples (Luke specifies that it was Peter) point out the obvious: "You see the crowd pressing on you, and yet you say, 'Who touched me?'" (Mk). The woman's touch was not simply the pushing and shoving of the crowd. It was a touch of faith. Jesus acknowledges this: "Daughter, your faith has made you

12. Jesus' ultimate priestly act is his sacrificial act upon the cross where he assumes unto himself death itself, but vanquishes death by lovingly offering himself to the Father. Such a perfect priestly act gives rise to the Father's raising him from the dead so as to live gloriously forever.

13. These very Gospels now present the church's authoritative account and not the parents' account.

well; go in peace, and be healed of your disease" (Mk). In this touch of faith, power came forth from Jesus by which she was healed. There is a twofold immediacy here. Upon touching Jesus, in faith she "immediately" perceives that she is healed, and Jesus perceives that he has been touched in faith because he "immediately" senses that power has gone forth from him. The cause of this twofold, simultaneous "immediate" perception is "the touching." The woman's bodily touch causes power to come forth from Jesus' body. Jesus' ability to heal is not some divine power extrinsic to his humanity, something divine that he calls upon from outside himself, but his ability to heal inheres within his fleshly humanity. This is again a priestly sacramental touching, which gives incarnational expression to who Jesus is as the Son of God. The woman acknowledges this, for when she realizes that her touching has been discovered, she "came in fear and trembling and fell down before him, and told him the truth" (Mk). In this falling down before Jesus, the woman confesses that the one whom she has touched possesses within his very humanity God's healing power. This healing also testifies that Jesus, in the totality of who he is, is Savior—even apart from his deliberate saving acts—he cannot circumvent the enactment of his name.

Power over Sin

Jesus not only confronted unclean spirits, the pollution of leprosy, the debilitation of sickness and the finality of death, but he also addressed their primordial source—the contamination of sin. Biblically, to sin is to enter an allegiance with Satan and so to suffer the consequences of such an adherence: sickness and death. The Synoptic Gospels narrate the event of Jesus healing the paralytic at his own home in Capernaum (Mt 9:1-8; Mk 2:1-12; Lk 5:17-26). The whole context of this miracle is important, for it manifests not only his power to heal but also his power to forgive, thus attending to evil's symptoms, body illness, and eradicating its very cause, sin. Because of the crowd within and outside Jesus' home, those who brought the paralytic were forced to lower him down into the house by making a hole in the roof. Jesus perceived in this determined action their faith. Jesus' first declaration was: "My son, your sins are forgiven" (Mk). This may have elicited surprise from the paralytic and those gathered because it was for healing and not for forgiveness that the man was brought to Jesus. Interestingly, in Matthew, Jesus says, "Take heart, my son; your sins are forgiven," as if the man were more troubled about his sin than about his paralysis. Nonetheless, Jesus, in making his decree of forgiveness, is marking the deeper theological connection between sickness and the ultimate cause of sickness: sin. Jesus recognized, if the paralytic did not, that the man's sin was of greater and deeper concern.

What Jesus' response did overtly elicit was a condemnatory response from the scribes for they questioned in their hearts: "Why does this man speak thus? It is blasphemy! Who can forgive sins but God alone?" (Mk). The scribes were not opposed to the forgiveness of sins. They knew that God could do such. What disquieted them was that "this man" spoke words of forgiveness, and such being the case, he neither had the power or the authority to forgive sins. Because only God possesses the power and authority to forgive, Jesus had blasphemously appropriated to himself such divine ability. Again, what causes consternation, like the negative response of his fellow townspeople in the synagogue at Nazareth, is not what is said and done, but who is alleging authority and power to say and do it—Jesus, the man. Jesus has nonetheless generated a scenario in which his true identity, who he is, is able to be manifested.

Perceiving their condemnation, Jesus responded, "Why do you question thus in your hearts?" (Mk). Matthew has Jesus say, "Why do you think evil in your hearts?" Why are the scribes thinking evil thoughts, since what they are saying is true—only God can forgive sin? Their thoughts are evil precisely because they have already precluded that Jesus could not possibly be God, and thus were not open to the revelation contained in the ensuing healing that will manifest that he is truly God with the authority and power to forgive. Jesus draws these two together—the ability to heal and the ability to forgive—by further asking, "Which is easier, to say to the paralytic, 'Your sins are forgiven,' or to say, 'Rise, take up your pallet and walk?'" (Mk). For someone who is merely human, neither is easy to say, much less to do. Jesus proceeded to heal the paralytic not merely to display his healing power, "but that you may know that the Son of man has authority on earth to forgive sins." The healing confirms Jesus' authority to forgive, an authority that is exercised not by God on high but by the Son of man on earth. Jesus, then, is not challenging the scribes' theology. They are thinking properly—only God can forgive sins. What is amiss is their "evil hearts." Their hearts are closed and hardened to the truth of who Jesus might be. They refuse to believe that Jesus the man is exercising divine power and authority and so, by these acts of healing and forgiveness, is revealing his divine identity. In the act of forgiving the paralytic's sins, Jesus manifested that he is able to act so as to vanquish the source of all evil and with it break the bond that ties humankind to Satan. Thus Jesus' healing act of forgiveness reveals that he is truly the one who not only heals in body but also saves in heart and mind.[14] Once again, Jesus is performing a priestly act, for it was traditionally the sacrificial acts of the priests—the animal sacrifices—that symbolized reconciliation with God and so a cleansing of sin. Jesus' act of healing and forgiveness is prophetic in that it anticipates the redemptive act of the cross, whereby Satan is decisively defeated and sin is definitively forgiven, and the restorative act of the resurrection whereby humankind is able, in communion with the glorious Jesus, to share, body and soul, in his re-created humanity.

The Questioning of John's Disciples and Jesus' Sending Out of His Apostles

In the light of all the above, we can perceive the significance of Jesus' response to John the Baptist's disciples when they, at his behest, came to him asking, "Are you he who is to come, or shall we look for another?" The one who is to come is he who would establish the everlasting Davidic kingdom of God. Significantly, Jesus does not respond by simply telling John's disciples: "Yes, I am." Rather, he said: "Go and tell John what you hear and see; the blind receive their sight and the lame walk, lepers are cleansed and the deaf hear, the dead are raised up, and the poor have good news preached to them. And blessed is he who takes no offense at me" (Mt 11:2-6); Luke notes that "in that hour [just prior to their questioning] he [Jesus] cured many diseases and plagues and evil spirits, and on many that were blind he bestowed sight" (Lk 7:18-23).

The kingdom of God must be real and tangible if Jesus' claim that the kingdom is at hand is to be believed and thus that the reason it is present is because he is present. The mere saying that it is present is insufficient. Thus Jesus' response to John's disciples does not directly answer their query as to whether he is the one who is to come. Instead, he tells them to report to John what

---

14. Although Mark and Luke conclude the story of the healing of the paralytic by noting the amazement of the crowd and their glorifying God, Matthew states that they "glorified God, who had given such authority to men." The Acts of the Apostles narrates that the same saving deeds that Jesus had done while on earth the apostolic church continues to do in his name and by the power of the Holy Spirit: exorcisms and healings. The fact that Matthew speaks of "men" in the plural may be a doctrinal ecclesial statement in that the church continues Jesus' ministry of forgiveness of sins. Because Jesus is the Lord and Savior of the church, the church exercises his authority and power to forgive. This is made evident in the Gospel of John, where the resurrected Jesus explicitly gives his Apostles authority to forgive sin in the power of the Spirit (see Jn 20:21-23).

Besides forgiving sin, Jesus demonstrates that his ministry is primarily to sinners, those in need of salvation, by his intimate association with them. This is another instance of Jesus enacting his name as the one who saves. See, e.g., Mt. 9:10-13 and Lk 7:34, 15:1-2.

they have heard and seen. The events that they have witnessed testify that the kingdom of God is present, and the reason it is present is because Jesus is present. What they have heard and seen—the healings, the exorcisms, the raising of the dead, the preaching of forgiveness to poor—were done by him. John needs no other response than this. These words and acts bear witness that he is the one who is to come. They manifest that he is the prophesied Messiah, the anointed son of David. This also accounts for Jesus' final comment, which encourages faith and implies a warning: "Blessed is he who takes no offense at me." It is Jesus of Nazareth, a man of little human earthly consequence, who is saying and doing all of this. Although what is said and done may be approved and applauded, the one who is doing the saying and the doing may indeed give offense. Thus blessed is the one who is not offended, for he sees beyond the appearance, and with the eyes of faith recognizes that the one who is present is indeed the one who was to come. In seeing Jesus, John's disciples need look no further.[15]

If Jesus tells John's disciples to take notice of what he has said and done so as to convince them that he is indeed the one who is to come, Jesus' approach to his own twelve Apostles is quite different. He sends them out to say and to do what he is saying and doing.[16] Within Matthew's account, Jesus first "called to him his twelve disciples and gave them authority over unclean spirits, to cast

15. The question perennially arises as to why John would send his disciples to Jesus and ask if he is the one who is to come when John already baptized him as the one who is to come, thus conferring upon him the fulfillment of this prophetic designation. While Luke tells us that John's disciples informed him of what Jesus had been doing—his miraculous deeds—Matthew appears to provide the clue to answering this question. He notes that "when John heard in prison about the deeds of the Christ, he sent word by his disciples." First, being in prison, John knew that his ministry had ended and that his death was near. Second, he heard about the deeds "of the Christ." Thus he knew already what marvelous deeds Jesus performed, and he also knew by what authority and power he did them. He knew Jesus to be "the Christ," and the reason that he knew this is precisely because it was within his baptizing of Jesus that the Father anointed Jesus to be "the Christ." Although John knew this, his disciples did not. Sensitive to their loyalty to him and his ministry, that of preparing for the one who is to come, John does not simply tell them that they need to move on to Jesus and abruptly abandon him in prison. Such a command they would find emotionally too difficult to fulfill. Rather, he wishes them to perceive for themselves that it is time to leave him and to now, willingly and rightly of their own accord, to follow Jesus. Once they see what John has already heard, they too will rightly see that Jesus is indeed the one who is to come, the very one for whom they, as disciples of John, were ardently preparing. They too, in hearing and seeing what Jesus is doing, will recognize what John already knew: Jesus is the Christ, the anointed one who has come. Then they will freely follow him in faith.

16. Although the Synoptic Gospels have similar narratives, here we follow Matthew's account (Mt 10:1-16; see also Mk 3:13-19 and Lk 6:12-16, 9:2-5).

them out, and to heal every disease and every infirmity." What immediately follows within the Gospel account is the presenting of the names of the twelve Apostles. After naming the twelve, the narrative continues with Jesus telling them that they are not to go to the Gentiles or to the Samaritans but only to "the lost sheep of the house of Israel." This is what they are to say and do: "'The kingdom of heaven is at hand.' Heal the sick, raise the dead, cleanse lepers, cast out demons" (Mt 10:1-16). Their message and their acts are the same as Jesus'.

Significantly, the acts of the Twelve, like Jesus' acts, testify to the truth of what they say, for their acts make real the kingdom of God. And Jesus, in sending them out to say and do what he says and does, is enacting an ecclesiology. The named Twelve, specifically chosen by him, are authorized to continue his ministry. Having first been chosen to be the authorized hearers and seers of the Gospel, they are now to be the authorized speakers and doers of the Gospel. Jesus, by his act of sending, has enacted a second foundational ecclesiology in act. For Jesus, the church is that authorized body which continues to enact his acts and in so doing continues to make present the kingdom that he established through his saving acts. The salvific acts of Jesus and the saving acts of his church are one and the same. Importantly, Jesus did not articulate an ecclesiology or write an ecclesial constitution. Rather, as he is the kingdom of God in act, so the church, as witnessed in the acts of the Twelve, is to be the continuance of the kingdom of God in act. It is this church-in-act that Jesus founded by conferring upon the Twelve his authority to proclaim what he proclaims and his power to enact what he enacts. As Jesus enacts his name as Savior in establishing the kingdom of God through his words and deeds, so the church, through her words and deeds, continues to enact Jesus' name as Savior, and so she continues to make real God's kingdom.

Jesus' Power and Authority over Nature

Beside his authority and power over demons, sickness, sin, and death, Jesus' authority and power also extend to his dominion over the forces of nature. All three Synoptic Gospels tell of one instance of Jesus calming storms upon the Sea of Galilee while Matthew and Mark tell of two. The first finds Jesus asleep in a boat with his disciples. A great storm arose and his disciples were fearful for their lives. They woke Jesus and he rebuked the wind and the sea saying, "'Peace! Be still!' And the wind ceased, and there was great calm."[17] Jesus con-

---

17. By way of humor, the fact that Jesus could sleep during a raging storm at sea in a relatively small boat, with furious waves crashing over the sides, testifies to his being either an

fronted his disciples by pointedly asking why they were afraid and by impatiently querying their lack of faith. The disciples, for their part, were "filled with awe" and questioned among themselves: "Who then is this, that even wind and sea obey him?" (Mk 4:35-41; see also Lk 8:22-25). Matthew has them ask: "What sort of man is this, even the winds and sea obey him" (Mt 8:23-27). The sea's obedient response to Jesus' human act of commanding again raises the issue of Jesus' identity: *who* is this man? Jesus, in his quelling of the storm, was exercising his ministry as Savior and so revealing his divinity, for, biblically, only God, as creator, sovereignly governs the created realm. The entire occurrence is almost a literal enactment of Psalm 107. It speaks of men going to the sea in ships doing their business. When God caused a storm, "their courage melted away in their evil plight; they reeled and staggered like drunken men, and were at their wits' end. Then they cried to the Lord in their trouble, and he delivered them from their distress; and made the storm be still and the waves of the sea were hushed. Then they were glad because they had quiet, and he brought them to their desired haven" (Ps 107:23-30).[18] Without realizing it, the disciples were crying out to "the Lord." Yet this ignorance is precisely why the disciples were afraid. Their questioning of who Jesus is testifies to their lack of faith that he is "the Lord." Although amazed at what they had just witnessed, they were yet to perceive the truth contained within their experience. Jesus' rebuke is his attempt to press his disciples to go beyond their amazement and perceive the deeper significance of what has occurred and so ascertain, in faith, the right answer to their own question as to who he might be.

The second calming of a storm enhances and so advances the revelation as to Jesus' divine identity. After the multiplication of the loaves and fishes, Jesus sets his disciples off on a boat while he remained behind to pray. As evening came, Jesus could see from shore that his disciples were encountering rough seas and high winds. Later he came to them walking on the water and was about to pass them by. His disciples, thinking they were seeing a ghost, became frightened. Jesus immediately reassured them, saying, "Take heart, it is I; have no fear." He proceeded to get into the boat and the wind ceased. Again, his disciples "were utterly astounded" (Mk 6:45-52; see also Mt 14:22-33).[19]

Matthew's account adds Peter's request to come to Jesus on the water, to which he accedes. Becoming fearful at the sight of the waves and the sound of

---

extremely tired man or simply God. On a more serious note, Mark's specifying that Jesus was "asleep on a *cushion*" lends to the historicity of the event.

18. See also Ps 65:77, 89:10, and 93:3.

19. The Gospel of John also contains this story (see Jn 6:16-21).

the wind, Peter begins to sink and cries out, "Lord, save me." Whereupon Jesus caught him and, by way of reproach, said: "O man of little faith, why did
you doubt." Upon entering the boat, the wind calmed and "those in the boat
worshiped him, saying, 'Truly you are the Son of God'" (Mt 14:28-33).[20]

The significance of this entire narrative is found in Jesus' words. He tells
his disciples to "take heart" and to "have no fear" for "it is I (*ego eimi*)." His disciples should not be afraid because he who is identifying himself as "it is I" is the
one with whom they are well acquainted—"It is me, Jesus, your friend, the one
you know very well and not a ghost of whom you should be afraid." Through
his human words, his human act of speaking, he identifies himself as the man
Jesus. Simultaneously, in these same humanly spoken words, "it is I," we hear
the echo of the Lord speaking to Moses—"'I AM who am' (*ego eimi ho on*).... Say
this to the people of Israel, 'I AM (*ego eimi*) has sent me to you'" (Ex 3:14). Jesus
has appropriated to himself the divine name, YHWH.[21] The identity of the "I
AM" who divinely spoke to Moses from the burning bush possesses the same
identity as the "I AM" who humanly speaks to his disciples. Thus Jesus in identifying himself as "It is I" is testifying to the Incarnation. From within his human self-consciousness, Jesus is identifying himself as "I AM" and the identity
of "the who," from whom the "I AM" is humanly spoken, is God.

The same human words and human act that identify him to be Jesus the
familiar man known to his disciples are the same as those that identify Jesus
to be the familiar God known to Israel. In a real sense this too is a sacramental
or *theandric* act, for through the same human act of speaking and within the
same spoken words, Jesus both identifies himself as a known friend of his disciples and simultaneously reveals himself to be God. The human act of saying
"It is I" is the causal incarnational act by which the one who is saying "It is I"
identifies himself to be the human Jesus who is the Son of God. The divine
calming of the storm corroborates that the same one who is man is the same
one who is divine: Jesus. As in all of Jesus' mighty deeds, the divine effect of
calming the sea was enacted in a human manner. In the human act of entering
the boat, the sea became calm. The disciples were now safe because the man

---

20. Mark's narrative does not have this profession of faith but rather notes the disciples'
lack of faith. "And they were utterly astounded, for they did not understand about the loaves
[the miraculous multiplication], but their hearts were hardened" (Mk 6:51-52).

21. The "I AM" sayings within the Gospel of John more fully develop this notion. There
Jesus speaks of himself (*ego eime*) as the bread of life (6:34), the light of the world (8:12), the resurrection and the life (11:24), etc. He even speaks of himself as simply "I AM" (see Jn 4:26, 8:24,
and 8:28).

who entered the boat, and so was now in communion with them, was Jesus—the one who saves from all evil, danger, and harm.

In the context of the miraculous calming of the storm, Matthew portrays the disciples as grasping the double identity within Jesus' "It is I." The disciples' response, unlike their questioning as to who this might be after the first quelling of a storm, was to worship him, saying, "Truly, you are the Son of God." Their bodily act of worship was offered to a man with whom they had lived on a daily intimate basis. They knew him to be Jesus. What made this act of worship fitting and right, and not an act of idolatry, is their simultaneous acknowledgment in faith that Jesus was indeed the Son of God. Thus the disciples' profession of faith brings nuance to Jesus' divine identity. He is not simply God in some generic divine sense, but the Son of God, and therefore they distinguish him from his Father and in so doing acknowledge his Father as well.[22] Thus what we doctrinally perceive here is that the "It is I" (*ego eimi*), the distinguishing and defining divine name "YHWH" that was divinely revealed within the Old Testament, now pertains to both the Father and to Jesus the Son, and as such both are equally and fully the *one* true God. Therefore Jesus is aptly named—YHWH-Saves.

Jesus' Healing on the Sabbath

Jesus often performed his acts of healing on the Sabbath, the most sacred day within the Jewish week, for it marked the day upon which God rested from his work of creation and in so doing set it aside, by his own command, as day hallowed by the Lord (see Gn 2:1-3 and Ex 20:8-11).

This being the case, the Pharisees were scandalized, on one occasion, at observing Jesus' disciples plucking grain and eating it on the Sabbath. Having confronted Jesus, he responds by countering with the story of David and his hungry men eating "the bread of the Presence which it was not lawful for him to eat nor those who were with him, but only for the priests." While unlawful,

22. Jesus warns his disciples that many will falsely come in his name. They will claim, "It is I" (*ego eimi*) (Mk: 13:6; see also Lk 24:8). False saviors/prophets will assume, like Jesus, the divine name and in so doing lead many astray. Their falsity resides precisely in their appropriating divinity unto themselves and in becoming anti-Christs, for only Jesus can rightly claim that "I am he" (see Mt 24:5 and 1 Jn 2:18). Jesus as the Son of God also identifies himself as "I am he" and thus that God is the Father and the Son, whereas the false prophets, in assuming the divine name "I am he," would identify themselves simply as God. This would manifest that they cannot possibly be God, for God is not a singular, isolated supreme being but the divine communion of the Father and Son.

they did so without incurring guilt (1 Sm 21:1-6). Jesus narrates another relevant occurrence about how "the priests in the temple profane the Sabbath, and are guiltless. 'I tell you, something greater than the temple is here.'"

Jesus draws a twofold conclusion. If the Pharisees understood the saying "'I desire mercy and not sacrifice,' you would not have condemned the guiltless. For the Son of man is lord of the Sabbath" (Mt 12:1-8; see also Mk 2:23-28 and Lk 6:1-5).[23] For the sake of mercy, David and his men were permitted to eat the sacred bread. For the sake of fulfilling their righteous duties, priests are permitted to offer sacrifices on the Sabbath. Jesus is also both greater than the temple and, as the lord of the Sabbath, has authority over the laws that govern the Sabbath. But what could be greater than the temple, since it is the most holy sanctuary where the Most High God dwells, and who could be the lord of the Sabbath when the Sabbath was established by God? The obvious implication is that Jesus is asserting divine authority over the Sabbath because he embodies the presence of God in a manner that even exceeds the temple. These conclusions are enacted within the healing that immediately follows.

Upon entering a synagogue, Jesus beholds a man with a withered hand. The same Pharisees, who queried the lawfulness of his disciples plucking grain and eating it on the Sabbath, ask Jesus: "Is it lawful to heal on the Sabbath?" Jesus notes that if a man finds that one of his sheep has fallen into a pit on the Sabbath he will surely lift it out, so "how much more value is a man than a sheep! So it is lawful to do good on the Sabbath." Having established once again that the demands of mercy exceed those of the law, Jesus performs the act of mercy. He said to the man, "Stretch out your hand." In response to the healing, the Pharisees took counsel as to how to destroy him (Mt 12:9-14; see also Mk 3:1-6 and Lk 6:6-11, 14:1-6). This healing confirmed that Jesus was indeed the merciful lord of the Sabbath and thus possessed divine authority.

Why did Jesus heal on the Sabbath? Was it simply to manifest his mercy and divine power and authority? If so, the observation of an indignant synagogue leader would be apropos: "There are six days on which work ought to be done; come on those days and be healed, and not on the Sabbath day" (Lk 13:14). There must be a more profound reason, because Jesus knew that his healings on the Sabbath would antagonize others, causing great discord and tension to the point of its being used as justification for his rightful condemnation and death.

23. In Mark, Jesus, instead of appealing to mercy as he does in Matthew, says, "The Sabbath was made for man and not man for the Sabbath" (Mk 2:27). Thus the Sabbath was given to men as a gift from God, allowing them to rest as he did, and in so doing, giving him glory. It was not established for its own sake but so that men would have to keep it sacred.

The answer lies in the nature of the Sabbath. The Sabbath marked the day that God rested after his six days of performing the work of creation, which he knew to be good. That good creation was now disfigured by sin and evil and scarred by death. By healing on the Sabbath, Jesus was demonstrating God's mercy by undertaking the new work of re-creation. In Jesus, God was no longer resting. In Jesus, God has initiated a new work of creation. Jesus is the merciful lord of the Sabbath because through his acts of healing he is inaugurating, making real, God's kingdom. In Jesus himself is found the new Sabbath—a new creation that knows no sin with its deadly effects, a kingdom of holiness and life. In Jesus, there is to be found a new hollowed day of rest.

In these acts of healing on the Sabbath, Jesus is again enacting his name. He is the Savior who, specifically through his Sabbath acts of healing, is unambiguously re-creating and making new God's good creation and in so doing manifesting that he is God's Son. Only as the Son could Jesus take upon himself such divine authority and assume the divine responsibility that would warrant his acting in such a merciful manner as lord of the Sabbath. Healing on the Sabbath was integral to the revelation of who Jesus is and to the nature of his ministry—the Son through whom the Father was once again making all of creation good.[24] Likewise, these Sabbath acts of healing are prophetic because they anticipate the cross and resurrection. Having enacted his final saving act on the cross, Jesus' resurrection on Sunday, the eighth day, will inaugurate the new hallowed Sabbath marking the dawn of the new creation. This, in turn, prophetically anticipates Jesus' coming in glory, when there will be a new heaven and new earth and all the faithful, fully healed of sin and death, will find eternal rest—the eternal Sabbath.[25]

The Multiplication of the Loaves

One last example of Jesus' power must be examined: his multiplication of the loaves and fish. This miracle is distinctive, for it is not the healing of some sickness or deformity or an exorcism or even the remedying of some natural

24. Jesus makes this understanding explicit within the Gospel of John. There Jesus heals a blind mind on the Sabbath. John comments that it was because of this that the Jews persecuted Jesus. Jesus responded: "'My Father is working still, and I am working.' This is why the Jews sought to kill him, because he not only broke the Sabbath but also called God his Father, making himself equal with God" (Jn 5:16-18). Jesus, as the Son of the Father, by healing on the Sabbath, is merely doing what his Father is doing: resuming the task of creation.

25. The Letter to Hebrews develops this theme (see Heb 4:1-11).

calamity such as a storm. There is no negative abnormality that needs to be rectified. That people become hungry and need food is normal, and there is a normal way of meeting this need. After Jesus had taught the crowd for a considerable time in a lonely place, the disciples (Luke designates them as "the Twelve") wisely suggested to Jesus, because it is evening, that he send them away so that they could buy food. But Jesus says that they should give them something to eat. Their response is one of frustrated if not irritated bewilderment. They vehemently point out that they have only five loaves and two fish, and besides, it would take two hundred denarii to buy enough bread to feed such a large gathering.[26] Jesus requests the loaves and fish and has his disciples sit the people down on the grass (Mark notes that it was "green" and thus lush), whereupon Jesus performs an act that is not normal from within a normal earthly setting.

Taking the loaves and fish, "he looked up to heaven, and blessed, and broke and gave the loaves to his disciples, and the disciples gave them to the crowds. And they all ate and were satisfied." Jesus has enacted a priestly liturgical act composed of a sequence of causal acts. First, he "looked up to heaven." Jesus' "look" is a looking up to God, a prayer of intercession to his heavenly Father, and a calling down of his Father's heavenly blessing. Through this causal act, Jesus imparted to the following acts a heavenly blessed causality that exceeded any normal earthly causality. Second, in communion with his Father, Jesus then "blessed" the bread, and so it was no longer simply normal bread of this earth but bread that now bore a heavenly blessing; it was heavenly bread. Third, this blessed heavenly bread Jesus "broke," which is the first act of multiplying the bread. Only because Jesus multiplied it in the breaking could it continue to be broken and so continue to be multiplied. Fourth, he "gave the loaves to his disciples." While Jesus multiplied the blessed heavenly bread, he gave the responsibility for its continued multiplication to his disciples. They are designated as the authorized distributors of the multiplied blessed heavenly bread, and so they perform their liturgical priestly act of distribution. The final liturgical act is performed by the crowd—"they ate." Only

26. The fact that a large sum of money is specified could call to mind Isaiah's prophecy. "Ho, everyone who thirsts, come to the waters; and he who has not money, come, buy and eat! Come, buy wine and milk without money and without price. Why do you spend your money for that which is not bread, and labor for that which does not satisfy? Hearken diligently to me, and eat what is good, and delight yourselves in fatness" (Is 55:1-2). Jesus, in providing an abundance of bread that costs nothing, is prophetically anticipating the heavenly bread that he will freely give in the heavenly banquet that is his Eucharistic risen body and blood, and that will eternally satisfy.

in their "eating," only in this participative priestly liturgical act, is the liturgical act completed, for they ate the heavenly bread that was broken and given
for them. The effect of all these priestly liturgical acts, each containing within
them their distinctive causality, is that the people—"about five thousand men,
besides women and children"—"were satisfied." The hunger of all was satiated.
Even with so many, the disciples collected "twelve baskets full of pieces left
over" (Mt 14:13-21; see also Mk 6:32-44 and Lk 9:10-17). There was an abundance of bread.

Several theological points need to be made. First, this liturgy finds its obvious prophetic prefiguration within the Old Testament where God said: "I will
rain down bread from heaven for you" (Ex 16:4).[27] This heavenly bread, manna, provided nourishment throughout the Israelites' sojourn through the desert to the Promised Land. Jesus fulfills this prophetic prefiguration through
his priestly multiplication of the new blessed heavenly bread, which itself is a
sign of God now nourishing his people within the true, and not simply prefigured, Promised Land of his kingdom. The apostolic church Jesus' priestly
liturgical act is also a prophetically looking forward to the Eucharistic liturgy
first enacted by Jesus at the Last Supper and continues to be enacted within
the present life of the church. The true significance of what Jesus did within
the multiplication only becomes transparent when interpreted from within its
Last Supper fulfillment. To properly interpret theologically the multiplication
of the loaves, both the Old Testament prefigurement and the Last Supper fulfillment must be considered.

Second, while God rained down manna upon the Israelites, Jesus' "looking
up" to heaven is his priestly "calling down" from heaven a heavenly blessing.
In this light, Jesus is now the one who is "raining down" bread from heaven,
for he through his heavenly blessing multiplies the loaves. There is now, within the person of Jesus, a communion between God in heaven and Jesus upon
earth, for the act of multiplication finds it source, its initial causality, in heaven
and finds its effect, the multiplication, upon earth. This communion of heavenly causality and earthly effect resides within the fact that he who is looking
up from earth to heaven and he who is calling down from heaven to earth
a heavenly blessing is the heavenly Son of God who exists on earth as man.
Within the Incarnation, within the priestly humanity of the Son, heaven and

27. Psalm 78 declares that God "rained down upon them manna to eat, and gave them
grain of heaven. Men ate of the bread of angels; and he sent them food in abundance" (vv. 24-
25; see also Ps 105:40). Paul speaks of the manna as "spiritual food" (1 Cor 10:3).

earth are one. Thus the prophetic Old Testament prefigurement of God raining down manna is fulfilled in Jesus, who, as the Son of God incarnate, rains
down the new manna upon the earth. If the above theological interpretation
of the multiplication is in keeping with and so fulfills the Old Testament type,
in what manner does the multiplication prophetically look to the Last Supper
and thus find its full significance within the Last Supper?

Third, what unites the present multiplication of the loaves with its future
fulfillment within the Last Supper, and so finds its full significance therein, is
Jesus' performing the act of multiplication as a priestly liturgical act. The acts
of "looking," "blessing," "breaking," and "giving" are priestly acts that conform
the multiplication into one liturgical act.[28] Within the Passover Liturgy of the
Last Supper, Jesus "took bread, and blessed, and broke it, and gave it to his disciples." The priestly acts of the Last Supper are the same as those within the
multiplication, and so Jesus, in his priestly actions, conjoins these two litur-
gies. Moreover, what Jesus declares within the liturgical actions of the Last
Supper fulfill its prophecy within the multiplication and so give it full meaning: "Take, eat; this is my body" (Mt 26:26 and Mk 14:22; Lk 22:19 adds, "which
is given for you"). The Passover bread that is blessed, broken, and given is Jesus' body. Thus the *heavenly blessed bread* within the multiplication is now considered the anticipation of *the blessed bread* of the Passover that is Jesus' body.
The *broken* heavenly blessed bread within the multiplication is now seen to
be the anticipation of the *broken* blessed bread of the Passover that is Jesus'
body. The *giving* of the broken heavenly blessed bread of the multiplication
in now seen to be the anticipation of the *giving* of the broken blessed bread of
the Passover that is Jesus' body. Jesus can provide the foreshadowed multiplied new heavenly bread because he is, as the bodily Son incarnate, the new
heavenly bread come down from heaven. The truly new bread that God rains
down from heaven is Jesus, his incarnate Son. Thus what the multiplication
ultimately prefigures is the raining down of the new heavenly bread of the
new Passover, which is Jesus' own body.[29] Because this new heavenly bread of
Jesus' body is the bread of the new Passover, the blessing, breaking, and giving
of the multiplication anticipate the blessing, breaking, and giving of Jesus, that

28. Within the Jewish liturgical tradition, it was common to bless and give to others that
which was blessed.

29. Here we see within the Synoptic Tradition the basis upon which Jesus, in the Gospel of
John, gives his bread of life discourse, that is, that he is the bread of life come down from heav-
en, which is his own flesh. In a sense, Jesus in John's Gospel is providing his own theological
commentary on his miraculous multiplication of the loaves (see Jn 6).

is, his blessed and broken offering of himself as the new Passover lamb of sacrifice and the new lamb through which a new covenant is made. Within the
multiplication, Jesus' priestly act of blessing the bread and the bread that was
blessed and broken are distinct. From within the Last Supper we perceive now
that Jesus is both the priest who offers the new bread and, because the blessed bread is his broken and given body, equally the sacrifice. What Jesus takes,
blesses, breaks, and gives is himself for many.[30]

Fourth, the final priestly liturgical act of the multiplication is the eating
of the taken, blessed, broken, and given bread. The final liturgical act within
the new Passover liturgy of the Last Supper is the eating of the taken, blessed, broken, and given bread that is Jesus' body. Both are interconnected causal priestly liturgical acts that conclude in eating. The effect upon those who
ate the multiplied bread is that they "were satisfied." We see now that those
who eat the bread of the Last Supper, the bread of the new Passover, are also
satisfied, for this is the broken bread of the new covenant, the new lamb of
sacrifice, the bread of the new kingdom of God—the body of Jesus. Although
the Apostles wanted to provide normal earthly bread to the gathered crowd,
we now perceive that the new "normal" bread of the kingdom of God, foreshadowed in multiplication, is the new bread that is Jesus himself. Jesus is the
heavenly nourishment and life within the new covenant that brings heavenly
satisfaction.

Furthermore, when Jesus proclaimed the passage from Isaiah to the people within the synagogue at Nazareth, he finished by saying that this passage
was fulfilled not in his "speaking" but in their "hearing." The word of God,
the word of Jesus, is fulfilled when those who hear it take hold of it in faith.
This taking hold, this fulfillment, is ultimately the taking hold of Jesus himself
in faith, for he is himself the word of God as the Son incarnate. Similarly, the
liturgy of the multiplication and its fulfillment within the Last Supper are not
fulfilled in Jesus' acts of taking, blessing, breaking, and giving but in the act
of receiving, in the act of eating, for only then does one become one with the
bread, only then does one become one with the bread that is Jesus' body. This
is the prefigured goal within the multiplication, and this is the actualized goal
within the Last Supper—a living and nourishing communion with Jesus.

30. Here I wish only to make the theological connections that pertain to the bread of the
multiplication and the bread of the Last Supper. I will provide a fuller theological and doctrinal interpretation of the Last Supper at the proper time in chapter 9. I do not present here how
the Last Supper is fulfilled within the Paschal Mystery, that is, Jesus passion, death, and resurrection. But one can already perceive how Jesus' death and resurrection fulfill all that is discussed here.

Fifth, the abundance of bread multiplied—the twelve leftover baskets—is fulfilled, for the new bread that is Jesus' body provides the abundance of life that is obtained and lived within God's heavenly kingdom here on earth. The miracle of the loaves was unique in that it was not remedial, as are Jesus' healings, exorcisms, and acts of forgiveness. We now perceive the difference. This miracle is an expression of the abundance of life that lies within the kingdom of God. Theologically, to live within the kingdom of God is both remedial and elevating, for in so doing one is both freed from all that enslaves, sin and all its consequences, and raised into the abundance of a never-ending holy life. To live in Jesus, who embodies the kingdom, is to be healed and sanctified. Thus God's Old Testament raining of bread upon the Israelites in the desert is fulfilled in Jesus raining down the multiplied bread upon the crowds sitting on lush green grass, and in turn this verdant raining down foreshadows the raining down of the new bread, his own life-giving body, upon members of the new covenant, which finds its fulfilled reality in the eternal raining down within the heavenly banquet of the Lamb, where the saints will eternally be satisfied, having their fill of Jesus' divine life—forever living within and forever being nourished upon the glorious incarnate Son's risen body (see Rv 19:9).[31] What we see from within the whole is, again, Jesus becoming Jesus. In the multiplication of bread and in its fulfillment within the Last Supper, Jesus is enacting his name, for to be Savior is not simply to bring freedom from evil but also to generate an abundance of life. To be in communion with him is to partake of the abundant and enduring life that is God's kingdom.

Lastly, just as Jesus' sending forth of his disciples to enact his saving acts of healing was an ecclesial act, Jesus' giving to his twelve Apostles the multiplied blessed and broken bread to distribute is an ecclesial act. They are the priestly distributors of Jesus' abundance. At the Last Supper, Jesus "gave it [the blessed and broken bread] to his disciples and said, 'Take, eat; this is my body'" (Mt 26:26). Jesus' priestly liturgical act of "giving" within the Last Supper fulfills his priestly liturgical act of "giving" within the multiplication. As the Apostles distributed the multiplied bread, so now they are to give the new blessed and broken bread that is Jesus' body. Thus Jesus' priestly liturgical act of giving within the Last Supper is an ecclesial act by which he establishes

---

31. Although the Israelites first rejoiced in and were satisfied with the abundance of the manna that God had rained down upon them, they later tired of it and complained that they were, literally, fed up with it. They did not even want to look at it, much less eat it (see Nm 11:4-6). The Israelites may have wearied of the manna, but those within the kingdom of God will never become weary of the bread that Jesus provides—the bread that he himself is.

his church in act. The church is the apostolic act, the living apostolic reality, wherein the priestly liturgical act of Jesus' giving of his body is continuously enacted.[32] And the faithful within the church in their receiving, in their taking, of the abundance enact their priestly liturgical act, for within them the abundance of life, Jesus, now dwells. To reside within the church, to reside wherein the abundant life-giving bread that is Jesus' body is given, is to reside within the abundant life of the kingdom of God, that is, to reside within Jesus himself. The church, then, is the apostolic church precisely because she continues to enact, as did the Apostles, the priestly acts of Jesus. She continues to proclaim the presence of the kingdom of God, which is present within and through her remedial priestly acts of healing and forgiveness and within and through her priestly acts of bestowing the abundance of heavenly life. To participate in the priestly saving acts of the church is to partake of the priestly saving acts of Jesus—it is simply to encounter Jesus being Jesus.

Jesus Speaks and Acts in the Holy Spirit

Jesus' mighty deeds provoked the question as to the source of his power and authority to heal, specifically as to his ability to cast out demons. As Jesus revealed through his acts of healing his divine authority and power, did he reveal something more than his own identity as the Son of God?

In Matthew's Gospel, having healed a blind and dumb demoniac, the crowds wondered in amazement whether Jesus could be the promised "Son of David." Reacting to this positive assessment, the Pharisees contemptuously declared: "It is only by Beelzebul, the prince of demons, that this man casts out demons." Jesus responds by noting that a house divided against itself cannot stand, and thus "if Satan casts out Satan," his kingdom cannot stand. Jesus concludes: "But if it is by the Spirit of God that I cast out demons, then the kingdom of God has come upon you" (Mt 12:22-30; see also Mk 3:22-27 and Lk 11:14-23).[33] Jesus is declaring that God's kingdom can only become a

---

32. Luke emphasizes that it was "the Twelve" who first came to Jesus encouraging him to send away the crowd so that the people could buy bread (see Lk 9:12). I would not want to make too much of this, but it may be of some significance that twelve is the number of baskets filled with leftover bread. One could see that the full abundance of life resides within the whole of the apostolic tradition. The Apostles individually (one basket each) and the twelve together (twelve baskets total) form the copious whole of the Gospel.

33. Jesus says, "But if it is by the finger of God that I cast out demons, then the kingdom of God has come upon you" (Lk 11:20). More than likely, Luke is the more historical. Because Luke emphasizes the presence of the Holy Spirit within his Gospel and Acts, it would be surprising

reality by the power of God's Spirit, for only such divine power is capable of vanquishing evil, including the dominion of Satan's kingdom, and only in the same divine Spirit can the bounteous life and goodness of God's dominion be secured. A kingdom that is divine in origin and in which the fullness of divine life is lived demands a divine causal agent both in its establishment and in its continuance. This divine causal agent, Jesus declares, is the Spirit of God. Jesus asserts that he is employing this divine causal agent, this power of God's Spirit, when enacting his mighty deeds of over powering evil. This confirms that God's kingdom has come into their midst—the Spirit engendered wholeness and newness of life.

The full significance of what is being done—the casting out of demons, and the claim of its effect, the presence of God's kingdom—is found in the person who is performing the act and making the claim. The Greek text has Jesus emphasizing, through a double "I" (the personal pronoun "I" followed by the first person singular verb), that he specifically is doing the casting out. It would then read in English: "But if it is by the Spirit of God that *I, I cast* out demons, then the kingdom of God has come upon you." Jesus, by specifically accentuating the "I," is emphatically designating himself as the one who is performing the acts by which demons are cast out, and so he is making present God's kingdom. Likewise, in accentuating the "I," he is equally emphasizing that he himself is doing so "by the Spirit of God." The emphatic "I" specifies both that Jesus is performing the act and that he is doing so by the Spirit of God, thus revealing that the act he is performing is done in communion with the Spirit of God. The "I" then testifies, once again, to the intrinsic abiding of the Spirit of God within Jesus, which is constitutive of who Jesus is as Savior, for only within this communion of the Spirit is he capable of performing those acts that are salvific. Without the indwelling Spirit, Jesus would be unable to enact the mighty deeds that make God's kingdom present, and without Jesus the indwelling of the Spirit of God would not be made manifest within these mighty deeds. Thus the Spirit of God inherently abides in Jesus, so that all that he says and does, and not just in this one instance of casting out the demon, is said and done in communion with the Spirit and so manifests the Spirit's presence.

This, in turn, manifests the entire Trinity of persons. If, when he acts in the Spirit of God, Jesus humanly manifests that he is God—that is, God's Son—

---

for him to change "Spirit" to "finger." Nonetheless, "finger" expresses an action of God himself, but one done through the instrumentality of his finger. Matthew's changing "finger" to "Spirit" expresses the same idea. Jesus acts by the "finger of God," that is, through the instrumentality of "the Spirit."

then, because he is acting in the Spirit of God, the God in whose Spirit he is acting is that of his Father. Thus Jesus' human actions bear witness to the communion of the Father, the Son, and the Holy Spirit. Jesus, the Son, always acts in communion with his Father, for his acts are always enacted through the Father's Spirit of Sonship.

Within Matthew's Gospel, the people respond to Jesus' healing of the dumb demoniac by querying whether Jesus might "be the Son of David." The question relates to God's promise to David that he would raise up an anointed Davidic heir who would establish an everlasting kingdom (see 2 Sm 7:12-16 and Is 7:9). Could Jesus be this promised Davidic heir who would establish this promised enduring kingdom? The clash between Jesus and the Pharisees began when the Pharisees refuted this claim by asserting that Jesus acted with the authority of Beelzebub. Jesus counters by denying this and asserting instead that "if it is by the Spirit of God that I cast out demons, then the kingdom of God has come upon you" (Mt 12:28). Thus the initial query is answered in the positive. By acting in the Holy Spirit and so bringing about the kingdom of God, Jesus manifests that he is the anointed Son of God and in so doing equally reveals that he is truly the anointed Son of David. Being simultaneously the Son of God and the Son of David, Jesus not only establishes the kingdom of God but also is himself the kingdom of God, for he humanly embodies, as Son of David, the divine Spirit of God, as Son of God.

In the light of all the above, we can understand why Jesus concludes this encounter with the Pharisees by saying that all sins and blasphemies will be forgiven, even "a word against the son of man," but whoever blasphemes and speaks against the Spirit "will not be forgiven, either in this age or in the age to come." To declare that Jesus casts out demons by Beelzebul, when in fact he is doing so by the Spirit of God, is not simply an attack against him but more fundamentally a blasphemous assault on the Spirit of God in whom he acts, for such a declaration identifies the Spirit of God as Satan and so the author of all evil. Such a sin is unforgivable, for the Holy Spirit who is the very goodness of God and in whom the merciful forgiveness of God is made manifest within the saving deeds of Jesus is now professed to be the embodiment of evil itself—Satan. This very act renders the act of forgiveness incapable of being enacted, for the one capable of enacting this act, the Spirit of God, is now identified as Satan, the one who is incapable of forgiving.

Theological Conclusions

Here we can articulate several theological and doctrinal summary conclusions. I want to highlight the logical interrelationship, the relational flow, within all that was examined above, hopefully sharpening the significance and enhancing the beauty of all that has been argued.

First, Jesus' acts of casting out demons, healing the sick, raising the dead, forgiving sins, calming storms, and multiplying bread are *theandric* acts and as such are priestly sacramental acts. They do not simply disclose that God has given to Jesus divine authority and power. Nor are they performed apart from his humanity as if they were merely exterior bodily symbols or signs of what Jesus is doing essentially, simply, and solely by his divine authority and power as God. Nor do these miraculous deeds even disclose, as in the traditional apologetic, that Jesus is God, as if this revelation is alone important. What is of the utmost importance is how these acts are performed, for how they are performed authenticates not only Jesus' divinity but also his humanity. The human acts—Jesus' willing, speaking, touching, blessing—are the causal acts through which and in which Jesus' divine power is exercised and so is efficacious. These human acts symbolize what they effect and effect what they symbolize: Jesus' divine authority and power. Thus they are important because they inherently testify to and so confirm the Incarnation. Because these human acts are the cause of a divine effect, they testify that the man who is performing these human acts is the Son of God. Only if Jesus is truly the Son of God truly existing as an authentic man can he, through his human words and acts, truly heal the sick, forgive sin, raise the dead, and multiply bread by his own personal divine authority and power. Thus these acts are *theandric* or sacramental acts precisely because they are incarnational acts, for through and in them the reality of the Incarnation is enacted—the Son of God *acting* as man and so revealing that the Son of God is man. This being the case, these acts are unique. No one but the Son of God existing as man could enact such acts.

Second, as incarnational acts, they manifest the intrinsic abiding presence of the Spirit of God within Jesus, and thus his performing of all such actions is founded upon Jesus being conceived by the Holy Spirit. The Holy Spirit is the causal agent through whom the Son of God becomes man within the womb of Mary, and this causal act intrinsically tethers all of his subsequent human causal actions to the Spirit of Sonship, by whom he was begotten as man. Jesus only speaks and acts by, with, and in the Holy Spirit. This finds confirmation and further expression within the baptism of Jesus, where the Father sends forth his Commissioning Spirit whereby Jesus is empowered to inaugurate God's kingdom. In and through this Commissioning Spirit, Jesus performs his priestly sacramental *theandric* acts that make the kingdom present. The Father is well pleased in his Son because the Spirit abides in Jesus, animating and empowering him always to act in accordance with his Father's will, that is, bringing about his kingdom.

Third, we perceive here more clearly the full priestly sacramental nature of Jesus' words and acts. Jesus performs his human sacramental acts of healing, exorcism, forgiving, and blessing as the Spirit imbued Son of God, through his Spirit of Sonship, and in so doing he is performing his salvific priestly ministry of overcoming evil and simultaneously engendering abundant life that only the Spirit brings—reconciliation with and so communion with the Father within the kingdom of God.

Fourth, this brings theological and sacramental depth to the importance of "touching"—fleshly touching is priestly sacramental touching. Those who Jesus humanly touches and those who, in faith, humanly touch him are in fleshly communion—the flesh of the incarnate Son of God and the flesh of other human beings. To be literally in touch with Jesus, the Son, is to be literally in touch with the very power and life of the Spirit of God—the Spirit of Sonship—and so to be in communion with—literally, in touch with—the Father. To be in communion with the Incarnate Son is to be in communion with the Father through the communion of the Holy Spirit. This is what the kingdom of God means and what it means to live in the kingdom of God. This is the kingdom promised to David, the everlasting kingdom of which Jesus, as David's son, is David's royal heir who will reign forever. This is why Jesus can truly and authoritatively declare: "But if it is by the Spirit of God that I cast out demons, then the kingdom of God has come upon you." Jesus as priest casts out demons and in so doing becomes the king of God's kingdom. Jesus, in enacting his name as Savior, is performing priestly acts and so is establishing himself as king. To be in touch with Jesus is to be in touch with the King. Therefore Jesus, as the incarnate Son of God, is the anointed Christ and so is the anointed Priest and King and thus the Savior—YHWH-Saves.

Finally, Jesus makes possible the continuance of this communion, this being in touch with him, through the commissioning of his Apostles to perform his same acts of healing and life giving. In this commissioning, Jesus enacts the church so that his priestly saving acts become ecclesial priestly saving acts. Thus the church continues to make the kingdom of God present and in so doing continues to make it possible for others to enter that kingdom where they will encounter Jesus' acts of healing and elevating—the remedy to sin and its effects and the procurement of eternal life. The apostolic church is, then, the continued literal embodiment of Jesus, for within the bodily priestly sacramental acts of the church, one is in touch with the bodily priestly sacramental acts of Jesus, the King. These ecclesial acts ensure the faithful's communion not only with Jesus but also with his Father and the Holy Spirit, for within these ecclesial acts Jesus unites the faithful to the Father in the communion of the Holy Spirit. Within and through the apostolic church, Jesus continues to be Jesus.[34]

34. Although this was not the main point of the above, I have essentially articulated the doctrinal basis for the Catholic understanding of the sacraments as manifested within Jesus' public ministry of healing, exorcising, forgiving, and blessing. The singular nature of Jesus' incarnational acts being sacramental in nature makes these acts, the acts of the Son of God incarnate, the primordial sacramental acts and Jesus, as the Son of God existing as man, the foundational sacrament. All ecclesial sacramental acts find their source and efficacy within Jesus' incarnational sacramental acts—the human saving acts of the Son of God.

Although the sacraments will only be conclusively instituted through Jesus' priestly sacrificial death and glorious resurrection, Jesus, during his public ministry, performs those priestly acts that prefigure and illustrate the saving benefits of the sacraments. These benefits come through Jesus' cross and resurrection—freedom from Satan's dominion, healing of sickness, forgiveness of sin, overcoming of death. These saving benefits also include initiation into and participating in the abundant life of God's kingdom—communion with the Father in Jesus his Son through the intimacy of the Holy Spirit.

This communion finds its preeminent sacramental expression within the church as the sacrament of Christ. Through the sacramental actions of his church, Jesus makes present his own saving sacramental acts. It is through faith and the sacraments of initiation—baptism, confirmation, and the Eucharist—that the faithful enter into and live within the church as the Body of Christ by entering into and living in communion with the risen Jesus as Lord and Savior, and so sharing in his life of the Holy Spirit, the Spirit that transforms the faithful into holy sons or daughters of the Father in the likeness of Jesus the Son, making them brothers and sisters to one another in Christ.

As within his earthly ministry, it is this being "in touch" with Jesus' risen humanity that is sacramentally essential. This sacramental touch of the risen Jesus exceeds that of the sacramental touch of the earthly Jesus. Through the church and the sacraments, the faithful are again literally in touch with, in communion with, the risen Jesus, the humanly risen and glorious Son of God incarnate, and within that living communion within the risen humanity of Jesus, they share with him communion with the Father in the life and love of the Holy Spirit. Paul professes that the faithful are one living body/flesh in Christ and so they are never out of touch with Jesus (see Rom 12:4-5; 1 Cor 12:12-13; Eph 2:15-16; Col 3:15), for they share with him, within his risen humanity, the one life of the Holy the Spirit, having one God as their Father. In Jesus the Christ, the faithful form one new man who comes to full maturity when Jesus the Head comes in the fullness of the Spirit as Lord and Savior at the end of time (see Eph 4:11-16). This presently finds its most mature expression and most vibrant source of growth in the Eucharistic Liturgy. There the faithful offer in union with Christ and participate in union with Christ his one sacrifice to the Father and so can be in communion with his Father through receiving and so sharing in his Spirit-filled risen body and blood. The Eucharist is then the fullest expression of literally being in touch with Jesus, for it is the fullest expression of the one living Body/Flesh of Christ, head and members. To be in sacramental communion with the risen humanity of Jesus, through the sacrament that is the church, is to be in communion with the Father, the Son, and the Holy Spirit.

The primary reason that the Protestant understanding of sacramental acts is erroneous is found in the above Catholic understanding. For Protestants, the sacraments are external symbolic acts that merely signify Jesus' spiritual and invisible acts. The Protestant notion of sacramental acts undermines the reality of the Incarnation, if it does not implicitly altogether deny it. Protestants have lost the sacramental equation: as Jesus acts as the Son of God within and through his humanity, so within the sacraments he acts in and through his humanity, the material symbolic action effects the acts symbolized. Moreover, Protestant sacramental theology has lost the whole theological importance of being "in touch" with Jesus, since the material symbolic acts are now detached from the living materiality of the risen Jesus. The sacramental acts no longer give expression to or intensify the one living reality of Christ and his Body—the church.

5 · JESUS' PROPHETIC SALVIFIC ACTS

Promulgating the Law of the Kingdom of Heaven

We have considered extensively the theological and doctrinal implications of Jesus' priestly acts in initiating the kingdom of God. It is now important to examine his unique prophetic authority, especially in promulgating the new law within God's kingdom. We will do this by examining Matthew's account of the Sermon on the Mount and particularly the Beatitudes.[1]

In his acts of healing and the like, Jesus manifested, as the Son of God, his priestly saving sacramental acts through which the kingdom of God is made present. In so doing, he revealed that he is also the son of David, the new and everlasting king of God's perpetual kingdom. The Sermon on the Mount as narrated in the Gospel of Matthew is the classic text that exhibits Jesus' unique authority within God's kingdom, as he now reveals that he is also the new prophet divinely promised to Moses. "I will raise up for them [the Israelites] a prophet like you [Moses] from among their brethren; and I will put my word in his mouth, and he shall speak to them all that I command him" (Dt 18:18). By ascending "up on the mountain" and proclaiming the new law of the kingdom of God, Jesus became the new Moses (Mt 5-7; see also Lk 6:20-49 and Ex 19:16-20:17). Here Jesus, as the new Moses, promulgates a law that supersedes the divine law previously proscribed. This is the new law of the everlasting kingdom of God, the law of the new and eternal covenant.

Before examining the Sermon on the Mount, particularly the Beatitudes, several preliminary points need to be made to set the theological context from which it can be properly interpreted. First, as Jesus initially made real the kingdom of God within his public ministry through his healings, exorcisms, forgiveness, blessings, and so on, so he must make real, again through his ac-

1. While focusing on the Gospel of Matthew, particularly the Beatitudes, I also take into account the other Synoptic Gospels where appropriate.

146

tions, the new law within that kingdom. He must be not only the promulgator of the new law, but also the enactor of what the new law commands. In enacting the Beatitudes, Jesus enacts the kingdom, making it a reality.

Second, just as the culminating acts will establish God's kingdom lie within his passion, death, and resurrection and subsequent outpouring of the Holy Spirit, the new law within God's kingdom, the Beatitudes, lie within Jesus' passion, death, and resurrection. Within the same acts by which God's kingdom comes to be, the Beatitudes, the new law of God's kingdom, are enacted.

Third, Jesus is not simply the exemplar of what is contained within the Sermon on the Mount, specifically the Beatitudes, but more so, in enacting the Sermon on the Mount and in so doing founding God's kingdom, he empowers the faithful who are united to him within the kingdom that he embodies, to live the holy life of the kingdom of God. Because Jesus embodies the kingdom of God, it is only in living in communion with Jesus and so in communion with the Spirit of God that the faithful are empowered to live within God's kingdom, a life that is inscrolled within the Sermon on the Mount.[2]

Fourth, to live a life appropriate to God's kingdom is, again, to live in communion with the Trinity. In Christ, through the Holy Spirit, the faithful live within the Father's kingdom and so live, as does Jesus his Son, as holy children of the Father, embodying his kingdom's blessed precepts and obeying its life-giving decrees.

Finally, as Jesus displays divine authority and power within his public ministry, he also, as the new prophetic Moses, in promulgating the new law of God's kingdom, appropriates to himself an exclusively divine prerogative. These above points are evident within the Beatitudes.

2. The theological and moral heart of the Mosaic Law is the Ten Commandments. To live in accordance with God's covenant was to live in accordance with these commands, for to do so was to live a holy life and so be holy as God is holy (see Lv 11:44, 19:2, 20:7, and 20:26). This law defined the holy covenanted kingdom of Israel and, with its law, was a prefiguration of the new covenant with its new law. Because the Law of Moses, particularly the Ten Commandments, defined the holy kingdom of Israel, so the Sermon on the Mount, the law of the new covenant, particularly the Beatitudes, defined the new holy kingdom of God. Thus the theological and moral heart of God's kingdom is the Eight Beatitudes. The fundamental difference is not simply that they enhance the significance of the Ten Commandments of the Mosaic Law, but that Jesus will enact the Beatitudes within his own life, and by doing so he will fulfill the Mosaic Law. Likewise, the faithful, who subsequently live in communion with Jesus and so live in God's kingdom, through their enacting of the Beatitudes will be empowered to obey God's commandments, which hitherto was impossible because the Law of Moses is no longer written in stone, a law imposed from without. Rather, the law of the new covenant resides within the newly created Spirit-filled hearts and minds of those who abide in Christ and so are empowered from within to fulfill them (see Jer 31:31-34 and Ezek 36:24-27).

The Beatitudes

Blessed are the poor in Spirit, for theirs is the kingdom of heaven.[3] Blessed are those who mourn for they shall be comforted. Blesses are the meek, for they shall inherit the earth. Blessed are those who hunger and thirst for righteousness, for they will be satisfied. Blessed are the merciful, for they shall obtain mercy. Blessed are the pure in heart, for they shall see God. Blessed are the peacemakers, for they shall be called sons of God. Blessed are those who are persecuted for righteousness' sake, for theirs is the kingdom of heaven.[4]

In the first and eighth Beatitudes, Jesus makes a declarative statement that pertains to the present. "Blessed are the poor in spirit." The reason is that "theirs *is* the kingdom of heaven." "Blessed are those who are persecuted for righteousness' sake." The reason is that "theirs is the kingdom of heaven." By what authority can the man Jesus make such assured declarative pronouncements? How can he emphatically and categorically declare what "is" concerning the kingdom of heaven? Within the remaining six Beatitudes, Jesus prophesies that those who live them *will* receive appropriate corresponding blessings. By what authority does Jesus make such prophetic claims, especially seeing as he does not preface them with the words: "God promises, blessed will be"? Jesus is not only promulgating the new law of God's kingdom but also asserting facts and promising specific rewards and blessings to those who keep the new law. Unlike Moses, who did not author the commandments but received them from God, Jesus is authoring the Beatitudes with their directives and respective promised blessings. Thus Jesus is appropriating to himself a divine prerogative both in promulgating a way of life, the new life within the kingdom of heaven, whose sanctioned legitimacy can only be divine in origin, and by pledging blessings for such a way of life that can only be fulfilled by God. This promulgation of the new law of the heavenly kingdom can only be authenticated in its prophetic fulfillment.[5]

This prophetic fulfillment will be definitively realized in Jesus himself. In

3. Within the New Testament, only Matthew employs the phrase "the kingdom of heaven" rather than "the kingdom of God." This may be because of his Jewish audience. Because of their reverence for the name of God, the Jews would speak of the kingdom of heaven rather than the kingdom of God. This designation will be employed within this chapter.

4. Mt 5:3-12. The Old Testament Wisdom literature and Psalms frequently use the phrase "Blessed are/is." See, e.g., Pss 1:1, 2:12, 32:1-2, 34:8, 40:4, 41:1, 106:3, 112:1; Prv 8:32-34; Dn 12:12.

5. Within the Old Testament, a prophecy is not true if it does not come to pass. "And if you say in your heart, 'How may we know the word which the Lord has not spoken?'—when a prophet speaks in the name of the Lord, if the word does not come to pass or come true, that

fulfilling the Beatitudes, by enacting them, he not only demonstrates his divine authority in promulgating them, but also reveals that he is the Son of God incarnate. Both the promulgating and enacting of the Beatitudes are incarnational acts. In promulgating, Jesus humanly speaks with the divine authority of the Son of God. In their human enactment, Jesus, as the Son of God, makes good on the divine prophetic promises within the Beatitudes because within his enactment he reaps them. Jesus promulgates the Beatitudes as man and enacts them as man, and in so doing he merits their blessings, but only because the one who is humanly preforming these acts by which the blessings are achieved is the Son of God. Jesus, as the Son of God incarnate, will enact these prophetic Beatitudes fully within his salvific death, and in so doing will fully procure for himself, within his resurrected humanity, their promised blessings, the blessings of the heavenly kingdom, the kingdom that he will establish and that he himself then is. Only then will the faithful, in communion with him, be empowered to live the Beatitudes and so, in communion with him, reap their blessings, which first accrued to Jesus and which he now shares with those within the heavenly kingdom. Thus Jesus, as the new Moses, not only prophetically promulgates the new law of the kingdom of God but also, unlike Moses, equally fulfills the new law and in so doing procures the promised blessings of the kingdom of heaven that were prefigured within the Mosaic Law and Covenant. All this said, we must now examine how Jesus, as the Incarnate Son, fulfills the Beatitudes, and so obtains their blessings, which will accrue to those in communion with him.

Blessed Are the Poor in Spirit, for Theirs Is the Kingdom of Heaven

In the incarnating act of the Holy Spirit, the divine Son of God assumed the poverty of a created humanity, which was not only frail and weak but also bore the birthmark of sin and death. This incarnating act is the first foundational poor-in-spirit act from which flows all succeeding poor-in-spirit acts. Through these salvific poor-in-spirit acts, performed in communion with the Spirit, Jesus will merit the kingdom of heaven by establishing the kingdom of heaven. He is therefore blessed by possessing the kingdom of heaven as its Savior and Lord. In becoming incarnate, Jesus does not simply place himself

---

is a word which the Lord has not spoken; the prophet has spoken it presumptuously, you need not be afraid of him" (Dt 18:21-22).

among those who are poor in spirit, feeble, or fallen and so obtain the blessing of the kingdom of heaven. Rather, by becoming poor in spirit among the
sinful, Jesus brings into being, through his poor-in-spirit salvific acts, the kingdom of heaven so that the sinful, those who recognize their poverty of spirit,
can be blessed in him—the blessing of the heavenly kingdom.

Within his public ministry, Jesus manifests his poverty of spirit.[6] From
within his poverty, Jesus relied completely on his Father. He humbly and obediently trusted his Father in all things. We recognize this both within his baptism and temptations. Jesus humbly came before John to be baptized and in
so doing humbly presented himself before his Father to assume obediently, in
the outpouring of the Spirit, his salvific task. The Father rejoiced in his Son's
humble and obedient poverty of spirit and so was well pleased. Similarly, Jesus, when tempted, arrogantly refused to employ his divine authority for his
own self-aggrandizement or to seek a rich and powerful kingdom that encompassed the entire world. Rather, he docilely remained faithful to the salvific
task that the Father conferred upon him in the descent of the Holy Spirit. This
inner recognition of being poor in spirit marks the whole of Jesus' ministry
and is expressed most fully within his passion and death. Jesus thoroughly
fashions his whole humanity into a living icon of poverty of spirit when he
offers himself, humiliated and beaten, to his Father upon the cross as a loving
Spirit-filled and so all-holy sacrifice for the forgiveness of sin. In the humble
love of the Spirit, Jesus, the Son, offers the paucity of who he is as man, simply his body and soul, to the Father. He keeps nothing for himself. In his utter
poverty of spirit, he commends, he hands over, in his last act, his lowly spirit
to the Father. In this utter expression of being poor in spirit, Jesus equally conforms himself into an all-consuming living icon of love for his Father and for
the whole of humankind. To be poor in spirit is to be rich in love, and in Jesus'
poverty the Father sees the riches of his Son's love.

The Father recognized that Jesus, by his complete love and absolute trust
in him alone, merited the kingdom of heaven and so raises his Son's poor and
lifeless humanity gloriously from the dead. He enthrones Jesus, his risen incarnate Son, as the King and Lord of heaven. Because Jesus literally embodied, in its totality, "poverty of spirit" within his earthly humanity, he comes to
embody, literally in its totality, the blessing of the kingdom of heaven within
his glorious humanity. Blessed is Jesus, poor in spirit, for *his* is the kingdom

---

6. The poor of spirit in the Old Testament (*anawim*) are the materially poor who place their
complete trust and hope in God alone (see Is 61:1 and Zep 2:3).

of heaven; blessed is Jesus for he *is* the kingdom of heaven. Here we perceive the significance of the "is" within the first Beatitude. Only within Jesus' humble and lowly poverty of spirit does the kingdom of heaven come *to be* and so come *to be* merited by him. Only in him does the kingdom of heaven exist. He *is* the present blessing, the forever existing *now* of the kingdom of heaven.[7]

Those who are poor in spirit, those who recognize the poverty of their own sinfulness, are those who come to faith in Jesus. In that faith they come to live in him and so are equally blessed in inheriting the kingdom of heaven. In Christ, through the Holy Spirit, the kingdom of heaven is theirs. Here also we perceive the significance of Jesus' Gospel command: "If any man would come after me, let him deny himself and take up his cross and follow me. For whoever would save his life will lose it, and whoever loses his life for my sake will find it. For what will it profit a man, if he gains the whole world and forfeits his life? Or what shall a man give in return for his life?" (Mt 16:24-26; see also Mt 10:38-39, Mk 8:34-37, and Lk 9:23-25). Those who trust in themselves, those who try to save their lives through the riches and glory of this world or attempt to give something of such value that they can buy and preserve their lives, such as surrendering their own integrity and veracity for worldly allurements, will forfeit their lives. But those who are poor in spirit, those who, like Jesus, trustingly surrender their poor lives to the Father and so, like Jesus, take

---

7. This understanding of being "poor in spirit" is beautifully taken up in the Pauline corpus. The Philippian hymn states that although Jesus was in the form of God, he did not arrogantly cling to his divine dignity, but in poverty of spirit emptied himself first in taking on the form of a servant, that is, being born as man. Within this poverty he further humbled himself by being obedient unto death, which found its culmination in being obedient even unto death on a cross. Because Jesus is poor in spirit, his Father highly exalted him by bestowing upon him a name that is above all others, such that at his name, Jesus, every knee in heaven, on earth and under the earth, must bow before him and every tongue confess that he, Jesus Christ, is Lord of all. This proclamation of the universal Lordship of the poor Jesus, now supreme over all, gives glory to God his Father. No one was poorer in spirit than Jesus, and thus no one is more exalted than Jesus. Not surprisingly, in keeping with this Beatitude, the hymn is prefaced by an exhortation that Christians should be of like mind—they too are to be poor in spirit after the manner of Jesus (see Phil 2:5-11).

Equally, Paul exhorts the Corinthians: "For you know the grace of our Lord Jesus Christ, that though he was rich, yet for your sake he became poor, so that by his poverty you might become rich" (2 Cor 8:9). The grace of salvation comes through the Lord Jesus Christ because, although rich in divinity, he became poor within our humanity, and he did so that we might share in the riches of his divinity. Now, if such riches came through such poverty, Paul concludes that surely the Corinthians, in their material wealth, can contribute to the poor in Jerusalem so that they can share in their riches. Again, Jesus' poverty of spirit is the model for the Corinthians to be poor in spirit themselves, and so share their earthly wealth as Christ, in his earthly poverty, shared with them his divine riches.

up their cross and lovingly offer up their lives for the sake of Jesus and his Gospel for the salvation of others, will save their lives. They will live in, and ultimately inherit, the kingdom of heaven. For this reason, they will be eternally blessed in communion with Jesus.

Significantly, Jesus within the Sermon on the Mount and throughout his public ministry frequently speaks of the need of being poor of spirit and exhorts others to embrace it. This testifies that Jesus sees being poor in spirit as the foundational Beatitude, the giving up of one's own life, necessary for entering and so living within the blessed kingdom of heaven.

Later in the Sermon on the Mount, Jesus elaborates on what being poor entails.[8] Those within the kingdom of heaven do not lay up "treasures on earth, where moth and rust consume and where thieves break in and steal," but rather they lay up "treasures in heaven," which endure forever. He reminds them that "where your treasure is, there will your heart be also" (Mt 6:18-21). Within Luke's account, Jesus is more proactive. There he says, "Sell your possessions, and give alms; provide yourselves with purses that do not grow old, with a treasure in heaven that does not fail.... For where your treasure is, there will your heart be also" (Lk 12:33-34). For Jesus, to accumulate the riches of this world, to seek the blessings of this world is incompatible with accumulating the treasures, the blessings, of the kingdom of heaven. Earthly riches, sought in selfishness and greed, only provide earthly blessings that decay as does the mortal body, but heavenly treasures, made rich by such acts as selling one's possessions and lovingly giving alms to the poor, are of eternal value. Upon these blessed treasures, being poor in spirit, the hearts of the faithful must cling.

Similarly, he tells his listeners that they are not to be anxious about their lives, what they are to eat or drink or wear. To be anxious about such worldly concerns is to act like the Gentiles. He tells them that the Father, who clothes the lilies of the field more splendidly than Solomon, knows their needs and so they are to "seek first his kingdom and his righteousness, and all these things shall be yours as well" (Mt 6:25-34; see also Lk 12:22-32). To be poor in spirit is to place one's trust, as did Jesus, in the Father alone knowing, as Jesus did, that he, in his love, is providentially caring for his own. To live in Jesus is to live within the benevolence of his loving Father—such are those blessed who possess the kingdom of heaven.

Later in the Gospel of Matthew, Jesus' disciples ask Jesus who is the great-

---

8. Although there is no set design, the remainder of the Sermon on the Mount, following upon the Beatitudes, at times seems to provide more detailed commands that build upon or provide concrete examples that elaborate on them.

est in the kingdom of heaven. He places a child before them and says, "Truly [Amen], I say to you, unless you turn and become like children, you will never enter the kingdom of heaven. Whoever humbles himself like this child, he is the greatest in the kingdom of heaven" (Mt 18:1-4).[9] When his disciples attempt to prevent children being brought to him, Jesus rebuked them by saying, "Let the children come to me, and do not hinder them; for to such belongs the kingdom of heaven. And he laid his hands on them and went away" (Mt 19:13-15). Mark narrates that Jesus "took them in his arms and blessed them, laying his hands upon them" (Mk 10:16; see also Lk 18:15-17). The kingdom of heaven belongs to those who become childlike, for children in their innocent humility are completely dependent upon the goodness and kindness of their parents and elders. They are naturally poor in spirit and so are blessed in being members of the kingdom of heaven. Jesus' own personal and affectionate blessing of them is the blessing of the kingdom, for in him is the kingdom embodied. This childlike poverty of spirit provides the humility necessary to recognize one's need for God and thus incites one to enter his heavenly kingdom.

In contrast to children to whom belongs the kingdom of heaven, the rich young man, whose story immediately follows, illustrates someone who rejects the kingdom even when it is offered to him. The rich young man asks Jesus what he must do "to have eternal life." Jesus tells him to keep the commandments and after further enquiry specifies what they are. The young man confirms that he has observed them and asks what then would he "still lack." Jesus

9. Mark and Luke note that the Apostles were arguing as to which of them was the greatest. See Mk 9:33-37 and Lk 9:46-48.

Jesus frequently prefaces his remarks or teaching with the word "Amen" or "Amen, amen" followed by "I say to you." Within the Jewish tradition, as within the Christian tradition, "Amen" meant "truly" (as translated above) and was employed as a response to prayers or doxologies by way of giving assent to what was just prayed. But Jesus singularly employed "Amen" (about sixty times in the Gospels) to emphasize that what he was about to say is truly of God. In declaring "Amen, amen, I say to you," Jesus is first emphasizing that what he is about to say is of divine origin and second emphatically accentuating that he ("I") is the one who is declaring it. In his use of "Amen," Jesus expressed his certainty, which is founded upon his own authority, that what he is about to say is not simply true but is true precisely because *he* is saying it. Although the man Jesus is saying "Amen" within a human self-conscious "I," who is humanly saying "Amen" and who is accentuating the "I" is the Son of God. Again, this is an incarnational act. Only if the Son of God exists as man can he speak with such divine authority in a human manner. In so expressing this truth as divine in origin, Jesus, by his own authority, placed upon his hearers an obligation to assent to this truth that exceeds that of human authority.

For other examples, see Mk 9:1, 10:15, 10:29, 14:25; Mt 6:16, 10:15, 11:11, 13:17, 25:40, 25:45, and parallels.

replies, "If you would be perfect, go, sell what you possess and give it to the poor, and you will have treasure in heaven; and come follow me."[10] The young man left in sorrow, unwilling to give up his "great possessions" (Mt 19:16-22; see also Mk 10:17-22 and Lk 18:18-23).[11]

Jesus is predicating perfection upon a twofold act: the utter abandoning of one's riches, the greatest expression of being poor in spirit, for in it is one is surrendering one's earthly life, and wholeheartedly committing oneself to following him, by which one gains heavenly life. This is ultimately the one good deed that ensures perfection and so eternal life. Perfection, then, is not obtained by obeying commandments over and above what God has already decreed, but by committing oneself entirely to Jesus. As within the Beatitudes, Jesus is making an extraordinary claim: perfection is found in him alone. No ordinary human being could reasonably demand that perfection consists in committing one's entire life to him, implying that he embodies perfection, which can only be achieved in communion with him. Jesus is a man, yet he is nonetheless declaring that perfection is found only in being intimately united to him. As with the Beatitudes, Jesus is not simply manifesting his divine authority, that is, revealing that who is making this human statement is the Son of God and so possessing the inherent authority to make such demands. More so, Jesus is offering the rich young man entrance into his own being poor in spirit to enter into the riches of the kingdom of heaven, which he himself embodies. To follow Jesus, in poverty of spirit, is to be ushered into the blessings of the heavenly kingdom. Jesus' authority is then founded upon his establishing the kingdom of heaven as the poor incarnate Son and so possessing the divine authority capable of ensuring others that the perfection of eternal life lies in following him alone in the same spirit of poverty.[12]

So essential is this poverty of spirit for entering the kingdom of heaven

10. Mark notes Jesus "looking upon him loved him" (see Mk 10:21).

11. The rich young man's response is unlike the man in the parable concerning the kingdom of heaven who finds a treasure hidden in a field. Whereas the rich young man went away sad, this man "in his joy goes and sells all that he has and buys the field." Similarly, he is not like the rich merchant who searches for fine pearls and, when having found the perfect pearl, he went and "sold all that he had and bought it" (Mt 13:44-45). Only in being poor in spirit—the giving up of all including the surrendering up of oneself—is one able to be blessed with the possession of the heavenly kingdom.

12. Similarly, whenever a man came and told Jesus that he would follow him wherever he goes, Jesus responds, "Foxes have holes, and birds of the air have nests; but the Son of man has nowhere to lay his head." To follow Jesus is to have nothing, being completely dependent in poverty of spirit upon God. Jesus makes similar responses to the man who wants to first bury his father and the man who wants first to say farewell to his home. If one looks back to the

that Jesus immediately tells his disciples: "Truly [Amen], I say to you, it will be hard for the rich man to enter the kingdom of heaven. Again, I tell you, it is easier for a camel to go through the eye of a needle than for a rich man to enter the kingdom of God." Even so, Jesus assures his "astonished" disciples that even such a seeming impossibility is possible with God's help (Mt 19:23-26; see also Mk 10:23-27 and Lk 18:24-27).

Having listened to this animated discussion with the rich young man and the ensuing query about who then can be saved, Peter, as usual not wanting to be outdone, exuberantly exclaims, "Lo, we have left everything and followed you. What then shall we have?" Jesus assures his twelve Apostles: "Truly [Amen], I say to you, in the new world, when the Son of man shall sit on his glorious throne, you will also sit on twelve thrones, judging the twelve tribes of Israel." He also promises that "everyone who has left houses or brothers or sisters or father or mother or children or lands, for my name's sake will receive a hundredfold, and inherit eternal life" (Mt 19:27-30; see also Mk 10:28-31 and Lk 18:28-30). Once again, Jesus is promising upon his own authority that his twelve Apostles will be enthroned as judges of Israel, but the promises are such that only one who possesses divine authority is able to fulfill them. The promise made to his Apostles is predicated upon Jesus assuming his own "glorious throne" in the "new world." This will only be achieved when Jesus, being poor in spirit as the incarnate Son of God, establishes the kingdom of heaven through his lowly death and glorious resurrection and so becomes its Savior and Lord. Thus, within this divine resurrected authority and in the light of these future salvific acts, he is "truly" able to assure his Apostles of their reward for leaving everything and following him, which will lead them into the blessed heavenly kingdom, where they will be gloriously enthroned astride him.[13] This accounts for Jesus' equally unprecedented promise that ev-

---

things of this world, if something takes precedence over following Jesus, then one "is not fit for the kingdom of God" (Lk 9:57-62). Only in being poor in spirit is one able to leave all and follow unreservedly Jesus within the kingdom of God.

13. Significantly, shortly thereafter within Matthew's Gospel, immediately following upon Jesus' prophetically telling his Apostles that they were going up to Jerusalem, where he will be delivered, condemned, mocked, scourged, crucified, and then rise on the third day, the mother of the sons of Zebedee, James, and John came kneeling before Jesus. One can surmise that her sons told her about Jesus, saying that they would be enthroned beside him when he is gloriously enthroned, for she now wants Jesus to enthrone her two sons immediately on his right and on his left. What was implied in his promise, which the sons did not fully grasp, Jesus now makes explicit. "You do not know what you are asking. Are you able to drink the cup that I am to drink?" (In Mark's account, Jesus also says, "or to be baptized with the baptism with which I am baptized.") Jesus had just revealed to them the cup he was to drink and the baptism he was

eryone who leaves all that is most dear to them—homes, families, and countries—for his sake will be blessed within the eternal life of the heavenly kingdom. Because of their blessed poverty of spirit, their giving up of all in order to possess Jesus, theirs too is the kingdom of heaven.

Jesus makes explicit the importance of being poor in spirit in an even more intense and provocative manner. Jesus not only says that those who leave their families for his name's sake will be blessed with eternal life within, but he also demands that they must love him more than their families. Jesus warns his followers that he has not come to bring peace but a sword—strife among family members. Singular love and supreme loyalty to Jesus will be the cause of this division. "He who loves father or mother more than me is not worthy of me; and he who loves son or daughter more than me is not worthy of me; and he who does not take his cross and follow me is not worthy of me" (Mt 10:37-38; see Mk 13:12 and Lk 12:51-5).[14] Within the Gospel of Luke, what Jesus demands is even more shocking in its negative expression. "If any-

---

to undergo when they come to Jerusalem, and only in drinking that cup and being baptized will he be gloriously enthroned. Such a cup and baptism the Apostles must drink and undergo if they too are to be enthroned. Although James and John affirm that they can drink from such a cup and Jesus confirms their affirmation, the Father alone has the authority to grant such a request. Not surprisingly, the other ten Apostles "were indignant at the two brothers." In response, Jesus again gives them a lesson on being poor in spirit, offering himself as the exemplar. Although Gentile rulers lord over others using their authority to achieve their own ends, such is not the case within the kingdom of heaven. Whichever Apostle wants to be great must be a servant, and whoever desires to be first must be a slave, because "the Son of man came not to be served but to serve, and to give his life as a ransom for many" (Mt 20:20-28; see Mk 10:42-45 and Lk 22:25-27). Jesus' lesson to his Apostles is a lesson first and foremost a lesson about himself. As he is poor in spirit and so will fulfill the commitment he made to his Father at his baptism and so humbly drink the cup of his passion and death, for the ransom for many, to be enthroned upon his glorious throne, the Apostles must be poor in spirit, humbly giving up their lives as servants so as to be enthroned.

14. Earlier within chapter 10 of Matthew, Jesus taught something similar. After choosing his twelve Apostles and giving them authority and power to cast out demons and to heal (signs of the in-breaking of the kingdom), Jesus sends them out to preach, saying, "the kingdom of heaven is at hand." Having been freely given the kingdom of heaven, they are to preach and heal without pay. And in their poverty they are to take no money or tunic or sandals or staff, but they are to receive whatever food they are given. Within this context of poverty, Jesus warns them that he is sending them out as sheep among wolves, and thus they will be delivered up to councils and synagogues to be flogged "for my sake." Within this context, members of one's own family—brothers, fathers, and children—will have one put to death for "you will be hated by all for my names sake." But "he who endures to the end will be saved" (Mt 10:1-22). Because of one's singular commitment to Jesus and to the preaching of the Gospel, persecution and hatred, even from within one's family, are inevitable. The world cannot tolerate those who reject its riches, giving up all for the sake of Jesus and the blessings of the heavenly kingdom.

one comes to me and does not hate his own father and mother and wife and children and brothers and sisters, yes, and even his own life, he cannot be my disciple. Whoever does not bear his own cross and come after me, cannot be my disciple.... So therefore, whoever, of you does not renounce all that he has cannot be my disciple" (Lk 14:26-26, 14:33).

Normally, no human relationship rightly demands more loyalty and love than a familial one. What is considered most distressing and heartrending is strife and hatred among family members. Yet Jesus is demanding a love and loyalty that far exceed anything human, even to the point of hating what is most thoroughly human: familial relationships. The interpretive key to these passages is found the phrases "not worthy of me" and "cannot be my disciple," and in the renunciation of oneself in the taking up of one's cross. To be worthy of Jesus is to recognize, in the spirit of poverty, that Jesus is worth more than even what one cherishes most—one's family. To be a disciple of Jesus, one must hate anything that is simply of human value here on earth for the sake of his name, for the sake of the kingdom of heaven that he embodies. All earthly values, even good earthly values, such as one's family, are now relativized. They render one poor, in the light of Jesus, for only in him does one obtain the rich and eternal blessing of the kingdom of God. The person of Jesus and having a loving personal relationship with him render all else relative.[15]

Thus Jesus' followers are not obliged to take up their cross on behalf of a just

---

15. Paul renders this principle in a similar manner. In the light of Jesus' return, everything must be judged in that light. Because of this, "from now on, let those who have wives live as though they had none, and those who mourn as though they were not mourning, and those who rejoice as though they were not rejoicing, and those who buy goods as though they had no goods, and those who deal with the world as though they had no dealings with it. For the form of this world is passing away" (1 Cor 7:29-31). Paul is not saying that spouses should not care for one another, or that those who mourn over evil and death and rejoice over what is good should not do so. Nor is he saying that Christians should not have any goods or be gainfully employed. Rather, he is graphically saying that all these earthly things—marriage, mourning, joy, buying the necessities of life, earning a living—while good and necessary, are nonetheless relativized in the light of Jesus' coming, for all these things will be passing away with the end of the passing world. They are not absolutes. Possessing Jesus, giving one's life to Jesus, is absolute, and everything else needs to be judged accordingly.

Paul puts all of this vividly when he declares, "But whatever gain I had, I counted as loss for the sake of Christ. Indeed I count everything as loss because of the surpassing worth of knowing Christ Jesus my Lord. For his sake I have suffered loss of all things, and count them as refuse [the English equivalent would be the slang for "dung"], in order that I may gain Christ and be found in him" (Phil 3:7-9). Everything—the Law, his good deeds, and the like—is mere rubbish to Paul compared to knowing Jesus his Lord and so possessing a personal relationship with him. Nothing is of real value but Jesus alone.

cause or to lay down their lives for some universally true principle. To him alone, to his very person, belongs this absolute loyalty and supreme love, and for his sake alone does one renounce all and take up one's cross.

In making these seemingly startling statements and inhuman demands, Jesus is revealing the uniqueness of his person and the centrality of his salvific work. He is revealing, through his humanity, that he is the Son of God and as such he can make such demands, for in and through him the kingdom of God is and will be realized. Only if Jesus is divine and only if he embodies the kingdom of heaven as the Son incarnate does the love and loyalty that he demands find their sanction and warrant—their rationality. In addition, the demands that Jesus is making are only those that he himself is fulfilling. He is asking nothing more than what he himself is doing. Within his incarnate poverty of spirit, he is giving himself completely for the sake of the kingdom of heaven. Those who wish to enter into this heavenly kingdom must then forsake all for his name's sake and give their lives and love to him, for in him alone does the heavenly kingdom reside.

We noted at the beginning of this examination of the first Beatitude—Blessed are the poor in spirit, for theirs is the kingdom of heaven—that its foundational Gospel principle resides in Jesus' mandate that if anyone wishes to come after him, he must "deny himself and take up his cross and follow me." Only in so doing will one lose one's life for the sake of saving one's life. It is not surprising that he concludes his teaching on loving him above all family members, even at the risk of their hatred, with the same exhortation. "He who does not take up cross and follow me is not worthy of me. He who finds his life will lose it, and he who loses his life for my sake will find it" (Mt 10:38-39). Jesus is worthy of the cost of all, even one's family, for even in losing one's family, one being poor in spirit finds one's life in loving Jesus, for in that love one gains the kingdom of heaven. This singular loyalty of love to Jesus is equally matched by his singular loyal love to those who do so. What Jesus promises—the commitment he personally makes to his followers—is equally singular. To those who endure all on his behalf, for the sake of his name, Jesus pledges that they will obtain eternal life within the heavenly kingdom. The nature of both the commitment and the promised recompense exceed the human. No simple human being can pledge such benefits. Again, only because Jesus is the incarnate Son of the Father, who establishes the kingdom of heaven within the poverty of the cross and merits its blessings in his resurrection, can such a pledge be fulfilled. Thus the commitment that Jesus demands of others and the pledge he makes to others for such a commitment are founded upon the truth, the doctrine, of the Incarnation. Thus Jesus, as the Son of God, is the universal Savior and definitive Lord of all.

From this extensive examination we readily perceive that being poor in spirit is the foundational Beatitude. First, Jesus, becoming poor as man, enacted within his lowliness those salvific acts whereby the kingdom of heaven came to be. Because of these blessed acts, the kingdom of heaven is his, for he now embodies the heavenly kingdom. Second, faith in Jesus, the key that unlocks the gate of the heavenly kingdom, requires one to be poor in spirit, for only in being poor does one recognize one's sinfulness and spiritual poverty. Having come to live in the heavenly kingdom through a faith-filled poverty of spirit, having given up all, one reaps its benefit by continuing to live as one who is poor in spirit.[16] Third, within Jesus' incarnational poverty, he enacts the next six Beatitudes, and equally the poor-in-spirit faithful, who abide in him, are then empowered to enact them as well. These Beatitudes flow from and, in various ways, give inborn and vital expression to being poor in spirit and so mark Jesus' manner of life in establishing the kingdom of heaven and the way of life of those who live within it. Fourth, living presently within the kingdom of heaven, for it *is* theirs, the faithful perform the next six Beatitudes, and for so doing they *will* receive the appropriate blessing that accrues to each. As the next six Beatitudes give varied expressions to being poor in spirit, so their distinctive blessings are the various ways one is blessed by being variously poor in spirit. These various blessings form the totality of the one blessing of being poor in spirit, for its blessing is living within the kingdom—all

16. "Being poor in spirit" is the foundational ecclesial Beatitude. It is the fundamental, the *sine qua non* theological, or doctrinal, Beatitude of the church. In poverty of spirit, Jesus founded the church, which gives concrete living historical expression to the kingdom of God. Moreover, the poor in spirit come to faith in Jesus and are baptized into him as their Savior and Lord, and so the church is composed of and gives expression to those who, in poverty of spirit, have given up all for him. The church, Jesus as her Savior and Lord and those in communion with him, is the living community of the poor in spirit. Likewise, those who become members of the church reap the blessings of the heavenly kingdom—forgiveness of sin and the Holy Spirit, who is the life of the kingdom and the soul of the church. In poverty of spirit, the members participate in the sacraments and so continue to reap the blessings of the kingdom as well as are strengthened to live the life of the kingdom. To live within the church is to live in communion with Jesus and so be blessed by possessing the kingdom of heaven. Equally, in this same poverty of spirit, the church proclaims the kingdom of heaven and makes it present within the world through all that she lovingly does, especially for her care of the poor and the marginalized. In her poverty, the church has nothing to offer but Jesus and his heavenly kingdom. In so doing, those inebriated with the world's riches and power continually persecute her, but this merely manifests and proves that she is faithful to the poor Jesus, following and serving him alone for the sake of the kingdom of heaven.

blessings flow from the one font of the poor and glorious Christ, the source and culmination of the heavenly kingdom. The blessings of the future are thus predicated upon and well up from within the present living within the kingdom of heaven, that is, the enacting of the new law of the heavenly kingdom.

Blessed Are Those Who Mourn, for
They Shall Be Comforted

Those poor in spirit who presently mourn within the kingdom of heaven will be blessed with comfort. The Son of God came into the world as a poor man and in so doing as one of *those* who mourns over sin with its deadly and everlasting condemnatory effects.[17] But Jesus' mourning, the incarnational mourning of the Son of God, was not the wailing of helpless grief. True compassion is not simply a suffering on behalf of or in communion with those who suffer and mourn. Rather, true compassionate mourning rises up to destroy the cause of such mourning. Jesus' mourning over sin, death, and the bondage of Satan aroused him, in love and pity, to rescue humankind from these curses. This is why he, in loving pity, befriended and forgave sinners (see Mt 9:10-13; Mk 2:13-17; Lk 5:27-32, 7:34, 15:1-2). This is why he raised the only son of the widow of Naim and the young daughter of Jairus (see Lk 7:11-17). Likewise, Jesus' mourning finds its fullest expression on the cross, but it is not a desolate cry of grief uttered in hopelessness but a powerful grieving cry steeped in a love for sinners, knowing that because of his death there will be no more sin or death—the gates of a bereaving hell will be thrust open, never to be closed. Because of Jesus' blessed mourning even unto death, he will, in his resurrection, be forever comforted in the joy and love of those with whom he shares his glorious heavenly kingdom—forgiven sinners once condemned.

Similarly, those who live in Christ and so within their poverty of spirit mourn over their own sin, and the sin and evil within the world will equally be comforted, for their mourning will be within the kingdom of heaven. Their mourning will spur them on to their own further and deeper need for repentance and will incite them to lovingly call others to repentance as well. The mourning over sin, over the prospect of everlasting condemnation, gives rise

---

17. The passage from Is 61:1-2 that Jesus read within the synagogue in Nazareth continues by declaring that in the year of the Lord's favor, the Lord will "comfort all who mourn; to grant to those who mourn in Zion—to give them a garland instead of mourning, the mantle of praise instead of a faint spirit" (Is 61:3). Jesus, as the Son of God, fulfills this passage in becoming man.

to the voice of evangelization. The mourning over sin finds its comfort in one's own salvation and in bringing others into the forgiving and loving kingdom of heaven through faith in Jesus. Similarly, although the followers of Jesus will mourn over death as he did, they will find comfort in knowing in faith that Jesus, through his death and resurrection, has conquered death, and so the mourning of this world will be turned to joy (see Jer 31:13 and Jn 16:20). Here on earth the faithful, who mourn over sin, evil, and death in all their horrendous and unspeakable forms, will be blessed in the comfort, even here on earth, of knowing that in living within the kingdom of heaven there is hope, which is fulfilled at the end of time. Then God will dwell with Christ's faithful, and he will wipe away every tear "and death shall be no more, neither will there be mourning nor crying in pain any more, for the former things have passed away. And he [Jesus] who sat upon the throne said, 'Behold, I make all things new'" (Rv 21:3-5).

Blessed Are the Meek, for They Shall Inherit the Earth

Jesus, as one poor in spirit, described himself as meek and humble. He told his disciples: "Come to me, all who labor and are heavy laden, and I will give you rest. Take my yoke upon you, and learn from me; for I am meek and humble of heart, and you will find rest for your souls. For my yoke is easy and my burden light" (Mt 11:29-30). Life upon earth is filled with labor, and life's multiple and various burdens are often demanding and disheartening. The meek, not because they lack moral conviction or inner strength but because they are not proud and willful but poor in spirit, often bear the brunt of the arrogant and strong. Jesus, in his meekness, bore the brunt of the haughty and the mighty even unto death on the cross. Yet his meekness was not one of passivity but the active will and power to undertake humbly the yoke that his Father had placed upon his shoulders. In so doing, he found eternal rest. In fulfilling all meekness, Jesus is blessed, for he has, in his resurrection, inherited the earth and all that dwells therein. As the crucified Savior of the world, he is the risen Lord of lords, not only of heaven but also the King of kings upon earth. The meek who undertake Jesus' yoke, because they are in union with him, will also find rest, for the earth that appears now to be the province of the proud and mighty will be their blessed inheritance.[18] In union with their Savior and

---

18. This fulfills Ps 37:10-11: "Yet a little while, and the wicked will be no more; though you

Lord, they will peaceably abide within the new heaven and will restfully inhabit a new earth, one that is their own.

Blessed Are Those Who Hunger and Thirst for Righteousness, for They Shall Be Satisfied

The poor Jesus, the Son, came into the world as the one who mourns over the lack of righteousness. Thus Jesus' whole life, all that he said and did as man, was his ardent attempt to alleviate his human hunger and satiate his human thirst for righteousness.[19] The making of what is right and just is manifest on many levels: the alleviating of injustice imposed upon the poor, weak, and marginalized; the establishing of a just and tranquil order among men and nations, founded upon the truth of human integrity and principled law; and, above all, the instituting of the proper righteous relationship between God and humankind. Although Jesus, throughout his public ministry, manifested his love for the poor and oppressed (see Lk 14:12-13, 14:21-24), he knew that true righteousness could only flourish within the world and among human beings when men and women were made righteous before God. This righteousness could not be established from without or imposed by law but demanded an inner righteousness that would transform the hearts and minds of people so that they could live in holiness and peace before God. Jesus' fundamental goal was to make righteous the unrighteous, to transform sinners into holy children of his Father. Jesus' hunger and thirst for this righteousness led him to the cross, for only then could the sin that made for unrighteousness and fostered unrighteous enmity and unjust strife among human beings and between races and nations be put to death. Only in his resurrection, only in his becoming a new man freed from the powers of sin and death, could Jesus send forth the transforming Holy Spirt of righteousness, who would re-create men and woman so as to be holy before God and act righteously toward one another.[20] In so doing, Jesus fulfilled God's promise: "A new heart I will give

---

look well at his place, he will not be there. But the meek shall possess the land, and delight themselves in abundant prosperity."

19. Malachi prophesies that there will come a day when all evil will be burned away and in the name of the Lord "the sun of righteousness shall rise, with healing in his wings" (Mal 4:1-2).

20. Again, Isaiah 61 speaks of the future "prophet" who will rejoice and exult in the Lord, "for he has clothed me with garments of salvation, he has covered me with a robe of righteousness" (61:10). Within the resurrection, the Father has clothed Jesus his Son in the salvific robe of righteousness.

you, and a new spirit I will put within you; and I will take out of your flesh the heart of stone and give you a heart of flesh. And I will put my spirit within you, and cause you to walk by my statutes and be careful to observe my ordinances. You shall dwell in the land which I gave to your fathers; and you shall be my people and I will be your God" (Ezek 36:26-28). The righteousness of the kingdom of heaven is the righteousness of the indwelling Spirit, in whom the righteous are made anew and so empowered to keep the new law of God's kingdom, whereby they are his people as he is their God.[21] In establishing this righteousness, Jesus was blessed, for his hunger and thirst were satisfied. This blessed satisfaction finds its eternal fulfillment in the heavenly kingdom where all men and women, peoples and nations will dwell together in righteous communion in him as holy Spirit-filled children of the Father, as they together inhabit the tranquil city of God.

For this righteousness, Christians, from within their poverty of spirit, are to hunger and thirst as they strive to promote justice and peace on earth, to alleviate the poverty inflicted upon the weak, to foster the inherent human dignity of all—their just claim to life, freedom, and well-being. To achieve this righteousness, the faithful perceive that they must hunger and thirst for the conversion of the world. They are compelled to evangelize all peoples and nations, for they recognize, from within their experience, that only within the righteousness that comes through faith and the transforming power of the indwelling Spirit can true righteousness and justice flourish among men and nations, as together they strive to live in righteous holiness with God. In this pursuit they will be blessed with satisfaction knowing that, among appalling injustice and unending strife, they have not labored in vain, for what they have achieved on earth, meagre as it may appear, will bear lasting fruit in Jesus' everlasting kingdom of peace and justice.

21. Speaking on behalf of God, the prophet Jeremiah tells of a future day when God will make a new covenant with his people. Unlike the old covenant, which was written on stone, the new covenant will be written upon their hearts. "I will put my law within then, and I will write it upon their hearts; and I will be their God, and they shall be my people. And no longer shall each man teach his neighbor saying, 'Know the Lord,' for they shall all know me, from the least of them to the greatest, says the Lord; for I will forgive their iniquity, and I will remember their sin no more" (Jer 31:31-34). Within the heavenly kingdom founded upon the new covenant enacted by Jesus, the Holy Spirit will dwell within the hearts of the faithful, cleansing them of sin and making them holy. Thus they will be interiorly enlightened to know God and so be empowered keep his law as his holy people.

Blessed Are the Merciful, for
They Shall Obtain Mercy

Mercy flows from poverty of spirit. Recognizing one's own spiritual poverty gives rise to acknowledging mercifully the poverty that resides within and among others. Jesus the Son, within the poverty of his humanity, came into the world to manifest the mercy of his Father—the mercy that resides within the heavenly kingdom.[22] His mercy and compassion are again evident throughout his public ministry as he manifests the in-breaking of God's kingdom through his healings, exorcism, and forgiveness (see Mt 4:23 and 9:35). His pity is ever present toward the hungry crowds that follow him like sheep without a shepherd (see Mk 6:34 and Mt 15:32). Later in the Sermon on the Mount, Jesus exhorts his listeners to love their enemies and to pray for those who persecute them. "You have heard that it was said, 'You shall love your neighbour and hate your enemy.' But I say to you, love your enemies and pray for those who persecute you, so that you may be sons of your Father who is in heaven."[23] The reason is that the Father mercifully makes the sun shine on the evil and on the good, and sends rain upon the just and the unjust. They are to love both those who love them and even those whom they would consider un-

---

22. Within the Old Testament, the Lord frequently manifests that he is a God of mercy, which is often expressed as his covenantal virtue of "steadfast love" (*hesed*). See, e.g., Ex 34:7; Pss 100:5, 106:7, 119:41. Paul in Ephesians speaks of God as "rich in mercy," and this is seen in his making us alive in the risen Christ (2:4-5).

23. This is one of six passages within the Sermon where Jesus declares what has been divinely promulgated in the past: "You have heard that it was said." He then elevates or nuances these commands, by his own authority, to a higher or distinctive moral standard: "*But I say to you.*" In Greek, "I say" contains an emphasis that is concealed within the English translation. Jesus employed not only the first person singular verb *lego* (I say), but he also prefaced it with the first person pronoun *egō* (I). If one were to translate literally the Greek, it would read: "I, I say to you." Jesus, by commanding that his followers must not even get angry with one another, or even look lustfully at a woman, or procure a divorce, and so on, has taken unto himself divine authority, and his emphasis of the "I" doubly accentuates this fact. Jesus, as the new Moses, has not simply promulgated the new law of the heavenly kingdom after the example of Moses, but promulgated it, unlike Moses, upon his own divine authority. Jesus, the man, is consciously acting in a human manner, but what he is consciously doing in a human manner is restricted to and the privilege of God alone, thus revealing that who it is who is humanly promulgating this new law is the divine Son of God. The act is an incarnational act, for only if the Son of God exists as man can he humanly promulgate a divine law.

Similar passages can be found within the Synoptics, where Jesus used the emphatic "I" (*egō*), all of which denote divine authority enacted humanly (see, e.g., Mk 9:25; Mt 10:16; Lk 11:20, 22:29).

lovable. The concluding principle is: "You, therefore, must be perfect, as your heavenly Father is perfect" (Mt 5:43-48). In his Sermon on the Plain, Luke significantly has Jesus conclude: "For he [the Most High] is kind to the ungrateful and the selfish. Be merciful, even as your Father is merciful" (Lk 6:35-36).

The divine perfection of the Father resides in his mercy. The perfection of Jesus resides in his mercy, and through such perfect mercy he reveals that he is the Son of his "Father who is in heaven." The perfect mercy of Jesus the Son reveals the perfect mercy of his Father. This mutual intertwining of divine paternal/filial mercy finds its perfection on the cross and in the resurrection. The mercy that defines God's heavenly kingdom is perfectly enacted upon the cross, for here Jesus mercifully lays down his life for the unjust enemies of God, the whole of sinful humankind, and in so doing manifests and obtains the perfect merciful forgiveness of his Father. In this most merciful act, Jesus will obtain mercy not only for himself but also for all people, and thus he and all of humankind will be forever blessed. The resurrection is the Father's merciful blessing bestowed upon his merciful Son, Jesus. All who come to live within the merciful Christ will obtain the same divine paternal mercy—the forgiveness of sins and a share in Jesus' heavenly human glory.[24]

Having recognized that, within their own poverty spirit, they have obtained the Father's mercy, Christians, living within the merciful risen Jesus, are also called to be humbly merciful. With compassion, Jesus' followers are to care for the sick, clothe the naked, feed the hungry, give drink to the thirsty, visit the imprisoned, and welcome the stranger, for the merciful Jesus identifies with them, the least of his brethren. Because of such mercy, they are the "blessed" of his Father and so will "inherit the kingdom prepared for you from the foundation of the world," that is, "eternal life" in Christ Jesus, the merciful Savior and compassionate Lord of the kingdom. To lack such mercy renders one unfit for the Father's kingdom, for one has not enacted the virtue that defines his very perfection—the mercy made manifest in his Son, Jesus (Mt 25:31-40).

---

24. Paul expresses the depths of Jesus' and his Father's merciful love when he writes that in our utter helplessness "Christ died for the ungodly." One can hardly imagine someone dying for a just man, though that is possible. "But God shows his love for us in that while we were yet sinners Christ died for us.... For if while we were enemies we were reconciled to God by the death of his Son, how much more, now that we are reconciled, shall we be saved by his life." The Father's mercy fully resides in the death of his Son, whose wholehearted mercy resides in his own willingness to die for us. In Jesus' death, we ceased to be ungodly enemies of God, and we now share in his resurrected life. In this merciful love, we "rejoice in God through our Lord Jesus Christ" (Rom 5:6-11).

Jesus' followers will obtain the mercy they seek when, in him, they love their enemies and pray for and do good to their persecutors. This mercy finds its ultimate expression in laying down their lives for the sake of Gospel, which means for the salvation of those who kill them. In so doing, like the merciful Jesus, they will "be sons of the Father who is in heaven." Becoming the merciful children of the Father, in union with Jesus his merciful Son, they too will become perfect in mercy as their Father is perfect in mercy. Their perfect mercy will obtain the blessing of perfect mercy.[25]

Blessed Are the Pure in Heart, for They Shall See God

The darkness of duplicity, iniquity, and vulgarity does not reside in God. He is the divine transparency of sheer light. He is the pure light of truth, goodness, and beauty. Thus "blessed are the pure in heart, for they shall see God."[26] Only those whose hearts are not contaminated by sin, poisoned by evil, and distorted by obscenity but rather infused with honesty, uprightness, and sensitivity

25. Within the Sermon on the Mount, there are other examples that illustrate the need for mercy. Jesus tells his disciples: "Judge not, that you be not judged. For with the judgment you pronounce you will be judged, and the measure you give will be the measure you get" (Mt 7:1-5). If one judges mercilessly, one will be judged mercilessly. The more one acts mercifully, the more one will obtain mercy. Mercy appears to be the virtue residing within the Golden Rule: "So, whatever you wish that men would do to you, do so until them; for this is the law and the prophets" (Mt 7:12). The law and the prophets are ultimately expressions of God's love, and within Jesus' merciful acts of redemption he fulfills them.

There are other instances within Mathew's Gospel where Jesus speaks of mercy. There is the shepherd who seeks out his one lost sheep and rejoices more at finding it than over the ninety-nine who did not stray. The point of the parable is that Jesus' Father in heaven does not wish that any "one of these little ones should perish" (Mt 18:10-14). Luke also has the parable of the woman who rejoiced over finding a small coin. Jesus concludes by saying, "Just so, I tell you, there is joy before the angels of God over one sinner who repents" (Lk 15:1-10). Immediately following is the parable of "the prodigal son," which illustrates the depths of the Father's merciful love for repentant sinners (see Lk 15:11-32). Also within Matthew's Gospel, Jesus responds to Peter's query as to whether he should forgive his brother seven times by saying that he needs to forgive seventy times. He then gives a parable of the kingdom of heaven where the king forgives his servant's huge debt, thus manifesting his pity and merciful forgiveness (see Mt 18:21-35). Obviously, all these parables demonstrate that the Father's perfection, and so that of the followers of Jesus' perfection, is found within the virtue, the Beatitude, of mercy.

26. Within the Old Testament, only he who "has clean hands and a pure heart" and so is not deceitful or false is able to ascend the hill upon which stood the temple (Ps 24:3-4). The Psalmist also speaks for his longing to behold "the face of God" (Ps 42:2). God is also good to the upright and "to those who are pure in heart" (Ps 73:1). To see God, who is the pure light of goodness and truth, one must be equally pure.

are able to see God. To be poor in spirit is to acknowledge that one needs the light of truth, goodness, and beauty that only a vision of God can provide.

Jesus, within the poverty of his earthly life, always sought and obtained the vision of his Father. In so doing, there was never any duplicity about him. Never did he deceive or mislead or manipulate. He never acted from an impure or selfish motive. He was transparent in the truth he spoke and in the good that he did. His character and bearing displayed a beauty and attractiveness. He simply possessed a pure heart. Even amid the darkness of the cross, where to all appearances, even to himself, the Father had abandoned him, he was assured, in faithful trust, of his Father's loving presence.[27] In the unshakable depth of his pure heart, he could still see God. The Father blessed such faithful and trusting purity of heart by raising Jesus from the dead and so pouring into his glorious heart and enlightened mind a Spirit-imbued paternal vision of himself that could not be exceeded. Jesus, the risen Son of God incarnate, now possessed a loving pure filial vision of his Father, filled with unutterable truth, inexpressible goodness, and ineffable beauty.

Within the deceit, violence, and deformity of the cross, Jesus dispelled the darkness of sin and death and so opened a way for God's pure light to shine upon the earth and within the hearts and minds of humankind. Those poor in spirit who come to live within the heavenly kingdom—having cast off the darkness of sin, the shadow of death, and the ugly deformities of this world— will live within the pure light of the Spirit of truth, goodness, and beauty and so be blessed with the sight of God. This vision of God resides in coming to faith in Jesus, who is his Son. To recognize Jesus as the Father's Son is to see in his human face the human face of the Father. To be incorporated into the risen Christ and so be transformed into his filial image through the Holy Spirit is to come into the living presence of the Father. As children of the Father, in their striving to be pure of heart, the faithful will be equally blessed with a filial vision of the Father, which begins and matures on earth and finds its fulfillment in their own glorious resurrection in Christ the Son at the end of time.[28]

Again, later within the Sermon on the Mount, Jesus gives examples of what purity of heart entails. "You have heard that it was said, 'you shall not commit adultery.' But I say to you that everyone who looks at a woman lustfully has

27. At the height of his agony in the garden, Jesus, when he is anguishing over his imminent passion and death, can still call God his Father—"Abba" (see Mk 14:36).

28. Paul takes up this understanding when he writes that because we are children of the Father, we are able to cry out, in union with Jesus, "Abba! Father!" (see Rom 8:14-17 and Gal 4:6-7).

already committed adultery with her in his heart" (Mt 5:27-28). Although purity of heart cannot be reduced to sexual purity, a chaste life is necessary for coming to know God himself. Because lustful passions and licentious acts are sins against one's very nature as a bodily person, they not only enslave the person but also deform the person's own heart and mind. They are not simply sins against someone else (though that often is the case) but sins against oneself, for one is misusing and attacking one's very body, which is inherently and integrally determinative of who one is as a human being.[29] Moreover, lustful acts—adultery, fornication, sodomy, masturbation, pornography, and the like—arise not of their own accord from without but from within one's heart and mind, from within one's very bodily being. This is why within the new law of the kingdom of heaven, a law that is now rooted in one's inner being, Jesus condemns both the act of adultery and the lustful thoughts and imaginings that arise from with one's heart, for it is from such a lustful heart that the adulterous act arises and proceeds. Likewise, these consuming lustful passions and enslaving sensuous acts darken one's heart and mind, for they have deformed the beauty of one's very humanity so that one is neither drawn to or capable of seeing the beauty that is God.

Therefore Jesus, following his condemnation of adulterous thoughts, speaks of doing violence against one's very body. "If your right eye causes you to sin, pluck it out and throw it away; it is better that you lose one of your members than that your whole body be thrown into hell. And if your right hand causes you to sin, cut if off and throw it away; it is better that you lose one of your members than that your whole body go into hell" (Mt 5:29-30). If all sinful sexual acts do violence to and so deform a human being, so the remedy must be equally as violent; that is, one must attack the very source: the lustful evil inclinations that lie deep within. Jesus, then, is not advocating the actual plucking out of eyes or the loping off of limbs, but rather he is graphically illustrating that

29. Paul expresses this truth within the life of Christian. "The body is not meant for immorality, but for the Lord, and the Lord for the body.... Do you not know that your bodies are members of Christ?" If one joins oneself to a prostitute, one becomes one flesh with her, "but he who is united to the Lord becomes one spirit with him. Shun immorality. Every other sin which man commits is outside the body; but the immoral man is against his own body. Do you not know that your body is a temple of the Holy Spirit within you, which you have from God? You are not your own; you were bought with a price. So glorify God in your body" (1 Cor 6:13-20; see also 3:16). For Paul, to engage in immoral sexual acts is not just a sin against one's own body but even more so a sin against Christ, to whom Christians belong and are joined, and thus they are sins against the very holiness of one's body, which is the very temple of the Holy Spirit.

if one does not wish to enter into the darkness of hell where no one sees God, then one must resolutely stand against and even violently attack the lustful sinful passions that virulently reside within one's heart and mind. The cancerous growth of lust must be excised from one's sensuous heart so that, with a pure heart, one is able to see God.[30]

A pure heart is not duplicitous. Following upon his articulating the new laws concerning sexuality and marriage, in the Sermon on the Mount Jesus declares: "Again, you have heard that it was said to you of old, 'You shall not swear falsely, but shall perform to the Lord what you have sworn.' But I say to you, Do not swear at all, either by heaven, for it is the throne of God, or by the earth, for it is his footstool, or by Jerusalem, for it is the city of the great King. And do not swear by your head, for you cannot make one hair white or black. Let what you say be simply 'Yes' or 'No'; anything more than this comes from evil one" (Mt 5:33-37). Truth, forthrightness, and honesty reside within the pure of heart. If the pure of heart see God, who is truth itself and so is always forthright and honest, then they, after the manner of God, will never swear falsely nor will they have any need to swear at all. The pure of heart will simply say "yes" or "no." To say otherwise is evil, for it is from the evil one, the father of lies, in whom no truth resides (see Gn 3:4 and Jn 8:44). Conformed into a liar and infectious with deceit, Satan is devoid of pure heart and so is blinded from the sight of God, and so will those be who are equally contaminated.[31]

Jesus provides the analogy of the eye. "The eye is the lamp of the body. So if your eye is sound, your whole body will be full of light; but if your eye is not sound, your whole body will be full of darkness. If then the light within you is darkness, how great is the darkness!" (Mt 6:22-23). If the eye of one's heart

30. Jesus does not bring this out, though it may be implied in his prohibition against divorce (see Mt5:31-32), but while sexual immorality blinds one from a pure vision of God, chaste sexual acts within marriage lead to a vision of God, for they are done in love for the begetting of new life. As God is a God of life and love, so married couples replicate that life and love and so they conform themselves together into his likeness, and in such likeness they together see God.

31. Other forms of duplicity are also found within the Sermon on the Mount. The hypocritical actions of those who pray to be seen, or those who fast in such a manner as to also be merely seen contain their own reward, that is, being thought to be holy. But while others may see them as holy, they will not see God, for he sees their duplicitous motives. Rather, those who pray in secret and those who hide their fasting will see God, for God sees the purity of their hearts and will reward them with the sight of him. See Mt 6:5-6 and 6:16-18. Likewise, the man who has a divided heart, who strives to serve two masters, who strives to serve God and mammon, will never see God, for only a man with a pure and undivided heart will see God. His heart and mind will be blind to the glitter of this world and so see the light of God's glory. See Mt 6:24.

is pure, the whole of who one is as a human being is filled with the living light of God. If the eye of one's heart sees only the darkness of deceit, evil, and depravity, then great is the darkness that dwells therein. The pure in heart, those who live within the kingdom of heaven and so live in Christ, will see God within the light of the Holy Spirit—the Spirit of truth, goodness, and beauty.

Blessed Are the Peacemakers, for They Shall Be Called Sons of God

Through his being poor in spirit, his mourning over sin and death, his meekness in the face of adversity, his hunger and thirst for righteousness, his mercy and purity of heart, Jesus, as the incarnate Son, was acting so as to be a peacemaker.[32] His acts of healing, raising the dead, casting out demons and forgiving sins, even his acts of quelling storms, were all acts of bringing peace to those suffering in distress. In these acts of peacemaking, he was making manifest the peaceful kingdom of heaven and so revealing that he was indeed the blessed Son of God. His Father was the first to call him his beloved Son. In this Sonship, Jesus is blessed, for in him the Father is well pleased. The Father's pleasure resides precisely in his Son's accepting his anointed commission to destroy the enemies of peace, especially sin and death, and so usher in a heavenly kingdom of peace—reconciliation between peoples and nations founded upon peace with God. Not by happenstance, at the moment of Jesus' death, his final earthly human act of peacemaking, does the centurion standing beneath the cross cry out in awe: "Truly this was the Son of God" (Mt 27:54; see also Mk 15:39). In so doing, the centurion is simply recognizing and echoing the truth that Jesus' Father first proclaimed at his baptism, for in his death his baptism is fully enacted. In a sense, the centurion is giving voice to the Father, for in his death Jesus accomplished the task with which his Father had entrusted him, and now in his Son's peacemaking death his Father is well pleased.

Within Jesus' peacemaking death, he reconciles humankind to God, for he has put to death a sinful humanity that was born at enmity with God (see Gn 3:8-10). Likewise, in his resurrection, Jesus has created humanity anew, one new man re-created in the Holy Spirit. In so doing, he has broken down

32. The Old Testament speaks of seeking peace and God giving peace. One is to depart from evil and "seek peace, and pursue it" (Ps 34:14). The Lord God speaks "peace to his people" (Ps 85:8). God desires peace for Jerusalem and Israel (see Ps 122:6-7 and 125:5). Isaiah prophecies that the child to be born and the son who is given will be called, among other titles, "Prince of Peace" (Is 9:6). What God desires is that his people make peace with him (Is 27:5).

the walls of enmity that exist between God and man, but also those that separate nations and races (see Eph 2:14-16 and Col 1:19-20).

To live in Jesus is to live in God's heavenly kingdom of peace, for in him one becomes a new creation whereby one is reconciled to God and so finds peace within oneself.[33] In this peace one can strive for peace with others, and in this peace peoples and nations can work for peace and reconciliation. Significantly, a person's identity as a son of God is founded upon his being a peacemaker and the recognition by others that he is a son of God because of his acts of peacemaking. The Father is then well pleased to call others his sons when they engage in acts of peace, as they live within the kingdom of heaven and so work in union with Jesus his peacemaking Son.

Once again, Jesus, within his sermon, expands upon what it means to be peacemakers. He declares:

> You have heard that it was said to the men of old, "You shall not kill; and whoever kills shall be liable to judgment." But I say to you that everyone who is angry with his brother shall be liable to judgment; whoever insults his brother shall be liable to the council, and whoever says, "You fool!" shall be liable to the hell of fire. So if you are offering your gift at the altar, and there remember that your brother has something against you, leave your gift there before the altar and go; first be reconciled to your brother, and then come and offer your gift. (Mt 5:21-24).

Peacemakers are not simply those who abstain from physical violence to others such as killing. Anger, insults, and invectives make for enmity and strife. So much is this the case that those who act in such a manner could be liable to everlasting condemnation. Importantly, Jesus sets the scene of reconciliation within the context of offering sacrifice to God, who is the source of

---

33. Before he departs from this world, Jesus in John's Gospel bestows peace upon his Apostles: "Peace I leave with you; my peace I give you; not as the world gives do I give to you. Let not your hearts be troubled, neither let them be afraid" (Jn 14:27). Worldly peace resides within worldly security—riches that dispel the fear of poverty and want, power that wards off threats and peril, authority that obtains what is desirous. Yet such things never achieve their aim— true peace. Peace resides in Jesus and the salvation that he brings. Therefore the first words that the risen Jesus speaks to his fearful Apostles on Easer Sunday evening are: "Peace be with you." His words were accompanied by his showing them "his hands and side." Gladness arose within the apostles as he reiterated, "Peace be with you." This peace is founded upon the forgiveness of sins and the new life of the Holy Spirit. Breathing upon the Apostles, he said, "Receive the Holy Spirit. If you forgive the sins of any, they are forgiven; if you retain the sins of any, they are retained" (Jn 20:19-23). In the Spirit, one is cleansed of sin and so reconciled to God. All who are in communion with Christ, through the indwelling Spirit, abide together in peace with their Father.

peace. It is incongruous to attempt to make peace with God through a sacrificial offering and remain at enmity with one's brother. Likewise, the responsibility for overcoming this enmity does not reside in the person who has been offended, but rather upon the brother who is charged with the offence. Even if the charge is groundless, he is obliged to make the first overture of peace. Only when peace resides among brothers can offerings of peace be then made to God. In this light, Jesus exhorts his hearers: "Make friends quickly with your accusers." If one does not, one could find oneself condemned (Mt 5:25-26).

The sons of God who work for peace upon earth will encounter much opposition, for many men and women are not of good will, and so the peace that Jesus came to bring in becoming man and that the angels heralded at his birth will be frustrated and actively thwarted. When Jesus, the peacemaker, comes in glory at the end of time, however, he will vanquish all enmity and strife and peace will reign, and those who strove for peace on earth with be eternally blessed, for they will forever be called sons of God.

Blessed Are Those Who Are Persecuted for Righteousness' Sake, Theirs Is the Kingdom of Heaven

This final Beatitude is the other bookend to the first. The poor in spirit are blessed, "for theirs is the kingdom of heaven." Those who are persecuted for righteousness's sake are blessed, for "theirs is the kingdom of heaven." To grasp the full significance of the first and last Beatitudes and what lies between them, we must perceive the logical causal order from start to finish, which was already present throughout the above examination. Or, what we want to perceive is the logical order that simply lies among the Beatitudes. In perceiving their interrelationship, we will also perceive the causal relationship between the Beatitudes that are enacted and the effected blessings that are obtained.

We have seen in every instance that Jesus is one of those who personifies, makes his own, each of the Beatitudes, and in so doing he is blessed in accordance with each. We have also seen that the foundational Beatitude, the first bookend, is that of being poor in spirit, for through being poor in spirit one obtains the kingdom of heaven. By enacting this first Beatitude, Jesus brings into existence the kingdom of heaven through his incarnation and his subsequent human salvific acts, and so becomes the Savior and Lord of the heavenly kingdom; that is, within his resurrected humanity, the Son of God literally embodies it. Thus the kingdom of heaven *is* his because he *is* the kingdom of heaven.

Now, within Jesus' poverty of spirit, by which he establishes the kingdom of heaven, he equally enacts the middle six Beatitudes and so he *will* obtain, within the future fulfillment of the heavenly kingdom, their distinct blessings. Being poor in spirit, Jesus mourned over the world into which he was born, and in his human meekness he hungered and thirsted for righteousness by being merciful toward those who were sick, poor, downtrodden, dying, and sinful, and so he brought them peace by providing to the pure of heart a vision of God—the seeing of his very face as the incarnate Son of God. He did so at the cost of being persecuted, even unto death, for the very righteous truth, goodness, justice, peace, and vision of God that he sought to establish. Jesus was therefore blessed, for within and through that persecution unto death he obtained the blessed heavenly kingdom, which he in his resurrection gloriously embodies, a kingdom blessed with comfort for the sorrowful, inheritance of the earth for the meek, satisfaction for those hunger and thirst for righteousness, mercy for the merciful, a vision of God for the pure of heart, and so divine Sonship for peacemakers. Because he enacts these middle six Beatitudes by which he, being poor in spirit, establishes the kingdom of heaven, he is "persecuted for righteousness' sake, the second bookend Beatitude, and so again, as in the first bookend Beatitude, his "is the kingdom of heaven." This final Beatitude brings to a summary culminating close the entire previous seven Beatitudes and so brings to a summary culminating close the entirety of Jesus' life.[34]

Jesus, as the one who, through his enactment of the Beatitudes, established the kingdom of heaven with its blessings, made it possible for others to become members of the kingdom and so obtain its blessings as well. To enter the kingdom of heaven and so live within its shared blessings, others must also enact the Beatitudes. The pattern is the same. By being poor in spirit, others recognize their need for the heavenly kingdom and so through faith in Jesus enter the kingdom by being united to the risen Jesus. In so doing, theirs too is the kingdom of heaven. From within that kingdom, through their mourning,

34. Almost immediately after his promulgation of the Beatitudes, Jesus says that he has "not come to abolish the law and the prophets ... but to fulfill them" (Mt 5:17-20). By enacting the Beatitudes, Jesus would fulfill the law that prophetically foreshadowed the heavenly kingdom, in that their purpose was to foster a holy life where one could see God and so live in righteous and peaceful communion with him. These ends have now been fulfilled in Jesus' enactment of the Beatitudes. Jesus has also fulfilled the prophets, for their continual message was both a call to being faithful to the law and covenant as well as a prophetic foretelling of a new law and new covenant through which one could be transformed. Within that transformation one would become holy and so see God and thus live righteously and peacefully in communion with him. These ends too are fulfilled in Jesus' enactment of the Beatitudes.

meekness, hungering, and thirsting for righteousness' sake, mercy, purity of heart, and peacemaking, they too, in union with Jesus, will be persecuted for righteousness's sake, some even unto death. Likewise, within and because of this righteous persecution, they too, in communion with Jesus, *will* ultimately be blessed through their sharing in his glorious resurrection, in their fully possessing the kingdom of heaven, and so reaping the blessings of all the other Beatitudes as well. Living in the kingdom of heaven, being in communion with their risen Savior and Lord, they too, within their own glorious resurrection, will embody all its blessings. Thus this final Beatitude also brings to a summary culminating close the entire previous seven Beatitudes for those who live within the kingdom of heaven and so brings to a summary culminating close all of the blessings they receive by living in Christ Jesus—"theirs is the kingdom of heaven."[35]

Therefore Jesus addresses, similar to the eighth, a "ninth" Beatitude directly to his audience. Jesus included himself within the first eight by using the designation "theirs." For those, including Jesus, who live the Beatitudes, "theirs is/will be." Now in the "ninth" Beatitude, he says (and one can imagine that he raised his eyes and directly looked them in the face when he did so), "Blessed are *you* when men persecute you and utter all kinds of evil against you falsely on my account. Rejoice and be glad, for your reward will be great in heaven, for so men persecuted the prophets who were before you" (Mt 5:21-21). Jesus is emphatically reiterating that his hearers will suffer persecution and not just some anonymous "others" on account of their faithful following of him. Yet Jesus categorically and prophetically assures them on his own authority that

---

35. At the end of the Sermon on the Mount, Jesus gives a twofold final exhortation. First, he warns his hearers that simply calling him "Lord, Lord" will not gain them entrance into the kingdom of heaven, but the doing of the heavenly Father's will. To those who do not do such, Jesus will declare: "I never knew you; depart from me you evildoers." It is in fulfilling the law of the new covenant, principally the Beatitudes, that one does the will of the Father as Jesus himself, as Son, has done and so only those who do so are recognized by him as also being children of the Father. Those who do not live the Beatitudes Jesus personally, by his own authority, casts away.

Second, those "who hear these words of mine and do them will be like a wise man who built his house upon rock; and when the rain fell, and the floods came, and the winds blew and beat against that house, but it did not fall, because it had been founded on rock." To enact the words of Jesus is to build one's life on the rock of Jesus, for in fulfilling his own words, the Beatitudes, he did not fall amid the driving winds of persecution or the floods of death that befell him, and neither will those who live within his house that is the kingdom of heaven. Those who build their house other than on the rock of Jesus will find their lives destroyed (Mt 7:21-27; see also Lk 6:46, 13:25-27, and 6:47-49).

they are blessed and so should even rejoice and be glad that such is the case, because within the heavenly kingdom their reward will be great.[36] They must keep in mind that such was even done to the holy prophets who preceded them. To suffer on account of Jesus manifests that one is worthy of Jesus, for one has conformed oneself into his likeness, and so one is joyfully blessed in him. To live in Christ is the blessed great reward of living in heaven.

What Jesus teaches immediately following his promulgation of the Beatitudes is noteworthy because it underlines their significance. Jesus' followers "are the salt of the earth" and "the light of the world." Jesus is "the salt of the earth" and "the light of the world" because in him the Beatitudes are enacted and in so doing the kingdom of heaven is established. Jesus' followers are equally "salt of the earth" and "the light of the world," for through their enactment of the Beatitudes—in their acts of mercy and kindness, of seeking righteousness and peace, of proclaiming the Gospel—they make the kingdom of heaven present to all upon the earth. They should not lose the saltiness that allows others to truly taste the blessings of the kingdom, but rather their deeds should be the light upon the stand for others to see the glories of the kingdom's blessings. As many rejoice at seeing the good salvific deeds of Jesus and so give glory to his heavenly Father, so must their light shine before all, and in seeing their good works they will "give glory to your Father who is in heaven" (Mt 5:13-16). In witnessing the good earthly works of the faithful, people rightly recognize that the heavenly Father is their Father and so give glory to him and for the good works his children have done. To do the good deeds of the Beatitudes not only reveals that Jesus is the Son of the Father, but also testifies that his Father is the Father of all who perform them.

Conclusion: Jesus Becoming Jesus

First, we clearly see now that Jesus enacted the Beatitudes, establishing the kingdom of God/heaven. The acts by which Jesus enacted the Beatitudes are the same acts by which he enacted the kingdom of God/heaven. In his public ministry, Jesus initiates God's kingdom through his acts of healing the sick, exorcising demons, raising the dead, forgiving sinners, multiplying the bless-

---

36. Within the Gospel of Luke, Jesus is even more exuberant in his exhortation. On the day one is persecuted, "Rejoice in that day, and leap for joy, for behold, your reward is great in heaven" (Lk 6:22-23). His followers should not simply rejoice "on" that day but rejoice "in" that day, for that day of persecution is itself a blessing. In that blessed day of persecution, they are even to leap for joy, for they have merited a great heavenly reward.

ed bread, and so on, and in these same acts he enacted the Beatitudes of poverty of spirit, mourning, meekness, seeking righteousness, mercy, and so on. To state it the other way around, within his poverty of spirit, mercy, meekness, seeking righteousness, and so on, he heals the sick, casts out demons, forgives sins, raises the dead, and multiplies the blessed bread. Within this convergence, the heavenly kingdom comes to be. Importantly, within the culminating act of his salvific death on the cross, Jesus embodies or enacts all the Beatitudes, and in the consequent act of his resurrection, Jesus embodies all their blessings. All the blessings are enacted in him. Likewise, through his act of dying, Jesus reconciled humankind to the Father, and so the Father in raising him from the dead empowered him to pour out the new life of the Holy Spirit, the new life of God's heavenly kingdom. Thus the blessings that accrue to the Beatitudes are one and the same as the blessings that accrue to living in God's kingdom. All the blessings of the kingdom of God, all the blessings that accrue to the Beatitudes, are therefore contained within the one outpoured Spirit. These blessings reside in Jesus the Spirit-filled Christ as the risen Savior and Lord of the kingdom, and those who are therefore in communion with him are empowered in the Spirit to live the Beatitudes within the kingdom so as to participate in the Spirit's blessings of the kingdom.

A more theological or doctrinal way of conceiving and articulating the above is to grasp that Jesus in enacting the Beatitudes enacted the kingdom, and in so doing he, as the incarnate Son, achieved full living communion with the Father in the communion of the Holy Spirit, thus accruing the full blessings of such a communion with the Father in the Holy Spirit. Those who live in communion with Jesus, and thus in communion with one another, through the communion of the Holy Spirit live in communion with the Father and so accrue to themselves, through him, the blessings of such a communion with the Father in the Holy Spirit. Through and in the risen Jesus, human beings come to share together in the one perichoretic communion of life and love of the Father, the Son, and the Holy Spirit. Sharing in this one intertwining or intermingling communion of divine life is the one consummate all-encompassing blessing of the Beatitudes. Eschatologically, this comes to its fulfillment when Jesus returns in glory and God's kingdom finds its definitive expression and so the blessings of the Beatitudes find their full actualization—the everlasting blessed communion with the Father within the everlasting blessed communion of Jesus, his Son, through the everlasting blessed communion of the Holy Spirit.

Second, in chapter 4, we stressed that Jesus' salvific acts of healing, exorcism, forgiveness, and the like were priestly acts. Within this chapter, Jesus' authoritative prophetic acts were examined—his promulgation and enactment of the Beatitudes. Within the simultaneous convergence of his prophetic acts within his priestly acts, we also find Jesus becoming Jesus, and in so doing he reveals that he is simultaneously the new Priest and the new Moses. Within the same salvific acts, Jesus, the Savior, manifests that he is both Priest and Prophet. Moreover, within these same salvific priestly and judicial acts Jesus, as Savior, is beginning to make real the kingdom of heaven and so is becoming the new King David of the everlasting kingdom. Likewise, Jesus is enacting these acts as the one interiorly anointed with the Holy Spirit. This Spirit first accrued to him as the Son of God within his conception. This same Spirit was newly conferred upon him at his baptism, where his Father commissioned him to found the heavenly kingdom as the new Priest and new Prophet. Therefore Jesus, the Christ, the Incarnate Son of the Father, through becoming the Savior, will come to be the new and everlasting Spirit-anointed Priest, Prophet, and King. All these titles and the realities they designate will find their ultimate expression within Jesus' death and resurrection, and thus they will find their consummate embodiment within the person of Jesus himself—YHWH-Saves.

Third, we find here the supreme significance of Jesus' humanity. All of Jesus' priestly saving works that spring from within his prophetic enactment of the Beatitudes are enacted through his humanity. They are incarnational acts in that Jesus as the Son of God performed them as man. Equally, then, all the blessings of the heavenly kingdom that flow from these priestly prophetic human salvific acts accrue to his humanity. As a risen man, Jesus, the Son, is the glorious king. To partake of the blessings of the kingdom of heaven, one needs to be in communion with the risen humanity of Jesus, for he alone, as the risen Son incarnate, literally embodies in his very person these blessings as the Spirit-anointed Priest, Prophet, and King. Again, to know truly the man Jesus is for one to know that he is all of the above, and to believe in him as Savior and Lord is to be blessed in him who embodies all priestly, prophetic, and kingly blessings. To be in communion with the risen humanity of Jesus, the Son, in whom all priestly, prophetic, and kingly blessings reside, is to be in communion with the Holy Spirit, within whom all priestly, prophetic, and kingly blessings are contained, and so be in communion with the Father, from whom all priestly, prophetic, and kingly blessings flow. To abide within Jesus is abide within the Trinity.

Finally, we saw in chapter 4 that Jesus sent out his Apostles, giving them the power and authority to perform the same acts that he was performing— the acts that enacted the kingdom. In so doing we perceived that Jesus, in this sending out, was enacting the church. Within the apostolic church is found Jesus' acts of healing, forgiveness, and the abundance of blessed life, all of which make up life within God's kingdom. In this chapter we see, within these ecclesial salvific acts, the enactment of the Beatitudes. Jesus, through the salvific acts of his apostolic church, continues mercifully to heal the sick, cast out demons, and forgive sins. Within the apostolic church, those who mourn are comforted, those seeking righteousness find satisfaction, and the poor are mercifully fed. Through these acts the church brings peace into the lives of individuals and seeks to spread concord among peoples and nations. These salvific acts, enacted within the Beatitudes, find their specific enactment within the church's sacraments, each containing their individual blessings—in baptism, one enters into the righteous kingdom of God; in confession, one finds merciful forgiveness of sin; in the Eucharist, one participates in the one sacrifice of Christ and so achieves reconciliation with the Father through communion with Jesus—the abundance of life of his real glorified bodily presence. Within all these acts, we find the church poor in spirit, for what she offers are not the riches of this world but simply the riches of the poor Jesus Christ—the whole of his Gospel. In so doing the church is the salt of the earth and the light of the world. The church enacts all these saving acts often amid persecution, and in so doing these ecclesial acts become even more radiant, for they become living icons in act of Jesus crucified, who laid down his life for the salvation of all. In this the church continues to rejoice. Most importantly, in making Jesus present, the church provides for those who are pure in heart a vision of God, for they see in the face of the church the face of Jesus who, as Son, manifests, in the love of the Holy Spirit, the face of his Father.[37] As stated before, to live within the life and love of the church is to live within the life and love of Jesus being Jesus.

---

37. The psalmist prays, "Lift up the light of your countenance upon us Lord" (Ps 4:6). In Jesus, this prayer is answered.

Paul reminds the Corinthians that Moses had to place a veil over his face because the Israelites were afraid to see the glory of God that radiated from him. But for Christians, this veil has been lifted, and "we with unveiled face, beholding the glory of the Lord, are being changed into his likeness from one degree of glory to another; for this comes from the Lord who is the Spirit" (2 Cor 3:12-18; see also Ex 34:29-35). The church ever reflects the radiance of Jesus, for the radiance of Jesus continuously transforms the church from one degree of glory to another.

6 · JESUS' FILIAL RELATIONSHIP WITH HIS FATHER

In chapters 4 and 5, we examined Jesus' public ministry, specifically his priestly ministry exercised within his miracles and his prophetic ministry particularly found within his promulgation of the Beatitudes. We noted the convergence of this twofold ministry in that, within his own enactment of the Beatitudes, through his acts of mercy and righteousness, he simultaneously performed his acts of exorcism, healing, forgiveness, and the like. Through his public ministry, Jesus was making real, making present, the initial in-breaking of God's kingdom. In so doing, Jesus was equally calling others into that kingdom, first by appointing his official witnesses, the twelve Apostles, by eliciting faith from others, and founding his future church, the assembly of the faithful. Jesus' twofold public ministry was prophetically anticipating the fulfillment of this twofold ministry within his passion, death, and resurrection, whereby he would definitively establish the kingdom of God in which would reside those who acknowledge him to be their Lord and Savior.

Within his priestly and prophetic public ministry, Jesus was also revealing that he was the Christ, that his priestly and prophetic deeds where done in and through the Holy Spirit, the Spirit of Sonship. This in turn manifested that Jesus was truly divine, not simply as identifying himself as "He who is" ("It is I"), but more specifically as the Son of God. Jesus is God as YHWH-Son and so distinct from God his Father, YHWH-Father. Because the salvific acts that he performed, by which he revealed that he was the divine Son, were done in the Spirit of Sonship, he equally revealed that the Spirit is divine as YHWH-Spirit. Likewise, Jesus, through his priestly and prophetic acts, was also manifesting that he is truly the Savior. Jesus was enacting his name, YHWY-Saves, and so Jesus was becoming Jesus.

Who Is Jesus' Father?

The first recorded event in which Jesus expresses a unique relationship to God as his Father appears in the Gospel of Luke, where he, as a youth of twelve years old, was found by Joseph and Mary in the temple "sitting among the teaching, listening to them and asking them question." Upon Mary's anxiously questioning him as to why he had separated himself from them upon their return to Nazareth after the Passover, Jesus responds by insinuating that they should have known where he was since: "Did you not know that I must be in my Father's house/about my Father's business?" (Lk 2:46-49). Significantly, Jesus is in the temple. He is in the presence of God. Moreover, he is in God's presence as the Father's Son going about his Father's business. Jesus' physical presence in the temple thus signifies, as the Father's Son, that he is always in the presence of his Father and that he is always and everywhere doing the will of his Father.

In this light, although Mary knew that her son was conceived by the overshadowing of the Holy Spirit, she was yet to grasp the full significance of this—that her son was the unique Son of the Father. We also saw that, at the beginning of Luke's genealogy, Jesus is identified as "the supposed" son of Joseph and that, at the onset of Jesus' public ministry, his fellow Nazarenes presumed his mother was Mary and his father was Joseph, the carpenter (Lk 3:23, 4:22). Although Jesus' subsequent miracles and teaching caused the crowds to be amazed and set them wondering as to who he might be, they took offense to him precisely because they "knew" him to be the mere son of a carpenter from Nazareth (see Mt 13:54-58, Mk 6:1-6, and Lk 4:16-30). Thus the fundamental question permeating the entire Gospel narratives is: Who is Jesus' father? To know who Jesus' father is to establish and so resolve who he is, his own identity. Although everyone presumes that he is the son of Joseph, his miracles and teaching with authority throughout his public ministry are not in keeping with his possessing such mere presumed human paternity, thus resulting in both the marveling and the taking of offense. Nor does it square with how Jesus himself speaks of his relationship with God as "my Father," and thus the future charge of blasphemy—of Jesus making himself equal to God (see Mt 26:63-65, Mk 14:61-64, and Lk 22:70-71). With this seeming paradox in mind—the authentic humanity of Jesus and yet his speaking and acting in a manner that is not in keeping with his being merely human—we must examine more closely his human self-conscious awareness that God is his Father. Jesus' own response to this seeming paradox is for him to speak of God as his own Father, and thus his justification for speaking with authority and for his ability to perform his mighty deeds.[1]

In this chapter, we examine Jesus' human consciousness and knowledge of his Father, for it is determinative of his own self-conscious identity as Son. The manner of this relationship defines who he is and thus determines how he speaks and acts.

"My Father"

Jesus spoke of his relationship with the Father from within the historical environment of the Old Testament. There the title "son of God" designated Israel (Ex 4:22; Hos 11:1), individuals (Dt 14:1; Hos 2:1), kings (2 Sm 7:14; Ps 2:7), and angels (Gn 6:2; Jb 1:6). The question that immediately arises is whether Jesus' consciousness and knowledge of God as his Father were such that his sonship differs only in degree—or, more radically, in kind—from the sonship of Israel, the kings, the angels, or other human beings. Did Jesus perceive himself as being the Father's Son in an adopted sense, or was he consciously aware that

---

1. Although the question of Jesus' identity within the Synoptics revolves around his father's identity, in the Gospel of John the issue is expressed as to where he is from. The people of Jerusalem speculated that Jesus might be the Christ, yet they concluded that he could not be the Christ because "we know where he comes from; and when the Christ appears, no one will know where he comes from." In response, Jesus ironically asks them, "You know me, and you know where I come from? But I have not come of my own accord; he who sent me is true, and him you do not know. I know him, for I come from him, and he sent me" (Jn 7:25-31; see 8:14). Later, when Jesus tells the crowds in the temple that from within the hearts of those who believe in him "will flow rivers of living water," some responded: "'This is really the prophet.' Others said, 'This is the Christ.' But some said, 'Is the Christ to come from Galilee? Has not the scripture said that the Christ is descended from David, and comes from Bethlehem, the village where David was?' So there was a division among the people over him" (Jn 7:37-39). When questioning the former blind man, the Pharisees assure him that Jesus is a sinner and not from God, for "we do not know where he comes from" (Jn 9:24-34). Jesus assures his faithful disciples that the Father loves them, for they love him and believed that he has come from the Father. "I came from the Father and have come into the world; again, I am leaving the world and going to the Father" (Jn 16:25-28; see also 17:20-26). This querying finds its culmination at Jesus' trial before Pilate. The Jews cry out for Jesus' crucifixion "because he has made himself the Son of God." Such an accusation instilled fear in Pilate, as he returns to the praetorium and asks Jesus, "Where are you from" (Jn 19:6-9). Although people think they know where Jesus is from and so know who he is, they truly know neither. Those who believe in him know that, although he was born in Bethlehem and lived in Nazareth of Galilee, he is truly from the Father and so he is the Father's Son.

he was the Father's Son in a truly divine sense—was he aware that he, as Son, was God as his Father is God?[2]

Jesus, within his ensuing priestly and prophetic public ministry, speaks exclusively in terms of "my Father." Thus Jesus does not directly reveal that he is "God the Son" by simply saying that he is such.[3] Rather, by speaking of "my Father," and so revealing his Father, Jesus manifests that he is the Father's Son. This is in keeping with his identity as the Father' Son; that he is only the Son of the Father by being the Father's Son. He has no identity of his own apart from his Father. As the Father's Son, being the perfect image and likeness of the Father, he is defined as the one who reflects perfectly and so manifests completely the Father. Jesus' very purpose as Son is not simply or primarily to reveal himself as Son, but rather, in revealing himself as the Father's Son, he reveals his Father. Actually, it is only in perfectly revealing the Father that he reveals that he is the Father's Son, for only one who is the Father's Son could perfectly reveal the Father. In the light of this, it is not surprising that Jesus, within the Synoptic Gospels, invariably refers to God as "*my* Father."

"My Heavenly Father"

Not infrequently, Jesus refers to "my heavenly Father" or "my Father who is in heaven" (see, e.g., Mt 15:13; 18:10, 18:14, 18:35). By employing such phrases, Jesus is designating not simply that God is his Father but also that his Father is "heavenly." He abides "in heaven." There is a twofold intertwined emphasis here. God is indeed Jesus' Father, and thus his Father is not an earthly father but one who dwells in heaven. This twofold emphasis reflects directly upon Jesus himself. Jesus is not simply the Son of the Father, but he is the heavenly Son of the Father. The term "heavenly" specifies that both the Father and Jesus, the Father's Son, exist together in an ontological manner that is distinct from the earthly, that is, in an utterly transcendent divine manner that befits the title "heavenly." Significantly, Jesus personally identifies himself, who he

2. I confine myself to those passages within his public ministry and not those within the Passion Narratives, which we will examine later.

3. Surprisingly, Jesus, within the Synoptic Gospels, never refers to himself as "Son of God." Therefore some have concluded, falsely, that he never consciously thought of himself as the Son of God but that it was a designation later allocated to him by the apostolic church. Yet such an argument misses the entire point. As Son, being the perfect image of the Father, Jesus, by the very nature of who he is, is to reveal the Father, and only in so doing does he reveal himself as the Father's Son. Thus Jesus is conscious of himself as God the Son, but only within his conscious awareness of God his Father.

personally is, only in relation to God as "my" Father and thus reveals to others that he is the Father's Son.

Pointedly, Jesus assures his disciples: "Again, I say to you, if two of you agree on earth about anything they ask, it will be done for them by my Father in heaven." Why is it that what Jesus' disciples agree to upon earth will be done by his Father who is in heaven, and why is Jesus, on his own personal authority ("Amen, I say to you") so assured of this? "For where two or three are gathered in my name, there am I in the midst of them" (Mt 18:19-20). To gather in Jesus' name—that is, to gather believing in him—is to gather in the midst of Jesus himself—he is present in the midst of those who believe in him. How is it that agreeing upon something, having gathered in Jesus' name, a gathering in which he is present, assures that what has been agreed upon on earth will be done by his Father in heaven? The reason that Jesus can give such personal assurance that his disciples' prayer will be answered lies in the fact that he is personally the Father's Son. They can also be assured that their prayer will be answered because they do not pray on their own apart from Jesus but in communion with Jesus, the Father's Son, who is in their midst. Thus their prayer to the Father is not simply made in the name of Jesus, the Father's Son, but also by Jesus himself, the Father's Son, on their behalf. For Jesus to exhort his disciples to bring their intercessions to "my Father" is for Jesus to bring his own intercessions to "my Father," for he has made their requests his own. The assurance of being heard by the Father resides in the assurance that Jesus is the Father's Son. The Father's hearing and answering the disciples' prayers therefore bears testimony to Jesus' Sonship. On the one hand, Jesus is primarily giving assurance to his disciples that his Father will hear them and thus focusing their attention not on himself but on his Father. On the other hand, his Father, in responding positively to the prayer of those gathered in Jesus' name and in his midst, reflects on Jesus, confirming that he is truly the Father's Son.

The reason his disciples gather in his name arises from their belief that he who bears the name Jesus is the Father's Son. If they did not believe that such were the case, there would be no reason for them to gather in his name rather than in the name of someone else. Likewise, for Jesus, as the Father's Son, to be in the midst of this gathering is for his Father to be present as well, for where the Son is so too is the Father. Here again, Jesus is enacting his name as Savior and in so doing revealing that he is the Father's Son, for the Father answers the entreaties made by Jesus on behalf of and in communion with those who have gathered in his name—believing him to be the Father's Son. Jesus, then, is giving expression to his church. The church is composed of those who gather in Jesus' name, the name of the Father's Son, and in so doing, in communion with him, make known their needs to his Father. Being in communion with Jesus, his Son, the Father is compelled to answer the church's requests.[4]

Likewise, Jesus' followers need not fear what may befall them because of their faithfulness. "So everyone who acknowledges me before men, I will also acknowledge before my Father who is in heaven; but whoever denies me before men, I will deny before my Father who is in heaven" (Mt 10:31-33; see also Mk 8:38; Lk 9:26 and 12:8-9). When one ultimately comes before the heavenly Father, the earthly acknowledgment of Jesus is crucial for entrance into the heavenly realm. Equally, not to have acknowledged Jesus while on earth results in his refusal to acknowledge such a denier. But what is one to acknowledge? The answer resides within the phrase "my Father." It is the acknowledgment that Jesus is the Son of the Father and it is precisely because he is the Son that his testimony, on behalf of his faithful followers, boasts singular standing with his Father. To acknowledge before men on earth that Jesus is the Father's Son and to be loyal to that acknowledgment in the face of innumerable trials provides assurance of entrance into the Father's presence precisely because Jesus, as Son, will confirm before his Father that such a person was indeed his faithful disciple. The Father cannot refuse such an acknowledgment, for to do so would be an act of refusal, his own act of denial, his own act of not acknowledging that Jesus is indeed his Son. Also, in his acknowledgment before his Father, Jesus is equally confirming that those so acknowledged have borne witness to the Father, for to acknowledge the Son is simultaneously to acknowledge the Son's Father. Jesus simply knows, and therefore he definitely declared to his followers what he did, that in the face of his filial testimony the only response available to the Father is that of responding accordingly. As his divine Son, Jesus enjoys privileged entrée to his heavenly Father to the eternal benefit of those who faithfully acknowledge him on earth. The church enjoys such divine benefits, for she and her members are those who acknowledge(d) on earth that Jesus is indeed the Father's Son. Jesus' acknowledgment before his Father is therefore a saving act. Jesus is enacting his name predicated upon his faithful followers' acknowledgment that he is their Savior precisely because he is the Father's Son.

---

4. Within the liturgy, the church offers her prayers to the Father in communion with Jesus in the unity of the Holy Spirit.

"The Will of My Father in Heaven"

Jesus admonishes his listeners that "Not everyone who says to me 'Lord, Lord' will enter the kingdom of heaven, but he who does the will of my Father who is in heaven." Although acknowledging Jesus as "Lord," and thus divine, is a prerequisite for entering the kingdom of heaven, it is not the only requirement. To enter the kingdom of heaven, one must also, here on earth, do the will of Jesus' Father, who is in heaven. Moreover, Jesus recognizes that "On that day [the last day] many will say to me, 'Lord, Lord, did we not prophesy in your name, and cast out demons in your name, and do many mighty works in your name?' And then will I declare to them, 'I never knew you; depart from me, you evildoers'" (Mt 7:21-23; see also Lk 6:46 and 13:25-27). Notice first that on the last day "many" will address Jesus personally as "Lord." They will not address God in general or even his Father, but Jesus himself. Jesus, as "the Lord," is to judge whether one is worthy of entering into the everlasting kingdom, and he will do so precisely because he, as the heavenly Father's Son incarnate, is the glorious risen Lord of the heavenly kingdom. But one can even have done mighty deeds in Jesus' name and so the same mighty deeds that Jesus himself has done, and yet Jesus will declare not only that he does not know such persons but will also designate them as "evildoers." Why such an utterly unsympathetic response on Jesus' part? Jesus establishes the kingdom of God and so becomes its Lord by doing the will of his Father and thus revealing that he is the Father's Son. To call Jesus "Lord" and to do mighty deeds in his name implies that the person, in so doing, is also doing the will of Jesus' Father and so is able to enter into God's kingdom—a kingdom Jesus established by doing his Father's will. Not to do the will of the Father entails not truly recognizing Jesus' authentic Lordship, because if one did understand what it means for Jesus to be Lord of his Father's kingdom, one would be obedient to his Father's will as he is as the Father's Son.[5] Jesus does not know such people because they are not in his filial image; they are not his brothers and sisters in that they have not done as he, as Son, has done—being the Father's Son he did his Father's will. For Jesus, the Son, not to do the will of his Father is to be an evildoer, despite appearances to the contrary, that is, calling him "Lord, Lord" and doing mighty deeds in his name. Thus, amid this admonition, Jesus is reveal-

---

5. In Luke's Gospel, Jesus makes this clear: "Why do you call me 'Lord, Lord,' and not do what I tell you?" (Lk 6:46). To acknowledge Jesus as "Lord" is to do what he says, and what he says is that one should do the will of the Father as he, as Son, does the will of his Father.

ing himself as the Father's heavenly Son by clearly inferring that he singularly does on earth his Father's will "who is in heaven," and for this reason he alone is "Lord" of his Father's heavenly kingdom.

Similarly, when Jesus is told that his mother and brothers wish to speak to him, he replies, "'Who is my mother, and who are my brothers?' And stretching out his hand toward his disciples, he said, 'Here are my mother and my brothers! For whoever does the will my Father in heaven is my brother, and sister and mother'" (Mt 12:46-50; see also Mk 3:31-35 and Lk 8:4-8). From a biological or physical perspective, mothers and fathers, brothers and sisters share the same family bloodline. This extends to grandparents, aunts and uncles, and cousins. All of one's immediate relatives physically compose, through the begetting of children, one family. Jesus' mother and brothers wished to speak to him. But Jesus raises the concept of family from that of an earthly bloodline to that of a heavenly one. Jesus does have an earthly family, but his true identity, who he truly is, is not ultimately founded upon it. He is the son of Mary, but who he is as the son of Mary is the Father's Son. Being the Father's Son, Jesus is humanly obedient to his Father's will. Jesus' utter perfect earthly obedience defines him as the heavenly Son of his Father in heaven. Thus, to be truly a member of Jesus' family, to partake of his heavenly bloodline, to share in his divine identity as Son and so to be his brothers and sisters, is to be obedient to his Father. As Jesus is Son only in relation to his Father, so his disciples are his mother, brothers, and sisters only in their relation to his Father, and to be such they are to be obedient to his Father as he, as Son, is obedient to his Father for, in that obedience they become his mother, brothers, and sisters.[6] All the above is predicated upon the phrase "my Father in heaven." Only if Jesus is singularly the heavenly Father's divine Son will his disciples, in obeying his heavenly Father, be his mother, brother, and sister. Jesus, as the Father's heavenly Son, is the bond that establishes the communion between his obedient disciples, his brothers and his sisters, and his heavenly Father. If Jesus is not the divine heavenly Son of the Father, then he has no ontological "familial"

---

6. Mary only became Jesus' earthly biological mother because she was first obedient to her son's heavenly Father. It was in doing the will of her son's Father, within her *fiat*, that Mary became the mother of the Father's Son. In one and the same act of obedience, Mary not only conceived Jesus within a human earthly family but also was taken up into, "conceived" within, her son's heavenly family, for his Father, in her act of motherly obedience, became her Father as well. Thus Mary is both mother and sister to Jesus, the Father's Son, for they are both obedient to one and the same Father.

foundation, no divine bloodline, for professing that those who are obedient to God are his brothers and sisters and so children of the same heavenly Father.

By way of summarizing the above two passages, we see that Jesus makes real the kingdom of God by doing the will of his heavenly Father and in so doing manifests that he is the Father's heavenly Son. His filial obedience, his absolute enacting the will of his Father, expresses Jesus' divine Sonship. To enter the kingdom, one must not simply call Jesus "Lord, Lord" and do mighty deeds, but one must do the will of his Father and in so doing manifest, as Jesus does, that one is a child of the Father, for this authenticates that one is truly Jesus' brother and sister. As Jesus reveals that God is his heavenly Father only through his filial acts of obedience as Son, so do others manifest, through their obedience to his Father, that they belong to the family of Jesus and thus members, in union with him, of his Father's heavenly kingdom. To profess in faith, then, that Jesus is truly one's Lord inherently entails the recognition that Jesus is the obedient Son of his heavenly Father, and such recognition equally entails that, if Jesus is one's Lord, one must also do the will of the Father as he does. Only then is Jesus not only one's Lord but also one's brother and so one is able to live under his brotherly Lordship sharing in his filial relationship with his Father.

"They Will Respect My Son"

Significantly, it is within a parable that Jesus clearly distinguishes himself as Son from all those who have gone before him—the prophets. Jesus tells of a vineyard owner who lent out his vineyard to tenants. At the appropriate time, he sent various groups of servants to obtain the fruit of his vineyard. But the tenants maltreated some and killed others. The vineyard owner "still had one other" and so in desperation he sent his "beloved son," saying, "they will respect my son." The tenants nonetheless said, "This is the heir; come, let us kill him and have his inheritance." So, the tenants "took him and cast him out of the vineyard, and killed him." In response, the vineyard owner will destroy the tenants and give his vineyard to others. Jesus then provides the interpretive key to the parable by quoting from Psalm 118:22-23: "Have you never read in the scriptures: 'The very stone that the builders rejected has become the head of the corner; this is the Lord's doing, and it is marvellous in our eyes'?" (see also Is 28:16). Within Matthew, Jesus adds: "Therefore I tell you, the kingdom of God will be taken away from you and given to a nation producing the fruits of it. And he who falls on this stone will be broken to pieces; but when it falls on any one, it will crush him" (Mt 21:43-44).[7] Knowing that the parable was aimed at them, "the chief priests and Pharisees tried to arrest him" but did not because they feared the multitude who "held him to be a prophet" (Mk 12:1-12; see also Mt 21:33-46 and Lk 20:9-19).

Jesus has added the word "very" when quoting Psalm 118:22, accentuating both that he is that "very stone" and thus that he is the very "beloved son" rejected by the Jewish leaders. The "very" also radically distinguishes him as the very "cornerstone," and so the very "beloved son," from those who had gone before who were merely stones—the servant prophets. In designating that the last to be sent was the vineyard owner's "beloved son," Jesus gives to the vineyard owner the identity of "father." In so doing, Jesus consciously confirms, within this parable, his own identity, distinct from the servant prophets, by specifying his unique divine relationship with the Father—that of beloved Son. Also, although Jesus is consciously aware that he is the Father's Son, within the parable it is his Father, as the vineyard owner, who designates him as his "beloved son." Jesus does not designate himself as Son within the parable, but his Father, the vineyard owner, designates him as such. Thus Jesus has his Father, through the voice of the vineyard owner, echo the words spoken at his baptism: "This is my beloved Son, with whom I am well pleased." As Jesus reveals himself as Son by speaking of "my Father," so the Father reveals himself as Father only by speaking of Jesus as "my beloved Son."[8]

Within the parable, Jesus not only reveals that he is consciously aware that he is the Father's beloved Son, but also intimates how he will die. Jesus, as the stone rejected by the builders, is the beloved son whom the tenants "took" and "cast out of the vineyard" and "killed." Likewise, "the chief priests and the Pharisees ... perceived that he was speaking about them." Although they could not arrest and kill him at the time, for fear of the multitude, they will come in darkness and arrest Jesus and cast him outside the vineyard (Jerusa-

---

7. Verse 44 is rather puzzling and difficult to interpret. It is not in most ancient Greek manuscripts.

8. Here we glimpse what will later become intrinsic to the traditional understanding of the doctrine of the Trinity. The Father is only the Father in relation to his Son—in the begetting of his Son. Thus it is proper to the Father to be the revealer of his Son. The Son is only the Son in relation to his Father, in his being begotten of the Father. Thus it is proper to the Son to be the revealer of his Father. The Father and Son never reveal themselves directly or apart from one another. They only reveal themselves in the other—the Father in the Son and the Son in the Father, and so only in communion with one another. Therefore the Father never says "I am the Father" but instead "You are my beloved Son." And therefore Jesus never says, "I am the Son," but instead, "my heavenly Father."

lem) and kill him. The killing of Jesus, though, is not simply a murderous act. Because within the parable the father says he is sending his "beloved son," we hear the faint words that God spoke to Abraham in the distant past: "Take your son, your only son Isaac, whom you love, and go to Moriah, and offer him there." (Gn 22:2). Here the Father is sending his beloved Son, and his beloved Son, in being rejected and killed on the cross, will give his life as a loving sacrificial offering, which will bring forth an abundance of fruit—the holy life of God's people. In addition, although the Jewish leaders killed Jesus so that they might maintain their tenancy over God's vineyard, "to have his inheritance," they, in rejecting Jesus the beloved Son, forfeited it.[9] The kingdom of God will be given "to other tenants who will give him [God the Father, the vineyard owner] the fruits in their seasons" (Mt 21:41 and 43), that is, the new people of God who will bear the fruit of holiness.[10]

9. Jesus, in presenting this parable, obviously has in mind God's love song in Isaiah 5:1-7. There God, through Isaiah, sings of his love for the vineyard he has planted. He lovingly planted his vineyard with the best vines and carefully nurtured it. "What more was there to do for my vineyard, that I have not done in it? When I looked for it to yield grapes, why did it yield wild grapes?" The vineyard, says Isaiah, "is the house of Israel, and the men of Judah are my pleasant planting; and he looked for justice, but behold bloodshed; for righteousness, but behold, a cry!" Jesus, within his own parable, is the living enactment of Isaiah's parable. The "wild grapes" of the Jewish leaders do not bring forth justice and righteousness but rather the cry for bloodshed. Nonetheless, in Jesus's death and resurrection, God's new planting, justice, and righteousness will flourish.

10. Those who reject and kill the beloved son are equated with "the chief priest and the Pharisees." They recognized that Jesus was exclusively addressing them. They contrast with the Jewish "multitudes" who consider Jesus to be a prophet. Thus, when Jesus interprets the parable by stating that "the kingdom of God will be take away from you and given to a nation producing the fruits of it," he is not implying that the kingdom of God will be taken away from the Jews as a whole and given to the Gentiles. Those (the "you") from whom the kingdom will be taken away are the specific Jewish leaders who have rejected him. The "nation" to whom the kingdom will be given could rightly be both a Jewish "nation" that does accept Jesus as well as a nation of the Gentiles.

This also appears within one of Jesus' confrontations with the Pharisees and the scribes. The confrontation concerned Jesus' disciples not obeying parts of the tradition, that of washing their hands before eating. Jesus calls the Pharisees and scribe hypocrites because even though they legally obey the precepts of God's law, their hearts are far from him. Peter notes to Jesus that Pharisees were offended by his words. In response, Jesus says, "Every plant which my heavenly Father has not planted will be rooted up. Let them along; they are blind guides. And if a blind man leads a blind man, both will fall into a pit" (Mt 15:1-14). Jesus speaks here, as he did within his vineyard parable, of "my heavenly Father" planting plants. Those plants that were not planted by his Father, however; here those Pharisees who do not accept him as the divine heavenly Son of the Father will be uprooted by his Father precisely because of their nonacceptance of Jesus, his Son. Thus it is not the Jewish nation as such that is rejected, but those who, in their blindness, fail to recognize the Father's Son.

Likewise, the stone, Jesus, that the Jewish leaders have rejected, the Lord (God the Father, the vineyard owner) will make the very cornerstone of his kingdom (see Mt 21:43). Implied in his making Jesus the cornerstone is the Father's raising him from the dead.[11] Thus Jesus will be the living cornerstone of a living building—the new temple of God's kingdom.[12] In so doing, "the multitude," which the Jewish authorities feared because they considered Jesus "a prophet," will rejoice, for they will recognize that this is "the Lord's doing, and it is marvelous in our eyes." They will rejoice not simply in Jesus being "a prophet," but also in his being, as the risen and living cornerstone of God's kingdom, the Father "beloved Son."

11. Although Jesus only quotes of Ps 118:22-23, the entire psalm is important. It first repeatedly professes that God's "steadfast love endures forever." It next tells of the man who is hated and encompassed on all sides yet will take refuge and triumph in the Lord. "I shall not die, but I shall live." It is in his being saved from his enemies and in his triumphant living that he is the stone rejected by the builders and yet has become cornerstone. This is the marvel that the Lord has done. Although Jesus does not quote it, the next verse is significant (so significant that one wonders why he did not quote it): "This is the day which the Lord has made; let us rejoice and be glad in it." The day of Jesus' triumph, the day of his resurrection, was made by God his Father, and in that there is rejoicing. Unsurprisingly, the refrain recited after the Scripture readings for Lauds, the minor hours, and Vespers for the Octave of Easter within the Roman Breviary is this very verse. We will also see that Psalm 118 plays an important role in interpreting Jesus' passion, death, and resurrection within the Passion Narratives.

12. In the Acts of the Apostles, Peter proclaims to Jewish rulers, elders, scribes, and high priests that although they crucified Jesus, "God raised him from the dead." In raising Jesus, God is declaring: "This is the stone [Jesus] which was rejected by you builders, but which has become the head of the corner. And there is no salvation in no one else, for there is no other name under heaven given among men by which we must be saved" (Acts 4:10-12). In that act of being crucified, Jesus became the universal Savior, and because of that very salvific act, God made him the definitive cornerstone—the Lord.

In his First Letter, Peter elaborates the point. He exhorts: "Come to him, that living stone, rejected by men but in God's sight chosen and precious; and like living stones be yourselves built into a spiritual house, to be a holy priesthood, to offer spiritual sacrifices acceptable to God through Jesus Christ." For Peter, God has fulfilled Isaiah 28:16 (though Peter somewhat changes the Isaiah text): "Behold, I am laying in Zion a stone, a cornerstone chosen and precious, and he who believes in him will not be put to shame." This stone is precious to believers because they recognize that, although it was rejected, it "has become the head of the corner." To those who disbelieve, Peter states, referring to Isaiah 8:14-15, that Jesus will be a stumbling stone: "'The stone that will make men stumble, a rock that will make them fall'; for they will stumble because they disobey the word, as they were destined to do" (1 Pt 2:4-8).

Whether Peter had Jesus' parable in mind when preaching and writing is debatable. But it is obvious that he has, in many ways, provided his own theological interpretation to that parable by employing the same text that Jesus used to interpret the parable: Ps 118:22-23. Moreover, in his Letter, he even interprets Jesus' enigmatic statement in Mt 21:44 about people being broken to pieces and crushed by the stone. For Peter, their unbelief is their downfall.

Here we perceive why Jesus on the one hand narrates a parable about a vineyard owner and on the other hand interprets it by means of a building analogy. The parable narrates the prelude of what is and will take place—God the Father has sent his beloved son to his Jewish people, his vineyard, to reap the fruit of that vineyard, the fruit of holiness, and yet he will be rejected and killed by the Jewish authorities. Jesus provides his Father's future and definitive response to this analogical parable by employing a new metaphor or analogy, that of his Father building a building—despite his Son being rejected and killed, he will make his beloved Son the living cornerstone of his kingdom (the new vineyard), and within that kingdom Jesus will be the living keystone of the new temple, in which the Father will receive the authentic and living fruit of true worship and honor. In a sense, Jesus, in becoming the new living cornerstone of God's kingdom, also becomes the new living vineyard, the new living vine, from which will grow an abundance of living fruit—the faithful who believe and live in him.[13] Although Jesus' interweaving of these different analogies makes for complexity, it does provide an abundance of revelation as to who Jesus consciously sees himself to be, the future narrative of his salvific acts, and his Father's eventual culminating response to whole future scenario. The truth that directs and governs both analogies is the truth contained in the Father's (the vineyard owner's) words: "my beloved son," that is, Jesus' conscious awareness that he is that beloved Son. Within his parable, Jesus reveals not only that he is conscious of being the Father's beloved Son but also how his love will be manifested—in his being rejected and killed. Yet he is equally aware that, precisely because he is rejected, his Father will establish in him, the living cornerstone, his everlasting vineyard/kingdom of his living and glorious heavenly temple that is the church.

This parable and its interpretation offer another example of Jesus becoming Jesus. Jesus, as his beloved Son, has been sent by the Father, and he will manifest his divine Sonship within the act of his being rejected as the Father's Son—through his condemnation, passion, and death. But this act of rejection will be the catalyst for the Father to designate him, in raising him from the dead, as the cornerstone, for within his saving acts, in his becoming Jesus, he has become the keystone of God's kingdom, wherein holiness will be attained and true worship will be offered to his Father. Only in his name, Jesus (YHWH-Saves), is there salvation.

13. In John's Gospel, Jesus refers to himself as the vine, of which his disciples are the branches. This living union between Jesus, the vine, and believers, the branches, will produce much fruit (see Jn 15:1-8).

"No One Knows Who the Son
Is Except the Father"

A passage that would fit easily within the Gospel of John makes its presence within the Gospels of Matthew and Luke notably significant. Luke tells us that Jesus "rejoiced in the Spirit" and so joyfully addressed this prayer to his Father: "I thank you Father, Lord of heaven and earth, that you have hidden these things from the wise and understanding and revealed them to babes; yea, Father, for such was your gracious will." In what was Jesus rejoicing, a joy induced by the Spirit dwelling within him? Jesus' Spirit-filled joy resided in his gratitude to his Father: "I thank you Father, Lord of heaven and earth." Jesus' joyful Spirit-imbued gratitude springs from his Father having hidden "these things" from the wise while having "revealed them to babes."[14] Now what has the Father willed to keep hidden from the learned but graciously willed to reveal to infants? What are "these things?"

Having concluded his Spirit-imbued prayer of joyful gratitude to his Father, Jesus proclaims: "All things have been delivered to me by my Father; and no one knows who the Son is except the Father, or who the Father is except the Son and anyone to whom the Son chooses to reveal him" (Mt 11:25-27 and Lk 10:21-22; see also Jn 3:35, 5:20, 6:36, 7:29, 10:15, 17:25). "All things" have been given to Jesus by his Father, the Father whom he just addressed in joyful prayer. The "these things" that the Father revealed to children is contained within the "all things" that the Father has given to Jesus. But why has the Father given "all things," including those "things" that he has revealed to children, to Jesus? The Father's relationship to Jesus contains the answer.

---

14. Jesus' use of the term "babe" does not designate physical infants, but rather those who have a child-like trust and openness to God. Thus they are unlike "the wise and understanding," who are confident in and so satisfied with their own learning. In their scholarly arrogance, they are not docile toward or trusting in God.

This is seen when Jesus' disciples ask him who is the greatest in the kingdom of heaven. He brings a child into their midst and tells them that unless they become like little children, they will not enter the kingdom of heaven. Humility, Jesus proclaims, is the key to being great in the heavenly kingdom. Therefore no one should despise children (and implied those who are like them, "for I tell you that in heaven their angels always behold the face of my Father who is in heaven" (Mt 18:1-11). Because the heavenly angels behold the face of Jesus' heavenly Father, to see the human face of Jesus is to see the earthly face of his heavenly Son. On earth, both the heavenly angels and the heavenly Son protect the Father's children.

The Father's Paternal Knowing of His Son

"No one knows who the Son is except the Father, or who the Father is except the Son." Jesus is professing that the relationship between he and the Father is absolutely and categorically singular. "No one" designates that only the Father has comprehensive personal intimate knowledge of his Son and no one but the Son has comprehensive personal intimate knowledge of his Father. "No one" specifies that their exclusive interrelated knowledge of one another differs in kind, and not simply in degree, from the knowledge that anyone else might have of the Father and the Son. Given that the Father is God, the Son must be God, for only if such is the case would such a one-of-a-kind manner of knowing be applicable. "No one" excludes everyone who is not God.[15]

Within the Father's exclusive knowing of his Son, he delivers all things to his Son. It is not because the Son first knows the Father that he receives all things, but rather because the Father first actively knows that his Father actively gives him all things. Being the Father necessitates that the Father originates—fathers—the exclusive mutual knowing between himself and his Son. The Son, because he is the Son, cannot initiate, cannot "father," the mutual knowing between him and the Father. The Father alone knows the Son, because he fathers his fatherly knowing of his Son. So, Jesus declares that only the Father knows the Son prior to his declaring that only the Son knows the Father. Within and through the Father's originate fatherly knowing of his Son, the Son simultaneously becomes aware of his being known by the Father as his Son. In the Son's knowing that he is known by his Father as the Father's Son, the Son simultaneously comes to know his Father, and within this "coming to know" his Father he simultaneously comes to know what his Father knows, that he himself is the Father's Son. In being known by the Father as the Father' Son, the Son knows the Father and himself as the Father's Son. Thus the Father's fatherly act of knowing his Son is the one and the same simultaneous act by which and in which the Father knows his Son and the Son knows his Father.

Now the Father, in his fatherly knowing of his Son, gives complete knowledge of himself to his Son. Only in this act, within his fatherly knowing of the

---

15. The fact that the "Father" Jesus is addressing is "Lord of heaven and earth" designates him as the one supreme Creator God and as such is heaven and earth's Lord. Thus, if that divine Father is his Father, then Jesus, as the Father's Son, is equally divine. Also, the mere fact that Jesus addresses "the Lord of heaven and earth" as "Father" intimates that he possesses a filial relationship with the Lord God that warrants such an intimate and informal address.

Son, is the Father actually being "Father," acting in a fully fatherly manner. Not to have given full paternal knowledge of himself to his Son would demand the Father is not authentically being fatherly toward his Son, and thus his Son, not knowing fully his Father, would not truly be his Son. The Father is "Father" precisely because in the knowing of his Son he is giving full paternal knowledge of himself to the Son. Only in receiving complete paternal knowledge of his Father, in his being fully known by his Father, is the Son actually the Son—knowing, as Son, all that his Father is. It is within this complete paternal fatherly knowing of his Son, through which the Son comes to know completely his Father, that the Father delivers "all things" to his Son, for to know fully the Father is to know all.

We now clearly perceive why "no one knows who the Son is except the Father, or who the Father is except the Son." Only within their exclusive mutual paternal and filial acts of knowing one another do they manifest completely who each is in relation to one another—the Father in knowing his Son manifests that he is truly the Father in relation to his Son, and the Son in knowing his Father manifests that he is truly the Son in relation to his Father. The Father and the Son only come to know their own distinct subjective identities as "Father of the Son" and "Son of the Father" in knowing one another. They do not know themselves apart from one another, as if they possessed identities independently from one another. Their identities are exclusively and completely predicated upon their interrelational knowing of one another. The Father only knows himself as Father, possessing his own identity, in knowing his Son and the Son only knows himself as Son, possessing his own identity, in knowing his Father.

The Father's Paternal Fathering of His Son

Because Jesus speaks of a divine manner of knowing, this divine manner of knowing bespeaks, by ontological necessity, a divine manner of being. Knowledge is only authentic knowledge if it is the knowing of what actually is. Epistemology must be metaphysically founded upon ontology. For this mutually exclusive divine knowing of the Father of his Son and the Son of his Father to be true, that they do comprehensively know the truth of one another, demands that the Father be the Father of his Son only in relation to his Son and that the Son be Son of his Father only in relation to his Father. These divine exclusive mutual relational acts of knowing between the Father and the Son explicitly comprise within themselves the divine exclusive mutual relational acts by which the Father is the Father of his Son and the Son is the Son of his Father, and thus they are who they are only as they exist in relation to one another. Thus "to know" and "to be" are one and the same act among the Father and the Son. The Father fathers his exclusive knowing of his Son in his ontological act of fathering the being of his Son. The Son's exclusive knowing of his Father is within the same ontological act of his being fathered by the Father as the Father's Son, for in being ontologically fathered by his Father, and so being known by the Father, the Son simultaneously knows his Father as the one in whom he is ontologically fathered. Epistemologically, the singular and exclusive manner in which the Father and Son alone know one another is ontologically founded upon the singular and exclusive manner in which the Father and Son exist in relation to one another—the Father being the Son's Father and the Son being the Father's Son.[16] Conceptually, the term "Father" contains the term "Son," for the Father only is Father in fathering his Son. And, conceptually, the term "Son" contains within it the term "Father," for the Son is only the Son by being fathered by his Father. Ontologically, being the Father of the Son the Father epistemologically only knows himself as the Son's Father. Ontologically, being the Son of the Father the Son epistemologically only knows himself as the Father's Son. The Father only knows himself as Father in knowing himself as the Son's Father. The Son only knows himself as Son in knowing himself as the Father's Son.[17] Therefore the Father and the Son onto-

16. An interesting question arises. If the Son perfectly knows the Father and thus knows all that the Father knows, how is it that he does not know the last day? Apparently, this would be one of "those things" the Son knows in that "all things" were given to him by the Father. Exhorting his disciples to be prepared for the last day, Jesus states: "But of that day or that hour, not even the angels in heaven know, nor the Son, but only the Father" (Mk 13:32). Not only do the angels living in heaven not know the day or hour (even though they would presumably have access to such knowledge), but also the Son, who surely should know, does not even know. Lacking such divine knowledge, it could then be concluded that the Son is not truly divine. But it is actually "*the* Son" who does not know that places the Son in a singular and exclusive relation to "*the* Father." The traditional interpretation of this passage, going back to the Fathers of the Church, is to acknowledge that "the Son" *as man* does not know the time of the last day, while "the Son" *as God* does. Such an argument would validate the authenticity of the Son living as a genuine human being. Jesus, as the Son, is given "all things" that pertain to the Father as Father, but not all things pertain to the economy of salvation and so not given to Jesus as man.

17. A human analogy might be helpful here. Only in knowing his wife does a husband know that he is her husband. Only in knowing her husband does a wife know that she is his wife. But men and women are more than just husbands and wives. They are not fully defined as who they are in being husbands and wives. A spouse may die, but that other partner continues to live as an unmarried spouse. This is not the case between the Father and the Son. The Father

logically constitute the one being or nature of the one God. Because the Father is the Son's Father and the Son is the Father's Son, and so only exist in relation to one another, the one being of God is constituted by their mutual interrelationship. And because the Father and the Son are constitutive of who the one God is, the terms "Father" and Son" are not predicated of God accidentally, that is, as mere traits or qualities predicated of the being of God. Rather, they are predicated properly of God, for they define God's ontological manner of existence. Thus the terms "Father" and "Son" are not simply human analogies that are employed by human beings to describe God, but analogical terms that define God's very being: God is ontologically the Father and the Son.[18]

The Father's Willing and the Son's Choosing

Having declared that no one knows the Father except the Son, Jesus concludes with an extremely significant "and." "And anyone to whom the Son chooses to reveal him." Being the Son, and so the perfect ontological image of the Father, possessing singular knowledge of the Father, he alone is so ontologically constituted as to reveal the Father in the Father's fullness.[19] Jesus, as the Son of

---

is fully who he is as Father only in fathering his Son and so existing in relation to his Son, and the Son is fully who he is only in being fathered as the Father's Son, and so existing in relation to his Father. Independent of their relationship, the Father not only would not be the "Father," but also "he" would also not exist and the Son not only would not be the "Son," but "he" would also not exist. Their very divine being as Father and Son is dependent upon one another.

18. This is why the title "Mother" cannot properly be applied to God. God may have some "motherly" traits, but the title "Mother" does not ontologically define how God exists. To be a "mother," a woman must receive from her husband and in so receiving becomes a "mother." God is "Father" because he never receives, but he is the absolute unqualified giver. It is in the act of giving himself in fathering his Son that the Father *is* Father. The Father gives himself completely to humankind in giving his Son. Although the Son receives all from the Father, receiving it as Son, he is the complete and unqualified active image of his Father. Being the Son, Jesus gives himself completely to humankind and in so doing reveals, makes present, the active giving of his Father to humankind. The Holy Spirit is the act in which the Father completely gives himself in love to the Son and the act in which the Son completely gives himself in love to the Father. The Father and Son completely give themselves to humankind within the love of the Holy Spirit. There is no passivity within the Trinity itself, nor is there any passivity within their salvific acts within the economy. Significantly, God revealed his ontological manner of existence, and he did so by ontologically defining himself as the Father, the Son, and the Holy Spirit. Human beings do not define who God is. God defines himself because only he knows who he truly is as the Father, the Son, and the Holy Spirit.

19. The Father, being the Son's Father, cannot reveal himself as Father apart from his Son because he is only ontologically the Father in the fathering of his Son, and so all that he does by way of revealing himself ontologically necessitates that it be done through his Son. Similar-

God incarnate, is the only one competent and capable of revealing the Father, for he alone, as the Son incarnate, truly knows the Father. Jesus, as the Son of God existing as man, humanly knows the Father in a singular filial manner, for he knows himself as his singular divine Son and so, as man, is fit to reveal his Father to others. This is why Jesus is prayerfully rejoicing.

This event began with Jesus rejoicing in the Spirit-filled gratitude that it was "the gracious will" of his Father that those "things" that were hidden from the learned were revealed to children. Jesus subsequently declared that "all things" were delivered to him by his Father, the entire whole of which is contained in his exclusive knowing his Father as Son. And now, as Son, Jesus can reveal his Father to whomever he chooses. What the Son chooses to do, in accordance with the gracious will of his Father, for which he is grateful and in which he rejoices in the Spirit, is to reveal to mere babes his exclusive knowledge of the Father. The Father wills to reveal hidden things to children, and Jesus, as Son, chooses to reveal to children what was hidden—his Father. Thus, for Jesus, in the joy of the Spirit, to say "I thank you Father" is for him to rejoice in gratitude for what the Father is doing through him, as Son—revealing his Father. To rejoice in his Father is for Jesus to rejoice in himself as Son, and this twofold act of joy is imbued by and in the Spirit.

Thus the Holy Spirit rouses and imbues Jesus' joyful gratitude to his Father for revealing to mere infants what is hidden to the learned. What the Father has chosen to reveal to children is his Son, and what the Son now wills to reveal to children is his Father. This twofold choosing and willing, that of the Father and the Son, is roused by and imbued with the Holy Spirit, for only in the enactment of this choosing and willing, the revealing of the Son by his Father and the revealing of Father by his Son, does the rejoicing in the Spirit come to be. Through, with, and in the Holy Spirit, the Father joyfully wills and the Son joyfully chooses to reveal one another, for in so doing, they bring their own joy to the merest children.

---

ly, the Son cannot reveal himself apart from his Father because he is only ontologically the Son in being the Father's Son, and so all that he does by way revealing himself ontologically necessitates that it be done through his revealing the Father as the Father's Son. Again, this is why Jesus never speaks of himself as Son but only speaks of "my Father." In revealing his Father, he reveals himself as Son. Likewise, the Father, within the New Testament theophanies, such as Jesus' baptism or transfiguration, never speaks of himself as Father but always speaks of "my Son." In revealing his Son, he reveals himself as Father.

The Holy Spirit's Joyful Loving Act

The Holy Spirit lies at the heart of the Father's joyful willing and the Son's joyful choosing. This outward expression manifests a prior interior joy. Within the Holy Spirit's joyful arousing and imbuing of the Father and Son to reveal one another to children lies the primordial eternal joyful arousing and imbuing of the mutual joyful love of the Father and the Son. The very act of the Father's fathering, which ontologically constitutes the Father as Father, is imbued with the joyful love of the Holy Spirit. Thus the Holy Spirit, within the very act of the Father's fathering, conforms the Father to be joyful loving Father of his Son. Likewise, the Son, in being fathered in the joyful love of the Holy Spirit, is conformed to be, in the same Holy Spirit, the joyful loving Son of the Father. Within the Father's one fathering act, the Holy Spirit conforms the Father to be the joyful loving Son's Father and conforms the Son to be the joyful loving Father's Son. Only in the Father fathering his Son in the joyful love of the Holy Spirit is he the loving Son's Father, and only in the joyful love of the Holy Spirit, the same joyful love of the Spirit in which he was fathered, is the Son the loving Father's Son—the Son who joyfully loves his Father in the same Spirit in whom he himself is lovely fathered. As the Father and Son lovingly rejoice in one another in the Holy Spirit, so now in their loving rejoicing they reveal, in the same joy of the Spirit, themselves to the merest babes so that such children can share in their mutual love and joy. This is the cause of Jesus' filial Spirit-filled rejoicing in prayerful gratitude to his Father.[20]

Jesus Becoming Jesus

Here we perceive the heart of who Jesus is and why he is called "Jesus." Jesus, as the Son of God incarnate, is to reveal his Father, as only he, as Son, can. And only in his fully revealing the Father does he fully reveal that he is the Father's Son. The revealing of his Father is therefore Jesus' consummate salvific act as Son. Jesus becomes Jesus when Jesus reveals his Father.

To know the Father as Jesus the Son knows his Father is to share in the divine life that Jesus possesses as his Son. What is of the utmost importance is

---

20. In the above lengthy section on the ontological relationships among the persons of the Trinity, I have attempted to provide, exclusively, a theological interpretation founded upon Mt 11:25-27 and Lk 10:21-22. It would be helpful to also read my *The Father's Spirit of Sonship: Reconceiving the Trinity* (Edinburgh: T&T Clark, 1995). What I propose there theologically and philosophically complements what is stated here.

that Jesus, as Son, does not and cannot reveal his Father by using words. Simply telling others that God is their Father would be insufficient, because they have little idea of what it means for God to be "Father." Simply to tell others that they are children of the Father would be of little help to them, since they would possess little self-awareness of what being a child of the Father encompasses or entails. Moreover, it would not be true. One's knowledge of the Father is predicated upon one's manner of being, that is, on one's being in a filial relationship with the Father. Jesus, being the Father's Son, provides him singular and exclusive knowledge of his Father. For others to know the Father comparable to Jesus' own filial knowledge of his Father demands that they too possess a similar singular and exclusive manner of being in relationship to the Father comparable to Jesus' own relationship to his Father as the Father's Son. To tell others that God is their Father or that they are his children without their having acquired and so participating in a new kind of relationship with the Father would be telling them a lie.

Only within and because of Jesus' salvific acts, enacted in the Holy Spirit, is it possible for human beings to share, in analogous manner, Jesus' own filial Spirit-filled relationship with his Father and so come to know his Father in a manner comparable to his own. Thus Jesus' saving acts not only manifest the fullness of who the Father is—the fullness of his paternal love and mercy—and so reveal himself as the Father's Son, but they also make it possible for others to share in a new relationship with the Father, comparable to his own, and so come to know truly the Father as their Father, comparable to Jesus' own knowledge of his Father. The same saving acts by which Jesus fully reveals his Father simultaneously make it possible for others to become children of his Father. These saving acts are first manifested within Jesus' public ministry. Jesus' loving and merciful priestly and prophetic acts—miracles, exorcisms, healings, forgiveness of sins—display, and so make real, his Father's love and mercy and manifest his own divine Sonship. Definitively, through his passion and death, Jesus overcomes those obstacles—sin and death—that render such an intimate personal relation with his Father, and so an intimate personal knowledge of the Father, impossible. In his loving sacrificial death, Jesus reconciles us to his Father. In his resurrection, within his own new Spirit-filled humanity, Jesus makes present a new holy humanity freed from sin and death and abounding in the love and life of the Holy Spirit. Through his outpouring of the Holy Spirit on Pentecost, Jesus makes possible for others to share in his risen Spirit-filled humanity. Those who come to faith in him and are baptized come to share in his risen humanity and so are transformed, through the indwelling of the Holy Spirit, into his filial likeness. Having been set free from sin and death and having been transformed into Jesus' filial likeness by sharing his own Spirit of Sonship, the faithful come to be children of his Father in a manner analogous to the manner in which he himself is the Father's Son. Precisely within this new living communion, Jesus, the Father's Son, reveals to the little ones his Father, for they now see the Father through his own filial eyes, and so together with him they rejoice in the Spirit that what has been hidden from learned and clever has now been revealed to them. Thus those infants to whom Jesus, the Son, has chosen to reveal his Father are no longer part of the "no one." In him they now truly know his Father.

This is what it means to be a member of the church, which gives expression to the kingdom of God. The church is composed of those who live in Jesus as the Christ and so in the same Spirit know his Father and reap the benefits of his Father's kingdom. Having been separated from the "no one" group and placed with Jesus, through his indwelling and transformative Spirit of Sonship, within a living divine communion with his Father, the babes now possess a filial knowledge of God as their Father that differs in kind and not simply in degree from those who are not Christian. Those who are not Christian still belong in the "no one" group who do not authentically know Jesus' Father because they do not share in his filial relationship with his Father. Thus, as Jesus, the Father's Son, possesses an exclusive and singular divine knowledge of his Father as the Father's divine Son, so Christians, in a comparable manner as "adopted" children of the Father, possess an exclusive and singular knowledge of their Father as the Father's children. Within the above, we now perceive the singular manner in which the term "adoption" is used when applied to those who come to faith in Jesus and are baptized in the Holy Spirit and are thus said to be adopted sons and daughters of the Father.

When a married couple adopts a child, they legally become the child's parents, with the corresponding rights, privileges, and obligations. The child, in turn, possesses all the rights and privileges (and obligations) of being their child. The parents strive to love their child as their own, as a true mother and father do; and the child strives to love his or her adoptive parents, as his or her true mother and father. But the parents are not the biological mother and father, nor then is the child biologically from them. The whole concept of adoption is founded upon this lack of a biological relationship. This is equally true of a man who marries a woman who has children from a previous marriage. The woman is the biological parent, but the father is not, though he can become the legal father of her children. He may love her biological children as his own, but they are not biologically his children. If that couple conceives a child, then both they and their child are biologically united, and that child becomes a half-brother or half-sister to the other children born of the same mother. Although analogous to human adoption, the Christian understanding of being adopted children of the Father is radically different.

Only the Son is ontologically God, for he possesses the same divine nature as his Father as the Father's Son. Human beings, unlike the Son, are not by nature sons or daughters of the Father, for they are by nature human beings and so not begotten of the Father. But to be "adopted" children of the Father does not mean, as within human adoption, that Christians do not participate in the very same divine life of Father as that of his only begotten Son. To be adopted as children of the Father means that Christians share the same divine life, the same "ontological" life, of the Son for they are begotten in the same Spirit as the Son.[21] The Holy Spirit, the Spirit of Sonship, does transform Christians into the likeness of Jesus the Son such that they, in union with Jesus the Son, share in the same divine filial life and so actually do have the same Father. To be in communion with the risen Jesus, through the indwelling and transforming presence of the Holy Spirit, is to share in his filial relationship with the Father and so to partake truly of his own Sonship. It is this actual sharing in the filial divine life of the Son, through transforming the Spirit of Sonship, that makes this adoption as children of the Father different in kind from human adoption. Thus the Christian notion of divine adoption simultaneously contains both a negative and a positive aspect. As adopted, Christians are not

21. Within the Gospel of John, Jesus brings out this same truth when speaking with Nicodemus. Jesus tells him: "Truly, truly I say to you unless one is born anew [from above], he cannot see the kingdom of God." Nicodemus responds, "How can a man be born when he is old? Can he enter a second time into his mother's womb and be born?" To this Jesus says, "Truly, truly I say to you, unless one is born of water and the Spirit, he cannot enter the kingdom of God. That which born of flesh is flesh, and that which is born of the Spirit is spirit." Human beings are naturally born of the flesh, but by being born of the Holy Spirit, one can enter the kingdom of God because one is born into a filial relationship with the Father—to live in God's kingdom is to see, to live with, the Father as the Father's children in union with Jesus, the Son. This is why, when Nicodemus again asks how this can be, Jesus responds, "Truly, truly I say to you, we speak of what we know, and bear witness to what we have seen; but you do not receive our testimony. If I have told you earthly things and you do not believe, how can you believe if I tell you heavenly things?" (Jn 3:1-15). What Jesus knows and sees and to which he is bearing witness is that human beings on earth, those born of the flesh, can be born of the Holy Spirit and be children of the Father within his kingdom. The reason he can testify to this is because he knows that he himself, in heaven, has been begotten, in the Holy Spirit, of the Father. If Nicodemus cannot believe that human beings can be born of the Spirit on earth, how is he ever going to believe that Jesus was eternally begotten as Son in heaven?

sons as the Son is Son but nonetheless do share, through the Holy Spirit, in his filial life and relationship to the Father as that of the Son, and so the Father is truly their Father as well. The negative aspect is in accord with human adoption—the adopted child's father is not actually his father, and so Christians are not begotten from the Father. The positive aspect accentuates that, although there is a difference between the Son and the adopted, the adopted do share in the Sonship of the Son and so his Father is theirs as well. It is this sharing in the Sonship of the Son that makes it both analogous to human adoption and radically different from human adoption. By sharing in the filial life of the Son, Christians, in a sense, are "ontologically" related to God the Father, for they are related to the Father in living communion with Jesus, his only begotten Son possessing the same Spirit of Sonship as the Son. Christians enter the communal, familial life of the Trinity because in communion with the Son, through the Holy Spirit, the Father is their Father. It is precisely because of the unique Christian form of adoption, different in kind from human adoption, that Christians possess both a singular filial relationship to the Father and a singular filial knowledge of the Father that is different from those who are not Christians.[22]

22. Paul develops this understanding beautifully, and it is founded upon the Synoptic tradition (particularly in the present discussion from Matthew and Luke). Jesus became man and died and rose "so that we might receive adoption as sons" (Gal 4:4-5). Thus those who are united to Christ are "a new creation; the old has passed away, behold, the new has come," for God has reconciled us to himself through Christ. "God was in Christ reconciling the world to himself" (2 Cor 5:16-19; see also Gal 6:15). This is founded upon the truth that those who are baptized die and rise with Christ, "so you must consider yourselves dead to sin and alive to God in Christ Jesus" (Rom 6:1-11). Being a living new creation in Christ, "God's love has been poured into our hearts through the Holy Spirit who has been given to us" (Rom 5:5). As God his Father poured out his love upon his Son, the Spirit of Sonship, so the Father now pours out his love upon those who abide in his Son. They know the Father's Spirit-filled love just as Jesus, the Son, knows the Father Spirit-filled love. This Spirit-filled paternal love in turn empowers his children to love their Father, being the loving Spirit of Sonship, as Jesus, the Son, loves his Father. The climatic conclusion comes in that, because we are sons of God, bearing the Spirit of Sonship, we in communion with Jesus can cry out, as does he, "Abba! Father!" (Rom 8:15). Because Christians are sons of God, "God has sent the Spirit of his Son into our hearts, crying, 'Abba! Father!'" (Gal 4:6). This ability to call God "Father" is "the Spirit himself bearing witness with our spirit that we are children of the God" (Rom 8:16). This cry "Abba! Father!" bespeaks a new filial relationship with God. Because Christians possess a new filial manner of being—that is, living in Christ and so sharing in his divine Sonship—they also possess a new filial manner of knowing God, that is, as Father. Christians are presently groaning "inwardly as we wait for adoption as sons, the redemption of our bodies" (Rom 8:23). This will be achieved when Jesus comes in glory and we share fully in his resurrected divine life and so share fully in the life of our Father. This is all in keeping with the Father's eternal plan in that "in love he destined us to adoption as sons through Jesus Christ" (Eph 1:5; translation slightly altered).

Paul's proclamation concerning adoption is founded upon his doctrine of the body of Christ.

Through and because of all of his Spirit-filled saving acts, Jesus is becoming Jesus because he is revealing the divine plenitude of his Father's Spirit-imbued love and mercy, and in so doing he is simultaneously revealing himself to be the Father's Spirit-imbued loving and merciful Son, for only the Son could express the fullness of the Father's love and mercy as witnessed, ultimately, in his own filial loving sacrificial death on the cross. And in raising Jesus gloriously from the dead through the Holy Spirit and enthroning him upon his own heavenly throne by making him now also "Lord of heaven and earth," the Father manifests the fullness of his paternal love for his Son, thus authenticating that Jesus is truly Jesus—YHWH-Saves.[23] This will find its full completion at Jesus' Second Coming, for only then will Jesus, the Son, fully reveal to those little ones who reside in him his full knowledge of his Father. Then all— the Father, the Son, and the little ones—will forever thankfully rejoice in the fullness of the Holy Spirit, the Father gratefully rejoicing in his Son, the Son

---

This doctrine also finds its basis within the Synoptic tradition in that by being in union with Jesus, through the Holy Spirit, one is in communion with his Father. Because Jesus is gloriously risen from the dead, Christians can share and live within his new humanity. Christians are "nourished and knit together" as one body with their one head, Jesus Christ (Col 1:18-19; see also Eph 1:23). "For just as the body is one and has many members, and all the members of one body, though many, are one body, so it is with Christ. For by one Spirit we were baptized into one body—Jews and Greeks, slaves and free—and all were made to drink of one Spirit" (1 Cor 12:12-13; see also Rom 12:4-5, Gal 3:28, Eph 2:13-18, and Col 1:15 and 3:15). Being one body in Christ, we have both (Jew and Gentile) "access in one Spirit to the Father" (Eph 2:18). Thus "there is one body and one Spirit, just as we were called into one hope that belongs to your call, one Lord, one faith, one baptism, one God and Father of us all" (Eph 4:4-6). We are not only one body *in* Christ, but we are the one body *of* Christ, for we share in his one life, that of the Holy Spirit (see 1 Cor 12:27). Because Christians are members of Jesus' body, they share in the divine filial life that befits him as their head and so in same breath of the one Spirit rightly and properly call out together with him "Abba! Father!" Thus Paul's doctrine of the body of Christ is not a metaphorical or figurative symbol. He is speaking of one living reality—Jesus, the head, in union with those who are united to him, sharing in the one life of the Holy Spirit. Precisely because it is a reality, Christians share in the filial being of the Son, the Holy Spirit, and so share in a personal filial vision and knowledge of his Father.

Therefore evangelization is such a loving imperative. Those who are not Christian are deprived of an intimate personal filial relationship with God as their Father in Jesus, his Son, through the transforming love of the Spirit of Sonship.

23. Obviously, once again, as Jesus, the incarnate Son, reveals himself as YHWH-Saves in revealing his Father, he also reveals his Father as YHWH-Saves, for his choosing to reveal his Father to children is in accord with the saving will of the Father. Likewise, because the joyful impulse of the Holy Spirit imbues the Father's willingness to reveal what was hidden and Jesus' choosing to reveal what was hidden, knowledge of his Father, the Holy Spirit is also salvifically acting as YHWH-Saves. Again, to rightly know who the man Jesus is as YHWH-Saves is to perceive the entire Trinity.

gratefully rejoicing in his Father, and the little ones gratefully rejoicing in their Father and in their brother, Jesus, the Father's Son.

Jesus' Human Self-Consciousness

Here we must bring this epistemological and ontological examination of the Father's and the Son's mutual and relational divine knowledge and being literally back to earth. Jesus declared, employing intelligible human words, "All things have been delivered to me by my Father." The "me" is Jesus and the "my Father" is the Father. It is Jesus *whom* only the Father knows as his Son in the joyful love of the Spirit, and it is Jesus *who* only knows the Father as his Son in the same joyful love of the Spirit. Jesus' declaration articulates the mystery of the Incarnation and, in so doing, the mystery of the Trinity. There are a number of pertinent conclusions concerning Jesus' conscious awareness that God is his Father in a singular and exclusive manner, and thus his own self-conscious awareness of being the Father's Son.

First, and most obvious, all the declarations of "my Father's house," "my Father," "my heavenly Father," and the like were spoken by the human Jesus. The "my" is a human "my," for it was spoken by a man and as such denotes Jesus' human self-consciousness and knowledge that he possessed a relationship with the Father that is reserved to himself alone and so enjoyed by no other human being.

Second, in humanly articulating "my" in relationship to his Father, Jesus synchronously gives expression to his own human self-consciousness awareness of who he is. To humanly say "my Father," Jesus consciously knows himself, in a human manner, to be the Father's Son. The "my," then, expresses a relationship that identifies the one to whom the "my" refers, the Father, and the one who is articulating the "my," Jesus, the Father's Son.

Third, the fact that Jesus exclusively identifies himself in relation to his Father, by using "my," means that he only became conscious of his own identity as Son through and within his human consciousness and knowledge of his Father. Jesus' human self-consciousness as Son does not originate from within the inner workings of his own human psyche, as if Jesus as Son simply discovered, through his own human introspection and self-analysis, his human identity as Son. Rather, it originates solely from within his becoming humanly self-conscious that God is his Father and thus attests to his own self-identity as Son. Thus, within the Incarnation, the Son of God becomes humanly conscious of himself as Son, and so knows himself as Son, only in being humanly conscious of his Father and so humanly knowing himself to be the Father's Son. Thus, as the divine Son knows himself as Son only in relation to his Father, so the incarnate Son is humanly conscious of himself as Son only in relation to his Father. It is being conscious of his filial relationship to his Father, in knowing the Father as "my," both as God and as man, that the Son perceives his own identity, for it is that filial relationship that ontologically constitutes his identity.

This accounts for why, within the Synoptic Gospels, Jesus never refers to himself as the "Son of God." He is indeed, but, precisely because he is the Son, Jesus wishes to focus attention not upon himself but upon his Father and so invariably refers not to himself as Son but to the Father as "my." Moreover, if Jesus referred to himself simply as the "Son of God," this would cause debate over what such a self-designation could mean, spawning confusion and erroneous conclusions. By identifying himself only in relationship to his Father, a relationship that is revealed to be singular and exclusive through his use of the word "my," Jesus clearly reveals the manner in which he is the Son—as the Father is God so he knows him as "my Father," that is, the Son, is equally God.[24]

Fourth, to humanly say "my" necessitates there being a human "I" who is saying it. In speaking of "my Father," by which he denotes his unique relation to and exclusive consciousness and knowledge of him, Jesus reveals the identity of the human "I" that lies within that human "my." The identity of that human "I" is the eternal Son of the Father. Who it is who is humanly saying "my Father" is the Son of the Father, and given that he is saying "my" in a human manner, the "I" from which this human "my" springs is the human "I" of the Son. Thus Jesus, in humanly saying "my" and in so doing divulging a human "I," personally articulates as a man the mystery of the Incarnation. Jesus can truthfully say, in an authentic human manner, "my Father," a human "my" that springs from a human "I," only if he who humanly says "my" is the *Son of God existing as man,* for only then is what is humanly said actually true.

Fifth, Jesus' saying "my Father" is similar to his walking on the water in the midst of the storm. But there is one significant difference. There he declared: "It is I" (*ego eimi*) and in so doing identified himself not only as their friend but also concurrently as God. The one who is humanly saying "I" is

---

24. Therefore Jesus silences the demon who says that he knows who he is: "the Holy one of God" (Mk 1:25; Lk 4:35). Such declarations, while literally true, only cause confusion because they are not set within the proper revelational context. Jesus' authentic identity as Son is only rightly understood in perceiving his singular relationship to his Father.

Jesus, and the identity of that human "I" is God. Here, through his humanly saying "my Father," Jesus specifies the exact manner in which he is God; he is identifying the divine subjective distinctiveness of who said, "It is I." Jesus humanly distinguishes his divine identity as the Father's Son and in so doing declares that he and the Father are both the one God, the one "I Am," revealed to Moses. In this light, when one is conceiving of God, one must now consider both the Father and the Son, for this is what Jesus has now revealed to be the case. In addressing God as "my Father," the one God must be the Father of the Son and Son of the Father.

Sixth, while we do not find many references to "the Spirit of God" or "the Holy Spirit," the two major places where the Spirit is mentioned are telling not only for the episodes in which we find them but also for the whole of Jesus' ministry. Jesus, as Son, rejoices in gratitude to his Father, a joy induced by the Spirit. Likewise, all of Jesus' actions and words are in the Spirit of God because he performs them as the Father's Son. Throughout the entirety of his public ministry, Jesus is manifesting that, as the Son, he acts in relation to and in communion with the Father and the Spirit. His acts, whether in deed or word, reveal the contributing communal associated acts of the Father and the Spirit.

Last, the same acts, words, and deeds by which Jesus reveals that he is the Father's Son, within the communion of the Spirit of God, are the same acts through which Jesus enacts his name as Savior. Through his saving word and deeds, Jesus evidences his identity as the Father's Son acting in the Spirit. And these saving acts, performed in the Spirit, provide, to those who believe Jesus to be the Father's Son and acknowledge him as such here upon earth, entrance to his heavenly Father. This is the goal and summit of salvation: to live with Jesus the Son in unity his Father within the communion of the Spirit. Those who do are the church. Thus to properly know in faith Jesus as Savior, and so be in communion with him, is to know the Father, the Son, and the Holy Spirit and to be in communion with them. The name Jesus is above all other names, and in no other name is there salvation.[25]

We now proceed to Part III, which examines the events that directly led to and so prefigured Jesus' passion, death, and resurrection. Part IV examines those saving events themselves: the Paschal Mystery.

25. This complements what I have proposed in "The Human 'I' of Jesus," *Irish Theological Quarterly* 62, no. 4 (1996/97): 259-68; "Jesus' Filial Vision of the Father," *Pro Ecclesia* 13, no. 2 (2004): 189-201; and "The Beatific Vision and the Incarnate Son: Furthering the Discussion," *Thomist* 70 (2006): 604-15. The last three essays are reprinted in my *Jesus: Essays in Christology* (Ave Maria, Fla.: Sapientia Press, 2014), 266-301.

꒦

PREFIGUREMENTS OF JESUS' PASSION, DEATH, AND RESURRECTION

*P*ART II examined some of the central theological elements surrounding Jesus' public ministry within the Synoptic Gospels—his mighty works of power, his authoritative teaching, and the revelation of himself as Son in relation to his Father. All that we have discerned will find its culmination in Jesus' passion, death, and resurrection.

Part III focuses upon the Christological, Trinitarian, and soteriological doctrines contained within those events that most approximately prefigure Jesus' passion, death, and resurrection. I first treat, in chapter 7, two events within Jesus' public ministry that provide an immediate anticipatory prophetic prologue to these events. The first is Peter's profession of faith, which not only proclaims who Jesus is, but also provides entrée into Jesus' teaching concerning his passion, death, and resurrection. To understand correctly who Jesus is as the Christ, the Son of the living God, one must also grasp that he is to suffer, die, and rise. Christology and soteriology are inextricably linked. Similarly, the Transfiguration prophetically prefigures, in a single act, the sequential saving acts of Jesus' passion, death, and resurrection, acts through which the Father transforms him, through the Holy Spirit, into the glorious Lord and Savior. Chapter 8 examines Jesus' triumphal entry into

Jerusalem. This event and what follows, up to his last supper with his disciples, also proximately prefigure Jesus' death and resurrection, specifically his triumphal entry as king into the new Jerusalem, where he will himself be the heavenly living temple. Thus this triumphal entry anticipates Jesus' founding the eschatological age, the everlasting kingdom of God his Father.

Both the Transfiguration and the triumphal entry into Jerusalem prophetically enact the manner in which Jesus, through his death and resurrection, will definitively become Jesus, YHWH-Saves, and in so doing manifests, as Peter professed, that he is truly the Christ, the Son of the living God. Within these foreshadowing events of the Paschal Mystery we also perceive the salvific roles that the Father and the Holy Spirit will play within Jesus' death and resurrection. Thus Peter's profession of faith, the Transfiguration, and the triumphal entry into Jerusalem all anticipate the full soteriological expression of the Incarnation and the Trinity.

Peter's profession of faith is the pivotal event within the Synoptic Gospels. First, Jesus asks about his own identity. Who do others say that he is, and more pointedly, who do his disciples believe him to be? Second, Peter, the soon-to-be designated leader of the Apostles, provides the answer. Third, although Peter on one level answers correctly, he does not fully fathom the significance of his own answer and so misconceives the meaning of his own declaration. Fourth, Jesus takes Peter's misconception as an opportunity to reveal more fully who he is and in so doing articulates more specifically the nature of his salvific ministry. Within this context, we now turn to the Synoptic accounts themselves.

Peter's Profession of Faith

Although Matthew (16:13-20) and Mark (8:27-30) specify that this event took place in "the district (Mt) or "villages" (Mk) "of Caesarea Philippi," Luke (9:18-21) simply begins his narrative by stating: "Now, it happened that as he [Jesus] was praying alone the disciples were with him; and he asked them."[1] Luke, as he did at Jesus' baptism, places this event within the context of Jesus praying and being in communion with his Father, and thus, as at his baptism, this communion is constituted in the Holy Spirit—their shared communion of love. On the one hand, Jesus is praying by himself. There is a singular "aloneness" about Jesus of which no one can share. He alone is the Son of his Father and so he alone, unlike his disciples, can pray, in the communion of the Holy Spirit, to his Father as his unique and exclusive divine Son. Within his prayerful worship of his Father, Jesus knows who he is; he is humanly self-conscious

---

1. All quotations in this section are from the above passages unless otherwise noted.

of his singular divine identity as the Father's Son. On the other hand, Jesus is not alone because "the disciples were with him." Although he alone can pray to God as his divine Father, Jesus' singular manner of praying is not apart from his disciples, for they "were with him." From within Jesus' prayerful "aloneness" with his Father and his incarnational "togetherness" with his disciples, Jesus first asks, "Who do the people say that I am?" and then "But who do you say that I am?" It is in knowing who Jesus is as the Christ, the Son of God, that one can come into communion with his Father. To be "with" Jesus is then to be taken into his "aloneness" and so share in his singular filial relationship with his Father through the communion of the Holy Spirit, and thus be identified as the Father's sons. The whole point of Jesus' enquiry is to lead his disciples into prayerful Spirit-filled communion with his Father through a proper knowledge of him as the Father's Son.[2]

Particularly within the first half of Mark's Gospel, Jesus' teaching and mighty works elicit wonder and amazement, causing many to question who he might be. This conjecturing as to Jesus' identity significantly finds its decisive expression in Jesus asking his disciples: "Who do men say that I am?" Jesus is obviously not asking, "Do people know my name?" Everybody knows him to be "Jesus." That is the mystery—who is Jesus? The question concerns his true identity, and this is the nature of Jesus' question—who do people think I truly am? Thus, although someone may know Jesus' name, only in knowing his authentic identity does one fully know Jesus and so grasp the full meaning of his name. To know who Jesus truly is to know fully the significance of his name— YHWH-Saves.

To the initial question as to who do others think he is, the disciples respond by saying that some people say he is John the Baptist, others Elijah or one of the prophets. Matthew adds Jeremiah. Luke specifies that "one of the old prophets has arisen." On one level, these designations seem rather bizarre because they all involve Jesus being identified as someone who has died and

---

2. Within the Gospel of Luke, Jesus is often found praying prior to or during decisive events—at his baptism and now in his querying his disciples as to who he is. Notably, Jesus also prayed before he chose the twelve Apostles. "In those days [Jesus] went out into the hills to pray; and all night he continued to pray to God. And when it was day, he called his disciples, and chose from them twelve, whom he named apostles." Significantly, his choice of Apostles, the future foundational leaders of his church, was done in accord with his Father's wishes. Jesus, as the incarnate Son, simply makes known what he has received from his Father. Also significant is not only that Simon is named first among the twelve, but also that Jesus, in choosing him, named him Peter. As the first named among the twelve, he is the rock in relation to the other eleven (Lk 6:12-16; see also Mt 10:2-4 and Mk 3:13-19).

who has come back to life.[3] On another level, these designations are revealing because they are all prophets and as such prophetically anticipate or foretell the coming of the Messiah. For Jesus to be one of these would then mean that he too is anticipatory to the coming of the Messiah. In this light, Peter's profession takes on its full significance. To the question as to who the disciples think he is, Peter responds, "You are the Christ." Jesus is not simply the reincarnation of an anticipatory prophet to the Messiah, but he is the actual Messiah, the Christ. In so doing, Peter is claiming that the entire previous biblical revelation, all that was foretold by the prophets of old, finds its culmination and completion in him.[4] Within Peter's profession of faith, the whole of the Old Testament, with Israel's full hope of redemption and long awaited deliverance, is subsumed within the very person of Jesus as the Messiah, and it is incorporated within him as its fulfillment. Jesus literally embodies the anticipatory and now being achieved in the Old Testament revelation, and so in this sense he is John the Baptist, Elijah, Jeremiah, or "one of the old prophets" who has arisen. Nonetheless, how did Peter (and the later apostolic church) understand such a designation—in what manner is Jesus the Christ?

In Mark's account, quoted above, Peter simply declares Jesus to be the Christ. In Matthew's account, Peter professes, "You are the Christ, the Son of the living God." Luke has Peter avowing, "The Christ of God."[5] Because it is

3. In Mark and Matthew, Herod believes that Jesus is John the Baptist come back to life, while others think he is Elijah or one of the prophets come back to life (see Mt 14:1-2 and Mk 6:14-15). In Luke, Herod is perplexed having heard that some think Jesus to be John raised from the dead or Elijah or one of the prophets. Herod thinks it cannot be John because "John I beheaded; but who is this about whom I hear such things?" (Lk 9:7-9).

4. Because within the Synoptic Gospels John the Baptist is perceived to represent Elijah, who according to tradition was to return prior to the coming of the Messiah, Jesus could not simply be another prophet or even the reincarnation of John or Elijah. He would have to be the Messiah himself.

5. This designation is in keeping with what is proclaimed at the onset of both Matthew's and Mark's Gospels. Matthew concludes his opening genealogy by stating that Joseph was "the husband of Mary, of whom Jesus was born, who is called the Christ" (Mt 1:16). Matthew is signaling that his Gospel concerns the long-anticipated Messiah, the anointed Savior. Mark opens his Gospel with the unadorned declaration: "The beginning of the gospel of Jesus Christ, the Son of God" (Mk 1:1). Interestingly, although Mark narrates that Peter simply called Jesus "the Christ," here he adds the phrase that is attached to Peter's declaration in the Gospel of Matthew, that "Jesus is the Christ, the Son of the living God." This confirms that even if Matthew enlarges on Peter's original profession, he does so, in keeping with Mark himself, to ensure the full understanding and proper meaning of the term "Christ," that to be the Christ is to be anointed specifically with the Spirit of Sonship.

Moreover, Martha, within the Gospel of John, responds to Jesus' query as to whether she believes that he is the resurrection and the life echoes Peter's Matthean profession: "Yes, Lord;

more likely that Matthew's and Luke's accounts would add explanatory phrases rather than remove such from Peter's original proclamation, Mark's version more likely expresses the historically verbatim account. But this does not imply that the meaning of these added explanatory phrases or words were absent from Peter's declaration. Rather, Matthew and Luke would have added them to ensure that the authentic and complete meaning of Peter's declaration would be fully understood by later Christian generations. Considering all three versions of Peter's profession of faith, since all are deemed canonical by the church, we can perceive the exact and inclusive understanding of that profession.

All three accounts agree that Peter professed that Jesus is the Christ and so he is the unique anointed one of God, that is, that God has singularly anointed him with his Holy Spirit. To be anointed as Messiah demands that Jesus' anointing exceeds the anointing of past prophets, priests, and kings. If his anointing was like theirs, Jesus would be reduced again to someone who is anticipatory to the Messiah and not the Messiah himself. For Jesus to be the Christ (Mark) means that he is anointed specifically as "the Son of the living God" (Matthew). He is "the Christ of God" (Luke) in that his anointing arises from within his very being as being "of God" himself. His anointing is not such then that it comes upon him from without as with the prophets, but rather his anointing springs from within and is integral to his very identity as the Son of the living God. He possesses the Spirit of God, and thus his anointing, his being the Christ of God, defines his very identity as the Son of the living God. Moreover, as God is "living" in that he eternally lives in and of himself and thus is the definitive expression of what it means to be alive, so the Son shares in that eternal divine life as Son—he is the eternal Spirit-anointed living Son of the eternal Spirit-anointing living God. Thus for Jesus to be anointed as the Messiah is for him to be anointed in a manner that differs in kind and not in degree from the prophets, priests, and kings of old. Although Peter within Mark simply confesses that Jesus is "the Christ," to grasp the full intent of that declaration is to know that he is Spirit-anointed as "the Son of the living God" and thus the very Christ "of God"—the one anointed of God as the Son of God.

Likewise, this question, "Who do you say I am," is asked by the man, Jesus. Thus the "I" is a human "I" spoken humanly, giving expression to a human self-consciousness. Jesus asked his disciples, in a human manner and so under

---

I believe that you are the Christ, the Son of God, he who is coming into the world" (Jn 11:27). Nathanael also declares, when called by Jesus, "Rabbi, you are the Son of God! You are the King of Israel!" (Jn 1:49).

the auspices of a human "I," to identify who the "who" is, the personal subject, who humanly asked "who am I." By answering Jesus' human question, Peter is professing that Jesus is the Christ, and as such he is the Spirit-anointed Son of the living God who is eternally of God. That is who Jesus is! Peter's proclamation is then a profession of faith in the Incarnation. The man Jesus asked, "who am I?" and for the correct answer to be "the Christ" (the Son of the living God/of God) demands that "the Christ" (the Son of the living God/of God) exist as man. If "the Christ" (the Son of the living God/of God) did not exist as man, Jesus could not be rightly identified as being such. Again, to know rightly the man Jesus as the Spirit-anointed Son of the living God is to know the Trinity—the Father, the Son, and the Holy Spirit.

What we perceive here, particularly within Matthew and Luke, is a harking back to Jesus' conception and baptism. The foundational ontological basis for Peter's profession—though he probably did not fully realize it at the time, but the later apostolic church, including Peter, would—is the manner of Jesus' conception. Jesus was conceived within the womb of Mary by the overshadowing of the Holy Spirit, and because of this Gabriel prophecies that "therefore the child to be born will be called holy, the Son of God" (Lk 1:35; see also Mt 1:21). As noted in chapter 1, Jesus, as the Incarnate Son, interiorly possessed, from within his very ontological constitution, the Spirit of Sonship, and so from the moment of his conception he is the anointed Messiah, the holy Son of the living God. Again, how Jesus is conceived is the hermeneutical principle that determines who the man Jesus is—the Spirit-anointed Son of the Father. Thus Peter's profession of faith is founded upon and gives expression to this incarnational hermeneutical principle.

In making his profession of faith, Peter is not only fulfilling Gabriel's prophecy that Jesus, having been conceived by Holy Spirit, would be called the Son of God, but also echoing God the Father's proclamation at Jesus' baptism. The Father is the first to call Jesus "Son," and he did so in his anointing him with the Commissioning Spirit, the power that activated his saving ministry. Significantly, within Matthew's Gospel, Jesus confirms Peter's profession of faith by stating that it was his Father who revealed his identity to Peter. "Blessed are you, Simon Bar-Jona! For flesh and blood has not revealed this to you, but my Father who is in heaven." Simon's profession is not of human origin and so does not express a compelling conclusion attained through human reason. Simon is blessed precisely because Jesus' Father revealed it to him.[6] Although Peter's dec-

6. This is also in keeping with Paul's own conversion and calling. He adamantly declares,

laration is human in that he as a man made it, what he humanly declared gives voice to what Jesus' Father has made known to him, and in so doing Peter's declaration echoes the Father's declaration made at Jesus' baptism. Pointedly, though Jesus addresses his question to his disciples, his Father provides the answer. Thus Peter's profession of faith bears within it not the human authority of Peter but the divine authority of none other than that of the Father.

In confirming the truth of Peter's declaration by stating that it was his heavenly Father who revealed it to him, Jesus does not simply approve Peter's response on the Father's authority alone but he himself also affirms it. Although he does not explicitly say "Peter, you are correct in professing that I am the Christ" (the Son of the living God/of God), Jesus, by implication, confirms Peter's response by specifying that it was "My Father who is in heaven" who revealed this. By stipulating that God is his heavenly Father, the source of Peter's declaration, Jesus is clearly identifying himself as the Father's heavenly Son, and in so doing he is acknowledging the truth of Peter's avowal that he is the Christ of God, the Son of the living God. This is in keeping with Jesus' filial relationship to the Father. Jesus never states directly that he is the Son, but only by way of speaking of "my Father." In keeping with being the Son, Jesus can only say "Father." The Father, in being the Father, can only say "Son." This is ultimately the reason why the Father revealed to Peter that Jesus was his Son and in so doing revealed that he was the Son's heavenly Father. Thus, in the Father revealing that Jesus is his heavenly Son and Jesus in affirming that he is the Father's heavenly Son, both the Father and Jesus are revealing that Jesus is of heavenly origin. Jesus, as Son, shares in the same ontological divine manner of being as that of his heavenly Father. He *is* the Father's Son as the Father is the Son's Father and so they live in communion with one another. This is also founded upon and confirmed in that Jesus, the Father's Son, bears the anointing of the Father's Spirit as the Messiah. What the Father reveals to Peter here on earth, that Jesus is the Christ, equally reveals what is true in heaven, that the Son eternally possesses the Father's Spirit of Sonship. This mutual possessing of the same Spirit, the Father as he who bestows the Spirit and the Son as he upon whom the Spirit is bestowed, is the Father and Son's perichoretic communion of life and love with one another. Thus Peter's profession of faith is not simply a declaration of who Jesus is on earth, the Christ

---

"But when he [God the Father] who had set me apart before I was born, and had called me through his grace, was pleased to reveal his Son to me, in order that I might preach him among the Gentiles" (Gal 1:15-16).

(the Son of the living God/of God), but also a statement of what is eternally the case. What unites the earthly truth with the heavenly truth is the heavenly Father. He eternally bestows upon his Son, in his very begetting of him, the Holy Spirit of Sonship, and he bestows this same Spirit of Sonship upon him in the incarnating act—his being conceived as man by the power of the Holy Spirit. The Father reveals to Peter this same twofold truth, that the earthly Jesus is his Spirit-anointed Christ, his heavenly living Son.

Luke initiates his account by remarking that Jesus was praying alone. The goal of Jesus' enquiry as to his identity was not simply to have his disciples come to know who he truly is but also, in knowing who he is, that they would come to share in his prayerful communion with his Father. Peter professed that Jesus is the Christ (the Son of the living God/of God) and in so doing correctly identified Jesus as the Father's anointed Son. Peter made an act of faith that did not consist in simply his professing what is true, but more so his act of faith was enacted under the revealing inspiration and power of the Holy Spirit. The same Spirit with which the Father anointed Jesus as the Messiah, the Son of the living God, is the same Spirit through whom the Father revealed to Peter that Jesus was the Christ, the Son of the living God. Thus Jesus and Peter share the same Spirit, which unites Peter, in the act of professing that Jesus is the Christ, with Jesus the Christ. Under the anointing guidance of the Spirit, Peter recognizes in faith the Anointed One—Jesus the Christ—and so within his Spirit-anointed proclamation comes into communion, within their mutually shared bond of the Spirit, with Jesus the Anointed One. Having come into communion with Jesus through sharing in the same Spirit, Peter comes into communion with his Father, for to be in communion with Jesus the anointed Son is to be in communion with the anointing Father. As the Father and Son are in communion with one another through the Holy Spirit, so Peter comes into communion, through his Spirit-anointed act of faith in Jesus, with the Father in union with his Son.[7]

---

7. I have emphasized a sequence of causal events—Jesus is in prayerful Spirit-filled communion with his Father, which leads to the questioning of his disciples as to who he is, which elicits Peter's Spirit-revealed profession of faith that Jesus is the Christ, which culminates in Peter coming into communion with Jesus and so coming into communion with his Father. I have also noted that, within the Gospel of Luke, Jesus is often depicted at prayer. Not surprisingly, then, the disciples in Luke's Gospel ask Jesus to teach them to pray, having witnessed him at prayer. And even less surprising is that he teaches them the "Our Father" (see Lk 11:1-4; Mt 6:9-15). The entire goal of Jesus' salvific work is to make possible for all the same communion with his Father that he possesses. The "Our Father" is the prayerful expression of that communion so that not only is Jesus rightly able to call God Father, but also all those who are joined to him

Similarly, Peter and Jesus, the Son, share the same common bond of the Holy Spirit and Peter and God, the Father, also share the same common bond of the Holy Spirit, for both now share a common knowledge, revealed to Peter by the Father through the Spirit, that Jesus, the Christ, is the Father's Son. As the Father fathered his Son in the Holy Spirit, so the Father fathered Peter's faith in the same Holy Spirit. Both the Father and Peter acknowledge, in communion with the Spirit, that Jesus is the anointed Son, and in so doing are in communion with one another. They share the same truth in the Spirit, and so are united in the same Spirit, that Jesus is the Spirit-anointed Son.

Although this union with the Father in communion with the Holy Spirit was the goal of Jesus' inquiry as to who he is and terminated in Peter's anointed profession, the Father was the initiator of the entire event. Again, the key is Luke's noting that the enquiry began when Jesus was "praying alone the disciples were with him." Jesus' enquiry as to who he is immediately follows this prayerful communion, and thus it is the fruit of his prayerful communion with his Father. Jesus, in communion with his Father, enquires concerning his identity, knowing that the Father wishes to bring Jesus' disciples into communion with him. The Father ensures that this will be accomplished not only in having Jesus initiate the questioning, but also in revealing the answer to Peter. The whole event is rightly orchestrated by the Father, obediently enacted by Jesus his Son, and appropriately concluded by Peter's Spirit-anointed profession of faith—all of which effects Peter's and his fellow disciples' union with the Father, just as the Father desired from the onset. What we perceive here is the Father acting as Father, the Son acting as Son, and the Holy Spirit acting as Holy Spirit, within this Trinitarian perichoretic act bringing all who believe in Jesus the Son through the inspiration of the Holy Spirit into communion with the Father.[8]

Within the Gospel of Matthew, having declared that Peter's profession was revealed to him by his heavenly Father, Jesus asserts: "And I tell you that you

---

in faith, having been transformed through the indwelling Spirit of Sonship into his likeness and so becoming children of the Father. This finds its fulfillment only within Jesus' death and resurrection and his subsequent pouring out of the Holy Spirit upon those who believe in him. Only then can believers, and only believers, pray in truth and reality the "Our Father." Paul takes this up. Only those who possess the Spirit of his Son, and so are sons of the Father, can cry out "Abba, Father" (see Rom 8:14–16 and Gal 4:6).

8. This is similar to what was discussed in chapter 6, that only the Father knows the Son and only the Son knows the Father and anyone to whom the Son choses to reveal him. This mutual revelation effects a communion to the one to whom such is revealed with the Father and the Son through the Holy Spirit.

are Peter, and on this rock I will build my church."[9] There is a causal relationship between Peter's Father-inspired profession of faith and Jesus' declaration that Peter is the rock upon which he will build his church. Peter is the rock upon which Jesus will build his church because his profession of faith, that Jesus is the Christ, the Son of the living God, is the rock mystery, the rock-solid foundational mystery, of the entire Gospel. Peter the rock and the rock mystery he professes cannot be separated. The Rock (Peter) is the rock because of what he professes, and what he professes is the rock of faith because it was professed by the Rock (Peter).[10] To attempt to build the church or to attempt to live the Gospel on anything other than Peter and his profession would be to build upon or live a specious fabrication, for it would not be the revelation of the Father nor inspired by the Holy Spirit. Thus, although Jesus will build his church on the rock of Peter and his profession, Peter possesses the authority not simply of Jesus but of the Father, who through the Holy Spirit inspired Peter to make his profession of faith, upon which Jesus would found his church. For Peter and the church to profess that Jesus is the Christ, the Son of the living God, is to speak with the definitive voice of the Father.

Jesus' speaking in terms of the future is significant because it makes his statement prophetic. Jesus will found and continue to build his church on Peter's faith, both as to what will be believed and what will be proclaimed. This prophetic element is first perceived within the Father's revelation to Peter that

9. Within the Gospel of John, Andrew brings his brother, Simon, to Jesus, telling him, "We have found the Messiah." "Jesus looked at him [Peter], and said, 'So you are Simon the son of John? You shall be called Cephas' (which means Peter)" (Jn 1:41–42). John accentuates the Greek meaning of the words "Messiah" and "Peter." He also notes that Jesus "looked" at Simon, which for John is not a casual glance but a penetrating knowing. What Jesus "the Christ" saw, in communion with the anointing Spirit, was "the Rock." As in Matthew, Jesus' statement is prophetic, for he declares that in the future Simon will be called the Rock because, as Jesus already perceived, within John's account, Peter will be the Rock upon which his church will be built, for it will profess, through the Holy Spirit, that he is indeed the Christ.

In the Old Testament, the Hebrew word *qahal*, of which *ecclesia* (church) is the Greek translation, specified the Israelites as the chosen people called together by God. The church that Jesus will now build will be those called together under his name as the Messiah, the Son of the living God.

10. Within our English translations, the emphatic nature of Simon being renamed Peter (Rock) is missed. For the Greek-speaking apostolic community, to say "Peter" would simply be saying "Rock." Rock said or did this, or Rock said and did that.

In Luke's Gospel, Jesus, knowing that Peter would deny him, nonetheless states: "I have prayed for you that your faith may not fail, and when you have turned again, strengthen your brethren" (Lk 22:32). Although Peter will fall, his faith will not fail, and so Rock (Peter) will still be the rock upon which his brethren can depend.

Jesus is the Christ, the Son of the living God. The Father revealed in embryo the entire mystery of the Gospel, for Jesus, as the Christ, the Son of the living God, contains within himself, and so within his salvific actions, this entire evangelical mystery. Thus the church that Jesus will continue to build upon the rock of Peter's faith will possess the full mystery, in all its saving facets, of Jesus as the Christ, the Son of the living God. The church will be defined as that body of people who profess and proclaim the same faith as Peter— that Jesus is the Christ, the Son of the living God. Similarly, to be in communion with Jesus, as the Christ the Son of the living God, one must be, by definition and so by necessity, in communion with the church professing the same faith as Peter, for the church is built by Jesus upon the foundation of Peter's profession. Likewise, only in being in communion with Jesus by being in communion with his church, and so professing in unison Peter's faith, is one in communion with the Father, for only by acknowledging that Jesus is the Christ, the Son of the living God, does one come into communion with the Son's heavenly Father. This entire interrelated communion is founded upon the communion of the Holy Spirit. The Holy Spirit reveals who Jesus is as the Christ, the Son of the living of God, and empowers the declaration of faith that Jesus is the Christ, the Son of the living God, and this revelation and declaration define the church. The Holy Spirit binds together the members of the church with Jesus and through him to his heavenly Father. To profess the faith of the church is to profess the faith of Peter and so to live and abide with the Father through Jesus the Son in the communion of the Holy Spirit.

Peter, and even the apostolic church, would not have fully grasped the complete meaning of Jesus' prophetic declaration concerning the future church, nor the ensuing corollaries and the subsequent implications that flow from it. Yet the church, to be true to the mystery of who Jesus is as the Christ, the Son of the living God, and so faithful to Peter's profession of faith, would gradually assume, under the same revealing light of the Holy Spirit in which Peter's own act of faith was made, the responsibility of proclaiming the full mystery of Jesus. In so doing, the church would continually ensure that the full truth of that mystery, in its entirety, would not be jeopardized by erroneous doctrinal understandings or mistaken moral practices. As Jesus, being the Christ, the Son of the living God, embodies the entire mystery of salvation, so the church, founded upon Peter's profession of that same saving truth, embodies the entire saving mystery that is Jesus.[11]

11. In Matthew's Gospel, Jesus intrinsically binds faith in him with Peter's profession and

Because Jesus will build his church on Peter's profession of faith, Jesus equally prophetically declares: "and the powers of death [Greek: "gates of Hades"] shall not prevail against it." "Hades" is the Greek translation of the Hebrew "Sheol." Within ancient Near Eastern literature and the Old Testament, Sheol is the shadowy abode of the dead and thus a place shrouded in darkness, gloom, desolation, and inactivity (see Ps 55:16, Jb 17:13-16, Is 14:9-11, and Ex 32:17-32). Conceived as a personified power, Sheol robs human beings of life and so seizes them from the land of the living with all its present joys and future opportunities. Sheol, who snatches them, is seen particularly as the home of sinners who dwell in the very depths of Sheol (see Ps 49:13-14 and Jb 24:19) To abide in Sheol meant that one could no longer experience the love and goodness of the living God and so respond in worship and praise (see Ps 6:5 and Is 38:18). Yet Sheol is not beyond the reach of God, who alone can deliver someone from its clutches (see Pss 16:10-11 and 49:16). Nearer to the time of Jesus, Sheol came to be seen as a place that was the exclusive domain of sinners and becomes synonymous with Gehenna, a place of fire and torment (see 1 Enoch 27:2 and 90:26).

The powers of death or the gates of Hades will not prevail against Jesus' church for, as Peter professed, it is the church of "the Christ, the Son of the living God." He who will build his church is the Christ, the Son of the living God, and he will build it upon the rock of Peter, who professed this very truth. The church will be the living embodiment of Peter's faith and so will be the living embodiment of who Jesus is as the Christ, the Son of the living God. Therefore no evil power, not even death itself, will ever prevail against it.

What is theologically important to grasp is that the heart of Jesus' prophetic declaration anticipates his own death and resurrection, for only in

---

then integrally ties Peter, the Rock, with the church. In so doing, Jesus did not conceive of a person having faith in him as the Christ, the Son of the living God, apart from the church. While one's faith may be personal in that each person must make his or her own personal act of faith, for it to be authentic it must bear some relationship to the church's profession of faith. There is no such thing as a "Lone Ranger Christian," that is, one who believes in Jesus as Lord and Savior but does not want to acknowledge the necessity of belonging to the church. This is a vitiated form of Christianity. Within the Acts of the Apostles, those who come to believe in Jesus become, in their act of faith, members of the church (see Acts 2:47). The apostolic church understands herself, and nonbelievers equally readily acknowledge her, to be precisely that body of people who believes in Jesus.

Because I am commenting on the theological significance of Jesus' words, I have purposely not attempted to define the church within the present-day context of a multitude of Christian denominations. My theological interpretation, which I would argue is objective, nonetheless would support the Catholic Church's later ecclesial theological and doctrinal development.

these saving mysteries is his prophetic declaration definitively fulfilled. Al-though Jesus is the Christ, as Peter declared, he will only conclusively enact his anointing through his death on the cross and in his glorious resurrection. On the cross, through the Spirit-filled offering of himself to his Father, he will reconcile humankind to his Father and so conquer all evil—sin, Satan, and death—thus depriving Sheol/Hades, even the fires of Gehenna, of its noxious dark power. As the resurrected Christ, Jesus will be empowered to pour out his Spirit and so give birth to his living Spirit-filled church, a gathering of people freed from the clutches of evil and the shadow of death and sharing in his indestructible risen life, that is, living in communion with his Father through the indwelling of his Spirit. Against these saving and live-giving acts, against the church that embodies these acts, the gates of Hell will not prevail for no evil can triumph over Jesus. Thus, in becoming Jesus, YHWH-Saves, Jesus tru-ly enacts his anointing as the Christ and so reveals, as Savior and Lord, that he is the Son of the living God. To be a member of Jesus' indestructible church, to live in him and so in union with his Father through the Holy Spirit, one must confess this truth of who Jesus is as the Christ, the Son of the living God. Al-though Peter's profession of faith is presently true, Jesus places it within the context of a prophecy that will only be fulfilled through his future death and subsequent resurrection, for only then will he have enacted his saving anoint-ed act as the Christ and so revealed himself fully as the Son of the living God.[12]

Jesus, within the Gospel of Matthew, concludes his series of declarations by stating, "I will give you [Peter] the keys of the kingdom of heaven, and whatever you bind on earth shall be bound in heaven, and whatever you loose on earth will be loosed in heaven." In the Book of Isaiah, God tells Shebna that he will give to Eliakim his kingly robe and authority. "And I will place on his shoulder the key of the house of David; he shall open, and none shall shut; and he will shut and none shall open" (Is 22:15-22). Jesus, who will establish David's everlasting kingdom, will give to Peter such authority over his heaven-ly kingdom. As Sheol or Hades has gates that imprison those within, so Peter will possess the power and authority to judge who is fit to enter through the

---

12. The Gospel of Matthew and Jesus within it speak almost exclusively of the kingdom of heaven and not of the church. Jesus has come to establish the kingdom of heaven. The church is nonetheless the living expression of the kingdom of heaven on earth. To abide in the church is to live and so experience the reality of the kingdom of heaven, for to reside within the church is to live in union with Jesus, who embodies the kingdom of heaven.

Besides the present event of Peter's profession of faith, the only other passage within the Gospels where the term "church" is employed is Mt 18:17, which we will examine shortly.

gates of the kingdom and to whom these gates will be locked.[13] Peter, because he is the rock upon which Jesus will build his church, stands guard over the church's teaching and practice. With the keys of the kingdom in hand, Peter approves of those who believe and live in accordance with the church's faith and practice and so grants them citizenship within the heavenly kingdom, and he rejects those who do not believe or live in accordance with the church's teaching and practice and so bars them from God's heavenly kingdom.

There appears to be a change of metaphor within Jesus' declaration, from that of "keys" to that of "binding and loosing." Although the giving to Peter the keys of the kingdom of heaven authorizes him to judge who is worthy to be a member of the church and so provides entrance into the heavenly kingdom and who is not, the giving to him the power to bind and loose, while conjoined to the power of the keys, pertains to his authority to impose or pardon disciplinary sanctions. The nature of the offense that would cause such disciplinary action or the reasons for a subsequent pardon is left unspecified. But it probably also pertains to sinful behavior within the church itself. This seems to be the meaning when Jesus, within the context of disciplining a recalcitrant sinner, declares to his disciples as a whole: "Truly, I say to you, whatever you bind on earth shall be bound in heaven, and whatever you loose on earth shall be loosed in heaven" (Mt 18:15-18).[14] Thus both the giving of the keys of the kingdom of heaven and the authority of binding and loosing pertain to Peter's leadership in governing, guiding, and guarding the apostolic nature of the church, that is, that it would always believe and live, under the anointing of the Holy Spirit, in accordance with his profession of faith that Jesus is the Christ, the Son of the living God.[15]

13. In the Book of Revelation, Jesus declares that because he is "the first and the last," the one who died and "behold alive forevermore," he has "the keys of Death and Hades" (Rv 1:17-18). The risen Jesus, having conquered sin and death, possesses the authority and power to release the sinful dead from the everlasting punishment of Hades and, by implication, provide them entrance into his everlasting heavenly kingdom.

14. This would also be in keeping with what Jesus declares to his Apostles when he appears to them on the first Easter evening when he breathed upon them and said, "Receive the Holy Spirit. If you forgive the sins of any, they are forgiven; if you retain the sins of any, they are retained" (Jn 20:22-23).

Although Jesus gave Peter the keys of the kingdom of heaven, the power of binding and loosing, as in his other declarations, is given to the Apostles as a whole. This would especially be the case with regard the apostolic authority to forgive sins.

15. From a theological and doctrinal perspective, it is somewhat frustrating that Jesus' declarations to Peter are so undefined and lacking in specificity. But being the wise lawgiver, he realized that he could not possibly delineate all the specific issues and circumstances under

Jesus' Foretelling of His Passion, Death, and Resurrection

At the conclusion of Peter, professions of faith all of the Synoptic Gospels speak of Jesus' prohibition: "Then he strictly charged the disciples to tell no one that he was the Christ." The reason for Jesus' embargo immediately follows. "From that time Jesus began to show his disciples that he must go to Jerusalem and suffer many things from the elders and chief priests and scribes, and be killed, and on the third day be raised" (Mt 16:21; see also Mk 8:31 and Lk 9:22). Peter's authoritative declaration has provided the doctrinal catalyst for Jesus to reveal

---

which such authority could and needed to be exercised. Peter and the Apostles would not and could not possibly comprehend prior to the events when such given authority should be employed. What is not ambiguous is that Peter and the Apostles did possess authority to judge the truth of revelation (what pertains to the church's doctrine and moral practice) and to oversee and administer the discipline within the church that accords with that revelation.

We find instances of Peter and the Apostles learning to exercise their authority in the Acts of the Apostles, for example, in choosing Matthias to take the place of Judas as one of the twelve (Acts 1:15-26) and establishing "the order" of deacons who would oversee the physical needs of the community (Acts 6:1-7). The nascent life of the apostolic community is summed up as: "They devoted themselves to the apostles' teaching and fellowship, to the breaking of bread and the prayers" (Acts 2:42). Such a communal life needed to be organized, administered, and governed. Paul lists the various offices and charisms that were and continue to be an essential part of the church's life (see 1 Cor 12:27-30 and Eph 2:20, 3:5, and 4:11).

Most significantly, at "the First Council of Jerusalem," the Apostles grappled with the issue, in relation to the Gentile converts, of what pertains to the heart of the Gospel and what Jewish practices do not apply to the Gentiles. Peter is the primary doctrinal arbiter, and James provides the practical disciplinary solutions to the doctrinal issues, to which all agreed. They knew they possessed the authority to judge this issue. In their letter, they noted that this judgment "seemed good to the Holy Spirit and to us" (see Acts 15:1-29). The Holy Spirit, who first revealed to Peter who Jesus is and, because of this Jesus bestowed upon him the keys of the kingdom, continues to guide Peter and the Apostles in the exercise of their apostolic authority.

An interesting example of binding and loosing is found in Paul's disciplinary authority over the church at Corinth. Paul learns that a member of the church in Corinth "is living with his father's wife." Paul is shocked by such behavior and demands that the Corinthian church, even though he is not present, "when you are assembled and my spirit is present, with the power of our Lord Jesus, you are to deliver this man to Satan for the destruction of the flesh that his spirit may be saved in the day of the Lord Jesus" (1 Cor 5:1-5). In his Second Letter to the Corinthians, Paul judges that the punishment he and the Corinthian Church imposed upon the sinner is sufficient and served its purpose of bringing the offender to repentance. "For such a [sinful man] this punishment by the majority is enough; so you should rather turn to forgive and comfort him, or he may be overwhelmed by excessive sorrow. So I beg you to reaffirm your love for him" (2 Cor 2:6-7).

We clearly perceive now why Jesus could not be specific on the execution of the authority and power he gave to Peter and the Apostles. Having given them such authority, the Spirit would need to guide them in the practical concrete exercise of its use.

more fully what it means for him to be the Christ. Peter's profession and Jesus' subsequent commentary introduces the forthcoming paschal mystery. For Jesus to be the anointed Son of God inherently contains the saving mystery of his passion, death, and resurrection. Within these acts Jesus fully enacts his name as Savior (YHWH-Saves) and in so doing manifests that he is truly the Father's Son.[16]

The necessity for such teaching is immediately evidenced in Peter's disavowal: "God forbid, Lord! This shall never happen to you" (Mt 16:22; Mark simply says that Peter "began to rebuke him" (8:32), and Luke does not narrate such a rebuke). It is reminiscent of Satan's words: "If you are the Son of God." Peter too holds that if Jesus truly is the Christ, the Son of the living God, then such evil cannot possibly befall him, but rather, in accord with who he is, he should display (flaunt) his glory and so obtain the accolades of all. Thus Jesus' stinging reproach to Peter: "Get behind me Satan! You are a hindrance to me; for you are not on the side of God, but of men" (Mt 16:23; see also Mk 8:33). Like Satan, Peter is a hindrance because he is luring him away from his commitment to doing his Father's will, a temptation to which Jesus himself interiorly recognizes that he is susceptible.[17] But Jesus must be faithful to the commission given to him by his Father at his baptism: to be the Servant-Son.

Jesus informs his followers what is demanded of them, but he also provides a further explanation as to what is demanded of him. "If any man would come after me, let him deny himself and take up his cross [Lk adds "daily"] and follow me. For whoever would save his life will lose it, and whoever will lose his life for my sake [Mk adds "and for the Gospel's"] will find it. For what will it profit a man, if he gains the whole world and forfeits his life? Or what shall a man give in return for his life?" (Mt 16:24-26; see also Mk 8:34-37 and Lk 23-25). This initial mentioning of the "cross" and its "being taken up" is referenced first in relation to Jesus' followers. But it is the taking up of one's cross that one becomes a follower of Jesus, for he has daily taken up his cross in embracing who he is as the Christ. By informing his followers what they must do, he is informing them what he is doing. If one refuses to take up one's cross in an attempt to save one's life (earthly life) one will lose his life (heavenly eternal life). Conversely, whoever is willing to lose his earthly life "for my sake,"

16. Jesus first speaks of his death and resurrection only after Peter's profession of faith. Only through his death and resurrection will Jesus fully reveal that he truly is the Christ/Messiah, the Son of the living God.

17. This vulnerability is seen in Jesus' own prayer in the Garden of Gethsemane: "My Father, if it be possible, let this cup pass from me" (Mt 26:39).

and so for the Gospel, will find his eternal life. This is exactly what Jesus is willing to do and is doing. He is willing to give up his life here on earth so that he might obtain eternal life, and the same is true for those who do the same for his sake, on behalf of and in union with him. Here again Jesus is making extraordinary demands of his followers—the laying down of their lives in the very manner of death by which he himself will die, the cross. This obligation is not imposed for the sake of some universal principle or some righteous cause but solely for the sake of Jesus himself—to be simply his follower and so to be in personal communion with him. To follow Jesus and so to live in communion with him is alone worth taking up one's cross, for in so doing one gains eternal life in him. Satan tempted and Peter wanted Jesus to gain the whole world, but he declares to his followers and so to himself that in such an attempt one forfeits one's own life and thus gains nothing for the price of his very life. Everything, Jesus is ultimately declaring, must be evaluated and judged in the light of himself and his cross, for only in him and through his cross will one rise with him "on the third day."[18]

In Mark and Luke, Jesus concludes with an appropriate warning: "For whoever is ashamed of me and of my words in this adulterous and sinful generation, of him will the Son of man also be ashamed when he comes in the glory of his Father with all the holy angels" (Mk 8:37-38; see also Lk 9:26). Peter's rebuke to Jesus testified to his embarrassment at the mere thought of Jesus' humiliating death. But Jesus is emphasizing that so much does the shame of the cross, the utter disgrace and ignominy of such a humiliating public display, enfold and embrace him that it actually defines who he is. Jesus is the Christ, the Son of the living God, as Peter proclaimed, only because he will be handed over and killed. And it is the very shame and disgrace of the cross that will gain Jesus access to the glory of his Father with all the holy angels. To be, as Peter is, ashamed of the cross's shame, to be disgraced by the cross's disgrace, to be humiliated by such a public display, is to be ashamed of Jesus himself, that is, to find him an utter disgrace, to consider him a humiliating embarrassment.[19]

18. Paul ardently acknowledges this truth. He says that he considers "everything as loss" and "refuse" compared to the "surpassing worth of knowing Christ Jesus my Lord." He only desires to share in Jesus' righteousness and in the power of this resurrection and so to "share his sufferings, coming to be like him in his death, that if possible I may attain the resurrection from the dead" (Phil 3:7-11). To be like Jesus in his death is to take up one's cross and in so doing come to share in his resurrection. For Paul, because everything in this world (marriage, mourning, rejoicing, buying, and the world itself) is passing away, everything should be judged in the light of eternal life with Christ (see 1 Cor 7:29-31).

19. Jesus crucified did prove to be an embarrassment to the early Christians. How could

Jesus does not say he will be angry or disappointed or even sorrowful toward those who are ashamed of him, but strikingly he will assume their shame. He will be ashamed of them precisely because they refused to perceive his glory in the shame of the cross, gracious dignity in the disgrace, and splendor and beauty within the public humiliation. The shame of their shame will be manifested when Jesus "comes in his glory," which he attained in and through the very the shame of the cross and which is the very divine "glory of the Father and of the holy angels." The crucified Jesus bears the glory of the whole heavenly realm. Implicit within Jesus' declaration is the corresponding response to those who are not ashamed of him—he will not be ashamed of them. Rather, they, in being Jesus' loyal followers, will share in his and his Father's glory, for they too will have borne the shame, disgrace, and public humiliation of their crosses at the hands of an adulterous and sinful generation.[20]

Son of Man

Before proceeding to the Transfiguration, we must examine Jesus' use of the title Son of man. Although Peter professes that he is the Christ, the Son of the living God, Jesus now refers to himself as the "Son of man." Much has been written and debated concerning this enigmatic title. I do not wish to enter directly into that discussion, but I do want to highlight what I believe is its partial theological importance.

Jesus alone employs this title within the Gospels—seventy times within the Synoptics and twelve times in the Gospel of John. The only other place in the New Testament where Jesus is referred to as the Son of man is in Acts 7:56, where Stephen states that he sees "the Son of man standing at the right hand of God." This testifies to the authenticity of Jesus designating himself as the Son of man, but why, and what did he wish to reveal?

---

he possibly be the Son of God and acknowledged to be the one Lord and universal Savior? Because of this, Christians were ridiculed and mocked. Paul, in his Letters, provides an apologetic founded upon Jesus' very teaching. The cross is the glory of Jesus and his followers. To be a Christian is to boast in nothing other than in Jesus and him crucified (see 1 Cor 1:18-25, 2:2; Gal 6:14). The Philippian Hymn exults in the humility of Jesus in not grasping at his divinity but humbly becoming man to the point of dying on the cross. Because of his humility/shame, God raised him from the dead and gave him a name above every other name. Before the crucified Jesus every knee is to bend and every tongue is to proclaim that he is the supreme Lord to the glory of God the Father (see Phil 2:6-11).

20. Here we find the echo of Jesus' earlier teaching concerning those who do or do not acknowledge him on earth—such an acknowledgment or denial will elicit a corresponding acknowledgment or denial before his heavenly Father.

Within the Synoptics, scholars divide this title into at least four categories. (1) As Son of man, Jesus designates his own humanness, such as having no place to lay his head (see Mt 13:37 and parallels), or coming, eating, and drinking (see Mt 11:19 and Lk 7:34). (2) Jesus also uses this title when speaking of his divine authority, for example, his ability to forgive sins (see Mt 8:6 and parallels) or being the Lord of the Sabbath (see Mt 12:8 and parallels). (3) Jesus calls himself the Son of man mostly when speaking of his approaching passion and death (see, e.g., Mt 12:40, 17:12, 17:22, 20:18, and parallels). (4) Finally, as he did in the passage above, Jesus employs this title in an eschatological sense, that is, the coming of the resurrected Son of man gloriously on the clouds of heaven at the end of time (see, e.g., Mt 10:23, 13:41, 16:28, 17:9, 24:17, 26:64, and parallels).

Given the various above uses, I argue that it is the last eschatological use of the title Son of man that is the hermeneutical key that holds all the various other uses together. Jesus' use of the title within his eschatological declarations most clearly references, though it can be present in the other uses as well, Daniel 7:13. Within Daniel's vision he sees coming on the clouds of heaven "one like the Son of man, and he came to the Ancient of Days and presented himself before him. And to him was given dominion and glory and kingdom, that all peoples, nations, and languages should serve him; his dominion is an everlasting dominion, which shall not pass away, and his kingdom one that shall not be destroyed" (Dn 7:13-14). God his Father, the Ancient of Days, will give to Jesus, his resurrected divine Son, an everlasting kingdom when Jesus comes in glory at the end of time. He will do so because his Son became man as are other men and so a Son of man. As a Son of man, Jesus offered up his sacred humanity as a loving sacrifice to his Father on humankind's behalf, thus obtaining forgiveness of sins and destroying death. For this reason, Jesus' Father raised him gloriously from the dead, making his divine Son now the glorious Son of man. At the end of this age, the Father will enthrone his Son, the glorious Son of Man, as the Lord of all peoples, giving him everlasting dominion over all nations.

Within Peter's profession of faith and Jesus' subsequent clarifying amplification of what it truly means for him to be the Christ, the Son of the living God, all the above elements pertaining to the title Son of man are expressed. First it is the *man* Jesus, a Son of man, who asks, "Who do you say that I am?" Second, Peter proclaims that this Son of man is the anointed Messiah, the Son of God. Third, the man Jesus professes that for him to be the Christ, the Son of God, necessitates that he must humanly suffer, die, and rise on the third day. Fourth, Peter finds this corollary unbecoming of one who is the Christ of God. Fifth, Jesus concludes his reprimand of Peter by stating that he who is ashamed of him because of cross, the Son of man will equally be ashamed of him "when he comes in the glory of his Father with all the holy angels" (Mk 8:37-38; see also Lk 9:26). This Son of God who became a weak Son of Man, through his human death and resurrection, will be transformed into the glorious Son of man, and this glory will be fully manifested when the Son of Man, who is the Son of God, comes upon the clouds of heaven and is given by his Father everlasting dominion and rule over heaven and earth.[21] The Father, in so doing, will conclusively reveal that Jesus, the Son of man, is truly the Son of God. Thus this eschatological revelation manifests that, as intimated in Daniel 7:13-14, the title Son of man is inherently a divine title as well as a human designation. To be the authentic human Son of man is simply to be the divine Son of God, for only if Jesus is the Son of God incarnate could he gloriously come down upon the clouds of heaven as the radiant Son of man. For Jesus to accrue the title Son of man manifests his own self-consciousness that he is the Son of God incarnate and that, as the Christ, he is to suffer and die so as to become the glorious Son of Man who will come upon the clouds of heaven as the universal Savior and definitive Lord. As the Son of God made man, all that pertains to being the Son of man is subsumed into Jesus as the Son of God, and all that pertains to Jesus being the Son of God is subsumed into his being the Son of Man. By employing the title Son of man, Jesus, as the Son of God, manifests, through his incarnation, death, resurrection, and second coming, the manner in which he is becoming Jesus—YHWH-Saves.

The Transfiguration

Jesus' amplification that for him to be the Christ means that he must suffer, die, and rise from the dead is enacted in the Transfiguration. What Jesus prophesied in words he prophetically embodied (literally) in the act of the Transfiguration. Although the Transfiguration is one event, there is an ordered sequence of acts contained within it, each succeeding act enhancing the revelational content of previous act(s). The following doctrinal commentary, for the sake of logical presentation and theological clarity, will follow closely the biblical narrative.

21. This is why Stephen in his Spirit-filled vision "saw the glory of God, and Jesus standing at the right hand of God; and said, 'Behold, I see the heavens opened and the Son of man standing at the right hand of God'" (Acts 7:55-56). Stephen sees the Son of God as he truly is: the glorious Son of Man reigning in heaven.

Jesus took Peter, James, and John up a high mountain. There "he was trans-figured before them, and his garments became glistening, intensely white, as no fuller on earth could bleach them" (Mk 9:1-2). Matthew states that "his face shone like the sun, and his garments became white as light" (Mt 17:1-3). Luke notes that they went up the mountain to pray and it was while Jesus "was praying, the appearance of his countenance [face] was altered, and his raiment became dazzling white" (Lk 9:28-29).[22]

What act does the word "transfigured" express? The transfiguring act is perceived in its effects. Mark emphasizes the radical change in the appearance of Jesus garments. So brilliantly white did they become that no earthly cause (fuller's bleach) could account for their radiant luminosity. The causal act of transfiguring is therefore of divine origin. Matthew and Luke draw attention to Jesus' face, or countenance. Luke simply notes that it was "altered," but presumably it too, like "his raiment," was "dazzling white." Matthew states that "his face shone line the sun." The sun is the most brilliant, dazzling, and luminous light that human beings experience. Its luminosity comes from within; it is self-generating. To say that his face was altered so as to be likened to the brilliant luminosity of the sun conveys the notion that the transfiguring act, the resplendent light radiating from his face, comes forth from within Jesus himself. Like the sun, the transfiguring radiance is self-engendered from within his very being. To say that the brilliance of Jesus' face is like the sun does not imply that the resplendent light of his face is a lesser or even an equal reflection of the sun's radiance, but indicates that the luminous intensity of his countenance exceeds that of the sun. Jesus' face is not compared to the sun, but the sun is compared to his face.[23]

22. Peter's Second Letter references the Transfiguration. Peter states that he does not preach empty myths but the power "of our Lord Jesus Christ." He was an "eyewitness of his majesty. For when he [Jesus] received honor and glory from God the Father and the voice was borne to him by the Majestic Glory, 'This is my beloved Son, with whom I am well pleased,' we heard this voice borne from heaven, for we were with him on the holy mountain" (2 Pt 1:16-18). Interestingly, Peter writes in such a manner that he presumes that his readers are already well acquainted with the Transfiguration, for he never explains the actual event. He is simply using it to illustrate his point, and so to remind his readers, that Jesus possesses authentic power and might as the glorious Son of the Father.

23. This is in keeping with God being the author of light. In the first Creation story, although he did not create the sun until the fourth day, light was the first good "thing" God did create. In first creating light, God dispelled the darkness of utter chaos—the dark void of nothingness (see Gn 1:3-5 and Is 45:7). Jesus is now the light that will dispel the chaotic darkness of sin and the lifeless void of death. The Prologue of the Gospel of John highlights this truth. God created all through his divine Word and therefore "in him was life, and the life was the

The fact that Matthew and Luke accentuate that it is Jesus' face that radiates this brilliance is also doctrinally significant. The human face, more than any other aspect of the human body, reveals and manifests the person's identity. (This is why portraits are painted, photo identification is often required, and police have criminal line-ups.) Peter, James, and John beheld the human face of Jesus, a face they recognized, and what they beheld was a face radiating from within a light more brilliant than the sun, and a light whose causal origin was not human but divine. The human face, unlike the "faces" of animals, manifests a human person—a rational being.[24] To behold the radiant human face of Jesus manifests that the luminosity emanating from that face springs not from some impersonal divine reality (a what) but from a personal divine rational being (a who). Because the cause of the transfiguring light is divine in origin and because Jesus' human face, the face of a rational being, particularly manifests the luminous brilliance of this divine light, the divine causal source of this luminous splendor shining forth from his human face must be a divine person (a who). Here we perceive the importance of Luke's noting that it was while he was at prayer that Jesus was transfigured.

The transforming brilliance of his face and garments came forth from within Jesus, but it was not apart from his prayerful communion with his Father, and thus the splendor emanating from within his humanity bears witness to the communion of the Father and the Son. The Father, being the Father, fathers his glory within his Son in the fathering of his Son. The Son's glory, then, is not his own for he does not "father" (is not the cause of) his own glory, but rather radiates the glory of his Father as the Father's fathered Son. Such is the brilliance and splendor that shine forth like the sun from the human face of Jesus, as he is in prayerful communion with the Father, that it luminously manifests and so vividly confirms that he is the Father's Son. Within the transfiguring act, Jesus, in keeping with who he is as Son, is manifesting the splendor of his Father and thus that he is the Father's Son. The primary

---

light of men. The light shines in the darkness and the darkness has not overcome it" (Jn 1:1-15). Paul also picks up this theme. He tells the Corinthians that the Gospel is veiled to those who are perishing, for the god of this world has blinded them "keeping them from seeing the light of the gospel of the glory of Christ, who is the likeness of God." Nonetheless, he preaches "Jesus Christ as Lord," for it is "God who said: 'Let light shine out of darkness,' who has shone in our hearts to give light of the knowledge of the glory of God in the face of Christ" (1 Cor 4:3-6).

24. The eye alone illustrates this. To be shown photos of two sets of eyes, one human and one animal, it is apparent which eyes are human. Human eyes radiate rationality—the being whose eyes these are is a rational animal—a person. An animal's eye bears no evidence of rationality. There is no personhood displayed in an animal eye.

task of Jesus as Son is to reveal the Father, and it is only within his revealing the Father that it reveals himself to be the Father's Son.[25]

Thus the transfiguring act manifests the Incarnation. The transfiguring act is a living icon of the incarnational act. To behold Jesus' radiant humanity is not like beholding the radiant beauty of stained glass, where the colored glass and the source of its splendor, the sun, are distinct. Rather, Jesus' human body itself is transfigured; his humanity is luminous from within. This is particularly evidenced in his face. The radiance and the source of the radiance are the same reality. The glorious brilliance that radiates from Jesus' human countenance could only be the radiance of the Father's Son if his Son existed as man, for only then could his humanity make visible the radiant glory of the Father's Son. To behold the luminous human face of Jesus is, literally, to behold the human face of the Father's Son and so too the face of the Father.[26]

Mark continues to state the next act: "And there appeared to them Elijah with Moses; and they were talking with Jesus. Peter said to Jesus, 'Master, it is well that we are here; let us make three booths, one for you and one for Moses and one for Elijah.' For he did not know what to say, for they were exceeding-

---

25. In the Old Testament, to be blessed is to have the light of God's face shine upon one (see Nm 6:24-26; Ps 67:2 and 89:15). The Son is most blessed because the entire light of the Father's face, the entirety of his being, shines upon him so as to conform his divine "face," his divine identity, to be that of the Father's Son. As the incarnate Son, Jesus is equally the most blessed, for the very light of his Father's face shines forth from him as his divine Son, thus conforming his human face, his human identity, to be that of the Father's Son.

Within the Old Testament, to have the light of God's face to shine upon one is to experience salvation. The Psalmist prays that the light of God's face would shine upon his people "that we may be saved!" (Ps 80:3; see also Ps 4:6, 119:135 and Is 60:1-3). To avoid the shame of defeat at the hands of his enemies, the Psalmist entreats the Lord, "Let your light shine on your servant; save me in your steadfast love" (Ps 31:16). These blessings and prayers are fulfilled in Jesus. As the Transfiguration will demonstrate, he is blessed because the light of his Father, his steadfast love, radiates in a singular manner from his face and thus, despite the cross, he will be saved. The radiating saving face of Jesus now shines upon his Apostles and will shine upon all Christians so that they too will be blessed and so saved. They will be blessed because the filial light of Jesus' face will shine upon their faces and so conform their faces into the likeness of his own. Christians will bear his filial likeness, his filial identity, as children of his Father. Both Jesus and his followers can thus confidently declare: "The Lord is my light and my salvation; of whom shall I be afraid?" (Ps 27:1).

26. The Gospel of John explicitly brings this out. In response to Philip's request that Jesus show them the Father, he responds, "Have I been with you so long, and yet you do not know me, Philip? He who has seen me has seen the Father; how can you say, 'Show us the Father'? Do you not believe that I am in the Father and the Father in me?" This unity is manifested in that Jesus only speaks by his Father's authority and only does the works of his Father, for the Father "dwells in me." "Believe me that I am in the Father and the Father in me" (Jn 14:8-11).

ly afraid" (Mk 9:4-6). Mathew's account is similar, but he does not comment on Peter's suggestion about the building of booths, thus saving him from embarrassment (Mt 17:3-4). Luke provides this account: "And behold, two men talked to him, Moses and Elijah, who appeared in glory and spoke of his departure [his exodus] which he was to accomplish at Jerusalem. Now Peter and those with him were heavy with sleep but kept awake, and they saw his glory and the two men who stood with him. And as the men were departing from him, Peter said to Jesus, 'Master, it is well that we are here; let us make three booths, one for you and one for Moses and one for Elijah'—not knowing what he said" (Lk 9:30-33).[27]

Within the act of the Transfiguration, Moses and Elijah appeared with Jesus. Luke notes that they too "appeared in glory," thus also reflecting the heavenly divine nature of the event. But their glory is not of a like kind to that of Jesus' radiance and brilliance. When Moses came down from Mt. Sinai, having spoken with God, "the skin of his face shone" such that he needed to veil his face when speaking to the people, removing it only when he spoke with God (Ex 34:29-35). Moses' face reflected the light of God's glory such as the moon reflects the brilliance of the sun. Whereas the light upon Moses' face came from without, the luminosity upon Jesus' face is like the sun, which radiates its own brilliance from within. This is not a triumvirate of equals. Jesus, as the Christ, holds preeminence in a manner that is radically different, for Moses and Elijah came into his divinely self-possessed glorious presence rather than him coming into their simply divinely reflected glorious presence.

Luke tells us that the conversation between Jesus, Moses, and Elijah concerned "his departure" (Greek: *exodus*) that "he was to accomplish at Jerusalem." This conversation alerts us to the Old Testament exodus event because Moses is one of the interlocutors. Within that event, God, through the instru-

---

27. Peter's desire to build three booths may reference the Feast of Booths or Tabernacles, a seven-day harvest festival that recalled the Israelites' forty-year sojourn in the desert, where they lived in tents before entering the Promised Land (see Lv 23:39-43). (Matthew introduces the Transfiguration with the phrase "After six days.") Peter's comment could then be interpreted as seeing the Transfiguration as Jesus passing through the desert of his passion (his exodus) into the glory of his heavenly resurrected dwelling. This would be in keeping with Jesus' triumphal entry into Jerusalem. As we will see in chapter 8, his triumphal entry is closely aligned to and interpreted within the Feast of Booths, for Jesus in triumphantly entering the earthly Jerusalem is prophetically anticipating his triumphal entry into the heavenly Jerusalem. Thus the Feast of Booths finds its prophetic fulfillment both within the Transfiguration and the triumphal entry, for they both anticipate Jesus' ultimate Transfiguration and triumphal entry into his resurrected glory.

mentality of Moses, freed the Israelites from their slavery in Egypt, ultimately by protecting them from death through the blood of the Passover lamb, and proceeding to guide them to a new life of freedom in the Promised Land. During their forty-year journey God (the Lord/YHWH) made a covenant on Mt. Sinai with the Israelites, thus fashioning them into his chosen people. They would be his people, and he would be their God. As such, the Israelites possessed a relationship with the Lord God that differed in kind from every other nation and people. They were also to live holy lives, the Lord God having given them the commandments and law, and so be holy as he is holy. The Israelites proved themselves unfaithful to the covenant despite God's continual merciful forgiveness and loving covenantal presence—this being primarily found in his sending to them prophets, such as Elijah, who called them to repentance and to renewed fidelity.[28]

Over the long history of Israel's frequent infidelity and the Lord God's reprimands, chastisements (culminating in the Babylonian Exile), and calls to repentance and fidelity, the prophets began to speak about and to look forward to a future covenant that God would inaugurate with and on behalf of his people. Although many prophets and prophecies could be examined, two are of particular relevance here.

Jeremiah prophesied that the new covenant would not be like the old covenant, which the Israelites broke. Unlike the old covenant, which was written on stone tablets and so imposed upon the people from without, the new covenant would affect an interior transformation. The Lord declared: "I will put my law within them, and I will write upon their hearts; and I will be their God, and they shall be my people." Within the new covenant, no one will need to be taught about God "for they shall all know me, from the least of them the greatest." God will "forgive their iniquity" and "remember their sins no more" (Jer 31:31-34). The new covenant is to be marked by this interior conversion. The Israelites' obedience will no longer be to an alien law to which they must grudgingly conform, but their obedience will be to a new way of life, founded upon their new interior personal knowledge of God. This new life will spring from within their own hearts, a life in which they, being cleansed from sin, will happily abide.

Ezekiel specifically prophesies the interior source of this new covenantal transformation. God failed in his first attempt to make his people holy, and

---

28. Ultimately, Jesus is the new Israelite who will be holy and in whom the Israelites will succeed in becoming holy as God is holy.

thus his holy name was profaned among the nations. Because of this, God will, "for the sake of his name," "sprinkle clean water upon you, and you shall be clean from all of your uncleanness.... A new heart will I give you, and a new spirit I will put within you; and I will take from your flesh the heart of stone and give you a heart of flesh. And I will put my spirit within you, and cause you to walk in my statutes and be careful to observe my ordinances" (Ezek 36:22-32). The Israelites will readily obey God's commands, which now reside within them (Jeremiah), for God will remove their hearts of stone and bestow within them a new heart of flesh, imbued and enlivened by the transforming power of his very spirit. The water of this spirit will cleanse them of their iniquity and empower them to live God's holy ordinances. In making his people holy, God will prove his own holiness and thus restore the integrity of his holy name. Moses and Elijah convey this entire salvation history, in the fullness of its prophetic meaning, into the Transfiguration, for they literally embody the all-inclusive revelation of the Old Testament.

For the sake of clarity, it must be recalled that the initial event, of which the Transfiguration is the culmination, is Peter's profession of faith that Jesus is the Christ, the Son of the living God. In this context, Jesus proceeded to instruct his disciples that this inherently entailed his passion, death on the cross, and rising on the third day. But Jesus did not say why this must be the case nor did he state what this would accomplish. The Transfiguration now provides the interpretive clue as to why Jesus, as the Christ, must die and rise and what his death and resurrection would accomplish.

Luke accentuates that the departure, the exodus, is an event that Jesus will "accomplish" at Jerusalem. He is going to enact those acts that would "accomplish" and so result in his exodus. Thus Jesus' Transfiguration pertains to his own exodus, which is placed within the former exodus and can only be understood within that context. The former historical exodus event here becomes the prophetic preparatory anticipation of Jesus' exodus event and so assumes its proper significance, a prophetic significance that it had hitherto never possessed.

This being the case, Jesus is portrayed within the transfiguring act as the new Moses, the new anointed prophet of God (see Dt 18:15). Jesus as the Christ, whose possession of the Spirit is inherently integral to and so defines his being the Son of the living God, will initiate his exodus by offering himself as the new Passover lamb, a holy lamb truly without the blemish of sin, to his Father through the shedding of his life-blood on the cross. As such, his sacrifice will bring freedom from sin, of which death is its chief consequence, and provide entrance into the true Promised Land of God's kingdom. In so doing, he will fulfill the historical former Passover's prophetic anticipation.

Jesus, as the Spirit-anointed Christ, is not only the new Passover Lamb but simultaneously also the sacrificial lamb that seals the new covenant. As God sealed the covenant with his people at Mt. Sinai through the act of Moses sprinkling the blood of a lamb upon the altar of sacrifice and upon the people (see Ex 24:3-8), so Jesus' anointed sacrificial act, the offering of his holy life's blood, will bring reconciliation with God and so seal the new covenant, the new Spirit-sealed relationship with his Father. As the sprinkled blood of the old covenant was the outward symbolic expression of God sanctifying his people, making them a consecrated nation unto the Lord God, so Jesus' blood interiorly sanctifies, in the Holy Spirit, those of the new covenant by making them truly a holy people unto his Father. In Jesus the prophesied effects of the new covenant are found.

The transfigured humanity of Jesus manifests, then, not the ignominy of the cross of which one (Peter) should be ashamed, but the glory of the cross, of which one should rejoice because through it humankind is reconciled to the Father and a new covenant is sealed. Moreover, the glory of the cross intrinsically bears within it the glory of the resurrection, which is the fruit of the cross. To behold the luminous transfigured humanity of Jesus is simultaneously to behold the true living and glorious Passover/covenantal lamb of sacrifice.[29] The Father's act of raising Jesus gloriously from the dead is his confirming act that testifies to the glory of the cross—its effecting forgiveness and reconciliation. In being raised from the dead, the glorious Jesus is the first fruit of his own sacrificial death and so embodies within his own risen humanity the new covenantal relationship with his Father. He therefore embodies within his own risen humanity the reality of the kingdom of God. To behold the luminous face of Jesus within the transfiguring act is to peer prophetically into the salvific future.

What Jesus, as the Spirit-anointed Christ, prophetically manifests within his Transfiguration is also the manner in which he will enact his own name as Savior (YHWH-Saves) and so reveal that he is, as the Christ, the living Father's Son. Jesus will truly become Jesus in accomplishing his own exodus— the passing over from his earthly life to his glorious risen life through the act of his sacrificial death and the act of his resurrection, for through these saving

---

29. This is vividly portrayed in the Book of Revelation in the image of the glorious living Lamb that was slain, who is worthy to receive all "power and wealth and wisdom and might and honor and glory and blessing" (Rv. 5:6, 5:9, 5:12, 5:13, and 13:8).

events he will provide entrance into the very presence of his Father. To live in communion with the risen Jesus, as the glorious Lord and universal Savior, is to live in communion with his Father. This act of communion with Jesus, which equally entails communion with the Father, is enacted within the Transfiguration.

The final act of the Transfiguration brings it to its crescendo and in so doing portrays its authoritative interpretation. As Jesus, Moses, and Elijah were conversing about the exodus he would accomplish at Jerusalem and as Peter was expressing his pleasure at being present, "when lo, a bright cloud overshadowed them, and a voice from the cloud said, 'This is my beloved Son with who I am well pleased; listen to him'" (Mt 17:5).

The whole transfiguring event is brought into this overshadowing cloud with the Father's concluding declaration and provides a vivid depiction of its meaning. The cloud that overshadowed Moses on Mt. Sinai is the prophetic anticipation of the same cloud that now finds its fulfillment in the overshadowing of Jesus. "Then Moses went up on the mountain, and a cloud covered the mountain. The glory of the Lord settled on Mount Sinai.... Now the appearance of the glory of the Lord was like a devouring fire on the top of the mountain ... and Moses entered the cloud" (Ex 24:15-18; see also 16:10). Within that cloud, the physical fiery symbolic representation of God's presence in his glory, God initiated his covenant with Moses. The bright cloud that now overshadows the transfigured Jesus, a cloud into which he enters, fulfills that first prophetic overshadowing, for it confirms that "the glory of the Lord," the very presence of the Father, has now settled on that mountain. It also prophetically confirms that Jesus will establish, through the acts of his death and resurrection, the new covenant. This in turn is confirmed in the Father's final declaration. As at Jesus' baptism, the Father has the last word, which, as at the baptism, provides the definitive interpretation of the whole transfiguring event. "This is my beloved Son with whom I am well pleased, listen to him." The Father is declaring that the one whose human shining face the Apostles behold in luminous brilliance is his beloved Son. In so doing, the Father corroborates his previous revelation to Peter that Jesus is indeed the Christ, the Son of the living God, and so confirms the Incarnation. To behold the glorious human face of Jesus is to behold the Father's glorious beloved Son. The Father is well pleased because Jesus, as his loyal Son, is proving to be true, in the course of public ministry, to his baptism pledge of being his faithful Servant/Son. The transfiguring event likewise foretells that Jesus, as the Christ, the Son of the living God, will be faithful until his sacrificial death on the cross. Thus, contrary to Peter's prognosis, the Father is corroborating Jesus' own declaration of what it means for him to be the Christ, that through his glorious saving passion and death he will merit his glorious resurrection and so embody, in his risen humanity, his Father's kingdom as its glorious King and universal Lord.[30] The Father is ultimately pleased simply because Jesus is, devotedly and decidedly, committed to becoming Jesus—YHWH-Saves. For this reason the Father adamantly insists that Peter, James, and John "listen to him." Without the entirety of this knowledge they will possess an inadequate, and even erroneous, understanding of Jesus and what it means for him to be, as Peter rightly professed, the Christ.

The Apostles must once more be placed within this concluding act. Peter states, "Lord [Matthew]/Master [Mark and Luke], it is well that we are here," not merely voicing their simple pleasure at being present, but more so gratefully affirming their privileged witnessing such a hallowing act. Mathew and Mark note that it was while Peter is still speaking that "a bright cloud overshadowed them." The "overshadowing" of the bright cloud, in these two accounts, may give the appearance that something is simply passively happening to them. But Luke makes clear that this "overshadowing" is an act by which "they entered the cloud." The "overshadowing" is "a being taken up into," an act of entering the transfiguring act itself, the very transfiguring act that Jesus entered when he entered the cloud. The three Apostles are no longer merely sleepy observers but now alert active participants within this holy transfiguring event, and thus the cause of their falling on their faces being filled with "awe" (Matthew) and "fear" (Luke). Their awe resided in their entering into this divinely hallowed event, which they could neither fully grasp nor anticipate its possible frightening consequences—who can see the face of God and live?

Nonetheless, what is being prophetically enacted here is the reality that Jesus' followers, the church, will be taken up into his glory, and this communion with him will be the act by which they will reap the benefits of his sacrificial death and glorious resurrection—the fulfilled promise foretold from of old as personified in Moses and Elijah.[31] In communion with Jesus, the risen

---

30. The Book of Isaiah prophesies that God will make his suffering servant a light to all nations (see Is 42:6, 49:6, 60:1-3). Ps 24:7-10 heralds that the King of glory, the Lord, strong and mighty, will triumphantly enter the gates of Jerusalem.

31. Paul beautifully expresses this truth. Unlike Moses, who had to veil his face, this veil is removed from those who come to faith in Jesus. Through the Spirit, "we all with unveiled face, beholding the glory of the Lord, being changed into his likeness from one degree of glory to another" (2 Cor 3:17-18). The divine light that shone upon Moses' face came from without, but

Christ, they will be purified of sin and share in his holiness, for his indwelling Spirit will transfigure their hearts of stone into hearts of flesh (Ezekiel). And in him, as the risen Son, they will enter into the new covenantal relationship with his Father—empowered, by the indwelling Spirit, to obey the new law written upon their hearts and so happily abide within the kingdom of God (Jeremiah). Thus they will become the new Israel—God's chosen people, possessing a new relationship, different in kind from any other relationship, with the Father as they now abide, through the Spirit, in his risen Son.[32]

This is why Matthew concludes the Transfiguration with these words: "But Jesus came and touched them, saying, 'Rise, and have no fear.' And when

---

the glory that resides within Christians is that of the indwelling Spirit, and this Spirit continually transforms Christians more and more into the glorious likeness of Jesus, in whose glory they now share.

32. The Apostles entering into the cloud and thus sharing in Jesus' glorious communion with the Father looks back to the Jewish temple and looks forward to Jesus as the new temple. When Moses had erected the tabernacle, "the cloud covered the tent of meeting, and the glory of the Lord filled the tabernacle. And Moses was not able to enter the tent of meeting because the cloud abode upon it and the glory of the Lord filled the tabernacle" (Ex 40:34-35; see Nm 14:10, 16:19, 20:6). When Solomon completed the temple and brought in the Ark of the Covenant, "a cloud filled the house of the Lord, so that the priests could not stand to minister because the glory of the Lord filled the house of the Lord" (1 Kgs 8:10-11). In the Gospel of John, the Jews confront Jesus asking by what authority he has cleansed the temple. Jesus responded, "Destroy this temple, and in three days I will raise it up." The disciples realized, after his resurrection, that Jesus was speaking of "the temple of his body" (Jn 2:18-22). As the Son of God incarnate, Jesus himself is the new temple, and to be united to the risen glorious Jesus is to reside in the presence of his Father.

The Letter to the Hebrews speaks of Jesus fulfilling Jeremiah's prophecy of a new covenant and so compares this covenant with that of the Mosaic covenant. Within the old covenant, only the high priest could enter the holy sanctuary once a year. But Jesus, the new high priest, enters the heavenly sanctuary, that is, into the very presence of his Father taking with him not the blood of goats, "but his own blood, thus securing an eternal redemption" (9:11-12). "Therefore, brethren, since we have confidence to enter the sanctuary by the blood of Jesus, by the new and living way which he opened to us through the curtain, that is, through his flesh, and since we have a great priest over the house of God, let us draw near with a true heart in full assurance of faith, with our hearts sprinkled clean from an evil conscience and our bodies washed with pure water" (Heb 10:19-22; see also 9:8). Hebrews is referencing the curtain in the temple that separated the outer temple from the Holy of Holies, the inner sanctum where God dwelt. When Jesus died, that curtain was torn from top to bottom, for through his sacrificial death he has gained for all who are in communion with him (with his risen flesh) entrance into the inner sanctum of heaven, into which all can now confidently draw near (see Mt 27:51). When the three disciples entered the cloud, they were prefiguring all Christians entering into the glorious presence of the Father, the heavenly sanctuary, in communion with the glorious incarnate flesh of Jesus the Son, having been purified by the sacrificial blood of Jesus and interiorly made new in the living waters of the Holy Spirit of which Ezekiel prophesied.

they lifted up their eyes, they saw no one but Jesus only" (Mt 17:7-8). The Apostles may have witnessed and participated in an extraordinary theophany, one that vividly and luminously portrayed the whole Gospel both in its prophetic anticipation and in its future fulfillment, but they need not fear, for the one who now touches them, the one in whom this Gospel resides, is simply Jesus—YHWH-Saves.[33]

According to Matthew, "as they were coming down from the mountain, Jesus commanded them, 'Tell no one the vision, until the Son of man is raised from the dead'" (Mt 17:9). Mark's account is similar, but adds: "So they kept the matter to themselves, questioning what the rising from the dead meant" (Mk 9:9-10). Luke simply states that "they kept silence and told no one in those days anything of what they had seen" (Lk 9:36). The need for silence until Jesus' resurrection is evident because they did not comprehend what it would mean for him to be raised from the dead, even though they had just witnessed a vision of it. Under these circumstances, for them to tell of their vision would cause nothing but confusion among those they told. More importantly, because the Transfiguration is prophetic in nature, in that it enacted the salvific meaning of Jesus' future passion, death, and resurrection, its true inherent significance could only be perceived in the light of its fulfillment. When the prophetic content of the Transfiguration is fulfilled, it then becomes the authoritative commentary that illuminates and enhances the meaning of the salvific events it prefigured.[34]

33. Within the smoke-filled and trembling temple, Isaiah experienced the glorious presence of the Lord, the seraphim proclaiming, "Holy, holy, holy is the Lord of hosts; the whole earth is full of his glory." Because of his sin and the sins of the people, Isaiah cried out, "Woe is me!" for he had seen "the King, the Lord of hosts!" The Lord purified Isaiah of his sin and so made him worthy to be in his presence (Is 6:1-5). Although the three Apostles beheld the glory of the Lord, the King, they did not need to fear, for Jesus, as his transfiguration portrays, will purify them of sin and thus they will abide in the presence of his Father.

Although the Transfiguration looks back to Moses and the Exodus and looks forward to Jesus' death and resurrection, it ultimately prefigures his second coming in glory. Then all the faithful will rise in glory and enter the eternal cloud of the Father's glory—heaven itself. "And I saw no temple in the city, for its temple is the Lord God the Almighty and the Lamb. And the city has no need of sun or moon to shine upon it, for the glory of God is its light, and its lamp is the Lamb." Because the faithful see the glorious and luminous face of Jesus, the risen Lamb who was slain, "they need no light or sun, for the Lord God will be their light, and they shall reign forever and ever" (Rv 21:22-23 and 22:4-5). Thus the prophecies of Isaiah will be wholly fulfilled. "The sun shall be no more your light, nor for brightness shall the moon give light by night; but the Lord will be your everlasting light, and your God will be your glory" (Is 60:19).

34. As the inherent prophetic meaning of the Passover lamb is only found in Jesus' sacrifice upon the cross, Jesus is perceived to be the new Passover lamb, so only when Jesus fulfills the prophetic content of his transfiguration does the transfiguration assume its full prophetic end as an interpretive commentary on what he has accomplished.

The Transfiguration contains a series of acts that express the doctrines of the Incarnation, the Trinity, and salvation. First, the whole event itself, concluding with the Father's authoritative declaration, is a revelational act of the Incarnation—beholding the luminous face of Jesus is to behold that of the Father's Son. Second, Jesus, as the Son of the Father, is equally revealed to be the Spirit-anointed Christ. Thus, within the luminous transfiguring of Jesus, the Trinity is made manifest—the Father, the Son, and the Holy Spirit. Third, Jesus as the transfigured Christ, the Son of the living God, prophetically anticipates those acts by which he will fulfill the entire revelation contained within the Old Testament, law, and prophets. Those acts will be his saving passion, death, and resurrection through which Jesus will enact the new covenantal relationship with the Father that is the kingdom of God. In communion with him as their glorious risen Savior, Jesus' followers will, through the indwelling of the Spirit, enter into communion with his Father and so share, in that communal act, their eternal life and radiant glory.[35]

Two More Predictions of Jesus' Passion, Death, and Resurrection

The Synoptic Gospels tell of two further occasions when Jesus told the Apostles of his future passion, death, and resurrection. They are significant in that they further enhance the anticipatory prophetic vision of the transfiguring act. They all occur as Jesus and his disciples are making their way from Galilee to Jerusalem. What Jesus tells his disciples is substantially the same on all occasions, although differing in some details.

Nonetheless, what Jesus foretells finds its significance in where he and the Apostles are going: Jerusalem. All three Gospels emphasize that there he will

---

35. I have attempted to demonstrate that the Transfiguration is a confirmation of Peter's profession of faith as well as a confirmation of Jesus' correction of Peter's misconceived understanding of his profession. Interestingly, the Gospel of John narrates neither Peter's profession nor the Transfiguration. I will argue later, however, possibly in a future volume, that the whole of John's Gospel is a doctrinal interpretation of both. The Gospel was written "that you may believe that Jesus is the Christ, the Son of God, and that believing you may have life in his name" (Jn 20:31). This declaration is that of Peter. The reason that such faith can be professed is that "the Word became flesh and dwelt among us, full of grace and truth; we have beheld his glory, glory as of the only Son of the Father" (Jn 1:14). The entirety of John's Gospel is the narration of Jesus revealing his glory (first in the book of signs, 1:19-12:50) and ultimately in his death on the cross and in his subsequent resurrection (the book of glory, 13:1-20:31), and in so doing manifesting his "transfigured" glory as the Christ, the Son of God. In so doing, for John, Jesus is becoming Jesus—YHWH-Saves—and so in his name we have eternal life.

be delivered first to the chief priests and then to the Gentiles to be mocked, spit upon, scourged, crucified and on the third day raised from the dead (see Mt 20:17-19). Mark deliberately states that "they were on the road going up to Jerusalem, and Jesus was walking ahead of them; and they were amazed, and those who followed were afraid" (Mk 10:32-34). Jesus, with determined resolve, eagerly strode toward Jerusalem.[36] Although those who followed were in awe of Jesus' keenness, they were afraid of what this journey forebode. As Jesus immediately states, "Behold, we are going up to Jerusalem; and the Son of man will be delivered up to the chief priests and scribes ... etc." (Mk 10:32-34). Luke notes that "when the days drew near for him to be received up, he set his face to go to Jerusalem" (Lk 9:51). As is the case in Matthew, Jesus accentuates this point. "Behold, we are going up to Jerusalem, and everything that is written of the Son of man by the prophets will be accomplished" (Lk 18:31).

On one level, Jesus is simply conveying the facts about what will take place in Jerusalem—his passion, death, and resurrection—and does not enlarge on the meaning and consequence of what will happen. On another level, there are now echoes of and allusions to the former transfiguring event, particularly of a soteriological nature. It is in Jerusalem that Jesus will be "delivered to" the chief priests and Gentiles. The "delivering into" the hands of those who will condemn and kill him will be his being "delivered up"—his being "taken up" into his passion and death so as to be "taken up" into the transfiguring glory of his resurrection (and ascension). As Luke stated above, Jesus would "accomplish," through his saving deeds, all that was written of him in the prophets—the fulfillment of the conversation that he had with Moses and Elijah when they spoke of "the departure, which he was to accomplish at Jerusalem." Although Jesus does not articulate a soteriology in the foretelling of what will take place in Jerusalem, he does allude to his transfiguring as the interpretive event that will soon take place within his saving actions. Through his being "delivered up," he will perform those saving acts, in accordance with the prophets, that will "accomplish" his being "taken up" into the glory of his

---

36. This is in keeping with what Luke records: "I came to set fire on the earth; and would that it were already kindled! I have a baptism to be baptized with; and how I am constrained until it is accomplished" (Lk 12:49-50). Jesus' mind and heart are ablaze with completing the task set before him by his Father, and he is unable to rest until it is fulfilled. Although Jesus then speaks of his being the cause of division within families, those divisions will be due to his having kindled the fire of the Gospel through his death and resurrection (his baptism), which in turn will demand either acceptance or rejection of him personally as Savior, thus making him the cause of divided households.

Father, and so his being the one in whom communion with the Father is secured.

The Apostles' reactions to Jesus' foretelling of what will take place in Jerusalem range from "distress" to "fear" to "incomprehension." Their apprehension and dread are understandable, but their lack of understanding initially poses a slight problem. One would think that after three verbal foretellings and the Transfiguration, they would begin "to see the light" and so have some understanding of what Jesus is persistently attempting to communicate. Yet their impregnable incomprehension gives rise to their anxiety and angst. Luke tells us that, having descended from the mount of the Transfiguration and having cast out the demon from a boy to the marvel of the Apostles, Jesus said, "Let these words sink into your ears; for the Son of man is to be delivered into the hands of men" (Lk 9:43-44). Emphatically, Jesus tells his disciples to be attentive to what he is about to say, to allow his words to sink deeply into the depths of their hearts and minds, and he does so immediately after his Father emphatically insisted that they listen to him because he is his beloved Son. "But they did not understand this saying, and it was concealed from them, that they should not perceive it; and they were afraid to ask him about the saying" (Lk 9:46; see also Mk 9:32). The disciples' incomprehension is not due to their slowness of wit or to the darkness of their hearts, but rather they were prevented from grasping the meaning and significance of what Jesus was saying, not simply in this instance but in all occasions, including the Transfiguration. Why would there be such a divine intervention when apparently the point of the exercise is to inform them of the meaning and consequence of Jesus' death and resurrection?

Jesus and his Father want the disciples to listen carefully and to keep in their minds and hearts a lively remembrance of what has been told them not so that they can comprehend the meaning now, but so that they can comprehend all that is said upon its being completed. Again, as with his transfiguring, Jesus' predictions of his passion, death, and resurrection are prophetic, and so their meaning can only be fully perceived when what is said is fulfilled. Only in the light of their fulfillment will Jesus be able to open their minds so that they may comprehend (see Lk 24:25-27), which is what Jesus ardently and repeatedly exhorted them to remember even though they did not understand what was being said at the time. The risen Jesus will remind them: "These are the words which I spoke to you while I was still with you" (Lk 24:44). Only then, in calling to mind what Jesus had already told them, are they prepared and so capable of comprehending what Jesus had "accomplished at Jerusalem" through his "being handed over" and in his "being given up" and in his "exodus/departure" and, ultimately in his being "received up" into glory—Jesus, the Spirit-anointed Christ, the Son of the living God, is Savior and Lord.[37]

Conclusion

I have attempted in this chapter to demonstrate the inherent connection between Peter's profession of faith and the Transfiguration. The Transfiguration is the enactment of Jesus being the Christ, the Son of the living God, and as such the enactment of his entrance into his glory through the salvific acts of his passion, death, and resurrection. This unity between Peter's profession and the Transfiguration are prophetic anticipations of what is about to take place: the enacting of the Paschal Mystery, to which we now turn. In so doing, we will observe Jesus definitively becoming Jesus—YHWH-Saves.

37. The above could be likened to parents telling their children things that they know they will not comprehend or appreciate at the time. They do so knowing that the time will come when, as adults, they will remember what was told them, appreciate their parents' wisdom, and act upon it.

8 · JESUS' TRIUMPHAL ENTRY INTO JERUSALEM

Within the Synoptic Gospels, Jesus' public ministry culminates with his triumphal entry into Jerusalem. This fulfills his thrice-proclaimed prophetic words that he must go up to Jerusalem, where he will be handed over, killed, and rise on the third day (see Mt 16:21, 17:22-23, 20:17-19, and parallels). Luke emphasizes that this journey to Jerusalem was a deliberative act on Jesus' part: "When the days drew near for him to be received up, he set his face to go to Jerusalem" (Lk 9:51; see also Mt 19:1-2 and Mk 10:1). When told that Herod was seeking to kill him, Jesus states that he must continue to heal and cast out demons, but "I must go on my way today and tomorrow and the day following, for it cannot be that a prophet should perish away from Jerusalem" (Lk 13:31-33). This purposeful striding up to Jerusalem, where Jesus will enact his passion, death, and resurrection, becomes the hermeneutical principle for interpreting his triumphal entry into Jerusalem. Within this soteriological context, the triumphal entry is a multifaceted enacted prophecy. It prophetically enacts and so anticipates Jesus' being "received up" into the heavenly Jerusalem, where he, as the risen heavenly king, will reign as the living heavenly temple giving full access to his heavenly Father. The triumphal entry prophetically anticipates that Jesus will be king! But between the day of Jesus' earthly triumphal prophetic entry and the day of his realized triumphal resurrection, Jesus will enact those salvific acts by which his own prophetic entry is fulfilled: his passion and death. Only because Jesus will be "received up" upon the cross in the earthly Jerusalem will he be "received up" into the heavenly Jerusalem. Jesus' death on the cross is the establishment of the heavenly Jerusalem, for his sacrificial death secures the forgiveness of humankind's sins and so merits his own resurrection. As the resurrected Savior and Lord, Jesus is literally the living embodiment of the heavenly Jerusalem, living in Spirit-filled communion with Father, and so he enters the heavenly Jerusalem by becoming the heavenly Jerusalem. Jesus is the triumphant king of God's kingdom because he is the supreme high priest who offers himself as the consummate sacrifice for the forgiveness of sins. Being the heavenly Jerusalem, Jesus equally becomes the living temple within it, for, in communion with him, humankind will have immediate access to his Father. Jesus' triumphal entry into Jerusalem is, then, a prophetic act that portrays and so proclaims him as the priest-king, and the fulfilling of this prophet act within the salvific acts of his death and resurrection becomes his consummate prophetic act. In his death he proclaims his priesthood, and in his resurrection he proclaims his kingship, and so Jesus is the living supreme everlasting Prophet forever professing himself, in his resurrected person, to be the living high priest-Victim who embodies, as King, his Father's everlasting kingdom. The triumphal entry into Jerusalem prophetically enacts that Jesus is and is to be Prophet, Priest, and King. Ultimately, what Jesus is prophetically enacting is his simply becoming Jesus—YHWH-Saves.

The prophetic triumphal entry also contains within it the three previously discussed pivotal prophetic events. First, the triumphal entry contains the Davidic kingly prophetic elements within the Infancy Narratives. Being the son of Mary as the Son of God incarnate, he will inherit the everlasting throne of his father David. Second, it contains the prophetic suffering servant elements contained within Jesus' baptism. As the Spirit-anointed Messiah and so as the Father's obedient beloved Suffering Servant/Son, Jesus will, through his sacrificial death, provide access, beyond the opened heavens, to his Father. Third and more explicitly, it contains the prophetic passing over of the Transfiguration. Having fulfilled the law and the prophets, Jesus, by way of his sacrificial death, will pass over into his resurrected kingly glory and so, with his disciples, live in communion with his heavenly Father in the new Jerusalem. This in turn will conclusively confirm Peter's proclamation of faith that Jesus is the Christ, the Son of the living God.

What we are going to find is that all that Jesus does and says between his triumphal entry into Jerusalem and his death and resurrection is both a looking back and a looking forward. What Jesus later says and does looks back to the triumphal entry by way of giving that triumphal entry a greater depth and clarity—a fuller understanding of its prophetic significance. In providing a fuller understanding of the triumphal entry, these later events and words also then look forward because, having increased the significance of his triumphal entry, they provide a clearer prophetic understanding what Jesus is about to accomplish through his salvific acts: the Paschal Mystery.

The event of Jesus' triumphal entry, which leads to and anticipates his death and resurrection, and all that takes place between these events, is eschatologically important. We will be witnessing the prophetic anticipation of the coming of God's kingdom, its present coming into being, and its prophetic future-awaited culmination at the end of time. With this in mind, we can now examine the biblical texts.

Preparatory Acts

Having purposely journeyed to Jerusalem to fulfill his foretold death and resurrection, all three Synoptic Gospels tell us that when he drew near to Bethphage and Bethany at the Mount of Olives, Jesus directed two of his disciples to the village to procure an ass or colt. By sending his disciples, Jesus not only sets the triumphal entry into Jerusalem in motion, but more importantly manifests that he is orchestrating the whole event and all that would follow upon it. This is also true for his passion and death. The Paschal Mystery is something Jesus will enact, and not something that will be enacted upon him. Jesus must enact his name YHWH-Saves if he is to be Jesus— YHWH-Saves. Similarly, only in so enacting his name do the Father and Holy Spirit enact, in communion with Jesus, their names as Father-YHWH-Saves and Holy Spirit-YHWH-Saves. By enacting the Paschal Mystery, Jesus enacts fully the Father's will, from which all saving acts flow, and he does so by acting in communion with the indwelling Spirit of Sonship, bringing the Spirit's saving work to completion. Within the Paschal Mystery the Father, Son, and Holy Spirit fully enact together, in accord with their personal distinctiveness, the complete work of salvation.

Jesus instructs his two disciples: If anyone queries their taking of the ass, they are to say, "The Lord has need of it."[1] Within Mark and Luke, the disciples are challenged upon untying the colt and respond, "The Lord has need of it." Although Jesus is yet to be the risen divine Lord, within the context of the triumphal entry, Jesus is prophetically anticipating the reality of his becoming "Lord," which his disciples are already unwittingly prophesizing. Matthew at this juncture notes that all of this took place to fulfill the prophecy: "Tell the daughter of Zion, Behold, your king is coming to you, humble, and mounted on an ass, and on a colt, the foal of an ass."

---

1. All quotations within this section are from Mt 21:1-6, Mk 11:1-6, and Lk 19:28-35 unless otherwise noted.

This passage is a compilation of two prophecies. Isaiah proclaims that the people should "go through the gates" of Jerusalem and "prepare the way for the people." They should "build up the highway" and clear away all stones. They are to "lift up an ensign over the peoples." The reason is that "the Lord has proclaimed to the end of the earth: 'Behold, your salvation comes; behold, his reward is with him, and his recompense before him. And, they shall be called The holy people, The redeemed of the Lord; and you will be called Sought out, a city not forsaken'" (Is 62:10-12). Zechariah proclaims: "Rejoice greatly, O daughter of Zion! Shout aloud, O daughter of Jerusalem! Lo, your king comes to you; triumphant and victorious is he, humble and riding on an ass, on a colt the foal of an ass."[2] This king will destroy the weapons of war, and "he shall command peace to the nations; his dominion shall be from sea to sea, and from the River to the ends of earth" (Zec 9:9-10).

These braided prophecies focus on Jerusalem, a specific geographical location. Isaiah emphasizes that its citizens should go through its gates so as to prepare the highway that leads to Jerusalem. This preparation harkens back to John the Baptist's ministry of preparing a way for the Lord, which is now being fulfilled in Jesus' entry into Jerusalem as the baptized Messiah who will enact his identity as the faithful Suffering Servant/Son. But this prophecy significantly first designates this preparation as an anticipation of the coming of "the peoples" to Jerusalem, not simply Jews but all nations, in the light of the Lord's coming. The reason lies in what the Lord has proclaimed "to the end of the earth" and thus to all peoples. "Your salvation comes," and this salvation is a person, for he brings "his reward" and "his recompense with him." Thus these peoples from the ends of the earth "shall be called The holy people, The redeemed of the Lord." All peoples, Jews and Gentiles alike, will be one holy people—the one redeemed people of the Lord. Therefore the Jewish people, specifically the city of Jerusalem, will be "Sought out, a city not forsaken." All peoples, seemingly greater nations with superior cities, will ardently seek out a city once thought forsaken and enter its gates once considered abandoned precisely because the Lord's universal salvation resides therein. The Gentiles will enter into salvation, into Jerusalem, through the Jews, for Jesus, as a Jew, fulfills the promises made to the Jews, and in so doing brings salvation to all

2. Because Matthew takes the colt and the ass in this passage to be two distinct animals—that is, the ass and her colt—he will have Jesus performing an acrobatic "miracle" of sitting on both simultaneously (see Mt 21:7). It appears that he did not grasp, at least here, the nature of Hebrew poetic parallelism, where the same point is successively expressed in two similar ways.

peoples. Salvation is predicated upon a primacy of place (Jerusalem) and a primacy of people (the Jews) into which the Gentiles enter. This is the city of Jerusalem, through whose gates Jesus is now entering, and so the daughter of Zion is to rejoice and the daughter of Jerusalem is to shout aloud, "Lo, your king comes to you; triumphant and victorious." Moreover, the Jews who joyfully accompany Jesus are the prophesied preparatory Jews entering Jerusalem, for in so doing they are preparing the way for all peoples and nations to enter within its saving walls.[3]

Furthermore, Jesus enters Jerusalem as a humble king, for he rides upon, of all animals, a mean ass. Although by entering the earthly Jerusalem he is prophetically enacting the truth that he will be king of the heavenly Jerusalem and thus a cause of rejoicing and shouting aloud, the humble ass upon which Jesus now rides through the gate into the earthly Jerusalem anticipates the humiliation of the cross that will carry him through the heavenly gate into the everlasting Jerusalem as its king. Through that humble salvific gate, all "The holy" and "The redeemed" jubilant nations, carrying "the ensign" of the cross above them, will enter a kingdom of peace, which will extend in this world "from sea to sea and from the River to the ends the earth" and culminate in the Father's everlasting and universal heavenly kingdom.

The Feast of Booths

Having brought Jesus the colt or ass, the two disciples placed their garments upon it, and upon it Jesus sat. Much of the crowd proceeded to place their garments as well as leafy branches upon the road before him. As they descended the Mount of Olives toward Jerusalem, the people cried out. Luke notes that they "began to rejoice and praise God with loud voice for all of the mighty works that they had seen" (Lk 19:37). (For this section, see Mt 21:7-8, Mk 35-36, and Lk 19:35-37.)[4] This enactment finds its antecedent in the Book of Levit-

---

3. I do not believe that it is insignificant that, over the centuries, the Gentiles continue, unabated to this day, to visit Jerusalem specifically to pray at the geographical location where their redemption was achieved—the spot of Jesus' death and resurrection. In so doing, they implicitly, if not explicitly, acknowledge the Jewish roots of their salvation and into which they have now been grafted (see Rom 11:17-24). They enact, yet sadly the Jewish people as a whole do not, the truth of Zechariah's prophecy: "In those days ten men from the nations of every tongue shall take hold of the robe of a Jew, saying, 'Let us go with you [to Jerusalem], for we have heard that God is with you'" (Zec 8:23). The God who is with them and of whom the Gentiles have heard is Jesus, Emmanuel.

4. The question might be asked: What mighty deeds had these people seen, presuming that

icus, where God commands Moses that on the seven-day harvest feast, or feast
of booths (which commemorates that while God made the Israelites dwell in
small booths or tabernacles in the desert, he was nonetheless leading them
to their "permanent" home), the people are to "take on the first day the fruit
of the goodly trees, branches of palm trees, and boughs of leafy trees, and
willows of the brook; and you shall rejoice before the Lord God seven days"
(Lv 23:40). This is to remind the people that God "made the people of Israel to
dwell in booths when I brought them out of the land of Egypt: I am the Lord
your God" (Lv 23:43). Likewise, when Jehu was anointed king of Israel, every
man in haste "took his garment, and put it under him on the bare steps, and
they blew the trumpet, and proclaimed 'Jehu is king'" (2 Kgs 9:13). Moreover,
when Maccabeus and his men, "the Lord leading them on, recovered the temple and the city," they cleansed and purified the temple and offered sacrifices
and burned incense. Because previously they were unable to celebrate properly the feast of booths, they did so now. "Therefore bearing ivy-wreathed
wands and beautiful branches and also fronds of palm, they offered hymns of
thanksgiving to him (the Lord) who had given success to the purifying of his
own holy place" (2 Mc 10:7; see 10:1-8 and 1 Mc 13:49-51).

The onset of Jesus' triumphal entry, then, prophetically enacts these earlier events and in so doing, again by knitting them together, gives those events
prophetic significance. First, the placing of garments upon Jesus' donkey and
before his path suggests the act of the men proclaiming Jehu king in that Jesus will be heralded, in the course of his garment-strewn path into Jerusalem,
as an anointed king. This act prophetically anticipates the obtaining, through
his passion and death, of his definitive Spirit-anointed Davidic kingship in his
resurrection and so will reign over God's everlasting kingdom. Second, within Jesus' entry there is a clear allusion to the feast of booths and the bounti-
ful Promised Land that would find its fulfillment in the eschatological harvest
feast. It was within their desert pilgrimage that God made a covenant with his
people, the Ark of the Covenant and the subsequent temple into which it was
placed being expressions of his steadfast loving covenantal presence among
them. Jesus, through his new covenantal death and resurrection, will lead the

they are mostly from the Jerusalem area (including Bethphage and Bethany), since, within the
Synoptic Gospels, this is supposedly Jesus' first journey to Jerusalem? Given that they are rejoicing over his mighty deeds, this might not have been his first time in Jerusalem. The Gospel
of John, which has multiple visits of Jesus to Jerusalem, specifies that the people were rejoicing
and proclaiming him king because "the crowd that had been with him when he called Lazarus
out of the tomb and raised him from the dead bore witness. The reason why the crowd went to
meet him was that they heard he had done this sign" (Jn 12:17-18).

new Israel from their earthly ramshackle homes where they ate their meager mortal meals into their palatial heavenly homes where they will, in communion with their living God, savor the harvest of the eternal banquet.[5] Third, their harvest/booth celebration, as portrayed in the Second Book of Maccabees, consisted of a liturgical procession, presumably within the temple or the temple area, wherein they joyfully carried fruit and beautiful branches from palm and leafy trees. Jesus will now lead his jubilant palm-laden liturgical procession to the temple where he will, like Maccabeus, symbolically cleanse it of all defilement. Thus Jesus' enactment of Maccabeus' act of cleansing the temple prophetically enacts the fruit of Jesus' death and resulting resurrection—a holy living temple, a temple undefiled, that is Jesus himself, in whom all will process into the presence of his righteous Father, jubilantly waving in worship their heavenly palms of victory. Jesus' liturgical procession into Jerusalem to worship in the temple anticipates the eternal liturgical procession that will comprise the heavenly liturgy of the new Jerusalem—the faithful surrounding the temple throne of God glorifying, in the Spirit, the Father, and his glorious crucified and risen Son.[6]

Hosanna in the Highest

Within the context of Jesus' prophetic liturgical enactment of previous intertwining prophesies and braided historical events, the Synoptic Gospels proceed to give various, but similar, renditions of what the crowds proclaimed. These proclamations confirm and further illuminate the prophetic significance of Jesus' triumphal entry into Jerusalem. The peoples' exclamations find their source in Psalm 118, and although only the concluding verses of this psalm are quoted or alluded to, the entire psalm is of the utmost theological significance for interpreting fully the implications of Jesus' triumphal entry. Jesus' thrice-proclaimed foretelling of his death and resurrection is the hermeneutical key for interpreting his triumphal entry into Jerusalem. In Psalm 118,

5. Isaiah prophesies on the Lord's behalf: "On this mountain [Jerusalem] the Lord will make for all peoples a feast of fat things, a feast of wine on the lees, of fat things full of marrow, of wine on the lees well refined" (Is 25:6).

6. The entire Book of Revelation can be interpreted as a heavenly liturgical banquet. Within that liturgy Jesus, the crucified and risen Lamb, is worshiped and adored as king. "'To him who sits upon the throne and to the Lamb be blessing and honor and glory and might forever and ever!' And the four living creatures said, 'Amen!' and the elders fell down and worshiped" (Rv 5:13-14). See also the whole of chapters 4 and 5 in the Book of Revelation.

we now find the prophetic content of this thrice-proclaimed prophecy, for it prophetically describes the acts that Jesus is performing presently within his prophetic triumphal entry and, in so doing, anticipating his future passion, death, and resurrection, acts through which he will fulfill both the content of Psalm 118 and what is being prophetically enacted in the triumphal entry. For this reason we must first examine the entire psalm.

The psalm is set within a liturgical procession into the temple that was composed of the king and his people. The psalm begins as a hymn of thanksgiving to the Lord for his goodness. Because of God's goodness, the people are to proclaim, "His steadfast love endures forever" (vv. 1-4). So much is this the case that even in the peoples' distress, they need not fear, for "the Lord is on my side to help me," and therefore it is "better to take refuge in the Lord than to put confidence in man" or even princes, for "I shall look in triumph on those who hate me" (vv. 5-9). Even if "all the nations surround me, "in the name of the Lord I cut them off," for "the Lord is my strength and my song; he has become my salvation" (vv. 10-14). This elicits "glad songs of victory" among the righteous, for they have witnessed the valiant right hand of the Lord. "I shall not die, but I shall live, and recount the deeds of the Lord." The Lord may chastise "me sorely, but he has not given me over to death" (vv. 16-18). Here the jubilant procession reaches the gates to the temple and the people cry out to the temple priests: "Open to me the gates of righteousness, that I may enter through them and give thanks to the Lord" (vv. 19-20). The hymn of thanksgiving is renewed, for the Lord "has become my salvation" in that he has chosen not the choice stone, but the stone rejected by the builders. It is this stone that "has become the head of the corner." "This is the Lord's doing; it is marvelous in our eyes." Therefore "this is the day which the Lord has made; let us rejoice and be glad in it" (vv. 21-24). We clearly perceive here that Jesus is prophetically enacting this psalm within his triumphal entry into Jerusalem that will conclude at the temple itself.

Jesus' triumphal entry into Jerusalem is a liturgical procession in which he is already prophetically giving thanks to his Father, for he is assured of his paternal enduring goodness and steadfast love. Amid his impending suffering and death, where he will be sorely chastised, surrounded by those who hate him, he need not fear, but he already confidently looks forward to his triumph over death, for his Father is his strength and his salvation. "I shall not die, but I shall live and recount the deeds of the Lord." He is presently entering the gates of Jerusalem and thence through the gates of the temple, and this entry prophetically anticipates his entry into the "gates of righteousness"—the heavenly Jerusalem. He may be the stone rejected by his fellow Jews and killed by the gentile Romans, but he will become the cornerstone, chosen by his Father, of the new living temple, which will be his risen humanity.[7] This will be the marvel for all eyes to see, and so the dawning of the new day which his Father has made and in which all will rejoice. All the above sequential liturgical acts with their appropriate liturgical responses contained within Psalm 118 are now prophetically being acted out by Jesus in his own liturgical procession into Jerusalem and will be fulfilled within the liturgical act of his own imminent death and resurrection—his triumphal entry into glory as his Father's faithful Son.

At this juncture within Psalm 118, we arrive at the words proclaimed by the people who have joined and compose Jesus' triumphal entry. "Save us, we beseech you, O Lord! O Lord, we beseech you, give us success! Blessed be he who enters in the name of the Lord! We bless you from the house of the Lord." Matthew renders this proclamation as: "Hosanna to the Son of David! Blessed is he who comes in the name of the Lord! Hosanna in the highest!" (Mt 21:9). "Hosanna! Blessed is he who comes in the name of the Lord! Blessed is the kingdom of our father David that is coming! Hosanna in the highest!" (Mk 11:9-10). "Blessed is the King who comes in the name of the Lord! Peace in heaven and glory in the highest!" (Lk 19:38).

Matthew and Mark have rendered the psalm's "Save us, we beseech you, O Lord!" as the acclamation "Hosanna!" which can be translated as either "O Lord grant salvation" or "May the Lord save." As the people surround Jesus on all sides, their jubilant cry enfolds him and rises to the highest heavens as he makes his way to and into Jerusalem. In so doing, they are both confidently petitioning that the Lord will grant them salvation in Jesus and also, within their hopeful faith, cheerfully acknowledging that in him the Lord is actual-

---

7. Within the Gospel of John, when Jesus is challenged by what authority he has cleansed the temple, Jesus responds, "Destroy this temple, and in three days I will raise it up." John notes that Jesus spoke not of the temple built with stone, "but spoke of the temple of his body. When therefore he was raised from the dead, his disciples remembered that he had said this; and they believed the scripture and the word which Jesus had spoken" (Jn 2:18-22).

Within the Gospel of Matthew, Jesus later quotes this passage from Ps 118:22-23. He concludes his parable on the vineyard owner who finally sent his own son to collect his produce and who is then killed by the tenants by stating in obvious self-reference: "Have you never read in the scriptures: 'The very stone which the builders rejected has become the head of the corner; this was the Lord's doing, and it is marvelous in our eyes'" (Mt 21:42; see also Acts 4:11 and 1 Pt 2:7). Jesus, as the beloved incarnate Son, is the rejected stone that will become the keystone to his Father's living temple.

ly saving his people. The reason for their confident request and hope-filled acknowledgment of its realization lies in Jesus being the Son of David who comes in the name of the Lord. This is clearly seen in Matthew, where the "Hosanna," the "O Lord grant salvation," is directly addressed to Jesus. "Hosanna to the Son of David! Blessed is *he* who comes in the name of the Lord. Hosanna in the highest!" The peoples' assurance of salvation lies in Jesus, for he comes in the name of the Lord as David's son and will, as such, establish according to the Lord's promise an everlasting kingdom. Thus the source of salvation, the Lord himself, is the highest; the cause of salvation, the prophesied son of David, is the highest; and therefore the hoped-for salvific effect will be the highest, the everlasting Davidic kingdom. Mark's rendering corroborates this: "Blessed is the kingdom of our father David that is coming! Hosanna in the highest!" The blessed promised kingdom of David is coming in the person of Jesus, David's son, and therefore the people can exclaim to the heights of heaven their joy in the Lord's salvation. These jubilant acclamations are prayerful worshipful praises and so are constitutive of the liturgical nature of this triumphal procession. But the cornerstone of this liturgical procession, what makes it a prayerful pageant, is Jesus, for he is leading them to the temple—his Father's house of prayer. He will then prophetically enact, through his cleansing of the temple, that he is the holy temple in whom, as its cornerstone, is found genuine worship of his Father.

Although Luke's rendering does not have the people exclaim "Hosanna," they do cry out: "Blessed is the King who comes in the name of the Lord! Peace in heaven and glory in the highest!" The people here echo the words of the angel Gabriel to Mary at the Annunciation: "He will be great, and will be called Son of the Most High; and the Lord God will give to him the throne of his father David . . . and of his kingdom there will be no end" (Lk 1:32–33). Jesus, the Son of the Most High, is the blessed king because he, in the Lord's name and by the authoritative initiative of his Father, was born into the world as the Son of God incarnate and now, in the name of the Lord, he is triumphantly entering into Jerusalem to establish the everlasting kingdom for which he was born and over which he will now reign as its king. Similarly, the people also echo the glorious choir of heavenly host who first heralded the announcement of Jesus' birth: "Glory to God in the highest and on earth peace to men with whom he is pleased" (Lk 2:14). The angels informed the shepherds that in the city of David a Savior, Christ the Lord, was born to them, and therefore all glory should be given to God on high for the heavenly peace that is being established on earth. Now this finds its culmination in the people proclaiming

Jesus to be their Davidic Savior, who is Christ the Lord, as he enters Jerusalem to inaugurate this kingdom of peace between God and men through his death and resurrection—the very saving acts that he was born to perform.

Confrontation and Weeping

Within the Gospel of Luke, Jesus was confronted by some Pharisees among the multitude (Lk 19:39-40). "Teacher, rebuke your disciples." Although the stones to which he refers may be those scattered about on the Mount of Olives, from Jesus' response to this confrontation it would more likely be taking place within the temple precincts and thus at the conclusion of his triumphal entry. "I tell you, if these were silent, these very stones would cry out."[8] The Pharisees clearly grasped the theological significance of Jesus' triumphal entry into Jerusalem, which culminated at the temple. Jesus' entry into Jerusalem was being heralded by his disciples as the entry of their king. Whether Jesus intended this or not the Pharisees were unsure, but they were certain that such homage should be immediately rebuked by Jesus, and so Jesus should dissociate himself from such zealous but totally unacceptable accolades. Instead of reprimanding his disciples for their false perception of what had just been enacted, Jesus intensifies the validity of their proclamation. Even if the people were to become silent, the stones of the temple, before which they now stood, would cry out: "Blessed is the King who comes in the name of the Lord!" The dead stones of the earthly temple would cry out that he is king, for even they would recognize that Jesus, as king, is the living heavenly temple, and in him his disciples are the living stones who exult in praise of him. This is in keeping with Psalm 118 quoted above: "Blessed be he who enters [the temple] in the name of the Lord! We bless you from the house of the Lord" (v. 26). Jesus enters the temple by becoming the living temple, and all those who are united to him, the living stones, bless him from within it, the very house of the Lord that he is.[9]

8. It is difficult to determine the exact sequence of these events. Although the stones above may refer to the stones of the temple, immediately after this Luke has Jesus weeping over Jerusalem. In light of Matthew's and Mark's narratives, such lamenting on the Mount of Olives took place after his triumphal entry and his cleansing of the temple.

9. The First Letter of Peter quotes the passage from Psalm 118:20 where the stone rejected by the builders has become the cornerstone. Within that context, Peter also exhorts his readers: "Come to him, to that living stone, rejected by men, but in God's sight chosen and precious; and like living stones be yourselves built into a spiritual house, to be a holy priesthood, to offer spiritual sacrifices, acceptable to God through Jesus Christ" (2:4-5; see also vv. 6-10). Jesus and those

Matthew narrates two scenes similar to that of Luke (Mt 21:10-11).[10] When Jesus entered Jerusalem, "all the city was stirred, saying, 'Who is this?' And the crowds said, 'This is the prophet Jesus from Nazareth of Galilee.'" What stirred the Jerusalem crowds was a man riding on an ass who was being proclaimed as the promised Davidic king who is bringing salvation. Significantly, within the same Gospel, the last time Jerusalem was in such an uproar was when the three wise men entered their city in search of the king of the Jews. While they were searching for a king, the priests and the scribes informed them that "the Christ" was to be born in Bethlehem, from which, according to the prophet (Mi 5:2), the ruler would come (see Mt 2:1-6). The three kings entered Jerusalem searching for the king of the Jews, and now the very king for whom they searched has just entered Jerusalem—the prophesied Savior born in Bethlehem is Jesus from Nazareth of Galilee. Although the village in which he was born and the town where he matured may be of little account, Jesus, humbly riding on an ass, now enters into the sacred capital of all of Israel, and he does so being proclaimed as the promised Prophet-Messiah-Savior-King. This inexplicable enactment is what scandalized the teachers in Luke's Gospel and now perplexes the unsettled befuddled crowds in Matthew's Gospel. And as king Herod sought to kill the king of Jews, so his failed wishes will now be fulfilled by those who, like Herod, refuse to perceive the truth of what is being enacted before their very eyes.

---

who believe in him form one living temple, and in him, the new high priest, they can truly offer, having been cleansed of sin, spiritual sacrifices.

This understanding becomes the major theme within the Letter to the Hebrews. Although the old covenant allowed for an earthly temple in which God dwelt and to whom animal sacrifices were offered, it was but a prefigurement of Jesus, "the mediator of a new covenant," one that will allow access to the true heavenly temple, that is, into the very presence of his heavenly Father (Heb 9:15). "For Christ has entered, not into a sanctuary made with hands, a copy of the true one, but into heaven itself, now to appear in the presence of God on our behalf" (Heb 9:24). "Therefore, brethren, since we have confidence to enter the sanctuary by the blood of Jesus, by the new and living way which he opened for us through the curtain, that is, through his flesh, and since we have a great priest over the house of God, let us draw near with a true heart in full assurance of faith, with hearts sprinkled clean form an evil conscience and our body washed with pure water" (Heb 10:19-22).

This finds its ultimate reality at the end of time, when Jesus comes in glory. Thus the concluding vision in the Book of Revelation: "And I saw no temple in the city [the new Jerusalem], for its temple is the Lord God and the Lamb" (Rv 21:22). In communion with Jesus, the ever-living Lamb of sacrifice, all the faithful will live forever in the presence of his eternal Father.

10. The first takes place prior to the cleansing of the temple and the second immediately after the cleansing. Although the subject matter of the second is more like that within Luke, we will wait until after treating the cleansing before we discuss it because its postcleansing setting is theologically significant.

Immediately after Jesus' confrontation with the Pharisees, Luke narrates Jesus' weeping over Jerusalem. As he left the unbelieving Pharisees behind and proceeded toward the city, Jesus "wept over it" because Jerusalem, as symbolically embodied in the Pharisees, did not know what makes for peace, for it was hidden "from your eyes." Because of this, the days are coming "when your enemies will cast up a bank about you [Jerusalem] and surround you ... and they will not leave a stone upon another in you; because you did not know the time of your visitation" (Lk 19:41-44). What the Pharisees and Jerusalem did not recognize, in keeping with Luke's Gospel, was the fulfillment of the opening proclamation of Zechariah's canticle: "Blessed be the Lord God of Israel for he has visited and redeemed his people, and has raised up a horn of salvation for us in the house of his servant David ... that we should be saved from our enemies and from the hand of all who hate us" (Lk 1:68-71). Jesus, as the Son of God, is the Lord God who is visiting his people and is now triumphantly visiting Jerusalem, and as the promised son of David he is the horn of salvation who would free Jerusalem of its enemies.[11] As Zechariah also proclaims, salvation is ultimately found in "the forgiveness of their sins," which manifests "the tender mercy of our God" that will destroy the "shadow of death." In so doing, God will "guide our feet into the way of peace" (Lk 1:77-79). This is what Jesus is prophetically proclaiming in triumphantly entering Jerusalem. He, the Father's Son, is guiding the feet of those who are singing his praises as David's kingly son into Jerusalem, where he will manifest God's divine mercy through his reconciling death and so establish, through his resurrection, true peace-loving communion with his Father. In the end, however, this day is the day that Jerusalem recognized as the day "of your visitation."[12]

The Cleansing of the Temple

We have now reached the culminating theological climax of Jesus' triumphal entry into Jerusalem. As noted throughout our discussion, this liturgical procession is not without a terminus. It is not a meandering political demonstra-

---

11. Whether Jerusalem would not have been destroyed had it accepted Jesus as the saving visitation of their Lord God cannot be answered. What we do know is that Jesus' prophecy was fulfilled in 70 AD, when the Romans destroyed Jerusalem and the temple.

12. Luke shortly after has Jesus twice prophetically reiterate the coming of Jerusalem's demise (see Lk 21:5-6 and 20). The second time is within the context of the coming of the eschatological end times and what will portentously precede it. This will be examined at the appropriate point.

tion consisting of a disaffected rabble hailing their partisan leader. From its on-set from the heights of the Mount of Olives, Jesus pointed his donkey in one direction and to one final location—the sacred city of Jerusalem and the most sacred site within that city—the temple of YHWH, the One, Holy, Most-High God. Matthew continues his narrative by stating, "And Jesus entered the temple of God and drove out all who sold and bought in the temple, and he overturned the tables of the money-changers and the seats of those who sold pigeons. He said to them, 'It is written "My house shall be called a house of prayer; but you have made it a den of robbers"'" (Mt 21:12-13; see also Mk 11:15-17 and Lk 19:45-46).[13] (Mark has Jesus say, "a house of prayer for all nations.") Although the activity in the outermost court of the Gentiles was to facilitate the purchase of animals for sacrifice and to obtain the proper coinage to make such purchases (see Ex 30:13 and Lv 1:14), Jesus perceived that such activity had turned into a profane business powered by greed. Thus the sacred prayerful character of the holy temple acquired the avaricious atmosphere of a common market.

The last recorded sordid monetary transaction to take place within the temple precincts prior to Jesus' death and resurrection is when Judas, the greediest thief within a den of thieves, betrayed Jesus to the chief priests for thirty pieces of silver. Historically, other monetary transactions were no doubt transacted after Jesus' resurrection, but what makes Judas' transaction ironic is that he "sold" to the chief priests the perfect lamb of sacrifice and they "bought" that lamb for thirty pieces of silver. Once Jesus offered his holy and innocent life to his Father, all the buying and selling of sacrificial animals within the temple precincts meant nothing—they were no longer of any authentic spiritual value other than the continuing prefiguring of what had now taken place. Jesus was the last lamb to be truly bought and sold, and the last lamb to be truly sacrificed, for his sacrifice cleansed all of humankind of sin and so made it possible for all to enter into the heavenly Holy of Holies as God's holy people.[14]

The words of Jesus' rebuke are again the intertwining of two prophetic passages, Isaiah and Jeremiah, the context of which is theologically signifi-

13. Although all three Gospels narrate the event similarly, Mark states that Jesus, while looking around at the temple upon the day of his entry, returned to Jerusalem the next day to cleanse it (see Mk 11:11).

14. The Letter to the Hebrews makes this point clearly: "Now Christ appeared as high priest of the good things that have come, then entered through the greater and more perfect tent (not made by human hands, that is, of this creation) he entered once for all into the Holy Place, taking not the blood of goats and calves, but his own blood, thus securing an eternal redemption" (Heb 9:11-12).

cant. The Lord, through Isaiah, proclaimed that the people are to be just and righteous, "for soon my salvation will come and my deliverance will be revealed." Because of this, neither the faithful foreigner nor the righteous eunuch should think that they are excluded, for all who "love the name of the Lord, and to be his servants, everyone who keeps the Sabbath, and holds fast my covenant—these I will bring to my holy mountain, and make them joyful in my house of prayer … for my house shall be called a house of prayer for all peoples" (Is 56:1-8). The daughter of Zion and the daughter of Jerusalem are to rejoice and sing for joy, for the Lord is proclaimed to all the earth, and thus all nations shall come to Jerusalem to be in the presence of the Lord. Jesus is now confirming this—the temple is to be, as Mark fully quotes Isaiah, a joyful "house of prayer for all nations," for salvation is near and deliverance is at hand; that is, Jesus the Savoir is standing upon the holy mountain, and he will attract all peoples to himself. Most importantly, although Jesus is quoting from Isaiah, he speaks now in his own person as the temple being "my house." The temple is God's (YHWH's) house of prayer, but as the Father's Son, it is equally Jesus' house of prayer as well. Jesus, as the Father's Son, is laying claim to the temple, and as the Father's Son he possesses the right and authority to cleanse his Father's dwelling place so as to make it a true house of prayer for all peoples.[15] In accordance with Luke's Gospel, Jesus is once again in his Father's house, where he is bringing his Father's business to conclusion—the cleansing of God's people from sin and so making them a holy people worthy to worship him in the new living temple that is Jesus himself. Here the passage from Jeremiah finds its importance.

God tells Jeremiah "to stand in the gate of the Lord's house," the very place where Jesus now stands. There Jeremiah is to proclaim to all who enter the temple gate to worship: "Amend your ways and your doings, and I will dwell in this place. Do not trust in these deceptive words: 'This is the temple of the Lord, the temple of the Lord, the temple of the Lord.'" God asks whether the people will persist in sinning and offering incense to Baal and yet continue "to

---

15. The Letter to the Hebrews contrasts Moses and Jesus in that "Moses was faithful to God's house as a servant, to testify to the things that were to be spoken later, but Christ was faithful over God's house as a son" (Heb 3:5-6a). Jesus was faithful to his Father's house as Son in that he not only cleansed the earthly temple of all unclean commerce, but also purified God's people of their sin, allowing them to enter into the true and living temple as his holy people. "And we [Christian believers] are his [God's] house if we hold fast our confidence and pride in our hope" (Heb 3:6b).The subsequent confrontation between Jesus and the Jewish leaders concerns who Jesus is and by whose authority he has cleansed the temple.

stand before me in this house, which is called by my name, and say 'We are de-livered!'—only to go on doing all these abominations? Has this house, which is called by my name, become a den of robbers in your eyes? Behold, I myself have seen it, says the Lord."[16] In this light, God tells the people to go to Shiloh, "where I made my name dwell first" and see the destruction of that first holy place because of Israel's sin. He will now do the same in Jerusalem what he did at Shiloh. "I will cast you out of my sight, as I cast out your kinsmen, all the offspring of Ephraim" (Jer 7:1-15).

Recall that the whole of Jesus' triumphal entry into Jerusalem is a prophet-ic act that foretells what salvific acts he is about to perform, and the salvific effects they will achieve. Here we perceive, in the act of cleansing the temple, the character of his yet-to-be performed saving acts and what they will accom-plish. Jesus has triumphantly entered Jerusalem to cleanse the people of their sins and so make them worthy to enter a new temple where they will be able to worship God in righteousness and holiness. This prophetic cleansing of sin will be fulfilled in Jesus' sacrificial death, for he will offer, as the all-holy high priest, the perfect unblemished sacrifice of his own holy life to his Father by which humankind will be cleansed of sin and so reconciled to God. Unlike the present sacrifices, often bearing only the marks of mere ritual formality and the half-hearted remnants of sin, Jesus' holy priestly sacrifice will be imbued with the perfect love of his Father and of his Father's beloved people, and in so doing he will establish a new living temple, that is, access to the heavenly tem-ple, and so be ushered into his Father's very presence. This living temple, the place where the Father's holy name dwells, will be the resurrected Jesus, the Father's Son, for only in him, sharing in his holiness, will those who believe in him, possessing in him his Spirit of Sonship, worship his Father as his sons and daughters. No longer will the people superstitiously recite "The temple of the Lord, the temple of the Lord, the temple of the Lord" as a hollow and so fu-tile religious mantra because, in being cleansed of their duplicity and unfaith-fulness, they will perceive Jesus as the true living temple of the Lord in whom they now possess God's protecting and saving presence.

On the one hand, Jesus will make the present temple redundant because, through his cleansing sacrificial death and sanctifying resurrection, he will be the living gate through and in whom all the righteous will enter to worship his Father in holiness. Although the Romans will soon destroy it, Jesus had already

---

16. As man, the Son of God, "the Lord," has now literally seen with his own eyes "these abominations."

made the temple superfluous. "My temple" is to be Jesus, for in him, as the glorious Father's Son, all will be able to enter into the presence of "my Father."[17] On the other hand, what cannot be forgotten is that this redundancy is not the mere tossing away of the old, the demise of something that is of no lasting value. In coming to the temple, Jesus is acknowledging that it is his Father's house of prayer, and in so doing he bears with his coming all that the temple rightly signifies and properly embodies: the ancient covenant with its liturgical rituals and sacrifices. This covenantal history, although it will be cleansed and fulfilled, is not repudiated. In Jesus, this covenantal history and all that the temple implies and denotes find their true and lasting meaning. Jesus raises their importance to a new level and so they are to be even more venerated, for they are now valued for what they were truly meant to be—prefigured anticipations of the new covenant that would be established within Jesus' death and resurrection and the new temple that he would embody. The whole of the Old Testament revelation is carried into the new revelation, for Jesus, as the new revelation, bears with him, within his very person, the old. Nothing is lost and all is fulfilled and so obtains its lasting treasured significance.

Immediately after the cleansing of the temple, Matthew places the second scene that closely echoes the one we already commented on from Luke. Matthew narrates that the blind and the lame came to Jesus in the temple to be healed. "But when the chief priests and the scribes saw the wonderful things that he did, and the children crying out in the temple, 'Hosanna to the Son of David!' they were indignant; and they said to him, 'Do you hear what these are saying?' And Jesus said to them, 'Yes; have you never read, "Out of the mouth of babes and sucklings you have brought perfect praise?"'" Significantly, while Jesus was cleansing the temple, "the blind and the lame came to him in the temple, and he healed them." When David first conquered Jerusalem, the Jebusites, thinking their stronghold was impregnable, taunted him by saying that even the blind and the lame could ward him off. In response, David sarcastically encouraged his men to smite the Jebusites, that is, "attack the lame and the blind, who are hated by David's soul." Because of this the saying arose: "The blind and the lame shall not come into this house/temple" (2 Sm 5:6-8).[18] Jesus' healing of the deformed blind and lame within the temple pre-

17. The Letter to the Hebrews corroborates this: "In speaking of a new covenant he [Jer 31:31-34] treats the first as obsolete and growing old is ready to vanish away" (Heb 8:13). The earthly temple is the visible expression of the old covenant, and after its destruction by the Romans, it has vanished.

18. Although the Hebrew has the word "house," the Septuagint Greek has translated it as

cincts, a pure sanctum where they are not permitted to be, further heightens the imagery of cleansing from evil and the sin that is the source of all evil and deformity. Within the Gospel of Matthew, these are the last of Jesus' miracles, and rightly so, for now he is about to perform the ultimate healing, the ultimate cleansing—the conquering of the deformity of sin and death through his own passion and death—and so initiate the new holy life that is God's kingdom. While the chief priests and scribes witnessed these "wonderful things" and the joyful acclamation of the children exclaiming, as did those who participated in Jesus triumphal entry, "Hosanna to the Son of David!" they were indignant. Like the Pharisees in Luke's Gospel who demanded that Jesus rebuke those who were proclaiming him king, the chief priests and the scribes now irately and accusatorially asked Jesus: "Do you hear what they are saying?" Jesus, as in his response to the Pharisees about the stones crying out, retorts: "Have you never read, 'Out of the mouths of babes and sucklings you have brought perfect praise'?" Jesus is quoting Psalm 8, which declares that the Lord's name is majestic over all the earth, and therefore his glory, which is above the heavens, "is chanted by the mouths of babes and infants." In these infants and babes the Lord has "founded a bulwark because of your foes, to still the enemy and the avenger" (Ps 8:1-2). Just as the irrational stones would cry out Jesus' kingship, so would the merest unlearned children chant out perfect praise of him and so silence his enemies and avengers. In the psalm the children are also glorifying God, and Jesus is condoning such children-given glory, implying, here in the very temple, he is deserving of divine worship. Jesus, as the son of David and the Son of God, will cleanse the temple and will eradicate all evil through his purifying salvific death and in so doing become the new holy living temple, in him and to him God's holy children will chant perfect praise.

Theological Significance

In the cleansing of the temple all the abovementioned biblical passages and events converge and find their full significance. As the one coming in the name of the Lord, Jesus' coming to Jerusalem, as he thrice foretold, is his coming to die and rise. This dying and rising, in keeping with his conception, is

---

"temple." This is in keeping with 2 Sm 7:1-7, where David observes that he dwells "in a house," but God "dwells in a tent." While David wanted to build God a "house," a temple, God remarks that it is to his credit that he has dwelt in a tent and so has traveled with the Israelites wherever they journeyed. See also 1 Chr 17:1-2.

the razing of the kingdom of evil and his inheriting of the everlasting "throne of his father David" as "the Son of the Most High" (Lk 1:32–33). This dying and rising, in keeping with his Spirit-filled baptismal commission, is his opening of the heavens as the loyal and faithful Suffering-Servant/Son in whom his Father is well pleased. Having opened the heavens, he will, as the risen Son, pour out from the heavens the Holy Spirit and so allow all who believe in him to enter into the heavens. This dying and rising, in keeping with his Transfiguration, is his passing over from the old earthly Jerusalem into the new heavenly Jerusalem. It is a passing over from the old earthly temple to the new heavenly temple. It is a passing over from the old covenant into the new covenant. It is a passing over from the earthly Promised Land into the heavenly Promised Land. This dying and rising is the passing over of Jesus' putting to death his fallen humanity inherited from Adamic and his rising into his new glorious humanity as the new Adam, becoming the father of a new humanity within a transformed new Creation. This is the true joyful palm-strewn liturgical procession, prefigured in Maccabeus's cleansing of the temple on the feast of booths with palms in hand, that will culminate in the liturgical action of Jesus' death, his offering as High Priest of his own holy life as a loving sacrifice to his Father, whereby humankind will be cleansed of sin and so be reconciled to his Father. This is the passing over from an earthly harvest festival into the heavenly banquet.

This liturgical procession anticipates Jesus' triumphal procession into his own risen glory, his full entrance into his Father's glory. It is the passing over of the "I shall not die, but I shall live and recount the deeds of the Lord." And all of this converges in reality and in symbol upon the temple in Jerusalem, for in all of the above Jesus, as the once-rejected stone, is prophetically enacting, as his Father's chosen cornerstone, the building of the new and living temple of a new and living Jerusalem that he will literally embody. In this new Jerusalem, Jesus, as now jubilantly and prophetically proclaimed, will be the everlasting king of God's eternal kingdom. This is the new and everlasting day that God has made and in which all will forever marvel.

These are all the prophetic palm-heralded hosanna-saving acts that are enacted as Jesus' donkey comes to a halt before the temple's door. Significantly, Palm 118, which lies at the heart of Jesus' triumphal entry, concludes: "Bind the festal procession with branches, up to the horns of the altar!" The palms that expressed jubilation upon entering the temple are to be bound to the altar of sacrifice. The palms that covered Jesus' triumphal path and that were jubilantly waved about him amid the loud proclamations of his being the kingly son of David who comes in the name of the Lord may not have been left bound upon the altar of sacrifice, but Jesus knew that his kingship, his palm of martyrdom, was bound to the altar of sacrifice and thus that he was bound to the altar of sacrifice. Yet he confidently knew the truth of the psalm's final verse, which replicates the first and so confirms all that is contained therein: "O give thanks to the Lord, for he is good; for his steadfast love endures forever!" (vv. 27-29).

Ultimately, what we behold in Jesus' triumphal entry into Jerusalem is Jesus, as the incarnate Messianic Son of the Father, prophetically enacting those salvific acts through which he will become who he is, Jesus—YHWH-Saves. Jesus is enacting the name prophetically given to him by his Father when he first entered the temple on the day of his circumcision, the day when he was first separated from all that was profane, the day when he was first dedicated to the Lord as a member of God's holy people, and so the day when he first shed his blood. And in initially becoming Jesus, in this same city of Jerusalem and in this same temple, Jesus is prophetically and dramatically enacting his becoming fully Jesus now—the great High-Priest, the supreme Prophet and the everlasting King.

From the Cleansing of the Temple to the Last Supper

Given the theological nature of our study, which does not aim at commenting on every scriptural passage, I want to highlight several theologically important events that lie between Jesus' triumphal entry into Jerusalem and his last supper with the Apostles. Their theological significance lies in their further clarifying and enhancing Jesus' triumphal entry and his cleansing the temple and so also evinces a fuller understanding of his forthcoming death and resurrection.

Although Luke and Matthew have the Pharisees (Lk) and the chief priests and scribes (Mt) scandalized by the jubilant crowds (Lk) and the exuberant cries of the children (Mt), Mark and Luke summarize the effect of Jesus' triumphal entry and cleansing. Because "the multitude was astonished at his teaching" (Mk) and so "hung upon his words" (Lk), the Jewish authorities "sought a way to destroy him" (Mk 11:18-19 and Lk 19:47-48). We now have in play two "destructions." On the one hand, we have Jesus already predicting in Luke the destruction of Jerusalem and so the temple as well, which will shortly be corroborated by Matthew and Mark and reaffirmed again by Luke, and on the other hand the Jewish authorities seeking to destroy Jesus. The theological irony is that in their "destruction" of Jesus a new Jerusalem and a new temple will arise in his resurrection, and so the spiritual symbolic destruction of the earthly Jerusalem with its temple, which will subsequently actually be destroyed, historically, by the Romans. This is exactly what Jesus prophetically enacted in his triumphal entry into Jerusalem and in his cleansing of the temple.

By What Authority?

Immediately following this, the Synoptic Gospels narrate that when Jesus returned to the temple, the chief priests, scribes, and elders challenged Jesus with the question: "By what authority are you doing these things, and who gave you this authority?" Jesus responds by telling them that he too has a question, and if they answer his, he will answer theirs. "The baptism of John, whence was it? From heaven or from men?" The Jewish authorities are now in a quandary. "If we say 'From heaven,' he will say to us, 'Why did not we believe him?' But if we say, 'From men,' we are afraid of the multitude; for all hold that John was a prophet.' So they answered Jesus 'We do not know,'" and so Jesus refused to tell them "by what authority I do these things" (Mt 21:23-27; see also Mk 11:27-33 and Lk 20:1-8). There are two sets of intertwining questions here, the answers to which have theological significance as to who Jesus is and what he is salvifically about.

The first set of questions is that the Jewish authorities want to know by what authority Jesus cleansed the temple and who gave him that authority. Beneath those questions is the real issue of whether Jesus cleansed the temple by divine or by human authority. The Jewish authorities are setting a trap. If by human authority, then Jesus' actions could be condemned, for no man has such authority over God's holy sanctuary, not even the Romans. If he said by divine authority, he could equally be accused of usurping the authority of God and so making himself out to be divine, which could easily be interpreted as a blasphemous act, for again only God has ultimate authority over his holy temple. Second, Jesus answers with his own question concerning divine and human authority, and his question harkens back to the onset of his ministry— the baptism of John. By what authority did John baptize, and who gave him that authority? Was John baptizing by divine authority, so that his baptism was from heaven? Or was John merely exercising his human authority so that his baptism was merely from men? Notice that Jesus' question focuses on the act of John's baptism and the authority from which that baptismal act originates. Within their huddle, the Jewish authorities are concerned that if they

reply that John's authority and baptism are from heaven, then Jesus would respond by saying, "Why then, did you not believe him?" They are focusing on
what John said and not on what John did—baptize. And what John said was:
"I baptize you with water for repentance, but he who is coming after me is
mightier than I, whose sandals I am not worthy to carry; he will baptize you
with the Holy Spirit and with fire" (Mt 3:11). What the Jewish leaders did not
want to believe then and do not want to believe now is that Jesus is the one
proclaimed by John and so is the anointed Messiah who comes to baptize in
the Holy Spirit. To affirm the heavenly origin of John's baptism is to affirm the
heavenly authority of his words concerning Jesus, and so to affirm John's past
words concerning Jesus would be a self-condemning act for their present lack
of faith in Jesus. Or, to put it another way, if the Jewish authorities confirmed
the heavenly origin of John's baptism, and therefore the heavenly nature of
his proclamation, they would be implying that Jesus' authority, as the divinely anointed Messiah, was given to him by God and thus his present acts of
cleansing the temple were in keeping with his divine authority.

In addition, although the Jewish authorities focused on the implications
of what John said, Jesus focused on what John did: baptizing. Ultimately, the
importance of John's baptism was not simply that it was a baptism of repentance but that it culminated in the baptism of Jesus. John's baptism was "from
heaven" and so bore divine authority because in the act of baptizing Jesus the
heavens were opened and the Holy Spirit descended upon him, commissioning him to be the Messiah who would baptize in the Holy Spirit. Here we also
perceive why Jesus did not ask whether John's baptism was "from God" but
rather "from heaven." While it may be "from God," the point that Jesus wanted to accentuate is that John's baptism of repentance culminated in his baptism of Jesus, and within that baptism the heavens opened because Jesus is the
one, as the Spirit-commissioned Messiah, through whom the heavens would
be opened and by whom and in whom all who believed in him, as John proclaimed, would be baptized in the Holy Spirit. Now we have come full circle.

Jesus was asked by what authority he cleansed the temple and from whom
he received such authority. Jesus in turn asked similarly by what authority did
John baptize and from whom he received such authority. Although neither Jesus nor the Jewish authorities directly answered the other's questions, the answer to the Jewish authorities' question is clear. Ironically, they are the ones
who answered their own question by not answering Jesus' question. By refusing to acknowledge that John's baptism was from heaven for fear that what he
said about Jesus was true, they unwittingly confirmed that Jesus, as the be-

loved Messianic Spirit-anointed Son of Father, possessed the divine authority to cleanse the temple. Moreover, the cleansing of the temple was a prophetic act foretelling the true cleansing—the purpose for which Jesus was first baptized by John. Through his death, Jesus, as the Messiah, would cleanse humankind of its sin and in his resurrection be empowered, as Savior and Lord, to baptize with the Holy Spirit those who believe in him. In so doing, Jesus would become the new living and holy temple through and in whom the faithful would be able to enter through the opened heavens into the presence of his heavenly Father. Thus there is an integral causal connection between the Spirit-filled commission that Jesus first received from his Father at his baptism, his cleansing of the temple, and his passion, death, and resurrection. In his baptism, he was commissioned and empowered to enact his death and resurrection, and the cleansing of the temple prophetically enacted what Jesus would effect through his death and resurrection: a new living temple in which God's people truly worship him in the Spirit of holiness.

Whose Son Is the Christ?

The Synoptic narrative continues with Jesus providing parables that contrast those who are faithful to God and those who are not: the parable of the two sons, one who did his father's bidding and one who did not (see Mt 21:28-32); the parable of wicked tenants who refused to give the vineyard owner his proper fruits even when he sent his own son (see Mt 21:33-46 and parallels); and the parable of a wedding feast at which the invited guests refused to attend and so the poor, blind, and lame were invited from the streets and the hedges (see Mt 22:1-14, but Lk places this parable earlier; see 14:15-24). In response to these parables, which the Jewish authorities realized were directed at them, they attempted various ways to trap Jesus in his speech, asking whether taxes should be paid to Caesar (see Mt 22:15-22 and parallels), whether there is a resurrection from the dead (see Mt 22:23-33 and parallels), and which is the greatest commandment (see Mt 22:34-40 and Mk 12:28-34, but Luke places this earlier in a more positive light; see 10:25-28). These attempts at entrapment climax when Jesus, turning the tables, asks the Jewish leaders a question and he does so, according to Mark, while teaching in the temple (see Mk 12:35).

Although all three Gospels are similar, Matthew renders the dialogue by having Jesus first ask what they think of the Christ. "'Whose son is he?' They said to him, 'the Son of David.' He said to them, 'How is it then that David, inspirited by the Spirit, calls him Lord, saying, "The Lord said to my Lord,

Sit at my right hand, till I put your enemies under your feet?" If David calls him Lord, how is he his son'" (Mt 22:41-45, Mk 35-37, and Lk 20:41-44; Jesus is citing Ps 110:1). While the Jewish authorities attempted to trap Jesus by asking questions that digressed from the real issue at hand—who is Jesus and by whose authority is he acting and speaking—Jesus brings them back to the central question by alluding to his triumphal entry into Jerusalem. While making his way into the temple, the crowds joyously proclaimed, "Hosanna to the Son of David! Blessed is he who comes in the name of the Lord! Hosanna in the highest" (Mt 21:9 and parallels). The crowds proclaimed him to be the long-awaited son of David who comes in the name of the Lord and as such would establish God's everlasting kingdom. This glad jubilation is given to God on high. To Jesus' "trick" question as to whose son the Christ is, the Jewish authorities confidently declare that he is David's son, thus echoing the jubilant crowds. So, the Spirit-anointed Christ is the son of David of whom the crowds acclaimed to be Jesus and the Jewish authorities do not. But Jesus wishes to intensify the issue.

If the Spirit-anointed Christ is the son of David, how can David, himself inspired by the Holy Spirit, proclaim in Psalm 110, "The Lord [i.e., God] said to my Lord [i.e., God], Sit at my right hand, until I put your enemies under your feet?" How can the Messiah be David's son if David calls him Lord [i.e., God]? Or how can the Messiah be David's God if he is David's son? Moreover, how can the Lord, who is speaking to David, speak of another "Lord" who, as David's son, is David's Lord? The only way that Jesus' seeming riddle can be resolved is if one perceives that Jesus is Lord as the Son of God incarnate who is humanly born of the lineage of the house of David. Jesus' riddle is the mystery of the Incarnation. The Messiah is the human son of David, and he is also David's Lord because he is the Father's divine Son, and so, as the Father's Son, both he and the Father equally share the same divine title "Lord." [19] The crowds proclaimed Jesus to be the expectant son of David, and now the Pharisees declare that the Messiah is the son of David. In so doing, Jesus has lured them into the trap where they are now faced with the reality that the Messianic son of David is equally the divine Son of God. This is Jesus' logic. Inher-

---

19. This double use of the divine designation "Lord" is similar to what we found in the Visitation. There Elizabeth speaks of Mary being "the mother of my Lord" and also of Mary being blessed because she believed "what was spoken to her from the Lord" (Lk 1:43-45). Mary is the mother of the Lord because her human son is the Father's Son, and she is blessed because she believed the Lord's word spoken to her through the angel Gabriel, that is, the word spoken by the Son's Father. Both the Father's Son and the Son's Father are "Lord."

ent within the cry "Hosanna, to the Son of David" lies the cry "Hosanna, to the Messiah," and within that cry lies the acclamation "Hosanna, to the Son of God"—David's anointed son and David's divine Lord. Jesus, following his triumphal entry into Jerusalem, has now revealed both who he is and by what authority he acts and speaks, prophetically anticipating his salvific death and resurrection. In those acts he, as the Messiah, will establish the everlasting kingdom of his ancestor David, the new Jerusalem, in which he, as the risen Son of God incarnate, will be the living heavenly temple.

In quoting Psalm 110, Jesus is not only bringing into relief the mystery of the Incarnation but also alluding to his salvific work. The Lord is announcing to David's Lord that he is to sit at his right hand "till I put your enemies under your feet." Later the same psalm he professes: "The Lord has sworn and will not change his mind, 'You are a priest for ever after the order of Melchizedek'" (Ps 110:4). Jesus, as the Messiah, in offering himself on the cross, becomes the ever living risen High Priest after the manner of Melchizedek. In so doing he has conquered every enemy—sin, Satan, and death—and so, as Lord, sits at his Father's right hand until his Father places all his enemies under his feet when he sends forth again his glorious Son Jesus at the end of time. In his second coming, Jesus, as the risen Christ and supreme Lord, will forever dispel sin, vanquish Satan, and triumph over death. Also, within his glorious coming, Jesus will conclusively manifest to all of his unbelieving "enemies," such as the present Pharisees, that he is indeed the Messianic son of David and thus David's Lord as the Father's incarnate Son.[20] After this questioning and confron-

20. The apostolic church takes up and furthers this theme contained in Psalm 110. In the Acts of the Apostles, Luke has Peter noting in his Pentecost sermon that David, knowing that God had sworn an oath to him that one of his descendants would inherit his throne, "spoke of the resurrection of the Christ" and that this Christ is Jesus. Although David did not ascend into the heavens, he did prophecy: "The Lord said to my Lord, Sit at my right hand till I make your enemies a stool for your feet." Peter vigorously concludes, "Let all of the house of Israel therefore know assuredly that God has made him both Lord and Christ this Jesus whom you crucified" (Acts 2:29-35). Here we perceive all the elements contained within the Gospel accounts of Jesus' dialogue with the Pharisees. Jesus, as David's son, is the Christ who, on the cross, offered his own life to his Father as High Priest. For this reason, his Father raised him from the dead as the glorious Christ and universal Lord. In so doing he is both David's Messianic son and David's divine Lord.

The Pauline corpus also takes up this theme. In 1 Corinthians, Paul professes that, as the risen Christ, Jesus is the first fruit of those who have died and now reigns "until he has put all of his enemies under his feet. The last enemy to be destroyed is death. 'For God has put all things in subjection under him'" (1 Cor 15:20-27; see also Eph 1:20 and Col 3:1).

This is most fully developed within the Letter to the Hebrews, where Psalm 110 forms the context of Jesus being the ever-living great High Priest. "When he [God's Son] had made puri-

tational dialogue between Jesus and the Jewish elders, Matthew notes that "no one was able to answer him a word, nor from that day did any one dare to ask him any more questions" (Mt 22:46; see also Mk 12:34 and Lk 20:40). Although the elders where silenced, Mark concludes "the great throng heard him gladly" (Mk 12:37). Here stubborn unbelief collides with rejoicing faith. And here Jesus' preaching takes on a new and ominous tone: the condemnation of the scribes and Pharisees.

Woes and Laments

Although all three Synoptic Gospels narrate Jesus' condemnation of the scribe and Pharisees, Matthew places here Jesus' lengthy litany of "woes" (Mt 23:1-36; see also Mk 12:37-40 and Lk 20:45-47).[21] This "woe to you, scribes and Pharisees" resides in their hypocrisy: "you hypocrites!" They enact all that is demanded by the law, and thus appear holy in their exalted station within the synagogues and in the market places, but this is mere empty show. They are actually "whitewashed tombs ... full of dead men's bones and all uncleanness. So you also outwardly appear righteous to men, but within you are full of hypocrisy and iniquity" (Mt 23:27-28). This litany of woes leads, within Matthew's Gospel, to Jesus lamenting over Jerusalem.

We saw earlier that Luke has Jesus weeping over Jerusalem during the course of his triumphant entry, but Matthew narrates Jesus' lamenting the state of Jerusalem (Mt 23:37-39).[22] And although Matthew has Jesus lament, all three

---

fication for sins, he sat down at the right hand of the Majesty on high, having become as much superior to angels as the name he has obtained is more excellent than theirs" (Heb 1:1-4). As his risen Son, the Father exalts, "Sit at my right hand, till I make your enemies a stool for your feet" (Heb 1:13). As the Christ, Jesus "offered for all time a single sacrifice for sins" and so "sat down at the right hand of God, thereto wait until his enemies should be made a stool for his feet" (Heb 10:12-13). Therefore we are to look "to Jesus the pioneer and perfecter of faith, who for the joy that was set before him endured the cross, despising the shame, and is seated at the right hand of the throne of God" (Heb 12:2). Because Melchizedek was without mother or father or genealogy, and thus "neither beginning of days nor end of life, but resembling the Son of God, he continues a priest forever" (Heb 7:3). Although Melchizedek, having no known human origin, resembles Jesus' eternal divinity as the Son of God, Jesus, as man, resembles Melchizedek in that his human priesthood, because of his resurrection, lasts forever after the order of Melchizedek (see Heb 5:5-10, 6:20, 7:15-17, and 7:21).

21. Luke places many of these woes earlier within his Gospel narrative (see 11:37-12:1).

22. It would appear from Matthew's and Mark's Gospels that, historically, the lamenting over Jerusalem with its foreseen demise probably took place after Jesus' triumphal entry and cleansing of the temple.

Synoptic Gospels have Jesus subsequently predicting the destruction of Jerusalem (Mt 24:1-2, Mk 13:1-2, and Lk 21:5-6). This is theologically significant because all three Synoptics sandwich this prediction between Jesus' denunciation of the scribes and Pharisees and his eschatological discourse. Thus Jesus' lament over Jerusalem (Mt) and his prediction of its destruction (Mt, Mk, and Lk) are both a response to the scribes' and Pharisees' rejection of him and a presaging of the new eschatological age he is about to establish: the inaugurating of the new Jerusalem with its heavenly temple.

Within Matthew, Jesus says, "Jerusalem, Jerusalem, killing the prophets and stoning those who are sent to you! How often would I have gathered your children together as a hen gathers her brood under her wings, and you would not! Behold, your house is forsaken and desolate. For I tell you, you will not see me again until you say: 'Blessed is he who comes in the name of the Lord'" (Mt 23:37-39). Despite Jerusalem's violent past, Jesus speaks of his heartbreaking love for the city, and he does so by employing a maternal metaphor, that of a mother hen fretfully gathering her young heedless energized chicks under her protecting and nurturing wings (see Pss 17:9 and 91:4). Interestingly, Jesus speaks of how often he would have protectively gathered Jerusalem's children and yet they relentlessly refused. Because this is Jesus' first and only presence in Jerusalem within the Synoptic account, his words could insinuate that he has been there multiple times. Alternatively, it could look to Israel's entire history, during which God continually attempted to gather his people back to himself, but they constantly refused by remaining stubbornly persistent in their sin. If this were the case, then Jesus, in the use of "I," is insinuating that he is that divine "I" who over the centuries lovingly longed to gather his Father's people. And his current presence among them, as the incarnate divine Son, is his ultimate and most ardent attempt, and thus the cause of his present acute sorrow. Nonetheless, Jesus continues by echoing what God spoke to Solomon upon his completing the temple. If the people do not keep his covenant and commandments, "then I will cut off Israel from the land which I have given them; and the house which I have consecrated for my name I will cast out of my sight.... And this house will be a heap of ruins" (1 Kgs 8:6-8; see also Jer 22:5). Because of the Jewish authorities' rejection, the temple will become a desolate heap of ruins. Yet their rejection will also be the catalyst for Jesus, through his death and resurrection, to usher in the eschatological age. Thus they will only see him again when they see him with eyes of faith, and so do then what they now would not, acknowledge him as their risen Savior and glorious King. Then they will add their voices to the jubilant chorus that proclaimed, upon his first triumphal visitation, "Blessed is he who comes in the name of the Lord."

The Destruction of the Temple and Eschatological Discourse

Matthew now comes into synchronization with Mark and Luke. Upon leaving the temple, after his confrontation with the Jewish authorities, all three Synoptics note that his disciples pointed out to Jesus the beauty and splendor of the temple and its surrounding buildings. Jesus responds, "Do you see these great buildings? There will not be left here one stone upon another, that will not be thrown down" (Mk 13:1-2; see also Mt 24:1-2 and Lk 21:5-6).[23]

Having, within the temple precincts, once again foretold the destruction of Jerusalem with its temple, Jesus and his disciples crossed over the Kedron Valley to the Mount of Olives. There his disciples (Mark specifies Peter, James, John, and Andrew) asked Jesus (Matthew and Mark specify that this was done privately), "Tell us, when will this be, and what will be the sign when these things all are to be accomplished" (Mk 13:3-4; see also Mt 24:3 and Lk 21:7). The disciples are querying about when Jerusalem and the temple will be destroyed, which Jesus had just foretold, and what manner of sign will precede such an event to mark its imminent coming. In response to their specific request concerning the destruction of the temple, Jesus begins his "eschatological discourse," that is, the intervening time between Jesus' resurrection and the period immediately preceding his coming at the end of time. Intertwined are both the manner of life the church will experience within that intervening period and the signs that presage Jesus' final coming. What I want first to emphasize here is that the catalyst that accounts for Jesus' eschatological discourse and the sign that specifies the advent of the eschatological age is the destruction of Jerusalem and the temple. To grasp the theological significance of this catalyst, we must recall the theological logic of the biblical narrative that we have been following.

The triumphal entry is the prophetic hermeneutical event that governs the interpretation of all that follows in that it looks back to and so reveals more fully the theological significance of Jesus' prophetic triumphal entry. In turn,

---

23. Although Luke previously has Jesus predicting the destruction of Jerusalem, where there will not be one stone left upon another, here it is specifically the temple that will be destroyed (see Lk 19:41-44).

there is a looking forward. In perceiving more clearly and fully the theological significance of the triumphal entry, we perceive more clearly and fully its theological prophetic nature, that is, how that triumphal entry will be fulfilled within the terminating acts of Jesus' death and resurrection. As the narrative progresses, we perceive more clearly both the prophetic significance of the triumphal entry and its fulfillment within Jesus' saving acts. This being so, we have discerned two interrelated truths: one concerns Jesus' identity and the other the nature of his salvific ministry. Jesus is the long-expected son of David who is the anointed Messiah, and as such he is the Lord—the Son of God. Because of who he is, Jesus possesses the divine authority to do what he is doing, particularly in cleansing the temple. This prophetic symbolic action will find its fulfillment in Jesus' death, which will cleanse humankind from sin, and in his resurrection, which will empower him to baptize his followers in the Holy Spirit. Thus these events will establish the heavenly kingdom, the new Jerusalem, for he will embody the new living temple in whom pure and holy worship will be given to his Father. These acts, then, initiate the eschatological age.

Now, although his death and resurrection are the positive historical events that inaugurate the eschatological age, the negative historical event that manifests the fulfillment of and so demise of the former age is the destruction of the temple. But the absence of the temple on Temple Mount is not simply a negative sign that bears witness to nonexistence but a positive sign that a new and living temple has been built upon the heavenly Mt. Zion—that is, the risen and glorified humanity of Jesus himself. The historical continued absence of a temple on Temple Mount is an enduring historical testimony to Jesus as the new living temple. The absence of the historic temple likewise confirms that the risen Jesus is the promised son of David who is the Christ and so the Son of God incarnate. He is the prophesied everlasting Lord of David's divinely promised everlasting kingdom. All the above manifests why Jesus' response to his enquiring disciples as to when this destruction of the temple would take place is the theological or revelational catalyst for embarking on his eschatological discourse. The absence of the temple is a positive sign that the eschatological age has dawned and that the risen Lord Jesus, the Davidic Messiah, is literally the living embodiment of that age.

This study is not the place to give a detailed account of Jesus' eschatological discourse and what follows upon it. Yet a summary and a few theological conclusions can be made. Prior to Jesus' coming at the end of time, many others will come in his name claiming to be the Christ and so lead many astray.[24] There will be wars among nations and the persecution of Jesus' followers. Being simply followers of Jesus, "for his name's sake," they will be hated by all nations. Yet his disciples, when dragged before the courts of both Jews and Gentiles, should not worry or be fearful, for the Spirit of their Father will be speaking through them.[25] So terrible will be the tribulations that they will exceed any distress experienced since creation or into the future. "And if the Lord had not shortened the days, no human being would be saved, but for the sake of the elect, whom he chose, he shortened the days" (Mk 13:20 and parallels; see also Mt 24:3-28, Mk 13:3-23, and Lk 21:7-24). Immediately following these tribulations, Jesus states that "the sun will be darkened, and the moon will not give its light, and the stars will be falling from heaven and the powers in the heavens will be shaken." Within this eschatological cosmological climax, "they will see the Son of man coming on the clouds of heaven with great power and glory. And he will send out his angels, and gather his elect from the four winds, from the ends of the earth to the ends of heaven" (Mk 13:24-27; see also Mt 24:29-31 and Lk 21:25-28).

Jesus' disciples specifically asked about the future destruction of Jerusalem and the temple. Jesus, on one level, addressed this question. But his response throughout his discourse is not simply addressing that question but also simultaneously addressing two interrelated issues: what his future disciples/ church will experience during the interim between his resurrection and his second coming, and what they will experience immediately prior to his coming in glory and power upon the clouds of heaven at the end of time. He interweaves these various issues because they are theologically or revelationally one entwined issue. The signs preceding the destruction of Jerusalem and the temple are the same signs that will accompany his disciples/church throughout their/her history, and these same signs will thus immediately precede Jesus' coming in glory. The reason is that all are eschatological. Because the destruction of Jerusalem and the temple with its foreshadowing tribulations are

---

24. While Matthew has Jesus saying that many will come professing to be "the Christ," Mark and Luke has him predicting that others will come, saying, "I am he!" (Mt 24:5, Mk 13:6, and Lk 21:8). This "I am he" is the Greek *ego eimi*, which alludes to God's divine name, "I Am Who Am" (see Ex 3:13-14). Jesus is the Christ because, as the Son of God, he exclusively possesses the Father's Spirit of Sonship, and therefore he alone can lay claim to the divine name. He alone is the Christ because he alone is "I Am He." See also Mt 24:23-24, Mk 13:21-23, and Lk 17:23.

25. Jesus' prophetic words find immediate fulfillment within the Acts of the Apostles, where his followers are persecuted by both Jews and Gentiles.

eschatological signs of the in-breaking of the new eschatological age, these same foreshadowing tribulations and signs will continue throughout history as the old order continues to war against the new eschatological age, reaching culmination at the dawn of Jesus' return in power, when his enemies will definitively be placed under his feet. Because Jesus had to suffer and die in order to inaugurate the new eschatological age in his death and resurrection, his disciples/church, while living within that new eschatological age, will experience hatred, suffering, and persecution, sharing in and meriting the fullness of his glory. Only then will the eschatological Davidic heavenly kingdom be fully realized, and only then will the new Jerusalem come down out of heaven, for only then will Jesus descend upon the clouds as the living heavenly temple in and with whom all glory and praise will be given to his heavenly Father in communion with the Holy Spirit.

By interweaving the destruction of the Jerusalem and the temple with the interim period and the coming of the son of man, Jesus is teaching his disciples that what is ultimately important is not simply linear time, or what will sequentially historically take place when. Rather, although linear historical time records events, more important is that to which linear historical time with its events is bearing witness—the reality of the eschatological age and that that new age knows no time but simply is the forever risen presence of Jesus and his kingdom. Jesus is verging upon his return, not simply into an always encroaching future but more so into the present now—the ever present today. Thus all the historical signs of his imminent return are always present. The future is always present because the risen Jesus who exists beyond time is ever present in time. In the risen Jesus, the present and future are one, for he literally embodies both, and so his faithful/church, and even Jesus himself, live this ever expectant simultaneity. Here we see the significance of what Jesus states, within the Gospel of Luke, at the end of his eschatological discourse: "Now when these things begin to take place [all of the signs and tribulations], look up and raise your heads because your redemption is drawing near" (Lk 21:28). Jesus' followers, in the very present, are to raise their heads and look up to heaven for he, their future heavenly redemption, is now drawing near.[26]

26. This simultaneity is enacted within the trial and death of Stephen, and it focuses again on the destruction of the temple. Because Stephen spoke with "wisdom and the Spirit," his accusers were confounded. He was therefore falsely accused of blasphemy and speaking against the temple and the law. "For we have heard him say that this Jesus of Nazareth will destroy this place [temple], and will change the customs which Moses delivered to us" (Acts 6:10-15).

Here we once again grasp the full prophetic significance of Jesus' triumphal entry into Jerusalem with its terminal cleansing of the temple, for it points not only to its fulfillment within the passion, death, and resurrection whereby he will inaugurate the new Jerusalem with its new holy temple that is himself, but also to its climactic consummation, the gathering of "his elect," in his coming gloriously at the end of time. In that glorious coming upon the clouds of heaven, he will fully enter into the new Jerusalem, for he will have completed the building of the heavenly temple—the consummate worship of his Father that is offered by Jesus and those who are in living in holy communion with him through the Spirit. Then he will be fully the son of David, the Spirit-anointed Christ, the Father's Son incarnate, for he will be fully Lord and Savior. He will have become what he was, is, and ever shall be named to be— Jesus, YHWH-Saves.

Jesus concludes his eschatological discourse with a parable. His disciples are to learn a lesson from the fig tree. "As soon as its branch becomes tender and puts forth its leaves, you know that summer is near. So also, when you see these things taking place, you know that he is near, at the very gates" (Mt 24:32-33; see also Mk 13:28-29). In Luke, Jesus says, "You know that the kingdom of God is near" (21:29-31). The future trials and tribulations are not signs of winter, lifelessness, and death, but rather signs of spring, hope, and

---

Jesus was accused at his trial of saying "I will destroy this temple that is made with hands, and in three days I will build another, not made with hands" (Mk 14:58; see also Mt 26:61 and Jn 2:19, where Jesus says, "Destroy this temple, and in three days I will raise it up"). Although Jesus spoke of the destruction of the temple, he never said that he would literally destroy the material temple. He would make it redundant, and this redundancy would be symbolized in the Romans destroying the actual physical temple. Jesus did, through his death and resurrection, build a heavenly temple made not with human hands, for in him true spiritual worship is now offered to his Father. Theologically significant is Stephen's vision at the conclusion of his sermon to his irate accusers. "But he, full of the Holy Spirit, gazed into heaven and saw the glory of God, and Jesus standing at the right hand of God; and he said, 'Behold, I see the heavens opened, and the Son of man standing at the right hand of God'" (Acts 7:54-57). Stephan was accused of saying that Jesus would destroy the temple, but what Stephen experienced in his vision, what he saw when he raised his eyes to heaven, was the eschatological heavenly temple that Jesus did build. He saw his redemption at hand. Stephen, here on earth, was taken up into the heavenly realm, for the heavenly realm is ever present on earth. As foreshadowed in Jesus' baptism, Stephen peered through the open heavens, an opening that Jesus made through the Paschal Mystery, and there witnessed and participated in the heavenly liturgy where Jesus, the glorious son of man, reigns with God his Father. Because Jesus offered his spirit and life to the Father and in so doing entered into the heavenly temple, Stephen could now offer his spirit and life to Jesus and so fully enter into the heavenly temple, in which he already dwelt here on earth, that is, his living Spirit-filled communion with the risen Jesus.

life, for they are the harbingers of summer, fruitfulness, and abundance. They are signs that Jesus is near, "at the very gates." This allusion to the gates of Jerusalem is significant because the eschatological discourse is in response to the disciples asking when Jerusalem and the temple would be destroyed. Thus, when one sees the Romans converging on the gates of Jerusalem to destroy it, what one truly sees is Jesus arriving to transform the city into the heavenly Jerusalem. The destruction of Jerusalem is the eschatological sign, the spring fig tree sprouting forth its leaves, announcing the age of the new Jerusalem, the kingdom of God. The mature summer fruit of Jesus' redemption is at hand. Nonetheless, "of the day and hour no one knows, not even the angels of heaven, nor the Son, but the Father only" (Mt 24:36; see also Mk 13:32). Although the demise of the old Jerusalem testifies to the rise of the new Jerusalem, no one knows when Jesus will come in glory on the clouds of heaven, not even Jesus, the Son. Only his Father knows. The Father is the originator and designer of all—from the begetting of his Son from all eternity to the sending of his incarnate Son in glory at the end of time. Therefore to him alone belongs the prerogative of knowing "the day and the hour" of his Son's coming. If the angels and the Son do not know the day or the hour, even less do Jesus' disciples. They are to "take heed, watch" and what Jesus says to them he says to all: "Watch" (Mk 13:33-37; see also Lk 21:34-36).[27]

Not surprisingly, Matthew immediately places after the eschatological dis-

---

27. Within the theological tradition, Jesus' specifying that not even the Son knows the last day is interpreted to mean that he, as the Son incarnate, as man, does not know the last day, but that the Son as God, being fully divine as the Father is divine, would know the last day. Although this interpretation is in accord with the reality of the Incarnation, a further question can be asked. Does Jesus, as the glorious risen Son of God incarnate, know the last day? Again, the theological tradition would say "yes." Although the Son of God knows all that his Father knows, I wonder, whether the risen Son of God *as man* knows all that the Father knows. The risen human Jesus now possesses the full filial vision of his heavenly Father, but I wonder whether it is appropriate for him, even as risen, to know when his Father will send him forth at the end of time. Jesus is now the Lord of heaven and earth, but he, as Son, is still under the authority of his Father, and as the incarnate Son, he too anxiously and expectantly awaits, along with his body the church, for his Father to bring all his enemies under his feet in the Father sending him forth in glory. I am concerned that if the risen Jesus knows the day and the hour of his coming, that knowledge would enfeeble the intensity of his own longing to return and of his intercession to the Father for his return, just as such knowledge would enfeeble the church's longing and intercession. No one can more longingly desire and anxiously await his return, no one can more prayerfully intercede in anticipation of his return than Jesus himself, but such yearning, expectation, and entreaty are nurtured in the assurance of hopeful ignorance—in the knowing of the not knowing. As he exhorts his disciples to be always prepared and watchful because they do not know the day or hour, so maybe Jesus too must keep his eyes fixed upon his Father, ever watchful for his paternal nod.

course Jesus' parables pertaining to watchfulness—of Noah, of the household-er, of the good steward as opposed to the negligent wicked servant, of the ten wise virgins in contrast to the ten foolish virgins—the parable of the talents and their proper use, and the parable of judging and separating the sheep from the goats (see Mt 24:37-25:46; Mk and Lk place some of these parables earlier within their respective Gospels, such as Mk 13:35 and Lk 17:26-36, 12:39-40, 12:41-46, 19:11-27). Even though each is making specific points concerning be-ing prepared, they all concern the need to be watchful, as most of them end with similar exhortations: "Watch therefore, for you do not know on what day your Lord is coming (Mt 24:42). "Therefore you also must be ready; for the Son of man is coming at an hour you do not expect" (Mt 24:44). "Watch therefore, for you know neither the day nor the hour" (Mt 25:13). Again, although there is a future element within all of these parables—the unknown future day or hour on which Jesus will return—being prepared is a constant duty because Jesus is always at the very gates. Being the risen Lord and Savior, he is ever pres-ent with those who are anxiously awaiting his impending return and always ready to greet him when he reveals himself in glory.

All of these parables are prophetic in that they cannot be fulfilled by Je-sus' followers until Jesus himself fulfills the conditions for his disciples to be prepared and watchful. Only through Jesus' death and resurrection do these parables of preparedness and watchfulness come into play, for only then is the new eschatological age present, an age that awaits his return on the clouds of heaven. Only then can his followers be prepared and watchful. Thus these parables look back, particularly in Matthew and Mark, to Jesus' prophetic tri-umphal entry into Jerusalem, where he prophetically enacts the coming of his triumphal entry into the new Jerusalem with its new cleansed and holy tem-ple. They also look forward to those salvific acts that will establish the new Jerusalem and the new temple that is himself—his death and resurrection with his subsequent ability, as the risen Savior and Lord, to send forth his holy and life-giving Spirit. To be prepared is to live the new life of the Holy Spirit, and in that Spirit one anxiously awaits and prayerfully anticipates Jesus' trium-phantly coming down out of heaven, his everlasting triumphal entry into the new Jerusalem, for he brings with and in him the new and eternal Jerusalem, in which he himself is the heavenly temple in whom all his faithful, together with him, forever give praise and glory to his Father.

Conclusion

Here I want to emphasize three overarching points and then comment, by way of introduction into the Passion Narrative, on the manner in which the Synoptic Gospels close the whole triumphal entry event.

First, as noted at the onset of this chapter, from the moment that he told his disciples to fetch him a donkey, Jesus orchestrated all that followed.[28] Amid this liturgical prophetic procession with its palm-waving accolades of praise and worship, within his confrontations with various groups of Jewish leaders, within his laments and weeping over Jerusalem, within his eschatological discourse and exhortations to be prepared and watchful, Jesus was ever revealing the theological significance of who he is and what he is about to accomplish. Jesus focuses solely on revealing himself, through his deed and words, as the kingly son of David, the Spirit-anointed Christ, and so the Son of God incarnate. In so doing, he focuses the attention of those who see and hear, both those who believe in him and those who do not, upon himself and what he is doing and saying.

Second, in revealing himself to be the Messianic son of David and the Son of God, Jesus has his eyes on the future and so again focuses the eyes of all on the future, when he will enact his priestly salvific deeds, his sacrificially offering of himself to his Father, whereby he will establish and so enter and thus become the new Jerusalem and in so doing establish, enter, and become the new living heavenly temple. Jesus is prophetically revealing and wants all to perceive what it means for him to be Jesus and the acts by which and through which he will become Jesus—YHWH-Saves.

Third, as this study has observed throughout the whole of his public ministry, Jesus' prophetic triumphal entry into Jerusalem and all that ensues from it is eschatological. It is most immediately eschatological in that it prophetically foreshadows Jesus' pending death and resurrection, through which he will initiate the eschatological age—his triumphal entering into the new Jerusalem with himself as its new temple. To this, Jesus is directing our gaze. Jesus is also directing our gaze to what lies within and beyond these eschatological events. His inaugurating of the eschatological age prophetically looks, by its very coming into existence, to the culmination of this eschatological age when

---

28. Although the authors of the Synoptic Gospels manifest differences, especially in some of their ordering of the events, they are not manipulating the material. Rather, their narration demonstrates that Jesus is directing the progression of the events and the flow of the narrative.

Jesus will enter the fullness of his glory at the end of time. Then Jesus the Son, as the Messianic King and heavenly high priest, will truly become Jesus, for in him all of creation will be fully re-created and all who have entered into him on earth will eternally enter into him in heaven and so abide with him, sharing fully in his risen Spirit-filled life as sons and daughters of the Father. When Jesus enters into his fullness as Jesus, when he becomes Jesus fully in act, and so truly becomes the promised Prophet, the great high priest and the everlasting Davidic King, all peoples and nations will fully enter God's Kingdom by fully entering God's holy city, the new Jerusalem, where they will fully enter God's living holy house of prayer, for all of these will be resplendently and everlastingly subsumed within the completeness of Jesus himself, YHWH-Saves. In the Lord Jesus Christ, the Son of the living God, will all peoples and nations, in the fellowship of the Holy Spirit, be fully one in glorifying his and their one God and Father.

At the beginning of this chapter I also noted that Jesus' triumphal entry into Jerusalem followed upon and was compelled by his thrice-told foretelling of his going to Jerusalem to be handed over, suffer, and die, and on the third day to rise. Having triumphantly entered Jerusalem and having prophetically revealed all that would take place with its eschatological significance, the Synoptic Gospels next provide, by way of concluding, Jesus' response and that of the Jewish leaders. "When Jesus had finished all of these sayings, he said to his disciples, 'You know that after two days the Passover is coming, and the Son of Man will be delivered up to be crucified.' Then the chief priests and the elders of the people gathered in the palace of the high priest, who was called Caiaphas, and took counsel together in order to arrest Jesus by stealth and kill him. But they said, 'Not during the feast, lest there be a tumult among the people'" (Mt 26:1-5, see also Mk 14:1-2 and Lk 22:1-2).

Inherent within Jesus' triumphal entry into Jerusalem is the shadow of the cross, for only through the cross will he enter triumphantly into the new Jerusalem. Jesus now reminds his disciples, who witnessed and participated in his jubilant entry, why he came to Jerusalem. First he reminds them of what they already know—"after two days the Passover is coming." Jesus, in reminding them that the annual feast is swiftly approaching, inherently conjoins its coming presence to his presence in Jerusalem. "And the Son of man will be delivered up to be crucified." Although Jesus will celebrate the Passover with his disciples, he will become, through his crucifixion, the new Passover. Jesus' Passover celebration with his disciples will be the liturgical enactment of his being the new Passover. Thus Jesus' concluding gloss on his triumphal entry into Jerusalem is that one must judge it in the light of the Passover, and ultimately the Passover that he himself is—his passing over through the crucifixion into his joyful entry into the new Jerusalem.

Matthew significantly continues his narrative with the word "then." After Jesus coupled his triumphal entry and the Passover with his own death, the chief priests and elders "then" gathered to scheme how they might surreptitiously arrest and kill him. This is their concluding gloss on Jesus' triumphal entry: Jesus must be killed. So Jesus and the Jewish leaders both speak, in the light of his triumphal entry into Jerusalem, of his death. What is fascinating is that Jesus inherently conjoins his death with the Passover, and the Jewish leaders want to ensure that his execution does not take place on the Passover, "lest there be a tumult among the people." What they want to avoid at all costs is another boisterous throng of Jesus' followers marching through the streets of Jerusalem, this time in righteous anger. As the orchestrator of all salvific events, particularly his own death, Jesus will again have his way, and the procession through the streets of Jerusalem will be that of Jesus carrying his cross—seemingly a procession of defeat, to the delight of the Jewish leaders. But what will actually be enacted, as seen prophetically within his triumphal entry into Jerusalem, is Jesus triumphantly entering, passing over into, the joy of the new and heavenly Jerusalem. Although the Jewish leaders' worst fears were seemingly avoided, they actually were not, for Jesus' followers would forever jubilantly process around his heavenly throne within the heavenly Jerusalem.[29]

With Jesus having woven his prophetic triumphal entry to his imminent death, we can now proceed to examine the Passion Narratives, where all of this is enacted and so becomes a reality.

---

29. The Book of Revelation provides this heavenly vision: "After this I looked, and behold, a great multitude which no man could number, form every nation, from all tribes and peoples and tongues, standing before the throne and before the Lamb, clothed in white robes, *with palm branches in their hands,* and crying out with a loud voice, 'Salvation belongs to our God who sits upon the throne, and to the Lamb!'" (Rv 7:9-11, emphasis added).

PART IV

⅓⁻

THE PASSION NARRATIVES

ALL THE PREVIOUS chapters have noted that from the very onset of the Gospel, beginning with his conception and throughout his public ministry—particularly in his baptism, Peter's profession, the Transfiguration, and his triumphal entry—Jesus' passion, death, and resurrection are prophetically anticipated and prefigured. The whole of Jesus' life and ministry forms one ever-emerging trajectory that points to and culminates in the Paschal Mystery.

Before examining the Passion Narratives, I review briefly four pivotal prophetic mysteries within the life of Jesus, highlighting this progressive revelational development that finds its cumulative termination in Jesus' passion, death, and resurrection: the conception, the baptism, the Transfiguration, and the triumphal entry.[1] I also emphasize a significant theological point at its conclusion, one that I made briefly in the introduction to this volume. While it has been present throughout our study, it has yet to be fully articulated. I have waited until this juncture to address this theological issue because it will now bear considerably

---

1. Although I focus on these prophetic events as portrayed within the Synoptic Gospels, these events are suffused with previous Old Testament prophetic events and words. Jesus always conveys within his very person and actions the whole of the Old Testament, and so who he is and all that he does within his public ministry not only prophetically looks to a future fulfillment, but also looks to a past prophetic prefigurement.

upon our examination of the Passion Narratives. By way of anticipating my theological conclusion, note that my review focuses upon prophetic actions.

The angel Gabriel prophesied that Mary would bear a son, whom she is to call Jesus (YHWH-Saves). The Lord God will give to her human son and the Son of the Most High the promised throne of David, his human paternal ancestor, and from this throne he will reign over God's everlasting kingdom. These prophecies will be fulfilled because the human child will be conceived by the overshadowing power of the Holy Spirit, and so he will be the holy Son of God. Here there is the interplay of the human and the divine. What brings together these two spheres, and so makes such statements true, is the incarnational act. That the Son of God is conceived by the Holy Spirit as man within the womb of Mary is the premise, the foundational act, upon which all of Gabriel's prophecies will be enacted and so fulfilled.

Having been conceived by the Holy Spirit as the Son of God incarnate, Jesus will singularly possess the Spirit of Sonship, and so the human acts by which he will establish God's kingdom will be performed by the power of that Spirit. By performing these Spirit-filled salvific acts by which God's kingdom will be established, Jesus will manifest that he is truly the Father's Spirit-filled Son. Jesus, as the Son of God incarnate, is YHWH-Saves because, as the Son of God (YHWH), he will enact salvific human deeds. Although the conception of Jesus contains the whole of the Gospel mystery literally in embryo, the deeds by which Jesus will establish God's kingdom, and so inherit his father David's throne, are not fully revealed, other than that they will be saving deeds performed by Jesus (YHWH-Saves). Anticipatory clues are found within the birth narratives and within his circumcision and presentation, but the light of Jesus' salvific ministry only truly dawns at his baptism.

In the context of John's baptism of repentance, Jesus actively steps forward as a sinner among sinners and so inserts himself within the fallen race of Adam. Within the baptismal act the heavens are opened, the Spirit descends upon him, and his Father declares him to be his beloved Son in whom he is well pleased. The baptismal act is both the Father sending forth his commissioning

Spirit upon Jesus and Jesus deliberately laying hold of that divine charge in the same commissioning Spirit. Because he accepts his Father's commission, the Father declares him to be his beloved Son in whom he is pleased, for he now embraces the task of establishing his Father's kingdom by being the Father's Suffering Servant-Son. By being in Spirit-filled communion with his Father, Jesus, as the beloved Servant-Son, will overcome sin and bring forth the new Spirit-filled life of God's kingdom; that is, he will baptize in the Holy Spirit as John the Baptist proclaimed. Thus Jesus' baptism and his ensuing public ministry manifests that he will destroy all evil—Satan, sickness, and death. He will equally bring forth an abundance of life, partaking in Jesus' Spirit of Sonship and so sharing in his filial relationship with his Father, the source of all life. Although Jesus' baptism further reveals the salvific nature of his ministry in that he is to be the Servant-Son, it does not reveal what that will fully entail. Only within Peter's profession of faith and in Jesus' response to it, followed by his Transfiguration, does the salvific purpose of his death and resurrection come more fully into the light.

Others see him as Elijah or one of the prophets come back to life, and so anticipatory of the Messiah, but Peter professes that Jesus himself is the Christ, the Son of the living God. This truth was revealed to him by Jesus' Father, yet Peter did not fully grasp the soteriological implications of his own profession. Jesus further specifies that his messiahship necessarily entails his being handed over to the authorities, suffering, dying, and rising on the third day. Here we perceive more clearly and fully the nature of Jesus' messianic mission, for which he was conceived and which he assumed at his baptism. For Jesus to be the anointed Suffering Servant-Son is for him to die on the cross for the salvation of all and subsequently to rise in glory from the dead. The transfiguring event, as a theophany, is an enactment of the full revelational content contained within Peter's profession of faith—what it means for Jesus to be the Christ, the Son of the living God.

In fulfilling the law (symbolized in Moses) and the prophets (symbolized in Elijah), Jesus, as the Son incarnate, will pass over, through his sacrificial death, from this earthly life into a life of radiant heavenly glory. This exodus will establish a new covenant that will allow others, portrayed by Peter, James, and John, to pass over within the cloud into God's luminous heavenly kingdom in communion with Jesus, their transfigured Lord and Savior, and so abide with his heavenly resplendent Father. This is why the Father reconfirms that Jesus is his Spirit-filled beloved Son to whom the Apostles need to listen. Thus Peter's profession of faith in union with Jesus' clarification, followed by Jesus' subsequent Transfiguration, provides a precise prophetic anticipatory enactment of the Paschal Mystery—what messianic salvific acts Jesus, as the anointed Son of the living God, is to perform to become truly Jesus (YHWH-Saves). The Transfiguration, then, by drawing into and intertwining the truths contained within Jesus conception and baptism, illuminates and amplifies them and so projects their future fulfillment within his passion, death, and resurrection.

We have examined most recently Jesus' triumphal entry into Jerusalem, where he prophesized his triumphal entry into the heavenly Jerusalem through his death and resurrection as its everlasting king. As anticipated in his cleansing of the temple, this passing over from the earthly to the heavenly Jerusalem involves the cleansing of sin and the establishment of the new heavenly living and holy temple. This prophetic entrance into Jerusalem with its subsequent cleansing of the temple in turn foreshadows Jesus' ushering in the eschatological age—the everlasting kingdom of God over which he will reign as its full embodiment.

I will now articulate my theological point. Throughout the whole of our theological study, what may have gone unnoticed is that Jesus never articulates a "theology" of his death and resurrection—*why* he must suffer, die, and rise. Nor then does he provide an explanation as to what these saving deeds will accomplish. Only through his actions—his baptism, Transfiguration, and triumphal entry into Jerusalem—does Jesus present, by way of a prophetic portrayal, the salvific meaning of his death and resurrection. I believe that the positive "theology" by way of prophetic acts and the absence of an articulated "theology" is doctrinally significant. Jesus did not give a verbal explanation of his death and resurrection, a verbalized "theology," precisely because salvation is not the mere obtaining of some new, and until now hidden, knowledge. Rather, salvation is founded upon causal acts, which are founded upon the primordial "conceiving" causal divine act of the Father sending his Son to be conceived as man by the Holy Spirit within the womb of Mary. This incarnating act contains the intertwined causal perichoretic acts of the Father, the Son, and the Holy Spirit. This is the inaugural Trinitarian saving divine act upon which all other causal saving acts flow: Jesus' human saving acts, enacted by the divine Son of God in communion with the Holy Spirit in accordance with the will of his Father. Why this emphasis on "causal acts," and why this emphasis at this juncture within our study? There are three reasons.

First, beginning with the Last Supper, Jesus is going to enact fully those saving acts that were previously prophetically enacted within his public ministry, four of which we just reviewed. The fulfilling of those prophetic acts consists in Jesus' death and resurrection. But these are not merely the terminating acts of his previous prophetic saving acts, but also the conveying into the acts of his death and resurrection all that those previous prophetic saving acts anticipated. In so doing, those anticipatory prophetic saving acts not only illuminate the salvific meaning of Jesus' death and resurrection, but also are elevated to their full prophetic meaning. We will perceive clearly, in the light of Jesus' death and resurrection, what their full prophetic significance entailed. Moreover, by "enacting" a "theology" of his death and resurrection through his previous prophetic acts, Jesus reveals more clearly the meaning of his future definitive saving acts and demonstrates that it is only through such saving acts that salvation is accomplished. As prophetically anticipated within the prophetic acts, salvation is obtained not through words but through actions.[2]

Second, and most importantly, Jesus' saving acts, as prefigured

2. Although the Prologue of John's Gospel emphasizes "the Word" and therefore would appear to highlight the verbal nature of the new revelation through "the Word," what is theologically significant is that "the Word became flesh." The Word will primarily reveal God's saving truth not through human words, but through human actions. The Word's revealing "words" are his fleshly acts, and seeing the glory of these enacted "words," he will reveal his glory as the only begotten Son of the Father—Jesus, the Word made flesh. The ultimate word that the Word enacts is the word of the cross and the word of the resurrection, for both constitute the hour of Jesus' glory, the acts of salvation through which we perceive the full glory of Jesus as the Father's Son.

in his previous prophetic acts, are causal saving acts in that they effect salvation, which is not simply the providing of information that was previously unknown, but the establishing, the bringing into being, a whole new salvific order that was not present prior to the causal salvific acts. Prior to Jesus' death and resurrection, humankind was not reconciled to his Father, sin could not be cleansed, the Holy Spirit could not be poured out, human beings could not be holy children of his Father living in communion with him, death was not conquered, and a glorious everlasting life was unattainable. As prophetically enacted and anticipated, only through the salvific causal acts of Jesus' death and resurrection could humankind be radiantly transfigured in him through the Holy Spirit and so pass through the opened heavens into the heavenly Jerusalem and, in communion with him who is the living temple, worship his Father—in short, abide in the heavenly kingdom of God.

Third, through these causal salvific acts a whole new salvific order comes to be and so offers a manner of salvation that differs in kind from what was possible before. This is because of what has changed and the manner in which it has been changed. Again, the change does not consist *only* of human beings coming to know something that they did not previously know—some new "saving knowledge"—though it certainly includes that. Rather, what has changed is how humankind can now salvifically relate to God, and this change is brought about by divine causal acts enacted humanly. This new relationship allows for a new experiential knowledge of God. Jesus, the incarnate Son, in communion with the Holy Spirit and in conformity with his Father's will, enacts the saving acts that make possible a new and unprecedented relationship with the very persons of the Trinity. Salvific revelation is not only a revelation of divine words spoken humanly, but also a revelation of divine deeds done humanly, for only those human salvific acts effect the manner of salvation needed to be truly saved—forgiving sin, conquering death, and sharing in the eternal communion of life and love with the Father, the Son, and the Holy Spirit. In other words, Jesus, by performing those saving acts by which salvation is obtained, is actualizing himself, and thus only through these causal salvific acts is Jesus becoming Jesus—YHWH-Saves. Without such saving acts, Jesus literally would not have lived up to his divinely given name, for humankind would have never attained salvation.[3]

With the above theological summary in mind, we can proceed to the Passion Narratives, which recount Jesus' definitive salvific acts. Evident from the onset is that we have moved, in a radically significant manner, from the realm of prophecy to the realm of fulfillment and so reality. All that has been prophetically anticipat-

3. Here I want to note two interrelated points. First, only Judaism and Christianity are founded upon a "revelation of act," that is, divine acts that bring about a new relationship with God. Within the Old Testament, God acted to establish through his covenantal act a distinct and exclusive relationship with the Israelites that differed in kind from the relationship he had with all other peoples and nations—specifically the primordial relationship that was established in the act of creation, the Creator/creature relationship. Jesus likewise acted to establish a new salvific order, a new covenant, that offered the ultimate saving relationship with God. Although this revelation is conveyed through words, the preaching of the Gospel, and although this verbal proclamation is to be believed, what is proclaimed and what is to be believed are the mighty works of God, and in believing in these mighty divine works, one comes to share in the salvific benefits made possible by them.

Second, "revelation" within all other religions, other than Judaism and Christianity, is a "revelation of words"; that is, the founder of the religion, such as Buddha or Mohammed, or the religion itself, such as Hinduism, purports to provide knowledge, and one obtains a correct understanding of god/gods as well as knowing how to properly respond to this understanding by knowing and practicing the requisite religious behavior. There is no divine action that makes possible a new kind of relation with "the divine," but simply the providing of "revelational" knowledge that allows one to relate to the divine properly. Therefore all religions, other than Judaism and Christianity, are Gnostic and the founders of all other religions are Gnostic Redeemers, for their sole purpose is to provide knowledge of what had previously been unknown until it was revealed. Once the Gnostic Redeemer provides "the saving knowledge," he loses his contemporary saving significance. He may be revered by those who believe what he has said, but what he "reveals" is ultimately salvifically important, not himself. Within Christianity, Jesus always maintains his contemporary salvific importance, for only in, with, and through him as the risen Lord and Savior does one reap his salvific benefits—everlasting unity with the Father in communion with the Holy Spirit.

Paul emphasizes this understanding within his notion of being and living "in Christ." For example, "In Christ all shall be made alive" (1 Cor 15:22); "Therefore, as any one is in Christ, he is a new creation; the old has passed away, behold, the new has come" (2 Cor 5:17); "For in Christ Jesus you are sons of God, through faith. For as many of you as were baptized into Christ have put on Christ" (Gal 2:26-27); God's plan was "to unite all thing in him [Christ], things in heaven and things on earth" (Eph 1:12).

ed within Jesus' entire life, particularly in the above four pivotal
events, is now enacted and so becomes actualized—the opening
of the heavens, the passing into glory, the entering into the new
Jerusalem, the building of the heavenly temple, and the establishing of communion with his Father through the outpouring of the
Holy Spirit—in short, the inaugurating of God's kingdom. What is
equally significant is that, although all previous events contained
an eschatological element, these events exclusively foreshadow
their ultimate eschatological fulfilment. Having established the
kingdom of God through his passion, death, and resurrection and
so having opened the heavens, having passed into glory, having
entered into the new Jerusalem, having become the living heavenly temple, and having established communion with his Father
in the Holy Spirit, Jesus, in his very person, prophetically and exclusively anticipates the future fulfillment of all that he has made
real when he comes in glory at the end of time. Jesus in becoming
Jesus (YHWH-Saves) through his death and resurrection prophetically anticipates the fulfillment of his name when he gathers all
believers into union with himself and so with his Father within
the loving and life-giving communion of the Holy Spirit. With this
in mind, we can now turn to the first two events of the Passion
Narrative: the anointing of Jesus and his final supper with his disciples. The first anticipates the second in that the anointing of Jesus prophetically portrays the church's future salvific relationship
to him and living in communion with him. The Last Supper enacts and so brings into reality Jesus' saving relationship with his
church and so her communion of life with him as Savior and Lord.

9 · THE ANOINTING OF JESUS AND THE LAST SUPPER

The Anointing: Preparing for Jesus' Burial

We concluded chapter 8 by noting that Jesus explicitly conjoins his triumphal entry into Jerusalem with his coming to celebrate the Passover and immediately speaks of his being "delivered up to be crucified." The Jewish leaders for their part gathered to plot his death, which they did not want to take place during the feast for fear of a tumult among the people (see Mt 26:1-5, Mk 14:1-2, and Lk 22:1-2). Within Matthew and Mark, the anointing of Jesus immediately follows, while Luke places this anointing earlier within his Gospel. Luke's placement may be more historically accurate, but by placing it as an immediate prelude to the Passion Narrative, Matthew and Mark indicate that it integrally bears upon the Paschal Mystery itself. Moreover, although Jesus has performed his last prophetic act, this anointing is uniquely theologically significant in that it is a prophetic act performed not by Jesus, as were all previous prophetic acts, but by someone else.

Matthew and Mark begin the narrative by stating, "Now when Jesus was at Bethany in the house of Simon the leper," while Luke says, "One of the Pharisees asked him [Jesus] to eat with him, and he went into the Pharisee's house and took his place at table."[1] Matthew informs us that, during the course of the meal, a woman came up to Jesus "with an alabaster flask of very expensive ointment, and poured it on his head, as he sat at table." (Mark also notes that

1. All quotations in this section are from Mt 26: 6-13, Mk 14:3-9, and Lk 7:36-50 unless otherwise noted. Although Matthew's and Mark's placing of this event at the onset of the Passion Narrative is more theologically significant for their purposes (and for ours), Luke's narrative contains more explicit theological depth. Also, Matthew and Mark immediately speak of "Simon the leper" and do not inform us that he is a Pharisee, and Luke initially only speaks of "the Pharisee" but will later specify that his name is Simon but not that he was a leper. Because all Synoptic Gospels appear to be narrating the same event, we will consider all three versions within our theological examination.

the woman "broke the flask.") Luke elaborates more fully: "Behold, a woman of the city, who was a sinner, when she learned that he was at table in the Pharisee's house, brought an alabaster flask of ointment, and standing behind him at his feet, weeping, she began to wet his feet with her tears, and wiped them with the hair of her head, and kissed his feet, and anointed them with the ointment."[2]

The woman's action within all three accounts is obviously a visible ardent display of her love for Jesus. According to Matthew and Mark (Luke will be treated separately below), she took what for her must have been her most precious and treasured possession and anointed not her own body, for which purpose she must have purchased it at great expense, but the head of Jesus, allowing the ointment to flow down his body.[3] The reaction of the disciples

2. As intimated in the previous note, the anointing of Jesus is an impossible narrative to sort out. Not only does Luke place it historically prior to its occurrence in Matthew's and Mark's accounts, but he also portrays the woman as sinful and describes more fully the manner of the anointing. In response to the anointing, Jesus forgives her sins. John's Gospel complicates this further (see Jn 12:1-8). As with Matthew and Mark, John's anointing takes place prior to the Passion Narrative but, unlike Matthew and Mark, before Jesus enters Jerusalem. Also, John's anointing takes place not in the house of Simon but in that of Martha, Mary, and Lazarus. Here Mary anoints Jesus, and John's Gospel describes her anointing in a way similar to Luke's portrayal of the sinful woman. Finally, Matthew states that Jesus' "disciples were indignant" over the expensive waste and that the money from the sale could have been given to the poor; Mark notes an ambiguous "some" were indignant for the same reasons; John emphasizes that it was Judas, the betraying thief, who protested the anointing for the same reasons; and Luke specifies that it was the Pharisee who had invited Jesus to his house and was scandalized that Jesus, a supposed prophet, would allow a known sinner to touch him, without making any mention of the waste of the ointment or of money being given to the poor. It is impossible to coordinate what historically happened when, where, and with whom. These various narratives could be the interweaving of two different anointings by two different women, one a "sinner" and one not, who both had flasks of expensive ointment, but that would seem highly unlikely. Whatever might be the case, the theological significance within all the Synoptic accounts is similar, though what is emphasized may differ.

Additionally, within Luke's Gospel, because the woman stood behind Jesus and anointed his feet, Jesus must have been reclining at table while eating, as was customary at the time. Matthew has the woman anointing Jesus' head while he is sitting at table. Although Jesus' eating posture may not be theologically significant, it does provide Matthew and Mark the opportunity to highlight that it was his head that was anointed. Luke emphasizes that Jesus' feet were anointed, and these two distinct parts of the body are theologically significant, depending on the doctrinal point that one wishes to make.

3. It is impossible to harmonize fully Matthew's and Mark's accounts with that of Luke's. Thus it may be the same woman in both accounts or two different women. From Luke's narrative, we can conclude that she was a sinner, and because the Pharisee in Luke is scandalized that Jesus would allow "that sort of woman" to touch him, we can also surmise that she was a prostitute. Thus the expensive ointment with which the woman anointed Jesus in the Gospels

(Matthew) or "some" (Mark) is one of indignation. "Why this waste?" The reason for this righteous ire is that the ointment could have been sold for a large sum of money (Mark specifies: "three hundred denarii," or three hundred days' wages) that could instead have been given to the poor. Undoubtedly, the disciples (or the "some") thought they were merely articulating Jesus' mind and reaction, thus endearing his approval, since throughout his public ministry he demonstrated a noteworthy love and concern for the poor.

While the woman is the one performing this prophetic act, Jesus is the one who theologically interprets its significance, which the woman probably did not overtly intend. Jesus, to the surprise of the righteous grumblers, asks, "Why do your trouble the woman?" (Mt). They should let her alone, "for she has done a beautiful thing to me. For you always have the poor with you, and whenever you will, you can do good to them; but you will not always have me. She had done what she could" (Mk). Jesus defends the action of the woman by first remarking that, because the poor are always nigh, kindness to them is an ever present option and thus summarily dismisses the righteousness flaunted by her incensed accusers. Second, and more importantly, Jesus affirmatively designates her action as "beautiful," for she did not simply do the best workable thing she could do but, given her options, the most comely and noblest thing she could do—unpretentiously and humbly displaying her dutiful love for him. In breaking open her flask and pouring out her most treasured and expensive possession, she is portraying her complete love and wholehearted affection for Jesus and simultaneously offering him worshipful homage—in prayerful adoration, she is breaking open and offering her entire self to him. In "sacrificing" her ointment, she is lovingly offering herself as a sacrifice to Jesus and so devotedly ministering or reverently attending to the one she loves. This is the beautiful act she is performing.[4]

Jesus notes that she did it during an opportune time, for he is not always going to be present for such loving actions to be performed upon him. Jesus is now at the heart of his theological interpretation of her prophetic act. "In

---

of Matthew and Mark, as well as in Luke's, could very well have been anointment plied within her trade, making herself even more seductive to her clients. That all three Synoptic accounts record that it was in "an alabaster flask" underscores not only its monetary value but also its stylish elegance. Even this scenario does not reconcile fully the various accounts.

4. This woman exemplifies what it means to love Jesus above all, even more than father or mother, son or daughter (and in her case even her expensive ointment; see Mt 10:37-39 and Lk 14:25-27). In a sense, as Jesus states here, one must even love him more than the poor. Only in loving Jesus above all will one come to love truly and properly one's family and the poor.

pouring this ointment on my body she has done it to prepare me for burial" (Mt).[5] Although the woman probably had no presentiment that Jesus was
about to be crucified and buried, Jesus did know that such was upon the immediate horizon: "two days the Passover is coming, and the Son of man will
be delivered up to be crucified" (Mt 26:2). That Jesus interprets her anointing
as a preparation for his burial, his "resting" interlude between his passing over
from death to life, means that the present anointing looks both to what will
be the past, his crucifixion and death, and to what will be the future, his resurrection. In her preparatory anointing the woman is not only anointing the
body/humanity of him who will be her crucified Savior but also anointing the
same body/humanity of him who will be her risen Lord—this is the meaning that Jesus gives to her prophetic act of love. In a manner unbeknownst to
her, she is expressing, pouring out, her prayerful love for one who deserves all
praise, worship, and honor: Jesus, her Savior and Lord.

Jesus concludes his interpretation of the woman's anointing by stating emphatically: "Truly, I say to you, wherever this gospel is preached in the whole
world, what she has done will be told in memory of her" (Mt and Mk). She will
be remembered for all time and in all places because she demonstrated an exclusive passionate love of and singular dutiful devotion to Jesus, her crucified Savior. Her undivided love for Jesus crucified will be the church's character-defining
love for and devotion to Jesus, a love that will be proclaimed, engendered, and
emulated by the whole church throughout the whole world for all ages. Thus,
in her prophetic anointing, she becomes a living prefigurement or icon of the
church, and as such, wherever the church is, "what she has done will be told in
memory of her," because what she has done so the living church, for all ages,
will do: profess her love for and worship of Jesus, her Savior.

Most importantly, she will only be remembered when "this Gospel" is proclaimed because the body she anointed for burial rose from the dead. Without
Jesus' glorious resurrection, there would be no "this Gospel," no good news, to
preach, and thus there would be no significance to, and thus no remembrance
of, "this woman's" anointing. In pouring the ointment upon Jesus' head, as traditionally practiced throughout Israel's kingly history, she prophetically designated him, in her unwitting love and worship, the everlasting Lord and King
of all nations, and for this she will be remembered wherever and whenever

---

5. Within Matthew's Gospel, we could see a reference to one of the gifts offered to Jesus by
the three wise men—myrrh, which, as noted at the time, can be seen as an ointment used for
anointing a human corpse.

Jesus is proclaimed until the end of the ages. Similarly, the church forever will profess that Jesus is the universal Lord and definitive king of all peoples. Thus this anointing of Jesus, within the Gospels of Matthew and Mark, is the prophetic theological prelude to the entire Paschal Mystery, for she has anointed he who, as the divinely anointed Christ, will become the crucified and buried Savior, and in so doing she has simultaneously anointed him as the everlasting risen King. To him she is worshipfully offering her life in adoration.

We now turn to Luke's lengthier narrative of the anointing. Luke specifies that Simon (the leper) was a Pharisee, which immediately alerts the reader to his strict observance of the Law. Simon invited Jesus to eat with him at his house, which would imply that they were acquainted and that Simon held Jesus in some, or at least guarded, respect. While they were reclining at table, Luke abruptly states, "And behold," which signals that something unusual is about to happen in this most unexpected setting—during a meal in the home of a Pharisee. The immediate implication is that what we are about to behold is something unseemly. What are we to focus our attention upon? We are to behold none other than "a woman of the city." Luke's description appears to be more a negative comment about her unbecoming living situation (the proverbial "red-light" district) than merely a comment about her geographical abode. This is confirmed when he adds, "who was a sinner." Now this sinful woman of the city, "when she learned that he [Jesus] was at table in the Pharisee's house, brought an alabaster flask of ointment, and standing behind him at his feet, weeping, she began to wet his feet with her tears, and wiped them with the hair of her head, and kissed his feet, and anointed them with the ointment." This is what we are to behold.

Immediately striking is the sensuous nature of the woman's actions—her weeping upon the feet of Jesus and her drying them with what must have been her long flowing hair, climaxing in her kissing and anointing his feet. Such a passionate display in the presence of others within a private home during a meal no doubt brought mortified embarrassment upon Simon and irate chagrin among the others in attendance. Most disturbing to Simon was Jesus' apparent toleration of such a sensuous exhibition, for he thought to himself: "If this man is a prophet, he would have known who and what sort of woman this is who is touching him, for she is a sinner." Ironically, Jesus did know exactly what sort of sinner this city woman was, thus proving that he was indeed a prophet. And what Jesus beheld was not a sensuality inflamed by lust but a sensuality imbued with love. She may have been a woman who habitually lived a sensuous life, and so knew no other way to express herself other than through her sensuality, but at this moment that sensuous obsession gave birth to her passionate ardor of love. Again, as in Matthew and Mark, Jesus becomes the interpreter of her actions. Although Jesus in the Gospels of Matthew and Mark interprets the woman's anointing in terms of preparing his body for burial, in Luke's Gospel, Jesus interprets her actions as those of a repentant sinner lovingly grateful for being forgiven.

Jesus tells Simon (the Pharisee, who is now named for the first time) that he has something to say. Simon replies, "What is it, Teacher?" Indeed, Jesus is a teacher, and he wants to teach Simon a lesson of truth. Jesus then tells of a creditor to whom two people owed money. One owed a large sum and other a small sum, and because neither could pay, he forgave them both. "'Now which of them will love him more?' Simon answered, 'The one, I suppose, to whom he forgave more.' And he said to him 'You have judged rightly.' Then turning toward the woman he said to Simon, 'Do you see this woman? I entered your house, you gave me no water for my feet, but she has wet my feet with her tears and wiped them with her hair. You gave me no kiss, but from the time I came in she has not ceased to kiss my feet. You did not anoint my head with oil, but she has anointed my feet with ointment.'" Jesus has now added his own personal "behold"—"Do you see this woman?" Jesus is looking at, beholding, the woman, but he is speaking to Simon because he wants Simon to see what he himself beholds. What Jesus wants Simon to perceive is that for every welcoming act that Simon neglected to do, this woman has fulfilled in a most extraordinary manner—washing his feet with her tears and wiping them with her hair rather than the ritual providing of water; the passionate kissing of his feet rather than the polite kissing of his cheeks, the humble anointing of his feet rather than the customary anointing of his head. What the woman did was not simply expected civility, but rather loving actions that sprang from an earnest heart.

Jesus now provides the genuine motive that lay within her loving actions. He first speaks to Simon. "Therefore I tell you, her sins, which are many, are forgiven, for she loved much; but he who is forgiven little, loves little." What is striking is that the woman is forgiven her many sins because she loved much, and not that she loved much because her many sins were forgiven. Her love for Jesus compelled her to seek him out and to do what she most wanted and needed to do, even if it must be done in a seemingly most inappropriate setting—obtain forgiveness from him. In Jesus, she perceived that she had found the mercy that she so ardently sought. Like the forgiven debtor, she may have loved Jesus more than the person who was forgiven little, yet her love first welled up within her heart from knowing, in faith, that Jesus could forgive her many sins. Thus Jesus now says to her: "Your sins are forgiven." Jesus' declaration of forgiveness affords for the others at the table a new cause for alarm. "Who is this, who can forgive sins?" Precisely! Only God can forgive sins. Inherent within the woman's lovingly seeking out Jesus was her faith in Jesus' ability to forgive her sin, and within that inherent loving-faith-recognition of Jesus' ability to forgive sin resides her faith in him as divine. This is why Jesus does not directly address his suspicious skeptics but simply addresses the woman, although the faithless would bend an ear to hear, "Your faith has saved you; go in peace." Faith in Jesus' divinity gave birth to her love of Jesus, and that faith-imbued love compelled her to seek him out at Simon's dinner table in her hopeful pursuit of merciful forgiveness. She found, in faith, what, in love, she was hoping to find and so now, as Jesus declared to her, she could go in peace because her many sins were forgiven.

What theological coherence is there between the accounts of the anointing of Jesus within Matthew and Mark and that within Luke?[6] There are two intertwining theological points: one concerns the woman who is enacting the prophetic act, and the other concerns Jesus, who is interpreting the prophetic act. The woman, in her anointing of Jesus, is obviously performing an act of love on his behalf. Matthew and Mark do not tell us what compelled her to do so. Given that Jesus interprets her act of love as a preparation for his burial, however, we perceive that his saving death and resurrection lay at the heart of her prophetic act of love, even if she was not fully cognizant of it. In an act of worship, she is lovingly anointing Jesus' head as her Savior and Lord. Luke emphasizes that her love was motivated by her knowing in faith that Jesus, being divine, could forgive her many sins. Jesus acknowledges that her loving faith was both the anterior cause of her forgiveness and in turn the subsequent cause of her grateful love. Thus, as in Matthew and Mark, the woman, in Luke, is also, in her loving anointing, acknowledging Jesus as her Savior and Lord. Although there is no reference to his burial in Luke, it will only be in his death and resurrection that he will achieve the forgiveness of sin and obtain a new reconciled life with his Father. Ultimately, the woman, in all three Synoptic Gospels, is a prophetic prefiguration of the church. The church, in communion with those who have entered and so abide within her, continually, in ar-

6. Interestingly, what "historically" unites these accounts is that they all narrate the same simple fact: while Jesus was at table with Simon (the leper Pharisee), a woman with a flask of expensive ointment anoints him.

dent faith and assured hope, humbly weeps over and anoints the feet of Jesus her Savior, ever beseeching his forgiveness and rejoicing in the forgiveness she has found. Equally, the church is always, throughout the ages, lovingly anointing Jesus' head and so worshipfully acknowledging, in adoration and praise, the sacred humanity of her crucified, buried, and risen Lord. This is her everlasting ministering, her prayerful attending, to him. Theologically, to tell the story of the woman's anointing of Jesus is to tell the story of the church itself, for the woman literally embodies the doctrine of the church. Jesus' interpretation of the woman's prophetic actions is, then, the words he speaks to his church: You have "done a beautiful thing to me" (Mt and Mk); therefore "your faith has saved you; go in peace" (Lk). Thus the whole enactment that includes both the acts of the woman and the acts of Jesus is a living prophetic icon of the interactive relationship, the dynamic communion, between Jesus and his church—Jesus mercifully offering himself in love as the Savior and Lord of his church and the church as composed of those who, having given themselves completely to Jesus in repentant faith and grateful love, worship and rejoice in him alone as their Savior and Lord. Again, what we perceive in this prophetic scenario is Jesus acting as Jesus and the woman (and the church) perceiving and acknowledging, through her actions, that Jesus is Jesus—YHWH-Saves.

Before proceeding to the Last Supper, a brief comment on Judas' betrayal is necessary (see Mt 26:14-16, Mk 14:10-11, and Lk 22:3-6). As the woman's anointing of Jesus is in keeping with Jesus informing his disciples that the Passover is close at hand, wherein he will be delivered up to be crucified, what immediately follows in Matthew and Mark is in keeping with the Jewish leader's plotting to kill Jesus, known as the betrayal of Judas. As the woman's anointing, imbued with the Holy Spirit, is the loving preparation for Jesus' burial, so Judas' betrayal, Satan having "entered into him" (Lk), is the unloving preparation for his burial. And as the woman lovingly poured out upon Jesus her most expensive treasure, Judas sells Jesus to the Jewish leaders for a mere "thirty pieces of silver" (Mt). As the woman sought out Jesus to express her love and achieve forgiveness, so Judas will now seek "an opportunity to betray him" and so commit what he believes is the unforgiveable sin (Mt, Mk, and Lk). Just as Jesus found the woman's action to be "a beautiful thing," so the Jewish leaders "were glad" (Mk) at Judas' proposal. The contrast between the actions of the woman and those of Judas could not be more stark—the self-giving of all to Jesus out of love versus the greedy marketing of Jesus for selfish gain. As the woman is an ever-living theological icon of the church's beauty so Judas, "one of the twelve" (Mt, Mk, and Lk), is the ever-deadly portrayal of the church's sin. The difference between the two is that loving repentant faithfulness keeps one in living ecclesial apostolic communion with Jesus, while deadly unrepentant sin separates one from that living ecclesial apostolic communion and from Jesus, as in the case of Judas who, because of his betrayal, is no longer numbered among "the twelve."

The Last Supper

Jesus' Theological Interpretative Enactment of the Paschal Mystery

I emphasized in the introduction to this section on the Passion Narratives that all that was previously prophetically anticipated within the Gospels now becomes a reality within the Paschal Mystery. The first instance of this is within Jesus' final Passover supper with his disciples.[7] When considering the relationship between the Last Supper and Jesus' death and resurrection, it can easily be presupposed that these future saving events provide the basis for understanding the Last Supper. Only in the light of the cross and resurrection do we perceive the significance of Jesus' Passover supper and in turn its theological and liturgical Eucharistic meaning. But in enacting the Last Supper, his final Passover, Jesus is enacting his own personal theological commentary on and doctrinal interpretation of his forthcoming passion, death, and resurrection.[8]

And even though the Last Supper is an anticipatory commentary in that Jesus provides it prior to the actual saving events, it is not a prophetic act. In the Last Supper, Jesus is not simply prophetically prefiguring, as he did in all his previous prophetic acts (such as his baptism, Transfiguration, and triumphal entry into Jerusalem), the meaning of his death and resurrection and the effects that they will achieve. Rather, the Last Supper is a true liturgical sacramental enactment of these saving events. He is sacramentally, through liturgical symbolic acts, making present his passion, death, and resurrection. Only within this liturgical sacramental enactment does Jesus reveal the intrinsic meaning and integral consequences of those anticipated saving acts. Likewise, because the Last Supper is a liturgical sacramental enactment of his fu-

---

7. I will not be commenting on Jesus' sending his disciples to prepare for the Passover meal nor on his foretelling of Judas' betrayal, which Matthew and Mark place immediately prior to the institutional narrative and Luke places immediately after (see Mt 26:17-25, Mk 14:17-21; Lk 22:7-14 and 21-23).

8. Note again that Jesus' theological commentary is not by way of words but by way of actions; his words declare the meaning of his acts.

ture salvific acts, and in so doing makes them real in the present enactment, the Apostles, who are participating in this liturgical sacramental enactment, are already taken up into those salvific acts, and so they become active participants within those acts. Being active participants within those salvific acts, they do not simply come to know the meaning of his passion, death, and resurrection, but having been subsumed within these very acts, they are united to them and partake of their saving effects. As inhabiting and partaking participants, the Apostles necessarily and properly realize the benefits constitutively contained within those salvific acts. The liturgical sacramental acts that are the Last Supper thus signify what they effect—Jesus' saving passion, death, and resurrection—and effect what they signify—the salvific benefits that accrue to Jesus' passion, death, and resurrection. With the above as a prologue, let us examine the liturgical sacramental acts that compose the Last Supper and in so doing perceive Jesus' enacted theological commentary on and interpretation of his passion, death, and resurrection.

Biblical Theological Setting

All three Gospels state that Jesus held his Last Supper "on the day [Mt and Mk specify that it was the first day] of Unleavened Bread." Mark and Luke note that it was on this day that "the Passover lamb had to be sacrificed" (see Mt 26:17, Mk 14:12, and Lk 22:7).[9] Thus the religious, and so theological, setting of the Last Supper is the traditional conjoined feast of Unleavened Bread and the Jewish Passover (see Ex 12:1-20, Lv 23:4-8, Nm 9:2-14, and Dt 16:1-8). The Passover commemorates the night when, at God's command, the Israelites killed a lamb without blemish and placed the blood of that lamb upon the doorposts and lintel of their homes. They were also to eat the lamb and unleavened bread in haste, with loins girt, sandals on their feet, and staff in hand. Although their attire and the unleavened bread that they ate convey a readiness to swiftly flee Egypt, the sprinkling of the blood upon the doors was to signify to God that theirs was an Israelite abode. Seeing the blood, the Lord would pass over their homes and not smite their first-born sons.

9. There is a well-known discrepancy as to the exact evening when Jesus ate the Passover meal with his disciples. The Synoptic Gospels place it on the day of the Passover, but the Gospel of John places the Passover on the day of Jesus' crucifixion. If this were the case, Jesus, within the Synoptics, would have eaten the Passover meal the day prior to the actual Passover. Scholars continue to debate this issue, but its resolution is not pertinent to our present discussion. John, for theological reasons, may have wanted to emphasize that Jesus is the new Passover Lamb and so has him crucified/sacrificed on the Passover, the day and time when the Passover lambs were sacrificed.

As he has done within the entirety of his ministry, Jesus, now within the commemorative enactment of the Feast of Unleavened Bread and Passover, embodies as the anointed Messiah the whole of the Exodus event. In so doing, all these Old Testament events, the entire Exodus narrative, are now recognized as prophetic events that Jesus is about to fulfill. Although these events thus give meaning to and so help interpret what Jesus is enacting, they simultaneously achieve their true inherent significance. The ultimate purpose of the Exodus events was not simply to achieve the goals obtained at the historical time of their enactment—freedom from Egyptian slavery and eventual entrance into the Promised Land. Rather, these events figuratively portray a future enactment that would achieve the eventual purpose that these prophetic events presaged. Thus, within his Last Supper, Jesus enacts the final commemorative Passover, for within his enactment of the old Passover he enacts the new Passover, to which the former Passover prophetically pointed—freedom from the slavery of sin and death and entrance into the Promised Land of God's Kingdom. What was prefigured in the Passover of old has now been fulfilled and thus becomes redundant as a commemorative feast. Its significance is not lost, however, but rather enhanced, for its true importance resides in its prophetic fulfillment. It must be remembered, however, that the ultimate fulfillment resides in the heavenly banquet when Jesus returns in glory. Jesus seems to allude to this when he proclaims, "I shall not drink of the fruit of the vine until the kingdom of God comes" (Lk 22:16).[10]

Now, if Jesus is enacting within his last Passover meal with his disciples the new Passover and so enacting his own interpretation of his death and resurrection, how will this new Passover be accomplished? How will he pass over from death to life, and how will his passing over allow his disciples to pass over from sin and death to communion with his Father? The answer lies within what Jesus enacts within the Passover setting. Within his celebration of the commemorative Passover meal, Jesus enacts the new Passover by establishing the new covenant.

The aim of God's freeing the Israelites from Egypt, the end toward which his passing over pointed, was the covenant he would make with them on Mt Sinai. He set the Israelites free from their slavery in Egypt to bind them to

10. Because Jesus fulfilled what was prophetically portrayed within the Passover, it is objectively no longer necessary to celebrate the traditional Jewish Passover. But for the Jews, who have not come to faith in him, to do so is not a superfluous religious commemoration. They continue to commemorate in gratitude the past mighty saving deeds of God and in so doing give him praise and worship. For them it remains a graced, though incomplete, celebration.

himself as his children, to make them his holy people, and so lead them in righteousness and freedom into the Promised Land. The entire Exodus event achieves its purpose in the covenant, which was constituted and ratified with the sacrifice of a lamb. "Half of the blood he [Moses] threw against the altar." Having then read aloud to the people the book of the covenant, all that they were faithfully to obey, "Moses took the [remaining] blood and threw it upon the people and said: 'Behold the blood of the covenant which the Lord has made with you in accordance with all of these words'" (Ex 24:6-8). The blood of the Passover lamb, which saved the Israelites from death, finds its completion in the blood of the covenantal lamb, which constituted a living communion with the living God—YHWH. As the blood of the Passover lamb initiated the Israelites' journey from slavery and death, so the blood of the lamb of the covenant terminated that journey, living freely in communion with the Lord in the Promised Land. Within the commemorative celebration of the Jewish Passover, Jesus enacted the new Passover by enacting the new covenant. He conjoined within himself both the Passover lamb and the covenantal lamb of sacrifice—he became the commencement and the terminus of the new journey—the new Exodus, the new covenantal journey from the condemnatory slavery to sin and death to living with his Father in righteousness and holiness as his free children within his heavenly kingdom.[11] Keeping the above in mind, we can now turn to Jesus' words and actions within the Last Supper.

Jesus' Words and Actions

Matthew informs us that while he and his disciples were eating, "Jesus took bread and blessed, and broke it and gave it to his disciples and said, 'Take, eat; this is my body.' And he took a cup, and when had given thanks he gave it to them, saying, 'Drink of it, all of you; for this is my blood of the covenant, which is poured out for many for the forgiveness of sins. I tell you I shall not drink again of this fruit of the vine until that day when I drink it new with you in my Father's kingdom'" (Mt 26:26-29). Mark's narrative is similar, though he has Jesus say simply, "Take; this is my body." He does not say that his poured-out blood is "for the forgiveness of sins," and he speaks of drinking the wine anew in "the kingdom of God" rather than "in my Father's kingdom," as does Matthew (Mk 14:22-25). Luke's narrative is somewhat different. "And when the hour came, he sat at table, and his apostles were with him. And he

---

11. Within the Transfiguration, Jesus spoke with Moses and Elijah about his Exodus, and thus about the new covenant that he would establish as the new Passover Lamb.

said to them, 'I have earnestly desired to eat this passover with you before I suffer; for I tell you I will not eat it until it is fulfilled in the kingdom of God.' And he took a cup, and when he had given thanks he said, 'Take this, and divide it among yourselves; for I tell you that from now on I shall not drink of the fruit of the vine until the kingdom of God comes.' And he took bread, and when he had given thanks he broke it and gave it to them, saying, 'This is my body, which is given up for you. Do this in remembrance of me.' And likewise the cup after supper, saying, 'This cup which is poured out for you is the new covenant in my blood'" (Lk 22:14-20).[12] Luke has Jesus simply giving "thanks" over the bread but adds that Jesus spoke of the "new covenant in my blood."[13] With these sacramental actions and accompanying words, Jesus is enacting his theological interpretation of his death and resurrection and in his so doing making the reality of his salvific death and resurrection present within his enactment.

Within the commemorative Passover meal, Jesus performs a series of liturgical causal actions: he takes bread, blesses the bread, breaks the bread, and gives the bread. Luke has Jesus simply give thanks over the bread. The Apostles would doubtlessly perceive that these liturgical causal actions replicate Jesus' actions when multiplying the loaves for the hungry multitude. Here, again, a prophetic act achieves its full significance. Although Jesus alleviated the physical hunger of the multitude, that was not the ultimate import of the miracle. Rather, its definitive significance, the end for which it was first enacted, resided in its becoming a hermeneutical event for interpreting the future blessing, breaking, and giving of Jesus' body as the abundant new blessed and broken bread-of-life given to all who reside within the kingdom of God.[14]

12. Luke, unlike Matthew and Mark, narrates that Jesus, prior to his "words of institution" over the bread and wine, distributes a blessed cup of wine to his disciples, informing them that he will "not drink of the fruit of the vine until the kingdom of God comes" (Lk 22:17-18). Although there is scholarly discussion concerning the significance of this, it does not bear upon our present theological interpretation. More significantly, Matthew's and Mark's rendition of Jesus' words of institution and Luke's and Paul's rendering of Jesus' words, while similar, do differ. For a comparison, see Mt 26:26-29 and Mk 14:22-25, and Lk 22:19-20 and 1 Cor 11:23-25. Paul's rendering would be the earliest written account. We will note the differences in due course.

13. Some ancient manuscripts of Matthew and Mark also have the word "new" prior to the word "covenant."

14. Within John's Gospel, the multitude, having had their fill of bread owing to Jesus' miraculous multiplication, search after him and find him the next day in Capernaum. Jesus reproaches them: "Truly, truly, I say to you, you seek me, not because you saw signs, but because you ate your fill of the loaves. Do not labor for the food which perishes, but for the food which

The nature of this abundant new life and the nature of the causal actions of taking, blessing/thanking, breaking, and giving are found in what results, what is effected, from the taking, blessing/thanking, breaking, and giving. In these actions, Jesus mandates his Apostles to eat it, for "this is my by body" (Luke adds: "which is given for you"). Similarly, Jesus takes the cup of wine and gave thanks (Luke, having Jesus give thanks over the bread, omits his thanks over the cup), and mandates the Apostles to drink it, for "this is my blood of the [new] covenant, which is poured out for many for the forgiveness of sins" (Mt). Here we must recall who the man Jesus is: the Messiah, the Son of the living God who possesses the singular Spirit of Sonship. As the Father's Spirit-anointed Son, Jesus takes bread and a cup of wine and calls down a Spirit-filled blessing from his heavenly Father and in so doing equally gives thanks to his Father for the bestowed blessing. What this "Messianic" blessing effects by the power of the Holy Spirit, and for which Jesus gives thanks, is the transformation of this bread into his body, the body of the Son of God, and the transformation of this cup of wine into his blood, the blood of the Son of God. Because of the blessing, the calling down from his Father of the Holy Spirit, *what* Jesus, the Son, picks up (bread) is different in kind from *what* he now breaks and gives: the human body of the divine Son. The wine within the cup that Jesus takes is different in kind from *what* is in the cup that Jesus now gives his disciples to drink: the human blood of the divine Son. The causal act of the thanksgiving blessing accompanied by Jesus' words has brought about a change of "whatness" or quiddity, a change from what was bread and wine into what is now his body and blood. Each word of Jesus' declarative sentence is then of the utmost doctrinal importance. "This" denotes what he is giving. "Is" specifies ontologically what he is giving, what the "this" actually "is." "My body/my blood" identifies what the "this" ontologically "is" that he is giving, his actual body and blood. Thus what is really broken and given to his disciples is no longer bread but Jesus' blessed body, that is, the Spirit-blessed body of the Father's Son. That is what they are mandated to eat. Similarly, what is really poured out and given to his disciples is no longer wine but Jesus' blood, the poured-out blood of the Father's Son that is the blood of the (new) covenant for the forgiveness of sins. That is what they are mandated to drink. Although the human senses of the Apostles still see, smell, taste, and touch what

---

endures to eternal life, which the Son of man will give to you; for on him God the Father set his seal" (Jn 6:26-27). Thus, in John's Gospel, Jesus interprets the multiplication of the loaves not as an act that is complete, the feeding of the hungry, but as a sign toward a future fulfillment—the providing of food for eternal life that he will give them.

appears to be bread and wine, in fact what they are taking, consuming, and touching is Jesus' body and blood.[15]

Of equal doctrinal significance inherent in the above is the sacrificial nature of Jesus' sacramental words and actions, for through them he is enacting and so theologically interpreting his own death as a sacrifice. As Jesus actively takes the bread and blesses and breaks it, he will, on the cross, actively take his Spirit-anointed blessed body and offer it, his now broken body, as a loving sacrifice to his Father. The "breaking" of his body is the "giving" of his body as a sacrifice to his Father. Within Luke, what is given to his disciples is what is "given up for you," that is, given up to his Father on their behalf. Thus the *giving* of his blessed broken body to his disciples is the sacramental act of his *giving up* his blessed broken body for them on the cross. Similarly, what his disciples are to drink is "my blood of the [new] covenant, which is poured out for many for the forgiveness of sins." The blood that Jesus gives to his disciples to drink is the blood that he, the Spirit-filled Son, offers to his Father for the forgiveness of sins and in so doing consummates the new covenant with his Father. Jesus interprets his actions and his words, both in the giving of his body and in the giving of his blood to his Apostles, as a sacrifice of himself that he will offer on the cross. Although the giving of his body and blood within the Last Supper is one liturgical sacramental act, the very sacramental distinguishing within this one act of two distinct acts accentuates the sacrificial nature of Jesus' death on the cross, for there Jesus' blood will be separated and poured forth from his body, this severance constituting the sacrificial nature of the act. Nonetheless, in and through the same act of giving up of his body on the cross, Jesus pours out his blood and so they are enacted together, the giving up as a pouring out,

---

15. I have attempted to interpret theologically the above biblical text in accord with how it was written and so how Jesus wished his actions and words to be understood. For this reason, I tried not to employ in my interpretation later theological or philosophical concepts and terms that grew up within patristic and medieval theology. Nonetheless, my interpretation is obviously in accord with the teaching of the Catholic Church, which was canonized at the Council of Trent and continues to be the doctrinal teaching of the church to the present. The Council stated that this change of the bread and wine into the body and blood of Jesus can be "fittingly and properly called transubstantiation," that is, that the substance of bread and the substance of wine are changed into the substance of Jesus' body and the substance of his blood (Trent's "Decree on the Most Holy Sacrament of the Eucharist," chapter 4 [DS, 1642]. See also chapter 1 [DS, 1636]). My expression "change of whatness" attempts to capture that biblical teaching in a less technical fashion. Both the terms "substance" and "whatness" express the notion that, after the change, Jesus is sacramentally present in the Eucharist in a way that he actually now exists, though under the appearances of bread and wine, and not in some lesser manner such as in a symbolic or spiritual manner or through the simple exercise of his power.

the one sacrificial act through which sins are forgiven and the new covenant is established.

We must also observe the Gospels' consistent use of transitive verbs when describing Jesus' actions within his sacramental enactment and so his sacramental interpretation of his death within the Last Supper, as well as Jesus' use of transitive verbs within his own actions. Jesus is said to take, bless/thank, break, and give. He speaks of the giving up of his body and pouring out his blood. Theologically, these transitive verbs within the sacramental actions of the Last Supper denote that Jesus' death is not something that he passively undergoes despite the appearance of his being arrested, judged, scourged, crowned with thorns, crucified, and so put to death. Such passivity would attain nothing of salvific value. Rather, all these transitive verbs denote the actions that Jesus is sacramentally performing within the Last Supper and thus will enact on the cross, and it is only in the performing of them that salvation is achieved and the new covenant constituted. As the Father's Son, only Jesus and Spirit-filled acts, his sacrificial giving up of his body and pouring out of his blood, merit salvation. His sacrificial passion and death are things he is doing, and not something he undergoing, and in the doing he is achieving salvation for many. The Last Supper, as the enacted interpretation of Jesus' death, makes clear that Jesus is the governing actor within the entire sacramental liturgy, and so manifests that he is the governing actor within his entire passion and death.[16]

We now must address the relationship between the commemorative Passover meal that Jesus and his disciples are celebrating and Jesus' enactment of the new covenant within that Passover meal. Within the Old Testament Exodus event, the Passover lamb inextricably leads to the sacrificial lamb of the covenant. God passed over the homes of the Hebrews so that he could set

---

16. John's Gospel highlights Jesus actively "directing" his passion and death. For example, within the Synoptic Gospels, Judas and the arresting crowd approach Jesus in the Garden of Gethsemane, but John's Gospel states, "Then Jesus, knowing all that was to befall him, *came forward* and said to them and said to them, 'Whom do you seek?'" (Jn 18:4). Jesus, as the governing actor, initiated the act of his own arrest. Similarly, within the Synoptics, the soldiers led Jesus out to crucify him, and Simon of Cyrene helped him carry his cross. John's Gospel states, "So they took Jesus, and *he went out bearing his own cross*" (Jn 19:17). Jesus is enacting his saving acts; they are not enacted upon him. John's account here does not contradict the Synoptic accounts wherein Simon of Cyrene helps Jesus carry his cross. The Synoptics wish to emphasize a different theological mystery.

This is also in keeping with his baptism. There, Jesus steps forward to be baptized by John, actively aligning himself with sinful humanity and actively assuming his Father's Spirit-filled commission to be the saving Suffering Servant-Son.

them free from the slavery of Egypt to make a covenant with them in the desert, and thence lead them to the Promised Land as his covenanted holy people. Within the commemorative Passover celebration, Jesus conjoins within himself the two lambs: the new sacrificial Passover lamb that will bring freedom from sin and death and the new covenantal sacrificial lamb that will establish the new covenant. Because Jesus offers himself as the sacrificial lamb of the new covenant, he can pass over from the slavery of sin and death into the promised land of God's kingdom. But this kingdom is not something that already existed and into which Jesus came to abide. Rather, as the sacrificial lamb of the new covenant, Jesus brings into existence the kingdom of God, for the new covenant is his new definitive abiding with his heavenly Father. This is Jesus' sacramentally enacted theological interpretation of his own death and resurrection—the new and living Passover of the new and living covenant.

Within the commemorative Passover, Jesus, through his sacramental words and actions, also configures himself into the new priest and constitutes himself as the new victim. As the new high priest, Jesus offers himself as the new Passover-covenantal lamb of sacrifice. In this sacramental enactment of his death, Jesus interprets his own death, wherein he, as the Spirit-filled priest, will on the cross offer himself completely as a loving and all-holy sacrifice to his Father. As the Son of God incarnate, possessing as Messiah the Father's Spirit of Sonship, Jesus is the new and sovereign high priest capable of offering the perfect sacrifice that would establish the new covenant and, simultaneously, for the same reasons, be the new perfect supreme holy sacrifice for the forgiveness of sins.[17]

We have been focusing exclusively upon Jesus' sacramental actions within the Last Supper. We emphasized that Jesus' terminating act following upon his taking, blessing/thanking, and breaking is that of his giving his sacrificed body and blood to his disciples. Jesus conjoins this "giving" with his mandate that his Apostles are to "take." Again, as with his own actions, Jesus employs transitive verbs when mandating what his Apostles are to do. They are to actively "take" and not passively "receive." Moreover, they are to take and "eat" and take and "drink." In the act of taking and eating and taking and drinking, the Apostles conjoin their actions with Jesus actions. They are also performing actions and so become acting participants within the liturgical sacramental enactment. Because of their actions, there is now one conjoined action

17. Jesus as the great high priest who offers himself as the one everlasting sacrifice to his Father is later taken up and theologically developed within the Letter to the Hebrews.

performed by Jesus and his Apostles. The hands of Jesus—by which he takes, blesses, breaks, and gives his body—are now conjoined with the hands of the Apostles, by which they take and eat what Jesus' hands are giving. Both sets of hands are in action, act to act, and in so doing both sets of hands are set upon the same "bread" that is his body. Similarly, Jesus' hands take the cup, and having given thanks, he gives it to his disciples commanding that they take it and drink. Conjoined to Jesus' act of giving is the Apostles' act of taking and drinking—both sets of hands are again in action, act to act, and in so doing both sets of hands are upon the same cup of "wine" that is his blood. Although Jesus' actions are distinct from the Apostles', there is simultaneity of acts in that their conjoined actions compose the one liturgical sacramental act of giving and taking. These acts of these respective hands may even be considered perichoretic in that there is an intertwining, a making of one, of Jesus' giving and the Apostles' taking. From this giving and taking as well as from all the above, I draw eight interrelated theological conclusions.

The Communion of Jesus and His Apostles

First, the doctrinal significance of the conjoined acts of giving and taking, the conjoined hands upon the same "bread" and same cup, resides in Jesus bringing his Apostles into communion, literally in life-giving touch, with him. In eating Jesus' body and drinking his blood, the Apostles and Jesus come into living communion with one another—Jesus actively giving himself as the bread of life and the blood of salvation, and the Apostles actively eating the living bread and drinking the cleansing blood of salvation. The Apostles become one in and with Jesus, of which their conjoined hands upon the "bread" and "wine" is a symbol. Similarly, being in living communion with Jesus, the Apostles partake of and so are taken into the one sacrifice that he is—the body that is given up for them and the blood that is poured out for them. In so being conjoined to Jesus and his salvific sacrifice, the Apostles partake of the benefits of that one sacrifice, a passing over with Jesus from the condemnation of sin and death into the new Spirit-filled covenantal life that is communion with his Father. Because they are in communion with Jesus, the Apostles, by necessity, are in communion with all the sacrificial benefits that accrue in, with, and through him—all the benefits that he literally embodies, for they are literally "embodied" in him through their eating his body and drinking his blood.

Second, although not explicitly stated but nonetheless necessarily inherent within Jesus' bringing his Apostles into communion with himself, and so into a new Spirit-filled covenantal communion with his Father, is the reality of Jesus' resurrection. Thus Jesus' sacramental actions during the Last Supper not only make present his saving sacrificial presence, but also his glorious resurrected presence. If the Father did not raise Jesus, his Son, from the dead, it would mean that there would be no passing over from death to life and that no new covenant with his Father had been established. And if Jesus is not gloriously risen, if he is not alive, there would be then no possibility of the Apostles coming into living communion with him, no coming in living touch with him, and so there would be no point in his giving his body and blood to his Apostles and no point in their taking and eating it, for his body and blood would be lifeless—the remnants of a cadaver. Thus, although the body that Jesus gives to his Apostles is sacrificially given up for them and the blood that he gives to his Apostles is sacrificially poured out for them, the risen sacrificed body that was given up and the risen sacrificed blood that poured out Jesus tells his Apostles to eat and drink, for only in partaking of the risen Jesus do they then share in that one sacrifice and so obtain its salvific benefits. Only in being in communion with the risen Jesus, in taking and eating his risen sacrificial body and blood, do the Apostles pass over in communion with him from death to life and share in communion with him, through the Holy Spirit, his new covenantal communion with his Father. Here is the full meaning of Jesus' multiplication of the abundant loaves: Jesus is the "bread of life" because the bread he gives to his Apostles and the bread that they eat is the risen, and so life-giving, Jesus himself. To be in living communion with the risen Jesus, the Father's Spirit-filled Son, is to be in communion with him who now is the fullness of eternal life.[18]

Third, the Apostles, in their taking and eating and taking and drinking

18. This is the point that Jesus makes within the Gospel of John. Because Jesus is the Son of God incarnate, he is "the living bread which came down from heaven; if any one eats of this bread, he will live forever" (Jn 6:51). Jesus' divine eternal life is also mediated through his risen glorified body. "Truly, truly, I say to you, unless you eat the flesh of the Son of man and drink his blood, you have no life in you; he who eats my flesh and drinks my blood has eternal life, and I will raise him up at the last day. For my flesh is food indeed, and my blood is drink indeed. He who eats my flesh and drinks my blood abides in me, and I in him. As the living Father sent me, and I live because of the Father, so he who eats me will live because of me. This is the bread which came down from heaven, not such as the fathers ate and died; he who eats this bread will live forever" (Jn 6:52-58). Jesus articulates a sequential causal relationship. As the Father's eternally begotten Son, he eternally lives because of the Father. So, to eat the heavenly bread that is Jesus is to share in his divine life. And that divine life is mediated through his resurrected humanity. By eating Jesus' risen body and blood—"he who eats me"—the faithful will share in his risen divine life, for he will abide in them and they will abide in him, and will therefore abide and so live forever in communion with his Father, the author of all life.

Jesus' risen body and blood, not only come into living communion with him but also equally come into living communion with one another. The twelve become one in him. Jesus is revealing to his Apostles that through his new covenantal death and resurrection he is creating one new holy people. This one new holy covenanted people are one and holy precisely because they are conjoined to him through their sacramentally partaking of his sacrificial risen body and blood, by being in communion with him, who literally embodies the new holy covenantal communion with his Father.

Our examination of his commemorative Passover with his Apostles has emphasized Jesus' liturgical sacramental enactment of his death and resurrection and so his theological commentary upon or interpretation of these saving mysteries. Fourth, within his sacramental enacted interpretation, something that is sacramentally portrayed throughout, Jesus manifests that his death and resurrection are for the sake of the Last Supper or, what I will now refer to (and purposely did not do so previously) as the Eucharistic Liturgy. On the one hand, Jesus' sacramental enactment of his death and resurrection within the Last Supper does interpret what Jesus will enact on the cross: the sacrificial giving of himself to his Father on behalf of humankind for the forgiveness of sins and for the instituting of the new covenant. For this end Jesus dies and rises. On the other hand, imbedded within that salvific end is a further end—the ultimate final cause, the definitive goal—that of the Eucharistic Liturgy. By sacramentally enacting within the Last Supper his saving death and resurrection prior to his actual death and resurrection, Jesus is revealing that the goal of his death and resurrection, the whole purpose of his death and resurrection, is ultimately to bring his Apostles (the church) into living communion, in living touch, with him and his sacrificial death and resurrection. Simultaneously, he is revealing that this living communion is most fully achieved within the sacramental enactment that he just enacted: the Eucharistic Liturgy. Without providing a means through which his Apostles and his apostolic church could participate in his sacrificial death and glorious resurrection—that is, being fully in communion with himself as their Lord and Savior—his death and resurrection would not have achieved their final goal or purpose. Within the Eucharistic Liturgy, his Apostles (and subsequently his church) most fully partake of the Paschal Mystery's benefits. Within the Eucharistic Liturgy they are most fully in communion with the risen Jesus, and the salvific benefits that he embodies and that they now embody as one holy people in him. Without Jesus' salvific death and resurrection, there would be no sacramental Eucharistic Liturgy, but without the Eucharistic Liturgy there would be no sacramental enactment of his death and resurrection, by which, through which, and in which his Apostles and the later church could be fully incorporated and so obtain the benefits of his saving ministry. Thus the Last Supper is not simply for the sake of understanding the salvific significance of Jesus' death and resurrection, but more so Jesus' salvific death and resurrection are for the sake of the Eucharist Liturgy, for within that sacramental liturgy the full fruit of Jesus' death and resurrection is manifested, made present, and so realized.

Fifth, this is why Jesus, within Luke's account, not only mandates his Apostles to take and eat his body and to take and eat his blood, but also to "Do this in remembrance of me."[19] The goal or purpose of this "remembrance" is not simply that of being a continual reminder of what Jesus did at the Last Supper or even as a perpetual recalling of his saving death, but the enactment of what Jesus himself enacted: the sacramental enactment, the making present, of Jesus' death and resurrection so that in being conjoined to the risen Jesus the fullness of the Paschal Mystery could be ever realized in his followers. The Apostles are to take, bless, and break bread, then give it to others, saying, "Take, eat; this is my body." They are to give thanks for the wine and give it to others saying, "Drink of it, all of you; for this is my blood of the [new] covenant, which is poured out for many for the forgiveness of sins." In this "remembrance," his Apostles will sacramentally make present, just as Jesus has done, his body and blood that were sacrificially given up for them. In so doing, they and others will be perpetually conjoined, in enacting that remembrance, to Jesus and his own act of sacrifice. Without this Eucharistic Remembrance, the full salvific effects of Jesus' death and resurrection would remain extrinsic to his followers, for they would not be in full living communion with him and his saving death and resurrection, and so would not be interiorly transformed by such a living communion—being truly cleansed from sin and made holy children of the Father by the indwelling Spirit of Sonship, in the likeness of Jesus, his Son. Without this Eucharistic Remembrance, there would not be one holy people, the church, living in the Christ of God.

Sixth, inherent within this "remembrance" is another essential theological truth, that of sharing within the priesthood of Jesus. If the Apostles are to enact what Jesus has enacted, their words and actions must contain the same

---

19. Within his account of the Eucharistic Liturgy, Paul twice states this mandate of remembrance. Jesus took bread, "and when he had given thanks, he broke it and said, 'This is my body which is for you. Do this in remembrance of me.' In the same way also the cup, after supper, saying, 'This cup is the new covenant in my blood. Do this, as often as you drink it, in remembrance of me'" (1 Cor 11:23-25).

effect as his. Jesus must give them the priestly ability, the sacerdotal power, to do so. But Jesus cannot simply give the Apostles the authority to bless, break, and give the bread as his risen sacrificial body and the cup of wine as his risen sacrificial blood. Although simple authority may authorize them continually to recollect what he did and said, it would not be the enactment of what he did and said. If the Apostles are to do authentically what Jesus did and authentically say what Jesus said—"This is my body given up for you" and "This is the cup of my blood poured out for you"—then they must be configured into Jesus' priestly likeness; otherwise, their deeds and words would be merely mimicking or imitating Jesus' deeds and words, not the actual doing of his deeds or actual saying of his words. The word "my" is of the utmost importance here. In the Apostles' taking of the bread and wine and in their blessing, breaking, and giving, it must be Jesus himself acting in the person of the Apostles, for only then could their saying "This is *my* body" and "This is *my* blood" be as literally true and real as it was when Jesus first proclaimed these words at the Last Supper. For Jesus to act truly in the person of the Apostles demands that they be personally conformed into his priestly likeness and share in his priestly authority and power, so that when they do and say what Jesus did and said, when they take the bread and wine and say "my," Jesus is actually doing the doing and saying the saying in and through them. This does not mean that Jesus is merely "residing" within the Apostles or is spiritually united to them and so performs the sacramental deeds and says the sacramental words in congruence with their deeds and words. Jesus and the Apostles are not simply two acting and speaking in unison. Rather, the Apostles are configured into the priestly likeness of Jesus so as to share in his priesthood. Being configured into Jesus' priestly likeness, their acts and their words are authentically Jesus' acts and words. This is what gives the word "my," when spoken by the Apostles, its ontological theological depth and efficacy. Only if the Apostles say "my" in the same way that Jesus does does the "this is" become ontologically "body given up for you" and "blood poured out for you." Within every Eucharistic Remembrance Liturgy, the Apostles and Jesus, as one acting priestly subject/person, perform the same actions and say the same words and so causally effect the same end—Jesus' actual risen sacramental sacrificial presence.[20]

20. The Catholic Church articulates this theological point, following upon the patristic and medieval theological tradition, through the idiom that the priest acts *in persona Christi*, or in the person of Christ. The word "in" is theologically significant. The priest does not act "as" the person of Christ because he is not Christ, nor does he simply act "in" the name of Christ because then he would not be acting in the person of Christ but only under his authority. He

Seventh, this Eucharistic enacted remembrance then entails that, although Jesus' sacrificial death is historically a one-time completed salvific act never to be repeated, it is not a completed act that has ended. The one-time saving act that Jesus enacted on earth, within time and history, does not terminate on earth, within time and history, but is perpetually enacted, is everlastingly in act, in the presence of his heavenly Father. As the risen Lord and Savior, Jesus is ever in the presence of his Father, ever offering himself on behalf of the many for their salvation. Because Jesus is the risen Lord, his salvific sacrifice, his being Savior, is always in act, and thus the salvific benefits of that saving act are always in act. Because Jesus' saving acts are always in act, they and their saving benefits can be sacramentally enacted throughout the whole of human history within the Eucharistic Liturgy. Jesus can, until the end of time, enact his saving acts with their saving benefits within the priestly sacramental acts of the Eucharistic Liturgy. Thus the faithful are never saved, apart from being united to the risen Jesus and his saving acts, whether on earth or even in heaven. Within the risen Christ Jesus, the saving act of the cross is forever in act, and so those who abide in him, whether on earth or in heaven, are forever saved.[21]

---

acts "in" the person of Christ in that he shares in Christ's priestly ministry because he has been configured into Christ's priestly image, and so he acts in the person of Christ as Christ himself acting. See the Catechism of the Catholic Church, §1548. See also my forthcoming article "In Persona Christi: The Catholic Understanding of the Ordained Priesthood in Relation to the Eucharist," in Come, Let Us Eat Together! Sacraments and the Unity of the Church, ed. George Kalantzis and Marc Cortex (Downers Grove, Ill.: InterVarsity Press, 2018).

21. This truth is beautifully developed within the Letter to the Hebrews. Because "we have a great high priest who has passed through the heavens, Jesus, the Son of God," his priesthood is that of the order of Melchizedek; that is, it lasts forever (Heb 5:1; see also 5:5-6:20). Unlike the former priests who have died, the risen Jesus "holds his priesthood permanently, because he continues forever. Consequently he is able for all time to save those who draw near to God through him, since he always lives to make intercession for them" (7:24-25). As the risen high priest, Jesus ever intercedes before his Father because he is the risen embodiment, the living transfigured act, of his saving sacrifice. The priests of old, along with the sacrifices they offered, were but the prefigurement of what was to come. "When Christ appeared as the high priest of the good things that have come, then through the greater and more perfect tent [not made with hands, that is, not of this creation] he entered once for all into the Holy Place, taking not the blood of goats and calves but his own blood, thus securing an eternal redemption" (Heb 9:11-12). "Therefore, he is the mediator of a new covenant" (Heb 9:15). Jesus' blood secures a new eternal redemptive covenant because he, the risen Savior, ever appears "in the presence of God on our behalf" (Heb 9:25). Because Jesus, the Son of God, willingly offered himself in obedience to his Father as the new high priest and the all holy victim, all "have been sanctified through the offering of the body of Jesus Christ once for all" (Heb 10:10). Thus the faithful "have confidence to enter the sanctuary by the blood of Jesus, by the new and living way

Eighth, within the above we perceive the absolute necessity of Jesus' real Eucharistic Presence. If the bread and wine do not truly become the risen body and blood of Jesus, if Jesus is not truly sacramentally present in how he now fully exists as the risen Lord and Savior—the risen and glorious Son of God incarnate—then it would not be possible to be in communion with him as he presently exists, and so it would not be possible to share fully in the saving benefits that accrue to his sacrificial death and glorious resurrection. For Jesus to be, in some manner, only symbolically present in the Eucharist demands that one's communion with him would only be symbolic, and thus that one's appropriation of the saving effects of his death and resurrection would merely be symbolic. This will not do! To share fully in the saving mystery of Jesus and so be truly saved demands that one share fully in the mystery of Jesus himself, and to share fully in the mystery of Jesus demands that he be truly and fully present. Jesus' true and full saving presence is only achieved within the Eucharistic Sacrifice, in the "This is my body which is given for you" and in the "This is my blood of the [new] covenant, which is poured out for many for the forgiveness of sins." To take and eat and to take and drink that saving presence is to consume, literally, the fullness of salvation by being in full communion with the Lord and Savior Jesus Christ, the Son of the living God. To be in living communion with the risen Jesus is, then, to be united to the life-giving saving humanity of the divine Son, sharing in, as his Father's children, his divine filial relationship with his Father through his Spirit of Sonship. Asserted many times previously in this study is that to know rightly who the man Jesus is is to know the Trinity itself. We now perceive that to be in living and loving communion with the risen man Jesus within the Eucharistic Liturgy is to be in living and loving communion with the Trinity itself—with the Father, through the Son, in the Holy Spirit. This will find its completion in the eternal heavenly "Eucharistic Liturgy," where the faithful are fully in com-

---

which he opened for us through the curtain, that is, through his flesh, and since we have a great priest over the house of God, let us draw near with a true heart in full confidence of faith" (Heb 10:19-22). What we perceive here is a twofold "once for all." Being the Son of God, Jesus, as perfect high priest, offers himself as the perfect all-holy victim once for all. His saving sacrificial act need not and so cannot ever be repeated. And because Jesus' self-offering is the once and for all perfect sacrifice, he entered into the sanctuary of his heavenly Father, whereas the risen Savior and Lord he forever intercedes on behalf of the all. In the risen Savior, the Lord Jesus Christ, the one sacrificial act is the ever saving covenantal act that is always in act. And it is within the Eucharistic Covenantal Liturgy that this one act is made present, whereby those who prayerfully conjoin themselves to it can confidently ever enter the Father's heavenly sanctuary in communion with the flesh and blood of Jesus the risen Son, "the new and living way."

munion with Jesus and so fully in communion with his Father by sharing fully in the communion of the Holy Spirit.[22]

Jesus Becoming Jesus

In every step of our study of the Synoptic Gospels, within every chapter, we have witnessed Jesus, through his words and especially in his prophetic actions, becoming Jesus. Within the Last Supper, which is the fulfillment, the full enactment, of all his previous prophetic actions, we find Jesus definitively actualizing his name, who he truly is—YHWH-Saves. He has fully enacted his name because within the commemorative Passover Supper he has sacramentally enacted his sacrificial death and glorious resurrection, making those definitive salvific acts present. And Jesus has done so in such a manner that the salvific benefits that accrue to those saving deeds are likewise made present such that the Apostles and the future church can partake of them. Through his giving of his risen sacrificial body and blood, Jesus has united his Apostles to himself and so brought them into communion with himself, who embodies the saving benefits, and into forgiveness of sins and a new Spirit-filled covenantal relationship with his Father. Through his crucifixion, death, and resurrection, Jesus will perform those saving acts that make the Sacramental Eucharistic Liturgy possible, in that his saving acts empower and imbue the Eucharistic Liturgy. Yet Jesus has also revealed, through his Last Supper sacramental enactment of those saving deeds, that the Eucharistic Liturgy is the purpose, the final goal, for which these saving deeds are enacted, for the sacramental symbolic actions performed within it symbolize what they effect (Jesus' salvific deeds), and effect what they symbolize (the fruit of Jesus' salvific deeds).[23] Thus, within the Sacramental Eucharistic Liturgy, Jesus has so actualized himself as Savior that he already has become truly and fully Jesus, and in truly becoming YHWH-Saves, he manifests that he is truly the Father's Spirit-anointed Son.

In becoming truly YHWH-Saves as Son, his Father truly becomes YHWH-

---

22. Both the Letter to the Hebrews and the Book of Revelation teach that this entrance into the heavenly sanctuary through the risen sacrificial body and blood of Jesus finds its completion when Jesus comes again in glory. See Heb 9:27–28 and 12:18–24 and Rv 21:22–26.

23. To say that the Eucharistic Liturgy is the final goal of Jesus' salvific acts is not to say that the kingdom of God is not also the final goal. The Eucharistic banquet is actually that new meal of which all who live in God's new kingdom partake. Both the Eucharistic Liturgy and God's kingdom will find their mutual fulfillment within the heavenly royal banquet of the new Jerusalem that will come out of heaven upon the new earth.

314 THE PASSION NARRATIVES

Saves as Father, and the Holy Spirit truly becomes YHWH-Saves as Holy Spirit. Within the enactment of the Eucharistic Liturgy, Jesus, his Father, and the Holy Spirit are conjoined. In blessing the bread and wine, he calls down from his Father the Holy Spirit, and in that Father-given blessing the Holy Spirit transforms them into his risen body and blood. Because he, as the risen Savior and Lord, is imbued with the fullness of the Holy Spirit, those who participate in these sacramental saving actions, who come into communion with Jesus, share in the Spirit that Jesus embodies. In giving himself to his Apostles, Jesus gives to them the principal all-encompassing fruit of his saving actions, the new sanctifying life of the Holy Spirit. Thus, as the Holy Spirit fully conformed Jesus into the risen Savior and Lord, so the Holy Spirit is ever more fully conforming those who receive Jesus, the Son, within the Eucharistic mystery into the likeness of Jesus, making them ever more fully children of his Father. In so doing the Holy Spirit is also ever Spirit-YHWH-Saves. Likewise, within the Eucharistic Liturgy, the Father, as the author of salvation, truly becomes the saving Father. Within the Sacramental Eucharistic enactment, the Father enacts his saving fatherhood, for he brings into communion with himself his children who now abide in Jesus, his Son, by sharing with them his Spirit of Sonship, and in so doing he truly becomes Father-YHWH-Saves. Thus, within the Sacramental Eucharistic Liturgy, the Apostles and subsequently the church are ever taken into the divine life of the Trinity, the ultimate salvific goal, through the perichoretic saving actions of the Father, Son, and Holy Spirit, all of whom as one are YHWH-Saves in accordance with their own distinct divine singular identities.

We perceive now why Jesus, within Luke's Gospel, declares to his Apostles at the onset of his Last Passover Supper, "I have earnestly desired to eat this passover with you before I suffer; for I tell you I shall not eat it [again] until it is fulfilled in the kingdom of God." Jesus has longed to eat this Passover from his baptism and so from the commencement of his public ministry. Jesus knew that it was for this very Passover that he was conceived by the power of the Holy Spirit within the womb of Mary his mother. In all his prophetic words and deeds, Jesus was purposely and progressively advancing toward this intensifying longed-for moment. And the simple reason is that Jesus knew that here, in his Last Passover Supper, he would definitively become who he was designated and anointed to be—Jesus, YHWH-Saves. Jesus eats this Passover with his Apostles at the Last Supper, and he will only do so again when he, as the risen Savior, continually eats it anew with his faithful, the church, until the end of time here on earth and then forever within the heavenly ban-

quet. There the earthly sacramental Eucharist Liturgy will come to an end because its heavenly fulfillment will have been achieved—the church's full and
everlasting worship of the Father, through Jesus the life-giving Son, in loving
communion with the Holy Spirit. For this final Passover, Jesus longs still to eat
with his risen brothers and sisters.

Fulfillment of Previous Prophetic Acts

As emphasized above, all that Jesus prophetically enacted during his public
ministry finds its fulfillment within the Paschal Mystery. This being the case,
Jesus' sacramental enactment of his saving death and resurrection within his
Last Supper brings all his previous prophetic acts into full act, that is, all that
his Incarnation, baptism, Transfiguration, and triumphal entry into Jerusalem
prophetically anticipated. Jesus becomes fully Jesus within the Eucharistic celebration and so doing fulfills the name that was divinely conferred upon him
at his conception and presentation in the temple. Likewise, within the Gospel
of Luke, the angel Gabriel proclaimed to Mary that, because her son would
be conceived by the Holy Spirit and so be called Son of the Most High and
the Son of God, the Lord God would give him the throne of his father David.
Through Jesus' death and resurrection, God's kingdom is established, and the
fullest expression of that kingdom and the most intense experience of living
within it is found within the Eucharistic Liturgy, where the faithful are most
fully conjoined with Jesus, their Lord and King, and so reside in the loving and
life-giving presence of his heavenly Father. Also, within the Eucharistic Liturgy, Jesus continues, in accordance with Matthew's Gospel, to be most fully
Emmanuel, God with us, for he, the risen Son of God incarnate, gives himself to his church in such a manner that the faithful become one with him
by partaking of his risen body and blood—by being in communion with Jesus himself. Jesus' transfiguration prophetically enacted his passing over from
the darkness of death into the light of his glory, and within that transfiguring
cloud, Peter, James, and John were taken so as to share in Jesus' glory of the
Father's beloved Son. The Eucharist most fully enacts and so completes that
Transfiguration here on earth, for here the faithful share most fully in and so
are transfigured by Jesus' risen glory, having exited the realm of sin and death
and entered into the radiant love of his Father as his luminous Spirit-filled beloved children. Equally, within his triumphal entry into Jerusalem, Jesus prophetically enacts his ultimate entry, through his death and resurrection, into
the new Jerusalem, wherein he will be the new cleansed and holy temple. The

joyful crowds that accompanied Jesus' triumphal entry into Jerusalem cried out in anticipation: "Hosanna [O Lord, grant salvation] to the son of David! Blessed is he who comes in the name of the Lord! Hosanna in the highest!" Within the Eucharistic Liturgy, Jesus, as the messianic Spirit-filled son of David, now comes in the saving name of the Lord God his Father and gathers the faithful unto himself, the living and holy temple of the new Jerusalem. In Jesus, as one holy people, the faithful thank, praise, adore, and worship their heavenly Father. Within the Eucharist, the faithful continually echo that jubilant proclamation, for what the crowd anticipated they now know has come to pass—their salvific entry into Jesus—the heavenly temple of the new Jerusalem.

In the above, the fulfillment of Jesus' baptism within the Eucharist Liturgy was purposely not mentioned because there is a unique theological relationship between Jesus' baptism and his sacramental enactment of the Paschal Mystery within the Last Supper. Jesus' baptism, as we saw when treating it in chapter 3, inaugurated his public ministry, for within it he laid hold of his Father's commissioning Spirit and in so doing his salvific task. As the Father's beloved Son, Jesus would be his Father's obedient and faithful Suffering Servant, who would ultimately tear open the heavens so that those whom he would baptize in the Spirit, his Father's Spirit of Sonship, could enter into communion with his Father. Jesus fulfills this commission within his sacrificial death and glorious resurrection, for within those salvific acts, access to his heavenly Father is achieved through the forgiveness of sin and the establishing of the new covenant.

The commission that Jesus received within his baptism and that he fulfills in his death and resurrection is actualized within the faithful, both in their sacramental baptism and in their participation in the sacramental Eucharistic Liturgy. Jesus' baptism obviously came chronologically prior to Jesus' death and resurrection and its sacramental enactment within the Last Supper. This sequential historical chronology contains within it a sequential sacramental theological chronology. Jesus was first baptized in the Holy Spirit so as to be empowered to enact his saving death and enter fully into the presence of his heavenly Father as the risen Savior and Lord. Similarly, Jesus must first baptize the faithful in the same Spirit of Sonship that he was first baptized, for in that baptism they come to share in his saving death and glorious resurrection and so are transformed from being unrighteous sinners into his filial likeness, sharing in his filial relationship with his Father. Having come to live in Jesus, as their Spirit-anointed messianic Savior and Lord, the faithful are thus empowered and so deemed worthy to share fully in his Paschal Mystery within the sacramental Eucharistic Liturgy, wherein they, together with Jesus, worship their Father in fitting gratitude and praise. As Jesus' baptism finds it end, its fulfillment, in his death and resurrection where he comes fully into his Spirit-filled communion with his Father, so the baptism of the faithful finds its end, its fulfillment, within the Eucharistic Liturgy wherein they come into full communion with the Father. As Jesus' baptism, death, and resurrection encompass one whole salvific mystery, so the faithful share in that salvific wholeness through their baptism, which finds its completion within the Eucharistic Celebration.[24] We perceive here that the salvific purpose of Jesus' sacrificial death and glorious resurrection finds its end not only within the sacramental Eucharist Liturgy first enacted at the Last Supper, but also in the sacrament of baptism, which was first prophetically enacted within Jesus' baptism. Within both sacraments, Jesus acts to embrace the faithful and subsume them within the saving mystery that he is, first by baptizing them in the Father's Spirit of Sonship, whereby they come to share in his filial Spirit-filled relationship with his Father, and second within the Eucharist by uniting them to himself as he actually is through their partaking of his risen body and blood, and so abide more fully in the living Spirit-filled communion with his Father. Thus Jesus acts as Jesus, YHWH-Saves, within the sacramental act of baptism as well as in the sacramental act of the Eucharistic Liturgy.

24. How Jesus acts and so is present in sacramental baptism differs in kind from the manner in which he acts and so is present within the sacrament of the Eucharistic Liturgy. This manner of acting and presence determine the different benefits that accrue to each of these sacraments. Within baptism, Jesus sacramentally acts, through the ministry of the baptizer, by way of his saving power—the pouring out of his Holy Spirit upon the baptized so as to die and rise with him and thus be cleansed from sin and freed from death. Moreover, the person is transformed into a child of the Father and thus a member of the church, sharing in the new covenant as a citizen of the God's kingdom. Simply put, the faithful are baptized into Christ, and so the Holy Spirit comes to dwell within the baptized, such that the baptized person shares in the divine life and love the Father and the Son. There is a true interrelated indwelling between the baptized person and the persons of the Trinity. Having been baptized into Christ, the faithful possess the right and privilege to then share more fully in the Paschal Mystery within the Eucharistic Liturgy. Here Jesus acts and so is present in a different manner than within the sacrament of baptism. Jesus acts to make himself personally present as he is in himself as the risen Savior and Lord. In so doing, the faithful share more fully in the Paschal Mystery because they are in communion with Jesus as he exists in himself by partaking of his risen body and blood. Therefore the saving relationship that was initiated at their baptism, the faithful's relationship to the Father in Jesus his Son through the indwelling of the Holy Spirit, finds its fullest expression and reality within the Eucharistic Liturgy.

Conclusion

In concluding this chapter, we must look back to its beginning—the anointing of Jesus by the penitent woman. In response to the criticisms leveled against her for wasting expensive ointment, Jesus said that she "has done a beautiful thing to me.... In pouring this ointment on my body she has done it to prepare me for burial." The "beautiful thing" that she did was to express her ardent wholehearted love for Jesus, the pouring out of herself in anticipation of and in response to Jesus' merciful forgiveness. In that "beautiful thing," she anointed Jesus for his burial. "Wherever the gospel is preached in the whole world, what she has done will be told in memory of her" (Mt 26:13).

Jesus' burial was the result of his sacrificial death, the giving up of his body for the forgiveness of sin and the pouring out of his blood, the blood of the new covenant. Wherever the Gospel is preached in the whole world, what Jesus has done will be told in memory of him because, as he told of the woman's perpetual remembrance so he told of his own, "Do this in remembrance of me" (Lk). As the church, in her proclamation of the Gospel, will always tell, in memory of her, of the woman's preparatory anointing of Jesus' crucified body, so will she, within the Eucharistic Liturgy, always, in remembrance of him, enact his saving sacrifice. These two "remembrances" are enacted together within the Eucharistic Liturgy.

Within the Eucharistic Liturgy, Jesus makes himself present in his crucified and risen body and blood; he is giving up his body and pouring out his blood; he is breaking open his dearest life for his church. Within that same Eucharistic Liturgy, the church ardently lays hold of Jesus, breaking open and pouring out herself in loving gratitude for his sin-forgiving death and life-giving resurrection. Within the Eucharistic Liturgy, Jesus continues to give himself wholly, without counting the cost, to his church, the repentant woman. And the church, the forgiven woman born anew, continues to give herself wholly, without counting the cost, to Jesus as her Lord and Savior. And for this they will both as one, in the love and life of the Holy Spirit, be eternally remembered to the glory of God the Father. For together and for one another, Jesus and his church, have done, are doing, and will always and forever do, "a beautiful thing."

Having examined the anointing of Jesus and his last Passover with his Apostles, we now proceed to the onset of Jesus' passion, beginning with his agony
in the Garden of Gethsemane. Matthew and Mark narrate: "And when they
had sung a hymn, they went out to the Mount of Olives. Then Jesus said to
them, 'You will all fall away because of me this night; for it is written, "I will
strike the shepherd, and the sheep of the flock will be scattered." But after I
am raised up, I will go before you to Galilee'" (Mt 26:30-32 and Mk 14:26-28).[1]

The hymns that Jesus and his Apostles sang, according to scholars, would
have been the thanksgiving psalms (Pss 114-18) that concluded the Passover.
These psalms look both back to the past and prophetically to the future. Psalm
114 proclaims the mighty deeds of the Lord when he led the Israelites forth
from their slavery in Egypt, and to which Jesus' presently celebrated Passover
commemorates. In the light of what is imminent—Jesus' passion, death, and
resurrection—it signals the new mighty deeds of the Lord that are on the horizon, the new mighty deeds that Jesus already just enacted within his last Passover meal. Psalm 115 declares the glory of the Lord's name because, unlike the
lifeless gods who neither speak, hear, or walk, the living Lord God blesses the
house of Israel. Therefore Israel, and now particularly Jesus, will trust in the
Lord, who is its/his shield and so they/he will trust in him and bless the Lord

---

1. In the light of chapter 9, Luke, unlike Matthew and Mark, places Jesus' foretelling of Judas's betrayal at the end of the Last Supper. Luke also places next the debate among the Apostles as to who is greatest, where Matthew and Mark have it earlier within their Gospels. Luke
also inserts Jesus telling of Peter's denial as well as a short farewell discourse that speaks of the
coming trials of the Apostles, where he also states, quoting Is 53:12, that he will be reckoned
among sinners in order that what is written of him might be fulfilled (Lk 22:21-38). Only then
does Luke state that after the Last Supper Jesus "came out, and went, as was his custom, to the
Mount of Olives; and his disciples followed him" (Lk 22:39). Thus Luke mentions neither the
singing of hymns nor the striking of the shepherd as in Matthew and Mark.

forever. Psalm 116 is particularly significant in the light of Jesus' impending death, for the psalmist professes that he loves the Lord "because he has heard my voice and my supplications" (v. 1). Jesus' heart and mind would have resonated, especially during his looming agony, with the words "the snares of death encompassed me; and the pangs of Sheol laid hold on me; I suffered distress and anguish. Then I called on the name of the Lord: 'O Lord, I beseech you, save my life'" (vv. 3-4). Jesus said that he could trust that his Father would deliver "my soul from death, my eyes from tears, and my feet from stumbling," for he has kept his faith even when afflicted (vv. 8-9). What Jesus would soon pray in the Garden of Gethsemane would echo the Psalmist's words: "What shall I [Jesus] render to the Lord for all his bounty to me? I will lift up the cup of salvation [the cup that he will drink and the cup of himself that he will lift up and pour out upon the cross] and call on the name of the Lord in the presence of all his people [on behalf of the salvation of all and in the midst of all to see, Jesus calls on the merciful name of the Lord]." Jesus would declare: "Precious in the sight of the Lord is the death of his saints. O Lord, I am your servant; the son of your handmaid." Jesus, the Father's Son, knew his death, the death of the humanity he received at his conception from his handmaid-mother, would be precious to his Father, for he would offer it within the sanctity of his Father's very Spirit of Sonship. He would do so as his Father's faithful suffering servant, the Spirit-filled commission he received at his baptism. In so doing, Jesus could be assured that "Thou [his Father] loosed my bonds." Therefore Jesus could pray: "I will offer to you the sacrifice of thanksgiving [the sacrifice that would thankfully redress the sin of humankind and so be a sacrifice of reconciliation] and call on the name of the Lord. I will pay my vows to the Lord [again, the commitment Jesus assumed at his baptism] in the presence of all his people, in the courts of the house of the Lord, in your midst, O Jerusalem" (vv. 15-19). Jesus will offer himself as a thanksgiving sacrifice not only before all the people in the sight of the temple that lay within the earthly Jerusalem, but also forever in the sight of all nations within the heavenly temple, the temple that is himself, within the new Jerusalem.

We already saw the significance of Psalm 118 when examining Jesus' triumphal entry into Jerusalem, where the jubilant crowds echoed the Psalm in proclaiming: "Blessed be he who enters in the name of the Lord! We bless you from the house of the Lord. The Lord is God, and he has given us light. Bind the festal procession with branches, upon the horns of the altar" (vv. 26-27). Moreover, the psalmist, and now Jesus, gives thanks for God's steadfast love even amid distress, where the nations surround him like swarms of stinging bees. Even though the Lord "has chastised me sorely" and "given me over to death," "I shall not die, but I shall live, and recount the deeds of the Lord" (vv. 10-12, 17). Jesus would have perceived the truth that he was shortly going to be "the stone which the builders rejected" and yet "become the head of the corner," the reason being that "this is the day which the Lord has made; let us rejoice and be glad in it" (vv. 22-25). The words of the Psalms would have continued to murmur within Jesus' heart and mind as he and his Apostles made their way to the Mount of Olives.

Entangled within these psalms of confident thanksgiving was Jesus' knowledge that once he, the shepherd, was struck, his Apostles, the sheep, would fearfully take flight. He could nonetheless end on a hopeful note: "But after I am raised up, I will go before you into Galilee." As the risen shepherd, he will lead his Apostles back to the pastures of Galilee where he first called them by name. Although Jesus recognizes, in his very praying of these Psalms, his mental and emotional state—wanting so much to possess trust in his Father in the face of the impending doom of his suffering and death—Peter has no such tentativeness. He will stand firm even if all the others fall. He will not deny Jesus but will die with him. And all the other Apostles parrot Peter's bravado. Jesus, in turn, assures Peter that before the dawn-cock crows, he will deny him three times (see Mt 26:33-35, Mk 14:29-31, and Lk 22: 31-34). Here Jesus and his Apostles arrive at the Mount of Olives "to a place called Gethsemane," where Jesus' prayerful anguish will be played out in full, while his Apostles will confidently slumber (Mt 26:36; Mk 14:32).[2]

Jesus' Agony in the Garden

According to Matthew and Mark, Jesus first told his disciples: "Sit, here, while I go yonder and pray" (Mt).[3] He took "with him Peter and the two sons of Zebedee" (Mk specifies James and John). Luke has Jesus telling his disciples as a whole, "'Pray that you do not enter into temptation.' And he withdrew from them about a stone's throw, and knelt down and prayed." Jesus' intention in coming to Gethsemane was that he and all the Apostles were now to pray and specifically, according to Luke, that they would not be tempted. Jesus knew well that he was being tempted and so needed to pray, but his self-assured

2. The ubiquity of the Psalms within the Passion Narrative should be noted. Many of them, as we will see, loom large within the theological background of the narrative events.

3. All quotations in this section are from Mt 26:36-46, Mk 14:32-42, and Lk 22:39-46 unless otherwise noted.

disciples were oblivious to the fact that they could be tempted, and so of their need to pray. That Jesus took Peter, James, and John with him looks back to the Transfiguration, where he took them with him, apart from the others, up the mountain. In the Transfiguration, they not only witnessed Jesus luminously transfigured but also entered the cloud with him and so passed over with him into the Father's presence. Although Jesus will ultimately pass over from death into the glory of his Father through his resurrection and so fulfill the prophetic Transfiguration, his desire is that Peter, James, and John, in a special manner, enter with him into the initial stage of his actual passing over—his agony.[4] To them, he manifests his troubled sorrow (Mt) and his great distress (Mk). He tells them, "My soul is very sorrowful, even unto death; remain here, and watch/keep awake" (Mk; Mt adds "with me"). Although Jesus will now proceed "a little further" (Mt and Mk) or "about a stone's throw" (Lk) from them, the three are to watch, that is, to stay awake with him in devoted prayer. They are to conjoin themselves to Jesus' deathly sorrow and his supplicating entreaty, thus prayerfully entering into his passion with him lest they succumb to temptation and flee, and so jeopardize their passing over with him into glory. As in the Transfiguration, Peter, James, and John are to prefigure the church, which who will suffer with her Savior so as to pass over with him into his glory and so testify that in him death has been vanquished and in him eternal life reigns.

Having gone a little farther, Jesus "fell on his face and prayed" (Mt); "fell on the ground and prayed" (Mk); "and knelt down" (Lk). In the falling on "his face" and in the falling "on the ground," Matthew and Mark portray the overwhelming agony of Jesus' plight. No longer has he the physical strength or the emotional will to remain standing—his agony is simply his sorrowful collapsing as though dead. Luke portrays Jesus as kneeling down—a deliberate controlled action, and one that expresses not so much unrestrained physical and emotional exhaustion, but rather reverence to the one to whom he is about to pray. Thus, although Jesus' distressed agony is "even unto death," the body that lies face down to the ground is imbued with loving revered deference to his Father, to whom he is about to offer his filial supplication. And so Jesus prays. Matthew immediately provides his prayer: "My Father, if it be possible, let this cup pass from me; nevertheless, not as I will, but as you will." Mark

---

4. Jesus also took Peter, James, and John with him into the room where Jairus's daughter lay dead (see Mt 9:18-26, Mk 5:35-43, and Lk 8:40-56). There too is a going from death to life, and Peter, James, and John were to bear witness to the authenticity of Jesus' life-giving miracle.

states that Jesus "prayed that, if it were possible, the hour might pass from him. And he said, 'Abba, Father, all things are possible for you; remove this cup from me; yet not what I will, but what you will.'" In Luke, Jesus prays: "Father, if you are willing, remove this cup from me; nevertheless not my will, but yours, be done."[5]

Luke simply has Jesus address God as "Father," but Mark emphasizes the filial and familiar manner of his address: "Abba, Father." This same understanding is captured within Matthew where Jesus addresses God as "My Father." The use of the Aramaic "Abba," as well as the use of "my," alerts the reader that Jesus is speaking to his Father in his own human language and thus in the manner to which he was accustomed. The Aramaic, as noted previously, denotes the familial and affectionate manner of Jesus' address—that of a child lovingly and confidently addressing his caring and ever watchful father. Again, this is also seen in the expression "My Father" for, as the Father's Son, the Father is his Father in a singular divine manner. As Jesus agonizes over his pending passion and death, he comes before his loving "Abba, Father" in humble supplication. Significantly, in addressing God as "Abba" or "my Father," Jesus manifests his awareness of his Father's paternal love for him as well as his expressing his filial love for his Father. Within the address "Abba," there is a perichoretic intertwining of a mutual interrelational love that binds Jesus, the Son, and his Father. Thus, although Jesus pleads to his loving Father that, be-

---

5. When asked by James and John that he grant that they sit one on his left and one on his right in his glory, Jesus responded, "You do not know what you are asking. Are you able to drink the cup that I drink, or be baptized with the baptism with which I am baptized?" (Mk 10:38). We perceive here that Jesus already had a premonition of his passion and death and that he even had formulated it within his own mind in terms of drinking a cup of suffering. And although James and John will drink the cup that Jesus drank, in the garden with Jesus they are not up to the task and fall asleep. Only after Jesus drinks the cup and so merits his resurrection will Peter, James, and John, being empowered by the Holy Spirit, drink the cup that Jesus drank.

Within the Old Testament, to drink the cup was a sign of drinking God's judgment. For example: "On the wicked he will rain coals of fire and brimstone; a scorching wind shall be the portion of their cup" (Ps 11:6). Or, "Rouse yourself, rouse yourself, stand up, O Jerusalem, you have drunk at the hand of the Lord the cup of his wrath, who have drunk to the dregs the bowl of staggering" (Is 51:17). Jesus, through his suffering and death, will drink the cup of his Father's wrath against sin and evil, but in so doing reconcile humankind. As seen within Jesus' last Passover Supper, having offered his life as a loving sacrifice to his Father, he will give to his faithful the cup of his blood, the blood of the new covenant. Jesus, through his death and resurrection, transforms the cup of God's wrath into a cup of God's salvation. Those who refuse to drink the cup of salvation, however, will be forced to drink the cup of God's wrath at the end of time (see Rv 14:10, 16:19, 17:4, and 18:4-8).

cause all things are possible for him, he might let pass this hour of his passion and death, this bitter cup that painfully looms before his consciousness, yet within such supplication Jesus never doubts his Father's love.[6] The assurance of his Father's love is not conditioned upon his Father removing the cup, nor is Jesus' love for his Father dependent upon the cup's removal. Despite the seeming appearance of his Father not being truly loving in his not taking away the cup of suffering, Jesus is confident that such is not the case. This is why Jesus could authentically beseech his Father to remove the cup of suffering, the hour of his passion and death from which his whole humanity recoils, yet earnestly say "not as I will, but as you will." He, as the loving incarnate Son, will faithfully do what his loving Father wills knowing that his loving Father always wills what is good, right, and just. The mutual love that binds the Father and the Son is the same love that binds their mutual wills.[7]

That human "will" is in play within Jesus' agony is of the utmost salvific theological importance. The Son as God eternally wills as Son what the Father as God eternally wills as Father. Within the Incarnation, however, Jesus, the Son of God as man, always needs, within the history of time, to conform his human will to the divine will of his Father. Importantly, within his agony,

---

6. Although John's Gospel does not actually narrate Jesus' agony in the garden, Jesus does allude to it. "Now is my soul troubled. And what shall I say? 'Father, save me from this hour'? No, for this purpose I have come to this hour" (Jn 12:27). Likewise, when Peter cuts off the ear of Malchus, the slave of the high priest, Jesus responds, "Put your sword into its sheath; shall I not drink the cup which the Father has given me?" (Jn 18:11). And although Mark is the only one of the Synoptics who mentions "the hour" within Jesus' agony, within the Gospel of John, the notion of "the hour" is a major theme. The whole Gospel trajectory looks toward Jesus ever coming closer to his "hour," which is both the hour of darkness as well as the hour of Jesus' glory. See Jn 2:4, 7:30, 8:20, 12:23, 13:1, and 17:1.

7. Because they are not found in the earliest manuscripts, scholars believe verses 43 and 44 of chapter 22 of Luke's Gospel were not part of the original text but added later. What is fascinating nonetheless is that while Luke first portrays Jesus as kneeling down in reverence during his agony, verses 43-44 portray the physiological effect of his agony: "And there appeared to him an angel from heaven, strengthening him. And being in an agony he prayed more earnestly; and his sweat became like great drops of blood falling down upon the ground." The sweat-like drops of blood testify both to the intensity of his agony, his desire for the cup to pass, as well as to the intensity of his resolutely standing firm against such temptation. Likewise, the appearance of the heavenly angel to strengthen him confirms just how excruciating his agony truly was, for it suggests that without such renewed heavenly aid he could have fallen. Likewise, the appearance of the heavenly angel manifests the heavenly Father's love for his Son. The Father has not abandoned him to his own devices, being insensible to what his Son is undergoing in his desire to fulfill his Father's will. Rather, the Father recognizes that only in his paternal strengthening love, his paternal Spirit of Sonship, can his love-strengthened Son lovingly fulfill, in the same filial Spirit of Sonship, his will.

Jesus is not attempting to align his human will to his own divine filial will, but rather, as his prayer to his Father attests, he, the Son incarnate, is configuring his human filial will to that of his Father's divine will. If Jesus were to be conforming his own human will to his divine will, he would be merely obeying himself. The "dialogical prayer" would be within himself and not between himself and his Father. Rather, within every historical event, within every human word and action, there is a truly human pondering of what his Father wills, and there must always be a truly human willful decision to do his Father's will. As the Son of God as God eternally wills what the Father wills, so the Son of God as man must temporally will what the Father wills. Jesus achieves salvation not through his enacting of what he wills divinely but through his enacting what he wills humanly, that is, humanly willing what his Father wills for humankind's salvation. The Son of God became man so that as man and on behalf of man he might obtain salvation for all men. This salvation could only be achieved if Jesus, the Son, humanly willed to offer his human life, a life imbued with human love, to his Father. This is exactly what Jesus does within his agony in the garden of Gethsemane. He, the Son incarnate, humanly did what his Father willed, that is, offered himself, the entirety of humanity, to his Father as a loving sacrifice of reconciliation in the face of human sin.[8]

What we perceive in his prayer to his Father is Jesus fully enacting his name, definitively defining himself as Jesus, for in his willing to do the will of his Father, even to undergoing his passion and death, Jesus has configured himself wholly into Jesus—YHWH-Saves. In accepting his Father's will, Jesus is conclusively and resolutely avowing, "I will be Jesus" and in so doing actually does definitively become Jesus. Having fully configured himself into Jesus, having enacted his name within his agony by conforming his will to his Father's saving will, Jesus is now able to enact those acts that will obtain humankind's salvation—his passion and death. In Jesus' agony we find the ultimate significance of Gabriel's words to Mary at his very conception and what was revealed to Joseph in his dream: "You shall call his name Jesus." Here is the full meaning of his eighth-day circumcision, where he shed his first blood and "was called Jesus, the name given by the angel before he was conceived in the womb." Here is the final confirmation that Jesus, the Son of God, assumed

---

8. The Letter to the Hebrews is emphatic on this theological point. When Christ came into the world, his Father prepared for him a body precisely whereby, as man, he could do his Father's will. "And by that will we have been sanctified through the offering of the body of Jesus Christ once for all" (Heb 10:10; see 10:5-9).

a humanity of the fallen race of Adam with all its fear, weakness, and vulnerability.[9] Here is the full import of Jesus, at the age of twelve, professing that, as the Father's Son, he must be about his Father's business. Here Jesus' baptism is consummated, for the salvific Spirit-anointed commission first bestowed by his Father finds its final and complete confirmation here.[10] Here the Transfiguration's prophetic colloquy between Jesus, Moses, and Elijah is fulfilled, for Jesus has determined that he will enact his exodus, his passing over, from this world of sin and death into the promised land of Father's life-giving glory.[11] Conjoined to all these prophetic anticipations, the agony itself now lends gravity, intensity, depth, integrity, and even solemnity to Jesus' words "not as I will, but as you will." Apart from his agony, without his fearful physical ab-

9. Again, the Letter to the Hebrews makes this point. Jesus shared in our human weakness and so could sympathize with our condition, for he "in every respect has been tempted as we are, yet without sinning" (Heb 4:14-15).

10. This is keeping with what Jesus says in Luke's Gospel: "I have a baptism to be baptized with; and how I am constrained until it is accomplished" (Lk 12:50; see also Mk 10:38-39 and Jn 12:27). Jesus' ultimate baptism, which was prefigured within his baptism by John, is his death and resurrection, for in those saving acts he will put to death sin in his own body and rise to the newness of life in his resurrected humanity. Only then will he no longer be constrained for the full effects of his initial baptism by John will be realized—his ability to baptize in the Holy Spirit.

11. Traditionally (going back to the early Fathers of the Church), the purpose of Jesus' Transfiguration was said to be for the strengthening of the Apostles' faith, so that they would not lose faith in the face of the cross but recognize that the cross would result in Jesus' glorious resurrection. If that was the purpose of the Transfiguration, it utterly failed, for nowhere within the subsequent Passion Narratives do the Apostles demonstrate any recollection of or express any allusion to the Transfiguration before, during, or even after their fearful fleeing. The reason is that they did not grasp the concept of the resurrection. On coming down from the mountain of the Transfiguration, Jesus "charged them to tell no one what they had seen, until the Son of man should have risen from the dead." This they did while "questioning what the rising from the dead meant" (Mk 9:9-10; see also Mt 17:9). Nonetheless, in accordance with the Father's words, they are to listen to his beloved Son, for in so doing they will come to understand the meaning of Jesus' death and resurrection. Peter realizes the significance later as he expresses it in his Second Letter (see 2 Pt 1:18).

In the darkness of Jesus' agony, the Transfiguration was primarily for the sake of Jesus himself and not for his Apostles. He was in dialogue with Moses and Elijah about his exodus; his own humanity, which he inherited from his sinful father Adam, was transfigured; he passed over from darkness into the luminous glory of his Father. The whole point of the Transfiguration was to strengthen Jesus so that he would not lose trust in his loving Father when the dark "hour" arrived and the light of the transfiguring glory of his resurrection was reduced to a future yet unseen hope. Here in the dark cloud of his agony, Jesus securely grasped in hope his prophetic transfiguring entrance into his Father's glory. As the Letter to the Hebrews declares, "who for the joy that was set before him endured the cross, despising the shame, and is seated at the right hand of the throne of God" (Heb 12:2).

horrence of and his inner emotional trauma at the approach of the impending hour, Jesus' resolute faithfulness would never have been manifested, nor his utter filial love for his Father, nor his unqualified brotherly love of human-kind. In the face of all that looms before him, Jesus nonetheless says "yes" to the will of his Father and in so doing stubbornly declares, "Damn it all, damned be Satan and all of his temptations I will endure; damned be sin and all of its vile consequences I will bear; and damned be death and all of its tor-ments I will brave. I will be true to who I am—Jesus Christ, the living Father's Spirit-filled Son—YHWH-Saves."

Having made his first supplication to his Father, Jesus returns to Peter, James, and John, only to find them sleeping. Matthew and Mark have Jesus ad-dress Peter: "So, could you not watch with me one hour? Watch and pray that you may not enter into temptation; the spirit is willing, but the flesh is weak." Jesus then returns again and, according to Matthew, prays: "My Father, if this cup cannot pass unless I drink it, your will be done." (Mark simply says, "And again he went away and prayed, saying the same words." Luke has Jesus pray-ing and returning to his disciples only once. Amid castigating them for sleep-ing and exhorting them to pray lest they enter into temptation, the crowd ar-rives.) Matthew and Mark narrate Jesus' second return to the threesome, and again he finds them sleeping, "for their eyes were heavy." In Mark, they awk-wardly attempt but could not offer any excuse. Again Jesus leaves them, pre-sumably in sad frustration, and prays a third time "in the same words" (Mt). Returning again to his disciples, Jesus, in discouraged resignation, says: "Are you still sleeping and taking your rest? [Mk inserts here "It is enough."] Be-hold the hour is at hand, and the Son of man is betrayed into the hands of sin-ners. Rise let us be going; see, my betrayer is at hand" (Mt).

Interestingly, within Jesus' agonizing thrice-prayed supplication to his Fa-ther, there is no recorded response. His Father is silent. There is no voice from heaven saying, "Yes, as my beloved Son, in whom I am well pleased, I will that you drink the cup." Despite his entreaty, Jesus appears to know the answer to his bidding even while making it three times. This is not surprising. Through-out the whole of his public ministry, beginning with his baptism, Jesus was consciously doing his Father's will. As noted above, he was aware of the bap-tism that he must undergo and the cup that he must drink. On three occasions, he foretold that in Jerusalem he would be handed over, suffer, die, and rise on the third day. What we witness, then, within his agony is not something that unexpectedly and inexplicably came upon him as if it never dawned on him what the outcome would be. And the initial temptations he experienced after his baptism continued to plague him, temptations contrary to the baptism he must undergo and the cup he must drink, contrary to his being the loyal and obedient Son of the Father. At the prospect of the imminent "hour" fast approaching, these temptations crushingly bore down upon him. As Luke noted at the conclusion of Satan's initial temptations, "And when the devil had ended every temptation, he departed from him [Jesus] until an opportune time" (Lk 4:13). Within Jesus' agony, Satan's opportune time had arrived. Yet as Jesus threw off these temptations from the onset of his ministry, so now he will be faithful to his baptismal commitment, to the commission that his Father had given him, and so he will willingly now do what he always knew he must do—his Father's will. There was no need for his Father to respond but only to strengthen. Thus when "the hour" was "at hand" because his betrayer was "at hand," Jesus without any begrudging acceptance of a loathsome predestined inevitability, but rather with an unencumbered freedom and an unwavering conviction, could declare: "Rise, let us be going." That short sentence contains both his Father's answer and Jesus' response. While Judas, his betrayer, was making his way with the sword-bearing and club-wielding crowd "from the chief priests and the scribes and the elders," Jesus is the one who takes the first step, as he did when he first approached John the Baptist, toward his passion and death (Mk 14:43). He has raised his fallen face from the ground and therefore has thrown himself into fulfilling his Father's will—the hour has arrived and he will drink the cup.

Notice too that Jesus not only tells his Apostles to "rise," but he also directs them to go with him—"let *us* be going." But unlike Jesus, who has prayerfully thrown off his agonizing temptation and now is straightaway "going" to fulfill his Father salvific will, they must sluggishly pull themselves up from their lethargic slumber and so, having never watchfully prayed with Jesus, will swiftly fall to the temptation that this hour abruptly brings.[12] The shepherd, having

12. According to Luke, when Peter, James, and John were on the mountain of the Transfiguration, they "were heavy with sleep, and when they wakened they saw his glory and the two men who stood with him" (Lk 9:32). Only the resurrected glorious Jesus will ultimately awake them from their present slumber. The Apostles presently live within the darkness of sin and the slumber of death, and only after Jesus awakes them through the outpouring of his risen Holy Spirit will they awake from their sin and arise to newness of life. Jesus, in telling them to stay awake and pray was asking them to do something they were incapable of doing—only in the Spirit, as Jesus is in the Spirit, could they stay awake with him and watchfully pray. Peter, James, and John prefigure the church in that until Jesus dies, rises, and sends forth his Spirit, it too is shrouded in the darkness of sin and the sleep of death. When Jesus awakes the Apostles on Pentecost, he will simultaneously give birth to his church, which they first embody.

been struck, "all of his disciples forsook him and fled" (Mt and Mk). Unlike Jesus, who watchfully prayed three times and so did not ultimately fall to his temptation, sleepy Peter, despite being warned three times to prayer "lest he enter into temptation," will succumb to his fleshly weakness and will deny Jesus three times.[13]

Fulfilling the Scriptures

Following upon the anointing of Jesus, the Synoptics, as we saw in chapter 9, narrate Judas plotting with the chief priests as to how best for him to betray Jesus and so allow them to arrest him (see Mt 26:14-16, Mk 14:10-11, and Lk 22:3-6). Jesus perceives Judas's action as the catalyst that initiates the fulfillment of the Scriptures.[14] At the onset of the Last Supper, Matthew and Mark narrate Jesus' foretelling his betrayal. (Luke places it immediately following Jesus' enactment of the Eucharistic Passover Liturgy.) Having told his disciples that one of them was about to betray him, Jesus concludes, "The Son of man goes as it is written of him, but woe to that man by whom the Son of man is betrayed!" (Mt 26:21-25 and Mk 14:18-21). Luke states, "For the Son of man goes as it has been determined; but woe to that man by whom he is betrayed!" (Lk 22:22). What determines Jesus' going to his passion and death is what has been "written of him" in the Scriptures. Judas' act of betrayal is a free act of the will and so a "woe" bearing act, but it is in accordance with what God had foretold and so predetermined as written within the Scriptures. Judas' betrayal commences a whole series of acts in which and through which Old Testament prophesies will find their fulfillment, acts that concern Jesus' passion and death.[15]

13. In the Gospel of John, Peter's three-time denial is reversed in his three-time expression of love for Jesus. Thus, as Jesus three times lovingly affirmed that he would do his Father's will, so Peter will now lovingly serve Jesus, his Lord and Savior, by feeding the sheep of the now risen shepherd, which will ultimately conclude with Peter's own cross of martyrdom (see Jn 21:15-19). Peter, when he has turned again, will "strengthen" his brethren (Lk 22:32).

14. Throughout our study of the Synoptic Gospels, we have seen that Jesus, through his teaching and actions, was fulfilling or anticipating the fulfillment of various Old Testament events and prophecies. This was especially the case within the Jesus' conception and birth, his baptism, transfiguration, and triumphal entry into Jerusalem. This chapter has already examined Scripture passages that pertain to Jesus. Jesus nonetheless perceives, in a particularly focused manner at the commencement of his passion and death, that all the Scriptures that awaited him will now be the fulfilled. The saving events of his passion, death, and resurrection are at the heart of the prophetic nature of the Old Testament. The whole trajectory of the Old Testament points to and anticipates these Messianic salvific events performed by Jesus, the Son of God incarnate.

15. Jesus previously told his disciples that they will fall before the night is over, "for it is

Nothing should hinder nor can stop "what was written of him." Although Judas' act of betrayal set in motion the fulfilling of the Scriptures, Peter tries to stop their fulfillment by taking up his sword and striking the slave of the high priest, cutting off his ear. Jesus responds to Peter's violent act by saying, according to Matthew, "Put your sword back into its place; for all who take the sword will perish by the sword. Do you think that I cannot appeal to my Father, and he will at once send me more than twelve legions of angels? But how then should the scriptures be fulfilled, that it must be so?" (Mt 26:52–54). Peter's sword wielding is not in accord with the fulfilling of the Scriptures. If such were the case, Jesus had close at hand something far better and more effective than Peter's clumsy attempt at a rescue: twelve legions of his Father's heavenly angels. Such an assured "victory," however, would nullify the fulfillment of Scripture—what "must be so."[16]

Similarly, Jesus asks the crowds why they have come with clubs and swords as if to capture a robber when he was daily in their midst teaching in the temple and they did not seize him. He answers his own question: "But all of this has taken place that the scriptures of the prophets might be fulfilled" (Mt 26:56). Mark has Jesus simply state: "But let the scripture be fulfilled" (Mk 14:49) and, in Luke, Jesus says: "But this is your hour, and the power of

---

written, 'I will strike the shepherd, and the sheep of the flock will be scattered'" (Mt 26:31 and Mk 14:27). Luke also has Jesus telling his disciples, "For I tell you that this scripture must be fulfilled in me, 'And he was reckoned with transgressors'; for what is written about me has its fulfillment" (Lk 22:37). Although these passages do not directly pertain to Judas' betrayal, Jesus is conscious that, following upon Judas' action, the Scriptures written about him are in the process of being fulfilled.

16. Peter's action betrays that he still does not grasp his own profession of faith that for Jesus, as "the Christ, the Son of the living God," means that he "must go to Jerusalem and suffer many things from the elders and chief priests and scribes, and be killed, and on the third day be raised" (Mt 16:16 and 16:21). Peter is still acting the role of a satanic tempter—"God forbid, Lord! This shall never happen to you." In telling Peter to sheath his sword, Jesus recalls his words to Peter: "Get behind me, Satan! You are a hindrance to me; you are not on the side of God, but of men" (Mt 16:22–23). Peter is a hindrance because his sword-wielding action is an attempt to thwart God's predestined word as foretold in Scripture. And Jesus' response to Peter harkens back to his initial postbaptismal temptations. There Satan exhorts Jesus to throw himself from "the pinnacle of the temple," for if he is the Son of God, God, as Scripture testifies, "'will give his angels charge of you,' and 'On their hands they will bear you up, lest you strike your foot against a stone.'" In response to Peter's "temptation," Jesus states the same truth, evocative of Satan, that if he wants he could call upon his Father and he would send for twelve legions of angels to rescue him. Jesus did not succumb to Satan's first temptation nor will he be hindered by Peter's, now for "how then should the scriptures be fulfilled that it must be so?" In other words, Jesus is telling Peter what he first told Satan: "Again it is written, 'You shall not tempt the Lord your God'" (Mt 4:5–7).

darkness" (Lk 22:53). The hour of the power of darkness is that time when those prophetic Scripture passages concerning Jesus' death will now be fulfilled. At this point, Jesus' disciples forsake him and flee, while the crowd seizes him and leads him off to the house of Caiaphas, the High Priest. From this point on, Jesus makes no further reference to the Scriptures being fulfilled, because from this point on he will fulfill them.

At the time of Jesus' proclamations, the Apostles would not have identified to which Scriptures and prophetic passages he was referring. While he was alerting them that such was going to take place, they would only understand what had been fulfilled after his passion and death. Significantly, Jesus resumes speaking, within the Gospel of Luke, of the Scriptures being fulfilled only after the resurrection, when he appears to his disciples. At this point they will have been fulfilled. When Jesus meets two disciples on the road to Emmaus, they were dispirited because the one whom they hoped would redeem Israel, "Jesus of Nazareth," was condemned and crucified by their own chief priests and rulers. They were now also befuddled "because some of the women of our company amazed us" by saying that they had not found the body in the tomb but rather saw "a vision of angels who said he was alive." Jesus reproaches the twosome: "'O foolish men, and slow of heart to believe all that the prophets have spoken! Was it not necessary that the Christ should suffer these things and enter into his glory?' And beginning with Moses and all of the prophets, he interpreted to them in all of the scriptures the things concerning himself." After Jesus revealed himself in the breaking of the bread, they exclaimed, "Did not our hearts burn within us while he talked to us on the road, while he opened to us the scriptures?" Likewise, after returning to Jerusalem, the two were informing the Apostles of their experience when Jesus appeared to the entire group. Jesus showed them his hands and feet, and ate a piece of fish, all in the interest of proving that he was truly physically risen, and said to them: "'These are the words which I spoke to you, while I was still with you, that everything written about me in the law of Moses and the prophets and the psalms must be fulfilled.' Then he opened their minds to understand the scriptures, and said to them, 'Thus, it is written that the Christ should suffer and on the third day rise from the dead, and that repentance and forgiveness of sins should be preached in his name to all nations, beginning from Jerusalem. You are witnesses of these things. And behold, I will send the promise of my Father upon you, but stay in the city, until you are clothed with power from on high'" (Lk 24:19-49).

The main point to be made at this juncture is that Jesus brackets his passion, death, and resurrection with references to the fulfillment of the Scriptures—before that they will be fulfilled, and after that they have been fulfilled. In the last quotation, the risen Jesus first reminds disciples what he had told them prior to his death and resurrection before elaborating more fully anew. What lies between this bracketing is the actual fulfillment: "everything that was written about me." The present theological task is to discern to which Scriptures Jesus is referring, especially since he is frustratingly vague, even within his postresurrection delineation—the Law of Moses, the prophets, and the psalms. What is important, however, is not simply that Jesus revealed to his disciples particular passages but that he opened their minds and hearts to reading the whole of the Old Testament in an entirely new and unprecedented manner; that is, he is the fulfillment of the Scriptures, and so they can only be read properly and interpreted correctly in the light of him and his salvific ministry. What is of help also is that, although his disciples did not grasp prior to his resurrection to which Scriptures Jesus was referring, after the resurrection, their minds having been open "to understand the scriptures," they would have gradually come to greater clarity as they pondered the Paschal Mystery and so would have interpreted and proclaimed the salvific significance of that saving mystery through the lens of the Scriptures being fulfilled. This greater clarity would especially be the case after the outpouring of the Holy Spirit at Pentecost, which Jesus tells them they must await in Jerusalem.[17] Thus the later authors of the Synoptic Gospels would have written their accounts of Jesus' death and resurrection so as to allude to or even make evident pertinent Old Testament passages. Moreover, the manner in which Jesus' trial, passion, death, and resurrection were enacted would manifest the fulfilling of the Scriptures—those prefigured events and those prophetic passages that find completion within Jesus' saving acts. In the following theological examination of the remainder of the Synoptic Passion Narratives, we must read these accounts with Old Testament eyes. Only then will we discern at least some of the most relevant passages that find fulfillment within Jesus' trial, passion, death, and resurrection for they are, as Jesus declared, the hermeneutical keys that allow us to perceive clearly and interpret properly the theological and

---

17. The use of the Old Testament to interpret Jesus' salvific acts appears within the Acts of the Apostles, the Pauline Corpus, the Letter to Hebrews, and the remainder of the New Testament Canon. See, e.g., Peter's sermon following the outpouring of the Holy Spirit on Pentecost (Acts 2:14-36), Philip's instruction of the Ethiopian eunuch (Acts 8:26-35), and Paul's address to the synagogue in Antioch (Acts 13:16-43).

salvific significance of these events. As Jesus knew well from the onset of his ministry, they were "written about me."

Jesus' Trial before the Sanhedrin

Having seized Jesus, the arresting crowds took him to the house of the High Priest.[18] The chief priests and the council sought "false witnesses" so that "they might put him to death," but they found none. According to Matthew, two finally "came forward" (Mk states that "some stood up") and claimed, "This fellow said, 'I am able to destroy the temple of God, and to build it in three days'" (Mt). Mark quotes the "some" as saying that they heard him say, "I will destroy this temple that is made with hands, and in three days I will build another, not made with hands." Jesus does predict the destruction of the temple, as we examined above, but he does not say, within the Synoptic Gospels, what he is accused of claiming.[19] Prophetically and ironically, however, the false accusation contains a truth that is theologically relevant. Although Jesus will not destroy the temple, "made with human hands," he will build another temple "in three days" that is "not made with human hands." The early church, as well as Matthew and Mark, would have recognized that the Jewish leaders, in collaboration with the Roman authorities, did destroy the real temple by killing Jesus, the Son of God incarnate, and that Jesus, through his resurrection, has become the new living temple that was made not by human

---

18. All quotations within this section are from Mt 26:57-68, Mk 14:53-65, and Lk 22:54-71 unless otherwise noted. Matthew specifies that it was Caiaphas's house. Although Matthew and Mark note that Peter followed, Luke places Peter's denial at this point, prior to Jesus' trial before the Sanhedrin. Matthew and Mark place Peter's denial after the trial. Luke also, prior to the trial, has the arresting party mocking and beating Jesus. They blindfolded him and asked sarcastically, "Prophecy! Who is it that struck you?" Unlike Matthew and Mark, who narrate a night trial, Luke places the trial before the Sanhedrin in the morning.

19. The accusation of destroying and rebuilding the temple could be based upon Jesus' statement within the Gospel of John, "Destroy this temple and in three days I will raise it up" (Jn 2:19). But even here Jesus does not say that *he* will destroy the temple. And as John's Gospel notes, "But he spoke of the temple of his body" (2:21). Jesus, being the Son of God incarnate, is the true temple of God, for in him dwells the fullness of God. If Jesus, "the temple," is destroyed, he will raise it up in three days through his resurrection, when he will become the everlasting living and indestructible temple.

When Stephen in the Acts of the Apostles was taken before "the council," he was accused of speaking "against this holy place [the temple] and the law" and of saying "that this Jesus of Nazareth will destroy this place" (Acts 6:12-14). Since such accusations had not worked against Jesus, one would have thought the false witnesses would have been more creative, but this account does corroborate the historicity of Jesus being so accused.

hands but by the divine hands of his Father.[20] Also, while Jesus is the Son of God existing as man, and so the true temple for he is the supreme embodiment of God's earthly presence, because the humanity that he first assumed is that of the sinful doomed-to-death race of Adam, he is not truly the fully cleansed and everlasting living temple until his resurrection, when he, as the Son of God, assumes his new risen and glorious humanity, which is freed from Adam's sin-cursed corruptible body.

Alas, even though all the testimony was false and thus that one would expect the various false accusations to corroborate one another, they did not, for as Mark derisively states, "Yet not even so did their testimony agree." To save this embarrassingly awkward situation, the High Priest turned to Jesus in the hope that his frightened rebuttal to these false accusations might produce some resolution to their conflicting falsity and so provide grounds for his condemnation. But Jesus, despite the high priest's anxiously urging him to respond, remained silent, thus not only leaving him to look even more the fool but also, by his mere silence, accentuating the humiliating travesty of the whole reprehensible event. Jesus was not going to bestow, by his attempted response, credibility and dignity to these fabricated allegations.

Jesus' very silence is the fulfillment of a prophetic word. "He was oppressed, and he was afflicted, yet he opened not his mouth; like a lamb that is led to the slaughter, and like a sheep that before its shearers is dumb" (Is 53:7).[21]

20. The Letter to the Hebrews takes up this theme. "But when Christ appeared as the high priest of the good things that have come, then through the greater and more perfect tent [not made with hands, i.e., not of this creation] he entered once for all into the Holy Place, taking not the blood of goats and calves but his own blood, thus securing an eternal redemption" (Heb 9:11-12). Or, again, "For Christ has entered, not into a sanctuary made with hands, a copy of the true one, but into heaven itself, now to appear in the presence of God on our behalf" (Heb 9:24). The risen Jesus both enters into the heavenly sanctuary not made by human hands and becomes the temple not made by human hands, for in him all have access to his Father's heavenly sanctuary.

This also fulfills what God had promised David. When David wanted to build God a house, he was forbidden to do so. Solomon would build the first temple. But God promised David that after he died he would build David a house that will last forever: "I will raise up your offspring after you, who shall come forth from your body, and I will establish his kingdom. He shall build a house for my name, and I will establish the throne of his kingdom forever. I will be his father, and he shall be my son" (2 Sm 7:11-15; see also 1 Chr 17:10-14). Jesus, as the son of David, will establish God's everlasting kingdom, in which he will build for his heavenly Father a house worthy of his name. Jesus will be that new house, that new holy temple, in whom his Father will be duly worshiped and glorified.

21. Similarly, "He will not cry or lift his voice, or make it heard in the street" (Is 42:2). We will treat the Suffering Servant Songs at greater length below.

Jesus by his mere silence has purposely inserted himself, for the first time after his arrest, within the Suffering Servant Songs—he is that servant who will
be the true lamb of sacrifice, the lamb that will suffer on behalf of all for the
forgiveness of sins and for the making of the new covenant. Thus Jesus is silently signaling that he is now fulfilling the Suffering Servant Songs and that
they are the interpretive key for discerning the meaning of his passion, death,
and resurrection.[22]

Jesus' silence forces the high priest to address the true issue at hand, which
he probably wanted to avoid since it strikes at the heart of why he and the Sanhedrin wanted Jesus dead. Better, politically and for the sake of their own conscience, for Jesus to be condemned for some alleged threat against the temple
than for them to expose publically the genuine reason for his condemnation,
for the real issue concerns the identity of who Jesus truly is, an identity that
would best be kept hidden. From Jesus' perspective, if he is to be condemned,
he must be condemned for the real charge laid against him and not for some
contrived indictment. And if he is ultimately to be vindicated, which his resurrection will in due course achieve, it must be because of the truth for which
he was falsely condemned and not for some charge that was never true from
the onset. The chief priest and Sanhedrin want to hide in the dark shadows of
deceit, lest their evil deeds be exposed. Jesus, who is orchestrating the whole
event, ensures that the light of truth shines forth, and he does so by forcing,
by his mere silence, the chief priest to ask, "I adjure you by the living God, tell
us if you are the Christ, the Son of God" (Mt). Mark renders the question, "Are
you the Christ, the Son of the Blessed?" In Luke, the chief priest says, "If you
are the Christ, tell us." This is precisely the issue—who is Jesus? Upon this issue Jesus will be condemned and crucified. And on the truth of this issue his
resurrection depends.[23]

22. Jesus also remains silent when being accused during his trial before Pilate. Although
there is much discussion as to whom "the servant" is within the Isaian context, whether a specific person such as Isaiah or a collective group such as Israel, the answer to this question is
both. Jesus as an individual who embodies the whole of Israel fulfills these songs in a manner
that is uniquely unanticipated.

23. Jesus' assuring that he would be condemned for what is true and not upon charges that
were false is theologically important, for Adam and Eve fell prey to the lies of Satan. Since that
first sin, Satan has attempted, to this very day, to infect truth with falsehood—lies that give
some semblance of truth. Thus Satan, the father of lies and the hater of all truth, would not
want Jesus to be condemned for the truth of who he is but for a lie that he is not. For Jesus to
be condemned for the truth of who he is highlights the truth of who he is. For him to be condemned falsely, for saying that he will destroy the temple, hides the truth of who he is. Satan
wants to wrap Jesus in lies and falsehood so that no one can truly recognize him for who he is:

The chief priest's framing of the issue or question is of the utmost theological and soteriological importance. Ironically and importantly, what we perceive here is the replay of Jesus asking his disciples, "who do you say that I am," only this time the chief priest is asking Jesus his own question: who do you say you are? When we treated Peter's response in chapter 7, we noted that the common element in all three Synoptic accounts was his declaration that Jesus was "the Christ." Similarly, what is common in all three accounts is the chief priest asking if he is "the Christ." We also found within Peter's declaration that to profess Jesus to be the Christ/Messiah is to affirm that he possesses the Spirit in a singular manner—that is, he possesses the Spirit of Sonship—and so in a manner that designates him alone to be the Son of God. Implied within the chief priest's question or concern is the issue of whether Jesus is the divine Son of God. With the above in mind, we will, for the sake of clarity, examine each account separately.[24]

Luke's account gives the shortest and most unembellished rendering of the chief priest's question: "If you are the Christ, tell us?" This question most resembles Mark's version of Peter's profession of faith—"You are the Christ—but similar to Luke's own simple account: "The Christ of God." If Jesus is the Christ, he is so because he is God's anointed with the implication that this makes him singularly special. The way Jesus singularly possesses the Spirit is found in the ensuing dialogue between Jesus and his inquirers. Jesus' response is: "If I tell you, you will not believe; and if I ask you, you will not answer. But from now on the Son of man shall be seated at the right hand of the power of God." If Jesus tells them that he is indeed the Christ, they will not believe him, for they have arrested him precisely because he was saying and doing things that gave rise to the belief that he is the Christ. It is this belief that the

---

the Christ, the Son of God. At his trial, Jesus would not allow Satan to cover him with and so hide him behind lies.

24. Although the respective Synoptic accounts are always similar, even using the same words and phrases, there are also frequent significant differences. This was evident when we treated Peter's profession of faith. All three accounts gave similar but different renderings of what he professed. The same is now true concerning Jesus' trial. The wording of the chief priest's question differs within the three accounts, as does Jesus' response. As with Peter's profession of faith, the difference of wording often is dependent upon the Gospel author wanting to ensure a proper understanding or to disclose the deeper meaning of what is being said, either by the chief priest or by Jesus. This does not mean that the authors "made up" the accounts or "put words" in the speakers' mouths, but rather they were attempting to ensure that the fullness of what is being revealed is made manifest. So, while we may not know for sure which account, if any, provides exactly what Jesus said "word for word," we do know "approximately" his exact words, and we certainly know the full truth of what he wanted to convey.

high priest and the Sanhedrin wish to suppress by killing him. If he asks them if he is the Christ, they will not answer, not because they do not believe that he is, but because they do not want their denial to be recorded for fear that it would jeopardize their standing among the people who do believe him to be the Christ and so incite an uprising in Jesus' defense.[25] Jesus' further response implies that they will know that he is the Christ because he, the Son of man, will "be seated at the right hand of the power of God." Being seated at the right hand of God will confirm his being the Christ because, having died as the promised salvific Christ, it is by the power of God that he will be raised up from the dead and so be seated in glory with God, thus attesting to his death's soteriological effect. The implication was not lost upon his hearers, for they ask a question that shows they have drawn the right conclusion: "Are you the Son of God, then?" To which Jesus responds, "You say that I am (*ego eimi*)." Jesus is the Christ and the way he is the Christ is witnessed in his being seated at the right hand of God; that is, he is seated as the Father's Spirit-anointed Son.[26] Jesus, by his enigmatic use of the phrase "you say that I am," rather than simply saying "I am" (as we will see in Mk), is thrusting their question back at them, transforming it into a declarative statement. In their question they are declaring him to be the Son of God. They have reached this conclusion. Nonetheless, the fact that Jesus employs the emphatic Greek expression *ego eimi* (I, I am), reminiscent of God's own divine name, accentuates the ontological density of the title "Son of God." Jesus has subsumed the divine *ego eimi* into his being the Son of God, and so he is the Father's Son, not in some adopted sense but as ontologically being God as the Father is God. Thus Jesus not only affirms the Sanhedrin's declaration that he is the Son of God, but also ensures that they understand its full ontological divine sense. Again, ironically, although the Sanhedrin could not condemn Jesus on the grounds of false testimony, it would condemn him on the grounds of his own true testimony, which is again what Jesus wanted—he will not die because of lies leveled

25. When the chief priests and elders first took council together to arrest Jesus, they wanted to do so "by stealth" and thus "not during the feast [Passover], lest there be a tumult among the people" (Mt 26:4-5), for "they feared the people" (Lk 22:2; see also Mk 14:1-2).

26. Jesus, in declaring that he will sit at God's right hand, is quoting Psalm 110:1: "The Lord said to my lord; 'Sit at my right hand, till I make your enemies your footstool.'" Jesus also quotes this passage when earlier arguing with the Jewish authorities. How can the Christ be David's son if David calls him Lord (see Mt 22:41-46, Mk 12:28-34, and Lk 20:39-40)? The implication is, as explained previously, that Jesus, as the Christ, is David's son as man, but he is Christ the Lord as the Father's divine Son. Thus Jesus, in quoting Psalm 110:1, is inferring that he is God's Son, which was not lost on his interrogators.

against him but for the sake of the truth he spoke. The significance of what Jesus professed was not lost upon his accusers. "What further testimony do we need? We have heard it ourselves from his own lips." They need no further false testimony because they have now heard the "truth," the "it," from his own lips that he is the Son of God, and so "the whole company of them arose, and brought him before Pilate."

While Luke's account has the chief priest simply ask if Jesus is "the Christ," Mark's rendering is "Are you the Christ, the Son of the Blessed?" This form immediately brings out more explicitly the intrinsic relationship between being "the Christ" and being "the Son of God." God, being all holy, is the blessed one and thus the source of all blessings. The greatest of all blessings is for God to bestow his own Spirit in a singular manner such that the bestowal would designate the person to be truly his Son and thus truly the Christ/Messiah, the anointed one. This is the heart of the chief priest's query—has God so anointed Jesus with his Holy Spirit such that he is the Blessed's blessed Son? Mark's rendering, like Luke's, also has the high priest's question echo Peter's profession of faith: "You are the Christ." Unlike Jesus' puzzling response in Luke, however, in Mark, Jesus' response is simply: "I am (ego eimi)," and in so doing Jesus clarifies that to be "the Christ, the Son of the Blessed" is for him to be truly and fully divine. Jesus continues, as he did similarly in Luke, "and you will see the Son of man seated at the right hand of Power, and coming on the clouds of heaven."[27] Importantly, Mark's rendering has the final clause that is absent from Luke. That Jesus is "the Christ, the Son of the Blessed," and so is truly divine, will not only be manifested in his sitting at the right hand of "Power—that is, of God, who possesses the plenitude of power—but also in his coming on the clouds at the end of time to manifest the divine governing power that he shares, as Son, with his Father. Again, this is an allusion to the Book of Daniel: "I saw in the night visions, and behold, with the clouds of heaven there came one like a son of man, and he came to the Ancient of Days and was presented before him, and to him was given dominion and glory and kingdom, that all peoples, nations, and languages should serve him; his dominion is an everlasting dominion, which shall not pass away and his kingdom is one that shall not be destroyed" (Dn 7:13-14). Jesus is informing his ac-

---

27. Luke has Jesus say "Power of God," but here Mark has Jesus simply say "Power." In both instances, as well as in the chief priest's use of the term "Blessed," there may be a conscious avoidance of the divine name "YHWH," because to use this most sacred and holy name was forbidden. But Jesus, in his declarative ego eimi, is not afraid to apply the divine name to himself as the Father's Son.

cusers that not only is he the Christ, and therefore the divine Son of God who will sit at God's right hand, but consequent upon such, his Father, the Ancient One, will endow him at his coming at the end of time with an everlasting and indestructible kingdom that will encompass not only the Jews but all peoples and nations. Mark records a more passionate and violent response to Jesus' claim than Luke: "And the high priest tore his garments and said: 'Why do we still need witnesses? You have heard his blasphemy. What is your judgment?' They answered, 'He deserves death.' Then they spat in his face, and struck him; and some slapped him, saying, 'Prophesy to us, you Christ! Who is it that struck you?'"[28] There is no further need of false witnesses because Jesus has now committed the capital crime of blasphemy—attributing to himself, a man, the dignity of God. In response, members of the Sanhedrin insult, mock, and strike him as though what he confessed was sheer arrogant madness, little realizing that it will be confirmed and come to pass in Jesus' resurrection. The next morning, the Sanhedrin held a final consultation and led the bound Jesus away to deliver him to Pilate. Again, in Mark, Jesus is condemned not on fictitious charges but for the truth that he had spoken.

Matthew's account of Jesus' trial before the Sanhedrin is almost the same as Mark's, yet there is one significant difference. We find in Matthew the fullest and most explicit expression of Peter's earlier profession of faith being reenacted. Within Matthew, what is utterly fascinating and of the utmost theological significance is that the chief priest, in asking his question, employs the same designations concerning Jesus that Peter employed when making his profession. The chief priest: "I adjure you by *the living God,* tell us if you are *the Christ, the Son of God.*" Peter: "You are *the Christ, the Son of the living God.*"[29]

---

28. Although I noted above that Jesus, in his silence, alluded to the Suffering Servant Songs, the trial before the Sanhedrin is the first of three scenes in which the Isaiah passages explicitly come into play. Is 50:6 states: "I gave my back to smiters, and my cheeks to those who pulled my beard; I hid my face from shame and spitting." And Is 53:3: "He was despised and rejected by men; a man of sorrows, and acquainted with grief; and as one from whom men hid their faces he was despised, and we esteemed him not." Having now woven themselves into the fabric of Jesus' passion, the Suffering Servant Songs will continue to thread themselves throughout Jesus' trials before Pilate and Herod and become a whole cloth within his crucifixion. A fuller examination of their theological significance will be made at the conclusion of the trial before Pilate and in our discussion of the crucifixion. Also, these Old Testament passages have become a major interpretative tool for understanding Jesus' passion, death, and resurrection, as Jesus prophetically claimed they would be, as well as passages to which Jesus opened the eyes of his disciples after his resurrection.

29. It is difficult to determine exactly what the chief priest asked and what Jesus answered. So it is hard to judge the word-for-word accuracy of Matthew's account. I am confident that

The high priest, within Matthew's parallelism, is, in a sense, asking Jesus, "Do you agree with what Peter said of you?" Here we must observe that the high priest strictly commands Jesus "by the living God" to tell them if he is "the Christ, the Son of God." It was "the living God," Jesus' Father, who revealed to Peter that Jesus was the Christ, the Son of God. Jesus is being commanded in the name of his Father to declare whether he is truly the Father's anointed Son. Moreover, his Father, in the first and principal instance, lovingly revealed himself to Jesus, and Jesus came to know that he is the beloved Father's Son. Similarly, the Father, at Jesus' baptism, poured out his paternal love upon Jesus, his Son, by anointing him with the Holy Spirit—the Father's loving Spirit of Sonship. This anointing of the Spirit configured Jesus to be the Christ. Likewise, his Father was the first, in fulfillment of Gabriel's prophecy to Mary, to declare: "You/This is my beloved Son, with whom I am well pleased" (see Lk 1:35, Mt 3:17, Mk 1:11, and Lk 3:22). Thus it would be impossible for Jesus, in responding to the high priest, to deny who he truly is, for to do so would be for him to deny his Father, and that he would never do because he, as the Christ, loves his Father in the same Spirit of Sonship as the Father loves him. Just as Peter professed what the Father revealed to him, Jesus is now called upon to affirm what his Father revealed to him—that he is the Father's Spirit-anointed Son. This is what Jesus does. Matthew renders Jesus' answer as "You have said so." Again, as in Luke, Jesus turns the high priest's question into the high priest's declaration, for his question contains within itself the precise correct answer—the same truth that the Father first made known to Jesus himself and subsequently revealed to Peter. The reaction of the high priest within Matthew's account is basically the same as in Mark and Luke—condemnation for blasphemy deserving of death followed by mocking, spitting, and physical abuse.

I have been stressing that Jesus' trial before the Sanhedrin is an enacted replay of Peter's profession of faith, though within a different enacted genre. It might first appear, however, that what is missing is Jesus' clarification or elaboration of Peter's profession. Ensuing upon Peter's declaration, "You are the Christ, the Son of the living God," the Synoptics state, "From that time Je-

---

Matthew purposely formulated or consciously modeled the chief priest's question to Jesus in the light of and after the manner of Peter's profession of faith. This is not to say that the chief priest, under the inspiration of the Holy Spirit, did not say what Matthew has him say. Nonetheless, Matthew wanted the reader to grasp that it was the truth of Peter's proclamation, the truth that was revealed to him by the Father, upon which Jesus was being questioned and the truth upon which he was ultimately going to be condemned and crucified.

sus began to show his disciples that he must go to Jerusalem and suffer many things from the elders and chief priest and scribes, and be killed, and on the third day be raised" (Mt 16:21; see also Mk 8:31 and Lk 9:22). This is the full meaning of what it means for Jesus to be the Christ, the Son of the living God. Now, Jesus' verbal explanation or amplification is absent from his trial because he is enacting it. In the very acts of his being arrested, mocked, spit upon, condemned, and sentenced to death, Jesus is enacting what it truly means for him to be the Christ, the Son of the living God. In their condemnation of Jesus for professing that he is indeed the Christ, the Son of the living God, the chief priests, elders, and scribes unwittingly ensure that he, the Son of the living God, truly enacts his salvific ministry as the Christ. Thus Jesus bears testimony to the truth of his own, and Peter's, profession of who he is within the context of that profession being fulfilled. Ironically, in its very act of condemnation, the Sanhedrin also bears testimony to the truth of its own questioning declaration. To behold the bound Jesus at his trial is to behold the Christ, the Son of the living God.[30]

Jesus' Trial before Pilate

Having concluded their trial and consultation concerning Jesus, the Sanhedrin took Jesus to Pilate. As Jews living under Roman occupation, the Sanhedrin did not have authority to execute anyone. Thus the Sanhedrin needed to convince Pilate that Jesus committed a crime deserving of death. Although all three Synoptic accounts of Jesus' trial before Pilate are similar, they do deviate at times, either by way of additions or absences.

The trial before the Sanhedrin focused on the claim that Jesus was the Christ, the Son of God, and it was upon this charge of blasphemy that Jesus was condemned. Within the trial before Pilate, this matter of Jesus being the Christ is now conjoined with his being the King of the Jews, but only within Matthew and Luke. Mark does not mention Jesus as the Christ, but instead fo-

---

30. Matthew and Mark place Peter's denial immediately after Jesus' condemnation (Luke places it immediately before). Assuming that Peter was near enough to see Jesus' trial take place, it is ironic that he was blind to the fact that what he was witnessing was the reenactment, granted in a wholly different context and manner, of his own profession of faith. More significantly, he shows no awareness that the very amplification and clarification that Jesus amended to his own profession were being enacted before his very eyes. Instead of being amazed, or even simply recognizing, that his own words were coming forth from the mouth of the high priest, he professes that he has no knowledge of the man—the Christ, the Son of the living God.

cuses exclusively on his being the King of the Jews. Also, although the Jews
will accuse Jesus of being "a king," they never, throughout the entire Passion
Narrative, use the phrase "King of the Jews," either by way of reference to Jesus or as a title attributed to him. They purposely remove themselves from or
completely ignore any such assertion. It only comes from the lips of Pilate.
Thus Luke introduces the trial before Pilate with a dialogue between the Jewish authorities and Pilate over this issue of Jesus being both the Christ and a
king.[31]

Having presented him before Pilate, the Jewish authorities accuse Jesus:
"We found this man perverting our nation, and forbidding us to give tribute
to Caesar, and saying that he himself is Christ a king" (Lk). Here are two intertwined charges, one religious and the other political. First, Jesus is faulted
for "perverting" the Jewish nation, but the way he is doing so is not specified.
Second, Jesus is accused of forbidding the Jews to pay taxes to Caesar. This,
of course, is not true. In the hope of trapping Jesus, the Jewish authorities
"sent spies, who pretended to be sincere, that they might take hold of what
he said, so as to deliver him up to the authority and jurisdiction of the governor." Thus "the spies" asked Jesus, insincerely remarking upon his habit of
"teaching rightly" and truly teaching "the way of God": "Is it lawful for us to
give tribute to Caesar, or not?" Jesus, "perceiving their craftiness," asked to
be shown a coin, upon which bore the likeness and inscription of Caesar. Jesus said, "Then render to Caesar the things that are Caesar's, and to God the
things that are God's" (Lk 20:20-25; see also Mt 22:15-21 and Mk 12:13-17). Having failed in their entrapment of Jesus, the Jewish authorities now nonetheless
falsely accuse him of saying what he did not say, though that is precisely what
they had hoped he would say. As in the case of accusing Jesus of wanting to
destroy the temple, the Jewish authorities have once again reverted to con-
cocting lies in order to condemn Jesus to death. The difference being that the
destruction of the temple would be of Jewish concern while the forbidding of
paying taxes would be of Roman concern, and therefore disquieting for Pilate
to hear. Third, these two accusations come together within the last charge:
"and [Jesus] saying that he himself is Christ a king." Within Luke's account,
Jesus never actually said "I am the Christ."[32] But he did say, "If I tell you, you
will not believe me." And to the further question as to his being the Son of

31. All quotations in this section are from Mt 27:11-31, Mk 15:1-20, and Lk 23:1-25.
32. The closest is in Mark's account, where, when asked if he is "the Christ, the Son of the
Blessed," Jesus responds, "I am."

God, he responded, "You say that I am." Nor did Jesus ever claim to be a king. What the Jewish authorities have done is specify why they believe he is "perverting our nation," that is, by claiming to be the divinely promised and now expected anointed Messiah, and so the Son of God. Moreover, they have integrated this Jewish claim and so a Jewish concern with Jesus claiming, because of his claimed Jewish messianic anointing, to be an anointed king as well, the implication being that he is a threat to Rome. What Pilate sees before him is a self-deluded religious fanatic who is not only disturbing the well-being of the Jewish nation but also presenting himself as a self-proclaimed king. In his obsession to gain political-messianic grandeur and notoriety, this man may also threaten the well-being of the Roman Empire and even the Roman emperor. The not-so-subtle implication is that this religious and political muddle can easily be resolved, to the advantage of the Jews and the Romans alike, in Jesus' condemnation and death.

When we examined the false accusation against Jesus during his trial before the Sanhedrin, that he would destroy the temple and rebuild it in three days, we saw that within it resided truth. By killing Jesus, God's presence on earth as the Son of God incarnate, they would destroy him, the temple of God, and in three days his Father would gloriously raise him up, making him the new and everlasting temple in whom true spiritual worship of his Father would be given. Now, here, in the trial before Pilate, the Jewish authorities accuse Jesus of saying he is "Christ a king." Their charge as it stands is libelous, but the lie itself contains an important theological truth. Jesus is the Christ, for he is the anointed Son of God, and he will become the king of God's kingdom, a kingdom that like the temple will not be made with human hands. Likewise, as the condemning and execution of Jesus are the very deeds through which Jesus becomes the living temple, so now the condemnation and crucifixion of Jesus will be the very deeds through which Jesus will establish God's everlasting kingdom, over which he will forever reign as king. Irony has once more raised its knowing head and opened its bemused eyes. In the act of attempting to have their lies achieve their poisonous effect—Jesus' condemnation and death—the Jewish authorities are fulfilling the truth hidden in their lies—Jesus, the Christ, becoming a king, the very thing they were hoping to bury once and for all.[33]

33. Theologically and historically significant, Peter, at the conclusion of his Pentecost Sermon, makes this same point. "Let the house of Israel therefore know assuredly that God has made him both Lord and Christ, this Jesus whom you crucified" (Acts 2:36). Paul also, in beginning his Letter to the Romans, professes that the Gospel is about God's Son, "who descended

We also saw that, during his trial before the Sanhedrin, Jesus refused to respond to the false accusations because, if he was going to be condemned, it must not be because of fabricated allegations but for the truth of who he is— the Christ, the Son of the living God. Similarly, now in his trial before Pilate, the Jewish leaders falsely accuse Jesus of "perverting our nation" and forbidding the payment of tribute. Yet it is not Jesus who brings truth to light amid the darkness of falsehood, but Pilate. The Jewish authorities state that Jesus presents himself as "a king," seemingly in a generic sense but in a manner that would raise Pilate's suspicion. When Pilate turns to Jesus, however, he asks, "Are you the King of the Jews?"[34] Pilate, a Gentile, has connected the dots—if Jesus is the Christ, then he must be the King of the Jews. This is the last thing the Jewish authorities wanted Pilate to do and the last thing they wanted to hear! As the Sanhedrin purposely wanted to hide the issue of Jesus being the Christ, the Son of the living God until Jesus forced them to bring it into the light, so now, before Pilate, they were attempting to avoid the issue of his being *their* king. Again, if Jesus were to be condemned and crucified, it was not because he was falsely accused of being some religious fanatic and political zealot, but because of the real issue at hand—the truth of his being the King of the Jews. The Jewish authorities may not have believed that Jesus was the Christ, the Son of God, nor their king, but upon the truth of those two issues, those two charges, he will now be judged, condemned, and executed. Again, this truth is dependent upon his resurrection. Jesus responds to Pilate's query, "You have said so." In answering the question as to whether he is the Christ, the Son of God, Jesus here also turns Pilate's question into an assertion—he has declared him to be "King of the Jews," to the vexation of the Jewish authorities.

While Jesus answered Pilate's question, because he was speaking the truth, Jesus remained silent in the face of the Jewish false allegations. Even when Pilate offered Jesus the opportunity to respond, he remained silent to Pilate's great wonderment (see Mt and Mk). At this point, Luke's Gospel narrates that Pilate finds "no crime in this man," but the chief priests vehemently protest that Jesus "stirs up the people, teaching throughout all of Judea, from Galilee even to this place." So the accusation moves from "perverting our nation"

---

from David according to the flesh and designated Son of God in power according to the Spirit of holiness by his resurrection from the dead, Jesus Christ our Lord" (Rom 1:4). Jesus, the Father's Son, is "made" or "designated" Christ and Lord/King precisely because of his death and resurrection.

34. With Pilate's question, Matthew and Mark come into sync with Luke.

to "stirring up the people." How is Jesus stirring them up? The people hope or believe that he is the promised Messiah, the Son of God, David's promised kingly heir. The Jewish authorities do not provide such an elaboration, for that is the truth that they wish to remain in darkness. Pilate, though, discovering that Jesus is a Galilean, gladly sends Jesus off to Herod, under whose jurisdiction Jesus would fall. Herod was "very glad" to see Jesus because he hoped "to see some sign done by him." When Jesus did not accommodate his and "his soldiers" frivolous curiosity nor answer their pointless questions, they "treated him with contempt and mocked him" by "arraying him in gorgeous apparel." Even though the Jewish authorities, amid this bizarre unfolding, stood by, "vehemently accusing him," Herod sent Jesus back to Pilate. Upon his return, Pilate addresses the Jewish authorities, noting that neither he nor Herod has found Jesus guilty of any of the charges brought against him, particularly anything "deserving death," and therefore "I will chastise him and release him." Jesus has now twice been contemptuously mocked and ridiculed because of the accusations that he is the Christ, the Son of God and a king, first by the Sanhedrin and then by Herod and his soldiers, but the culpability of these charges cannot be proven and so a judgment of guilt cannot be made.

Theologically important, Jesus will not ultimately be condemned and executed because of the accusations made against him or for performing any action that deserves death. He will be killed for being the Christ, the Son of God, and so the King of the Jews, but he will not be proven guilty and formally sentenced for being the Christ, the Son of God, and so the King of the Jews. Thus Jesus will die for the truth of who he is, and not because of some fabricated accusation. He will not die because that "truth" has been proved to be false. Rather, in dying for that truth, he will manifest that he truly is the Christ, the Son of God, and so become the risen King of the Jews. Truth, not lies, will ultimately win the day and so will dispel the darkness of deceit.

From this point on within Jesus' trial, irrational envy, born of fear at Jesus' success and standing among the people, will drive the condemnatory process to its inevitable deadly conclusion.[35] Thorough hatred of Jesus will so inflame

---

35. The Book of Wisdom declares that "God created man for incorruptibility, and made him in the image of his eternity, but through the devil's envy death entered the world, and those who belong to his party experience it" (Wis 2:23-24). To ensure death's continued and everlasting reign within the fallen world, Satan's envy ignites and fuels the envy of the Jewish authorities—"those who belong to his party." To kill Jesus, the eternal Son of God, in whose eternal image humankind was fashioned, would provide death its ultimate irreversible triumph. Little did Satan realize that, in killing Jesus, sin would be forgiven, humankind would be reconciled to his Father, and thus the curse and reign of death would be forever vanquished. In the

and empower "the will" of his accusers that that "will" will not be denied—
that "will," by its sheer force, will ensure that Jesus dies. What transpires next
in the Passion Narratives is the triumph of the sin-darkened "will," which is
devoid of any rationality. What we will see is sinful Adam and the sinful race
he conceived come to full term—Satan's definitive attempt to have evil's darkness snuff out good's light. What we will also see is Jesus' holy, good, and loving will triumphing over the ungodly, hateful, and evil will of his accusers, for
Jesus has, within his agony in the garden, definitively committed his will to do
the will of his holy, loving, and good Father. In freely offering himself in love
to his Father on behalf of humankind, Jesus will put to death the sin-enslaved
humanity that he inherited from Adam and in so doing free humankind of
its sin-enslaved will and its sin-darkened mind. In his resurrection, Jesus, the
Son of God, will rise as the glorious new Adam in whom all who believe in
him and are re-created in his Holy Spirit, which he will pour out as the Saving
Lord, will come to share in his new humanity. Thus, although it may appear
that Satan's lying evil will has triumphed, in fact Jesus' truth-bearing will, as it
has from the onset of his arrest, rules the day. With the above in mind, we can
move on to the next stage of Jesus' trial before Pilate.

With the failure of having Jesus condemned for claiming to be the Christ,
the Son of God, the King of the Jews, both by Pilate and Herod (Lk), the trial takes a different course. It is somewhat ambiguous as to who initiated this
new round of negotiations. Matthew has Pilate do so. Introducing the custom
that on the feast of the Passover the governor would release "any one prisoner whom they wanted.... Pilate said to them, 'Whom do you want me to release for you, Barabbas or Jesus who is called Christ?'" Matthew tells us that
the reason he did so was because "he knew that it was out of envy that they
[the Jewish authorities] had delivered him up."[36] Although Mark has the Jew-

---

risen Lord Jesus, human beings would once more assume incorruptibility and so be restored to
the image of God's eternity. Satan may be the embodiment of falsehood, but he has never been
able to master the art of paradoxical irony, for in irony truth shrewdly lies.

36. Here Matthew also inserts an incident that is unique to his Gospel. He narrates that
"while he [Pilate] was sitting on the judgment seat, his wife sent word to him, 'Have nothing
to do with that righteous man, for I have suffered much over him today in a dream.'" Pilate,
as judge, should pronounce this "righteous man" innocent and thus remove himself from the
whole affair. In proposing to release either Barabbas or Jesus, Pilate is diplomatically attempting to do just that, hoping that the Jews will agree to his releasing Jesus.

Also, some ancient manuscripts have Matthew's Gospel giving Barabbas's full name as
"Jesus-Barabbas," so the translation of his entire name would be: Jesus (YHWH-Saves), son of
the father. If that is the case, we have two men being judged with the same name: a "notori-
ous prisoner" (Mt) who "committed murder in the insurrection" (Mk and Lk) who is named

ish crowds remind Pilate of the custom, perceiving, as in Matthew, "that it was out of envy that the chief priests had delivered him up," Pilate asks the question in such a manner that he makes plain his hope that they will want him to release Jesus, for he only gives them one option: "Do you want me to release for you the King of the Jews?" Both in Matthew and Mark, the "for you" is Pilate's attempt at wanting to do the crowds, and not the Jewish authorities, a favor, for they would probably look more favorably upon Jesus, not being envious of him. His attempt at currying the crowd's favor is accentuated in his designating Jesus as "Christ" (Mt) and "the King of the Jews" (Mk), the one playing to their Judaic pride as God's chosen people to whom the Messiah was divinely promised and the other to their political jingoism in the face (his face) of Roman rule. The common thread being that if Jesus is the promised Christ, he would also be their promised salvific king, the one who would free them from Roman rule, and thus, to the mind of the crowd, the last person they would want this pagan idolatrous Roman gentile to execute. Luke simply narrates, without any question being asked, that the crowd, upon hearing that Pilate would simply "chastise him [Jesus] and release him," "cried out together, 'Away with this man, and release to us Barabbas.'" Although Pilate may have thought his customary releasing of a prisoner of their choosing would release him from his dilemma (Mt), the Jewish authorities manipulated the custom so as to force Pilate to execute Jesus. For when he asked the Jews, "Do you want me to release for you the King of the Jews?" (Mk) or "Jesus who is called Christ" (Mt), all three accounts agree that the crowd demanded that he release Barabbas. At this point, Luke narrates that Pilate addressed them, again expressing his desire "to release Jesus." Here we witness the contest of "wills." Pilate wants to release Jesus because he has found no guilt in him, even though he is charged with claiming to be Christ, the Son of God and so the King of the Jews, but the Jewish authorities and the crowd they have now commandeered no longer show any interest in the indictments. They simply "will" that Jesus be put to death. When Pilate, having acceded to their desire to release Barabbas, asks them, "Then what shall I do with Jesus, who is called Christ?" (Mt)

"YHWH-Saves" and is "son of the father" and Jesus "YHWH-Saves," who is "Son of the Father." The contrast is obvious. Jesus-Barabbas has attempted to establish an earthly kingdom, a kingdom born of "man," with its ever illusive political freedom and justice, through a violent murderous uprising, and Jesus, who will establish a heavenly kingdom, a kingdom born of his Father, in which true freedom and justice will reign, through his death and resurrection. Oddly, Jesus-Barabbas and Peter are basically of the same mind—in the sword lies the answer—though Peter is innocently naive, whereas Barabbas is callously ruthless.

or "Then what shall I do with the man whom you call King of the Jews?" (Mk); "they all said, 'Let him be crucified'" (Mt) or "Crucify him" (Mk).[37] When Pilate pleads for some rationale or justification for such a sentence—"Why, what evil has he done?" (Mt and Mk)—they provide none. Rather, they just "shouted all the more, 'Let him be crucified'" (Mt) or "Crucify him" (Mk). Although the trial began with false Jewish accusations against Jesus, and Pilate next brings to light the "true" accusations that Jesus purports to be or is said to be the Christ, the Son of God and so the King of the Jews, at the climax of the trial, the Jewish authorities and the crowd not only demonstrate no interest in what might be true, but they also no longer manifest even any interest in leveling further lies. Their shout "Crucify him" is merely the expression of their "will" devoid of all rationality—even a rationality that would be underwritten by falsehood. Jesus will now be executed for no other reason than the wholly perverse will of an irrational mob. Thus Matthew narrates, "So when Pilate saw that he was gaining nothing, but rather that a riot was beginning, he took water and washed his hands before the crowd, saying 'I am innocent of this man's blood; see to it yourselves.'" Although Pilate wants to be free, as he attempted to do all along, from any responsibility for Jesus' death, his lack of "will" allowed evil's "will" to prevail. As Mark states, "So Pilate, wishing to satisfy the crowd, released Barabbas; and having scourged Jesus, he delivered him to be crucified." Pilate's "wish," his will, to release Jesus has now changed to his "wish," his will, "to satisfy the crowd." As Luke summarily states, "And their voices prevailed." "Voices" and not words, neither words of truth nor even words of falsehood, just the empty clamor of riotous vacuous noise, prevailed. Pilate is no longer concerned about the truth but has conjoined his will to, and so has taken on, the irrational destructive sentiments of the rioting crowd.

Matthew alone narrates that Pilate symbolically washes his hands of Jesus' innocent blood. When Pilate concludes his ablution and tells the Jewish authorities to "see to it themselves," "All the people answered, 'His blood be on us and on our children!'" While Pilate wishes to disclaim any responsi-

---

37. Upon to this point, Pilate has consistently called Jesus "the King of the Jews." Within Mark, Pilate says, "Then what shall I do with the man *you call King of the Jews?*" Now the emphasis is not upon what Pilate calls Jesus, but upon what the Jews themselves call Jesus—their king. Pilate apparently wants to appeal once again to their political nationalistic instinct—they do not want to execute their king. Pilate is aware of the envy of the chief priest's, but he does not fathom the depth of that envy, which is so deep that they want to kill this man for the same reason that they do not want him to be their king. Better they live under Imperial Rome than under the kingship of Jesus.

bility for Jesus' death, "all the people" willingly assume responsibility for his death. It was their doing from the onset of Jesus' arrest, and now that they have achieved their purpose, they are ready to release Pilate of any responsibility, which would hardly soothe his conflicted conscience, and take upon themselves the weight of Jesus' blood. This was the intent of their declaration, which cannot be denied. But what the Jewish crowd, the Jewish authorities, and the people as a whole have done is not call down a divine curse and an everlasting condemnation upon themselves, but a divine blessing and an everlasting righteousness upon themselves and the whole of their future posterity. The innocent blood of Jesus, the Spirit-anointed blood of Christ, the Son of God, will wash them clean of all sin and in so doing will transform them into Spirit-anointed citizens of God's kingdom, in which the risen Lord Jesus will reign as their beloved King.[38] Unbeknownst to them, they achieved the promise God swore to fulfill on their behalf, a promise first made from the time of Abraham: to make them a righteous, holy nation in his sight and a blessing to all the nations (see Gn 12:1-3, 8:18, and 22:18). Contrary to their intent, the will of Jesus, the filial will of the Father's Son, and not their own, prevailed.[39]

Having released Barabbas, Matthew and Mark narrate that Pilate had Jesus scourged. The soldiers took Jesus into the praetorium and, along with the whole battalion, "stripped him and put a scarlet robe [Mark has "purple robe"] upon him, and plaiting a crown of thorns they put it on his head, and put a reed in his right hand. And knelling before him they mocked him say-

---

38. The interpretation of this passage has long had a contentious and often sad history, filled with antisemitism. Since publication of the Second Vatican Council's *Nostra Aetate*, the church has rejected the notion that "all Jews indiscriminately at that time [at the time of Jesus' death], nor Jews today, can be charged with the crimes committed during his passion" (n. 4).

Although the Jews called down upon themselves the full blessings that come through the salvific acts of Jesus, specifically his crucifixion and resurrection, they have yet to attain those blessings as a whole people. Many Jews over the centuries down to the present have come to faith in Jesus and have been baptized, yet the church still awaits the full complement of the Jewish faithful (Rom 11:11-16).

In contrast to the crowd taking the responsibility for Jesus' blood, the Jewish authorities accuse Peter and John of filling "Jerusalem with your teaching and you intend to bring this man's blood upon us" (Acts 5:28). Ironically, as when the crowd accepted responsibility for Jesus' blood, so now Peter and John want "to bring this man's blood upon them," not to condemn them but save them through the blood of Jesus.

39. When Simeon prophesied to Mary that her son "is set for the fall and rising of many in Israel" so that "the thoughts out of many hearts may be revealed," he also rejoiced in the Lord, for his own eyes "have seen your salvation which you have prepared in the presence of all people, a light for the revelation to the Gentiles, and for the glory to your people Israel" (Lk 2:28-35). Both the negative and positive prophetic aspects of Simeon's declaration are fulfilled in the "prevailing" of the Jewish authorities and in the "prevailing" of Jesus.

ing, 'Hail, King of the Jews!' And they spat upon him, and took the reed and struck him on the head. And when they had mocked him, they stripped him of the robe, and put his own clothes on him, and led him away to crucify him" (Mt; see also Mk). The heart of the soldiers' mocking resides in Jesus being the King of the Jews—dressing him in a military (scarlet) or royal (purple) robe, crowning his head with thorns and placing a reed (a mock scepter) in his right hand, climaxing with their taunting obeisant fealty, their scornful regal salutation, and their demeaning spitting. This scarecrow caricature may not befit the Christ, the Son of God, the King of the Jews, but such dishonor bears testimony to why Jesus is the Christ, the Son of God, and so the King of the Jews, for because of and within such degradation, Jesus will fulfill his Messianic anointing, manifest his divine Sonship, and so establish his Father's kingdom, over which he will reign as the everlasting king. This scene of mockery, belittlement, and humiliation actually depicts Jesus' splendor, grandeur, and even beauty. This scene is but a prelude to the glory of the cross and the wondrous scene that will unfold beneath it.[40] We can now fruitfully examine the Suffering Servant Songs.

Jesus and the Suffering Servant Songs

Beginning with Jesus' silence before the Sanhedrin, continuing throughout Jesus' trial before Pilate and Herod, and now culminating in the actions of the soldiers, the Suffering Servant Songs of Isaiah have become ever more manifest and thus Jesus is fulfilling them.[41] At Jesus' baptism, God the Father spoke the first verse of the first Servant Song: "Behold my servant, whom I uphold, my chosen, in whom my soul delights; I have put my Spirit upon him, he will bring forth justice to the nations" (Is 42:1-2; see also Mt 3:17, Mk 1:11, and Lk 3:22).[42] Thus the Father is the first, at the onset of Jesus' salvific mission,

40. As was noted above, the Gospel of John makes this explicit. The "hour" of darkness is actually the "hour" of Jesus' glory.

41. The Suffering Servant Songs will not be completely fulfilled until Jesus' death and resurrection, yet I discuss them here because most of what they foretell is enacted within the context of his trials before the Sanhedrin and Pilate. These songs therefore become the lens through which we can properly look upon Jesus' impending death and his anticipated resurrection. Peter, within the Acts of the Apostles, employs the Suffering Servant Songs to interpret Jesus' death (see Acts 3:18 and 4:27).

42. Also, within the first Servant Song, God declares that his servant "will faithfully bring forth justice. He will not fail or be discouraged till he has established justice on the earth; and the coastlands wait for his law" (Is 42:3-4).

to affix the Suffering Servant Songs to the person of his Son and so proclaim that they are to be fulfilled within his Son's saving acts. The Father is also declaring to all that his Son's saving work can only be rightly understood and interpreted in the light of these songs. As the Father's Spirit-filled Servant-Son, Jesus is presently, amid his passion, enacting justice upon all nations and so fulfilling his Father's saving will. Shortly thereafter, God addresses his servant: "I am the Lord, I have called you in righteousness, I have taken you by the hand and kept you; I have given you as a covenant to the people, a light to the nations, to open the eyes that are blind, to bring out the prisoners from the dungeon, from the prison those who sit in darkness. I am the Lord, that is my name, my glory I give to no other, nor my praise to graven images. Behold, the former things have come to pass, and new things I now declare, before they spring forth I tell you of them" (Is 42:6–9). By his divine name, YHWH, God has chosen Jesus to be the righteous one, whom he has nurtured and guarded like a child, hand in hand. Jesus, as we saw within the Last Supper, will give up his body and will pour out his blood as the new covenantal sacrifice for Jews and Gentiles alike, thus releasing all from the darkness of sin and dungeon of death into the light of life. Jesus will be the new covenant, for to abide in Jesus as the risen Christ, the Son of the living God, is to live in Spirit-filled communion with his Father. Being "the Lord," God alone possesses the fullness of glory, and although he jealously guards his glory and does not praise idols, he will share his glory with his Servant and allow his praises to be bestowed upon his Son, for now in and through Jesus he is enacting the new work of salvation. This is what is being enacted within Jesus' passion, and this is what his Father wishes us to perceive and understand and so to sing the praises of his Son and give him glory.

In the second Servant Song, Isaiah prophesies that the Lord called his servant "from the womb, from the body of my mother he named me" (Is 49:1), and the Lord "formed me from the womb to be his servant" (Is 49:5). Within his very conception within the womb of Mary, the Father named his Servant-Son Jesus—YHWH-Saves. Jesus, as the Father's Son, would save God's people by being God's suffering servant and in so doing inherit David's everlasting kingdom, as Gabriel promised. His trials enact this fulfillment, for Jesus will be killed because he is the anointed Messiah, the Son of God, and so merit to be king of his Father's kingdom. In so doing, the Father will definitively declare: "You are my servant, Israel, in whom I will be glorified" (Is 49:3). Jesus embodies the whole of what it truly means for Israel to be the true Israel, the faithful servant of God, and so in Jesus, in the whole new Israel, his Father will be glorified, for in Jesus, God's people will truly become a holy people and nation unto the holy God. Jesus may be tempted to think, "I have labored in vain, I have spent my strength for nothing and vanity," yet he can be confident that "my right is with the Lord, and my recompense with my God" (Is 49:4). Thus Jesus can declare: "I am honored in the eyes of the Lord" for "my God has become my strength." And the Lord will say, "It is too light a thing that you should be my servant to raise up the tribes of Jacob and to restore the pre-served of Israel; I will give you as a light to the nations, that my salvation may reach to the ends of the earth" (Is 49:5-6). In saving Israel, Jesus merits to be the saving light to all nations, as Simeon prophesied at his circumcision—the first shedding of his blood (see Lk 2:29-32). Although Jesus, the Lord's servant, is "deeply despised, abhorred by the nations, the servant of rulers," "kings shall see and arise; princes, and they shall prostrate themselves; because of the Lord, who is faithful, the Holy One of Israel, who has chosen you" (Is 49:7). As Jesus, the suffering servant, has been faithful to his Father, so his Father will be faithful to him, and thus the rulers of world who considered Jesus of little account will see the glory bestowed upon him by his Father and so lie pros-trate before him in worship.

The third Suffering Servant Song reiterates the same pattern as the first two. Jesus may be mocked and his face spit upon and so covered in shame, but he can say, "I have not been confounded, and I know that I shall not be put to shame; he who vindicates me is near.... Behold, the Lord God helps me; who will declare me guilty? Behold all of them will wear out like a garment; the moth will eat them up" (Is 50:6-9). Jesus will be killed, but he is not con-demned because he is not found guilty. Being the Father's beloved Son, Jesus, despite all appearances, will not be defeated nor ultimately will he be morti-fied, for his Father is ever at hand to help him and to justify him, to raise him up as his all-holy and glorious Son. Those who refuse to believe in him will decay in their unbelief.

The last of the Suffering Servant Songs most vividly portrays the present plight of Jesus. Jesus, "my servant shall prosper, he shall be exalted and lifted up and shall be very high," but at present many will be astonished at Jesus' appearance, being scourged and crowned with thorns, for he no longer bears any human resemblance (see Is 52:13-15). Even though he grew up before the Lord "like a young plant," he had "no form or comeliness that we should look at him, and no beauty that we should desire him. He was despised and rejected by men; a man of sorrows, and acquainted with grief; and as one from whom men hide their faces he was despised, and we esteemed him not" (Is 53:1-3).

Here the Servant Song imparts theological meaning to Jesus' suffering. Although "we esteemed him stricken, smitten by God, and afflicted," "surely he has borne our grief and carried our sorrows." Again, it appears to be Jesus as the beaten and tormented outcast of God, yet it was not his own condemnation that he bore, but the grief and sorrow of humankind. The reason is that Jesus "was wounded for our transgressions, he was bruised for our iniquities; upon him was the chastisement that made us whole, and with his stripes we were healed ... the Lord has laid on him the iniquity of us all" (Is 53:4-6). In becoming man, the Son of God assumed the flesh of his father Adam, and in that assumption he took upon himself the sin and the iniquity and the guilt of Adam's posterity. Now, in the city of Jerusalem, when Caiaphas is high priest and Pontius Pilate is governor, Jesus, in loving faithfulness to his divine Father and as a loving member of his human father's race, bore the just punishment of humankind's sin. In so doing, he transformed the justly imposed punishment into an act of loving sacrifice to his heavenly Father and so healed and made whole his human father's sinful race. The Suffering Servant Song is here providing an essential soteriological interpretive point, of which "love" is the hermeneutical key. On the one hand, Jesus, the Son of God, in lovingly assuming humankind's fallen and sin-marred nature, inherited within his own humanity and so the guilt and punishment that inhered within that humanity. On the other hand, by living a holy life without sin, Jesus, as the Spirit-filled Father's Son, was concurrently empowered, within his very suffering of humankind's sinful condemnation and deadly punishment, to transfigure or convert that punishment into an act of sacrificial love. This act then is twofold: love for humankind and love for the Father. First, this death is a loving act performed on behalf of humankind and in the stead of humankind; that is, Jesus lovingly assumed humankind's punishment in the place of humankind and in the aid of humankind, for humankind, lacking the fullness of love was incapable of aiding itself on behalf of itself. Second, having lovingly assumed on behalf of humankind and in the stead of humankind man's punishment, Jesus offered himself, on behalf of humankind and in the stead of humankind, as a loving all-holy sacrifice to his loving all-holy Father, a loving offering that sinful humankind was incapable of making. Thus the death that was a punishment for sin became a death that was the forgiveness of sin, for Jesus transformed death into a sacrificial act of loving forgiveness, both on behalf of humankind and on behalf of his Father. Jesus' death was simultaneously both a punishment for sin and the saving sacrifice for sin. He assumed the punishment in love for humankind and offered himself in love to his Father, and in that twofold love

Adam's race was redeemed from the curse of sin and death and reconciled to God. As the Suffering Servant Song states shortly after, "Yet it was the will of the Lord to bruise him; he has put him to grief; when he makes himself an offering for sin, he shall see his offspring, he shall prolong his days; the will of the Lord shall prosper his hand; he shall see the fruit of the travail of his soul and be satisfied; by his knowledge shall the righteous one, my servant, make many to be accounted righteous; and shall bear their iniquities" (Is 53:10-11). Because Jesus offers himself as a sacrifice for sin, bearing the iniquities of humankind, his Father ensures that he will see the saving fruit of his grief and travail, the prospering of his hand: the making righteous of his new offspring who share in the everlasting prosperity of his resurrection. Through his saving passion, death, and resurrection, Jesus puts to death the sinful race of the old lifeless Adam whose image he bore and becomes the new living Adam of a new righteous race re-created in his own now Spirit-filled resurrected image.

By way of concluding our examination of the Suffering Servant Songs, two summary points must be highlighted. First, evident throughout is the primary role of God, the servant's Lord. Within their present fulfillment, the Lord God is the Father of Christ Jesus, his Son. The Father wills all that Jesus does, and in so doing Jesus wills all that his Father wills. In accordance with the Father's will, Jesus, his anointed servant, is mocked, despised, abhorred, spit upon, smitten, bruised, stricken, scourged, and killed. In accordance with the Father's will, Jesus, his anointed servant, assumes humankind's guilt, transgressions, iniquity, and death. In accordance with the Father's will, Jesus, his anointed servant, is glorified, honored, restored, vindicated, exalted, lifted up, and so will prosper. Thus, within his whole of the passion and death, his Father is the source of all the saving acts, and Jesus, as his anointed suffering servant and faithful Son, enacts all these salvific acts. Therefore he is the first to reap the benefits of these saving acts. The Sanhedrin, Herod, Pilate, and even Satan may appear to be the controlling actors in whose presence Jesus stands helplessly bound and confoundedly silent. Yet the Suffering Servant Songs poignantly intone a different song. They sing a glorious tale—the divine drama of salvation orchestrated by the Father and performed by the Father's Spirit-anointed Son, and as such this ballad narrates the truth.

Second, as this study has emphasized throughout, the Suffering Servant Songs narrate a series of salvific causes that effect saving benefits. Again, the Father is the source of these soteriological causes, for they flow from the act of his divine will. Although the Father divinely wills all the causal saving actions, Jesus enacts these divinely willed causal saving actions not through his

divine filial will but through his human filial will. Jesus, the Son of God incarnate, humanly wills to do the divine will of his Father. And all that Jesus wills
and does as Father's Son is willed and done in communion with the Holy Spirit. This conformity of Jesus' human will, the human filial will of the incarnate
Son, to his Father's divine will infuses his human Spirit-imbued saving actions
with their authentic human salvific value. Likewise, the Son of God as man is
to save the whole of humankind, and he can do so only if, as man, he humanly wills to save man and humanly enacts those acts that are causally salvific.
Although the Son of God saves humankind, he does so as man, for only if he
saves humankind as man is humankind actually saved. Thus the human causes that effect humankind's salvation are the same actions we witness within
Jesus' passion and death as perceived through the lens of the Suffering Servant
Songs. These actions are not simply those of Jesus being mocked, spit upon,
scourged, crowned with thorns, and crucified. Rather, what is salvific within
these actions is Jesus' own Spirit-filled human acts: his willingly assuming in
love; his actively appropriating into his own humanity humankind's iniquity,
transgressions, and punishment; and lovingly offering his human life to his
Father on humankind's behalf. The mockery, scourging, crowning, and crucifying testify not merely to what is being brutally imposed upon Jesus, but
more significantly to what Jesus is actively doing, that is, performing those human acts that causally achieve humankind's salvation. Because Jesus willingly
enacted these human salvific acts, he merits his and humankind's resurrected
glory. These human saving acts elicit or cause the Father to respond positively
by raising Jesus, his Son, gloriously from the dead. The Father's resurrecting
act not only verifies that Jesus' human Spirit-empowered saving acts achieved
their saving purpose by being soteriologically efficacious, but also that his
Spirit-filled bodily resurrection is the saving effect, that is, that the risen Jesus
and those in Spirit-filled communion with him abide in everlasting live-giving
intimacy with his eternal Father.

It may appear that we have gotten theologically ahead of ourselves since,
within our own narrative, we have yet to treat Jesus' actual death and resurrection. But from the onset of Jesus' fulfilling the Suffering Servant Songs
within his trials before Sanhedrin and Pilate, the songs themselves, within
the Synoptic Passion Narratives, and also the Passion Narratives, have forced
us to focus on both what is taking place as well as where these events are
leading and will culminate: Jesus' death and resurrection. In accordance with
the Suffering Servant Songs, Jesus' present suffering is but the prelude to his
death, and his death is but the prelude to his resurrection—the prospering of

the Father's Suffering Servant-Son. Most importantly, Jesus, from the time of Judas' betrayal, forewarned his disciples of which the Synoptic have now duly taken account, that the Scriptures must be fulfilled. As Jesus declared to sword-brandishing Peter, "But how then should the scriptures be fulfilled, that it must be so?" (Mt 26:52-54). Or, to the arresting crowd, "But all of this has taken place that the scriptures of the prophets might be fulfilled" (Mt 26:56). Or to Mark, "But let the scripture be fulfilled" (Mk 14:49). What Jesus knew must be so, and so the Suffering Servant Songs are fulfilled.

Conclusion

As one would expect, what we perceive within Jesus' agony in the Garden, within his arrest and subsequent trials, is Jesus fully emerging as Jesus—YHWH-Saves. Importantly, he is doing so primarily by conforming himself completely into the likeness of his Father's Spirit-filled Servant-Son—by enacting the Suffering Servant Songs. To see Jesus in agony and then successively being mocked, ridiculed, spat upon, smitten, scourged, and crowned with thorns is to see Jesus increasingly configuring and so constituting himself, literally in body and spiritually in soul, into the living icon of Jesus—YHWH-Saves. Jesus is becoming Jesus because, as the Father's beloved Son, he is the Father's beloved Servant who, through his humiliating suffering and cruel death, will become humankind's beloved glorious Savior and the universe's beloved risen Lord.

Now we can move on with Jesus to his crucifixion, death, and resurrection, for, his trials being concluded, "they led him away" (Mt 27:31, Mk 15:20, and Lk 23:26).

11 · JESUS' CRUCIFIXION AND DEATH

Our study, in conformity to the whole trajectory of the Gospels, has come to its climax: Jesus' death and resurrection. All the prophetic words and actions within the Synoptic Gospels treated in previous chapters will now come to their fulfillment. All the prophetic words and actions within the Old Testament, many of which we have already examined, will now also find their completion—"that it must be so" (Mt 26:34; see also Mt 26:56 and Mk 14:49). Considering all that we have previously studied, we should be prepared to perceive the theological import and soteriological significance of Jesus' death and resurrection. This chapter focuses on Jesus' crucifixion and death, and chapter 12 focuses on his resurrection.

On the Way to Golgotha

As they led Jesus away, the soldiers "compelled" (Mt and Mk) or "seized" (Lk) Simon of Cyrene to carry the cross of Jesus.[1] Here we perceive a simultaneous twofold enactment. After Peter's profession of faith that Jesus is the Christ, the Son of the living God, Jesus expounds the fuller implications of this truth. He tells his disciples that this means that he must go to Jerusalem, be rejected by

---

1. All quotations in this section are from Mt 27:31-44, Mk 15:20-32, and Lk 23:26-43 unless otherwise noted. Mark informs the reader that Simon "was coming in from the country" and designates him "the father of Alexander and Rufus." "Coming in from the country" implies that it was by happenstance that he was compelled to carry Jesus' cross, and so he was probably unaware who Jesus was or why he was being crucified. This lack of awareness would be corroborated by the fact that Cyrene is in North Africa, and so Simon would not be a Jew who would have had a stake in the whole gruesome affair. Nonetheless, that he was the father of Alexander and Rufus implies that Mark's readers would know, or at least have heard of, his sons if they did not know their father, who presumably had died by the time Mark wrote his Gospel, as he was no longer personally known. This then implies that Alexander and Rufus, sons of their now "celebrity father," became followers of Jesus and so known to members of the apostolic community. That Simon's sons became Christians might imply that Simon became a Christian, but this would be mere unprovable speculation.

357

the elders, suffer, and be killed. He does not mention that he will be crucified, just that he will "generically" be killed. After Peter's protest that this should not be and Jesus' rebuke that such a proposal was satanic, however, Jesus declared: "If any man would come after me, let him deny himself and take up his cross and follow me. For whoever would save his life will lose it, and whoever loses his life for my sake will find it. For what profits a man, if he gains the whole world and forfeits his life? Or what shall a man give in return for his life" (Mt 16:24-26; see also Mk 8:34-37 and Lk 9:23-25). Jesus is now carrying his cross, he is suffering and being killed, and so is enacting his own prophetic words to his disciples. He is losing his life on the cross, and in so doing he will find his true life in his resurrection.[2] Simultaneously, Simon is now also carrying Jesus' cross, and Luke notes that he was doing so "behind Jesus." Jesus' cross and Simon's cross are one and the same, the difference being that Jesus is leading and Simon is following.[3] Because the Synoptics use the words "compelled" and "seized," one can presume that Simon did not volunteer to help Jesus—although he is carrying the cross for Jesus' "sake," it is not an act of charity. Nonetheless, Simon becomes the living icon of reluctant Christians, the reluctant followers of Jesus, who during their lives, in the ordinary affairs of "coming in from the country" (Mk), find themselves in situations where they, if true followers of Jesus, must take up their crosses and follow him. In a sense, all Christians and the church, as in the case of Jesus himself, would prefer to forego the cross, but their integrity of faith, "for my sake [Jesus'] and the gospel's" (Mk 8:35) will compel them to take it up. The Gospels do not inform us

2. In the desert, Satan offered Jesus "all of the kingdoms of the world and the glory of them" if only he would "fall down and worship" him. If Jesus had done so, he might have saved his earthly life, but he would have lost his life as the Father's Son. But Jesus thwarts such a temptation by declaring, "You shall worship the Lord your God and him only shall you serve" (Mt 3:8-10; see Lk 4:5-8). Jesus is presently serving the Lord his God by offering himself as a loving sacrifice of worship and in so doing will find his eternal life as the Father's resurrected Son.

3. Although all three Synoptics appear to imply that Jesus' cross was transferred from him to Simon, leaving Jesus empty-handed, yet this does not mean that Jesus did not carry the burden of the cross—the sin of the world with its just condemnation of death. Thus both Jesus and Simon carry the cross even if Simon alone actually carries the actual wooden cross. This has been traditionally depicted, especially within the Stations of the Cross, as Jesus carrying the crossbeam section of the cross and Simon lifting up and carrying the base end of the cross. The Gospel of John has no mention of Simon, but instead emphasizes that while the soldiers "took Jesus," "he went out, bearing his own cross" (Jn 19:17). John is obviously highlighting that, although it may appear that Jesus was passively being led out and put to death, Jesus was actively undertaking the work of salvation—he was not led, but went out and he carried the cross upon which he would offer his life to his Father.

about Simon's subsequent life or the effect of carrying Jesus' cross might have
had upon him. But we do know that those who take up their crosses and follow Jesus do not carry it reluctantly, but find in it, as Jesus declared, their very
life. For to carry one's cross is to conjoin one's cross to Jesus', as portrayed by
Simon, and so to share in Jesus' resurrected life and glory.

Luke alone now tells the reader that following Jesus was "a great multitude of the people, and of women who bewailed him and lamented over him."
Although many Jews followed Jesus on his way to Golgotha, it appears that
only the women did so in pronounced agonizing grief, for Jesus says to them:
"Daughters of Jerusalem, do not weep for me, but weep for yourselves and for
your children. For behold, the days are coming when they will say, 'Blessed
are the barren, and the wombs that never bore, and the beasts that never gave
suck!' Then they will say to the mountains, 'Fall on us'; and to the hills, 'Cover us.' For if they do this when the wood is green, what will happen when it is
dry?" These women were "daughters of Jerusalem," and so they are like Anna,
the prophetess, who lived her widowhood within the temple and spoke about
Jesus "to all who were looking for the redemption of Jerusalem" (Lk 2:36-
38). These Jerusalem women believed Jesus to be their redemption, but now
lamented and bewailed his apparent demise. But Jesus declares that they need
not weep for him (a sign of Jesus' confident assurance that he is under the care
of his loving Father), but rather their concern should be for themselves and
their children. Now the immediate reason is the impending destruction of Jerusalem. Upon approaching Jerusalem, Jesus "wept over it," for "the days" are
coming when Jerusalem will be destroyed and the enemy will "dash you to the
ground, you and your children within you," for "you did not know the time of
your visitation" (Lk 19:41-45). When Jerusalem is surrounded by armies, "alas
for those who are with child and for those who give suck in those days! For
great distress shall be upon the earth and wrath upon this people ... and Jerusalem will be trodden down by the Gentiles, until the times of the Gentiles are
fulfilled" (Lk 21:20-24). When Jerusalem falls, these bemoaning women will
be with suckling children, who are dashed to the ground along with the children in their wombs. Jesus is also alluding to Hosea's prophecy that because
of Israel's unfaithfulness God will bring down his devastating judgment. God's
condemnation will be so destructive and its effects so shocking that the people
will "say to the mountains, Cover us, and to the hills, Fall upon us" (Hos 10:8;
see also the whole of chapter 10). The very crushing of mountains and hills
is the last hope of protective cover against the even greater havoc of God's
wrathful judgment. Although Jesus may, in the first instance, be forewarn-

ing the destruction of Jerusalem and the suffering that these women and their children will endure, he is also signalling the mayhem that will occur at the end of time. The destruction of Jerusalem and the temple portends the current eschatological age, always on the threshold of its consummation. Then sin and evil will consume the world, and God's righteous judgment, in the fullness of its ferocious might and fearful power, will equally fall upon the earth. It may not appear so to the lamenting women, but what they are experiencing is a sinful evil event when the wood is green, when men have not yet reached the full depth of their depravity. There will come a time when the wood is dry, and for that time they should weep in suppliant prayer lest they (their future prodigy) be devoured by the evil that surrounds them—the final eschatological temptation.[4]

Luke then informs the reader that two criminals were led away with Jesus "to be put to death with him." Matthew and Mark will give notice of them later, but Luke, because he alone informs us of the "good thief," wants to accentuate that they were together with Jesus and so alerts us that all three shared a common death but all will not share the same end.

The Crucifixion

Having arrived at Golgotha, which means "the place of the skull," Matthew and Mark narrate that the soldiers first offered Jesus "wine to drink, mingled with gall" (Mt), or "myrrh" (Mk), "but when he tasted it, he would not drink it" (Mt). This implies, especially in Mark, that the soldiers wished to offer Jesus wine that was drugged so as to lessen his awareness of the pain. But the counter-implication is that Jesus, having tasted it and refusing to drink it, did not wish in any way to diminish the alertness of his mind nor to alleviate the severity of the pain. He was about to offer himself as a loving sacrifice to his Father, and for this offering to be soteriologically efficacious, Jesus must do it with complete clarity of mind and the full free consent of his will. He must consume the fullness of death, with the fury of its agony, if death itself was to

---

4. This final all-consuming conflict between the forces of evil and good is graphically portrayed in the Book of Revelation. (There the author also alludes to Hos 10:8.) Then there will be a great earthquake, the sun will become black, the stars will fall upon the earth, the sky will vanish, and every mountain and hill will be uprooted. Everyone will hide in caves and among the rocks—kings and generals, rich and poor, slave and free. All will cry out to the mountains and the rocks: "Fall on us and hide us from the face of him who is seated on the throne, and from the wrath of the Lamb, for the great day of their wrath has come, and who can stand it" (Rv 6:12-17).

be put to death. The poison of sin must be flushed out by the cleansing anti-
dote of pure love and, in that act of pure love, death, the ultimate effect of sin's
toxin, dies.

Matthew and Mark state next that "they crucified him" and "divided his
garments among them, casting lots." Matthew notes that the soldiers "then sat
down and kept watch over him there," while Mark notes that "it was the third
hour, when they crucified him." Luke again highlights immediately that Jesus
was crucified with "the criminals, one on his left and one on his right," while
Matthew and Mark tell of this just prior to Jesus being mocked. Luke then
also has Jesus speak his first words from the cross: "Father, forgive them, for
they know not what they do." Only then does Luke narrate that "they cast lots
to divide his garments." The order of narration may vary among the Synoptic Gospels, but the basic facts remain consistent and merit some theological
comment.

First, surprisingly, there is no description of the actual crucifixion—no
stripping of garments, no placing on the cross, no hammering of nails, no
hoisting up of the cross. The Gospel authors may have thought such a description unnecessary, since everyone at the time would have known the gruesome
protocol for crucifying someone. It was the cruelest and most humiliating of
all Roman punishments, reserved for slaves and the vilest criminals. Yet in
Matthew the crucifixion is reduced to an introductory clause ("And when they
had crucified him") to the declarative sentence ("they divided his garments").
Apparently the dividing of Jesus' garments is more important than Jesus' actual crucifixion. Mark has a compound sentence: "And they crucified him and
divided his garments," thus giving "the crucifixion" and "the dividing" equal
significance, but would not the crucifixion be more significant than the custom of soldiers laying claim to a criminal's garments? The dividing of Jesus'
garments holds such a preeminent position, for within this action resides the
hermeneutical key for interpreting the crucifixion. The "dividing" is the first
allusion within Jesus' crucifixion to Psalm 22: "Yea, dogs are round me; a company of evildoers encircle me; they have pierced my hands and feet—I can
count all of my bones—they stare and gloat over me; they divided my garments among them, and for my raiment they cast lots" (v. 16-18). Although
the Synoptics do not provide a descriptive narrative, this psalm prophetically
and vividly portrays what is now being enacted. Significantly, it does so as if
it were coming from the mouth of Jesus himself—He is the "I" and the "me"
and the "my." Jesus, not the evangelists, is imparting, through the psalm, the
detailed narrative of his own crucifixion. He describes the encircling of hard-

ened cynical soldiers and the mockery of denouncing Jewish leaders; he tells of the nail-piercing hammer blows of his hands and feet, and the indifferent, casual, and almost callous, distribution of his most personal possessions, the very clothes that hid his nakedness and lent honor to his body, clothes that he needs no more, for naked he is about to die. Most importantly, this psalm provides the theological and soteriological lens through which Jesus' crucifixion and death must now be read, and it will do so through Jesus' voice, as this psalm becomes his prayer.[5]

Second, Luke provides Jesus' first words from the cross: "Father, forgive them; for they know not what they do." On one level, it would seem that "they" do know what they are doing—Pilate knows he is allowing the death of an innocent man, and the Jewish leaders know that they have obtained the crucifixion of a man they feared because he presented himself as, and others believed him to be, the Christ, the Son of the living God. They achieved this even though Jesus was never legally convicted for any actual wrong doing. Yet within the invincible darkness of their minds and hearts, neither Pilate nor the Jewish leaders really knew what they were doing. Pilate may know that Jesus was innocent, but he surely did not believe that Jesus was some anointed Savior, or some kind of designated "son" of the Jewish God, or that he was the actual king of the Jews who would be a threat to the Roman Empire or to Caesar. Likewise, the Jewish leaders wanted Jesus killed precisely because they did not believe that Jesus was who he presented himself to be and others thought him to be—the Christ, the Son of the living God.[6] So, because of this very darkness, which was presently impossible to dispel, Jesus prays that his Father forgive them.[7] The irony is, presuming that those beneath the cross

5. We found a similar instance with the birth of Jesus. Matthew, simply mentioning that Jesus was born, moves immediately to the arrival of the magi. The magi manifest the significance of Jesus' birth—the newborn king of the Jews (see Mt 2:1-12). Similarly, in Luke, after Jesus is born, the action immediately shifts to the appearance of the angels to the shepherds. The glorious theophany of the angels and their message interprets the significance of the child wrapped in swaddling cloths and lying in a manger—in Bethlehem is born a Savior, Christ the Lord (see Lk 2:8-20).

6. Paul alludes to the invincible ignorance of the Jewish and Roman leaders. "None of the rulers of this age understood this [that God's wisdom is found in Jesus crucified]; for if they had, they would not have crucified the Lord of glory" (1 Cor 2:8). The odd thing is that if the rulers of this age had understood God's wisdom, and therefore would not have crucified the Lord of glory, then God's wisdom would not have been enacted, and humankind would not have been saved. But Paul seems to be stating a counterfactual. If the rulers knew Jesus was the Lord of glory, then there would really be no need to redeem them. Because they, and all of humankind, are sinners, they could not know the wisdom of God.

7. Jesus prays for their forgiveness, but it does not imply that the actions to which Pilate

heard him speak, that Jesus, in his very act of forgiveness, is revealing the truth for which he is falsely accused and the real reason for his crucifixion. The act of petitioning his Father's forgiveness on behalf of those who crucified him is a self-testimony that Jesus is indeed the Christ, the very Son of the living God, who is crucified so that sins may be forgiven. As the angel of the Lord spoke to Joseph, "You shall call his name Jesus, for he will save his people from their sins" (Mt 1:21). The very Jews who crucified him, "his people," are the first to benefit from his being "their" Savior—Jesus. This petitioning act of forgiveness, then, manifests that Jesus on the cross is lovingly offering himself as a petition to his Father for the forgiveness of all of humankind's sin, for in saving "his people" he is saving all of humankind. That sin, unbeknownst to every sinner of Adam's fallen race, was ultimately responsible for his death— no one knew what they were doing.[8] Thus this petitioning act of forgiveness is Jesus' first testimonial act within the crucifixion, whereby he bears witness to his becoming Jesus—YHWH-Saves.

The Mocking of Jesus

There is now an inversion within the Synoptic Gospels. Matthew and Mark first inform the reader of the inscriptive charge placed over Jesus' head and then narrate the crucifixion of the two thieves, followed by Jesus being mocked and ridiculed by the Jewish leaders. Having already noted the crucifixion of the two thieves, Luke first tells of the mocking and then concludes with the inscription. For the sake of clarity and emphasis, Luke's order will be followed. Matthew states:

> And those who passed by derided him, wagging their heads and saying, "You who would destroy the temple and build it in three days, save yourself! If you are the Son of God, come down from the cross." So also the chief priests, with the scribes and elders, mocked him saying, "He saved others; he cannot save himself. He is the King of Israel; let him come down now from the cross, and we will believe in him. He trusts in God; let God deliver him; for he said, 'I am the Son of God.'"

---

gave consent or the actions that the Jewish leaders insisted upon—Jesus' death—were not evil or entirely free of guilt. Although both may have been invincibly ignorant of who Jesus truly is, and so not subjectively guilty, both Pilate and the Jewish leaders knew Jesus was innocent of any wrongdoing. For that they are both justly guilty, and Jesus prays for their forgiveness.

8. In his Letter to the Romans, Paul demonstrates that all have sinned, Jew and Greek alike, and thus all are guilty and in need of salvation (see Rom 1:18-31 and 3:1-26).

364 THE PASSION NARRATIVES

Mark, while similar, has a couple of important differences:

> And those who passed by derided him, wagging their heads, and saying, "Aha! You who would destroy the temple and build it in three days, save yourself, and come down from the cross!" So also the chief priests mocked him to one another with the scribes, saying, "he saved others, he cannot save himself. Let the Christ, the King of Israel, come down from the cross, that we may see and believe."

Luke more briefly states:

> And the people stood by, watching; but the rulers scoffed at him saying, "He saved others; let him save himself, if he is the Christ of God, his Chosen One!" The soldiers also mocked him, coming up and offering him vinegar, and saying, "If you are the King of the Jews, save yourself!"

This scene is replete with theological and soteriological significance. First, what we observe beneath the cross was first choreographed within Psalm 22, a scene in which Jesus now narrates the action. "But I am a worm, and no man; scorned by men, and despised by the people. All who see me mock me, they make mouths at me, they wag their heads; he committed his cause to the Lord; let him deliver him, let him rescue him, for he delights in him!" (vv. 6-8). Although "worm" is a metaphor, its significance is not simply that others are treating Jesus as if he were a "worm" and not a "man." Rather, Jesus sees himself as a worm and not a man. In utter disgrace and humiliation, Jesus, on a purely human level, psychologically and emotionally perceives himself as worthless. The sarcastic scoffing of those below and the cynical scorning of the passersby, contemptuously mouthing "Aha" and satirically saying "Alas," and the vindictive wagging of snickering heads simply intensify and reinforce Jesus' own self-perception: "I am a worm."[9]

Second, the content of the mocking and scoffing is telling. First, "Aha! You who would destroy the temple and build it in three days, save yourself, and come down from the cross" (Mk). Matthew inserts: "If you are the Son of God, come down from the cross." The old false accusation of Jesus destroying the temple now has turned into ridicule. Hanging from a cross, Jesus is in no position to destroy anything, much less the temple, and having only three hours

---

9. While we are presently focusing on Psalm 22, it should not be forgotten that the Suffering Servant Songs, which we treated in chapter 10, are also relevant here. As was depicted within Jesus' trials, so once again here Jesus is the Suffering Servant who is "marred beyond human resemblance and his form beyond that of the sons of man," or crudely put, Jesus looks like a "worm." Again, Jesus is "despised and rejected by men, a man of sorrows, and acquainted with grief" (see Is 52:13-53:1-12).

to live, he does not have at his disposal the requisite three days to rebuild it—a temple that took forty years to complete. Nonetheless, if Jesus still thinks he can accomplish such a ludicrous feat, all he needs to do is come down from the cross and save himself, and then he will have all the time in the world to destroy and rebuild the temple. This would be especially so "if you are the Son of God." Residing in such ridiculing mirth again lies the irony of truth. Those who have just crucified Jesus are the ones destroying the old temple, for by killing Jesus, the incarnate Son of God, they are unwitting collaborators in his building the new temple in three days. Jesus, the Father's Son, on this cross, is configuring himself into the new high priest who is offering a holy and loving everlasting sacrifice of himself that will give entrance into the most holy place—the abode of his very own Father.

Third, the chief priests and scribes continue their mocking jibes. "He saved others; he cannot save himself. He is the King of Israel; let him come down now from the cross, and we will believe in him; let God deliver him, if he desires him; for he said, I am the Son of God'" (Mt). Mark is the same except for the Jewish leaders' designation of Jesus: "Let the Christ, the King of Israel, come down from the cross." Luke's rendering is: "He saved others; let him save himself, if he is the Christ of God, his Chosen One!" Luke also has the soldiers taunting Jesus: "If you are the King of the Jews, save yourself!" The ridicule is now shifting away from the mockery concerning the temple and toward Jesus being able to save himself and others. The shift revolves around who Jesus purports to be or what others believe him to be—the Son of God, the King of Israel, the Christ, the Chosen One of God and the King of the Jews.[10] Interestingly, in all three Synoptics, Jesus is said to have "saved others," but the manner is not specified. Presumably, the Jewish leaders have in mind Jesus' healings, exorcisms, and miracles. If this is the case, while they are ridiculing Jesus for being able to do such deeds and yet not be able to "save himself," they are admitting that such saving deeds were done. Thus their mockery redounds upon themselves, for if they acknowledge that Jesus did such saving deeds, their lack of faith in him is then self-condemnatory, for these deeds bear evidence to his being what is claimed concerning him. Moreover, those very saving deeds—curing the lame, blind, deaf, and dumb; casting out demons; raising the dead; multiplying the loaves—prefigured and anticipated the

10. The obvious should not be overlooked. All the titles for which Jesus is mocked find their source in Peter's profession of faith: "You are the Christ, the Son of the living God." As the Christ, Jesus is God's Chosen One, who will establish the messianic kingdom over which he will reign as the living Father's glorified Son.

saving deed that Jesus is presently enacting: freedom from sin with its deadly bodily consequences as well as procuring anew an abundance of everlasting life, even bodily life.

Nonetheless, having been able to save others, Jesus is taunted for now not being able to save himself. Unlike the saving of others, how Jesus can save himself is specified—by coming down from the cross. This saving of self is scornfully predicated upon who Jesus either supposedly claims to be or whom others claim him to be. Gazing sneeringly upon Jesus crucified, the Jewish leaders and the soldiers lampoon him as "King of Israel" (Mt), "the Christ, the King of Israel" (Mk), "the Christ of God, his Chosen One" (Lk), or "the King of the Jews" (Lk), sarcastically goading him to come down from the cross so that they might believe in him, and thereby acknowledging that their present taunts are true. Of course, all of this is, for them, laughable because they "know" that Jesus cannot come down and save himself, and therefore he is not any of those things for which they mock him. So they need not worry about ever having to believe in him. For the mockers (the Jewish leaders) and the scorners (the Roman soldiers), "salvation" resides in being unfettered from the cross, to leap miraculously down as the anointed Messiah, the Chosen one of God, thus demonstrating, for all to behold in believing amazement, that he is the King of Israel, the King of the Jews. Once again, the temptation that has haunted Jesus from his initial encounter with Satan has returned. "If you are the Son of God turn stones into bread, throw yourself down from temple's pinnacle and all of the kingdoms of the world will be yours if only you worship me" (see Mt 4:1-11 and Lk 4:1-13). Jesus can once more hear Peter's seductive words rising up from the deriding crowd below. "You are the Christ, the Son of the living God, the chosen one of God, far be it that you should be handed over, suffer and be crucified." But the taunt that strikes most deeply into Jesus' tempted heart and the one most likely to unnerve and demoralize him is the last: "He trusted in God; let God deliver him now, if he desires him; for he said, 'I am the Son of God'" (Mt). This is Jesus' final temptation—the eschatological temptation. Can he trust in his Father? Will his Father deliver him? Does his Father, could his Father, really desire a disgraced, rejected, lacerated, and crucified worm? The crowd below believes that such questions would be merely rhetorical—God's answer would be a resounding "No!" which plagues Jesus too.

Fourth, this final eschatological temptation must be read in the light of Psalm 22, which by making it his own prayer Jesus is both enacting and so interpreting his own crucifixion. Jesus sees himself as a worm, but his mockers, echoing Psalm 22, say, "He committed his cause to the Lord; let him de-liver him, let him rescue him, for he delights in him!" (Ps 22:6-8). Though "he delights in him" is said cynically by the Jewish leaders, it is precisely because Jesus has "committed his cause" to his Father that he can be assured, despite appearances, that he will be delivered and rescued, for he knows that he is do-ing that in which his Father delights—saving his Father's children. Similarly, the Jewish leaders are making their own the actions and words of the "ungod-ly" from the Book of Wisdom. They have laid in wait for the innocent man because he "is inconvenient to us" and "reproaches us" for our sins against the law. The just man claims to have knowledge of God and "calls himself a child/servant of the Lord." The righteous man's very life is a reproach and a burden. Yet he claims that the end of the good man is "happy," and "boasts that God is his father." So they wish to test him: "if the righteous man is God's son, he will help him, and will deliver him from the hand of his adversaries. Let us test him with insult and torture, that we may find out how gentle he is and make a trial of his forbearance. Let us condemn him to a shameful death, for, ac-cording to what he says, he will be protected" (Wis 2:12-20). Yet the wise man knows that wickedness has blinded the ungodly, for "they do not know the secret purposes of God." But Jesus, who embodies the very wisdom of God, knows that "the souls of the righteous are in the hands of God, and no tor-ment will ever touch them."[11] They just may look foolish and their death "an affliction" and a "destruction," yet "they are at peace" because, "having been disciplined a little, they will receive great good, because God tested them and found them worthy of himself; like gold in the furnace he tried them, and like a sacrificial burnt offering he accepted them. In the time of their visitation they will shine forth, and will run like sparks through the stubble. They will govern nations and rule peoples, and the Lord will reign over them forever" (Wis 2:21-3:9). What the Book of Wisdom describes is being visibly played out both beneath the cross and upon the cross, and so fulfilled in its fullest sense and in its most focused manner. The Jewish leaders and the Roman soldiers personify the ultimate blind folly of the ungodly, and Jesus embodies the per-fect expression of divine wisdom and holy goodness, which can only be found within the definitive manifestation of righteous suffering. Jesus, the gentle

---

11. Paul articulates the singular wisdom of God. "For Jews demand signs and the Greeks seek wisdom, but we preach Christ crucified, a stumbling block to Jews and folly to Gentiles, but to those who are called both Jews and Greeks, Christ the power of God and the wisdom of God. For the foolishness of God is wiser than men, and the weakness of God is stronger than men" (1 Cor 1:22-25).

servant Son, confidently knows that he is being disciplined and tested, and yet
that his pure sacrifice will be accepted by his Father, and thus that he will be
found worthy in his Father's presence.[12] As king of the nations, he will shine
forever forth like resplendent gold.[13]

Fifth, although ridicule, sneering, and mocking rise up to Jesus from beneath his cross, above his head silently hangs an inscription. Matthew and
Mark, prior to the onslaught of the mocking, inform the reader that this inscription recorded the "charge against him," which is not unusual since such
was done for all crucifixions. But Luke, after the mocking, says simply that
there was "also an inscription over him," with no mention of it being an accusation. Matthew and Mark are historically accurate, but Luke more clearly
makes a significant theological point, for in all three Synoptics, the inscription is a declarative sentence. "This is Jesus the King of the Jews" (Mt), "The
King of the Jews" (Mk), "This is the King of the Jews" (Lk). The mocking and
taunting of the Jewish leaders and the Roman soldiers always contain a sneering "if"—"If you are the Son of God" (Mt)—or a mocking that implies, "You
can't possibly be, but if you are, ha, ha, 'the King of Israel' or 'Christ, the King'
or 'the Chosen One of God' come down from the cross and save yourself."
There may be "if's" and the deriding mockery of unbelief from below, but
from above there are no "if's" and no hint of disdainful unbelief, nor even the
implication that what is stated is a criminal offense. There is only a straightforward statement of fact. Such is the significance of Matthew's and especially
of Luke's "This is" or Mark's even more direct "The." Who we have hanging on
the cross is "Jesus the King of the Jews." The declarative statement that comes
down from above also divests the denunciations of their mockery and unbelief, for they converge upon Jesus crucified, who hangs between and in him
the purity of truth. The cross irrevocably separates the darkness of falsehood
from the light of truth. Jesus is the King of the Jews/Israel precisely because
he, as the Son of God, is the Christ, the Chosen One of God, and he is such

12. The Letter to the Hebrews states, "Although he was Son, he learned obedience through
what he suffered" (Heb 5:8). Jesus learned what it truly meant to be the Father's incarnate obedient Son through his obedience to the will of his Father, even suffering death on the cross.
See also Heb 12:3-11, where it speaks of God disciplining his sons so that they may bear much
fruit—Jesus is the perfect exemplar of his Father's discipline.

13. So as not to lose sight of one of our significant theological concerns, at this point within
the Passion Narrative we now have three Old Testament passages in play, all of which are being
fulfilled and so are essential intertwining hermeneutical keys for properly interpreting Jesus'
crucifixion: the Suffering Servant Songs from Isaiah, Psalm 22, and chapters 2 and 3 from the
Book of Wisdom. These will coalesce and crescendo momentarily upon Jesus' death.

precisely because of the cross upon which he hangs. Upon the cross, Jesus, as the Spirit-filled Christ, the Chosen one of his Father, is transfiguring himself into the King of Israel by offering himself as a loving sacrifice to his Father for the forgiveness of sin, thus destroying the satanic kingdom of death so as to give birth to the messianic kingdom of life. While the wagging heads of boisterous guffawing, mocking, and taunting have long since fallen into silence, the silent inscription tacked upon a dead tree continues to echo throughout the ages and will find its full voice when Jesus returns in glory.[14]

The Two Thieves

Matthew and Mark next narrate the crucifixion of the two thieves on either side of Jesus, while Luke alone, having already spoke of their crucifixion, tells of their dialogue with Jesus.[15] While Matthew and Mark state that both the thieves "reviled Jesus" in the same manner as the Jewish leaders and the Roman soldiers, Luke has a much more nuanced version. One thief, parroting the mockery that was taking place beneath Jesus, said, "Are you not the Christ? Save yourself and us!" This "bad" thief obviously did not believe that Jesus was the Christ (though the manner of his opening question may imply that he had heard about him), but in sordid desperation he was willing to harass Jesus in the frantic hope that he just might do something that would get the threesome released. But the "good" thief (really he is a "bad" thief who becomes "good") rebuked him, "Do you not fear God, since you are under the same sentence of condemnation? And we indeed justly; for we are receiving the due reward of

14. John's Gospel accentuates the theological significance of the inscription, for "the Jews" wanted it changed: "Do not write, 'The King of the Jews,' but, 'This man said I am the King of the Jews.'" Pilate responded, "What I have written I have written" (Jn 19:19-22). Pilate here expresses the final prophetic word of the Father. It is Jesus' Father who has designated the crucified Jesus to be King of the Jews, and what he has written will not be changed.

The voices of jeering Jewish leaders and taunting Roman soldiers are no longer heard, yet unbelievers throughout the centuries and to this day continue to mock the crucified Jesus, ridiculing the notion that such could be the Savior of the world and the Lord of all. Often this takes the form of mocking the church and Christian believers, even to the point of overt persecution. But the Book of Revelation depicts the saints and heavenly hosts as forever giving praise and glory to the crucified and risen Jesus (see, e.g., Rv 5:12-14).

15. That Jesus was crucified amid two criminals fulfills Isaiah 53:12, that the Suffering Servant would be "numbered with transgressors; yet he bore the sin of many, and made intercession for the transgressors." Within Luke, Jesus quotes this passage upon his arrest and in response to Peter's attempted rescue: "For I tell you that this scripture must be fulfilled in me, 'and he was reckoned with transgressors, for what is written of me must be fulfilled'" (Lk 22:37-38).

our deeds; but this man has done nothing wrong." Both thieves face the same condemnation as Jesus, but they justly for the criminal deeds they have done, and thus they should fear God's judgment. Unlike the "bad" thief, the "good" thief perceives the truth, even though he too heard the mocking and sneering. The juvenile inanity of the heckling, the inherent vileness within the hissing, and above all the pitiless vulgarity of the gloating over the crucifixion itself, may have led him to grasp the truth within the sneers and taunts—Jesus is the Christ, the Chosen Son of God and therefore is the King of the Jews/Israel. Certainly, the "good" thief knew that the man next to him upon a like cross was innocent. So, he made this simple but heartfelt request: "Jesus, remember me when you come into your kingdom." Jesus responds: "Truly, I say to you, today you will be with me in Paradise."

In his use of the word "Paradise," Jesus provides the theological interpretive key to this whole scenario. "Paradise" is the word used within the Greek Septuagint for the Hebrew word *gan*, meaning "garden"; thus the Garden of Eden is a Paradise—devoid of evil and filled with abundant life with its beauty, joy, and blessedness. Within the Book of Genesis, this is portrayed as Adam and Eve walking together with God amid the bounteous goodness of God's creation. This abruptly ended when Adam and Eve ate from the forbidden tree of knowledge of good and evil. In so doing, they suffered God's promised consequence: death. God cast them out of "Paradise" lest they should eat of the tree of life and placed a "cherubim, and a flaming sword which turned every way, to guard the way to the tree of life" (see Gn 2:15 to 3:1-24).

Portrayed before us are three crucified men, each hanging from his respective tree. Two are justly condemned to death because of their crime, their deadly sin. The other man is "condemned" to death but is innocent because he has done no deadly deed, no deadly sin. The "good" thief asks Jesus, the innocent man, to remember him when he comes into his kingdom, thus acknowledging that Jesus is indeed a king. Jesus does not simply say that he will remember him, but promises him that he will be with him in Paradise this very day. Both thieves are of the sinful race of Adam, justly suffering the consequences of their sin—death—and so now they are nailed to the tree of good and evil, of which all of Adam's race have eaten. The "bad" thief remains crucified to his "bad" tree. But the "good" thief, because of his repentant plea, is taken from his "bad" tree and placed upon Jesus' "good" tree—the tree of life. Ironically, while the Jewish leaders and Roman soldiers were mocking Jesus, taunting him to come down off the cross and so save himself as he had saved others, Jesus does save another, the "good" thief, by staying on his own cross.

Only because the innocent Jesus, who is also a son of Adam's fallen race, remains upon his cross does his cross become the tree of life, for only in dying does Jesus enter the heavenly paradise that is God's kingdom, of which he will be king.

Remarkably, Jesus is once again enacting the very theological meaning of the cross upon which he is crucified—not by his words but in his actions. Within the story of the "good" and "bad" thieves, then, is the whole history of salvation enacted in one short vignette: the reversal of the fall of Adam and Eve and the re-creation of the whole of humankind, restoring humankind into God's image and likeness after the manner of Jesus, the eternal and perfect likeness of the Father in whom and through whom all was initially created. But it must not be overlooked that the "bad" thief remains one of Adam's condemned children suffering the punishment of his sin—everlasting death— while the "good" thief becomes a child of the new Adam—Jesus—and so enters into everlasting life. Only those who repent of their sin, like the "good" thief, and believe in Jesus, partaking of him, who is the tree of life, can enter God's kingdom, where they attain communion with God his Father. Before the gate of Paradise, the cherubim has been discharged from his sentinel post, and the flaming sword has been extinguished, and once again the fallen but now redeemed race of Adam can walk with God in union with Jesus, the son of Adam and the Father's Son and eat of the tree of life.

What we also witness in this event is Jesus enacting his name. He is becoming Jesus—YHWH-Saves. Because Jesus places the saving of the "good" thief within the context of Adam's sin within the Garden of Eden, he is revealing that he, as the Father's Suffering Servant/Son, is assuming the sinful history of all humankind; that is, in assuming humankind's sinful nature, he has assumed, taken into his very humanity, the totality of humankind's sin: he "was numbered with transgressors; and yet he bore the sins of many, and made intercession for the transgressors" (Is 53:12). Not only is Jesus saving the good thief, but in so doing he is also prophetically portraying, in this present salvific event, that he is saving all humankind, for he is transforming his evil cross, the tree of good and evil, into the paradisial tree of life, for on the cross he is transfiguring himself into Jesus—vanquishing the sin of all with its condemnatory death and so restoring life to all. In becoming Jesus, the tree of death upon which he was crucified becomes, upon his death, the tree of life. Only then does Jesus come down off his cross as the mocking Jewish leaders, the taunting Roman soldiers, and the desperate harassing "bad" thief goaded him to do, for only in dying on the condemnatory tree of death did he become the saving tree of life. And in so doing, Jesus did what all his hecklers and scoffers deemed impossible of a belittled man hanging on a cross: he fully saved others by not saving himself.[16]

The Death of Jesus
Psalm 22

All three Synoptics now inform us that at the sixth hour "there was darkness over the whole land until the ninth hour."[17] Luke provides the reason: "while the sun's light failed" or "the sun was eclipsed." This darkening of the sun at its zenith, even if it is of natural causes and not a miraculous phenomenon, fulfills God's prophecy in the Book of Amos. There God decries the sins of the people and foretells a day of punishment. "'And on that day,' says the Lord God, 'I will make the sun go down at noon, and darken the earth in broad daylight. I will turn your feasts into mourning, and all of your songs into lamentations.... I will make it like the mourning for an only son, and the end of it like a bitter day'" (Am 8:9-10). The Jews are on the threshold of celebrating their most sacred feast, Passover, and yet the darkening of the noonday sun upon its approach augurs lamentation as upon the death of an only son—a bitter day. On this darkened bitter day, the Father's only Son will die, occasioning lamentation from those who love him—then, now, and until the end of time. Yet such mourning will turn to joy, for on this festival Passover the new and final lamb of sacrifice is offered for the forgiveness of sins. While Luke adds "and the curtain of the temple was torn in two," Matthew and Mark place this rending of the temple's curtain at the moment of Jesus' death. The theological significance of this darkening and rending will be treated in accord with their accounts. For Luke, there is a causal relationship here between the darkening of the sun and the rending of the temple's curtain. It is enough to state that the dark death of Jesus allows light to enter into the darkness of the temple—into the once forbidden darkness of the Holy of Holies.

Luke proceeds immediately to the death of Jesus, but Matthew and Mark narrate Jesus speaking his last words: "And about the ninth hour Jesus cried

16. Jesus is here fulfilling his own Gospel principle—he who denies himself, loses his life, by taking up his cross will save it (see Mt 16:24-6; Mk 10:38-39; Lk 14:27 and 17:33; Jn 12:25). Because Jesus did not "save himself," he will be raised gloriously from the dead, and thus he will find his true life.

17. All passages in this section are from Mt 27:45-56, Mk 15:33-41, and Lk 23:44-49 unless otherwise noted.

out with a loud voice, 'Eli, Eli, lama sabachthani?' that is 'My God, my God, why have you forsaken me?' And some of the bystanders hearing it said, 'This man is calling Elijah.' And one of them ran and took a sponge, and put it on a reed, and gave it to him to drink. But others said, 'Wait, let us see whether Elijah will come to save him'" (Mt). Mark, upon whom Matthew is dependent, is similar with a few variations. While Matthew uses the Hebrew "Eli," Mark retains the original Aramaic "Eloi." Again, while Matthew narrates that some wanted to wait to see if "Elijah will come to save him," Mark has them say, "Wait, let us see whether Elijah will come to take him down." Because Jesus' cry of dereliction is theologically more complex, I first discuss the crowd's mishearing of his words.

Although the confusion of what Jesus says stems from the similarity between "Eli" (Mt) or "Eloi" (Mk) with "Elijah," one wonders whether Jesus at this point in his agony is finding it difficult to speak, especially in the light that crucifixion caused death by asphyxia—the weight of one's hanging body finally making inhalation physically impossible. The fact that the Gospels speak of a "loud cry" may suggest that Jesus was not only vocalizing the emotions that lay in the deepest recesses of his heart, but also attempting, with his last, most physically imperiled effort, to render clearly those innermost thoughts and feelings. The cumulative effect was that he was no longer able to speak clearly, even with his utmost physical exertion, and so slurred or garbled his words and was thus misunderstood. The man Jesus, the Son of God incarnate, is undergoing an excruciating death nailed to a cross. This is not a Hollywood production.

The way Jesus is mistaken is theologically significant. Because Elijah was taken alive up to heaven, it was commonly believed that he would return as the harbinger of the messianic kingdom, for according to Malachi, "Behold, I will send you Elijah the prophet before the great and terrible day of the Lord comes" (Mal 5:4; see 2 Kgs 2:11). Although those beneath the cross may have misheard Jesus, the readers of the Gospel know that Elijah had already come in the person of John the Baptist. Jesus himself stated, "and if you are willing to accept it, he [John] is Elijah who is to come. He who has ears to hear let him hear" (Mt 11:14-15). Ironically, those beneath him did not have ears to hear and so now mishear Jesus, believing that he was calling upon Elijah to come. In stating again that John is Elijah, Jesus also says that John's enemies "did to him whatever they pleased. So also the Son of man will suffer at their hands" (Mt 17:11-13; see also Mk 9:11-13). Those who refused to pay heed to John's call to a baptism of repentance, not only Herod but also the Jewish leaders, will be the same ones who crucify Jesus, a scene that is now being enacted. While one fellow scurries to give Jesus a drink of vinegar, presumably to perk him up with its sour taste and so ensure that he does not die before Elijah's anticipated appearance, others irritably stop him lest he obstruct Elijah's coming. Because the readers of the Gospel know that Elijah has already come, they perceive this chaotic bustling as mad foolishness—Elijah cannot come because he has already come. More importantly, they realize that because Elijah has already appeared, what is presently being enacted is precisely the reason that Elijah did appear—the in-breaking of God's messianic kingdom as well as the great and terrible day of God's eschatological judgment. In their wanting to see if Elijah will come and save Jesus by taking him down from the cross, thus fulfilling their own goading of Jesus, the Gospel readers perceive that, again, it is precisely in Jesus staying upon the cross that the purpose of Elijah's antecedent appearance is being served. Thus the mishearing of Jesus' words and the brief madcap muddle that ensues highlights what is really taking place: Jesus is the Messiah, of whom Elijah is his harbinger, who is inaugurating God's eschatological kingdom. The cross is not something from which Jesus needs to be saved but is the very instrument upon which he is saving God's people from sin and death and so procuring his ability, through his resurrection, to baptize in the Holy Spirit—the very thing that John, the true Elijah, prophetically proclaimed that he would do.

We have already observed that Jesus' crucifixion is being theologically read through the lens of Psalm 22, through which Jesus offers his own first-person interpretation. This now finds its fullest climatic expression in Jesus' final words, the Psalm's opening verse: "My God, my God, why have you forsaken me?" By taking it out of its full context, that first verse could be understood as Jesus giving expression to his experiencing the abandonment of his Father, of his being utterly forsaken in his most needy hour, and so a cry of absolute despair. But a much more nuanced interpretation is necessary, one that considers not only the entirety of the psalm but also the Suffering Servant Songs as well as the Book of Wisdom, chapters 2-3, all of which conjoin at this decisive salvific moment.[18]

On one level, Jesus genuinely exclaims, "My God, my God, why have you forsaken me? Why are you so far from my groaning? O my God, I cry by day, but you do not answer; and by night, but find no rest" (Ps 22:1-2). From the time of his lonely agony, through his humiliating arrest and bogus trials, through his scourging and crowning with thorns—and now within the bar-

18. For further theological treatment of Jesus' cry of abandonment within the contemporary discussion of whether God suffers, see my *Does God Suffer?* (Edinburgh: T&T Clark, 2000), 172-213.

rage of vile mocking, cynical sneering, callous taunting, and tittering gloat-ing—Jesus humanly feels emotionally shattered and psychologically dehu-manized: "I am a worm and no man." Added to this is the sheer physical pain of the crucifixion itself—the throbbing of vein and convulsing of muscle and the escalating inability to keep erect in order simply to breathe. His body has reached the point of total shock and complete exhaustion, with every vital or-gan desperately struggling to function and yet fast failing within him. Thus Je-sus makes his own the lament of Psalm 22: "I am poured out like water, and all my bones are out of joint; my heart is like wax, it is melted within my breast; my strength is dried up like a potsherd, and my tongue cleaves to my jaws; you lay me in the dust of death" (vv. 14-15). This suffering, however, is but the physical expression of an even deeper suffering—Jesus' bearing the weight of sin and its condemnation—separation from God. No earthly human being ever experiences or knows the full evil of sin, nor does anyone anticipate the sheer horror and doomed despair of being separated from God, yet Jesus now, having assumed humankind's sinful humanity, endures sin's full force and the absolute evil that resides therein, and so experiences its attending helplessness in the face of divine condemnation.

Within all this anguish and travail, there still lies Jesus' unsatisfied desire, his deepest longing, to be with his Father. Jesus, as the Father's Son incarnate, from the time of his youthful consciousness of being the Father's Son, longed to experience the fullness of that reality, the fullness of being the beloved Son. He self-consciously knew, possessing the Father's Spirit of Sonship, who he was, but the full human experience was yet to be fulfilled. Thus Jesus grew, impelled and inflamed by his inner Spirit of Sonship, in his ardent yearning to experience fully his Father's love, to experience fully his filial communion, as the Father's only Son. Equally and concomitantly, Jesus so longed to love and glorify his Father in the fullness of his Spirit of Sonship and in the totality of his humanity as the Father's only Son. What hindered this full paternal/filial experience of love is that Jesus, as the Son incarnate, still lived as a member of Adam's fallen race; his humanity was Adam's, and as such he was incapable of abiding fully in the presence of his Father and so experience the totality of his Father's love for him, nor could he express fully and adequately his love for his Father. What is being enacted on the cross, just moments before his death, is a clash, a colliding, of Jesus attempting to love his Father fully as Son and so experience fully his Father's love for him, but the very act by which Jesus is attempting to do this appears to be hindering its fulfillment. In his sacrificial death, in his drinking the cup, Jesus desired to love his Father with the fullness of his human love, yet in his dying, his Father's love for him appears to be totally absent. Death appears to be the insurmountable wall that separates Jesus, the Father's Son, and God, the Son's Father, and in a true sense it was; death, separation from God, was but the consequence of sin—the inability to abide with the all-holy God. In the face of death, Jesus felt helpless in his forsakenness, for the thing he desired most—fully abiding with his loving Father—appeared doomed, slain by death itself. This precipitates Jesus' loud cry: "My God, my God, why have you forsaken me?" To all appearances, even to Jesus himself, this is what his Father has done—he has abandoned Jesus to sin-condemning death with every humanly possible evil that accompanies it.

Now, on another level, what must be first observed and is often never noticed is that Jesus is asking a question: "why?" "Why, my God, have you forsaken me?" In verse 2, Jesus bemoans the fact that, while he cries and groans to his God all day long, "you do not answer." The question that Jesus is asking is on his own behalf—his needs to know why he has seemingly been abandoned by his Father. Second, what is also often not appreciated is that Jesus, in quoting the psalm, addresses God as "my God." Jesus is not calling upon God as a distant deity with whom he has little or no relationship, but a God who personally is his. This "My God" coming from Jesus' mouth echoes his last night's "Abba, Father," "My Father," in Gethsemane. There he asked his Father to take the cup from him; now Jesus is asking his Father, having willingly drunk the cup, why he seemingly has abandoned him. When treating Jesus' agony, we noted that the Father never responded to him. He never said to Jesus, "I will that you drink the cup." There was simply silence, and yet Jesus knew, a knowledge that resided within him from his baptism, that he, as the Father's faithful Servant-Son, must drink the cup in accordance with his Father's will, and so in the garden he purposely strode forward to meet the arresting crowd. So now here again, while drinking the cup, his Father is also silent. The Father's very silence is the dregs of the ultimate cup of suffering that Jesus must drink to the very last drop. To experience his Father's silence is to experience his Father's seeming abandonment. This is Jesus' final temptation! As within his agony, however, Jesus addresses God within the assurance of their mutual intimacy. It is "my God," Jesus' "Abba-Father" who appears to have forsaken him. That "my" deprives the "forsaken" of its ultimate reality and transforms it into a mere "appearance." Yes, all the physical suffering is real. All the debilitating emotions are authentic—even that of experiencing God's damning judgment of sin. The inner human sentiment of complete forsakenness is tangible, and its sense of utter helplessness is unfeigned. Yes, death itself is the gulf that separates Jesus, the Son, from God, his Father. But this genuineness does not rob the "my" of its truth. The suffering of abandonment may be real, but the reality of being forsaken is not. Amid real suffering and genuine tormenting feelings, "my God," my "Abba-Father," has not actually abandoned "me," precisely because of the "my." That "my" expresses the personal, intimate, unbreakable, and ever anchored Spirit-of-Sonship communion of love between Jesus, the Father's Son, and God, the Son's Father. As will be made manifest in the resurrection, the Spirit's bond of love between Jesus and his Father shatters the separating wall of death. The deadly cross does not slay the love between the Father and Jesus, his Son. Rather, the Spirit-filled love between the Father and Jesus, the Son, a love that is enacted fully on the cross, slays death, allowing Jesus and his Father to experience fully their mutual communion of Spirit-filled love. And in praying the remainder of Psalm 22, Jesus answers, in the presence of his silent Father, his own heartrending question. As Jesus stepped forward to meet the arresting crowd, he moved forward in his prayer, not stopping at his abandoned cry to his silent Father.

The Father's silence gives rise to Jesus' assured hope, a supreme trust that could only be fully expressed and wholly manifested within the Father's "forsaken" silence. The Father's voicelessness elicits Jesus' uttered hope: "Yet you are holy, enthroned on the praises of Israel. In you our fathers trusted; they trusted, and you did deliver them. To you they cried, and were saved; in you they trusted, and were not disappointed" (Ps 22:3-5). The silent Father is holy, the destroyer of all evil and the maker of all holiness, and him Jesus is presently enthroning within his own praises as the embodiment of the soon to be new Israel. As his Jewish fathers were saved when they cried, so he, who embodies their whole history, will not be disappointed either. Jesus may think of himself as "a worm, and no man," but "you are he who took me from the womb; you did keep me safe upon my mother's breast. Upon you was I cast from my birth, and since my mother bore me you have been my God. Be not far from me, for trouble is near and there is none to help me" (vv. 6-11). From his conception by the overshadowing of the Holy Spirit and since his birth from Mary, Jesus has been kept safe by his Father, for Jesus has always acknowledged him to be "my God." In his present trouble, then, he is assured that his Father is near even when there is no one else to aid him. So Jesus can confidently petition his Father: "But you, O Lord, be not far off! O you my help, hasten to my aid! Deliver my soul from the sword, my life from the power of the dog! Save me from the mouth of the lion, my afflicted soul from the horns of the wild oxen!" (vv. 19-22).

If Jesus did not truly experience what appeared to be his Father's abandonment, humankind would have never known the depth of Jesus' love for his Father and how much he cherished the Father's love of him. Nor would humankind grasp the trust that Jesus had in his loving Father, that amid seeming abandonment he never faltered in doubt of that love. Nor would humankind have perceived Jesus' love on its behalf, for he was willing to embrace that level of human suffering so that humankind might never experience being separated from his Father owing to sins condemnation. In so doing, Jesus not only becomes the exemplar of humankind's needed love and trust in God in its suffering, but also the source of that loving trust, for by living in him, the Father's never-abandoning love is ever present.

Although Jesus has focused his passion and death upon his praying Psalm 22, that prayer is in keeping with and corroborated by the other two major interpretive Scriptures: the Suffering Servant Songs and the Book of Wisdom, chapters 2 and 3. All three Scriptures portray the same unvarying soteriological pattern—the unjust suffering of the righteous is in accord with God's will and, because the righteous one is doing God's will, God is ever present within the very evil suffering he endures. And while the righteous one may be scorned and mocked and thought abandoned by God, God will rescue his holy one, lifting him up into reigning glory and making his name remembered forever. Likewise, the rescued suffering servant exults in God, who rescued him and saved him the grip of his enemies.[19] Various personal examples of righteous suffering, Jeremiah for instance, permeate the Old Testament and so exemplify the truth of this scriptural pattern, but Jesus crucified now fulfills both the exampled personages and the relevant prophetic passages. The

19. Many psalms follow this pattern (see, e.g., Psalms 3, 5, 6, 7, 13, 17, 23, 27, 30, 31, 34, 37, 38, 54, 55, 56, 57, 59, 61, 64, 69, 70, 86, 88, 102, 107, 109, 116, 130, 142, and 143). Additionally, Psalm 35 must be particularly noted, for it reiterates and complements Psalm 22. The psalmist calls upon God to "contend" with his foes and to say "to my soul, 'I am your deliverance.'" His foes seek his life and entrap him, but upon being rescued, "my soul shall rejoice in the Lord" along with "all of my bones." Although his enemies "mock me more and more, gnashing at me with their teeth," upon God's aid, "I will thank you in the great congregation; in the mighty throng I will praise you." Even though they say "Aha, Aha!" the Lord will not be silent nor be far away. Thus he concludes by rejoicing, "'Great is the Lord, who delights in the welfare of his servant!' Then my tongue shall tell of your righteousness and of your praise all the day long."

Regarding Psalm 35 and the other examples noted, it must be remembered not only that they would have been prayed by Jesus, but also that they are prayed definitively only by Jesus, for only he prays them in the most comprehensive manner, voicing the fullest and deepest articulation of their intent. Similarly, only those who presently abide in Jesus can pray them, in union with him, fully in harmony with their inspired purpose and meaning.

righteous men and women prefigured Jesus, and these prophetic Scriptures ultimately had only Jesus in mind, for only he fully embodies the innocent righteous man, only he fully takes upon himself the sin of the world, only he dies on behalf of humankind, only he fully suffers for righteousness's sake, only he fully offers himself to God as a sacrifice of reconciliation. That these anticipatory personages and prophetic passages find their total enactment in Jesus is found in how God, his Father, responds, in a way he never acted previously. The Father raises him gloriously from the dead and in so doing testifies that all that prophetically went before has now been enacted and so accomplished in Jesus, his Son.[20]

Therefore Jesus could rightly pray, in expectant anticipation, the closing verses of the Psalm. "I will tell of your name to my brethren; in the midst of the congregation I will praise you" (v. 22). His congregating brethren will be his future church. To his faithful, he will forever sing the glory of his Father. In so doing, Jesus will equally be exhorting them: "You, who fear the Lord, praise him! All you sons of Jacob, glorify him, and stand in awe of him, all you sons of Israel! For he has not despised or abhorred the affliction of the afflicted; and he has not hid his face from him, but has heard, when he cried out to him" (vv. 23-24). The whole Jewish nation is to glorify God and stand in awe of him because he has not despised nor abhorred Jesus, for to Jesus his Son, God has shown his face as Father. Likewise, because of what his Father has done for him, "All the ends of the earth shall remember and turn to the Lord; and all the families of nations shall worship him. For dominion belongs to the Lord, and he rules over the nations" (vv. 27-28). In Jesus the Son, all "posterity shall serve him [his Father]; men shall tell of the Lord to the coming generation, and proclaim his deliverance to people yet unborn, that he has wrought it" (vv. 30-31). Significantly, although God the Father will hear and answer his prayer and so raise him up because of the salvation Jesus has wrought, the conclusion of Jesus' prayer is not the praise of himself for what he has done, but rather the praise of his Father for what he has done through him—those who abide in Jesus, Jews and Gentiles alike, will, together with one voice, forever sing with him the praises of the Father.[21]

20. In the Gospel of John, Jesus' last words are: "It is finished" (Jn 19:30). Jesus' salvific work is finished, and contained within that finished work are all God's previous saving deeds. Jesus embodies the whole of salvation history and will bring it to full conclusion when he comes in glory at the end of time.

21. This is likewise seen in the Ephesian hymn, where God the Father is praised and glorified for all that he has accomplished in Christ through the Holy Spirit (Eph 1:3-14). See also the Philippian hymn (Phil 2: 5-11).

Simultaneous to this most acute temptation, which gives rise to his praying Psalm 22, Jesus also perceives, in the inner recesses of his Spirit-filled heart and mind, that it is on account of his being the Christ, the Chosen One, that he, as the Father's Servant-Son, is to remain upon the cross, for that cross is to be the throne from which he will reign as King of Israel and so be Savior of the world. He will truly save others through his sacrificial death, and in so doing he will save himself through his glorious resurrection, which will manifest his Father's deliverance and testify to his Father's desire for him, thus confirming that Jesus, this worm and no man, is indeed his beloved Son in whom he is well pleased.

Here we also observe that while Jesus, in praying Psalm 22, was seeking an answer to his own dire situation and finding it in the very prayer he was praying, he also forced those who would be told of his death, either by others or in reading the Gospels, to ask: "Why has God forsaken this man?" By vocalizing the opening verse for all to hear, Jesus was revealing to all, in every age, the reason for his god-forsaken abandonment, which first appears to be irrational and so absurd. To answer their own present question, Jesus directs them to pray the psalm, for in so praying it they will not only receive the answer to their question, as did Jesus, but also give glory and thanks with Jesus to the seemingly silent Father for the saving death of his only Son, their now Lord and Savior.[22]

The Loud Cry

Within Matthew and Mark, the telling of the frenzied reaction to Jesus' possibly calling upon Elijah to save him abruptly ends with the death of Jesus. "And Jesus cried out again with a loud voice and yielded up his spirit (*pneuma*)" (Mt). "And Jesus uttered a loud cry, and breathed his last" (Mk). Having narrated the eclipse of the sun and the rending of the temple's curtain (not having Jesus loudly intone Psalm 22), Luke states, "Then, crying out with a loud voice, said, 'Father, into your hands I commit my spirit (*pneuma*)!' And having said this he breathed his last" (Lk).[23]

All three Gospels indicate that Jesus cried with a "loud voice" or uttered a

---

22. Paul is aware of the scandal of the cross. "For the Jews demand signs and the Greeks seek wisdom, but we preach Christ crucified, a stumbling block to Jews and folly to Gentiles, but to those who are called, both Jews and Greeks, Christ the power of God and the wisdom of God" (1 Cor 22-25).

23. All quotations in this section are from Mt 27:45-56, Mk 15:33-41, and Lk 23:44-49 unless otherwise noted.

"loud cry" immediately prior to his death, Matthew noting that this was the second time, the first being his crying out "My God, my God, why have you forsaken me." The cry was that of Jesus' final and most acute temptation—the seeming abandonment of his loving Father, his drinking fully of his cup of suffering. The second cry, only seconds later, is that of Jesus breathing his last breath (Mk) or, more deliberately, his "yielding up his spirit" (Mt). If the first loud cry gave expression to Jesus' great distress in not experiencing the presence of his Father at this most critical of all times, the second loud cry gives expression to Jesus casting off his distress, the vanquishing of his final satanic temptation, and the giving up of himself to his Father wholly in love. If Jesus, with all the physical energy that he could muster, cried out to his Father in agonizing desolation, so now Jesus—ardently rallying the last of his bodily strength and urgently marshalling his whole inner being, human mind, and will—intentionally and freely surrenders himself to his Father with one last loud cry. Jesus' loud cry is the act of his "giving up" of his sacred body "for you" and the act of his "pouring out" of his innocent blood "for you," the act that is the forgiveness of sins and the act that is the new covenant (see Mt 26:26-28, Mk 14:22-24, and Lk 22:19-20). This loud cry is the sacrificial act that simultaneously constitutes Jesus as the supreme high priest and configures him into the pure and holy sacrificial victim. This loud cry expresses his complete love for both his Father and for all men and women, for he is lovingly offering himself to his Father on the loving behalf of all humankind. Thus, in this love-imbued sacrificial loud cry, Jesus, the Son of God, is humanly breaking free from his sin-scarred humanity that he inherited from his father Adam and breaking into, through the darkness of sin's condemning death, the light of God, his Father. As Luke narrates, "Then Jesus with a loud voice, said, 'Father, into your hands I commit my spirit!' And having said this he breathed his last." The "loud cry" is the "breathing of his last" (Mk) and so the "yielding up of his spirit" (Mt), which is the committing of his spirit "into the hands" of his Father (Lk). Interestingly, while Matthew and Mark give Jesus' last words as "My God, my God, why have you forsaken me?" Luke instead narrates Jesus' last words, which are absent in Matthew and Mark, as "Father, into your hands I commit my spirit!" From this perspective, the two "loud cries" become bookends. In the first, Jesus expresses the depth of his suffering, the seeming abandonment of "my God." In the second, Jesus expresses the reality that he can confidently entrust, his very life-engendering spirit, to his loving "Father." Between those two loud cries, only moments apart, Jesus discards the final temptation to despair in the face of death, and in so doing fully constitutes himself as Jesus—YHWH-Saves, for the loud cry of death's condemnation becomes the loud cry of humankind's salvation.[24]

It appears at first glance that the Holy Spirit is absent from the Gospels' Passion Narratives. We asserted above that the Holy Spirit is the unbreakable bond of love between Jesus, the Son, and his Father during his experience of his Father's seeming absence, but even there the Spirit is not explicitly mentioned. Again, at the moment of Jesus' death, the Holy Spirit is not named. But Jesus, as the Father's incarnate Son, uniquely possesses, as the Christ, the Spirit of Sonship. This is soteriologically significant, for only in possessing the Holy Spirit, in being the Christ, can Jesus wholly give himself as a loving sacrifice to his Father, and only in the love of the Spirit can he do so on humankind's behalf. Although Jesus, the Son incarnate, is the lead active salvific actor, he is not the sole salvific performer, for the Holy Spirit is also acting within him so as to empower him to give himself entirely in love. Jesus, as the new high priest, may be offering himself as the new sacrificial victim, but what makes him the new high priest and what makes the sacrifice of himself efficacious is the Holy Spirit. The Holy Spirit empowers his loving and holy high priestly act, thus making him the supreme high priest, and simultaneously the Holy Spirit imbues the sacrificial offering of himself, his last Spirit-filled breath, to his Father, making him the supreme loving and holy sacrifice. Thus Jesus' saving death, his breathing forth of his spirit into the hands of his Father, is a perichoretic act, the communal intertwining one saving act of Jesus,

---

24. The Gospel of John narrates neither Jesus' loud cry of abandonment (Mt and Mk) nor his loud cry commending his life to his Father (Lk). Rather, John tells us that "knowing that all was finished, Jesus said [to fulfill the Scripture], 'I thirst.'" In response "they," presumably the soldiers, held a sponge soaked in vinegar to his mouth. "When Jesus had received the vinegar, he said, 'It is finished,' and he bowed his head and gave up his spirit (*pneuma*)" (Jn 19:28-30). Jesus' physical thirst manifests his inner spiritual thirst—his passionate thirst to finish the work of salvation. Although the soldiers compassionately give Jesus vinegar to relieve his thirst, what they gave him to drink is the cheap bitter or sour wine that is hardly palatable unless spiced. For John, in drinking the vinegar, Jesus is drinking the final sour drop of his cup of suffering that, in the light of Matthew and Mark, is the bitter suffering of his Father's apparent absence. Having drunk fully this final suffering, his redemptive suffering "is finished," and so he simply and calmly "bows his head and gave up his spirit." John's use of *pneuma* implies not only that Jesus breathed his last, but also that he gave up his Spirit, his full self in his Spirit of Sonship, to his Father. As Son, having been eternally conformed into the Father's loving Son through the Holy Spirit, Jesus, who was conceived as the Son of God incarnate through the power of the Holy Spirit and anointed as the Christ at his baptism in the same Holy Spirit, now gives himself as man completely as the loving Son, in the same Spirit of love, to his Father. Although John has neither loud cry, he does articulate a clear theology of both—the "vinegar" cry of suffering (Mt and Mk) and the loving cry of "giving up" into the hands of his Father "his spirit" (Lk).

the Son, and the Holy Spirit. As Jesus truly becomes Jesus, Son-YHWH-Saves, in the sacrificial act of his death, so too does the Holy Spirit fully become Spirit-YHWH-Saves in that very same saving act.

Unlike the Holy Spirit, the Father is explicitly present within Jesus' saving act, even in his apparent absence, and in a twofold manner. First, being the Father, he is present as the author of the entire salvific work that is now being conclusively enacted upon the cross. The Father wills that Jesus, his Son, be the saving sacrifice for sin, and he initiated this by pouring out his Holy Spirit upon Jesus, his Son, within the conceptional incarnational act and by commissioning him, as the Christ, to be his saving Servant-Son. Evident throughout the entire Passion Narrative is Jesus actively doing the will of his Father from his agony in the Garden of Olives to his last breathing forth his spirit into the hands of his Father. Second, the Father is not only the author of the whole salvific economy, but also the end to which all is progressing. The Father is he into whose hands Jesus, his Son, is committing his spirit in the love of the Holy Spirit. And the Father grasps Jesus' spirit in his paternal hands, imbued with the love of the same Holy Spirit and into which Jesus handed his filial soul. The Father's reception of his Son in the Holy Spirit is the Father's decisive saving act by which he fully becomes Father-YHWH-Saves. Thus we perceive now a Trinitarian perichoretic salvific act, which would not be saving without the contributive and collaborative acts of each of the persons of the Trinity. Jesus, the Son, humanly gives himself in the Holy Spirit to his Father, and the Father, in the same Holy Spirit, receives Jesus, his Son, unto himself, and within that one intertwining act of Trinitarian giving and receiving, humankind's salvation is achieved. The Father will complete his saving contributing act by raising Jesus, his Son, glorious from the dead by the Holy Spirit, thus making him the risen Spirit-filled Lord and Savior. Thus the salvific "loud cry," which initiated this entire discussion, gives voice to the Trinity. Vocally we hear the human voice of Jesus, the Father's Son, and that voice rides on the loving breath of the Holy Spirit and enters the loving Spirit-imbued ears of the Father, who receives Jesus' spirit, which inhabited the loud cry. The loud cry, then, which began as a cry of dereliction, having been transformed into a loud cry of sacrificial self-giving, terminates as a loud cry of joy, for Jesus, the Son, now resides within his Father's Spirit-filled bosom.

This threefold perichoretic act is enacted within the man, Jesus. Only as a man does Jesus, the Son, sacrificially "yield up his spirit" to his Father in the love of the Spirit. Moreover, it is the Son's human "spirit" that the Father lovingly receives in the same love of the Spirit. Only within and through the earthly humanity of Jesus does the Trinity enact their saving acts precisely because Jesus is the Father's Spirit-filled incarnate Son, thus truly enabling all human beings to partake, within the risen humanity of Jesus the Son, in the divine life of the Father in the love of the Holy Spirit.

The Tearing of the Temple's Curtain, the Proclamation of the Centurion, and the Women Looking from Afar

Within the Synoptics, the narrating of Jesus' death is concise, except for Luke's providing Jesus' brief last words. There is no theological explanation as to its soteriological significance. If Jesus' death were not being read through the lens of the Suffering Servant Songs, Wisdom's chapters 2 and 3, and Psalm 22, its salvific importance would be entirely hidden or even nonexistent. Like Jesus' birth and crucifixion, the soteriological significance of his death is clearly perceived not simply in the act of dying itself, but in the immediate narrated effects of his death. Invoking a principle employed previously, we can perceive the significance of a cause in the effects that it achieves. Matthew and Mark directly state: "And behold, the curtain of the temple was torn in two, from top to bottom" (Mk does not have the "behold"). Luke places this rending of the temple's curtain prior to his death and in conjunction with the darkening of the whole earth, and he does so precisely to alert the reader to the soteriological importance of what is about to take place in Jesus' imminent death.[25]

For Matthew and Mark, the cause of the curtain of the temple being torn in two is directly related to Jesus' death. Matthew makes this explicit with his "and behold." What one is beholding is the salvific effect of Jesus' death. Now the temple, and specifically the Holy of Holies, was the dwelling place of God. God dwelt therein as the effect or consequence of the covenant he made with Moses and the Israelites. Because of the covenant, God would dwell among his chosen people. Moreover, because the temple was the dwelling of the most high and holy God, only the high priest could enter the Holy of Holies, and then only once a year on the Day of Atonement. To enter the Holy of Holies, the high priest had to pass through the curtain that separated this most holy place of God's dwelling from the rest of the temple (see Ex 26:31-36 and Lv 16:1-19). As we saw when commenting on his Last Supper, Jesus embodies both the new Passover lamb and the new covenantal lamb of sacrifice, and in so doing he is presently also the new atoning lamb of sacrifice for the for-

---

25. All quotations in this section are from Mt 27:45-56, Mk 15:33-41, and Lk 23:44-49 unless otherwise noted.

giveness of sins. There is here an interlacing sequential causal relationship. As the new high priest, Jesus willingly and lovingly offers himself as the ultimate Passover lamb and so passes over from the sinful world of death into the life-giving abode of his Father, and he does so because through his holy sacrificial death, his being the atoning sacrificial lamb, he redresses the sin of the world and in so doing becomes the covenantal lamb of the new and everlasting covenant. Here again, Jesus' human freedom and love are what cause his priesthood and make his threefold self-offering salvifically efficacious. In giving himself freely in love to his Father as a *loving sacrifice* on humankind's behalf, he offers to his Father the holy and loving gift of himself, which both abolishes, as an *atoning sacrifice*, humankind's ungodly and odious sinful history and simultaneously, as the new *covenantal sacrifice,* establishes the new relationship with his Father, allowing all, as the Passover lamb of sacrifice, to enter into his Father' presence in communion with him. Because the temple was the covenantal effect of God's relationship with his people, the place in which they had access to God, Jesus, being the Passover and atoning lamb of sacrifice of the new covenant, gives everyone access to the very presence of God, who is his Father. Jesus, then, is the new high priest who offered himself as the definitive atoning sacrifice in which all of humankind can pass over into the heavenly temple by means of the new covenant.[26] The old temple with its priesthood therefore becomes redundant for the covenant, and the priesthood it represents has been fulfilled by Jesus enacting the new covenant. Jesus is now the living priest and victim of the new living temple of the new covenant in whom all of mankind has admittance to the heavenly sanctuary where his Father dwells. Thus, unlike the old temple with its restricting curtain, Jesus, the new temple, provides open and unencumbered entrée to God. Therefore Luke links the darkness that covered the earth with the rending of the temple curtain. Although the darkness of Jesus' death covered the earth, his dark salvific death destroys death's darkness by unsealing the light of his Father's glory now made visible to all who believe. The darkness of the curtain-enclosed Holy of Holies has been transformed by the Father's glory that shines forth from the resurrected face of Jesus—the new Holy of Holies. The faithful

---

26. The Letter to the Hebrews expresses this theological point clearly. "Therefore, brethren, since we have confidence to enter the sanctuary by the blood of Jesus, by the new and living way which he opened for us through the curtain, that is, through his flesh, and since we have a great priest over the house of God, let us draw near with a true heart in full assurance of faith, with our hearts sprinkled clean from an evil conscience and our bodies washed with pure water" (Heb 10:19-22).

can now look directly into the heavenly temple by abiding in the risen Jesus, the living glorious light of his Father's presence.[27]

The fact that the curtain of the temple was "torn in two, from top to bottom" highlights that this rending is a divine act coming forth from the heavens, the top, and finds its effect on the earth, the bottom. Salvation, the enabling of earthly man to enter God's divine heavenly presence, is not something that human beings can achieve. Only the Father could enact such an act, and he has done so through his Son, the man Jesus, through the power of the Holy Spirit. This tearing of the curtain is the fulfillment of what was prefigured within Jesus' baptism. There the heavens were torn open, from top to bottom, from heaven to earth, when the Father, through the descent of the Holy Spirit, bestowed his salvific task upon Jesus, his Son, and Jesus undertook that commission as his faithful Servant-Son through the power of the Holy Spirit. This theophany has now been fulfilled, for in the tearing open of the heavens through his death, Jesus will now be empowered, through the same Spirit he received at baptism, to pour out the Holy Spirit upon all who believe, baptizing them in the Holy Spirit. The faithful, having been configured into the likeness of Jesus, the Son, by the indwelling Spirit and so made holy, will now have access in the same Spirit to their heavenly all-holy Father as his adopted children. Similarly, this tearing open of the temple's curtain is the fulfillment of the Transfiguration. There the luminous Jesus prophetically passed over from the darkness of sin and death, in the company of Elijah and Moses, into the glory of his heavenly Father, taking with him Peter, James, and John. Here Jesus' death tears open the heavens, having fulfilled the Law and prophets, so as to be transfigured in the glory of his resurrection, and in so doing allows all of humankind, in union with him, to enter into the transfiguring glory of his heavenly Father. Last, this is the true triumphal entry into the new Jerusalem, which terminates not at a stone temple built by human hands but at a living temple that comes out of heaven upon earth: Jesus himself, in whom all can abide with his Father and, in union with Jesus, offer proper worship and fullness of praise. This tearing of the temple's curtain testifies that God's kingdom, the new Paradise, is present and into which, with Jesus, humankind can triumphantly enter, waving the palm branches of a new creation and singing new hymns of praise to their risen Savior and glorious

27. The Book of Revelation states that there will be no temple in the new Jerusalem, "for its temple will be the Lord God Almighty and the Lamb. And the city has no sun or moon to shine upon it, for the glory of God is its light and its lamp is the Lamb. By its light shall the nations walk" (Rv 21:22-24).

King: Jesus—YHWH-Saves. The tearing open of the temple's curtain confirms, then, that Jesus is the anointed Messiah, the Chosen one of God, the King of the Jews. Here the soteriological importance of the centurion's proclamation is discerned, that Jesus is the Son of God.

The respective Synoptic narratives now diverge somewhat, particularly within Matthew. Following the rending of the temple's curtain, Mark states, "And when the centurion, who stood facing him saw that he breathed his last, he said, 'Truly this man was the Son of God!'" Luke, who already spoke of the tearing of the curtain prior to Jesus' death, moves directly from Jesus breathing his last to: "Now when the centurion saw what had taken place, he praised God, and said, 'Certainly this man was innocent!' And all of the multitudes who assembled to see the sight, when they saw what had taken place, returned home beating their breasts." Matthew conjoins the tearing of the curtain with "and the earth shook, and the rocks were split; the tombs were opened, and many bodies of the saints who had fallen asleep were raised, and coming out of the tombs after his resurrection they went into the holy city and appeared to many. When the centurion and those who were with him, keeping watch over Jesus, saw the earthquake and what took place, they were filled with awe, and said, 'Truly, this was the Son of God!'" For the sake of clarity, I first treat the centurion's proclamation and then examine Matthew's rather lengthy diversion.

I have stated throughout this study that the more Jesus enacts his name, YHWH-Saves, the more he reveals that he is the Son of God, for only someone who is truly divine could enact the saving deeds that he was enacting, such as working miracles, healing, performing exorcisms, and especially forgiving sins. The centurion, a Roman soldier, and thus not a Jew and someone who probably never heard Jesus preach nor witnessed his mighty wonders, is the first, upon Jesus' death, to recognize that "this man was the Son of God" (Mk). The sign above Jesus' head read "The King of the Jews" (Mk), but a Gentile is the first to identify this Jewish King is God's Son, and so, in a sense, he is not only the first Gentile convert, but the first convert.[28] Peter may have first proclaimed Jesus to be the Christ, the Son of the living God, but he is yet to grasp the full significance of his own declaration, even after Jesus' attempt at clarification. For Jesus, to be the Christ, the Son of God, and so the King of the Jews

---

28. It could be rightly argued that Mary is the first convert, as she exemplifies the faith of the church and so the faith of all Christians. Yet Mary may not be so much a convert as the ever faithful disciple from Jesus' conception to his death. Within the Gospel of John, she too stands beneath the cross of Jesus as a faithful believer in her crucified son as Savior and Lord (see Jn 19:25-27).

388 THE PASSION NARRATIVES

is for him to suffer and die. Here Mark's descriptive clause is significant: "who stood facing him." The centurion is standing as a sign of respect, facing Jesus and so beholding Jesus crucified and dead, yet in this beholding he recognizes the truth that Jesus is the Son of God. Although there is no hint of this, other than the echoing of Peter's words, it was seemingly the Father who revealed this fact, as with Peter, to the centurion. But the difference is that the centurion beholds the entire soteriological portrayal and believes it to be true, that in his cruciform, death Jesus is the Christ, the Son of the living God. Moreover, the centurion is professing the incarnation. It is "this man" who is "the Son of God" and the "truly" (Mt and Mk) accentuates that his Sonship exceeds that of any other man who may have been previously designated a son of God. The centurion may not have fully grasped the entire theological content of his declaration, though perhaps he did recognize that Jesus was truly divine. But the early apostolic community certainly would have, and it would have perceived, particularly slow-to-understand Peter, the significance that it was facing and beholding in the dead body of Jesus that such a declaration was first made.[29]

In Luke, however, the centurion does not declare Jesus to be the Son of God but rather, having "praised God," said, "Certainly this man was innocent/righteous!" The "certainly" matches the "truly" of Matthew and Mark. The question remains: Can the centurion's declaration in Luke be reconciled with his declaration in Matthew and Mark? The key to resolving this discrepancy may be found in the centurion first praising God immediately prior to his declaration. Why was the centurion praising God? Apparently, such divine praise arose because this man was innocent or righteous, implying that no other man was or is truly innocent or righteous. That this man was righteous, and thus innocent of all sin, means that for this man to be such is a singular salvific work of God, the source of all righteousness. Jesus, by God's doing, is the righteous one, and because "this man" just died innocently on the cross, he must have performed, in his death, the supreme deed of righteousness on behalf of God. But what is the supreme deed of righteousness that Jesus preformed through his death on the cross? Jesus, the righteous, holy innocent man free of all sin, through his death on the cross, achieved all righteousness by lovingly offering his holy life to God, thus making the whole of humankind righteous, and for this, God, the author of all righteousness, deserves praise.

29. The Book of Mark begins: "The beginning of the Gospel of Jesus Christ, the Son of God." The whole of Mark's Gospel is to manifest this truth, which comes to its culminating revelation in the centurion's proclamation beneath the crucified Jesus: "Truly, this man was the Son of God."

It may be a step too far to conclude that therefore, within Luke's account, the centurion is declaring that Jesus is the Son of God, but implicit within his declaration innocence lies the gloss of Jesus' divine Sonship, for only if Jesus is the Son of God incarnate would he be truly righteous and wholly innocent of all sin and thus capable of enacting the supreme deed of righteousness, the making holy God's unrighteous sinful people.

What immediately follows corroborates this interpretation. "And all the multitudes who assembled to see the sight, when they saw what had taken place, returned home beating their breasts." Are "the multitudes" the Jewish leaders and Roman soldiers (except for the centurion)? That is highly improbable. The Synoptics tell of various women who were present, but they would be too few to compose a "multitude," much less multiple multitudes. More than likely they are Luke's "great multitude of people," some of whom were women, the "daughters of Jerusalem," "who bewailed and lamented him [Jesus]." Thus they were not mere gawking onlookers, but those, having seemingly arrived somewhat later, "assembled to see the sight." That is, they purposely came together and proceeded, maybe, in a solemn and reverent manner. What "sight" did they want to see? They came to see Jesus dying on the cross or Jesus already dead, and "when they saw what had taken place," they "returned home beating their breasts." What did they see that "had taken place" that caused them to respond this way? Breast beating is a sign of sorrowful repentance for sin, often performed when one discerns that one is in the presence of the all-holy God.[30] Thus this "assembled multitude" saw Jesus hanging dead from the cross and perceived that, in accord with the centurion's declaration, they were in the presence of an innocent man who had just performed, in his death, the ultimate righteous act that procured God's forgiveness. Sensing that they were now in the presence of the all-holy God, the Father's Son, they, in deep bent-over sorrow and with remorseful hearts, beat their breasts in repentance, pleading for the mercy that they just beheld upon the cross, the sight they had assembled to see, "what had taken place."[31] Their "returning

30. The tax collector in Jesus' parable in the Gospel exemplifies this: "But the tax collector, standing far off, would not even lift up his eyes to heaven, but beat his breast, saying, 'God be merciful to me a sinner!'" (Lk 18:9–14).

31. Matthew's account may provide further evidence for the above interpretation. "When the centurion and those who were with him, keeping watch over Jesus, saw the earthquake and what took place, they were filed with awe, and said, 'Truly, this man is the Son of God.'" The "keeping watch over Jesus" appears to imply a "caring watch," much as one would attentively watch at the bedside of a dying friend. In their considerate watching, the centurion and the others saw the earthquake predicated upon Jesus death and, being "filled with awe," declared, "Truly, this is the

home" signals that what they just saw would continue to be quietly pondered and that the humble repentance within them would continue. The centurion, then, along with Luke's "assembled multitudes" portrays the proper response of the church's assembled multitudes to Jesus' salvific death—repentance of sin and faith in Jesus Christ as the righteous Son of God, who is Savior and Lord.

Matthew alone, in consort with the tearing of the temple's curtain, narrates the shaking of the earth with the splitting of rocks and "tombs were also opened, and many bodies of the saints who had fallen asleep were raised, and coming out of the tombs after the resurrection they went into the holy city and appeared to many." The coming of the great day, the eschatological day, of the Lord is here being portrayed. With Jesus' death, entrance into God's presence is achieved and the in-breaking of his everlasting kingdom is accomplished. The physical sign of God's impending judgment is the shaking of the earth and the splitting of rocks. When God comes marching into the presence of his people, "the earth will quake, the heavens will pour down rain, at the presence of God; you Sinai quaked at the presence of God, the God of Israel" (Ps 68:7-8; see also 77:18). As Mt. Sinai shook upon the appearance of God at the onset of the first covenant (see Ex 19:18), so now with the making of the new everlasting covenant through Jesus' sacrificial death the earth quakes at the sight of God's definitive presence. The eschatological nature of God's new presence is depicted within Matthew's account with the rising of the dead from their tombs. Here Matthew has conflated Jesus' death with his resurrection, for the tombs appear to have opened as a consequence of the earthquake upon Jesus' death, and yet "the saints" only came out of their tombs and walked about "after his resurrection." The theological point being made is that Jesus' death and resurrection constitute one salvific event: through the cross sin is forgiven, a new covenant is ratified, and this is confirmed in the Father raising Jesus back to life and so conquering death and sealing God's living presence among his people. This is prophetically anticipated in the Book of Daniel, where God shows Daniel in a vision his day of eschatological judgment. "At that time shall arise Michael, the great prince who has charge of your people [Jewish people]. And there shall be a time of trouble, such as never has been since there was a nation till that time; but at that time your people shall be delivered everyone whose name is written in the book. And many of those who sleep in the dust of the earth shall awake,

---

Son of God." Matthew's "those who were with the centurion" could be Luke's "assembled multitudes," Matthew's responding with "awe," and Luke's with the "beating of their breasts," all clearly perceiving that Jesus was a righteous man and reverently acknowledging him to be the Son of God, for they both saw "what took place" (Mt and Lk)—Jesus dying on the cross.

some to everlasting life, and some to shame and everlasting contempt" (Dn 12:1-2). Jesus' salvific death gives rise to his salvific resurrection, and the success of this one saving event finds it testimony in the resurrection of "the saints," their rising from "the dust of the earth," and who now enter not merely "the holy city" of Jerusalem at the time of Jesus' death, but "the holy city"—that is the new Jerusalem—founded upon his resurrection and which will come down out of heaven at his glorious coming at the end time. For Matthew, all of the above is predicated upon the proclamation of the centurion, who, having witnessed the earthquake and the spitting of rocks, immediately professes: "Truly, this was the Son of God." Only Jesus, as the Son of God, could, through his death and resurrection, issue forth the eschatological age, the great day of the Lord.

The Synoptics next speak of women who were closely associated with Jesus and who were present at his crucifixion and death. They speak of women "looking from afar," and Matthew and Luke specify that they were from Galilee. Besides the women, Luke also tells of "all of his acquaintances," but neither is specified or named. Matthew and Mark narrate that these Galilean women "ministered" to Jesus having come to Jerusalem with him. Unlike Luke, Matthew and Mark provide the names of a few. "Among them were Mary Magdalene, and Mary the mother James and Joseph, and the mother of the sons of Zebedee" (Mt). "Among whom were Mary Magdalene, and Mary the mother of James the younger and of Joses, and Salome" (Mk). That these women "ministered" to Jesus and traveled with him from Galilee to Jerusalem bespeaks their affection for Jesus personally and their commitment to his perceived salvific ministry. In addition, two of the women are mothers of three of Jesus' twelve Apostles. James, the younger, is the son of Mary, and earlier within Matthew he and Joseph are designated known relatives of Jesus (brothers/cousins/brethren; see Mt 13:55).[32] Also present is the mother of the Apostles James and John, the sons of Zebedee.[33] That these women were mothers of Apostles also

32. Joseph (Mt) or Joses (Mk) would then also be Jesus' close relative. Salome is not mentioned by name in Matthew, but he does speak of Jesus' "sisters" in conjunction with James and Joseph, and thus the Salome, mentioned in Mark, would be one of them. Interestingly, that these were known to be relatives of Jesus, as well as his being "the son of a carpenter," led to the question "where did this man get this wisdom and these mighty works?" (Mt 13:54). The wisdom and might of Jesus, as the Son of God, is now manifested upon the cross, for he is fulfilling the wise will of his Father and establishing God's kingdom. That Mark specifies that James is the younger distinguishes him from the other Apostle James, later designated "the Greater." According to tradition, James the Younger became the first "bishop" of Jerusalem.

33. One of the supreme ironies within the New Testament is that the mother of James and John was present at Jesus' crucifixion and her sons were not. She is the one within Matthew's Gospel who asks, to the consternation of the other Apostles, Jesus to command her two sons

suggests that they had concern not only for their own sons, but also for all the Apostles who traveled with Jesus and so ministered to them. In other words, they were manifesting their "motherly" care for Jesus and his Apostles.[34]

For Matthew and Mark, there is also a further theological importance in naming Mary Magdalene and Mary, for they would be witnesses to Jesus' burial as well as would bring spices to the tomb to anoint his body after the Sabbath ended and thereby witness the empty tomb and Jesus' resurrection (see Mt 27:61 and 28:1-8; Mk 15:48 and 16:1-8). Luke does not name the women who "saw these things" (Jesus' crucifixion and death), but he does also narrate that they "saw the tomb, and how he was laid" (Lk 23:55). Later, having found the tomb empty and meeting the risen Jesus, Luke informs us that these women were "Mary Magdalene and Joanna and Mary the mother of James and the other women with them" (Lk 24:10). Thus these women not only verify that Jesus was dead and buried but also testify that his tomb is now empty, and that he is risen from the dead. Their witness alone forms a continuity of testimony. That they are women, and simple women at that, will ultimately give the utmost credence to their testimony. Their testimony would be judged suspect

---

to sit on each side of him when he comes into his kingdom. Jesus asks if they can drink the cup that he is to drink, to which they answer yes (see Mt 20:20-24). But at the time when Jesus did drink his cup of suffering and does enter his kingdom, they are nowhere to be found, though their mother is "looking on from afar." James and John would later drink Jesus' cup, yet one can imagine that this mother would presently have "words" with her absentee sons. Within Mark's Gospel, Jesus designates James and John the sons of thunder, but their blustering bravado needed time to mature into true and firm commitment (see Mk 4:17).

There may be in this scene an allusion to Psalm 38:9-11. "Lord, all my longing is known to you, my sighing is not hidden from you. My heart throbs, my strength fails me; and the light of my eyes—it also has gone from me. My friends and companions stand aloof from my plague, and my kinsmen stand afar off." This passage would give a negative interpretation to the women "looking on from afar" as though they too had abandoned Jesus in his moment of greatest need. Yet the Synoptics do not appear to portray them in a negative light, but rather as faithful women who, with reverent reticence, watch with loving concern at what is enacted before them. This is borne out by their vigilant observance of where Jesus is buried and their being the first to come to his tomb immediately after the Sabbath to anoint properly his body. If there is an intimation that this passage from Psalm 38 is fulfilled in these women, it is only in that they are companions and relatives of Jesus who are standing and observing from afar his crucifixion and death and not that they are standoffishly avoiding him as one infected by a contagious plague.

34. Luke narrates early in his Gospel that as Jesus was traveling through cities and villages preaching with his disciples, there were also "some women who had been healed of evil spirits and infirmities: Mary, called Magdalene, of whom seven demons had gone out, and Joanna, the wife of Chuza, Herod's servant, and Susanna, and many others, who provided for them out of their means" (Lk 8:1-3).

and unacceptable within their culture, yet, precisely because they are women, no one would concoct or fabricate a story about Jesus' resurrection wherein women would be its first witnesses. Their greatest testimonial weakness— womanhood—becomes their greatest testimonial strength. Jesus also rewarded their faithfulness. While his Apostles fled in fear at the onset of his arrest, these faithful women fearlessly followed him to the cross, and thus they rightly earned the honor to be the first to see him alive and risen and so the first to proclaim the Gospel—Jesus Christ, the Son of the living God, has died and now is risen from the dead.

The Burial of Jesus

The Synoptic Gospels proceed to narrate the burial of Jesus. Matthew and Mark note that it was "evening," with Mark stating that "since it was the day of Preparation, that is, the day before the Sabbath, Joseph of Arimathea, a represented member of the council, who was also himself looking for the kingdom of God, took courage and went to Pilate, and asked for the body of Jesus."[35] There is urgency here because, with the onset of the Sabbath, a day of holy rest, no work could be done, including the burial of Jesus. Joseph of Arimathea is the central acting agent in ensuring that Jesus is buried before the Sabbath begins. Matthew refers to him as "a rich man" who "was a disciple of Jesus." Mark and Luke designate him as member of the council or Sanhedrin, Luke specifying that he "was a good and righteous man, who had not consented to their purpose and deed, and he was looking for the kingdom of God," thus corroborating Mark's portrayal. That Joseph was rich and a member of the council designates him as a man of some standing. That he was also a follower of Jesus who was looking for the kingdom of God, and thus did not concur with his fellow council members in their condemnation of Jesus, shows him to be his own man. That he was good and righteous indicates the inner source of his conviction as well as his love for Jesus and his present courageous resolve to provide for Jesus a proper Jewish burial.

Matthew and Luke state simply that Joseph "went to Pilate and asked for the body of Jesus" and that Pilate "ordered it to be given him" (Mt) and he "took the body, and wrapped it in a clean linen shroud" (Mt and Lk). Mark provides further detail, for having noted that Joseph "took courage" in going to Pilate

---

35. All quotations in this section are from Mt 27:57-61, Mk 15:42-47, and Lk 23:50-56 unless otherwise noted.

to ask for the body, he observes that Pilate did not indifferently and perfunc-torily agree to his request. "And Pilate wondered if he was already dead; and summoning the centurion, he asked him whether he was already dead. And when he learned from the centurion that he was dead, he granted the body to Joseph. And he brought a linen shroud, and taking him down, wrapped him in the linen shroud." In providing this scenario, Mark is conclusively establish-ing on the authority of the Roman governor, the emperor's delegated repre-sentative, as well as the testimony of a Roman centurion, that Jesus was dead. Presuming that this centurion is the same one who affirmed that Jesus was the Son of God (Mt and Mk) who was an innocent man (Lk), this centurion has now testified twice to his death, once upon his demise and now before his Roman superior. He, along with Pilate, then provides secular objectivity to the indisputable death of Jesus. This is important not merely to authenticate Jesus' subsequent resurrection rather than a simple resuscitation, but also to confirm that Jesus offered his life to the Father as a loving sacrifice. If Jesus did not truly die, he would not be the new Passover lamb, or the ratifying sacrifice of the new covenant, or the atoning sacrifice for sin. Jesus' salvific death is not authoritatively confirmed by Jews nor even by his disciples, but by Gentile pa-gans. Thus Jesus' death objectively enters the annals of factual history, just as the saving effects of his death enter into human history—the sins of historical men and women can be forgiven and they can be transformed, in this histor-ical world and within their historical lives, into holy children of God by the in-breaking of the Holy Spirit into world of time and history. The kingdom of God is not an ethereal mythological kingdom, but one that is firmly rooted in this present world, for it is here on a rocky crag outside the walls of Jerusalem that Jesus' cross was firmly planted, and upon that cross he died. In the resur-rection, the corpse of Jesus will bud forth the new creation, the eschatological new heaven and the new earth, that will find its mature growth and fruition when Jesus returns in glory, ending the present age of time and history. All this is predicated upon Pilate's wonder as to the truth of Jesus' death and the centurion's testimony that it was indeed so.

Having been granted Jesus' body and taken it down from the cross, Joseph wraps it in a linen shroud and lays it in a tomb. All the Synoptics agree that the tomb was hewn from a rock. Matthew designates it as Joseph's "own new tomb," and Luke thus notes it was a tomb "where no one had yet been laid." Upon burial, Mark and Matthew specify that Joseph "rolled a stone [Mt "great stone"] against the door of the tomb [Mt "and departed"]." Although Jesus was buried in a tomb typical of the time, Matthew and Luke emphasize that it was a new tomb in which no one previously had been buried. Jesus died and was buried as are all the sons of Adam, but he was not laid in a tomb that was already corrupted or infected by death, nor will his "borrowed" tomb be contaminated by death. It will forever remain a new tomb unpolluted by death, for he will rise gloriously from the dead, leaving his tomb devoid of death's corruption and contamination. Jesus' tomb is not Adam's old tomb of death but Adam's new tomb of life. That he borrowed it from Joseph of Arimathea manifests that while Jesus died as one of Adam's race, he does not possess his own tomb as one of Adam's race for he will be the new risen Adam, the father of a new race, and as such he will empty the tombs of all his Adamic brothers and sisters by raising them from the dead and so sharing fully in his resurrection. With Adam Jesus died and is buried, but in his resurrection, Adam comes to life and is raised up. Thus the lifeless body of Jesus lying in this dark and dank cold stone tomb is a "living" icon of Jesus becoming Jesus, for that body-filled tomb testifies that Jesus has truly offered his holy and innocent life to his Father, even unto death, for the forgiveness of sins, and, having accomplished his Father's will as the anointed Father's Son, he quietly awaits his Father's response. Having become the dead Jesus, the lifeless YHWH-Saves, Jesus eagerly waits for his Father to enthrone him as the living Jesus, the glorious YHWH-Saves, thus constituting him to be truly Jesus, the name his Father first gave him at his conception and that now will be fulfilled in his second birth, for he will be the Spirit-empowered Savior and life-giving Lord of all.

Having narrated the burial of Jesus, the Synoptics again mention the women who stood from afar at Jesus' crucifixion and death and who now witness his burial. Having already examined the theological importance of the women's testimony, we will only note here that Matthew emphasizes that Mary Magdalene and the other Mary were present and were actually "sitting opposite the sepulcher," leaving no doubt as to their knowledge of the exact location of Jesus' tomb and allaying any future doubt that the tomb they later found empty was not his.

Matthew alone next narrates another scene of what is now obviously becoming a progressive argument as to the authenticity of Jesus' resurrection. "Next day, that is, after the day of Preparation, the chief priests and the Pharisees gathered before Pilate and said: 'Sir, we remember how that impostor said, while he was still alive, "after three days I will rise again."[36] Therefore,

---

36. Jesus never says verbatim what is here attributed to him. He did prophetically thrice state that the son of man must suffer, die, and rise on the third day (see, e.g., Mt 16:22) and he was accused of saying that if the temple was destroyed he would raise it up in three days (see

order the sepulcher to be made secure until the third day, lest his disciples go and steal him away, and tell the people, "He has risen from the dead," and the last fraud will be worse than the first.' Pilate said to them, 'You have a guard of soldiers; go, make it as secure as you can.' So they went and made the sepulcher secure by sealing the stone and setting a guard."

What the chief priests and the Pharisees have done, in a sense, is to have fallen into the literary trap that Matthew had set for them. Historically they may have gone to Pilate, but within Matthew's account, their sealing the tomb and setting a guard is the final piece that assures that Jesus' resurrection is a reality and not some kind of hoax. Jesus' actual death has been authoritatively authenticated by Pilate, Joseph of Arimathea actually buried his body and sealed the tomb with a great stone, the women know the exact location and so they are positioned to be the unlikely official witnesses to it being later empty, and now the Jews secure the great stone with a seal so that if someone should enter the tomb and take the body, the seal would be broken, and lastly military guards are set in place to ward off any would-be intruders. For Matthew, if the tomb should be found empty, it cannot be due to any natural or human causality. The possibility of any or all such causes coming into play has been thoroughly eliminated. Should the tomb be found empty, then god must be the cause, for only he could perform an act, given the security, whereby the tomb is empty and the body gone. The subsequent appearances of the risen Jesus verify that the reason for the empty tomb is indeed due to divine causality—the Father has raised his Son Jesus gloriously from the dead by the power of the Holy Spirit. The fact that the women are the first to witness both the empty tomb and the risen Jesus lends credence, for Matthew, to their testimony because a fabricated resurrection story, if believable, would never be proffered by the likes of women. Ironically, although the chief priests and Pharisees wanted to ensure that "the impostor's" declaration that "after three days I will rise again" is not fraudulently fulfilled by his disciples stealing his body and subsequently proclaiming that he is indeed risen, they have ensured that Jesus' resurrection is authentic, for they have themselves eliminated all other possibilities. In wanting to safeguard, by securing the tomb, that the impostor's first fraudulent claims that he was the Messiah, the Son of God, and the king of the Jews would not be made worse by his disciples stealing the body and then proclaiming that he is risen, they have actually ensured that Jesus'

Mk 14:58). Throughout the Passion Narratives, the chief priests and Pharisees have a knack for putting words into Jesus' mouth to suit their immediate concerns.

resurrection is authentic and thus that he truly is the messianic Son of God who is the Jewish king of God's kingdom. They have orchestrated a scenario that guarantees that the "second" so-called fraud is worse than the "first," for what they feared most and wanted to ensure did not happen has taken place—Jesus rising from the dead after three days—and now the chief priest and Pharisees have no grounds, having themselves eliminated them, for claiming that it was a duplicitous affair. They have been hoisted upon their own petard.[37]

Conclusion

Jesus' resurrection is the decisive conclusion—his death cannot be separated from his resurrection because they form one saving event. But before theologically examining the resurrection narratives in Matthew, Mark, and Luke, I would like to highlight and develop a few key theological points and then append an addendum.

First, the crucifixion and death of Jesus bring to the fore the full theological significance of the Incarnation. All the Passion Narratives focus on the man Jesus—he carries his cross; he is crucified, mocked, and taunted; and he finally dies. His human corpse is taken down from the cross and buried in a stone-hewn tomb. Everyone's eyes—whether they be of the soldiers, Jewish leaders, or women nearby or far away—are fixed on him. There is no doubt in anyone's mind that a man, Jesus by name, has been hung upon a cross, was dying, and is now dead. Yet who this man Jesus is makes this crucifixion and death salvifically significant. Most of those present would either not know or fully grasp who he is, though the apostolic church of Matthew, Mark, and Luke would recognize that the centurion's proclamation of faith was now their proclamation as well—the man Jesus truly is the Son of God, and it is this incarnational truth that makes this the saving event within all human history, past, present, and future. This was not simply the death of a man by crucifixion but the Son of God incarnate offering himself, his whole human life, his entire humanity, to his Father for the forgiveness of sins. What makes this sacrificial act causally efficacious is not only that it was offered by the Father's Son but also that it was offered within the love and sanctity of the Father's and Son's Holy Spirit. What makes this death salvific is that Jesus, as the great high priest and the su-

---

37. As we will see later, the chief priests attempt to make the best of a bad situation by having the guards say, "His disciples came by night and stole him away while we were asleep" (Mt 28:11-15). The obvious rebuttal is: "If you were asleep, how would you know what happened?" Lies, unlike truth, are always devoid of rationality.

preme sacrificial victim, is the anointed Messianic Son of his Father, and so he is the universal Savior and definitive Lord. The focus is rightly upon the man Jesus, for what is being humanly enacted by this man is a Trinitarian act, a humanly enacted perichoretic salvific act of the Father, the Son, and the Holy Spirit. In accord with the Son's Father, Jesus, the Father's Son, is saving his Father's people within their Holy Spirit-imbued communion of love and in so doing Jesus has become Jesus—YHWH-Saves.

Second, I want to amplify, in a more systematic and theological manner, the salvific causality inherent within Jesus' death on the cross. Jesus, as the Son of God incarnate, is the efficient cause of humankind's salvation in that, as man, the Son of God achieves salvation through his death on the cross. And the foundational efficient causal act, the principal efficacious causal act that Jesus enacts, is the act of sacrifice, which is simultaneously a threefold act—an *atoning act,* a *covenanting act,* and a *passing over* act.

1. By willingly offering his Spirit-filled life to his Father as the Father's Son, Jesus atoned for, made reparation for, or compensated for humankind's sin, for his self-offering more than redressed or satisfied mankind's sinful acts against the perfect goodness, holiness, justice, and love of God. In so doing, Jesus' sacrificial act redeemed and set free humankind from the slavery to sin and sin's condemnatory death with its just punishment of hell. In short, Jesus' sacrificial death liberated and so redeemed humankind from the bonds of Satan. Through his atoning sacrificial act, Jesus simultaneously made humankind righteous before his Father; that is, he made it possible for humankind to once more possess a right and proper relation to God, which had been impeded by humankind's unrighteous, unholy, unloving acts of sin. Thus Jesus' *atoning sacrifice* is an efficient redeeming and reconciling cause, for it effects humankind's freedom from all evil and reunites it to his Father.

2. Having done away with all that impedes humankind's relationship to his Father, thus allowing it to relate justly to his Father through the atoning nature of his sacrificial death, Jesus simultaneously inaugurates the new and everlasting covenant with his Father. It is a *covenantal sacrificial act* for, as in the atoning nature of the sacrifice, Jesus, in his one sacrificial death, freely offers, in perfect love, his holy and innocent life to his Father on humankind's behalf and in so doing establishes, in him, an everlasting holy covenantal relationship with his Father. It is this covenantal aspect that establishes humankind's proper relationship with his Father, which is constituted upon humankind sharing in the very holiness of the Father. Thus Jesus' sacrifice is an efficient atoning covenantal cause, for all who are united to him are cleansed of sin,

made righteous before God, and so enter his Father's presence in Spirit-filled covenantal communion with him.

3. Within this atoning and covenantal sacrificial act, Jesus simultaneously merits for himself and for humankind the privilege of *passing over* from the realm of sin and death into God's kingdom of holiness and eternal life. Through his sacrificial death, Jesus establishes God's kingdom and so merits his own kingship. Those who come to live in God's kingdom through faith in Jesus, their king, share in his merits and so reside, in communion with the Holy Spirit, with his Father. Thus Jesus' sacrifice is an efficient atoning, covenantal, and meritorious cause, for all who are united to him and his one sacrifice are reconciled to his Father, and thus merit in him to pass over into his Father's kingdom through and within his new Spirit-filled covenant of everlasting life.[38] Being the efficient atoning, covenantal, and passing-over cause of humankind's salvation, Jesus has transfigured himself into Jesus—YHWH-Saves.

Third, here we find the conjoining of Jesus incarnational conception with his redemptive death—the conjoining of Gabriel's prophetic message and Pilate's fulfilled declaration. "The Lord God" will give to the Spirit-conceived son of Mary "the throne of his father David, and he will reign over the house of Jacob forever; and of his kingdom there will be no end" (Lk 1:32-33).[39] On the cross, the same Lord God, now through the words of Pilate, declares: "This is the King of the Jews" (Lk 23:38). The crucified Jesus, the son of David, is King of the Jews for in his death he has established his Father's kingdom—a

38. Paul would similarly develop this notion within his understanding of Jesus being the head of his body and the faithful being the members of his body. To live in God's kingdom is live in Spirit-filled communion with Jesus, the king, and so reap the Spirit-filled blessings of that godly kingdom. To be a member of Christ's body through sharing in the same life of the Holy Spirit means that one is in a living communion with Jesus, the head, and thus forming one living reality in union with him (see Rom 12:4-8; 1 Cor 12:12-30; Eph 1:23, 4:1-16, 5:21-33; and Col 1:18, 2:19). To abide in the body of Christ with Jesus as head and so share in the blessings of Jesus the head, thus forming one living reality head and members, is to live in God's kingdom, for one shares within Christ's body the holy life of that kingdom and reaps the benefits of that kingdom. Although Paul's understanding of Christ and his body denotes more metaphysical depth than that of Jesus and his kingdom in that it emphasizes the living oneness of Christ and his body, both articulate that it is only in living in communion with Jesus that one can share in the salvific benefits that Jesus, as king, embodies as head.

39. The crucifixion of Jesus also fulfills the seeking of the wise men. They were in search of the king of the Jews and were told that the Christ is to be born in Bethlehem. The murder of the Innocents prophetically anticipates the killing of innocent Jesus, but in so doing he becomes the king of the Jews by establishing God's kingdom (see Mt 2:1-18). Where one truly finds Jesus, the king of the Jews, is on the cross.

Spirit-filled kingdom of merciful forgiveness and everlasting life—and there-fore Jesus has become Jesus—YHWH-Saves.

Fourth, as we previously anticipated while treating the Beatitudes, Jesus in his death enacts and so fulfills the Beatitudes and in so doing reaps their benefits. The cross bears witness to Jesus' poverty, the extreme poverty of the Son's humanity, and for this he is blessed by establishing and so inheriting the kingdom of heaven. His suffering testifies to his mourning over sin and the deadly state of humankind, and for this he will now be blessed with the comfort of his resurrection. His physical thirst is a longing cry for righteous-ness—for truth, justice, and holiness—and for this he will now be blessed with the satisfaction that comes with his new resurrected ability to send forth the Spirit of all righteousness. The cross is the icon of mercy, and he will not only obtain divine mercy for all but also be blessed by his merciful Father by being taken up into glory. With purity of heart, Jesus offered himself innocently to his Father, and for this he will blessed because he will see what he yearned to look upon from his youth, the glorious face of his Father. On the cross, Jesus brought peace between his human brethren and his heavenly Father, and so he will be blessed by rightly being acknowledged to be the Son of God. The cross attests that Jesus, more than any other, was persecuted for righteous-ness's sake, for he is the fullness of all righteousness and in him all are made righteous, and because of this he will be blessed by obtaining the heavenly kingdom of his Father's divine righteousness. By enacting the Beatitudes and so obtaining, in his very person, their blessings, Jesus has made it possible for all who live in communion with him to also enact the Beatitudes and so reap their heavenly blessings, which he fully embodies. In enacting the Beatitudes, Jesus has become Jesus—YHWH-Saves.

Although more theological points could be developed that follow upon Je-sus' crucifixion and death, I think it best to treat them in the light of the res-urrection, for they only find their full theological importance in communion with Jesus' resurrection.[40] Here I offer what I believe is Jesus' own definitive interpretation of his death, one not given in words but, as is his customary manner, through actions—his enacting the Our Father.

---

40. I have in mind Jesus' baptism, the Eucharist, the Transfiguration, and Jesus' triumphal entry into Jerusalem.

ADDENDUM

Breathing His Last: Enacting the Our Father

There is no evidence that Jesus prayed the Our Father while hanging on the cross.[41] Unlike Psalm 22, for example, there is no overt verbal allusion to the Our Father. But I want to argue that Jesus, as the Father's Son, did not simply pray the Our Father, but he enacted, in the Holy Spirit, the Our Father, and in so doing his whole humanity was configured into the realities of which the Our Father speaks. Only because the crucified Jesus incarnated the Our Father did it assume its most profound soteriological significance and acquire the fullness of its revealed truth. Jesus taught his disciples the Our Father during his public ministry, but only by enacting the Our Father on the cross does it become the prayer that it was meant to be, and only because it became an authentic prayer within the reality of the cross could it then be properly prayed by his disciples. If Jesus did not enact the Our Father on the cross, while remaining a "wonderful" prayer, it would not embody and so speak the authentic truth that it expresses. Moreover, everyone who prays the Our Father does so only in union with and in imitation of the crucified Jesus, with it having been imbued with the meaning and authority that the cross has indelibly conferred upon it. With this in mind, we can examine the Our Father itself.

Our Father, Who Art in Heaven

We saw earlier that Jesus, at the time of his death, first cried out "My God, my God, why have you forsaken me?" (Mk 15:34 and Mt 27:46). While experiencing what appeared to be God's act of abandonment, Jesus referred twice to God as "my God" and so acknowledged that, despite appearances, God is truly his God to whom he is loyal and who, reciprocally, is also faithful to him as his God. This cry of "abandonment" immediately becomes a new loud cry of lovingly offering his life to his Father. "Jesus cried again with a loud voice and yielded up his spirit" (Mt 26:50).

---

41. I have previously written an article on this same theme. See "The *Our Father*, Prayer of the Crucified: In Tribute to Ralph Del Colle, Who Prayed the *Our Father* with Jesus His Savior," in *A Man of the Church: Honoring the Theology, Life and Witness of Ralph Del Colle*, edited by M. R. Barnes (Eugene, Ore.: Pickwick, 2012), 96-106. This was later published as a slightly edited version in my "The 'Our Father': Prayer of the Crucified," in *Jesus: Essays in Christology* (Ave Maria, Fla.: Sapientia Press, 2014), 357-68. This present addendum is a substantially altered version of this thesis. Previously, I emphasized that Jesus "prayed" the Our Father while hanging upon the cross. The truth of what I wrote remains, but I have since come to realize that what Jesus actually did upon the cross is "enact" the Our Father, and in this sense he "prayed" the Our Father. It is the theology of this enactment that I am articulating here. So I have purposely waited until now to treat the Our Father, for the cross cannot be understood apart from the Our Father and vice versa, and thus the Our Father can only be authentically prayed in the light of Jesus' saving death.

"And Jesus uttered a loud cry, and breathed his last" (Mk 15:37). "Then Jesus, crying with a loud voice, said: 'Father, into your hands I commit my spirit!' And having said this he breathed his last" (Lk 23:46). The "my God" is Jesus' own Father, his own *Abba*, and into his loving hands Jesus yielded up, entrusted, in his last breath, his very spirit. In this single momentary act, Jesus enacted the entirety of the Our Father and in so doing gave it life, made it real, and so constituted it as true.

Having been eternally begotten in the loving Spirit of Sonship, Jesus is the Father's (*Abba's*) Son in a singular and definitive divine manner, and so only he can righly address God in such an intimate and filial fashion. Jesus nonetheless taught his disciples to pray "our Father," and the Aramaic word he spoke for "father" would have been *abba*, thus designating their filial loving intimacy with the Father and his paternal loving intimacy with them.[42] That Jesus could teach his disciples to address God as "our" *Abba*/Father, and not simply "his" *Abba*/Father, is founded upon his offering, on humankind's behalf, his life as a loving atoning sacrifice for sin, thus establishing a new covenant with his Father and so allowing all who believe in him to pass over from the realm of deadly sin into a living holy communion with his Father. Thus the crucified Jesus, by handing over his spirit to his *Abba*/Father on humankind's behalf, establishes that his *Abba*/Father is humankind's *Abba*/Father as well, and so empowers all who abide in him to address, rightly and authentically, God as their *Abba*/Father in his Spirit of Sonship. Jesus, then, is giving his life to *his* Father and even more so to *our* Father, for in giving his life to *our* Father, Jesus, on our behalf, constitutes *his* Father as *our* Father and constitutes us as the Father's *own* children.[43] By enacting the Our Father, in completely giving himself to his Father, Jesus enables God to be our *Abba*/Father and in so doing empowers the faithful to pray the Our Father in union with him, for they, sharing in his Spirit of Sonship, have been transfigured into his filial likeness.[44] Without Jesus offering his life to "our Father," and so enacting the Our Father on our behalf, we would not be able to call God our *Abba*/Father and so not be able to pray the Our Father as Jesus taught us.[45]

42. I use Matthew's rendition of the Our Father. See Mt 6:9-13. See also Lk 11:2-4.

43. Here I use the word "constitute" in two different senses. God is not "constituted" as humankind's Father by way of a change in him, that is, by changing him from not being "Father" to making him be "Father." The Father is eternally Father because he eternally begets his Son. What Jesus changes through his death on the cross is humankind's relationship with the Father, and because of that changed relationship, the Father is constituted as humankind's Father. And because of Jesus' death on the cross, humankind can be changed from not being the Father's children to becoming the Father's children and thus, through faith in Jesus and the transforming work of the indwelling Spirit, human beings are constituted as the Father's children, and so the Father becomes their Father.

44. This notion is in keeping with the Pauline understanding that Jesus is the head of his body and all his members are united to his Father through and in him. Partaking of his Spirit of Sonship, the faithful can now cry out, in union with him, *Abba*/Father (see Rom 8:14-17 and Gal 4:4-7).

45. Although those who are not Christians can "pray" the Our Father, they do not do so in

Upon the cross, Jesus gave over and so entrusted his spirit to his "heavenly" Father; thus the Our Father specifies further both the divine nature of his Father and his own divine filiation. As heavenly, his Father exists distinct from the created earthly order and so in a manner that differs in kind from of all else that exists, and thus as the Father's Son, Jesus exists in the same divine manner as his Father. Further, by dying on the cross on behalf of humankind, Jesus established that his heavenly Father is our heavenly Father, thus affirming that, because of his death, the faithful have access to and so share in the divine communal life that he shares with his heavenly Father. The faithful no longer have a relationship with God that is simply founded upon the act of creation, as being creatures, but upon their being taken up into the heavenly divine realm. They now partake of the uncreated divine life as children of the Father by abiding in Jesus, his Son, through the transforming indwelling communion of the Holy Spirit. In the light of the cross, Jesus' disciples can truly address God as "Our Father, who art in heaven," for they now abide with their heavenly Father.

Furthermore, by entrusting his life to his Father, the crucified Jesus is acknowledging that his heavenly Father providentially governs all earthly events, even his own crucifixion, and so his loving protective hand is upon him. Upon the cross, Jesus is teaching his disciples that they too can trust their now Father in heaven. When the faithful pray the Our Father, in union with Jesus, they are confessing with him that they too trust, in all circumstances even amid their own suffering and death, that they reside in the providential safety of their heavenly Father's hand.

Hallowed Be Thy Name

Because the Father is the heavenly Father, his name is to be hallowed; that is, the name "Father" designates him to be the all-holy God who is separated from all that is profane, and as such, God, as the named "Father, is to be acclaimed as holy. God is not holy simply because he is God, but rather his holiness is predicated upon his being the all-holy Father. God's fatherhood constitutes his holiness. To be the Father is simply to be the full expression of holiness in act and thus the source of all holiness. The Father's name is hollowed in the very fact that he is the Father of all that is good and holy, primordially and eternally in his begetting, in the hallowing love of the Holy Spirit, his all-good and all-holy Son. Because the fullness of divine holiness was eternally bestowed upon him in the Holy Spirit, the divine Son eternally hallows the name of his Father. Being the Son, bearing that name, implies that, as Son, he hallows—confesses, reverences, exults, and acclaims as holy—he

---

a true authentic manner. Only Christians can properly pray the Our Father, for only they have been transformed into his children through the power of the indwelling Holy Spirit. Only they have a relationship with God such that he truly is their *Abba*/Father. This is obviously why becoming a Christian is so salvifically important and why to evangelize is such a loving deed.

who bears the name "Father." Within the hallowing communion of the Holy Spirit, the Father and Son reciprocally hallow one another; that is, the Father paternally hallows the Son he has begotten in the love of the Holy Spirit, and the Son filially hallows the Father in the same hallowing love of the Holy Spirit in whom the Father lovingly begot him.

The Father, in creating human beings in the divine image and likeness of his Son, also lovingly desired to share his holy divine life, the communion of the Holy Spirit, with human beings. In so doing, human beings were to hallow—acknowledge, confess, and worship—the Father in the Son through the Holy Spirit. They were to hallow the Father as the source of all holiness, and they were to do so after the manner of his Son as his children, and they were to do so from within the very holiness of the Spirit. As human beings were divinely hallowed, so they were to hallow the Father, the Son, and the Holy Spirit. Such would only be loving, just, and proper. But the act of sin by its very nature is an unholy act and thus contrary to the holiness of God the Father. Sin is a desecrating act, one that defiles and violates the Father's holy name. Sin is a blasphemous insult to the very holy name "Father." From the time of Adam and Eve's sin, from the time of their despoiling the Father of his rightful hallowing, human beings, in their unholy sinfulness, were rendered incapable of hallowing the God who bears the name Father. Thus this incapacitation of rendering holy the Father's name meant that humankind's very relationship with the Father was defiled and desecrated, and thus rendered null and void. Humankind, which now bears the name "unholy," was incapable of fellowship with he who bears the name "holy"—God the Father. Humankind was therefore unable to pray to God as "Father," for as unholy sinners, God was no longer their Father whose name they could hallow. Here we perceive the theological importance and soteriological significance of Jesus enacting the Our Father in his very death on the cross.

In assuming humanity from the sinful race of Adam, Jesus, the Father's all-holy Son, took upon himself sin's condemnation: death. Yet on the cross Jesus transfigured or transposed that condemnatory death into a prayerful hallowing act of worship by offering himself on humankind's behalf as an all-holy and loving sacrifice to his Father, and so perfectly hallowing his Father's name as the all-hallowed Father. When Jesus lovingly placed his spirit in the hands of his Father, when he breathed his last, he who bears the name "Son" perfectly hallowed him who bears the name "Father," and in so doing made reparation or satisfaction for humankind's sinful un-hallowing acts, which desecrated and violated his Father's holy name. In so doing, Jesus reconciled sinful and unholy humankind to his Father, thus reestablishing humankind's holy relationship to his all-holy Father, restoring humankind's holiness. In Jesus, as the all-holy Spirit-filled Christ, the faithful are now empowered to once more hallow their Father's name both in holy worship and through their holy acts. In enacting the Our Father upon the cross, Jesus made it possible for humankind to hallow his Father's name, for in communion with him they can now truthfully pray: "Our Father, who art in heaven, hallowed be thy name."

We have been treating "hallowed be thy name" as a declarative statement. Likewise, Jesus' death on the cross is a declarative action—of hallowing he who bears the name Father. Those who now live in union with Jesus are also able to hallow the Father through their worship, as in the Our Father itself, and in their holy virtuous actions. But "hallowed be thy name" can also be interpreted as an act of petition, a request that the Father's name be hallowed, that all creation might come to hallow the name of the Father and so give to him the praise, honor, and glory that he deserves as the all-holy Father. In his death, Jesus is not only hallowing his Father and so making it possible for all who will come to abide in him to hallow their Father as well, but also petitioning the Father to hallow him and all his future brothers and sisters so that they, in their holiness, might always hallow the Father—a growing community of faithful, both on earth and in heaven, who testify in prayer and deed, to the Father's holiness.

Hidden, then, within this request is also the entreaty that Jesus' own name, as the incarnate Son, be hallowed. As the Son eternally hallows his Father and the Father eternally hallows his Son, so now upon the cross, specifically in his death, Jesus is requesting, through his hallowing of his Father, that his Father hallow him. Jesus' entreaty is answered. In his all-holy and all-loving sacrificial death Jesus, the Son, hallows his Father, but simultaneously the Father is hallowing—displaying, affirming, and proclaiming—the holiness of his Son. Within the act of Jesus' hallowing all-holy death, the Father hallows the all-holy name of Jesus, his Son.[46] Thus those who abide in Jesus and so pray, in union with him, the Our Father are not only declaring the holiness of their Father, but also petitioning to be hallowed, declared, and made holy, by their Father. They too desire that their names be hallowed, for they abide with Jesus, he who bears the all-holy name, YHWH-Saves, he who makes the faithful holy.

Now, this salvific efficacious simultaneous enactment of Jesus' hallowing his Father's name and the Father hallowing his Son's name, Jesus, is found within the Eucharistic Liturgy. There, first enacted in the Last Supper, the faithful are unit-

---

46. Jesus' high priestly prayer within the Gospel of John can be seen as his "expanded version" of, and so his "commentary" on, the Our Father. Jesus prays: "Now is the Son of man glorified, and in him God is glorified; if God is glorified in him, God will also glorify him in himself, and glorify him at once" (Jn 13:31-32). As the Father's perfect Word, the Father eternally hallows and glorifies the name of his Son, for the Son expresses his own name in its entirety. Moreover, the Son eternally hallows and glorifies his Father, from whom he was begotten as the Father's perfect Word and Image. The event of the cross is the earthly historical act by which and in which the Father and Son mutually hallowed and glorified one another. "Father, the hour has come; glorify your Son that the Son may glorify you, ... I glorified you on earth, having accomplished the work which you gave me to do; and now, Father, glorify you me in your own presence with the glory which I had with you before the world was made" (Jn 17:1 and 17:4).

ed to Jesus' salvific sacrifice and so share in his perfect hallowing of his Father's name. By sharing in Jesus' perfect act of hallowing the Father, they too share in the Father's hallowing of Jesus. In Jesus, the faithful participate in the one holy saving sacrifice for sin and in so doing in Jesus reap the benefits of that one holy saving sacrifice by being made holy themselves. As they hallow their Father in Jesus his Son, so they are hallowed by their Father in Jesus his Son. By enacting the Our Father through his hallowing death, Jesus hallows the Eucharistic Liturgy—the supreme act of holy worship in which the worshippers themselves become holy. This hallowing finds it climactic realization in the reception of Jesus' risen body, that holy body that was given up to their Father for them, and in the reception of his risen blood, that holy blood that was poured out unto their Father for them, for by being in living communion with the all-holy Jesus the faithful hallow their Father who simultaneously hallows them his holy children.[47]

Thy Kingdom Come, Thy Will Be Done, on Earth as It Is in Heaven

In breathing his last, in yielding up of his spirit, in committing his life into the hands of his Father, in this one hallowing act of sacrificial love and worship, Jesus definitively petitions his Father to send forth his kingdom. Simultaneously within that same petition, Jesus establishes his Father's kingdom, for the petition itself is the first perfect holy act of sacrificial worship of his Father, an act of hallowing worship that embodies, expresses, and so constitutes the very kingdom of God. In that same act of establishing his Father's kingdom, Jesus becomes its king, for his all-hallowing act of sacrificial worship is the foundational kingly act upon which the kingdom is founded. As king of his Father's kingdom, Jesus destroyed the kingdom of evil and vanquished the reign of death—all that desecrates his Father's hallowed name—and he simultaneously opens the gates of his heavenly Father's kingdom, which is freed from sin and death and is filled with life, holiness, and love. It is a kingdom that is imbued with the Holy Spirit. Likewise, in establishing his Father's kingdom, Jesus is petitioning the Father on behalf of all who would enter into his kingdom—all those who acknowledge and profess him to be their all-holy king—so that they too would live with him the holy life of his Father's kingdom. By enacting the Our Father in his death, by establishing his Fa-

47. I do not know when the Our Father was placed as it is within the Eucharistic Liturgy. But it strikes me as properly placed. It is right and just that having participated in the holy sacrificial offering of Jesus' body and blood, the faithful, as the Father's holy children, are able to pray truly the prayer that Jesus taught them. Having prayed the Our Father, the faithful, by partaking of Jesus' risen body and blood, can then rightly and justly come to abide in full communion with their Father through their being in communion with Jesus, his Son, within the communion of the Holy Spirit.

ther's kingdom, Jesus made it possible for all who abide in him to live in that kingdom and as its citizens to pray to their Father, petitioning him to make evermore present his kingdom in their midst until it comes to its fulfillment at the coming of their glorious king at the end of time—Jesus Christ, the Lord of the kingdom, and the Savior of the world. Jesus, by enacting the Our Father through his death on the cross, fulfills Gabriel' prophecy that the son born of Mary would inherit the kingdom of his ancestor David over which he would reign forever. Likewise, Jesus fulfilled the prophetic acts of his baptism, his Transfiguration, and his triumphal entry into Jerusalem, for to enter into God's kingdom, the new Jerusalem, is to enter into his Father's presence and so be transfigured into his glorious likeness and thus empowered to baptize in the Holy Spirit all who profess him to be their king.

The coming of the heavenly Father's kingdom through the sacrificially hallowing of his name is predicated upon Jesus doing his Father's will. Although Jesus obediently assumed in the Holy Spirit his Father's commission to be the Suffering Servant-Son at his baptism, it was within his agony in the Garden that he fully and definitively embraced that will.[48] There Jesus called upon his *Abba*/Father to remove, if possible, his cup of suffering, but "not what I will, but what you will" (Mk 14:36). In his sacrificial death, in his lovingly handing over his spirit to his *Abba*/Father, Jesus perfectly fulfills his Father's will, and so this act of all-hallowing obedience is the causal act that effects the coming of his heavenly Father's kingdom.[49] From all eternity, the heavenly Son "obediently" willed the will of his Father, and so now on earth, Jesus, the Father's Son, obediently freely wills and enacts his Father's will, and in so doing effects the coming of his Father's kingdom and thus establishes himself as its everlasting king. By enacting the Our Father, Jesus made it possible for all who enter God's kingdom through him to be empowered, through the Holy Spirit, to do the Father's will. To live in Jesus the king is to live in the Father's kingdom, and so in him to do the Father's will. Thus the faithful can now rightly pray in and with Jesus—he who eternally obeyed the Father in heaven and on earth—that they on earth, and all of humankind, may always obey the Father, as his will is always obeyed by his Son, angels, and saints in heaven.[50] This desire will find its completion when Jesus, the king, comes in glory,

48. Throughout his public ministry, Jesus did the will of his Father. This is especially seen in John's Gospel (see Jn 5:19, 30, 6:38, and 8:16). The Letter to the Hebrews states that the Son became man to do the will of God and so offer the perfect sacrifice once for all (see Heb 10:10). Significantly, only those who do his Father's will are Jesus' brothers and sisters, for then they too will be acting as children of the Father (see Mk 3:35).

49. Paul articulates this theological point within his Philippian hymn: "And being found in human form he humbled himself and became obedient unto death, even death on a cross." Also, because Jesus was humbly obedient even unto death that his Father "highly exalted him and bestowed on him the name which is above every name, that at the name of Jesus every knee should bow, in heaven and on earth and under the earth, and every tongue confess that Jesus Christ is Lord, to the glory of God the Father" (Phil 2:8-11).

50. The Our Father then expresses, unlike Adam and Eve, the desire to be obedient to

for then all of creation and all human beings, both condemned and saved, will do the Father's will, either in hatred or in love, within the new heaven and the new earth, the new creation that is the Father's everlasting kingdom.

Give Us This Day Our Daily Bread

After Adam sinned, God said to him, "In the sweat of your face you shall eat bread" (Gn 3:19). When in the desert the Israelites were incapable of providing bread by the sweat of their brows, God freely gave them manna, bread from heaven (see Ex 16:4). This not only prophetically anticipated the Father sending down from heaven Jesus, his Son, as the new bread, but also demonstrated that only God could release Adam's race of his original curse. Thus the Father freed humankind from his imposed curse by sending down from heaven his Son, who literally embodies, as man, the Father's eternal life. As the Father's incarnate Son, Jesus is the new bread of life. In sending his Son, the Father also lovingly provided the means by which humankind could be released from his curse. Only upon the cross, through his Adamic sweat and blood, did Jesus, the new Adam, free Adam and his descendants (which included Jesus himself) from the curse and procured for them the new bread of life that his Father would send down from heaven—Jesus' own risen body and blood. Through his enacting of the Our Father, Jesus again simultaneously obtains that for which he petitions his Father. In giving himself to his Father as an all-hallowing sacrifice on humankind's behalf, Jesus transforms himself into the new living bread of his Father's kingdom, for all who eat of him, the risen holy sacrificial victim, and so abide in him, will partake of his eternal and incorruptible life. Moreover, by enacting the Our Father and so becoming the bread of life, Jesus makes possible the enactment, the making present, the new eschatological meal that is the Eucharistic banquet—the everlasting Last Supper—which the faithful can already partake of here on earth. Because of Jesus' enactment of the Our Father, the faithful who live in his Father's kingdom here on earth are able confidently to petition their Father daily, within the Our Father, for the living bread that nurtures life within his kingdom and makes it flourish, that is, the living bread that is the risen Jesus himself.[51]

---

the Father's commands. Likewise, Jesus' obedience undoes the disobedience of Adam. As Paul states, "Then as one man's trespass led to condemnation for all men, so one man's act of righteousness leads to acquittal and life for all men. For as one man's disobedience many were made sinners, so by one man's obedience many will be made righteous" (Rom 5:18-19).

51. Obviously, the faithful in praying the Our Father are also praying for "earthly" daily bread. But they do so knowing that only in receiving the "heavenly" bread that is Jesus will they live unto eternal life. This is keeping with Jesus' own teaching within the Gospel of John, chapter 6, where Jesus says that he is the true bread that comes down from heaven, and this true heavenly bread is his flesh and blood. Those who eat his flesh and drink his blood will have eternal life (see Jn 6:54). Significantly, Jesus articulates a threefold communion. "As the living Father sent me, and I live because of the Father, so he who eats me will live because of

And Forgive Us Our Trespasses as We Forgive Those Who Trespass against Us

In breathing out his spirit, his last breath, and so putting his life into the hands of his Father as an obedient sacrificial hallowing of his Father's name, Jesus obtained, on behalf of humankind, the forgiveness of sins. Jesus' atoning death was a petition to his Father for forgiveness, and so holy and loving was Jesus hallowing death that the Father heard and answered his suppliant plea. By entering into God's kingdom through faith in Jesus as its king and savior and so being baptized in his Holy Spirit, the faithful are cleansed of sin and made holy. Only by enacting the Our Father, in obtaining the forgiveness of sins, did Jesus make the truth of the Our Father actual, and in so doing he empowered the faithful to pray, in union with him, for the forgiveness of their sins. Without the cross, the faithful's petitioning of the Father's forgiveness would be pointless and futile.[52]

The faithful's plea for the forgiveness of their trespasses is also predicated upon the next phrase, "as we forgive those who trespass against us." As the faithful forgive others, so they are asking the Father to forgive them. This is in keeping with Jesus' teaching within the Sermon on the Mount. "For if you forgive men their trespasses, your heavenly Father also will forgive you; but if you do not forgive men their trespasses, neither will your Father forgive you your trespasses" (Mt 6:14-15). Again, Jesus, on the cross, perfectly fulfilled this prerequisite. "Father, forgive them; for they know not what they do" (Lk 23:34). Although the primary referents were those who had condemned and crucified him, Jesus was forgiving all who sin because, ultimately, all sinners do not fully grasp the horrendous evil of their sinful actions. The perfection of the Father also resides precisely in his merciful forgiveness (see Mt 5:48 and Lk 6:36). The Father is the source of all mercy, and only Jesus is as perfect as his Father, for only he is as merciful as his Father. The faithful, then, are to pray, in unison with Jesus, as he prayed. Likewise, in communion with the Father and the Son, sharing in the merciful love of the Holy Spirit, the faithful too are able mercifully to forgive those who have sinned against them.

---

me" (Jn 6:57). As the eternal Son, Jesus shares in the eternal life of his Father. Also, those who eat of his risen flesh and drink of his risen blood are in communion with not only the living Jesus but also with his Father, the source of all life, and so, in and through Jesus, partake of the same eternal life that Jesus possesses.

Praying the Our Father immediately after the Eucharistic Prayer is appropriate. Within Jesus' once and for all sacrifice, the faithful can rightly request from their Father their daily bread that is Jesus himself—the gift of heavenly bread given to them by their heavenly Father.

52. Although God did forgive sins prior to Jesus atoning death, he did so only in anticipation of Jesus' atoning death.

Lead Us Not into Temptation, but Deliver Us from All Evil

We know that Jesus on the cross prayed Psalm 22. He cried out, "My God, my God, why have you forsaken me?" Jesus had committed himself to drink the cup of suffering during his agony in the Garden, but on the cross he suffered the emotional experience of being abandoned by his Father. In trusting faith, Jesus humanly knew that this is not true, but this was also his greatest human temptation—the loss of his loving *Abba*/Father. "Why are you so far from helping me, from the words of my groaning?" (Ps 22:2). Jesus' cry of dereliction was inherently a petitioning cry. In enacting the Our Father, the crucified Jesus, amid feeling abandoned, was enacting the plea that his Father would not lead him into an insurmountable temptation, that his Father would free him from the grip of this lying fear and deceitful anguish. He was praying that the Father would send upon him the comforting love and enduring strength of the Spirit. In handing over his spirit to his *Abba*/Father, Jesus overthrows his temptation confident of his Father's loving acceptance.

Jesus is enacting the Our Father on behalf of all of humankind, especially the faithful—the "us." Thus, when the faithful presently pray "lead us not into temptation," they do so in the light of the cross and in union with Jesus, he whom the Father freed from temptation. The faithful are joining themselves to the prayer that Jesus is always praying on their behalf. He is ever interceding in communion with them. He is petitioning his Father to always send forth his Holy Spirit, his Spirit of truth and courage, so that all his disciples would overcome every temptation—the incessant lies of Satan. And amid the church's suffering, cares, and concerns, she too prays that, as one with Jesus her Savior and King, the Father will free her from the greatest of all temptations: the seemingly hopeless eschatological temptation of being forever abandoned by the Father. The faithful too at times feel that they no longer reside in the loving presence of their Father, and yet with Jesus they know in confident faith and unwavering trust that this temptation, despite it seeming reality, is simply that—a temptation. If the Father never abandoned his crucified Son, he will never abandon the church or any of those who now live in communion with his risen Son.

The ultimate resolution to being led into temptation is to be delivered from evil, from which all temptations arise. On the cross, within the all-hallowing self-offering as the perfect atoning sacrifice, Jesus petitioned his Father to deliver himself and the whole of humankind from all evil—the dominion of Satan, the enslavement to sin, and the condemnation of death. Again, the nature of the petition contains its end. The cross is the petition to be freed from all evil, and it is the means by which all evil is vanquished. In being reconciled and so united to the Father, living in his kingdom, the faithful obtain their authentic human freedom to live holy lives. Without the cross, there is no deliverance from evil, but in Jesus, because he enacted the Our Father upon the cross, Jesus' disciples can confidently pray to their Father as he, the Son, taught them: "deliver us from evil." We perceive here the conjoining of the beginning and end of the Our Father—the causal relationship between "thy kingdom come" and "deliver us from evil," for in the coming of God's kingdom there is the deliverance from all evil. The act that brings about God's kingdom and so delivers "us from evil" are one and the same: the all-hallowing obedient sacrificial death of Jesus.

Conclusion: The Resurrection

Throughout our examination of Jesus' enacting the Our Father upon the cross, the reality of the resurrection is evident. Jesus' enacting of the Our Father upon the cross precipitates the Father raising him glorious from the dead. Again, there is a causal relationship. Because Jesus freely did his Father's will in giving his life as an all-hallowing atoning sacrifice for sin, his Father responded by raising him gloriously from the dead. The resurrection is the Father's enacted answer to Jesus' enacted cruciform plea, thus making Jesus the answer to his own prayer. As Jesus, upon the cross, breathed forth his human Spirit-filled spirit into the hands of his Father, so his Father breathed forth his resurrecting Spirit into Jesus' spiritless humanity, and in this communion of enjoining S/spirits, the Our Father was simply enacted. The Father's act of raising him from the dead is conjoined to Jesus' priestly act of sacrifice, and their conjoined acts are what established God's kingdom, of which Jesus is the risen king; constituted Jesus as the heavenly daily bread of eternal life; assured the forgiveness of trespasses; and inaugurated the deliverance from evil. Conformed by the Spirit of Sonship into the likeness of Jesus, the Son, the faithful, then, in union with Jesus, can daily pray the Our Father knowing that what they pray is indeed efficaciously true and the realities of which they pray can be lived out in their daily lives.

To conclude, by enacting the Our Father in his breathing out his Spirit-filled spirit into the hands of his Father, Jesus became Jesus—YHWH-Saves. In so doing, he empowered all the saved to pray, in the same Spirit, the Our Father.

12 · JESUS'S RESURRECTION
AND ASCENSION

Throughout this study, the resurrection and the cross have loomed large, for the entire Gospel finds its culmination in these two conjoined mysteries. From Jesus' conception and birth, from his baptism and the onset of his Spirit-filled public ministry, the Gospels point in one direction, to Jerusalem, where Jesus would die and rise from the dead and so fulfill his Father's plan of salvation. All that goes before prophetically anticipates and so antecedently interprets these two salvific events. As was evident in chapter 11, it is impossible to speak of the theological and soteriological significance of that mystery without conjoining it to the resurrection, for Jesus' death inextricably leads to his resurrection. His resurrection not only validates his saving death but also bestows its salvific blessings. Nonetheless, within this final chapter, we examine the resurrection texts within Matthew, Mark, and Luke. Our purpose is not to attempt to sort out their historical and narrative complexity, a task no scholar has accomplished, but to discern further the theological importance and soteriological significance of Jesus' resurrection and in so doing advance and corroborate what we have already observed.[1]

The Women Return to the Tomb

Having seen where he was buried, the last to leave the scene of Jesus' crucifixion and death are Mary Magdalene and Mary the mother of Joses (see Mt 27:61 and Mk 15:47). Significantly, the first to return to the tomb are "Mary Magdalene and the other Mary" (Mt; Mark specifies that it was Mary the mother of James,

---

1. Various accounts of Jesus' resurrected appearances within the Synoptic Gospels do not entirely agree. Nor are they in total harmony with the Gospel of John. Paul's brief delineation of the sequence of Jesus' resurrected appearances adds even greater muddle to an already confused state of affairs (see 1 Cor 15:3-8).

and adds Salome). Luke initially refers to the generic Galilean women but later specifies that they were "Mary Magdalene and Joanna and Mary the mother of James and the other women with them."[2] Thus the women who witnessed his burial and his tomb are the same women who will find the same tomb empty. In neither case is their presence happenstance. They are purposely positioned as credible witnesses to the tomb being "full" and to its being empty.

Now these women, the Sabbath having ended, came to the tomb "early on the first day of the week" (Mk; Mt specifies "toward dawn" and Lk states "when the sun had risen").[3] This manifests that the women were anxiously awaiting the end of the Sabbath so that they could quickly return to the tomb with their spices and anoint the body of Jesus. In this act they were expressing their ardent love and devotion for Jesus even though he was now dead.[4] In addition, given that this is the dawn of a new day, the first day of a new week, the day upon which Jesus, having himself observed the Sabbath rest, has arisen, this solar dawn gives soteriological expression to a new dawn, a new day, that of a new creation where the light and life of the Holy Spirt has now appeared upon the horizon, vanquishing the darkness of sin and death. This is the eschatological eighth day, the dawning of God's everlasting kingdom in the rising of the kingdom's glorious king, the Father's luminously transfigured Son, Jesus Christ. Although the women thought they were rushing off at the crack of dawn to anoint the body of a dead loved one, a body of the death-

---

2. All quotations in this section are from Mt 28:1-15, Mk 16:1-12, and Lk 24:1-12 unless otherwise noted. Within the Gospel of John, Mary Magdalene goes to the tomb alone and finds the stone rolled away. She immediately runs to tell "Simon Peter and the other disciple" that "They have taken the Lord out of the tomb, and we do not know where they have laid him" (see Jn 20:1-2). Mary's words imply that the tomb is empty because the body is gone. Although Mary is portrayed as going alone, she tells Peter and the other disciple that "we" do not know where Jesus' body is now laid. The "we" could be those mentioned in the Synoptic Gospels.

3. Mark tells of their discussion along the way. "Who will roll away the stone for us from the door of the tomb?" This again confirms that the stone, as Mark later notes in accordance with Matthew, "was very large," making it impossible for "the weaker sex" to physically accomplish its removal. The fact that they found this large stone already rolled away heightens the fact that this being so was not because of the women.

4. The Synoptic Gospels tell of Joseph of Arimathea wrapping Jesus' body only in a linen shroud prior to burial (see Mt 27:59, Mk 15:46, and Lk 23:53). With the impending onset of the Sabbath, he apparently did not anoint Jesus' body for lack of time. Thus the women now come with spices to properly anoint Jesus' body, as was the Jewish custom. In the Gospel of John, however, Joseph of Arimathea and Nicodemus, who brought spices, do anoint the body of Jesus before burial. John's Gospel does not then tell of Mary Magdalene bringing spices with her to the tomb on the morning following the Sabbath (see Jn 19:38-20:1).

cursed race of ancient Adam, they were actually rushing off at the crack of dawn to meet the true light of an everlasting day, the life-blessed new Adam.

The Angels

The Synoptics provide similar though variant accounts of what the women found upon their arrival. The women, in Mark's account, having discussed their dilemma of the large stone in need of removal, looked up and found that the stone had already been rolled away. In entering the tomb, "they saw a young man sitting on the right side, dressed in a white robe; and they were amazed." Mark's is the simplest and most straightforward account. While not explicitly stating that the "young man" is an angel, his surprising presence and his white attire suggest that he is such. He is quietly sitting as if expectantly awaiting their arrival.[5] The fact that the stone had been rolled away and that the women "were amazed" upon seeing him supports this interpretation. Luke also says that the women found the stone rolled away, "but when they went in they did not find the body. While they were perplexed, two men stood by them in dazzling apparel; and as they were frightened and bowed their faces to the ground." Here the women first observe that Jesus' body is gone. The absence of the body thus becomes the cause or reason for what they saw next. In their perplexity at not finding Jesus' body, they saw not one (Mk) but "two men" dressed, not simply in white (Mk) but "in dazzling apparel." The "amazed" women in Mark become "frightened" in Luke, and so they bow their faces to the ground in reverence rather than look upon the alarming appearance of the two dazzlingly appareled men. A theophany is being enacted here.

On the one hand, there is the conundrum of "the great stone." Who will roll it away? But it is found to be rolled away. Moreover, there is no body, even though its presence within the tomb is the reason for the women's crack-of-dawn dash. This is the "natural" discovered scene. On the other hand, entwined within the issues of the unrolled/rolled stone and the absence of the body is the unaccountable and surprising presence of a "young" man or two men within the tomb and his "white robe" or their "dazzling apparel," which bespeaks the presence of the divine. Importantly, the totality of this scene now signals divine causality. The reason why the great stone is rolled away

---

5. That Mark specifies that he was sitting "on the right side" adds credence to the historicity of the event.

and why Jesus' body is not found is because God has acted in a way that accounts for both, and the presence of the mysterious "divinely" appareled man/men tells of that divine causal connection. Before examining what is said, however, it is first necessary to turn to Matthew's account.

In keeping with his cataclysmic earthquake upon Jesus' death, Matthew states: "And behold, there was a great earthquake; for an angel of the Lord descended from heaven and came and rolled back the stone, and sat upon it. His appearance was like lightning, and his raiment white as snow." This twofold "earthquake," for Matthew, conjoins Jesus' death to his resurrection. As the first earthquake signaled the tearing of the temple curtain, so the second earthquake signaled the rolling back of the of the tomb's stone—as the death of Jesus gave unencumbered access to the Father, so the resurrection gives unencumbered access, no obstructing great stone, to the living Jesus. To have access to the risen Jesus is to have access to the living Father. And just as the temple curtain was rent top to bottom, giving entrance into the Holy of Holies, the descent "from heaven" of "an angel of the Lord" testifies to this access to Jesus, this angel is now responsible in Matthew for rolling away the stone. He regally sits upon it in proud triumph of his divinely accomplished work. Thus no human being rolled back the great stone but God himself, through his messenger angel, and he did so in raising his Son Jesus from the dead. The true opening was made from a divinely bursting forth from within the tomb and not simply a rolling back from without. The great stone may have secured death in the tomb, but the resurrection unchained the great stone of death's tomb, making it a liberated tomb of life. The heavenly angel is the Father's personal presence and manifest sign that the tomb is now open, just as the heavens are.

That Matthew portrays this heavenly angel as appearing "like lightning" with "his raiment white as snow" alludes to Jesus' own transfiguration, where "his face shone like the sun, and his garments became white as light" (Mt 17:2). For the women to behold the man "dressed in white" (Mk) with "dazzling apparel" (Lk) is to see a heavenly angel of the Lord appearing as "lightning" with garments "white as snow" (Mt). And to behold such a being is but a prophetic declaration of the glory and splendor of the resurrection and an anticipatory vision of beholding the even more dazzling and lightning-white resurrected humanity of Jesus—the risen Son of God incarnate. It is not that Jesus, in the fullness of his risen humanity, is like a radiant spirit angel of light, but rather that the spirit angel of light is like the radiant Spirit-filled humanity of the risen Jesus, and so Jesus is the exemplar of the image and likeness of God's own radiant being, not the angels.[6]

Also, in keeping with his account of setting the security guard before Jesus' tomb, Matthew first relates the reaction of the soldiers upon the onset of the earthquake and the descent of the radiant heavenly angel. "And for fear of him [the angel] the guards trembled and became like dead men." Unlike the now "living" tomb they were to guard, the soldiers become "dead," having been stunned into stone-cold fear. Matthew has also already unmasked the falsity of the soldiers' later public testimony that they were asleep when Jesus' body was stolen.[7] But the angel pays them no mind and immediately turns to speak to the women who had arrived at the onset of the earthquake and his luminous appearance. Here the Synoptics come back into sync.

The Message of the Angels

Within Mark, the angel states to the astonished women, "Do not be amazed; you seek Jesus of Nazareth, who was crucified. He has risen, he is not here; see the place where they laid him. But go, tell his disciples and Peter that he is going before you to Galilee; there you will see him, as he told you." In Luke's account, the two men say to the women who had bowed their faces to the ground: "Why do you seek the living among the dead? He is not here but risen.

6. I later treat this theological and soteriological issue, but here I note that although the gleaming angel bears testimony to the divine act of Jesus being gloriously raised from the dead, he never appears to any human being in his radiant splendor within the Gospels, including John. He always appears as a "normal" human being, though with the uncanny resurrected ability to appear and disappear at will, whether along a road or within a locked room, and at times in a manner where he is not recognized until he reveals himself. Why? One would think that it would be to Jesus' "resurrected advantage" and to the "faith advantage" of those to whom he appeared that he would display his risen glorious humanity.

Jesus' appearance to Paul is a significant exception because he does not appear to him as a "normal" man as in the Gospel appearances. "Now as he journeyed he approached Damascus, and suddenly a light from heaven flashed about him" (Acts 9:3; see also 22:6 and 22:13). Although this light is not explicitly identified with the risen Jesus, it is within that heavenly light that Jesus spoke to Paul. In 1 Cor 18:8, Paul states, "Last of all, as one untimely born, he [Jesus] appeared also to me." Presumably that resurrected appearance was radiant in keeping with the heavenly light. The reason Jesus appeared to Paul in his glory is, I think, because this appearance is a "post-Ascension" appearance and one in which Jesus wanted to assure Paul that he is his glorious Lord and Savior.

7. Despite having experienced the earthquake and seen the radiant angel, the guards, at least within Matthew's Gospel, do not come to faith in Jesus, and there is no extrabiblical tradition in which they ever did. Rather, they accepted a bribe and told a lie (see Mt 28:11-15).

Remember how he told you, while he was still in Galilee, that the Son of man must be delivered into the hands of sinful men, and be crucified, and on the third day rise." In Matthew, the angel says, "Do not be afraid; for I know that you seek Jesus who was crucified. He is not here; for he has risen, as he said. Come, see the place where he lay. Then go quickly and tell his disciples that he has arisen from the dead, and behold, he is going before you to Galilee; there you will see him. Lo, I have told you." The angel's words within Matthew and Mark can be divided into two points. First, there is the message of Jesus' resurrection and, second, the charge to tell the Apostles and then to proceed to Galilee, where they will see Jesus. Luke does not narrate the second point as a message from the angels, but the women within his Gospel inform the disciples. Thus all three contain both points, and we will examine each topic in turn.

The women are not to be "amazed" (Mk) or "frightened" (Mt), for the angel knows of whom they seek "Jesus of Nazareth, who was crucified" (Mk) or simply "Jesus who was crucified" (Mt). In coming to the tomb, the women are seeking a historical person who was crucified—Jesus by name who is geographically from Nazareth. By providing this "down-to-earth" data, the angel deprives what he states next of any mythological or ethereal interpretation. Thus Jesus of Nazareth, whom the women knew to have been crucified here in Jerusalem, "has risen, he is not here; see the place where they laid him" (Mk) or he who "is not here; for he has risen as he said. Come see the place where he lay" (Mt). The reason the women do not see Jesus' corpse is because Jesus is not in the tomb. The women can see for themselves the empty place where his body once lay. The body is absent precisely because Jesus is risen. Significantly, the absence of the body, and so the reason for Jesus not being "here," is conjoined to his being risen—the conclusion to be drawn is that Jesus has risen bodily. Jesus, the man from Nazareth who was historically bodily crucified, is the same historical man who has now bodily risen, and thus the humanity with which he died is the same humanity with which he now lives. There is a full ontological and anthropological historical identity between the man who died and the man who is risen—his name is Jesus, and he hails from Nazareth. This is of the greatest soteriological significance. Jesus, the Son of God, lovingly offered his human life to his Father as an atoning sacrifice for humankind's sin, and the efficaciousness of that sacrifice is achieved only if Jesus, the Son of God, is raised gloriously from the dead, possessing the same humanity with which he died. If that same humanity was not now raised, if the Jesus who died does not presently possess the same humanity with which he was crucified, then humankind is not saved by and through that humanity. In short, salvation is predicated upon the same Jesus who died, the same Jesus who was raised, and this sameness is historically, ontologically, and anthropologically constituted by the risen Jesus possessing the same humanity, the same body, that died. Thus the humanity that the Son of God assumed for humankind's salvation in his incarnation must be the same humanity that was raised for humankind's salvation.

Herein lies the significance of the angel not literally speaking the truth from within the perspective of the women: "You seek Jesus of Nazareth, who was crucified" (Mk) or "I know that you seek Jesus who was crucified" (Mt). The women did not come to the tomb seeking Jesus of Nazareth. They came to the tomb seeking *the body* of Jesus for the sole purpose of anointing it. They presumed that Jesus would not be there because they knew he died. But the angel realized that in desiring, in love, to anoint Jesus' body, the women mourned for his loss and in their grief longed for him to still be alive—though they "knew" he was not. The angel speaks to their innermost desire—they are not merely seeking the body of Jesus but the man Jesus himself. The angel proclaims to them the truth that Jesus is not "here" but risen, and the absence of his body, which was constitutive of his historical humanity, testifies to his being truly humanly alive. Herein too lies the significance of the angels' words within Luke: "Why do you seek the living among the dead? He is not here, but has risen." The women did not come to the tomb seeking the living among the dead. They purposefully came seeking the dead among the dead. But while coming to the tomb in a mistaken search, the women, within their inner longing, are also mournfully seeking Jesus, who they hoped would be their Messiah, Savior, and Lord. Luke's angels simply admonish the women for seeking Jesus in the wrong location and so bring to life the women's dormant hope. They announce to the women that the historical man Jesus, whom they loved and still love, does not abide among the dead, as the women presumed, for he, the same Jesus, is risen, and so abides, as the women had hoped, among the living.

Within Matthew, the angel confirms this proclamation of Jesus' resurrection by stating, almost as an aside, "as he [Jesus] said."[8] In Luke, the angels elaborate more fully. "'Remember how he told you, while he was still in Galilee, that he must be delivered into the hands of sinful men, and be crucified,

---

8. The angel appears to be referring to Jesus' telling his Apostles on the way to the Mount of Olives: "You will all fall away; for it is written, 'I will strike the shepherd, and the sheep will be scattered.' But after I am raised up, I will go before you to Galilee" (Mk 14:26-28).

and on the third day rise.' And they [the women] remembered his words."
What the angels are reminding the women is Jesus' own thrice-proclaimed
prophecy (see Lk 9:22, 9:44, and 18:31-33), and in so doing confirming their
own proclamation that Jesus, who was crucified and died, has risen on the
third day and so is alive. Within the angels' reference to Jesus' own words,
the word "must" is theologically significant. Jesus said that he *must* suffer, die,
and rise, and he did so recognizing that such *must* be the case so that what was
written of him in the Scriptures would be fulfilled, and specifically within the
Suffering Servant Songs within Isaiah (see Lk 22:37; Is 53:12). Thus the angels,
in recalling Jesus' prophetic words concerning his death and resurrection, are
equally recalling his statement that the whole of Scripture must be fulfilled in
him. This in turn alerts the women, and subsequently all interpreters of Jesus'
death and resurrection, to search for appropriate passages that provide salvific
meaning to Jesus' death and resurrection, many of which we treated in chapter 11, on Jesus' death, for example, Psalm 22 and similar psalms, the Suffering
Servant Songs from Isaiah and the Book of Wisdom, chapters 2 and 3. Luke's
Gospel continues this emphasis of Jesus fulfilling the Scriptures, with Jesus
providing the emphasis.

Having treated the first of the angel's topics, we will now treat the second,
remembering that although Luke provides it, it is not part of the angels' proclamation. Within Matthew the angel tells the women "to go quickly and tell
his disciples that he has risen from the dead, and behold he is going before you
to Galilee; there you will see him. Lo, I have told you" (Mt). In Mark the angel says, "But go, tell his disciples and Peter he is going before you to Galilee;
there you will see him, as he told you" (Mk).[9] Having found Jesus' tomb empty
and having been told by the angel that Jesus is risen, the women are now commissioned to proclaim this news to his disciples and, in Mark, specifically to
Peter.[10] These women, particularly Mary Magdalene, become the first fully authorized evangelists—proclaiming that Jesus, who was crucified, died and was
buried, is now risen. And they have rightly deserved this honor, for only they,
in their love, were present at both his death and burial, and so only they, in

9. The angel's concluding remark in Matthew—"Lo, I have told you"—is his sign-off. As he
triumphantly sat upon the great stone that he had rolled away, he jubilantly accentuates that
he has completed what he was divinely commissioned to do: exhibit the empty tomb and proclaim the resurrection of Jesus.

10. That the angel directs the women to tell Peter that Jesus is risen could support the notion that Mark's Gospel is based upon Peter's own historical recollections and proclamation.

their loving desire to anoint Jesus' body, could testify that that same tomb was now empty. And only they are now able to give the reason why: Jesus is risen!

Jesus' Appearance to the Women and Their Proclamation of the Message

Here the Synoptic Gospels diverge in their presentation of Jesus' resurrected appearances.[11] Within Matthew's Gospel, having received the angel's message, the women "departed quickly from the tomb with fear and great joy, and ran to tell his disciples." But "behold Jesus met them and said, 'Hail!' And they came up and took hold of his feet and worshiped him. Then Jesus said to them, 'Do not be afraid; go and tell my brethren to go to Galilee, and there they will see me.'" This would appear to be the same story that is included in what scholars presently call Mark's "Longer Ending," and thus is not connected to the previous inexplicable ending.[12] Mark's Gospel states: "Now when

11. Mark's Gospel here becomes particularly jumbled and so difficult to interpret. Having been instructed by the angel to tell his disciples and Peter that Jesus is risen and that he is going before them into Galilee, where they will see him, Mark states that the women "went out and fled from the tomb; for trembling and astonishment had come upon them; and they said nothing to any one, for they were afraid." This is an awkward, if not a strange, ending. It gives the impression that the women were so overwhelmed by their experience that they bolted from the tomb in flustered panic and, being so beside themselves with fear, never told anyone what had happened and what the man dressed in white told them. Although this passage may be part of the canonical Gospel, its historical veracity is questionable, for it is neither congruent with the women's previously described demeanor and character nor does it harmonize with the other Gospels, including John's. It also appears to have no theological relevance or soteriological significance; therefore I offer no comment.

Scholars believe that Mark's Gospel originally ended at this point. But because of the inexplicable manner of this concluding verse (v. 8), some scholars have suggested that Mark's original ending was lost and subsequently this passage was added. This may be so, but it does not account for why the added passage is so alien to the trajectory of the narrated event. Its author may have thought that what he was narrating was true, but his inability to perceive its incongruity with the preceding account is baffling, as is his inability to recognize that it is not in keeping with broader Gospel tradition.

12. Following upon "the awkward ending," some ancient manuscripts have what is known as the "Longer Ending" (Mk 16:9-20), which at the Council of Trent was declared to be canonical. Some later manuscripts contain a "Shorter Ending," which follows Mk 16:8 and so what came before the Longer Ending, though these later manuscripts do not have the Longer Ending. This Shorter Ending seems to contradict what immediately goes before concerning the women's response to the angel. "But they reported briefly to Peter and those with him all that they had been told. And after this, Jesus himself sent out by means of them, from east to west, the sacred and imperishable proclamation of eternal salvation." It is not considered canonical.

he rose early on the first day of the week, he appeared first to Mary Magdalene, from whom he had cast out seven demons. She went and told those who had been with him, as they mourned and wept. But when they heard that he was alive and had been seen by her, they would not believe it." Luke has the women "returning from the tomb" and telling "the eleven and to all the rest," "but these words seemed to them an idle tale, and they did not believe them. But Peter rose and ran to the tomb; stooping and looking in, he saw the linen cloths by themselves, and he went home wondering at what had happened."

Matthew's and Mark's respective narrative of the women (Mt) or Mary Magdalene (Mk) encountering the risen Jesus is the first appearance recorded within the Synoptic Gospels. Mark specifies that Jesus "appeared first to Mary Magdalene." Although Mark narrates no dialogue or actions, he does note that Jesus had previously "cast out seven demons" from Mary, highlighting both the "evil" that previously inhabited Mary Magdalene as well as the mercy shown to her by Jesus in expelling the demons. The previous encounter between "evil" and "mercy" likewise finds its fulfillment in the risen Jesus. This soteriological conjoining is the consequence of Jesus' death and resurrection, the efficacious outcome of Jesus becoming Jesus. Thus this first appearance is a living icon of the "Communion of the Savior and the Saved." This living icon is more graphically depicted within Matthew.

Matthew accentuates this meeting with the words "And behold." What is to be beheld is Jesus' unanticipated meeting the women and his exclaiming, "Hail!" This "Hail!" is not simply Jesus' attempt to attract their attention, but rather his joyful greeting, alerting them to his risen reality. It is his "Oh, there! Here I am! I am alive!" Likewise, it is Jesus' jubilant invitation to the women to rejoice with him. As the "Hail!" implies, the women must have been at some distance, for "they came up" and then "took hold of his feet and worshiped him." They also must have emotionally conveyed some trepidation because Jesus tells them that they need not fear, instead telling them, reinforcing what the angel had already commissioned them to do, "to tell my brethren to go to Galilee, and there they will see me." The women immediately recognize Jesus, for their unhesitant response, despite their fear, is to bow down in worship, humbly grasping his feet.[13] This is the first post-resurrection act of Christian

13. Within the Gospel of John, when Jesus appeared to Mary Magdalene, she first thought he was the gardener. Upon hearing Jesus call her "Mary," however, she recognized him, calling him "Rabboni!" Jesus immediately says, "Do not hold on to me, for I have not yet ascended to the Father." Although Mary is not said to have grasped Jesus, his rebuke implies that she was at least attempting to do so—not just physically but also emotionally. This could be in accordance

worship of the risen Jesus recorded within the Synoptic Gospels. The women's reverent physical bowing before Jesus and their humbly laying hold of his feet manifest, within an act of worship, that they acknowledge him, this risen man Jesus, to be their divine Lord and Savior. Present as well, though not overtly acknowledged, is the Father and the Holy Spirit. Only the Holy Spirit, sent forth from the Father, could engender within the women a faith-filled knowledge and worship of Jesus as the Father's Son. Again, this is a living icon, a living theological and soteriological portrayal, of the faithful, living, and everlasting church, abiding in joyful Spirit-filled communion with and expressing Spirit-filled reverent worship of their glorious Lord and risen Savior, Jesus Christ, the Father's incarnate Son.

Within Luke's Gospel, the women go to the disciples, without being interrupted by Jesus' appearance, and tell them what they had seen and heard. But the Apostles did not believe them, for it "seemed to them an idle tale."[14] This appears to conform to what we read above in Mark's narration. When Mary Magdalene told the weeping and mourning disciples that she had seen Jesus alive, "they would not believe it." Evident here is a lack of faith among Jesus' disciples. This is immediately accentuated again in Mark. After Jesus' appearance to Mary Magdalene, "he appeared in another form to two of them [disciples], as they were walking into the country." Although it is unclear what the words "in another form" might mean, since no earlier appearance was narrated and no other "form" was previously described, the incident is obviously the same appearance of Jesus to the two men on the road to Emmaus within Luke's Gospel.[15] Unlike Luke's account, when the two "went back and told the

---

with Matthew's account, where the women do actually grasp the feet of Jesus, though there Jesus does not admonish them.

14. Luke says that the Apostles thought the women's story was an idle tale, but he continues, "But Peter rose and ran to the tomb; stooping and looking in, he saw the linen cloths by themselves; and he went away wondering at what had happened." Peter is able now to confirm as well that the tomb is empty, but not believing the women's report that Jesus is risen, he continues to wonder.

This scene must be the same as in the Gospel of John where Peter and the other disciple run to the tomb after hearing Mary Magdalene's troubled report that Jesus' body is missing. "They both ran, but the other disciple outran Peter and reached the tomb first; and stooping and looking in, he saw the linen cloths lying there, but he did not go in. Then Simon Peter, following him, went into the tomb." While "the other disciple" then "went in, and he saw and believed," it would appear, because there is nothing to the contrary, that Peter did not come to faith but left wondering, as portrayed in the Gospel of Luke (see Jn 20:3–10).

15. The fact that Mark specifies "in a different form" implies that there must have been a previous appearance that his Gospel did not narrate, or if it did, it is no longer present within the text.

rest" that they had seen the risen Jesus, "they did not believe them."[16] Jesus will soon upbraid his disciples because of their lack of faith, but why do Mark and Luke emphasize their lack of belief? Doubtlessly, it is historical, but the early church, and so the Gospel authors, would seemingly not want to feature this embarrassing lack of faith, especially the Apostles disparaging the women's words as an "idle tale." One might add: "An idle woman's tale."

Besides their simple inability to conceive that a dead man could rise gloriously from the dead, the Apostles were captives of their own cultural zeitgeist. If Jesus rose from the dead, if he wanted this to be authoritatively witnessed, and if he wanted to ensure proper testimony of his risen appearances, which would be respected by those from whom respect is most desired, then he would never have first appeared to women, and thus the Apostles' refusal to believe the women. But this is now the point. The early church, and so the Gospel writers, realize that being women, far from an embarrassment, is now their strong suit, and they are playing it for all its evangelistic and apologetic worth. First, the Apostles' lack of faith demonstrates that they are not gullible fools who will believe anything, especially what comes from the mouths of women. Second, that the women are the first to see and proclaim the risen Jesus demonstrates that what they say is not an idle tale, for if the resurrection were an idle tale, the first witnesses would have been portrayed as men, for only men would garner the respect needed for their naive listeners to believe the idle tale they told. For the early and present church, the women's testimony and the Apostles' lack of faith is a win-win combination: the Apostles are not gullible fools, and the fact that women are the first to confirm the resurrection attests that their "tale" is not an idle contrived story but actually the truth—Jesus is risen!

Following the emphasis on the Apostles' lack of faith within Mark's Longer Ending, Jesus appears "to the eleven themselves as they sat at table," which accentuates Jesus' reprimand of the Apostles. "He upbraided them for their unbelief and hardness of heart, because they had not believed those who saw him after he had risen" (Mk 16:14). Again, that the early church would be willing to tell of Jesus' reproaching the leaders of their group demonstrates the authenticity of both the appearance and the rebuke. Moreover, that the leaders of this nascent Christian community were scolded by its founder for their disbelief encourages and reassures those who also may now find it difficult to

---

16. This contrasts with Luke' account, where the disciples not only believe the report but also tell of Jesus' appearance to Simon (see Lk 24:34).

believe in the resurrection for, if the disinclined and obstinate Apostles now believe, so can they. Although the disbelief of the Apostles may be reprehensible, as Jesus noted, it ultimately serves a good theological and evangelistic purpose, for it both contributes to the authenticity of the claim that Jesus is truly risen and also facilitates the faith of others.[17]

Jesus' Appearance on the Road to Emmaus

Mark mentions that Jesus appeared to two disciples "as they were walking in the country." Mark does not elaborate, but Luke's Gospel gives a fuller account.[18] After the women bring word of Jesus' resurrection and the Apostles reject it as an idle tale, Luke states that on this same day "two of them" (I refer to them as "the two men") were going "to the village named Emmaus, about seven miles from Jerusalem and talking with each other about these things that had happened." The "these things" were not merely that Jesus had been crucified and died, but that the women had reported that he was alive. During their discussion, "Jesus himself drew near and went with them," implying that he came up from behind and was eager to catch up with them. But "their eyes were kept from recognizing him." This inability to recognize Jesus is more than some inherent "physical impairment or psychological blindness" on their part, but rather an act whereby they are prevented from recognizing him, pre-

17. The same can be said of Thomas' disbelief within the Gospel of John. Jesus first appears to the Apostles on Easter Sunday, though Thomas is absent. When told that Jesus appeared, Thomas says, "Unless I see in his hands the print of the nails, and place my finger in the mark of the nails, and place my hand in his side, I will not believe." Thomas wants to be assured of two facts. First, that Jesus is truly bodily risen; he demands to touch Jesus. Second, he wants assurance that that the man he is touching is the same man who was crucified, so he wants to see and touch Jesus' wounds. Others may be blessed, as Jesus states, for believing without seeing, but Thomas' unbelief is a great godsend to those who do come to faith without seeing. By Jesus acquiescing to Thomas' demands, Thomas can now authoritatively bear witness that Jesus did bodily arise and that the Jesus who was crucified is the same Jesus who is now alive. Thomas allays the doubts of others. Significantly, Thomas is the only person in the entire New Testament who gazes upon the risen Jesus and exclaims, "My Lord and My God!" No other person, not even Mary or Peter, has expressed the incarnational reality of Jesus' resurrection more clearly and resolutely than Thomas. The risen man Jesus, whom he has seen and touched, is indeed his divine Lord and his saving God. Thomas has been traditionally maligned as "the Doubting Thomas," when he should be lauded, to the benefit of all, as "the Man of Faith."

18. All quotations in this section are from Lk 24:13-35 unless otherwise noted. Luke's resurrection narrative at this juncture becomes a continuous interlocking series of appearances culminating in Jesus' ascension. Therefore will treat the whole of his account to the end and then return to Matthew and Mark to examine the rest of their resurrection accounts.

sumably an act willed by Jesus himself. Thus Jesus has not changed his appearance, and so who he is, in being risen. He is the same person, the same identifiable human being, as he was prior to his resurrection. This is theologically important and soteriologically necessary: the same Jesus, the same *Son of God* incarnate, who died must be the same Jesus, the same identifiable risen *incarnate* Son of God, who has arisen if humankind is to be saved.[19]

Upon his arrival at their side, Jesus asks, "What is this conversation which you are holding with each other as you walk?" Jesus perceived "this conversation," which the two have yet to conclude, and Jesus wants to know not simply its content but also, and maybe more so, the manner, the emotional tenor or cognitional mood, in which "this conversation" is being conducted. The two immediately give themselves away. They "stood still, and looking sad." Jesus' question stops them in their tracks, for they are so sad that they hesitate to share with Jesus the source of their sadness. Jesus, a stranger, is intruding into their own shared personal sorrow, which presumably he does not share with them. Cleopas (the only one now named) nonetheless tersely replies with an impatient smidgeon of irritated sarcasm at Jesus' butting into their personal conversation: "Are you the only visitor to Jerusalem who does not know the things that have happened there in these days?" Cleopas presumes that Jesus came to visit Jerusalem to celebrate the days of the Passover and so should have some knowledge of what transpired during his time there. But Jesus, playing dumb, asks in return, "What things?" Again, Jesus is not simply wanting to know the facts, which he obviously already knows since he is the "things" that have happened. What he really desires is their rendition, their understanding, their take on the "things" that have happened in Jerusalem during "these days" of the Passover.

So "they said to him." Although Cleopas alone asked Jesus the question,

19. This inability to recognize Jesus may account for Mark's remark, "he appeared in another form" (Mk 16:12). Presuming that Mark either knew of an appearance prior to the two men but did not tell of it, or that he did narrate it but it is now lost, the previous "form" would be the one in which he appeared to the women, as in Matthew's account, where the women recognized Jesus immediately upon seeing him. Now, as in Luke's Gospel, he does appear to the two, but in a form such that they are not able to recognize him. This might contradict what I proposed above, as it could imply a change in Jesus' appearance and not a change in the two men—their inability to recognize him. In response, I would say that "different form" means "not being able to recognize," and the inability "to recognize" Jesus was an impediment on the part of the two men and not a change in Jesus whereby he no longer truly looked like himself.

Jesus' appearance to Mary Magdalene in the Gospel of John may be similar. There Mary does not at first recognize Jesus but thinks he is the gardener. It is only when Jesus speaks her name that she realizes she is speaking to Jesus (see Jn 20:14-18).

what comes next comes from both of them—not only their mutually con-joined statement of the facts, but also their mutually conjoined personal in-terpretation of the facts. "Concerning Jesus of Nazareth, who was a prophet mighty in deed and word before God and all the people, and how our chief priests and rulers delivered him up to be condemned to death, and crucified him. But we had hoped that he would redeem Israel." What we have here is the making of a creed! They believed the man Jesus of Nazareth to be a mighty prophet because of the works they saw him perform—the miracles, healings, exorcisms—and because of the words they heard him speak—preaching by his own authority—and he performed these mighty prophetic acts and spoke these mighty prophetic words before the all-holy God and so on behalf of God, and he did all this publicly before all the people. That was their creed, but now their creed appears to lie in ruins, for this mighty prophet, Jesus of Nazareth, was delivered up by none other than their own chief priests and handed over to their despised Roman rulers for the sole purpose of having him condemned to death and crucified. This is their creedal disconnect—their "but." They are intellectually and emotionally incapable of conjoining their initial profession of faith with the most recent events. They do not know how to change their "but" to an "and"—"*and* our chief priest and rulers delivered him up to be con-demned to death and crucified him"—so they cannot conclude that Jesus is the redeemer of Israel. They "had hoped" that "he would redeem Israel" because of what they saw him do and heard him say "before God and man," "*but*" that redemption of Israel did not happen because of what has taken place in "these days" of the Passover in Jerusalem. They do continue, however, "Yes [*alla je kai*, or "whereas"], and besides all of this, it is now the third day since this happened. Moreover, some women of our company amazed us. They were at the tomb early in the morning and did not find his body; and they came back saying that they had even seen a vision of angels, who said that he was alive. Some of those who were with us went to the tomb, and found it just as the women had said; but him they did not see."

Their "yes" or "whereas" gives expression to the truth of what they just narrated, both to the facts and to their own interpretation of these facts; their expression of faith-filled hope and now to their inability to make sense of it all; and so to their present befuddled despair and sorrowful remorse at Jesus' death. But that "yes" or "whereas" does not just look to what they have just said, but also to what they are about to say, which appears to deviate unex-plainably, "and besides all of this, it is now the third day since this happened." Are the two men simply stating a fact—what happened three days ago is that

Jesus was crucified and died? Or are they also calling to mind what Jesus stated? "'Behold, we are going up to Jerusalem, and everything that is written of the Son of man by the prophets will be accomplished. For he will be delivered to the Gentiles, and will be mocked and shamefully treated and spit upon, they will scourge him and kill him, and so on the third day he will rise.' But they [the Apostles] understood none of these things; this saying was hid from them, and they did not grasp what was said" (Lk 19:31-34; see also Lk 9:22, Mt 20:17-19, and Mk 10:32-34). They may be inadvertently recollecting what Jesus previously said. But at present "their eyes were kept from recognizing him," so their minds are still presently kept from understanding the prophets—that on the third day the crucified Son of man will rise from the dead. Only when Jesus opens the eyes of their minds so as to understand the Scriptures will their eyes physically be opened so as to recognize Jesus. Their use of "the third day" nonetheless prophesizes what they narrate next—that Jesus is said to be alive, and so this "the third day" resurrects, amid their sorrowful bewilderment, their own dead hope.

The men tell of "some women" (left unnamed because this stranger would not know them even if they were named) "of our company" (again left unspecified because their present ill-informed inquirer probably is not aware of Jesus' followers) "amazed" them. They went to Jesus' tomb early in the morning but "did not find his body." However, they returned saying that they had seen "a vision of angels" and these said that "he was alive." Once again, we find an intrinsic connection between the absence of Jesus' body and his being alive. If Jesus is alive, it is with the same body (humanity) with which he died and was buried. The continuity of the dead Jesus with the risen Jesus must be soteriologically maintained, and that continuity resides in possessing the same body that Jesus had before his death must be the same body that was buried and the same body that is now risen, for then he is the same man, the one Lord and Savior, Jesus Christ.

"The vision of angels" once more accentuates, and so confirms, that if Jesus is alive, his resurrection is predicated upon divine causality alone. "Some of those who were with us," again unnamed but presumably Peter, whom this present fellow would not know from Adam (see Lk 24:12), also found the tomb empty but did not see Jesus.[20] That "the some" thought they could see the risen Jesus presupposes that there is a "bodily" Jesus to be seen. They instinc-

---

20. Although Lk 24:12 speaks only of Peter going to the tomb, the two men speak of "some" going to the tomb. This could include John, the beloved disciple, in the Gospel of John (see Jn 20:3).

tively make the connection that the absence of the body demands that the living Jesus is alive in that same body. Thus concludes the summary of "this conversation," the conversation about which their now fellow companion first enquired.[21] Here Jesus enters into "this conversation," and he does so precisely to enable the two men to change their incomplete creedal "but" to an "and."

"O foolish men, and slow of heart to believe all that the prophets have spoken! Was it not necessary that the Christ should suffer these things and enter into his glory?" Their foolishness did not reside in their falsely believing that Jesus of Nazareth was "a prophet mighty in deed and word before God and all the people." Rather, it resided in their inability to grasp that, because of what they believed—not simply because he was "a prophet mighty in deed and word" but more so because he was "the Christ"—Jesus must be handed over by their own Jewish leaders and crucified by the Romans. The men failed to grasp the "was it not necessary," and because of their failure they are forced to say "but." The cross should not be the cause their despair, but the assurance of Jesus being, as the Spirit-anointed Son of God, he who would "redeem Israel." The two men, like their foolish and slow-of-heart companion Peter, are thinking as men think and not as God. If they thought like God, they would grasp the truth that if Jesus is the true prophet, if he is the Christ, the Son of the living God, then, as Jesus prophesied, the meaning of which was still hidden to his disciples, he must suffer, die, and rise so as to fulfill the Scriptures, all of

21. Here I offer two rather "humorous" comments. First, what compelled the two men to set out for Emmaus in the first place? One would think that, having just heard their story, they would have stayed in Jerusalem with the Apostles to better keep abreast of the latest breaking news on this ongoing saga. We will only know why it was so crucial for them to go to Emmaus when we query them in heaven. Whatever the reason was, it was easily superseded when they realized that it was Jesus who had appeared to them, for they forget Emmaus and dash back to Jerusalem with their own news. Second, despite the rebuke he will give, one cannot help but imagine that, as the two men narrated their "conversation," Jesus was charmingly amused, since they were speaking to him as if he did not have a clue as to what they were talking about when in fact he knew far better than they the "entire" story, as he is the subject of "this conversation." The comic irony would not have escaped him. (There is a Shakespearean quality to this event.) More seriously, Jesus did achieve his purpose, for he provoked them to express their "faith" as well as their present befuddled despair, and in so doing allowed him to dispel the latter and to correct and expand the former.

On a more serious note, the summary nature of the two men's story adds credibility to its historical veracity. If this event was invented, the men would probably have added particulars—the names of people, for example—to add to its "credibility." But the Lucan account shows that the men spoke to Jesus as someone who was completely ignorant of Jesus and his companions, so it would be natural for them not to give specifics because such detail would mean nothing to him—he would not have an inkling as to the significance of Mary Magdalene, Mary the Mother of James, or Peter.

which ultimately pertained to him alone (see Mt 16:21-23, 26:51-56; Mk 8:31-33, 14:48-49; Lk 9:18-23). Instead, their foolishness overwhelmed their hearts, for Jesus' death brought them sorrow instead of joyfully confirming their faith. He is indeed "the one to redeem Israel," and he has done so because he was handed over by the chief priests and crucified by the Romans. Thus Jesus is informing the two men that, if they rightly understood the Scriptures, they would readily change their "but" to an "and."

Luke narrates next that "beginning with Moses and all of the prophets, he interpreted to them in all the scriptures the things concerning himself." One may wish that someone would find a papyrus containing Jesus' verbatim account, but we do know, and this may be the real point, is that the whole of Scripture, beginning with the Pentateuch and concluding with the prophets, concern him. All that God did in the past, all that was previously revealed by mighty deeds and words, prophetically anticipates and finds it ultimate fulfillment in him, "the Christ," and so it is the Old Testament that is the hermeneutical key to understanding Jesus and his salvific work.[22]

Here the conversation concludes with Jesus having brought the two men from a state of sorrow and confusion to a state of clarity and faith. So, when "they drew near to the village" and Jesus "appeared to be going further," the two men "constrained him saying, 'Stay with us, for it is toward evening and the day is now far spent.'" This is simply a pretext for getting Jesus to remain with them, as they are now enthralled with his words. The impression is given that the two men were not simply asking him to stay with them out of courtesy, but that they were almost physically forcing him—tugging at his sleeve—to enter their house. And while Jesus continues to play with them, acting as if he wants to continue, he readily agrees. The real reason the men want Jesus to stay is because he clarified their confusion by enabling them, through the Scriptures, to understand properly who Jesus is as the Christ and why his death was not a disaster but the very means of Israel's redemption. Likewise, Jesus really wanted to stay, for his purpose in appearing to them was only half-completed. Up to this point Jesus has been enacting a "liturgy of the word." He has preached the Gospel to the men, and in so doing they have come to faith in Jesus, the Christ. But the men do not yet personally know the risen and living Jesus, even though they have been walking and conversing with him, so they are not yet in full communion with the Christ. That is yet

---

22. I will comment more fully on his opening the Scriptures when I shortly comment on Jesus' later and last appearance to his disciples within Luke's Gospel.

to be achieved but it is now to be realized, made real, by Jesus enacting "the liturgy of the Eucharist."

"When he was at table with them, he took the bread and blessed it, and broke it, and gave it to them." Obviously, these acts employ the same causally efficacious words that were enacted both in the multiplication of the loaves and at the Last Supper (see Lk 9:16-17 and 22:19). The bread that is now blessed and broken is Jesus' resurrected body, which was given up and broken upon the cross, and it is this bread that is now his body that Jesus presently gives to the two men. They now share in that one atoning and covenantal sacrifice and so pass over into communion with the risen Jesus. Having taught them to understand fully the mystery of the cross through his interpretations of the Scriptures, Jesus now takes them into that mystery to reap its benefits—his very own Spirit-filled risen humanity. By coming to share in that sacrifice and so coming into personal communion with the living Jesus, the two men come to know personally Jesus. "And their eyes were opened and they recognized him; and he vanished out of their sight." Thus the conversation that began with the two men being sad because the one they believed to be a prophet, Jesus of Nazareth, "mighty in deed and word," had been crucified and was dead, now concludes joyfully because he was crucified and died. Ironically, by being taken up into the mystery of the cross in receiving Jesus' crucified and risen body, they came to recognize the crucified and risen Jesus—their hoped for redeemer of Israel. This sadness was turned to joy precisely because of the mighty word that Jesus spoke to them, the salvific mystery of the cross, and precisely because of the mighty deed that Jesus performed for them, the taking them into the very mystery of the cross whereby they could share in his resurrection.

We see here the inherent integral soteriological relationship between word and sacrament; neither is salvifically complete without the other, for only together does each find its distinct yet related saving fulfillment. Without the Eucharist, the word of God does not achieve its goal: full communion with Jesus. The spoken word of God always leads to and terminates in a sacramental act, for in that act one is incorporated into the mystery of which the word of God speaks. Without the word of God, the Eucharist does not achieve its ultimate goal: a living personal knowledge of Jesus. Sacraments, here the Eucharist, only achieve their full potential, their taking one into the mystery enacted, when those participating in the sacramental enactment are imbued with a living knowledge of the enacted sacrament, a living knowledge of Jesus—the living Word of God and the primordial enacted sacrament. Thus to denigrate either is to denigrate both. To enhance one necessarily entails the enhancement of the other, and if this mutual enhancement does not occur, then there is merely an exaggerated emphasis of one to the detriment of the other.

Having completed his mighty word and deed, by opening the eyes of the two men through his interpretation of Scripture and through his enactment of the Eucharist, Jesus vanishes from their sight. This "vanishing," like his "appearing," denotes the resurrected reality of Jesus; that is, although he is physically risen as an authentic human being, he now possesses properties and powers that are beyond that of a nonresurrected human being. Yet it is difficult to describe positively what these properties and powers are because they exceed those of a nonresurrected person, that is, everyone but Jesus (and Mary). It is possible to know the effects of these properties and powers—vanishing and appearing, for example—but the causal nature and source of these properties and powers remain a mystery that only the resurrected comprehend.[23]

Jesus having vanished, the two "said to each other, 'Did not our hearts burn within us while he talked to us on the road, while he opened to us the scriptures.'" This "heart burning" is the fire of the Holy Spirit—the divine flame of truth and love sent by their fellow traveler's Father. As they progressed in their journey, the men, through the Holy Spirit, were coming to perceive, in Jesus' words, the truth of Scripture and thus that it was necessary that "the Christ should suffer all of these things and enter into his glory." In this knowledge their hearts equally began to burn in love for Jesus, the Christ. So, off they went in "that same hour and returned to Jerusalem," little concerned as to why they went to Emmaus in the first place.

---

23. Paul was confronted with this conundrum. "But someone will ask, 'How are the dead raised? With what kind of body do they come?' You foolish man!" Paul gives the example of seed giving rise to a "body," and so there "are celestial bodies and there are terrestrial bodies." "So it is with the resurrection of the dead. What is sown is perishable, what is raised is imperishable. It is sown in dishonor, it is raised in glory. It is sown in weakness, it is raised in power. It is sown a physical body, it is raised in a spiritual body" (1 Cor 15:35-44). Although Paul speaks of a "celestial body" that is imperishable and glorious and powerful, and so a "spiritual body," other than knowing that it is still a "body," the nature of that resurrected body remains a mystery. We do not fully comprehend what it means to be imperishable, which only means that it will not die. Nor do we know what it means to be glorious, other than it will be far better than the one that is presently available. Nor do we know what it means to be powerful, other than it will be able to do things that presently it cannot do. The positive content of these descriptive concepts is still mostly unknown. The joyful hope, established in firm faith, is that such comprehension will be obtained upon the resurrection of one's own imperishable, glorious, and powerful body. In the meantime, all that can be done is to imagine what it will be like, knowing that one's imagination will fall exceeding short of reality.

When they arrived, their adrenaline running high, "they found the eleven gathered together and those who were with them." But even before they had a chance to tell, breathlessly, their story, their Jerusalem companions excitedly burst forth: "The Lord has risen indeed, and has appeared to Simon!" So, no longer is the women's story merely an "idle tale." Even the initially bewildered Simon Peter could now proclaim the truth that Jesus is indeed risen, for he saw him with his very own eyes![24] Only after the Jerusalem crowd finished sharing their latest good news were the two men able to share theirs. "They told what had happened on the road, and how he was known to them in the breaking of the bread." What the two men shared, something their Jerusalem companions may not have known, was how Jesus interpreted the Scriptures, thus teaching them how the Scriptures must now be seen and understood in the light of Jesus' death and resurrection, for they are the interpretive key to these saving events. Thus the cross is not a cause of shame and despair but the source of joy and hope, for through the cross, Jesus the Christ became the hoped-for risen redeemer of Israel. Moreover, these two men, and they are the first, now possess a post-resurrection "theology" of the Eucharist, the Last Supper. From their own experience, they could articulate, in some rudimentary manner, that it is in entering Jesus' atoning and redeeming sacrifice that one comes into covenantal communion with him and in so doing truly comes to know the risen Jesus personally.

Jesus Appears to the Apostles and the Gathered Jerusalem Community

The Gospel of Luke, as a continuous narrative, next states: "As they were saying this [the disciples and the two men], Jesus himself stood among them and said to them, 'Peace to you!' But they were startled and frightened, and supposed that they were seeing a spirit."[25] Even though the risen Jesus bestows upon the startled disciples his "peace," they are frightened because they think

24. Paul also makes mention of this appearance (see 1 Cor 15:5). Again, one would wish that Jesus' appearance to Peter contained more content other than that it simply happened. What transpired in the event? Was there any significant conversation? Since the Scriptures are inspired, the Holy Spirit judged that answers to such questions were unimportant. Also, the two men having found on their return to Jerusalem that Jesus had appeared to Peter and that everyone now believed that Jesus is alive is in stark contrast to Mark's summary remarks: "And they went back and told the rest, but they did not believe them" (Mk 16:13).

25. All quotations in this section are taken from Lk 24:36-43 unless otherwise noted.

they are seeing a spirit or ghost.[26] Jesus' greeting of peace, the only such narrated greeting within the Synoptics, signals not simply that his disciples should not be disconcerted at his appearance but more so that through his death and resurrection he has established true peace. Before his sacrificial atoning death, sinful humanity was at enmity with God, with one another, and within themselves. Through Jesus' death and resurrection, however, human beings are now reconciled to God as their Father and so reunited to one another as brothers and sisters in Christ his Son. This arises from their ability to share with the resurrected Jesus the new healing and elevating life of the Holy Spirit, thus making them new creations in him.[27] That the disciples "supposed" they were seeing a spirit or ghost allows Jesus to emphasize further his actual bodily resurrection, which permeates the whole of Luke's resurrection narrative. For Jesus next states, "'Why are you troubled, and why do questionings rise in your hearts? See my hands and my feet, that it is I myself (*ego eimi autos*); handle me, and see; for a spirit has not flesh and bones as you see I have.' And when he had said this, he showed them his hands and his feet."

The disciples are "troubled" precisely because they "suppose" that they are seeing a ghost, which leads them to "question" whether Jesus is truly risen. To alleviate their troubled questioning, Jesus shows them his hands and feet and assures them that it is he (*ego eimi autos*). Why would gazing upon his physical hands and feet give assurance that it is actually Jesus? Why not look at his face, which is more readily identifiably distinctive than his hands and feet?

---

26. This appearance may be out of order, since Luke's Gospel has already narrated Jesus' appearance to Mary Magdalene and the other women, the two men on the road to Emmaus and to Peter. If Luke's order were to be correct, one would think such surprise and fear and the "supposing" of seeing a ghost would have by now ended, as Jesus' appearing to people has become somewhat "routine." Thus the depiction of this appearance gives the impression that it may have taken place earlier.

This appearance in Luke's Gospel is similar to Jesus' evening appearance on Easter Sunday within the Gospel of John (see Jn 20:19) as well as his week-later appearance when Thomas was present (see Jn 20:24-29). But Luke has it taking place sometime either late on Easter Sunday night or early on the following day. Within John, there is no "fright" and no supposing that Jesus was a ghost, though he does show them his hands and side as in Luke. More will be said on this similarity below.

27. In the Gospel of John, the risen Jesus thrice greets his Apostles on two different occasions with the words: "Peace be with you" (see Jn 20:19, 20:21, 20:26). This is in keeping with Jesus' previous declaration: "Peace I leave with you; my peace I give to you; not as the world gives do I give to you" (Jn 14:27). Jesus' peace differs from what the world gives, for his peace is not simply the absence of conflict or the transitory comforting joys of this life, but an inner everlasting peace that is founded upon reconciliation with God the Father, through forgiveness of sin in Jesus his Son and in the loving communion of the Holy Spirit.

Only the actual marks of the nails imprinted upon his hands and feet, while not mentioned, provide conclusive proof that it is Jesus.[28] Likewise, so physical or material is he that his disciples cannot only see him but also "handle" him, place their fleshly hands upon his flesh, for he has "flesh and bones," and in so doing they will "see" that their eyes are not deceiving them. Thus "the flesh and bone" man who was crucified, died, and was buried is now standing before them, and they can see and touch him. Jesus identifies himself as "I am he" (*ego eimi autos*), just as he had done previously when the disciples were "frightened" and "supposed" they were seeing a ghost. When Jesus came to the disciples walking upon the turbulent storm-tossed waters, the Apostles "were terrified, saying, 'It is a ghost!'" But Jesus immediately responded by saying, "Take heart, it is I (*ego eimi*); have no fear" (Mt 14:22-27; see also Mk 6:45-52 and Jn 6:15-21). Now as then, Jesus is not simply identifying himself as someone they know and should easily recognize, but more so he, the flesh and bone Jesus, is identifying himself as God, "I myself" (*ego eimi autos*). Jesus has once again appropriated God's name: YHWH, I Am Who Am. Thus Jesus is revealing first that he is truly physically risen, after being crucified and buried, and second that he is the Lord God YHWH. Now, because the crucified risen Jesus is the Lord God YHWH, Jesus is ultimately manifesting that he is truly Jesus— YHWH-Saves, for through his death, sin and death have been vanquished, and in his resurrection, the new Spirit-filled life has dawned.[29]

28. In Luke's narrative, Jesus not only begins by telling his disciples to look at his hands and feet, but also Luke concludes "that when he had said this, he showed them his hands and his feet." The purpose of showing his hands and his feet is so that his disciples would see the wound marks left by the nails; otherwise, there would be no purpose in showing them and Luke emphasizing it.

29. One is assured that the Holy Spirit is guiding the authors of the Gospels, but it is somewhat perplexing that although Jesus, within Luke's Gospel, says the same thing to his disciples in his resurrected appearance as he does when walking on the water and quells the storm, Luke does not narrate that event. They are parallel stories, the first pre-resurrection and the second post-resurrection. The "take heart" in the quelling of the storm event is like Jesus' greeting of peace in Luke's appearance story. In both instances, the Apostles/disciples are frightened and suppose they see a ghost. So it is difficult to believe that Luke was not aware of the quelling of the storm even though he does not narrate it, but why does he not? Maybe this resurrection appearance was, for Luke, the real quelling of the storm—the true bringing of peace, of taking heart, to sinful humankind—and so for him a theological commentary on that previous event, one that he thought he need not narrate since it was well known within the apostolic community.

One may also wonder why Matthew, Mark, and John narrate Jesus' quelling of the storm but not the appearance story that is in Luke. In Matthew and Mark, the Apostles/disciples are frightened in supposing they are seeing a ghost, and Jesus assures them that they need not fear because "it is I myself?"

Luke next states, "And while they [the disciples] still disbelieved for joy, and wondered, he said to them, 'Have you anything to eat?' They gave him a piece of broiled fish, and he took it and ate before them."[30] The "disbelieved for joy" may appear to be an intellectual (disbelieve) and emotional (joy) disconnect. But what Luke is attempting to express is the disciples' sheer joy at the unbelievable yet true revelation that Jesus is risen. Their "wonder" is their "how can this all be possible and true?" amid beholding Jesus in the flesh and blood. Jesus' appearance is more than their minds could fathom, and in unison their feelings could express and emote. To give them further assurance and to bring them back to earth mentally and emotionally, Jesus asks for a piece of fish, which he ate in their presence, thus conclusively attesting that he is physically risen with actual flesh and bones—he who is the Lord God YHWH.[31]

Jesus' Last Words and His Ascension

Within this same appearance story, Luke's Gospel continues with Jesus now addressing another subject and concludes with Jesus ascending into heaven.[32] "Then [after revealing that he is truly risen as a physical human being and that he is "He who is"], he [Jesus] said to them, 'These are my words which I spoke

30. That the disciples do not give Jesus just a piece of fish but rather a "broiled" (not fried, baked, or boiled) one adds credibility to this event's historicity.

31. There are some fascinating similarities between Luke's narrative and that of John's two appearances: Easter Sunday and the Sunday after Easter. Thomas is not present at the first but is at the second. All three begin with Jesus bestowing peace upon his disciples. In both Luke's appearance and John's "first appearance," Jesus shows the disciples his hands and feet. But in John's account, Thomas states, "Unless I see in his hands the print of the nails, and place my finger in the mark of the nails and place my hand in his side, I will not believe." Now, what Thomas desires in John's account actually takes place in Luke's account. Jesus shows them his hands and feet and encourages them to "handle me." If they wish, they can place their finger in the nail marks. So, the disciples in Luke's account can do what Thomas wants to do and ultimately does in John's account of Jesus' "second appearance." Likewise, in Luke's account, Jesus, in showing his disciples his hands and feet which they can handle, declares: "it is I myself." He proclaims his divine identity as the Lord God YHWH. In John's account of Jesus' "second appearance," where Thomas is present and is bidden by Jesus to touch ("handle") him and place his finger and hand in the wound marks, Thomas declares, "My Lord and my God!" In Luke's Gospel, Jesus declares, "I am he"; I am the Lord God. Thomas, in John's account, echoes Jesus perfectly. What Jesus reveals in Luke's Gospel Thomas proclaims in John's Gospel. This once again manifests, that Thomas, far from being the doubter, is only asking for the proof that Jesus gives in Luke's Gospel so that he can truly profess in faith what Jesus revealed about himself, that he is truly God—He who is.

32. All quotations in this section are from Lk 24:44-53 unless otherwise noted.

to you, while I was still with you, that everything written about me in the law of Moses and the prophets and the psalms must be fulfilled.' Then he opened their minds to understand the scriptures."

The words that immediately stand out are "while I was still with you." Jesus is among his disciples and he is so in a physical manner, which he has just accentuated. Yet "while I was still with you" now distinguishes the manner of his being present to his disciples prior to his resurrection and the manner of his being present to them after his resurrection. What is this difference, and what is its theological and soteriological significance? In one sense, Jesus is saying, "I am no longer with you." Jesus is no longer with his disciples as one of them insofar as they are not gloriously risen from the dead and he is. He has overcome sin and death, and they have yet to achieve that goal. They continue to exist in this created world, but Jesus no longer exists in the created order of this world as one of its members. In this sense, he is no longer with them. Yet he is *still* with them, for his risen presence among them is manifest. So, although the manner of his presence has changed, not being with them in an earthly manner, he is present in a new way—as their risen Savior and Lord, as the risen Son of God incarnate.

Soteriologically significant, what differentiates his manner of presence with his disciples (his *not* still being with them) and simultaneously makes it possible for him to be present to them (his *still* being with them) is one and the same—his risen physical humanity. That his new humanity is gloriously risen separates him from his disciples. That his humanity is nonetheless "physical" and "material" continues to unite Jesus with his disciples. This is the "incarnational principle." In becoming man, the Son of God became one with humankind, and in rising from the dead as a full and complete man, the same Son of God continues to be with humankind, though now as a risen man, and so as humankind's Savior and Lord. Thus on the one hand Jesus is not still with his disciples, and on the other hand he is still with his disciples but in a different manner than prior to his resurrection. And by not still being with his disciples, Jesus, as the risen Savior and Lord, still can be with his disciples in a way that is far more intimate, far more salvific, than in his pre-resurrection state. As risen, Jesus is now fully empowered to save all who come to him in faith by uniting them to himself within the communion of the Holy Spirit, thus making them children of his Father. Being transfigured into the likeness of the risen Jesus through the indwelling Spirit, his disciples and all the faithful are thus united to Jesus in a new manner, for they now share in his risen humanity, and in so doing Jesus continues to be intimately present to them. Again, the risen humanity that "separates" Jesus from his disciples is the same risen humanity that "unites" them, for by sharing in his risen humanity, they become one with him. The fulfillment of this new living presence will be achieved when Jesus comes in glory and fully transforms his disciples into his perfect risen likeness, his full and complete humanity. Then Jesus will still be with them forever, for they will be fully like him in every way.[33] In summary, keeping with the major premise of our study, prior to his resurrection, Jesus was with humankind as "Jesus *becoming* Jesus." After his death and resurrection, Jesus is present to humankind as "Jesus *being* Jesus"—YHWH-Saves.[34]

The main point that Jesus wants to make is that "while he was still with" them, he told them that "everything written about me in the law of Moses and the prophets and psalms must be fulfilled." The whole of the Old Testament finds its ultimate purpose and fulfillment in Jesus. What previously may have served a purpose in its own time is but a prelude to its being fulfilled in Jesus. Without Jesus there is no final end, no final cause toward which all revelation is inextricably tending and upon which all revelation is resolutely converging, for no one but Jesus is the Spirit-filled Christ, the Father's Son incarnate. Thus Jesus is telling his disciples, and all future Christians, that when they read the Scriptures, the Old Testament, they must do so in the light of himself, for only then will they fully grasp who he is and the full nature of his salvific work, for they will be reading it as it was ultimately meant to be read and understood.

As he had already done for the two men on the road to Emmaus, Jesus now "opened their minds to understand the scriptures, and said to them, 'Thus it is written, that the Christ should suffer and on the third day rise from the dead, and that repentance and forgiveness of sins should be preached in his name to all nations, beginning from Jerusalem. You are witnesses of these things.'" Here Jesus is transitioning from the past to the present and on into the future. Jesus, as the Spirit-filled Christ, fulfilled the ancient Scriptures through his suffering, death, and resurrection. This is what his disciples must clearly grasp,

---

33. This is in keeping with the traditional principle that "grace" does not destroy nature but elevates it. The resurrection of Jesus does not destroy his humanity but perfects it, and, similarly, those who are united to him are perfected in their humanity, which was once subject to sin and death but now transfigured by being taken up in union with Jesus, the Son, through the indwelling Spirit, into the divine life of the Father.

34. Although the risen Jesus is present to all of humankind, he is only fully salvifically united to those who come to faith in him and are baptized, for only the faithful are one in him, sharing in his risen humanity, through the communion of the Holy Spirit, who transforms them into children of the Father.

and they will only do so by understanding properly the Scriptures.[35] Also in keeping with the Scriptures, his disciples are then to preach repentance and forgiveness of sins to all peoples and nations, and they are to do so "in his name." Repentance and forgiveness are to be preached to all in his name, for only Jesus has, through his death and resurrection, in fulfilling the Scriptures, obtained forgiveness for those who repent of their sins. In other words, Jesus is accentuating the importance of his name—Jesus, YHWH-Saves—and thereby underscoring the definitive and universal soteriological importance of who he is. He is also accentuating that repentance is necessary to receive forgiveness in his name, for only in sorrowfully turning away from sin and believing in him can one reap the salvific benefits that accrue to Jesus because of his death and resurrection. The disciples are commissioned to be the bearers of this Gospel because they "are witnesses of these things" and now per-

35. Because the Gospels express the faith of the apostolic community, they were written in the light of its members' minds having been "opened." Thus the Gospels often make clear which Scripture passages Jesus is fulfilling or has fulfilled. This was evident when treating the Passion Narratives with regard to Psalm 22 and other Scriptures. In addition, the Acts of the Apostles, especially in the apostolic sermons of Peter, Stephen, and Paul, will demonstrate how Jesus fulfills the Scriptures (see, e.g., Acts 2:14-36, 7:1-53, 13:16-41). We also see this in Philip's interpretation of the passage from Isaiah to the Ethiopian eunuch (see Acts 8:26-40), in the Pauline corpus (see, e.g., 1 Cor 10:1-5; 2 Cor 3:12-18), and in the Letter to the Hebrews (see, e.g., Heb 1-2, 7, 8:8-13, 10:5-10). The Book of Revelation is suffused with passages from and allusions to the Old Testament. This is not surprising—only when Jesus reigns in glory with all the saints and angels will the Old Testament find its complete fulfillment. For the Jewish apostolic community, reading and studying the Old Testament must have been an exciting and marvelous adventure, for it now blossomed into a whole new "book" blooming flowers and bearing fruit that they never conceived or imaged lay dormant within.

Although many of the passages we already examined—such as Psalm 22, the Suffering Servant Songs, and the chapters from the Book of Wisdom—emphasize the grief and ridicule that God's anointed would undergo, they all conclude with a "resurrection" theme, that is, that God's anointed will be vindicated. Thus Jesus' resurrection also fulfills these passages and others. There are also some psalms that, in the light of Jesus' resurrection, find their fulfillment. See, e.g., Psalm 3, which first speaks of David's foes who say that he has no hope in God, but he then says: "I lie down and sleep; I awake again, for the Lord sustains me" (Ps 3:1-4). The mockery of the crucifixion and sleep of death leads to Jesus' awaking when his Father raises him to life. Also, in Psalm 30, David extols God, for "you have drawn me up, and have not let my foes rejoice over me. O Lord my God, I cried to you for help, and you have healed me. O Lord you have brought up my soul from Sheol, and restored me to life among those gone down to the Pit" (Ps 30:1-3). (Psalm 16, which Peter quotes in his Pentecost sermon—see Acts 2:23-28 and 2:31—is similar. See vv. 9-11.) The Father heard Jesus' cry from the cross by raising him from Sheol and giving him life. The whole of Psalm 68 tells of God's defeat of the wicked and his protection of the righteous. Therefore "Blessed be the Lord, who daily bears us up; God is our salvation. Our God is a God of salvation; and to God, the Lord, belongs escape from death" (Ps 68:19-20). The Father bears Jesus up into heaven, and in so doing Jesus escapes from death.

ceive their theological and soteriological significance, their minds having been "opened" by Jesus. Primarily they are witnesses to Jesus' death and resurrection, but they are also witnesses to the whole of Jesus' public ministry, which also bears upon Jesus' death and resurrection, his destroying of all evil, and his giving of new and abundant life.[36] And while Jesus' disciples are to preach the Gospel in his name to all nations, they are to begin in Jerusalem. That the Gospel is first to be preached in Jerusalem underlines the city's soteriological and historical centrality, for here the whole of God's previous saving acts converge and find their fulfillment. Likewise, that the Gospel will be preached first in Jerusalem acknowledges the centrality of the Jews, God's covenanted chosen people, and it is in and through them, as found first in Jesus and subsequently his Apostles, that salvation will reach to the ends of the earth. The Gentiles will become followers of Jesus the Christ, but only by entering God's kingdom, the renewed Israel, the "capital" of which is not the "New Rome," but the New Jerusalem.[37]

Jesus next speaks about the immediate future. "And behold, I send the promise of my Father upon you; but stay in the city, until you are clothed with power from on high." His disciples are to "behold" that Jesus will be sending "the promise of my Father" upon them, and in so doing they will be "clothed with power from on high." Jesus is the one who will be sending "the promise," which is not his but that of his "Father." The promise, as becomes evident in Luke's Acts of the Apostles, is the Holy Spirit. The Father promised this gift of the Holy Spirit through John the Baptist, who prophesied that, although he baptized with water, there is one coming after him; "he will baptize you with the Holy Spirit and with fire" (Lk 3:16; see also Mt 3:11, Mk 1:8, and Jn 1:32-34). The Holy Spirit is the Father's promised gift, which will be sent by Jesus, the Son, and what the Holy Spirit, the Father's promised gift given by the Jesus, the Son, will do is clothe with power the disciples who will be staying in Jerusalem. Herein Jesus once again gives expression to the Trinity, not simply as

36. This is Luke's brief narrative of Jesus "commissioning" his Apostles. Below we will examine shortly Matthew's and Mark's commissioning narrative.

37. Luke, as is commonly recognized, sees the whole of salvation history converging on Jerusalem where Jesus enacts the supreme salvific act: his passion and death, and where the supreme salvific fruit of that act is born—his glorious resurrection. From Jerusalem, salvation history continues because the Gospel of salvation is from thence to be preached to the whole world. In Acts, Jesus' parting words to his Apostles, more fully expressed than in Luke's Gospel, are: "But you shall receive power when the Holy Spirit comes upon you; and you shall be my witnesses in Jerusalem and in all of Judea and Samaria and to the ends of the earth" (Acts 1:7-8).

it is found within the economy of salvation but also within the very life of the Trinity.

By saying that he will send "the promise of my Father," Jesus is designating himself as the Father's Son and simultaneously designating "the promise," the Holy Spirit, as proper to his Father alone. But because Jesus, the Father's Son, is sending that which is proper to his Father, the promised Holy Spirit, this implies that it is his privilege to do the sending and in turn that the Father has given to Jesus, his Son, the Holy Spirit in a manner in keeping with his being the Father's Son, that is, the full Spirit of Sonship. Having bestowed upon Jesus, his incarnate Son, the Spirit of Sonship, the Father has given him the proper capacity to send forth that Spirit which properly belongs to the Father, but which he has bestowed fully upon Jesus as his Son. Jesus, as the Father's Son, has also equally merited to "send" the Father's promised Holy Spirit, for it was through his death that he reconciled humankind to his Father and in his resurrection became humankind's Savior and Lord, who possesses the fullness of the Father's promised Holy Spirit. By sending the Holy Spirit upon his disciples and all the faithful, Jesus, the Father's Son, will unite them to himself and so, in union with him, will come into living Spirit-filled communion with his Father.

Jesus' sending of the Father's promised Holy Spirit also provides us a window into the life of the Trinity. The Father is the eternal wellspring of the Holy Spirit, whom he eternally bestows fully upon his Son in his eternal begetting of his Son. Thus the Father begets his Son in the Holy Spirit, and so the Son possesses the Holy Spirit, as Son, in the same divine manner as the Father. The Father and Son, then, equally share the fullness of the Holy Spirit, for the Father is only the Father by giving his Son the fullness of his Holy Spirit, and the Son is only the Son by sharing fully the Father's Spirit as Son. The Spirit is never foreign to the Son because the Son is never foreign to his Father. Reverting to the economy of salvation, because the Father is the source of the Holy Spirit, it is his divine prerogative to bestow this promised gift of the Spirit upon humankind. Because the Father eternally bestowed the gift of the Holy Spirit upon his Son, it is Jesus, the Son, who is rightly and properly the one through whom the Father bestows his promised gift of the Holy Spirit upon humankind. Thus there is a harmonious symmetry between how the persons exist as the one God within the Trinity and how they act within the economy of salvation. The Father begets his Son in the Holy Spirit so as to unite himself and his Son in the love of the Holy Spirit, and so the Father sends forth his Son into the world, having been conceived as man in the womb of Mary in the same Spirit in whom he was eternally begotten. In turn, Jesus, the incarnate Son, in communion with the Holy Spirit, achieves salvation through his passion and death. In becoming the risen Savior and Lord, Jesus, the Son, is now empowered by his Father to send forth the same Holy Spirit upon the faithful so as to incorporate them into the divine life of the Trinity itself—one with the Father in union with his Son within the communion of the Holy Spirit.

In sending the Holy Spirit, the Father's promised gift, his Apostles will be "clothed with power from on high." To be "clothed with power" implies more than just an outer dressing of power or an assuming the mere appearance of power, but a power that will transform them, clothe them interiorly, for that power is from "on high," the heavenly power of the Holy Spirit. Thus the Apostles, on being clothed with this heavenly power, will be able to do what they were incapable of doing prior to being so clothed: to live holy lives and to proclaim the Gospel with power, all of which Luke will narrate in the Acts of the Apostles. And the Father's promise, the Holy Spirit, whom Jesus will send is not simply for the good of the Apostles, but in being conferred upon the Apostles the Holy Spirit is the Father's gift to the whole apostolic church and to her members throughout history, for Jesus, as Savior and Lord, will continually pour forth the Father's Spirit until the end of time.[38]

Luke next narrates: "Then he [Jesus] led them out as far as Bethany, and lifting up his hands he blessed them. While he blessed them, he parted from them, and was carried up into heaven. And they worshipped him, and returned to Jerusalem with great joy, and were continually in the temple blessing God." From Jerusalem Jesus led his Apostles to Bethany, which sits just beyond the top of the Mount of Olives, and so they passed through the Garden of Gethsemane. Three days previously, Jesus knelt there in agony, petitioning his Father to remove the cup of suffering. Now, having drunk the cup to its bitter end in accordance with his Father's will, Jesus climbs the mount to ascend gloriously to his Father's throne. Upon arriving, Jesus lifts his hands, risen hands that bear the marks of the nails, in blessing and is simultaneously "carried up into heaven."[39] Jesus' blessing is both his last "earthly" act and

38. The Holy Spirit who comes upon the Apostles at Pentecost comes upon others in a similar manner upon their conversion (see, e.g., Cornelius' and his household's conversion; Acts 10:34-48).

39. The end of Luke's Gospel transitions into the opening of the Acts of the Apostles. As Luke now ends his Gospel with Jesus' ascension, so he begins Acts with the ascension. Though his Acts narrative is much fuller, it is not entirely in agreement with the Gospel. In his Gospel, Luke has Jesus ascending into heaven either late on Easter Sunday evening or early the next morning. In Acts, Jesus ascends "forty days" after his resurrection, during which time Jesus

his first "heavenly" act, for the blessing he bestows, upon being lifted up from the earth, is a heavenly blessing that is the fruit of the cross and in keeping with his being their risen Savior and Lord. Likewise, Jesus' blessing signifies his ever-enacted heavenly blessing, his continual bestowal of the Holy Spirit, upon them and his future church, for he is ascending to his Father, where he will assume his heavenly kingship sitting at the right hand of his Father's throne. This being "carried up into heaven" by his heavenly Father is the fruit of the cross. Having passed through the agony in the garden on his way to the cross, Jesus now passes through that same garden to ascend not upon the cross but to be carried up joyfully into his heavenly glory upon reaching the summit of the Mount of Olives.

Finally, Jesus' ascension into heaven is an icon of his no longer being with his disciples as well as his everlasting blessed presence among them. He is now present as their heavenly Savior and Lord, and as such he is now empowered to pour out upon them what he could not when he was in their earthly midst—the Holy Spirit. In sending forth the Holy Spirit, the risen and ascended Lord Jesus finally fulfills his Father's promise, and in so doing he will be ever present within his church.

Luke concludes by stating that the disciples then "worshiped him [Jesus], and returned to Jerusalem with great joy, and were continually in the temple blessing God." The Apostles' worship of him is their acknowledgment, their profession of faith, that Jesus is truly the living Father's Son, the anointed Christ, and their Lord and Savior. Worship of Jesus is the supreme proclamation that he is He Who Is—YHWH-Saves. The ascension of Jesus brings them "great joy" as they return to Jerusalem, for they now comprehend, their minds now open to the truth of Scripture, that he who died upon the cross for their salvation is now their risen life-giver. There, waiting for Jesus to send the Father's promised Holy Spirit, they continually abide in the temple "blessing God" for the marvelous things the Father has done for them through Jesus Christ his Son by the power of the Holy Spirit. As the Gospel of Luke began

---

repeatedly appeared to his Apostles, giving them "many proofs" of his being alive and speaking to them about "the kingdom of God" (see Acts 1:1-3). In the light of the Acts account, one can perceive in Luke's compact resurrection narrative the possibility that he has compressed multiple appearances into one continuous narrative. This may be evident in Jesus first manifesting the bodily nature of his resurrection (appearance one) and then immediately speaking about his death and resurrection fulfilling the Scripture and the opening of the Apostles' mind (appearance two), and concluding with his commissioning of the Apostles and the promise of sending the Holy Spirit immediately prior to his ascension (appearance three).

with the angel Gabriel appearing to Zechariah within the temple in Jerusalem, it now concludes in Jerusalem with the Apostles in the temple. What has transpired in the interim is the making of the new temple, the risen Son of God, Jesus Christ, in whom the whole of humankind can now come into the presence of the Father in the communion of Holy Spirit.

The "Longer Ending" within the Gospel of Mark

Mark's Gospel may have originally ended at 16:8, though some further ending may have also been lost. The present "Longer Ending" continues with the theme of the Apostles' unbelief. Our previous examination of Mark concluded with Jesus' appearance to the Apostles, where he upbraided their unbelief because of their "hardness of heart." Jesus nonetheless immediately commissions his Apostles: "Go into all the world and preach the gospel to the whole of creation. He who believes and is baptized will be saved; but he who does not believe will be condemned."[40] For clarity, it is necessary to pause here. Like Luke (and as we will see in Matthew as well), Jesus mandates that the Apostles go throughout the world and preach the Gospel to "the whole of creation." Luke and Matthew have Jesus speak in terms of converting nations and making disciples throughout the world, which connotes "people." Jesus' "the whole of creation," within Mark, if taken literally, means that human beings should hear the Gospel and everything that exists within the created order. Does this mean that bears, giraffes, great white sharks, turkeys, vultures, termites, and mosquitoes, and even trees, plants, rocks, planets, and stars, are to hear the Gospel? The latter group and many in the animal "kingdom" do not even have ears. Although Jesus obviously has human beings throughout "the whole of creation" as the primary recipients of the Gospel, the rest of creation, animate and inanimate, is not foreign to it. Ultimately the Gospel is about a new creation, a new heaven and a new earth, and not just the rebirth of men and women, but also the re-creation of the whole created order. Nothing of God's good creation will be lost, even if presently the whole of creation is marred by human sin. As humankind is made new in Christ through the transforming power of the Holy Spirit, so the whole of creation will be made new in Christ in that same Spirit, and that apparently includes hyenas, clams, fleas, oak trees, the moon, the sun, and everything else. So, yes, the Gospel is to be preached to the whole of creation, for as human beings come to share

40. All quotations in this section are from Mk 16:9-20 unless otherwise noted.

more fully in the risen Jesus so will the whole of creation reap the risen benefits.[41]

That Jesus, in the first instance, is concerned with human beings is found in what he states next, that those who believe and are baptized will be saved. The preaching of the Gospel serves the purpose of engendering faith in Jesus as the Father's incarnate Son who died to free humankind from sin and rose to give them the new life of the Holy Spirit. This new life is obtained in baptism, for those who believe are taken up into the divine life and love of the Father, the Son, and the Holy Spirit. We perceive here, beginning with Jesus' own words, the centrality of faith and the necessity of the sacrament of baptism, for together one comes to live within the risen Lord Jesus and so reaps the benefits that accrue to him alone—the filial holiness of everlasting life. However, "he who does not believe will be condemned." This condemnation is founded upon the refusal to both repent of sin and believe that Jesus is the Savior from sin and the Lord of God's life-giving kingdom. In other words, if one willfully remains in the fallen and sinful created order, haughtily seeking and egoistically rejoicing in its alluring indulgences and glamorous grandeur, then one necessarily reaps its satanic reward: God's everlasting condemnation.

Jesus continues, saying, "And these signs will accompany those who believe: in my name they will cast out demons; they will speak in new tongues; they will pick up serpents, and if they drink any deadly thing, it will not hurt them; they will lay their hands on the sick, and they will recover." Although Mark's is the only Gospel in which Jesus speaks of these signs, for the most part they are acts that are found within the apostolic church and that Jesus performed during his public ministry, casting out demons and healing the sick. As Jesus did mighty works by the power of the Holy Spirit, so now the apostolic church, in the same Spirit and in the name of Jesus, continues to per-

---

41. We previously commented on this point where we referenced Paul: "For the creation waits with eager longing for the revealing of the sons of God; for the creation itself will be set free from its bondage to decay and obtain the glorious liberty of the children of God" (Rom 8:19). At the end of time, when human beings become fully resurrected sons and daughters of the Father, in communion with humankind, the whole of creation will obtain incorruptible life. The Old Testament frequently speaks of the whole of creation giving praise to God (see, e.g., Pss 147, 149; Dn 3:52-90). This praise will reach its everlasting crescendo within the new heavens and new earth.

Also, many of the saints have already exemplified this new relationship with the created order. A lion is said to have been a "friend" of St. Jerome. St. Francis preached the Gospel to the birds and tamed the wolf of Gubbio. North Sea seals warmed the freezing feet of St. Cuthbert when he was a hermit on the Farne Islands. A goose was a constant companion of St. Hugh of Lincoln.

form these same life-giving deeds, testifying to Jesus' risen presence within their midst (see, e.g., Acts 3:1-10, 5:12-16). They are not simply signs of God's now present kingdom but partially constitute the reality of living within God's kingdom. As they were integral to Jesus' ministry, so they continue to be vital to life in his kingdom and not merely marginal curiosities.

They also evangelistically bear witness to Jesus being the risen Savior from all evil and the powerful life-giving Lord. Speaking new languages or in tongues is another sign of the Spirit's presence within the apostolic community and the church (see Acts 2:1-13).[42] The signs that seem most peculiar are the "picking up of serpents" (presumably of the poisonous variety) and the drinking of poisonous drinks, without the deadly effects that would normally follow. There is one instance within Acts where Paul, having been shipwrecked but landing safely on the island of Malta, was welcomed by the natives who built a fire to warm him. When Paul fetched more sticks for the fire, a viper came out and "fastened on his hand." The people thought this was a sure sign that Paul was "a murderer." Though having escaped from the sea, he was now being justly punished. But Paul shook off the viper into the fire, and when he did not swell up and die, the people concluded he "was a god." This miracle along with Paul's further healing of the sick brought about many conversions (Acts 28:1-10).[43] Jesus, in first announcing at the onset of his public ministry that the kingdom of God is at hand, manifested its reality though his mighty works of exorcism, healing, and raising the dead. If that same divine kingdom continues to be a reality, then it must manifest these same mighty deeds. In Mark's Gospel, Jesus is assuring his disciples that such mighty deeds will be part of their ministry and so manifest the enduring reality of God's Kingdom in their midst.

Mark's Longer Ending concludes by stating, "So then the Lord Jesus, after he had spoken to them, was taken up into heaven, and sat down at the right hand of God. And they went forth and preached everywhere, while the Lord worked with them and confirmed the message by the signs that attend-

42. In his First Letter to the Corinthians, Paul lists the spiritual gifts of the Holy Spirit some of which Jesus speaks of in Mark's Gospel: "gifts of healing," "the working of miracles," and "various kinds of tongues" (1 Cor 12:4-11).

43. In the New Testament, there are no stories of anyone drinking poison and not dying. But in the apocryphal "Acts of St. John," there is the story of Emperor Domitian persecuting the Christians. Having heard of John's peaching in Ephesus, Domitian sent for him. John was forced to drink poison but was unharmed. A criminal was forced to drink the remainder and died, whereupon John raised him back to life. Here we find both the sign of "drinking poison" and not dying, and the sign of raising someone from the dead.

ed it. Amen." Mark accentuates here that Jesus is the Lord precisely because he is risen, and being risen, he now abides gloriously with God, sitting in authority at his right hand. The Apostles, in turn, the Lord Jesus having been "taken up into heaven" by his enthroning Father, deliberately set forth, as Jesus commanded, to preach the Gospel "everywhere," that is, to "the whole of creation." Nonetheless, the heavenly Lord Jesus "worked with them" in their divinely commissioned endeavor to convert the whole world, and he did so through the very signs that he enunciated prior to his ascension. These attending signs "confirmed" the truth of the Gospel that they were preaching. Again, we perceive the integral relationship between "the signs" and the Gospel itself. It is the same inherent relationship that existed during Jesus' own ministry, where his casting out of demons and his healing of the sick manifested that he, through his death and resurrection, was overcoming all evil and establishing God's kingdom of life. As Jesus was becoming Jesus, YHWH-Saves, while on earth, so he now continues to act in, with, and through his disciples as the Lord Jesus, YHWH-Saves. On this triumphal truth, Mark's Gospel concludes with a confirming "Amen."[44]

The Ending of the Gospel according to Matthew:
The Great Commission

When the angel spoke to "Mary Magdalene and the other Mary" at the empty tomb, he told them to "go quickly and tell his disciples," for "behold he is going before you to Galilee; there you will see him. Lo, I have told you" (Mt 28:5-7). On their way, Jesus appears to them and says, "go and tell my brethren to go to Galilee, and there they will see me" (Mt 28:10). Jesus previously had

---

44. The Shorter Ending of Mark's Gospel, which is not considered canonical, concludes: "But they [Mary Magdalene and the other women] reported briefly to Peter and to those with him all that they had been told. And after this, Jesus himself sent out by means of them, from east to west, the sacred and imperishable proclamation of eternal salvation." Although this ending contradicts the "original" ending, it does have similarities to the longer one. Here, Jesus is the primary actor in the proclamation of the Gospel, for he "sets out." The Apostles are simply "the means" that he uses. In the Longer Ending, Jesus works in unison with the Apostles. Moreover, Jesus sets out, by means of the Apostles, "east to west," thus going from Jerusalem and Israel (east) to Asia Minor and Europe (west) and thus to all nations, "to the whole of creation." What is unique to the Shorter Ending is that what Jesus, the Son, and his disciples proclaim is "sacred," for it is the Father's Spirit-imbued message. It is "imperishable" because it is the Gospel of "eternal salvation," which is founded upon Jesus' salvific death and enduring resurrection.

told his Apostles as they journeyed to the Mount of Olives after the Last Supper: "After I am raised up, I will go before you to Galilee" (Mt 26:32). So, Matthew concludes his Gospel with "the eleven disciples" going to Galilee, "to the mountain to which Jesus directed them" (Mt 18:16).[45] Now, in Mark, the angel tells Mary Magdalene and the women to go "tell his disciples and Peter that he is going before you to Galilee," but the women "said nothing to any one" (Mk 16:7-8). In the Longer Ending, Jesus appears to the disciples, presumably in Jerusalem. After this appearance, Jesus "was taken up into heaven" (Mk 16:19). This again makes Mark's narrative confusing. Luke, in his Gospel, has Jesus leading his disciples to Bethany, which is just over the Mount of Olives; from there, he "was carried up into heaven," and Luke's Acts confirms this location (Lk 24:51; Acts 1:9-12).[46] There is, then, a seeming discrepancy as to the location of Jesus' ascension—Matthew places it in Galilee, Mark's narrative is ambivalent, and Luke definitely places it just outside Jerusalem at Bethany. So it is difficult, if not impossible, to verify historically at which location Jesus actually ascended. From a theological perspective, Matthew may want to emphasize that Jesus was assumed into heaven in the same region in which he began his saving ministry—Galilee. Luke, more assuredly, in keeping with his view of the whole of salvation history, wants to emphasize that all converges on Jerusalem and from which the saving Gospel goes forth.[47] Thus Jesus completes his salvific work in Jerusalem, and his last "earthly saving deed," immediately prior to his ascension, is to send forth from Jerusalem his disciples to preach the Gospel to all nations—to the ends of the earth.

Surprisingly, in Matthew's resurrection narrative, although Jesus appears to Mary Magdalene and the other women, he never appears to the Apostles prior to his ascension. Rather, at some indeterminate time, the Apostles, having gone to the mountain "to which Jesus directed them" (though no specific mountain was ever identified by Jesus within Matthew), "when they saw him they worshiped him; but some doubted." This absence of a prior appearance may account for Matthew's noting that some doubted Jesus' resurrection, for this "doubting" within Mark and Luke was occasioned by either an earlier ap-

---

45. All quotations in this section are from Mt 28:16-20 unless otherwise noted.

46. The Gospel of John has Jesus' last appearance taking place at the Sea of Galilee, but there is no narrative of any ascension taking place there (see Jn 21). In John's Gospel, Jesus does make reference to his ascension. "Then what if you were to see the Son of man ascending where he was before?" (Jn 6:62). "I shall be with you a little longer, and then I go to him who sent me" (Jn 7:33). See also Jn 8:21, 12:35, 13:1, 13:33, 14:19, 16:16, and 20:17.

47. In the Acts of the Apostles, Luke suggests that Jesus will return to the same place from which he ascends (see Acts 1:11).

pearance or by the unbelieved reports from the women. Upon beholding the risen Jesus, however, "they worshiped him." As in Luke, where the disciples worship Jesus as he is carried up into heaven, so this present worship also testifies to the Apostles' belief that Jesus was truly God (see Lk 24:52). It also replicates the response of Mary Magdalene and the other women who worshipped Jesus upon his appearance to them (Mt 28:9). Jesus' resurrection confirms for the Apostles and the apostolic community their belief that Jesus is the Spirit-anointed Christ, the Father's Son.

Matthew next states that "Jesus came and said to them, 'All authority in heaven and on earth has been given to me. Go therefore and make disciples of all nations, baptizing them in the name of the Father and of the Son and of the Holy Spirit, teaching them to observe all that I have commended you; and lo, I am with you always, to the close of the age.'" That Jesus "came" to them denotes that he is the initiator of his resurrected appearances and so is the primary controlling actor of all post-resurrection events. Simply put, Jesus is the risen Lord who directs all of history. This is confirmed by what Jesus immediately declares. In having been raised from the dead by his Father, he has been given, in that very act, "all authority in heaven and earth."[48] Jesus' words suggest what is portrayed within Daniel's vision: "Behold, with the clouds of heaven there came one like a son of man, and he came to the Ancient of Days and was presented before him. And to him was given dominion and glory and kingdom, that all peoples, nations, and languages should serve him; his dominion is an everlasting dominion, which shall not pass away, and his kingdom one that shall not be destroyed" (Dn 7:13-14). Jesus, the son of man who is the Son of God, is about to ascend upon the clouds into heaven, but that ascending, that being "presented" to his heavenly Father, the Ancient of Days, is but the manifestation that he has already been given, within his being raised by his Father, all dominion, glory, and power—"all authority in heaven and earth." Such authority, which spans both heaven and earth and a dominion that will last forever and will not pass away or be destroyed, is divine, for only the eternal all-powerful God possesses such authority. The risen Jesus, the Father's Son, now possesses such authority, but he possesses it as man, within

---

48. This is in accord with what Jesus declared earlier: "All things have been delivered to me by my Father; and no one knows the Son except the Father, and no one knows the Father except Son and any one to whom the Son chooses to reveal him" (Mt 11:27). Because Jesus knows the Father as the Father's Son, he will choose to commission his disciples to baptize disciples from all nations so that they can be taken up into the life of the Trinity and so know the Father in the Son through the communion of the Holy Spirit.

his risen humanity. This is theologically and soteriologically significant. The Son of God became man, and he offered himself, his humanity, as the atoning and saving sacrifice for the forgiveness of sins, and because of that sacrifice, he possesses as a risen man "all authority in heaven and earth." As the risen Lord, Jesus' dominion will last forever, and as the risen king, his kingdom will not be destroyed. Here we perceive the primacy and supremacy of the historical man Jesus, He Who Is: YHWH-Saves.[49]

Because God his Father has given to Jesus all authority, he mandates the Apostles to make disciples of all nations, that is, to go and preach the Gospel and bring all peoples to faith in Jesus—the same apostolic faith that they possess.[50] Thus there will be a unity of faith between the Apostles and the new multinational disciples. In bringing all nations to faith in Jesus through the preaching of the Gospel, the Apostles are then to baptize them. Again, we perceive the integral relationship between faith and baptism. In coming to faith in Jesus, converts can be taken up, with the ascended Jesus, into heavenly communion with the Trinity. This communion of divine life and love is predicated upon their being baptized "in the name of the Father, and of the Son and of the Holy Spirit." The convert's being immersed in water is the efficacious sign of

49. This is marvelously expressed in both the Ephesian and the Philippian Hymns. The Father's great might is "accomplished in Christ when he raised him from the dead and made him sit at his right hand in the heavenly places, far above all rule and authority and power and dominion and above every name that is named, not only in this age but also in that which is to come; and he put all things under his feet and has made him the head over all things for the church, which is his body, the fullness of him who fills all in all" (Eph 1:19-23). Because of Jesus' humility as the Son of God incarnate, even to death on the cross, "God has highly exalted him and bestowed on him the name which is above every name, that at the name of Jesus every knee should bow, in heaven and on earth and under the earth, and every tongue confess that Jesus Christ is Lord, to the glory of God the Father" (Phil 2:9-11).

Jesus' supreme authority is also seen in the Book of Revelation. There no one is found worthy to break open the seven seals. Because of this John wept. But one of the elders said, "Weep not; lo, the Lion of the tribe of Judah, the Root of David, has conquered so that he can open the scroll and its seven seals." The Lamb who was slain, who sits on the throne, "Worthy are you to take the scroll and to open its seals, for you were slain and by your blood did ransom for God from every tribe and tongue and people and nation, and has made them a kingdom and priests to our God, and they shall reign forever." Thus "Worthy is the Lamb who was slain to receive power and wealth and wisdom and might and honor and glory and blessing!" (Rv 5:12).

50. Previously, within Matthew's Gospel, Jesus tells his disciples not to go among the Gentiles or to enter the towns of the Samaritans, but "go rather to the lost sheep of the house of Israel" (Mt 10:5-6). Also, Jesus states that he "was sent only to the lost sheep of the house of Israel" (Mt 15:24). Only after Jesus has saved the whole of humankind through his death and resurrection does he now commission his disciples to proclaim the Gospel to all nations and peoples.

their being cleansed of sin and their being taken up into the divine life of the Trinity. Thus the convert becomes a new creation in Christ Jesus. By being united to Jesus, the Father's Son, through faith, they are transformed though baptism into his filial likeness by the power of the indwelling Spirit of Sonship, and so become holy children of the Father. This is only possible because Jesus died for their sins and, as the risen Lord, is now empowered to baptize with the Holy Spirit those who come to faith in him, a baptism that is now enacted by Jesus' apostolic church. We also perceive here the living personal relationship between the risen Lord Jesus and his church. Jesus continues to act salvifically, continues to be YHWH-Saves, through the sacramental actions of his church, for those ecclesial acts are Jesus' acts through which he unites the faithful to his church and so with himself.[51] Moreover, by being united to Jesus as YHWH-Saves, the baptized faithful enter into the heavenly Jerusalem, which the risen Jesus now embodies, and so, together with him, as the new and living temple, worship the Father in the Holy Spirit.

Having been united to Jesus through faith and having come to participate in the very life of the most Holy Trinity through baptism demands that the faithful now live holy lives in accordance with Jesus. Thus the Apostles and his church are to teach the baptized faithful "to observe all that I have commanded you." Through his public ministry, Jesus taught the new law that is to be lived within God's kingdom. Within Matthew's Gospel this is primarily articulated within Jesus' Sermon on the Mount and particularly within the Beatitudes. As Jesus, the Christ, enacted the Beatitudes and so established his Father's kingdom, so those who are now transformed into his likeness by the Holy Spirit are now empowered to live the Beatitudes as children of their Father.

Although Jesus does not ascend into heaven within Matthew's Gospel, his final words allude to his immediately being taken up into heaven. "And lo, I am (*ego eimi*) with you always, to the close of the age." Jesus may not be present visibly, but he is nonetheless "with" them, and he is present because of what the risen Jesus has just commissioned his disciples to do. Because he is alive as their risen Lord and Savior, he is present to them. Because of their faith in him, they are united to him and he is united to them, and so he is present to them. Because the baptized are immersed into the life of the Trinity, the risen and ascended Jesus is present to them, and he is present to them "to the

---

51. Baptism initiates the new disciple into this unity with Jesus, finding its fullest expression in the Eucharist.

close of the age" precisely as He Who Is (*ego eimi*), as the living Son of God. Thus Jesus is present to them as he now is, as YHWH-Saves. This will be so until this "age" closes at his return, for then he will be with them, and with all the "this-age" faithful, in all his glory, and they in turn will be glorified in his bodily risen likeness.

But of what "age" is Jesus speaking? Within Matthew's Gospel, this is an age in which Jesus sows the seed of the Gospel while the devil simultaneously sows the seed of evil. This age will end when Jesus reaps the harvest of the righteous and condemns the unrighteous. When interpreting to his disciples the parable of the sower, Jesus says that the Son of man sows in the world the good seed of "the sons of the kingdom." But the weeds are "the sons of the evil one, and the enemy who sowed them is the devil; *and the harvest is the close of this age*, and the reapers are angels." At the "close of this age," Jesus, the Son of man, will "gather out of his kingdom all causes of sin and all evildoers, and throw them into the furnace of fire. . . . Then the righteous will shine like the sun in the kingdom of their Father" (Mt 13:36-43). Similarly, the kingdom of heaven is like a fishing net that contains good and bad fish; the good are kept and the bad are thrown away. "So it will be at *the close of this age*. The angels will come out and separate the evil from the righteous, and throw them into the furnace of fire; there men will weep and gnash their teeth" (Mt 13:47-50). Within this world of sin, Jesus sows "the sons" of God's kingdom, the good seed, and nurtures their growth within that kingdom, while the devil sows offspring of his like, who cultivate evil.[52] At "the close of this age," Jesus will condemn the sons of Satan and bring to glory the sons of his Father. At its end "the Son of man is to come with his angels in the glory of his Father, and then he will repay every man for what he has done" (Mt 16:27). It is during this precarious yet Spirit-filled age that Jesus, YHWH-Saves, promises to be with his disciples, and so they need not fear. Rather, they are to long for its "close," when Jesus will return with his angels, resplendent in his Father's glory.[53]

---

52. Jesus does not refer to "this age," but he speaks of "an evil and adulterous generation" who seek a sign. The only sign will be that of Jonah, that is, Jesus' death and resurrection or ultimately his coming in glory (Mt 16:1-4). He also bemoans a "faithless and perverse generation," rhetorically asking in frustration, "How long am I to be with you? How long can I bear with you?" (Mt 17:17). He will bear with them until "the end of the age," at which time, if they continue in their faithless perversion, they will be condemned.

53. Jesus declares that the coming of "the close of this age" is the time of great tribulation (see Mt 24, esp. v. 3).

Three Theological Conclusions

Other theological issues could be treated by way of summary, but here I want to address only three. First, we need to see the theological and soteriological importance of the Father raising Jesus from the dead and taking him up into heaven. In the resurrection and ascension, the Father not only confirms all that Jesus has revealed but also actively establishes Jesus as Savior and Lord, setting into motion the benefits that accrue to Jesus' saving deeds. Second, I want to demonstrate that the resurrection and ascension, while chronologically portrayed as distinct events, are actually one and the same event. The Father, in raising Jesus gloriously from the dead, simultaneously lifted him up into his heavenly throne. Third, I return to a topic discussed throughout this study: that the Father in raising his Son Jesus into his glorious presence empowered him, in the Holy Spirit, to see him face to face. The risen Jesus, as the Father's Son, obtained the fullness of his filial vision of his Father. In all three topics, we see that in Jesus' resurrection and ascension the Father has made Jesus to be fully Jesus, YHWH-Saves, for the Father has given to him the fullness of his paternal Spirit of Sonship.

The Theological and Soteriological Effects of the Father Raising Jesus from the Dead

When Jesus was baptized by John, a baptism in which the Father commissioned him to be his Spirit-filled Suffering Servant-Son, "the heaven was opened, and the Holy Spirit descended upon him in bodily form, as a dove, and a voice came from heaven, 'You are my beloved Son; with you I am well pleased'" (Lk 3:21-22). And within Jesus' Transfiguration, the prefigurement of his passing over from the darkness of death into the glory of his ascended resurrection, the Father again declared, "This is my Son, my Chosen; listen to him!" (Lk 9:34-35). Now, in raising Jesus from the dead, the Father is definitively declaring that Jesus is his divine Son. In the act of raising Jesus, the Father is conclusively fulfilling Gabriel's prophecy to Mary: "Therefore the child to be born will be call holy, the Son of God" (Lk 1:35). The Father is also decisively tearing open the heavens by taking Jesus, the Son in whom he is well pleased, up into the heavens. The Father is also acknowledging that Jesus, through his saving death, as his Spirit-filled Suffering Servant-Son, has completed his baptismal commission and so has merited to reign gloriously, luminously transfigured before his Father forever. In so doing, the Father has given to Jesus the authority and power to baptize in the Holy Spirit all who believe in his Son, thus fulfilling his own prophecy first proclaimed by John the Baptist. Thus the Apostles and the church, now more than ever, are to listen to the ascended Jesus, for the Father has constituted him to be the *Prophet* fully in act, for the Spirit-filled words he will speak give full voice to his heavenly Father, at whose right hand he now sits. By establishing the risen Jesus, his beloved Son, as the Prophet, the Father has equally established himself as the source of all truth and the Holy Spirit, who now fully imbues Jesus' every word, as the Spirit of truth.

In raising Jesus from the dead and assuming him into heaven, the Father has likewise constituted him as the supreme *high priest*, for he offered the most perfect sacrifice of himself. In raising Jesus and taking him up into glory, the Father attests that Jesus' sacrificial, atoning, and covenantal death, his priestly offering of himself as victim, is efficacious, for its effect is witnessed in Jesus' own risen humanity, which is free from the effects of sin and death, and literally embodies the new Spirit-filled life of God's new and everlasting covenant. Therefore Jesus' risen humanity will always bear the marks of the nails, for they everlastingly testify to their efficacious effect—Jesus' risen humanity itself with its ascended heavenly glory. There is an everlasting enduring causal unity, a causal conjoining oneness, between Jesus' sacrificial act on the cross and the Father's act of raising Jesus from the dead. Jesus' salvific sacrificial act of redemption moves or causes the Father to reciprocate by his own causal act of raising Jesus from the dead. Each of their causal acts is conjoined and so meets within the humanity of Jesus; the humanity that Jesus offers becomes the humanity that the Father raises. Thus Jesus' redeeming act on the cross and his Father's reciprocal act of the resurrection is one mutually conjoining act, the effect of which is humankind's salvation. By raising Jesus, his Son, from the dead, the Father forever accepts his Son's atoning sacrifice as efficacious and so seals its saving effect within Jesus' own risen humanity, that is, the new and everlasting covenant. Importantly then, within the resurrection, Jesus' crucified humanity is forever transfigured in glory, and within that transfigured humanity resides his forever act of sacrifice with its forever saving effect. Although historically Jesus' sacrificial saving act is past, within his risen humanity that once-for-all saving act is still in act, for it is causally constitutive of Jesus' risen humanity. That sacrificial act is what still constitutes the risen Jesus to be Jesus—YHWH-Saves. It is not simply that in the resurrection the redemptive effects of Jesus' death are present, but that within the risen Jesus his very redemptive act is still in act, for the saving act itself embodies the saving effects, forgiveness of sins, and Spirit-filled life with the Father. Thus the saving effects of Jesus' death on the cross are always actively present because the risen Jesus always literally embodies the saving act from which they, by necessity, everlastingly flow. Jesus is forever the living Savior, Savior in act, for within his risen humanity his saving act with its saving effect is forever in act. In other words, the saving act by which Jesus constitutes and so conforms himself to be Savior, YHWH-Saves, is forever in act, for his Father, in the act of raising him from the dead, equally co-constitutes and so conforms Jesus, the now great high priest, to be forever Jesus—YHWH-Saves. The cross ever radiates from the gloriously transfigured Jesus.[54]

Here a Trinitarian point must be made. What motivates and empowers the causal conjoining acts of the Father and the Son is the Holy Spirit, for it is in the full love of the Spirit that Jesus offers himself to the Father and, in the same Spirit-filled love, the Father conjoins his resurrecting act to Jesus' sacrificial act. Thus the constituting of Jesus as the risen Savior and Lord is the co-inhering acts of the Father, the Son, and the Holy Spirit. Within these co-inhering acts, not only is Jesus definitively constituted to be Jesus as Son-YHWH-Saves, but also the Father as Father-YHWH-Saves and the Holy Spirit as Spirit-YHWH-Saves. The

54. I would like to make two points here. First, what I have proposed concerning Jesus' sacrificial act on the cross being forever in act within his risen humanity is similarly found within "normal" human beings. Men and women constitute who they are through their earthly acts. Thus holy acts constitute holy men and women. Those holy acts are not lost upon their entrance into heaven. Those holy acts are still in act, for it is these very holy acts that constituted them to be the holy heavenly persons that they are. Jesus' sacrificial act on the cross fully constituted Jesus as Savior, and that defining act is still in act because the Father raised Jesus gloriously from the dead precisely because that once-for-all act defined Jesus as Jesus, and in so doing constituted him the universal everlasting Savior. Therefore Jesus' priesthood is after the order of Melchizedek. As Melchizedek is never said to have died and so his priesthood is everlasting, so Jesus is forever the risen and ascended high priest because he forever, within his risen humanity, offers the once-for-all salvific sacrifice of himself to his Father (see Ps 110:1, 110:4; Heb 5:6, 5:10, 6:20, 7:11, and 7:21). Equally, then, the Father, in raising Jesus from the dead, forever accepts this once-for-all saving sacrifice. This is also why the covenant constituted by Jesus' sacrifice is an everlasting covenant, for it is constituted by the everlasting sacrifice embodied in the risen transfigured humanity of Jesus.

Second, because Jesus' saving sacrificial act is always in act, he can act as Savior within the sacraments. Being salvifically in act, he can salvifically act within the sacraments. As the in-act risen Savior, he can baptize in the Holy Spirit those who believe in him, thus allowing them to die to sin and rise to newness of life. Within the Eucharist, as we saw when treating the Last Supper, Jesus makes present his saving sacrifice precisely because that saving sacrifice is still in act even though it took place once and for all within history. Because this saving sacrifice is still in act within the risen Jesus, the saving benefits that accrue to it can be appropriated by those who are united to that in-act sacrifice within the Eucharist. To reap the benefits of the cross, one must be in communion with the cross, and this is possible within the sacraments because the risen Jesus embodies both the cross and its benefits—the new Spirit-filled life of the resurrection.

Father, in constituting Jesus as YHWH-Saves, has equally forever conformed and constituted himself as Father-YHWH-Saves. Similarly, because the constituting of Jesus as Son-YHWH-Saves and the Father as Father-YHWH-Saves is through the power of the Holy Spirit, the Holy Spirit forever conformed and constituted himself as Spirit-YHWH-Saves. In the resurrection and ascension, the whole Trinity, the one God, is constituted as YHWH-Saves.[55]

Having seen that, within his resurrection and ascension, Jesus, as the beloved Son, is constituted as the supreme Prophet and great high priest, we now perceive that he is also the risen and enthroned everlasting King. The Father, within the resurrection and ascension, constitutes and so confirms that Jesus, his crucified Son, is, as Pilate wrote, "the king of the Jews," and thus that he has established the promised everlasting kingdom of David. "I [God] will raise up your offspring after you [David], who shall come forth from your body, and I will establish his kingdom. He shall build a house for my name, and I will establish the throne of his kingdom forever" (2 Sm 7:12-13; see also 7:16 and Pss 89:2-4 and 132:11).[56] In addition, Gabriel's prophetic words to Mary at Jesus' conception are fulfilled. "The Lord God will give to him [Mary's son] the throne of his father David, and he will reign over the house of Jacob forever; and of his kingdom there will be not end" (Lk 1:32-33).[57] Without the resurrection Jesus would not reign forever, and without his ascension his kingdom would not be everlasting. Thus the Father, by raising Jesus from the dead and taking him up into heaven, establishes Jesus as the absolute King of heaven and earth. While Jesus is the everlasting king of the kingdom, it is God, his Father, whose kingdom it is. And as king of God's kingdom, Jesus pours out the life that is lived within his Father's kingdom—the Father's promised Holy Spirit.

We perceive in the above that the constituting of Jesus as Prophet, Priest,

---

55. By saying that the Father, the Son, and the Holy Spirit each constitute themselves as YHWH-Saves, I do not mean that they constitute themselves as a Trinity of persons. Their eternal relations, subsistent relations fully enact, ontologically constitute their distinct identities within the one God. Yet they each constitute themselves as YHWH-Saves within the economy of salvation by their distinct saving acts in relation to humankind.

56. Although God's promise to David that his offspring would build him (God) a house in his name (God's) is fulfilled in Solomon, his act of building the temple is a prophetic act. Jesus, the king of David's everlasting kingdom, builds the true house for his Father, by himself, in his resurrection, becoming the everlasting living temple in whom all, through the Holy Spirit, can come into the presence of his Father.

57. Establishing Jesus as the promised king of David's everlasting kingdom also fulfills the prophetic nature of Jesus' lineage. Jesus is a royal son of David, whose "father" was Joseph, "the son of David," and who was born in "the city of David" (see Mt 1:1, 1:20; Lk 2:4, 2:11).

and King through his resurrection and ascension always involves the distinct acts, though co-inhering acts, of the Father, the Son, and the Holy Spirit. If God had not raised Jesus from the dead, Jesus would not be the Father's Son and God would not be the Son's Father, for they would not be bound by the love and life of the Father's Holy Spirit of Sonship. Without the resurrection and ascension, the revelation of the Trinity would collapse and with it the truth of its existence. If the Father had not raised Jesus from the dead through the Holy Spirit, Jesus' cry of abandonment would be forever left unheard; it would have been met with everlasting divine silence. But Psalm 22's concluding hoped-for assurance is found in the Father silently raising Jesus, his Son, from the dead and by enthroning him in his heavenly ascension. Similarly, without the resurrection and ascension, the taunting ridicule of the mocking Jewish leaders, their guffawing head-wagging "if you are the Christ, the Son of God" would have then been true. And Jesus would rightly be remembered, if remembered at all, as a religious fiend out to destroy the Jewish faith and an impious fraud who attempted to deceive YHWH's chosen people. Again, the Father's silent act of raising Jesus, the Spirit-anointed Christ, from the dead and lifting him up into heaven silences forever not only the Jewish leaders of his day but also the blasphemous mocking leveled against his beloved Son, in whom he is well pleased.

The Resurrection and Ascension Are One Act
Though Portrayed Separately

Within the Synoptic Gospels, Jesus distinguishes his resurrection from his ascension. The risen Jesus first appears to his disciples and then, at some later point, is taken up into heaven and so unlike his post-resurrection appearances becomes invisible to their sight. The resurrection and the ascension are one and the same act, however. The Father's act of raising Jesus gloriously from the dead by the power of the Holy Spirit is the same act by which the Father makes him the risen Lord and Savior, the one who possesses all authority in heaven and on earth, and so the same act by which the Father gloriously enthrones Jesus forever at his right hand. Because this is theologically and soteriologically the case, why does Jesus distinguish them by separate events—the resurrection by his appearances and the ascension by his later visibly being take up into heaven, wherein he becomes invisible? This answer to this question lies, I believe, in first answering a theological and soteriological conundrum, one that is evident but normally not recognized. Why does Jesus, within the Gospels, never appear to anyone after his resurrection in his resurrected glory, but always in a physical bodily form that would appear to be not unlike that of a "normal" non-resurrected person? Why does Jesus not appear instead as he did during his Transfiguration—with his face shining like the sun and his garments glistening in light and dazzling white (see Mt 17:2, Mk 9:1-2, and Lk 9:29)?[58] To address fully this issue, we must first return to the scene of the women finding the tomb empty.

When Mary Magdalene and the other women arrive at Jesus' tomb, they find it empty, signaling that the humanity that was crucified is the same humanity that is now risen. Also, they see a "young man ... dressed in a white robe" (Mk), or "two men ... in dazzling apparel" (Lk) or an "angel" whose "appearance was like lightning, and his raiment white as snow" (Mt). The stark contrast is unmistakable—the dark empty tomb versus the brilliance of the man/men/angel dressed in luminous while apparel. The empty tomb denotes the resurrection of the man Jesus, the resurrection of the incarnate Son of God's humanity, and the glorious and radiant presence of the man/men/angel conveys the marvelous and resplendent nature of that resurrection.[59] Each separately emphasizes two essential, though conjoined, theological and

---

58. Traditionally, many artists portray Jesus coming forth from his tomb in exactly this manner. His visage radiates glorious light, and his tunic is luminously white. But he never appears to anyone in this fashion.

59. Within the Gospel of Luke, a similar contrast appeared within the birth of Jesus. At Jesus' birth, "an angel of the Lord appeared to them [the shepherds], and the glory of the Lord shone around them." The reason for this glorious theophany is that a child is born "this day in the city of David as Savior, who is Christ the Lord." But amid this heavenly fanfare, what the shepherds will find is "a babe wrapped in swaddling cloths and lying in a manger" (Lk 2:8-14). The angel signals Jesus' divinity, his being Christ the Lord. What the shepherds see is a normal infant lying in a manger. The scenes are distinct but conjoined, for what the shepherds see is a babe who is the Son of God—a human child divinely heralded by heavenly angels. Similarly, the women see an empty tomb while the angel(s) proclaims the glorious resurrection of the Savior, Christ the Lord, Jesus the risen Incarnate Son. Something similar can be perceived in Gabriel's appearance to Zechariah announcing that he will have a son and his appearance to Mary that she will conceive by the Holy Spirit and so her son will be the Son of the Most High God. In both instances, but particularly regarding the conception of Jesus, Gabriel's presence denotes a heavenly divine action, but the effect of that action is found here on earth.

Within the Acts of Apostles, Luke narrates that as the Apostles were "looking on, he [Jesus] was taken up, and a cloud took him out of their sight. And while they were gazing into heaven as he went up, behold, two men stood by them in white robes, and said, 'Men of Galilee why do you stand looking up into heaven? This Jesus, who was taken up from you into heaven, will come again in the same way as you saw him go into heaven'" (Acts 19-11). Luke's two graveside angels at Jesus' resurrection are the same twosome at Jesus' ascension. In both instances they fulfill the same role: declaring that Jesus, whose tomb is empty, is the risen and ascended heavenly Lord of glory. The earthly enactment of this one event may be separated in time, first the resurrection and then the ascension, but it is actually one event.

soteriological truths. The empty tomb emphasizes the genuine reality of Jesus' bodily resurrection, that the humanity that died on the cross for the remission of sins is the same as the humanity that is now risen. The presence of the radiant angel(s) testifies to the efficacious nature of that death, that of bringing forth of a glorious living humanity that is purged of sin's toxin with its venomous death. Only by separating these two soteriological facets is each properly emphasized, which allows them to be properly soteriologially conjoined. Yes, the crucified Jesus is bodily risen as a true and authentic man (the empty tomb), and that true bodily man Jesus ascended gloriously into heaven (the radiant appearance of the angel).

Now, Jesus, in his post-resurrection appearances, reveals the truth of the empty tomb, that he is risen as an authentic human being. Jesus accentuates, focuses upon, the reality of his risen humanity. His humanity holds center stage. Jesus humanly speaks; he can be physically seen; he can be bodily touched; he bears in his flesh the marks of the nails; and he can even, in Luke, chew and swallow a piece of broiled fish. The risen Jesus leaves no doubt about the authenticity of his humanity. Within this emphasis, Jesus is revealing that it was through his humanity that he both wrought salvation and the whole of humanity is saved from sin and death, and obtains life. Jesus, in his ascension, in his being taken up into heaven, reveals the truth of the radiant and luminous tombside angel(s). The actual man Jesus is the glorious heavenly man—the resplendent Son of God incarnate, the radiant Lord and the luminous Savior.[60] Within this emphasis, Jesus is revealing that, as the enthroned Lord, he is empowered through his risen humanity to bequeath to all the salvific benefits of his death and resurrection. Thus, although unbeknownst to them, what Mary Magdalene and the other women witness in one composite scene at Jesus' gravesite is both his resurrection and his ascension, for they are

60. In 2 Peter, the Transfiguration becomes the prophetic hermeneutical key for interpreting Jesus' resurrection, ascension, and coming in glory at the end of time. Peter does not follow clever myths, but he makes known the "coming of our Lord Jesus Christ," for "we were eyewitnesses of his majesty. For when he received honor and glory from God the Father and the voice was borne to him by the Majestic Glory, 'This is my beloved Son, with whom I am well pleased,' we heard this voice borne from heaven, for we were with him on the holy mountain." The coming in glory of the Lord Jesus Christ is assured because Peter beheld such glory in the Transfiguration, and Jesus' glory is confirmed by his Father's own words, for Jesus is his beloved Son in whom he is pleased. The glory of the Transfiguration, the glorious anticipation of Jesus' resurrection and ascension, is "a lamp shining in a dark place, until the day dawns and the morning star rises in your hearts" (2 Pt 1:16-19). For Peter, the final transfiguring event, founded upon Jesus' present heavenly glory, is Jesus returning gloriously to earth at the dawn of the eternal day when all the faithful will be transfigured into his luminous likeness.

one reality—the raising up of Jesus from the dead is the raising up of Jesus into heavenly glory.[61] As a good teacher, Jesus distinguishes them by means of his post-resurrection appearances and his portrayal of being lifted up into heaven so that both intertwining facets of one truth can be fully understood and appreciated, both in their distinctiveness and in their unity.[62]

Jesus' Resurrected Filial Vision of His Father

The Father, in raising Jesus to his ascended resurrected glory, has established him as the perfect Prophet, high priest, and King. The Father has accom-

---

61. In the Gospel of John, when Jesus appears to Mary Magdalene on Easter Sunday, she does not first recognize him, thinking he was the gardener. Jesus then rebukes her: "Do not hold me, for I have not yet ascended to the Father; but go to my brethren and say to them, I am ascending to my Father and your Father, to my God and your God" (Jn 20:17). Jesus appears to Mary in such a manner that she could physically lay hold of him, but not in that manner, for it bespeaks her desire to relate to him as she did prior to his resurrection. She is now to lay hold of him, in faith and love, as he now truly is—as resurrected. Mary will grasp this new manner of "laying hold" of Jesus when she recognizes that Jesus has ascended to his Father and so is now her glorious Lord and Savior. When she lays hold of Jesus in that manner, then Jesus' Father will be her Father and his God will be her God. Thus Jesus' appearance to Mary contains both the truth of his physical resurrection and his glorious ascension into heaven.

62. Interestingly, Jesus appears to Paul on his way to Damascus not in visible bodily form but in his glory. "Suddenly a light from heaven flashed around him [Paul]." While Jesus spoke to him, Paul did not recognize him and asked, "Who are you, Lord?" Paul, because of the heavenly light, knew he was in the presence of the divine Lord, but he did not know who the divine Lord was. Jesus had to identify himself: "I am Jesus, whom you are persecuting" (Acts 9:3-5). Unlike Jesus' appearance in the Gospels, his appearance to Paul combines both the reality of his resurrection and his ascension, and this is what confuses Paul. Deprived of Jesus' risen physical appearance, Paul is unable to identify the "Lord." But by designating himself as the man, Jesus, Jesus reveals that he is the glorious "Lord," and so conjoins his physical historical resurrection with his ascended heavenly glory.

Some translations (see, e.g., the New American Bible, revised edition) have Paul ask: "Who are you, sir?" This is an erroneous interpretative translation. *Kyrios* can be translated as "sir" when used as an honorific title for a gentleman. But Paul is not using it here in this way. He is not addressing some unknown human person as "sir." Rather, he is addressing someone whom he knows to be divine (*Kyrios*, Lord), but the identity of the divine "Lord" is unknown to him. It is this identity that he desires to know.

The Gospel of John has neither Jesus' Transfiguration nor his ascension. But the whole of John's Gospel is a narrative of Jesus' glory shining forth from his human flesh (*sarx*). "And the Word became flesh and dwelt among us, full of grace and truth; we have beheld his glory, glory as of the only Son from the Father" (Jn 1:14; see also 1 Jn 1:1-4). Through the weakness of Jesus' humanity, his divine glory as the Father's Son is made manifest. This will find its fulfillment in Jesus' death, where the full weakness of his humanity is displayed, yet this is the hour of Jesus' glory, which will be confirmed in his glorious resurrection. And the whole of Jesus' life, culminating in his death and resurrection, is a prophetic portrayal of his ascension (see Jn 6:62 and 7:33).

plished this through the Holy Spirit, through which the risen and ascended Jesus becomes fully the Christ and so fully Prophet, Priest, and King. Thus the Spirit of Sonship that Jesus received when he became the Son of God incarnate at his conception and the commissioning Spirit that he obtained at his baptism now find their completion in his resurrection, in which he has completed the purpose of his incarnation and fulfilled the divine commission he received at his baptism. Because he now possesses the fullness of the Holy Spirit as the risen Lord and Savior Jesus Christ, he can do what previously he could not— baptize in the Holy Spirit. The Father, then, in raising Jesus from the dead and sitting him at his right hand, perfected, through the Holy Spirit, his Son's humanity. While remaining a son of Adam, Jesus no longer possess Adam's fallen humanity, but as the new Adam, he possesses a new and living humanity freed from the bondage of sin and death. The perfecting of his humanity through the Holy Spirit means that Jesus, as the risen Son of God incarnate, now possesses the full filial vision of his Father, which he could not have possessed as simply Adam's son.

Having argued this notion throughout this study, I want here to address more fully a few issues concerning this position because it is not a part of the received theological tradition and may even be contrary to it. The tradition argues that Jesus, from the moment of his conception, possessed the "beatific vision"; that is, he possessed an objective vision of God that is reserved only to the blessed in heaven. But I want to say that Jesus, as the incarnate Son, never had a vision of God as if God were someone other than himself, an object to be known that differs from himself. Rather, as the Father's Son, Jesus' human vision of the Father must always be that of being his Father' Son and so it must integrally be a "filial vision." He humanly perceives his Father and in so doing perceives himself as the Father's Son. Jesus humanly recognizes that his own divine identity as Son—who he is—is dependent upon his eternal personal relationship with his Father. Thus Jesus, the incarnate Son, perceives his Father not as someone independent and apart from himself but as someone with whom he is eternally united as the Father's Son.

And because the Son of God truly became man, and so existed fully in accord with other human beings, his personal filial vision of his Father must be in harmony with his earthly humanity. If he possessed the "beatific vision" or even a full "filial vision" of his Father from the moment of his conception, it would not be in accord with how he presently existed as man. There is a true epistemological principle—something can be known only in accordance with the capacity of the knower, or what is known is in the knower in accord with the mode of the knower. For example, animals may perceive singular objects, but they do not actually know them. They may see a tree or water, but they do not know that what they see is a tree or water. Animals are incapable of knowing what something is, even themselves. Human beings can know finite reality in a universal manner. They know what a tree or water or a dog actually is. They know themselves to be human beings. Similarly, human beings can possess knowledge of God, such as his being eternal, all-knowing, and all-powerful, but they are not capable of knowing God as God knows himself. Such divine knowledge is beyond the capacity of human beings. Human beings can only know God in a human manner, in accordance with their manner of knowing. Thus Jesus as a non-resurrected man is, in principle, incapable of possessing a full filial vision of his Father prior to his resurrection, for to possess a full filial vision of his heavenly Father would, by the very fact that it is a full filial vision, make him resurrected.

Some argue that Jesus intellectually within his soul did possess the beatific vision while on earth, but that its effect upon his body was divinely impeded, and so while his soul possessed the heavenly vision, his body remained earthly. It strikes me that any time one must impede or disallow the normal effect of a cause—in this case, the beatific vision not glorifying Jesus' body—one has not properly conceived the issue. No cause should or can be denied its effect without another cause more powerful than itself impeding it, but Jesus' body is not a cause such that it could impede the beatific vision's effect. To introduce divine causality to bring about this impediment is a sure sign that something is amiss within one's fundamental conception. Also, to argue that Jesus did possess the beatific vision prior to his resurrection without it affecting his humanity implies some form of kenotic Christology where those divine attributes that are perceived to be incompatible with Jesus' humanity, such as omniscience or omnipotence, are either given up completely ("emptied" as in "kenosis") or rendered inoperative during the Son's earthly incarnate state. But how is it possible for the Son of God to become non-omniscient or non-omnipotent without simultaneously ceasing to be God, and how then can God not be God? Nonetheless, because the beatific vision is incompatible with Jesus' earthly body, it is thought that it must be rendered inoperative or not fully operative during his earthly life. But, again, how can the beatific vision be rendered inoperative or not fully operative any more than the Son's omniscience or his omnipotence be rendered inoperative? Similarly, that the earthly Jesus possesses the beatific vision without it affecting his body also implies a subtle form of Platonism where the soul and body are not only distinct but separate. A Platonist could argue that because the soul merely inhabits a body and so is ontologically isolated from it, Jesus' soul may possess the beatific vision, but his body, being isolated from his soul, is not affected by the beatific vision. But Christian revelation and philosophy reject such Platonic notions. The whole human being, created in the image and likeness of God, is constituted by the ontological union of the body and soul. A human being, body and soul, is one living ontological reality. Ultimately, to attribute to Jesus the beatific vision prior to his resurrection implies a misconception of the Incarnation—the metaphysics or ontology inherent within the Incarnation.

For the Son of God to become man means that the Son of God actually came to be man. Neither his divinity nor his humanity is jeopardized in the incarnational becoming nor is his humanity or divinity separated, for the Son of God in coming to be man came to exist as man and so the Son of God possessed all that pertained to his humanity. As an earthly man, Jesus, the Son of God, then came to know God as his Father, and so in that filial vision of his Father he became conscious of himself as the Father's Son. In and through his filial vision of his Father, founded upon his filial relationship with the Father, Jesus came to know his own identity as the Father's Son. Jesus' filial vision grew and matured, through the indwelling of the Spirit of Sonship, throughout the course of his life so that during his public ministry he could reveal his Father and in so doing manifest that he is the Father's Son.[63] Yet never did Jesus' filial vision of his Father, as the Son of God incarnate, exceed his earthly human capacity, precisely because his earthly human capacity was incapable of such a "surpassing." Jesus could receive the light of the Holy Spirit such that he knew his Father as the Father's Son, but within his earthly capacity he could not possess a full filial vision of his Father because his present humanity was incapable possessing the Spirit in that manner. A knower can know only in accordance with its manner of knowing. Jesus knew his Father and knew himself to be the Father's Son, and precisely because of this conscious knowledge he ever longed for its fulfillment, which he knew could only be achieved through his passion, death, and resurrection. Jesus longed to possess the full filial vision of his Father, but the full filial vision demanded that he become a resurrected man possessing a new humanity, one capable of knowing his Father fully. Thus Jesus knew that he could possess a full filial vision of his Fa-

63. As noted in chapter 2, Jesus was conscious of being the Father's Son by the age of twelve, though undoubtedly it was even earlier, as many children become aware of their identities at younger ages (see Lk 2:41–52). Jesus never knew his own self-identity apart from being the Father's Son.

ther, but he also realized it could not be achieved within his earthly state. But after Jesus fully becomes Jesus, YHWH-Saves, through his salvific death, the Father perfected his humanity, both body and soul, by gloriously raising him from the dead and in so doing gave to him the perfect ascended vision of himself.[64] Jesus' full filial vision of his Father inherently resides within his becoming the resurrected incarnated Son of the Father. Through his death, he merited his resurrection, in which he obtained the supreme Spirit-filled goal of that resurrection, full and complete union with his Father, which is embodied in his full Spirit-filled filial vision of his Father as the Father's glorified Son.

Here is the chief soteriological point: through Jesus' resurrection, through his becoming a perfect ascended glorified man and so possessing the full filial vision of his heavenly Father, he obtained for the whole of humankind the capacity to be gloriously resurrected and so to possess in him, by sharing fully his Father's Spirit of Sonship, a filial vision of his Father. By Jesus fully becoming Jesus, through his passion, death, and resurrection, he made it possible for each human person to become who he or she is fully meant to be: a child of the Father, possessing in the Spirit a full filial vision of the Father in communion with Jesus, the Son, a vision that is both the cause and the effect of their full filial union with their Father. In seeing fully their Father the faithful become fully their Father's children, and in becoming fully their Father's children they behold fully the face of their Father.

By way of concluding, we clearly grasp now that the Father, in raising Jesus gloriously from the dead and taking him up into heaven, fully revealed that Jesus is truly his divine Son and so the anointed Spirit-filled Christ. Similarly, the Father confirmed that his Son's saving death inaugurated the new and everlasting covenant in which human beings could come into communion with him through his risen Son, for Jesus is now empowered to pour out his

64. This in keeping with Heb 2:10, where it is said that Jesus was made perfect through what he suffered. It is not just his body that was made perfect, but the entirety of who he is as the Son of God incarnate. Moreover, the faithful are to look to "Jesus the pioneer and perfecter of our faith who for the joy that was set before him endured the cross, despising its shame, and is seated at the right hand of the throne of God" (Heb 12:2). Just as Jesus endured the cross to obtain a joy that he did not yet possess prior to his resurrection—that is, full filial communion with his Father accompanied with its joyful filial vision of his Father—Christians should persevere in their faith so that they too can share in that same joy. Also, within the Gospel of John, Jesus prays, "Father, glorify me in your presence with the glory which I had with you before the world was made" (Jn 17:5). The glory that Jesus, the Incarnate Son, longs to possess is the full filial glory that he, as Son, possessed from all eternity. That filial glory consisted of his complete union with the Father and with it his full filial vision of his Father as the Father's only begotten Son.

Spirit of Sonship upon all who believe. The Father thus constituted Jesus as the universal Savior and definitive Lord and in so doing elevated him to be the supreme Prophet, the great high priest, and the everlasting King. Likewise, his Father, in the love of the Holy Spirit, bestowed upon Jesus the supreme gift of that Spirit—the full and complete filial vision of himself. In the Holy Spirit, the Father and Jesus share forever the joy of their mutual love and life. They do so knowing that, together in the Spirit, they achieved the salvation of the world. Finally, a point not previously made: the Father, in taking the risen Jesus into his glorious presence, prophetically anticipates Jesus' eschatological future coming in glory at the end of time. As Jesus became Jesus through his incarnation, life, and saving death and as the Father constituted Jesus to be the glorious Jesus in his ascending resurrection, so the Father will send forth his Son upon the clouds of heaven at the end of this age, whereupon Jesus will bestow his heavenly Spirit-filled glory upon all the saints, for they will become like him in every way. Then Jesus Christ, the Father's Son, will be fully and everlastingly Jesus—YHWH-Saves—to the everlasting glory of God his Father. Amen.

CONCLUSION · THE
THEOLOGICAL FOUNDATION
OF JESUS' SALVIFIC ACTS

Here we have concluded our theological or doctrinal interpretation of the Gospels of Matthew, Mark, and Luke. A detailed summary is unnecessary, for it would entail repeating points already made many times over. Yet I want to highlight this book's major overarching theme and in so doing articulate its theological foundation.

I have emphasized throughout this study, beginning with the introduction, the theological importance of "acts." I have done this by primarily, almost exclusively, focusing on the salvific acts that Jesus performs: the major saving events within the life of Jesus as portrayed within the Synoptic Gospels. Jesus becomes Jesus only through the saving actions, which are definitively enacted through his saving death and resurrection and find their full completion when Jesus comes in glory at the end of time. God's revelation, the history of salvation, is an ever emergent, sustained, and purposeful series of divine acts that leads to and culminates in the salvation of humankind through Jesus Christ. Although God's acts are obviously divine in nature in that only he can perform them, the effect of those acts takes place within the material created order of time and history. The divine revelatory acts of God always have a material component and effect because they terminate with the created order—they can be seen, heard, and often even touched. They are all, in various ways, sacramental acts. The Incarnation of the Son is the consummate act that validates this truth—to see, hear, and touch Jesus is literally to see, hear, and touch the Son of God, for that is who the man Jesus is. It is precisely this ability to be humanly perceived that makes these divine actions revelatory.

In addition, these divine acts—like all acts—are causal acts in that they not only reveal more clearly and truly who God is but also either establish a new

465

salvific relationship, a new salvific order, with humankind or attempt to further and nurture humankind's relationship with God. There is no act, divine or finite, that is not causal in nature. Thus, for example, within the Old Testament history, God acts to establish a unique relation with Abraham and the nation that he would father. He makes a covenant with Moses and the Hebrew people so that they might be singularly his people and he might be singularly their God. He anoints kings, prophets, and priests with his Spirit so that they might lead the people in holiness; speak his words of condemnation, correction, and admonition as well those of forgiveness, comfort, and encouragement; and so gather them together in worshiping and glorifying him as the one true Lord God of Israel. Amid this long history of revelatory acts, God was advancing the future when he would reveal himself fully by making a new covenant with his people whereby they would be truly cleansed of their sin and interiorly sanctified in his Spirit and so be empowered to live holy lives within his kingdom. Now, as is evident from the Gospel, all these revelatory divine acts find their climax and end in the Father sending into the world his Son, who became incarnate in the womb of Mary through the overshadowing power of the Holy Spirit.

I have focused upon God's revelatory acts primarily to enhance the dynamic nature of God's revelation as well as to enrich the salvific significance of Jesus' acts, that through Jesus' saving acts, Jesus becomes who is—YHWH-Saves. In so doing, I also wanted to demonstrate that revelation cannot simply be placed under the theological rubric of God speaking his word. It is commonly said that the Bible is the "Word of God," and when the Scriptures are read within a liturgical setting, they are often closed with the proclamation "the Word of the Lord." The Bible is indeed God's anointed word, but the words that it speaks are not simply the words that God provides to tell us things we did not know. The biblical narrative, the Bible's story, is primarily an account of God's saving actions within the created order of history. Thus the words of the Bible principally are words that convey the meaning, and so the saving significance, of God's revelatory actions. Importantly, actions contain within themselves their own inherent meaning, and the concepts and words that we employ give voice to that inherent meaning. When we see a girl moving swiftly across a field, we say that the girl is running. When we hear a small bird, we say that the bird is chirping. The human mind grasps and its words express the meaning of the action. Within revelation, God acts, and the anointed words of Scripture provide the meaning inherent within those divine actions. And it is by divine actions and not by divine words that God brings about new salvific relationships that were not possible prior to God's actions. Amid these divine actions, humankind gains a deeper knowledge of God because the actions are revelatory of who God is. The Bible informs us as to who God is because the Bible narrates the acts that he performs, enabling a more intimate relationship with him.[1]

Now, this history of God's revelatory acts raises a theological and philosophical issue, which arises from within the revelatory acts themselves. This issue has been present throughout our study, and while alluded to at times, it was never brought into the fullness of light. I have waited until the conclusion because it can only be fully grasped and appreciated after having examined the mystery of Jesus as the incarnate Son and the divine mysteries that he embodies and humanly enacts as the Spirit-filled Christ. Why does God reveal himself through acts? More specifically, if God does reveal through divine acts, what is the metaphysical foundation from which these divine acts spring? The answers to these questions are found in what the divine acts reveal. First and foundationally important, the fact that the eternal God does act within time and history reveals that he is a personal purposeful God capable of acting within the created order of time. He is not some transcendent inert, passive, impersonal being incapable of interacting with the finite order, specifically with human beings. Second and ultimately, the divine revelatory actions manifest that the one God is the Father, the Son, and the Holy Spirit. This final revelation, made visible through the saving acts of Jesus Christ, demonstrates fully why God is a personal purposeful God capable of acting and why he reveals himself through his divine actions.

By revealing himself through his Son in the communion of the Holy Spirit, the Father manifests that he is the eternal wellspring of all acts, for as Father he eternally begets his Son in his loving act of the Holy Spirit.[2] The Father is the act of fatherhood fully in act, for he is ontologically configured to be "Father" in his simultaneous perichoretic twofold act of begetting his Son in his loving act of the Holy Spirit. He is utterly and entirely ontologically defined

---

1. Although God does reveal through his divine word and although the Bible is the word of God, the distorting emphasis of this truth arose within Protestantism, where sacramental actions were either deemphasized or misconstrued. The incarnational and sacramental nature of God's saving actions was lost. Salvation was exclusively dependent upon hearing and believing the word of God. What was forgotten was that the words that one was hearing were those that told of God's saving actions, and that saving faith was achieved when one believed in God's saving acts.

2. Here I am developing the theme discussed in chapter 6.

as "Father" in this very twofold act. The eternal act of the Father's fathering, then, eternally establishes a metaphysics, what it means "to be," founded upon "act." One cannot "be" without acting and one cannot "act" without being—"to be" is "to be in act." To be "Father" is simply to beget the Son in the loving act of the Holy Spirit. Thus the act of the Father's fathering, the act that totally constitutes and so defines himself as Father, eternally establishes him as the author of all life (the Son) and the source of perfect love (the Holy Spirit). For the Father *to be* Father is to be the perfect paternal act of live-giving and love-giving. We employ the noun "Father" to designate the Father, but he is actually a verb, the eternal act, the eternal springing forth, of begetting his Son in the Holy Spirit. The Father is fathering fully in act. Thus all subsequent acts, both eternal and temporal, are founded upon him. When the Father wishes to reveal, that revelation must be by way of "acts," for all revelation, by metaphysical necessity, must come forth from the Father, who is the eternal primordial act and so the sole source of all further acts. Equally, then, in eternally fathering his Son in his love of the Holy Spirit, the Father eternally establishes a metaphysics, an order of *being*, that is imbued with life and love, for from him eternally comes both his living Son who is his exact likeness and the Holy Spirit who is the fullness of his paternal love.

Because the Father is the twofold act of fully giving life and love, the Son and Holy Spirit are also fully in act. The Son, as the Father's perfect image, is the Father's filial image fully in act—he is the eternal fully-in-act-image of his Father. Therefore he is defined as "Son." If he were not the fully-in-act image of the Father, he would not be the perfect image of the Father who is fully in act as Father. Being the fully-in-act image of the Father, the Son simultaneously loves his Father in the same love of the Holy Spirit that he himself is loved. As the Father is the Father in the act of begetting his Son in the loving act of the Holy Spirit, so the Son is the Son in the act of perfectly imaging his Father, in whom he is begotten and so in the simultaneous act of loving his Father in the Holy Spirit. If the Son did not perfectly love the Father in the Holy Spirit, he would not be the perfect image of the Father who loves him in the Holy Spirit. The Son is Sonship fully in act, or simply the act of "Son-ing," for he is simply the act (the verb) that reflects the Father, and he does so in perfectly loving the Father as the Father perfectly loves him.

The Holy Spirit is also fully the perfect act of the Father's paternal love for his begotten Son and the Son's perfect act of filial love for his Father. He is the act of perfect paternal love of the Father for his Son and the act of perfect filial love of the Son for the Father. In being the perfect act of love of the Father for his Son and of the Son for his Father, he is simultaneously the act that conforms, co-constitutes, the Father to be the loving Father of his Son and conforms, co-constitutes, the Son to be the loving Son of the Father. The Holy Spirit is love fully in act because he is simply the act (the verb) by, through, and in which the Father and Son mutually love one another in their intertwining paternal and filial perfecting love.

Here is the answer to our question as to why God the Father, the Son, and the Holy Spirit reveal through acts. They do so because they are eternally mutually co-inhering perichoretic acts. They can reveal themselves only in the manner in which they exist as acts fully in act: the Father as fatherhood fully in act, the Son as sonship fully in act, and the Holy Spirit as love fully in act. Importantly, as the Son and Holy Spirit eternally proceed from the Father as mutually inhering perichoretic acts, so they come forth from the Father, throughout the course of revelation, to act within time and history. The Father as Father is the author and fount of divine revelation, for he is the eternal source of his Son and Holy Spirit, the eternal act of being Father. The Son as Son is he through whom the Father reveals, for he is the perfect image of the Father, the eternal act of perfectly reflecting the Father. The Holy Spirit as Holy Spirit is he in whom the Father lovingly reveals through his Son, for he is the eternal act of love that proceeds from the Father and the Son. Thus the perfect acts that the persons of the Trinity are, in relationship to one another are the very same perfect acts that act within the acts of revelation. The Trinity—the mutually inhering interrelational perichoretic acts of the Father, the Son, and the Holy Spirit—metaphysically demands that all revelation be by way of divine acts, for that is the manner in which the Trinity is. Therefore, within the economy of salvation, the Father acts through the acts of his Son in the loving acts of the Holy Spirit.

Although the above revealed metaphysical understanding of the Trinity is founded upon the revelatory acts of the Trinity within salvation history and not on some arbitrary or philosophical a priori principle, we recognize in hindsight why revelation always consists of divine acts. We also perceive why all divine revelatory acts are causal. Within the Trinity, the Father does not, strictly speaking, cause the existence of his Son or the existence the Holy Spirit, for neither exist as separate beings, as external effects, different from the divine being of the Father. Rather, they proceed inextricably from the Father's fatherhood. They are all equally God, for the Son and Holy Spirit share in the same divine being with the Father from whom they proceed. Yet the divine actions within revelation are causal acts in that they bring about a salvific effect within the created historical order; that is, through these causal revelatory acts, human beings, and in some manner the whole of creation, are taken up into the very life, the very divine acts, that constitute the life and being of the Trinity. The whole point of these revelatory causal acts is to allow human beings to participate in the eternal divine relationships that exist between the Father, the Son, and the Holy Spirit. The Father acts through his Son in the love of the Holy Spirit so that human beings through the Son and in the love of the Holy Spirit can come into relationship with him. Thus the revelatory acts within salvation history replicate the eternal divine acts within the Trinity, for through them human beings are assumed into the eternal divine acts, that is, into the relational perichoretic acts that constitute the Father, the Son, and the Holy Spirit as the one eternal living and loving God. If God were not the Father, the Son, and the Holy Spirit, there would be no metaphysical basis for God to act so as to assume humankind into relationship with him, for he would be neither a God of life nor a God of love, for he would not have an eternally living Son whom he eternally begot in the eternal love of the Holy Spirit. Thus there is a salvific intertwining of acts—those acts that constitute the Trinity and those acts that constitute humankind's life within the Trinity. The Father is the wellspring of both, for as he eternally begets his Son in the love the Spirit so he temporally begets sons through his Son in the love of the Holy Spirit.[3]

This theological and metaphysical exposition of the Trinity as the persons of the Father, the Son, and the Holy Spirit being perichoretially fully in act may seem far removed from the concrete and down-to-earth Gospel narratives. Yet such an understanding arises from the Gospels themselves, that is, from the full revelation of the Father, through his Son, Jesus Christ, in the love of the Holy Spirit. Here my theological exposition finds its terminal purpose. What we have perceived in this study of the Synoptic Gospels is the definitive acts of the Father, the Son, and the Holy Spirit within time and history—caus-

3. Although the divine act of creation is the primordial divine act of God outside himself, the Synoptic Gospels do not touch upon this issue. So I have purposely not addressed the act of creation. This divine act of creation, however, normally and traditionally examined under the rubric of the "one God" being existence itself and thus pure act, could only have been enacted if the one God is the Father, the Son, and the Holy Spirit. Only if God is the life-giving and love-giving Father who begets his Son in the Holy Spirit would it be possible for the Father to create other beings, particularly human beings, through his Son in the love of the Holy Spirit. Although the act of creation does not explicitly reveal the Trinity, once the Trinity reveals itself, it is possible to see that the act of creation could only be enacted if the one God is the Father, the Son, and the Holy Spirit, for only then would God be life giving and love giving.

al acts that establish the fullness of salvation, all of which are found in and focus upon the man Jesus and the human causal acts that he performs. This is
the marvel and the beauty of the Incarnation and so the marvel and beauty of
Jesus becoming Jesus. In the human acts of Jesus are found the divine acts of
the Father, the Son, and the Holy Spirit. As the Father, the Son, and the Holy
Spirit are eternally in act, so now they do, in accordance with who they are,
within the earthly temporal human acts of Jesus—the reason being that Jesus
is the incarnate Son of God!

In the Incarnation, the Father enacts his supreme revelatory act of sending
his Son into the world so as to become man in the womb of Mary through the
overshadowing power of the Holy Spirit. In becoming man, the Son enacts his
supreme revelatory act and all his subsequent human acts through the Holy
Spirit, by whose power he was made incarnate. In overshadowing Mary, the
Holy Spirit enacts his supreme revelatory act, which within the incarnating act
makes present the full love the Father and the Son in the man Jesus. In the Annunciation, we see the Father's fatherhood fully in act, the Son's sonship fully
in act, and the Holy Spirit's love fully in act, for the Father, in the full love of
his Spirit, gave to humankind the fullness of himself in giving his Son, his perfect image.[4] All that Jesus does humanly as the Father's Son, all of his human
salvific acts beginning with his conception and birth and culminating in his
death and resurrection, give expression to his Father's complete fatherly love
for humankind because he performs them in full loving communion with his
Father's Holy Spirit. All that we have examined in this book, all the advancing
saving acts of Jesus throughout his public ministry, reveal and give expression
to the Father being fully the Father through the Son being fully the Son in
union with the Holy Spirit being fully the Holy Spirit. By Jesus (YHWH-Saves)
ever becoming Jesus through his salvific acts, he was also manifesting, enacting, as Son, his Father becoming truly humankind's Father (YHWH-Saves),
for he was performing the very acts the Father willed him to do through the
loving acts of the Holy Spirit (YHWH-Saves). The conjoined salvific act of the
cross and resurrection therefore fully enact, and so complete, Jesus' conception, where the Father poured out his Spirit of love upon the world through
the incarnation of his Son. In the saving act of his death, Jesus, as the Father's
Son, enacted the fullness of his Sonship, for he enacted the fullness of his Father's will and he did so in the fullness of his Father's Spirit of Sonship. In rais-

4. This is in keeping with the Gospel of John: "For God so loved the world that he gave his
only Son, that whoever believes in him should not perish but have eternal life" (3:16).

ing Jesus, his Son, from the dead, through the life-giving action of the Holy
Spirit, the Father fully constituted Jesus as Jesus (YHWH-Saves) and in so doing fully constituted himself as Father (YHWH-Saves), for he did so through
the loving act of the Spirit and so fully constituting the Holy Spirit as the Holy
Spirit (YHWH-Saves). Thus, in the death and resurrection of Jesus, the Father, the Son, and the Holy Spirit became fully in act as the one saving-God—
YHWH-Saves—thus replicating what they were and are from all eternity—the
Father fully in act, the Son fully in act, and the Holy Spirit fully in act. In so
doing, they made it possible for human beings to share in the divine acts that
they are. By being united to Jesus, the Son, through the communion of the
Holy Spirit, human beings become divine children of the Father. What was
from all eternity is now available to humankind—sharing in the loving and
life giving acts that are the Father, the Son, and the Holy Spirit.

What was not possible prior to the salvific acts of Jesus, the Son, in accordance with the will of the Father and in the love of the Holy Spirit, is now
possible. The Father, through the Spirit-filled human acts of Jesus, his Son, has
established a new salvific order, a whole new manner in which human beings
could relate to him through his Son in communion with the Holy Spirit. But
what is now possible demands reciprocal human acts. Only through the act
of faith and the ecclesial act of baptism are human beings united to the risen
humanity of Jesus, the Son, in the love of the Holy Spirit so as to obtain communion with the Father as his children. This is most fully expressed in the
Eucharistic Liturgy, for there the full saving benefits of Jesus' sacrificial death
and glorious resurrection are made present. In Spirit-filled communion with
Jesus, the Son, the Father's children are ushered into his heavenly presence,
his everlasting heavenly kingdom, and in so doing the whole of humankind
becomes brothers and sisters to one another. Thus we perceive that the divine
saving acts fully residing within the risen humanity of Jesus and the reciprocal
human saving acts, human acts empowered by the Holy Spirit, are conjoined.
In this intertwining of divine and human acts, salvation is fully achieved—a
living and loving union with the persons of the Trinity. To know rightly in
faith the man Jesus, and so to be in communion with him, is to know rightly,
and so be in communion with, the Trinity—Father, Son, and Holy Spirit.

Throughout this book we have witnessed Jesus becoming Jesus as
the Spirit-anointed Christ, the Son of the living God. In becoming Jesus
(YHWH-Saves), he became our definitive Savior and universal Lord—the Davidic King of his Father's everlasting kingdom. Now we only need eagerly to

anticipate, in resolute faith, enduring hope, and steadfast love, Jesus' coming at the end of time. Then Jesus will be Jesus fully in act—YHWH-Saves—for we will become fully in act, sharing in his Spirit-filled risen glory and so becoming wholly children of his Father. Then, upon hearing the Father pronounce the holy name of Jesus, we, on bended knee, will eternally proclaim, in the hallowed joy of the Holy Spirit, "Jesus Christ is Lord to the glory of God the Father." Amen.

SUGGESTED FURTHER READING

Albright, W. F., and C. S. Mann. *Matthew.* New York: Doubleday, 1971.

Bauckham, Richard. *The Gospel for All Christians: Rethinking the Gospel Audiences.* Grand Rapids, Mich.: Eerdmans, 1998.

———. *Jesus and the Eyewitnesses: The Gospels as Eyewitness Testimony.* Grand Rapids, Mich.: Eerdmans, 2006.

Bovon, Francois. *Luke: A Critical Commentary on the Gospel of Luke.* 3 vols. Minneapolis: Hermeneia, 2000-2009.

Byrne, Brendan. *The Gospel of Mark: A Commentary.* Collegeville, Minn.: Order of St. Benedict, 2015.

Collins, A. Yabro. *The Beginning of the Gospel: Probing Mark in Context.* Eugene, Ore.: Wipf and Stock, 2001.

Davies, W. D., and Dale Allison. *Matthew.* 3 vols. Edinburgh: T & T Clark, 1988-97.

Fitzmyer, Joseph. *Luke.* 2 vols. New York: Doubleday, 1981-85.

France, R. T. *The Gospel of Mark.* Grand Rapids, MI: Eerdmans, 2002.

———. *Matthew: An Introduction and Commentary.* Downers Grove, IL: InterVarsity Press, 2008.

Gadenz, Pablo. *The Gospel of Luke.* Catholic Commentary on Sacred Scripture. Grand Rapids, Mich.: Baker Academic, 2018.

Giambrone, Anthony. *Creditor Christology and the Economy of Salvation in Luke's Gospel.* Tübingen: Mohr-Siebeck, 2017.

Harrington, Wilfred. *Luke: The Gracious Theologian. The Jesus of Luke.* Dublin: Columba Press, 1997.

Healy, Mary. *The Gospel of Mark.* Catholic Commentary on Sacred Scripture. Grand Rapids, Mich.: Baker Academic, 2008.

Hurtádo, Larry W. *Lord Jesus Christ: Devotion to Jesus in Earliest Christianity.* Grand Rapids, Mich.: Eerdmans, 2003.

Lagrange, Marie-Joseph. *The Gospel of Jesus Christ.* Westminster, Md.: Newman Press, 1958.

Leim, Joshua. *Matthew's Theological Grammar: The Father and the Son.* Tübingen: Mohr-Siebeck, 2015.

Leiva-Merikakis, Erasmo. *Fire of Mercy, Heart of the World: Meditations on the Gospel of Matthew.* 3 vols. San Francisco: Ignatius Press, 1996-2012.

Luz, Ulrich. *The Theology of the Gospel of Matthew.* Cambridge: Cambridge University Press, 1993.

Marcus, Joel. *Mark.* 2 vols. New Haven, Conn.: Yale University Press, 2001-9.

Mitch, Curtis, and Edward Sri. *The Gospel of Matthew.* Catholic Commentary on Sacred Scripture. Grand Rapids, Mich.: Baker Academic, 2010.

Ratzinger, Joseph (Pope Benedict XVI). *Jesus of Nazareth: From the Baptism in the Jordan to the Transfiguration, Part 1.* New York: Doubleday, 2007.

——. *Jesus of Nazareth: From the Entrance into Jerusalem to the Resurrection, Part 2.* San Francisco: Ignatius Press, 2011.

——. *Jesus of Nazareth: The Infancy Narratives.* New York: Image, 2012.

Watson, Francis. *Gospel Writing: A Canonical Perspective.* Grand Rapids, Mich.: Eerdmans, 2013.

Watts Henderson, Suzanne. *Christology and Discipleship in the Gospel of Mark.* Cambridge: Cambridge University Press, 2006.

Weinandy, Thomas G. *Does God Change? The Word's Becoming in the Incarnation.* Still River, Mass.: St. Bede's, 1985.

——. *In the Likeness of Sinful Flesh: An Essay on the Humanity of Christ.* Edinburgh: T & T Clark, 1993.

——. *The Father's Spirit of Sonship: Reconceiving the Trinity.* Edinburgh: T & T Clark, 1995.

——. *Does God Suffer?* Edinburgh: T & T Clark, 2000.

——. *Jesus the Christ.* Huntington: Our Sunday Visitor, 2003. Republished by Ex Fontibus, 2017.

——. *Jesus: Essays in Christology.* Ave Maria, Fla.: Sapientia Press, 2014.

INDEX

Adoption as children of the Father/ deification, 198-204
Agony in the garden, 319-29
Anointing, 289-97
Arrest of Jesus, 329-33
Ascension, 435-43; great commission, 446-52; Longer Ending (Mark), 443-46; one act with resurrection, 456-59

Baptism of Jesus, 80-101
Birth of Jesus, 35-40, 48-60
Burial of Jesus, 393-97

Church: founding of, 113-15, 216-21; Mary and, 12-13; Peter the Rock on which it is built, 216-18; sending out of the disciples, 126-28
Circumcision of Jesus, 40-42
Conception of Jesus, 7-17
Crucifixion, 360-63
Cry of dereliction, 380-84

Death of Jesus: Psalm 22, 372-80; women looking from afar, 391-93
Dei Verbum, ix-xi, xvi-xviii

Father's Son, Jesus as, 179-98
Finding Jesus in the temple, 61-64
Foretelling of passion, death, and resurrection, 222-25, 239-42

Genealogy of Jesus, 14-15, 101-4
Golgotha, on the way to, 357-60

Healing on the Sabbath, 131-33
Holy Spirit, Jesus acts in the, 139-41
Human consciousness of Jesus, 204-6; human "I," 205-6, 212-13

I AM, 130-31
Incarnational act, 18-21

John the Baptist: birth, 31-35; conception, 3-7; ministry, 72-80

Last Supper, 297-313

Mary: purification, 42-48; virginity and motherhood, 11-12; visitation, 21-27. See also Conception of Jesus
Mocking of Jesus, 363-69
Multiplication of loaves, 133-39

Our Father, 401-11

Peter's profession of faith, 207-21
Power of Jesus: over death, 122-24; over nature, 128-30; over Satan, 119-20; over sickness, 120-22; over sin, 124-26
Priestly ministry of Jesus, 116-18
Proclamation of the centurion, 387-91
Prophet, priest, and king, Jesus as, 91-98
Prophetic acts: Beatitudes, 146-75; fulfilled, 315-18; leading to the passion, 281-88

Resurrection: the angels, 414-20; appearance on the road to Emmaus, 424-32; appearances to the apostles,

Resurrection: (cont.)
    432-35; appearances to the women,
    420-24; one act with ascension, 456-59;
    resurrected filial vision of the Father,
    459-64; women return to the tomb,
    412-14

Sacramental acts. See Theandric acts
Saving acts, xviii-xix
Scripture and tradition, xi-xii
Son of Man, 225-27
Suffering Servant Songs, 350-56

Tearing of the temple curtain, 384-87
Temptations of Jesus, 104-9
Theandric acts, 130, 142-43
Theological interpretations and summaries:
    foundation of Jesus' salvific acts, 465-73;

infancy narratives, 64-69; passion and
    death, 397-400; public ministry, 142-45,
    175-78; resurrection, 452-56
Transfiguration, 227-39
Trial of Jesus: before Pilate, 341-50; before
    Sanhedrin, 333-41
Trinity, 27-30, 98-101, 179-98, 214-16
Triumphal entry into Jerusalem: after-
    math of cleansing of the temple, 270-76;
    cleansing of the temple, 255-62; de-
    struction of the temple/eschatologi-
    cal discourse, 270-76; Feast of Booths,
    247-49; preparatory acts, 245-47; Psalm
    118, 249-53
Two thieves, 369-72

Jesus Becoming Jesus: A Theological Interpretation of the Synoptic Gospels was designed in Yoga with Veljovic Script display type and composed by Kachergis Book Design of Pittsboro, North Carolina. It was printed on 60-pound House Natural Smooth and bound by Sheridan Books of Chelsea, Michigan.